A HISTORY OF RUSSIA

VOLUME III

THE MONGOLS AND RUSSIA

A HISTORY OF RUSSIA

THE MONGOLS AND RUSSIA

BY

GEORGE VERNADSKY

PROFESSOR EMERITUS OF RUSSIAN HISTORY
YALE UNIVERSITY

New Haven and London: YALE UNIVERSITY PRESS

SOMERSET COUNTY COLLEGE
LIBRARY
North Branch, New Jersey

© 1953 by Yale University Press.
Fourth printing, November 1966.
Printed in the United States of America by
Vail-Ballou Press, Inc., Binghamton, N.Y.
and reprinted by The Murray Printing Company,
Forge Village, Massachusetts.
All rights reserved. This book may not be
reproduced, in whole or in part, in any form
without written permission from the publishers.

Library of Congress catalog card number: A43–1903

FOREWORD

THE MONGOL PERIOD is one of the most significant epochs in the whole course of Russian history. The Mongols dominated all of Russia for about a century, and even after the disintegration of their power in West Russia in the middle of the 14th century they continued to exercise control over East Russia—although in a milder form—for another century. This was a period of profound changes in the whole political and social setup of the country, especially of East Russia. Directly and indirectly, the Mongol invasion contributed to the downfall of the free political institutions of the Kievan age and to the growth of absolutism and serfdom.

Russia's position was further aggravated by the fact that simultaneously with the Mongol onslaught from the East she was subjected to the Teutonic *Drang nach Osten* from the West. Caught between two fires, the Russians had temporarily to accept the suzerainty of the khan in order to have their hands free to stop the Teutonic crusade. The Mongols at least did not interfere with the religion of their subjects, while the Germans tried to impose their own faith on the conquered "schismatics." While the danger of German invasion was forestalled, it proved not so easy to get rid of the "Mongol yoke" once it had been imposed by the khans with ruthless efficiency. The process of emancipating the Russian people from Mongol domination was long and tortuous. Unable, at first, to muster sufficient force to oppose the invaders, the Russian princes had to show subservience and to use cunning as the only weapon left to them. But the spirit of the people was never broken, as was evidenced by a series of daring, even if unsuccessful, revolts of the townspeople against the Mongol officials.

On the whole the historian, contemplating the events of that remote age, cannot but be impressed with the unyielding tenacity the Russian people displayed in their struggle for survival. In spite of all the calamities and disruptions of normal life, they went on with their usual work, restoring what could be restored and building anew what they might. By 1350 many of Russia's wounds were healed, and the nation was once more in position to expand her economic resources and reassert her culture. By the close of the century Russia's industrial and military technique was more advanced than that of her conquerors, and her emancipation was only a matter of time. And indeed, in the middle of the 15th century the grand duke of Moscow became independent of the khan de facto and in 1480 de jure.

Mongol rule came thus to an end, although it left scars on Russia which remained visible for a long time after the downfall of the Golden Horde. It was, of course, inevitable that in their struggle against the Mongols the Russians should absorb many features of Mongol politics and of the Mongol system of government and administration. At the same time Russia's hard experiences toughened her people and made them better fit for survival in the further trials the future had in store for them.

Because Russia was part of the Mongol Empire and the regional Khanate of the Golden Horde for a century, and part of the Khanate of the Golden Horde alone for another century, the course of Russian history in this period cannot properly be understood without adequate examination of the whole Mongol background. Many important political decisions, or administrative orders which deeply affected Russia were made by the great khan residing in Mongolia or in China. As long as the Mongol Empire existed the grand duke of Moscow, a vassal of the khan of the Golden Horde, was a subvassal of the ruler of Peking. The general principles of government and administration on which the Golden Horde operated and to which Russia was also subjected were established by the founder of the Mongol Empire: Chingis-Khan, the guiding spirit of the Mongol nation, whose followers believed that he had received a mandate from Heaven to rule the earth. Obviously, a study of Chingis-Khan's institutions is a prerequisite for an analysis of the system of administration which the Mongols established in Russia. Russia, in her turn—although not as a free agent—contributed much to the strength and prosperity of both the Golden Horde and the Mongol Empire as a whole. Russian conscripts in the Mongol armies played an important role in the campaigns of the khans of the Golden Horde, as well as of the great khans. In the 1330's a Russian Guards Division was organized in Peking, apparently an important prop of the imperial regime in China at that time. Russia's best craftsmen were requisitioned for the khan's service and a number of them worked in the Golden Horde and in Mongolia. Characteristically enough, Khan Guyuk's throne as well as his imperial seal was manufactured by a Russian goldsmith. Furthermore, gold and silver collected in Russia as tribute or customs duties constituted an important source of revenue for the khan of the Golden Horde, helping him to pay for his share of the "presents" the regional khans sent to the great khan in China. And the importance of that share for the well-being of the empire should not be underestimated. Hence it may be said that knowledge of this period of Russian history in turn is of considerable importance for the student of the Mongol Empire as a whole and of the Golden Horde in particular.

With these considerations in mind I am offering the reader in this volume not just a history of Russia during the Mongol period but a study of the Mongols and Russia in their interrelations during that time. I am convinced that this is the only road to proper understanding of the basic trends in Russia's political and social development in that epoch. I also believe that my approach may be useful, to a certain extent, to students of Mongol and Turkish history as well. The disadvantage of my plan, of which I am well aware, is that no room has been left, within the framework of this volume, for a balanced picture of Russian social, economic, and cultural life under the Mongols. This is especially true of West Russia and Novgorod. I hope to be able to make up for the deficiency in the next volume of this series, by means of a retrospect.

It is my pleasant duty to express my gratitude to all those friends and colleagues who showed interest in my work, helped with advice, and sent me reprints of their valuable studies, and especially to Francis Woodman Cleaves, Serge Elisséeff, Roman Jakobson, Akdes Nimet Kurat, Nicholas N. Martinovitch, Vladimir F. Minorsky, and Johannes Rahder. Years ago, when I first approached the problem of Mongol-Russian relations, I received much encouragement from the late Wladyslaw Kotwicz whom I would like to remember here with warm sympathy and deep respect. It saddens me to think that the late Boris A. Bakhmeteff, the original sponsor of this series, will not see the present volume.

My warm thanks are due to the staff of the Yale University Library for their kind cooperation; and to the editorial department of the Yale University Press, in particular to Roberta Yerkes and Ella Holliday, for their assistance in preparing the manuscript for the printers. I am also greatly indebted to Michael Karpovich who generously helped me read the proofs in spite of being overburdened with his own work; and to my wife, Nina Vernadsky, who prepared the indices. The maps have been drawn by Robert L. Williams of the Cartography Laboratory at the Sterling Memorial Library.

Acknowledgment of their courtesy in granting permission to quote from books published by them is made here to Sir Rupert B. Howorth, K.C.M.G., K.C.V.O., C.B., for permission to quote from Volume 1 of Sir Henry H. Howorth's monumental *History of the Mongols* (Longmans, Green & Co., 1876); to the Cambridge University Press for E. G. Browne's *History of Persian Literature under Tartar Dominion;* and to the Princeton University Press for A. C. Krey's *The First Crusade.*

The publication of this volume would not have been possible without the financial support of the Humanities Fund of New York City, and the author wants to express his gratitude to that organization.

G. V.

New Haven, Connecticut
  February 6, 1953.

CONTENTS

MAPS

THE MONGOLS AND RUSSIA

CHAPTER I

THE MONGOL CONQUEST

1. THE WORLD ASPECTS OF THE MONGOL EXPANSION

THE MONGOL expansion of the 13th century was one of those crucial and fateful eruptions in the history of mankind which from time to time change the destinies of the world. In range of impact on world history it may be likened to the barbarian invasions of the 5th century which overthrew the Roman Empire, putting an end to the ancient world, and to the triumphal march of Islam in the 7th century. In spite of all their importance for the cultural and economic history of Europe, the Crusades, which represented the reverse movement—a counterattack of the Christian West against Islam—achieved much more limited objectives and brought about fewer territorial changes than the Arabian offensive, not to mention the Mongol deluge.

It has been said that the Mongol invasion "may be truly described as one of the most dreadful calamities which ever befell the human race." [1] And indeed when we think of such fruits of Mongol victory as the devastation of the countries with old cultures like China and Persia, the turning of parts of the flourishing realm of Khorezm (Turkestan) into a desert, the ruin of the blossoming Russian cities with their advanced civilization, and above all, the wholesale slaughter wherever nations dared to oppose the invaders, it is not difficult to understand the horror the Mongols inspired in Moslems and Christians alike. Even if the number of men, women, and children slain along the paths of their invasions has been exaggerated by the chroniclers, the total casualties of the Mongol wars may have reached several millions.

The score is staggering. No other place and period have known such a concentration of wholesale killing. Yet it should be remembered that the Mongols' opponents were not averse to bloodshed. With all their lofty ideals and rising civilization, both medieval Eu-

1. Browne 3, p. 4.

rope and the medieval Near East present in the long run a sad record of cruelty and barbarism, not only in the wars between nations but in the suppression of religious and other minorities within each nation. Moreover we know, as witnesses of two world wars and two revolutions, the Red and the Brown, that along with technological progress there has been considerable progress in wholesale killing. Indeed our "enlightened" generation has outdone the records of Chingis-Khan and his marshals. And are we not, to judge by our daily press, gradually acquiescing in the idea that the death toll of the second World War will be far surpassed in a global war fought with the new sources of energy accessible to us?

Be this as it may, the Mongol invasion was certainly a dreadful calamity for the countries involved. But describing the tragic results of human cruelty and folly is not the only duty of the historian; he has to study the over-all effects of wars and revolutions on the life and history of mankind. The historians of the second World War are now engaged not only in counting the casualties and costs but also in extensive study of wartime governmental and military policies and of the effect of the war on the world. In the same way, the historian of the Mongol expansion has to consider both the grim terror it brought to mankind and its impact on Asiatic and European nations. It would not be an exaggeration to say that the greater part of the Old World—the immense reach from the shores of the Pacific Ocean to the Adriatic coast, from China to Hungary—was engulfed by the Mongols for a longer or shorter period, depending on the strength of the Mongol grip. The course of history of a number of mighty Asiatic and European nations was changed abruptly, and the effects and aftereffects of Mongol rule were felt for centuries, in China, in Persia, and in Russia.

While the nations of the West trembled at the first news of the Mongol invasion of Russia, and even more so when the tidal wave reached Poland and Hungary,[2] Western Europe was one of the few corners of the Old World spared the horrors of the Mongol raids. Nevertheless, West European politics and economics could not but be deeply affected by the upheaval elsewhere. Moreover, the westward drive of the Ottoman Turks in the late 14th and 15th centuries was, historically speaking, a by-product of the Mongol expansion.

2. Here is an excerpt from Emperor Frederick II's letter to the King of England on the appearance of the Mongols: "Hence fear and trembling have arisen amongst us, owing to the fury of these impetuous invaders." See Matthew Paris, *1*, 343.

The Ottoman conquest of Constantinople (1453) impressed the Western nations vastly more than the sack of Kiev by the Mongols two centuries before. While the Mongol horsemen had come close to the gates of Vienna, they did not camp there for long; but the danger to Vienna from the Ottoman Turks lasted until the late 17th century. In this indirect form, then, the aftereffects of the Mongol drive threatened Western Europe almost as long as they harassed Russia. And it will be recalled that Constantinople—now known as Istanbul—is still in Turkish hands. To be sure, by the strange irony of fate, Istanbul is today considered a bulwark of the Western world, while "Holy Moscow" has become, for many a Westerner, the capital of infidels and the stronghold of the abominable East.

The picture of history is not all black and white, however. In every conflict of nations not all the villains are on one side nor all the heroes on the other. There are objective forces affecting the policies of good and evil rulers alike. The elemental forces of the historical process make use of every channel available. As Sir Henry Howorth puts it, the Mongols were "one of those hardy, brawny races cradled amidst want and hard circumstances, in whose blood there is a good mixture of iron, which are sent periodically to destroy the luxurious and the wealthy, to lay in ashes the arts and culture which only grow under the shelter of wealth and easy circumstances . . . Like the pestilence and the famine, the Mongols were essentially an engine of destruction; and if it be a painful, harassing story to read, it is nevertheless a necessary one if we are to understand the great course of human progress." [3] In Sir Henry's opinion the drastic methods applied by the Mongols served the purpose of renovating the decadent societies subjected to invasion. The prosperity of those peoples "was hollow and pretentious, their grandeur very largely but outward glitter, and the diseased body needed a sharp remedy; the apoplexy that was impending could probably only be staved off by much blood letting, the demoralized cities must be sown with salt, and their inhabitants inoculated with fresh streams of vigorous blood from the uncontaminated desert." [4]

This is an example of the "blood and iron" argument which has served for centuries in interpreting the sociological function of wars in history. There is, however, a more positive aspect of the historical role of the Mongol expansion. By unifying most of Eurasia under a

3. Howorth, *1*, x.
4. *Idem, 1,* xi.

single government the Mongols succeeded, if only for a comparatively brief period, in assuring the safety of the great overland route from China to the Mediterranean. The Pax Mongolica naturally resulted in a degree of cultural exchange between China, the Middle East, and Europe. "I have no doubt myself," says Howorth, ". . . that the art of printing, the mariner's compass, firearms, and a great many details of social life, were not discovered in Europe, but imported by means of Mongol influence from the furthest East." [5] As the Turkish historian A. Zeki Validi Togan puts it, "The invasion of the Turks and the Mongols . . . was not a universal catastrophe. It accented a moment in history [*un moment historique*] during which new regions entered the orbit of civilization." [6]

Sociologically, the Mongol expansion was the last great wave of the westward migrations of the Eurasian nomads. The Mongols followed the path of the Scythians, the Sarmatians, and the Huns; [7] they were preceded in the Pontic steppes by the Patzinaks and the Cumans.[8] The Arab expansion of the 7th century was a parallel drive of a different group of nomads.

Taking into consideration the vastness of the territory conquered by the Mongols, we may say that the Mongol phase of the nomadic expansion constituted the climax of all those drives. And yet the original Mongol tribes united by Temuchin (Chingis-Khan) were not stronger numerically than the Patzinaks and the Cumans. What were the causes of the overwhelming success of the Mongol drive? How did it happen that a nation of no more than a million people conquered a multitude of other nations with a total population of around one hundred million? One incentive for the Mongol warrior was his share in the war booty, but that motive applied equally to the wars of other nomad tribes. Among the chief reasons for the Mongol success were the unpreparedness of their opponents, the disunity of the non-Mongol world, and the inability of the outsiders to understand the determined character of the Mongol drive. Another reason was the perfection of the army organization achieved by Chingis-Khan. Prior to the invention of powder and firearms few nations could raise and maintain a force tactically and strategically equal to the Mongol cavalry or that rivaled it in spirit and will to conquer.

5. *Ibid.*
6. A. Zeki Validi [Togan], "Considérations sur la collaboration scientifique entre l'Orient islamique et l'Europe," *REI* (1935), p. 269.
7. See *Ancient Russia*, chaps. 2–4.
8. See *Kievan Russia*, pp. 224–225.

The sudden outburst of aggressive energy among the Mongols in the early 13th century still remains a psychological riddle. To use an analogy with the physical sciences, a sort of psychic explosion took place. It is generally admitted that the initial force of the 7th-century Arab expansion, psychologically speaking, was derived from the fervor and fanaticism of a new religion. But Chingis-Khan did not belong to any of the great established churches; he was called a heathen by both Moslems and Christians. His religious policy was toleration of all creeds. The traditional beliefs of the Mongols were a mixture of shamanism and reverence of the Sky. At all critical moments of his life Chingis-Khan invoked the "Eternal Blue Sky." But he did not let the shamans interfere with affairs of state. So we cannot say that Chingis-Khan belonged to a shamanist "church"; on the contrary, he felt that the link between him and the Sky was personal. And this feeling was combined with the sense of a mission: to conquer the world in order to establish universal peace. This was his message; and at least some of the peoples of the Islamic Middle East and Christian West, weary of internal strife and constant wars, must have been impressed. A 13th-century historian, Gregory Ab-ul-Faraj, commented on Chingis-Khan's guiding idea: "in such behaviour as this the Mongol's confidence in the Lord showeth itself. And by that they have conquered and will conquer." [9]

To sum up, we may say that Chingis-Khan was inspired by religious feeling intermingled with the ideal of the universal state. His cannot be called a state religion, however, since psychologically the link between him and God was direct, not through any established church. On this ground Gibbon even found it possible to characterize Chingis-Khan's religion as "a system of pure theism and perfect toleration." Comparing it with Chingis' laws, he says: "It is the religion of Zingis that best deserves our wonder and applause." [10]

2. THE MOSLEM AND CHRISTIAN WORLDS ON THE EVE OF THE MONGOL ONSLAUGHT

In November 1095, at the church council in Clermont, France, the spiritual head of the Western world, Pope Urban II, urged the Christian nations to "take the cross" against the infidels and to "liberate" the Holy Land, assuring them that such was God's will.

9. Ab-ul-Faraj, p. 354.
10. Gibbon, 2, 1203.

Within a few weeks all Europe knew about it, and before long the Moslems in the Levant—at whom the attack was aimed—were also informed of the plans of the Christians. This is an instance of the close connection between the Christian and Moslem worlds in the Middle Ages. Whether enjoying peace or locked in war, these two worlds were linked together. As everybody knows, the First Crusade was victorious: Jerusalem fell in 1099. What we are apt to forget whenever we talk of the lofty aims of the crusade is that the capture of the Holy City was accompanied by terrible slaughter. According to Fulcher of Chartres, the crusaders did not spare even the women and children. Another chronicler, Raymond of Agiles, relates that "in the Temple and porch of Solomon men rode in blood up to their knees and bridle reins. . . . The city was filled with corpses and blood." And yet he thought it "a splendid judgment of God that this place should be filled with the blood of the unbelievers, since it had suffered so long from their blasphemies." [11] The city was retaken by the Moslems in 1187; the Third Crusade failed to wrest it from them. As a result of an involved game of diplomacy and the commercial imperialism of Venice the Fourth Crusade was directed against the Byzantine Empire and not against the Moslems. Jerusalem was not "liberated," but Constantinople was taken instead and mercilessly sacked by the crusaders (1204).[12]

While Christians fought Moslems and the Christians of the West attacked the Christians of the Near East, clouds were gathering in the Far East. In 1206, in far-away Mongolia, the assembly of clan leaders (*kuriltay*) proclaimed one of their kinsmen, Temuchin, Emperor of the Earth and gave him a new name, Chingis-Khan. The Mongol crusade was about to start.

This momentous event passed entirely unnoticed by Moslems or Christians. Nobody in the West at that time knew of the existence of Mongolia. Even as late as A.D. 1241 many an educated European argued that "there are only seven climes in the whole extent of the world; namely, those of the Indians, Ethiopians or Moors, Egyptians, Jerusalemites, Greeks, Romans, and French." On this ground they refused to believe that the Mongols actually came from the Far East.[13]

11. Fulcher of Chartres, E. McGinty, trans., University of Pennsylvania "Translations and Reprints," 3d ser., p. 69; Raymond of Argiles as quoted in A. C. Krey, *The First Crusade* (Princeton University Press, 1921), p. 261. Both excerpts cited by La Monte, p. 342.

12. See H. Grégoire, "The Question of the Diversion of the Fourth Crusade to Constantinople," *Byzantion, 15* (1940–41), 158–166.

13. Matthew Paris, *1*, 348.

The Moslem Middle East was of course much closer to Mongolia than the European West. Khorezmian merchants traded with the Uigurs in eastern Turkestan, and Uigur merchants used to send their caravans to the Mongols. Nevertheless, several years passed before the decisions of the 1206 kuriltay became known in Khorezm and even then their ominous significance was not at once realized.

The Khorezmian Empire was at that time the strongest Moslem power in the Middle East. The authority of the Khorezm-shah was recognized in most of Turkestan and Persia.[14] Farther south, the Abbasid Caliphate in Iraq was in a state of decay. Egypt and Syria were ruled by the sultans of the Ayyubid dynasty founded by the famous Saladin (Salah ad-Din) in 1169. In Asia Minor the Seljuq Sultanate was the strongest power.[15] Wedged in between these large states were a number of smaller ones, among them the Christian kingdoms of Georgia and Armenia. A peculiar Islamic religious group in Persia, with a branch in Lebanon, enjoyed influence and power out of proportion to the small number of its adherents. Founded in the late 11th century, it belonged to the so-called Ismailian movement in the Shiite division of Islam. The group was bound by strong discipline and loyalty to their sheikh, "the Old Man of the Mountain" as the crusaders called him. The latter's basic method of dealing with his opponents was secret murder. No one who offended him seems to have been safe from the daggers of his agents; their fanaticism was heightened by the use of hashish, from which comes their name— and our term—"assassin." [16] The Assassins waged perpetual under-cover war against the Abbasids, the crusaders, and the Seljuqs. Among their victims were a king-elect of Jerusalem, Conrad (killed in 1192), and the famous vizier of the Seljuqs, Nizam al-Mulk, author of a remarkable treatise on government, "Siyaset-nama," who was murdered in 1092.[17]

There was no more unity in the Christian world than in the Islamic. Two institutions claimed to be universal in the West: the Roman

14. On the Khorezmian Empire see W. Barthold, "Kwarizm-shah," *EI, 2,* 913–914; *idem., Turkestan,* chap. 3; Tolstov, *Po sledam,* pp. 273–289; cf. *Kievan Russia,* p. 236. For a survey of the sources of Khoresmian history see Togan, pp. 206–207.

15. On the Seljuqs see Gordlevsky; cf. *Kievan Russia,* pp. 235–236, 361–362. For a survey of the sources of Seljuq history see Togan, pp. 204–206.

16. On the Ismailites and Assassins see "Assassins," *EI, 1,* 421–422; C. Huart, "Ismailiya," *EI, 2,* 549–552; W. Iwanow, *Studies in Early Persian Ismailism* (Leyden, 1948); *idem, The Alleged Founder of Ismailism* (Bombay, 1946).

17. *Siyaset-nama;* see also K. E. Schabinger, "Zur Geschichte des saldschuqen Reichskanzlers Nizamu'l Mulk," *Historisches Jahrbuch, 62* (1949), 250–283.

Catholic Church and the Holy Roman Empire of the German nation. Their authority was not recognized in all of Eastern Europe, however, most of that being Greek Orthodox. Moreover, a historical extension of the original Roman Empire—the Byzantine Empire—centered around Constantinople until 1204.

Even before the overthrow of the Greek Empire at the Bosporus and the establishment of the Latin Empire there, the authority of the pope of Rome was immensely strengthened by the Crusades. The popes now had an army at their disposal which they eventually were tempted to use as they pleased.[18] The Crusades gradually acquired a new meaning, being directed not only against the Moslems but against the schismatics (Greek Orthodox) as well. The attack on Constantinople represented the southern route of the Roman Catholic drive; simultaneously a northern route was opened by German missionaries and knights in the Baltic area. The Order of the Sword Bearers was created in Livonia in 1202. The Teutonic Order in Prussia was to follow (1229).[19] Thus the anti-Orthodox crusade was rapidly assuming shape. Combined with it there started, in 1209, the internal crusade which aimed at the "heretics" at home, the Albigensians and the Cathari.[20] While the authority of the pope tended to rise rapidly, its growth was greatly undermined by the dissensions between Rome and the "Roman Empire" of the Germans. The protracted conflict between emperors and popes sapped the forces of both sides. The dramatic struggle of Frederick Barbarossa (1155–90) against the pope ended in the defeat of the former's ambitious plans and in compromise. Frederick's son Conrad kept truce with the pope, at least outwardly, but during the reign of his son Frederick II (1215–50) there was a new violent clash between the church and the empire. Besides, the emperor had to face opposition on the part of some of his powerful vassals as well as from some cities; there were also mighty states like France and England outside of the pale of the empire.

The political and religious dissensions within the Moslem and the Christian worlds, as well as the conflict between the two in Palestine,

18. La Monte, pp. 335, 413.

19. In 1237 the two orders merged, the Teutonic Order taking control; see *Kievan Russia*, p. 235.

20. On the Albigensians and Cathari see La Monte, pp. 411, 413–416, 505; D. Obolensky, *The Bogomils* (Cambridge, Cambridge University Press, 1948), pp. 156, 157, 215, 216, 242–246, 286–289. These "heresies" represented a western extension of Manichaeism. For a recent study of Manichaeism see H. C. Puech, *Le Manichéisme, son fondateur, sa doctrine* (Paris, 1949).

weakened the potential of their resistance to any outside danger, such as was to come from Mongolia. In social organization there were many similarities between the feudalism of the West and the *ikta* (fief) regime of the Near and Middle East.[21] While the emperors and kings were supported by powerful aristocracy, from time to time they also had to check claims of their unruly vassals which seemed excessive to them. The peasants were oppressed either by their lords or by the tax collectors, depending on the nature of the regime in each case. The towns were in the ascendant; crafts and commerce thrived both in Europe and in the Middle East, from Khorezm to Italy.[22] As regards learning and technology, in spite of the so-called "12th-century renaissance" in Europe the Moslem East was probably still on a higher cultural level at that time than the West. All told, life in both Europe and the Near and Middle East was easy only for the few. The despotic caprices of the Oriental rulers affected even some of the few; and the rulers of the West could be tyrants too. A number of prosperous north Italian cities were destroyed by the emperors; and when the internal crusade started both actual and suspected "heretics" were killed indiscriminately; the task of saving the souls of the innocent was left to God.

The rapid spread of the "heresies," in both the West and the Near and Middle East, was in itself an indication of the dissatisfaction of the common man with his lot. It emphasized one more aspect of the internal weakness of both Christian and Moslem worlds.

So far, in order not to complicate the argument, I have abstained from any reference to Russia. The reader will find a picture of the political, economic, and cultural situation in Russia of the late 12th and early 13th centuries in the preceding volume of this series.[23] Suffice it to say here that, like Western Europe, Russia, in spite of political dissension among her princes, was making steady economic and cultural gains. Moreover, her free political institutions made her

21. On the *ikta* see M. Sobernheim, "Ikta," *EI, 2*, 461–463; Siyaset-nama, chaps. 5, 22, 23, and 27. Cf. M. Fuad Köprülü, "Le Féodalisme Turc-Musulman au Moyen-Age," *Belleten, 5* (1941), 335–350; A. N. Poliak, *Feudalism in Egypt, Syria, Palestine, and the Lebanon, 1250–1900* (London, The Royal Asiatic Society, 1939); Minorsky, *Tadhkirat,* pp. 27–28.

22. On Khorezmian crafts and industries see W. Barthold, *Istoriia kulturnoi zhizni Turkestana* (Leningrad, 1927), pp. 74–81; A. Iu. Iakubovsky, "Feodalnoe obshchestvo srednei Azii i ego torgovlia s vostochnoi Evropoi v x–xv vekakh," *Materialy po istorii Uzbekskoi, Tadzhikskoi i Turkmenskoi S.S.R.* (Leningrad, 1933), *1,* 4–9, 27–36; Tolstov, *Po sledam,* pp. 285–287.

23. *Kievan Russia,* chaps. 8–10.

position between the Oriental monarchies and the Western feudal states a unique one. Nevertheless, the internecine struggles of her princes and the rising danger of the crusade from the West seriously imperiled Russia's chances of stemming the flood about to engulf her from the east.

3. The Mongol Tribes in the Late 12th Century

Mongolia may be considered the easternmost section of the Eurasian steppe zone which stretches from Manchuria to Hungary. From time immemorial that steppe zone was the home of various nomad tribes of Iranian, Turkish, Mongol, and Manchu descent.

The nomad society was highly mobile and nomad policies highly dynamic. In their efforts to exploit the neighboring settled peoples and to control the overland commercial routes, the nomads combined from time to time into huge hordes capable of launching an offensive against far-away lands.[24] In most cases, however, the empires they built were not very solid and disintegrated as easily as they had been created. Thus periods of unity of the nomads and concentration of their power in one particular tribe or group of tribes alternated with periods of fractionation of power and lack of political unity. It will be recalled that the western section of the steppe zone, the Pontic steppes, was controlled first by the Iranians (the Scythians and Sarmatians) [25] and then by a succession of Turkish peoples (Huns, Avars, Khazars, Patzinaks, and Cumans).[26] It was also the Turks who, in earlier periods, controlled Mongolia itself: the Huns from ancient times to around the 2d century after Christ; the so-called Eastern Turks from the 6th to the 8th centuries; and the Uigurs in the late 8th and early 9th centuries. Presumably, Mongol elements intermingled with Turks in many of the latter's campaigns, and at times the Mongols succeeded in forming a comparatively strong

---

24. On the role of the nomads in history see W. Kotwicz, "O rolę ludow koczowniczych w historji," *Pamietnik IV Zjazdu historikow polskich w Poznaniu* (1925); A. J. Toynbee, *A Study of History* (Oxford, Oxford University Press, 1934; 2d ed. 1935; 3d impression, 1945), *3*, 393, 395, 399–402. 421, 431; G. Vernadsky, "The Eurasian Nomads and Their Art in the History of Civilization," *Saeculum, 1* (1950), pp. 74–85; *idem*, "Sarmat. Hintergrund," pp. 340–392.

25. M. I. Rostovtzeff, *Iranians and Greeks in South Russia* (Oxford, Clarendon Press, 1922); *Ancient Russia*, chaps. 2 and 3. For further references see G. Vernadsky, "Sarmat. Hintergrund," pp. 340–346.

26. See Moravcsik; F. Altheim, *Attila und die Hunnen* (Baden-Baden, 1951); *Ancient Russia*, chaps. 4–6; *Kievan Russia*, pp. 224–225.

state of their own (the Sien-pi in eastern Mongolia from the 1st to the 4th centuries; the Khitan in Mongolia, Manchuria, and North China in the 11th century); [27] but on the whole prior to Chingis-Khan the Mongols failed to play any leading role in steppe politics at large.

There was no centralized state in Mongolia in the 12th century. A number of tribes and combinations of clans lived in various sections of the country without any definite boundary lines between them. Most of them spoke the Mongol language, except in the western region where Turkish was used too. In their more remote ethnic background there was a strong admixture of Iranian blood in both Turks and Mongols. It is supposed that people belonging to the Caucasian race inhabited Central and Eastern Asia, including China, from time immemorial. To this race, according to G. Grum-Grzymailo, the name Dinling mentioned in Chinese chronicles must apply.[28] In spite of this somewhat vague background, it may be stated in more precise terms, that during the last centuries before the Christian era the north Iranians whose historical center was in the Khoresm region expanded both west and east of that center. Both linguistic and archeological data testify to this expansion. Pictures of horsemen engraved on the rocks along the Enisei River are strikingly similar to the representations of the Alanic horsemen in the wall paintings of the Crimea.[29] In an inscription of the early 8th century found in Mongolia, wars between the Turks and the As (Alans) [30] are mentioned.[31] Later we find the "Asud" (i.e. As) incorporated into the "right wing" of the Mongol nation, that is among the west Mongol tribes.[32]

Whatever the ethnic origin of the tribes populating Mongolia in the 12th century, they all were similar in their way of life and social organization and thus may be said to have belonged to the same

27. See McGovern; W. Barthold, *Turkestan;* Wittfogel, especially appendix 5 (Qara-Khitay); W. Eberhard, "Kultur und Siedlung der Randvölker Chinas," *TP, 36,* Suppl. (1942).

28. Grum-Grzymailo, *2,* 5–27; Menges, p. 3. P. A. Boodberg's study, "Ting-ling and Turks," *Sino-Altaica, 2,* No. 5 (Berkeley, Calif., 1934) has not been accessible to me.

29. See M. Rostovtzeff, "The Sarmatae and the Parthians," *CAH, 11,* 100; A. M. Tallgren, "Inner Asiatic and Siberian Rock Pictures," *ESA, 8* (1933), 174–210, especially p. 204. Cf. A. P. Okladnikov, "Kon' i znamia na lenskikh pisanitsakh," *Tiurkologicheskii sbornik* (Moscow and Leningrad, 1951), *1,* 143–154.

30. On the identity of the As and the Alans see *Ancient Russia,* pp. 105–106; H. W. Bailey, "Asica," *TPS* (1945), pp. 1–2.

31. See W. Kotwicz and A. Samoilovitch, "Le Monument turc d'Ikkekhuchotu en Mongolie centrale," *RO, 4* (1928), 15 (of the reprint); Bernshtam, p. 47.

32. Vladimirtsov, p. 131.

cultural sphere. There was no generic name at that time however to denote the totality of these tribes and clans. The name Mongol originally referred to only one small tribe. That tribe came to prominence early in the 12th century, but in the middle of the century was defeated by its neighbors, the Tatars, and all but disintegrated. The Tatars then became in their turn one of the leading tribes in Mongolia.[33] The Merkits, the Keraits, and the Naimans were the three other prominent tribes.[34] It will be recalled that in Western Europe the word Tatars, in the form of Tartars, was applied as a generic name to all the Mongol invaders. This form of the name was partly a play on the likeness of the original name to the classical Tartarus. As the chronicler Matthew Paris explains it: "That detestable race of Satan, the Tartars . . . rushed forth, like demons loosed from Tartarus (so that they are well called Tartars, as it were inhabitants of Tartarus)."[35] In Russian the name was kept in the original form (*Tatary*). A considerable part of the soldiers of the Mongol armies which invaded Russia were Turks under Mongol leadership, and therefore the name Tatars was eventually applied in Russia to some of the Turkish tribes which settled there after the Mongol invasion, like the Kazan Tatars and the Crimean Tatars. In modern times the Russian Orientalists coined the name Turko-Tatar to denote all the Turkish peoples. As for the name Mongol, it was saved from oblivion by a whim of history—the accident of the future emperor Chingis-Khan having belonged to one of the Mongol clans. With his rise to power all the tribes of Mongolia were united under his leadership, and a new "nation," known as the Mongols, was created. For the sake of simplicity we shall call all of these tribes Mongol even in speaking of the 12th century.

It should be noted that while the leading Mongol tribes lived in the steppe zone, other tribes or clans lived in the northern fringe of the steppes or even well within the forest zone, in the Baikal, upper Enisei, and Altai regions. The division of the original Mongol tribes into forest tribes and steppe tribes is very important for a better understanding of the early Mongol background.[36] The steppe tribes

33. It is P. Pelliot's opinion that the Tatars belonged to the Mongol group rather than to the Tungus; see Grousset, p. 25.

34. According to Pelliot, the Keraits and the Naimans represented a mixture of Turkish and Mongol elements; see Grousset, p. 28. On the anthropology and ethnology of the tribes of western Mongolia see Grum-Grzymailo, *3*, Pt. 1, and chap. 1 in Pt. 2.

35. Matthew Paris, *1*, 312.

36. See Vladimirtsov, pp. 33–36.

were mostly horse and cattle breeders, as might be expected; hunting was their second occupation. The men of the forest, on the other hand, were mainly hunters and fishermen; there also were skillful smiths among them. Economically, the two sections of the Mongol tribes supplemented each other. The steppe people were especially interested in the Siberian furs supplied by the inhabitants of the forest zone; they also needed the services of trained smiths to forge their weapons.

In religious belief the forest tribes were essentially shamanists; the steppe people, although influenced by shamanism, were primarily worshipers of the Sky; among both groups the cult of Fire was widely spread. Both groups had totem animals and taboos. Both used crudely carved figurines, some having human features, others representing animals. These were not "idols," as early European travelers used to call them, or "fetishes" in the common sense of the word, but rather religious or magic symbols of veneration; they are known as *ongon*.[37]

Among the forest tribes the shamans eventually acquired considerable political authority. In the steppe milieu a powerful lay aristocracy was rapidly developing, among whom both Buddhism and Nestorian Christianity [38] found a number of adepts in the course of 12th century. According to the chronicler Ab-ul-Faraj the whole tribe of Keraits was converted to Nestorianism as early as the 11th century.[39] The Nestorian faith reached Mongolia from the Near East via Turkestan. The Uigurs, a Turkish people who settled in eastern Turkestan (now known as Sin-kiang) in the middle of the 8th century and achieved a comparatively high level of culture, served as intermediaries between the Near East and Mongolia on this as on many other occasions.

Mongol society of the 12th century was based on patriarchal clans.[40] The Mongol clan (*obog*) consisted of agnates and was exo-

37. On the "ongon" see Rashid *1*, pp. 24, 198; Vladimirtsov, p. 50; D. K. Zelenin, *Kult ongonov v Sibiri* (Moscow and Leningrad, 1936). On the old religion of the Turks which was close to that of the Mongols see Schmidt. See also N. Veselovsky, "O religii tatar po russkim letopisiam," *ZMNP*, N.S., *64* (1916), 81–101; Poppe, "Opisanie."

38. On the spread of Nestorianism in Central and Eastern Asia see W. Barthold, *Zur Geschichte des Christentums in Mittel-Asien bis zur mongolischen Eroberung* (Tübingen and Leipzig, 1901); P. Y. Saeki, *The Nestorian Documents and Relics in China* (Tokyo, 1937); J. Dauvillier, *Le Droit chaldéen* (Paris, 1939; inaccessible to me).

39. Pelliot doubts the authenticity of Ab-ul-Faraj's story in this case; see Grousset, p. 29.

40. See Vladimirtsov, pp. 46–59.

gamic; marriage between its members was prohibited and thus brides were solicited or bought from other clans. As polygamy was a traditional institution among the Mongols, each of them needed several wives, which made the problem even more involved. All this often resulted in abducting future wives and consequently in many clashes between clans. To keep peace, some of the clans concluded mutual agreements about marrying their children on a basis of a regulated exchange. When, with the natural growth of families, a clan became too large to remain a unit, branches of it split off to form new clans. The new clans, however, recognized their descent from the common forefather; they were said to belong to the same "bone" (*yasun*).[41] Marriages between the children of all these clans were also forbidden. Each Mongol was taught, in early childhood, his genealogy and clan relationship, and this knowledge was sacred to him. The historian Rashid ad-Din compares the strength of clan ties among the Mongols to that among the Arabs.[42]

The unity of the clan was based not only on blood relationship but on religious feeling as well. Each clan, including both living members, dead ancestors, and future descendants, was a self-sufficient religious group, and in this sense was considered immortal. The clan's, and on a smaller scale the family's, spiritual life centered around the cult of the hearth. To be excluded from the right to take part in the clan's rites and worship meant to be expelled from the clan itself. The eldest son of the senior branch of the clan leaders was traditionally in charge of the clan cult. Those most venerated were given the title of *beki*. On the other hand, the youngest son in the family was considered the keeper of the hearth (*ochigin*) and inherited the basic share in his father's estate.[43] This duality of functions and rights seems to be an evidence of two different concepts in the system of religious and blood relationships of clans and families.

To pasture their herds and gain a measure of protection against sudden attack by other clans or tribes, several clans usually combined into a larger unit at the time of the seasonal migration. Such a unit camped together, its tents, which sometimes numbered over a thousand, being pitched in a huge circle known as *küriyen*.[44]

41. On the bone (*yasun*) see also W. Kotwicz, "Contributions à l'histoire de l'Asie centrale," *RO, 15* (1939–49), 161; cf. Cleaves, Inscription III, p. 75.

42. Rashid 1A, p. 8; cf. Vladimirtsov, p. 46.

43. See Vladimirtsov, pp. 49–51.

44. The Russian word *kuren'* (in Ukrainian, *kurin'*) is a borrowing of this Mongol term, although with a different connotation. In the Zaporozhie Cossack host the barrack

The wealthiest and strongest clans preferred, however, to graze their herds by themselves. The camp of such a group, consisting of a comparatively small number of tents, was an *ayil*. It must be noted that some of the wealthy clans were accompanied each by a vassal or serf clan (*unagan bogol*), serfdom in this case being the result of defeat in a tribal war. The ayil way of tending herds constituted the economic foundation of the wealth and power of the outstanding clans. On this basis an aristocratic society established itself among the Mongols, comparable to the feudal society of medieval Europe. The Mongol knight was known as *bagatur* (brave; compare the Russian *bogatyr'*) or *sechen* (wise). The head of a group of knights was called *noyan* (lord).

Below the knights were the commoners, who although free were now considered socially inferior (*kharachu*, literally "black").[45] On the lowest level were the serfs. Most of these in this period were not bound individually to the person of the lord but were members of a conquered clan, bound as a clan to serve the victor clan. With the formation of the class of knights a process of feudal integration started, the strongest noyan in the vicinity assuming the authority of a suzerain over other knights, his vassals. Intercourse with the Chinese helped to formulate the grades of vassal relationship, as some of the noyans looked to the emperor of China for investiture and received Chinese titles such as *taishi* (duke) and *wang* (king). In the 12th century China was divided into two empires: South China was ruled by a native dynasty, the Sung; in the north reigned the Manchu invaders, the Jurjen (in Chinese, Nuchen), who had established themselves in Peking in 1125. Theirs was known as the Golden Dynasty (Chin). Continuing the traditions of the earlier Chinese emperors, the Chin watched events in Mongolia closely with the aim of preventing the creation of a united state there. Chin agents tried to keep a balance of power between individual Mongol tribes. As soon as one tribe grew dangerously strong the Chin supplied arms to a neighboring tribe to fight the upstart, or tried to organize a coalition of tribes against it. This diplomacy toward the "northern barbarians" was based on the principle which guided Rome and Byzantium in regard to their northern neighbors: (*Divide et impera*). It

---

of a Cossack company was known as kurin'. In modern Russian kuren' means a hut (such as lumbermen or garden watchmen use).

45. Vladimirtsov, pp. 70, 118; for a similar term in Muscovite Russia (*chernye liudi*) see below, chap. 5, sec. 4, p. 375.

was with the assistance of the Chinese that the Tatars were able to defeat the Mongols in the middle of the 12th century. In 1161 a strong Chinese army was sent to Mongolia to support the Tatars. The Tatars, by treachery seized the Mongol khan Ambagai and sent him to the Chin capital, Peking (then known as Enkin). There he was executed by being nailed to a wooden donkey, which was considered a particularly humiliating method of disposing of a criminal. The Chin government now hoped that the Mongol danger was eliminated. As events proved, it was only temporarily held off.

4. THE RISE OF TEMUCHIN

The power of a steppe aristocrat depended on the support both of his retinue and clan and of other clans of the same "bone." His wealth consisted chiefly in his herds, as well as in the booty obtained during his forays on rival clans or tribes. After a successful raid his rival's herds were added to his own. An unsuccessful razzia leader lost prestige with his kinsmen and his retainers, some of whom might even leave him and go over to a stronger noyan. If his horses and cattle were decimated by epizootics or taken away by a successful rival, it might cost him his life. Should he survive, he and his kinsmen might become serfs of the conqueror. If he managed to escape serfdom, he faced poverty and had to subsist on what he could get by hunting or fishing. As by that time he was, more likely than not, abandoned by all his retainers and even most of his kinsmen, he had no men for a battue, could not bag big game, and had to content himself with catching marmots and field mice. This is precisely what happened in his youth to the future conqueror of the world. Only men of iron do not succumb to despair in such circumstances but continue scheming for eventual revenge, even with small chance of success. Temuchin proved to be such a man. He was supported in his perseverance by the traditions of his clan with which he was imbued in childhood, and by faith in his destiny.

By birth Temuchin belonged to the Borjigin clan of the Mongols.[46] He was a greatgrandson of the mighty Kabul-Khan who dared to attack not only the Tatars but the Chinese as well. After their defeat

46. The basic sources for Temuchin's biography are the following: the Secret History of the Mongols; the Chinese story of Chingis-Khan's campaigns; and Rashid ad-Din's Collection of Chronicles. For editions and translations of these works see Sources. For Chingis-Khan's biographies see Bibliography. See also the Mongol inscription of 1362, Cleaves, Inscription I, pp. 83–85.

by the Tatars, the power of the Mongol clans was considerably diminished. Temuchin's father Esugay-Bagatur was a petty chieftain in comparison with his grandfather, but in the smaller world in which he revolved he enjoyed the prestige of a brave warrior and champion of chivalrous society, a worthy representative of the traditions of his clan. As was customary among the Mongols, Esugay memorized the genealogy of his clan and later had his sons do so. In 1240 that genealogy was written down and incorporated into the official history of the Mongols, the so-called Secret History, a heroic poem rather than a learned treatise, although based in part on actual facts.

According to this genealogy, the Mongols descend from a pair of totem animals: the gray wolf (Borte Chino) and the doe (Qoa-Maral).[47] It must be noted in this connection that the wolf and deer (or doe) were among the totem animals of the Turks and north Iranians as well.[48] In addition to Qoa-Maral the Mongols venerated the memory of another ancestress, Alan-Qoa, wife of the knight Dobun-Mergan, a descendant of the original ancestral couple. The name Alan-Qoa deserves special attention. "Qoa" means "beautiful." "Alan" is, in all probability, an ethnic name—that of the mighty Iranian people, the Alans. As has been already mentioned, there were clans of Alanic origin among the Mongol tribes. It seems that, as in some other Mongol clans, there was an admixture of Alanic blood in the Borjigins. Significantly, the Mongol word for "glory" (*aldar*) is a borrowing from the Alanic.[49] In Ossetian [50] "aldar" means "chieftain," "prince." [51] Very likely the Alanic knights of old impressed the forefathers of the Mongols with their glorious deeds. Incidentally in Mingrelian *alani* (Alan) means a "hero," a "brave." [52] In sum the name Alan-Qoa may be translated as "the Alan Belle."

According to Mongol tradition, the last three sons of Alan-Qoa (one of whom was Chingis-Khan's forefather) were born long after her husband's death. A legend was created about it, and the conception of these three sons was ascribed to supernatural interven-

---

47. "Maral" (*Cervus maral*) is the Altaic deer which also inhabits western Mongolia. See Grum-Grzymailo, *1*, 517–518.

48. On the wolf and the deer as totem animals among the north Iranians (Alans) see Abaev, p. 49.

49. *Idem*, p. 85.

50. The Ossetian language is considered to be derived from the Alanic.

51. Abaev, p. 85.

52. *Idem*, p. 45.

tion.[53] This legend was incorporated in the Mongol genealogy and a variant of it was included by the Persian historian Rashid ad-Din in his *History of the Mongols*. With praiseworthy caution Rashid put the responsibility for the authenticity of the story on his source— the Mongol tradition in this case.[54] According to both the Secret History and Rashid ad-Din, Alan-Qoa herself explained to her relations and later to her sons, the miracle which had occurred. "Every night in my dream I used to see somebody with blond hair and blue eyes enter noiselessly, come close to me, and then go away.[55] When they grow up . . . these children I have born will be emperors and khans of your people and of other peoples." [56] The Secret History mentions the beam of light emanating from Alan-Qoa's mysterious visitor.[57]

What is the origin of the story? The late Ernst Herzfeld suggested that the Mongol legend is but a variant of the story of the supernatural birth of Alexander the Great.[58] Herzfeld points out that the Alexander legend was widely spread in the Islamic world; he even considers the name Alan-Qoa (which he spells Alongoa) a corruption of Olympias (the name of Alexander's mother) and attempts to explain how the corruption could have occurred through the Arabic way of spelling Olympias. While Herzfeld's theory seems ingenious and tempting, his argument is not convincing and is partly based on sheer misunderstanding. That the Alexander legend was popular in the Islamic world, including Persia, is true, but there is no trace of it in early Mongol literature. To attribute any role to Arabic texts and Arabic spelling in transmission of a name from the Near East to the Mongols is to disregard the fact of the illiteracy of the Mongols prior to Chingis-Khan as well as the whole background of Mongol folklore. As a matter of fact, Herzfeld seems not to have been sufficiently familiar with the original Mongol genealogy. His whole argument refers to the inscription on Timur's tomb of the early 15th century.[59]

---

53. It is not clear from the context of the legend whether the three sons of Alan-Qoa were triplets or born at intervals.

54. Rashid 1A pp. 7, 9.

55. It should be noted that, according to Ammianus Marcellinus, the hair of the Alans "inclines to be blond"; see *Ancient Russia*, p. 90. Some of the Ossetians, their descendants, are also blond; see V. Miller, "Osetiny," *ES, 43,* 263.

56. Rashid, 1A, p. 10.

57. Kozin, p. 81.

58. E. Herzfeld, "Alongoa," *Der Islam, 6* (1916), 317–327; cf. E. Blochet, "Les Inscriptions de Samarkand," *RA* 3d ser., *30* (1897), 67–77. Arnold J. Toynbee, *A Study of History, 6,* 268 and n. 4, accepts Herzfeld's theory.

59. On Timur (Tamerlane) see below, Chapter 4, sec. 2, pp. 247–248.

This inscription contains a genealogy of Timur and, since Timur considered himself a descendant of Alan-Qoa her story is told. Timur was a Moslem, and consequently in the inscription the legend assumed an Islamic appearance, with quotations from the Koran. The two verses of the Koran given in connection with Alan-Qoa (19.17 and 19.20) actually deal with the Virgin Mary.[60] Here we seem to have the key to the true origin of the Alan-Qoa legend. In view of the considerable spread of Nestorian Christianity among some of the Mongol tribes it seems quite probable that the story of the Virgin Mary was adapted to Mongol notions and eventually incorporated into the Secret History.

We are now faced with another problem: at what time was the legend of the supernatural birth of Alan-Qoa's last three sons incorporated into the Mongol genealogy? Was it only after Temuchin became emperor, or before it? The question has bearing on Temuchin's spirit and mentality. If we consider that the legend had been part of Mongol tradition before his birth, then we must recognize its full impact on the mind of the boy Temuchin. In this case the legend must have constituted part of the foundation of Temuchin's belief in his great destiny. While the question cannot be answered categorically, the mere fact that not only the son of Alan-Qoa from whom Chingis-Khan descended but two others of her sons as well were said to be born in a supernatural way is an indication that the legend was created long before Temuchin became emperor and probably long before his birth.[61] The legend obviously was intended to glorify not only the Borjigin clan (which was Temuchin's clan) but the whole group to which it and the clans associated with it belonged.

As we have seen, Esugay-Bagatur enjoyed great popularity in steppe society; he must have been admired by the women as well as by the men of his clan. However, when he decided to marry he had to reckon with clan customs which prevented his marrying within his "bone." Esugay thus had the problem of getting a bride outside, which he solved by kidnaping a beautiful girl of the Olqonout tribe who was being carried by a Merkit to his home as his fiancée.[62] Her

60. In this form the story of Alan-Qoa is repeated by the biographer of Timur, Sharaf ad-Din Ali Yazdi in his *Zafar-nama;* see Blochet (as in n. 58), pp. 202–221.

61. According to *Yüan-shi* only one of Alan-Qoa's sons was born in a supernatural way. See Krause, *Cingis Han,* p. 8; Iakinf, p. 2.

62. The Olqonouts were a branch of the Ungirats who lived in the eastern part of Mongolia. For interesting comment on this episode see L. Olschki, "Ölün's Chemise," *JAOS, 67* (1947), 54–56.

name was Oelun (Ölün). A protracted feud between the Merkits and the Borjigins was a result of this episode.

Temuchin was Oelun's and Esugay's first child. There is some uncertainty about the date of his birth. According to Rashid ad-Din's computation, Temuchin was born in the month of Zulkada, 549 A.H., which corresponds to the period between January 7 and February 5, 1155 A.D.[63] On the other hand, in the extant copies of the Chinese history of the Yuan (Mongol) dynasty it is stated that Chingis-Khan died at the age of sixty-six.[64] Now the year of his death is firmly established as 1227, from which it was computed that Temuchin was born in 1162.[65] As a matter of fact, 1162 is impossible as it cannot be correlated with the cycles of years in the Mongol chronology. Each such cycle consisted of twelve years; each year was known under the name of an animal.[66] According to Rashid ad-Din, Chingis-Khan was born in the Year of the Pig.[67] A.D. 1155 happened to be such a year, but 1162 was the Year of the Horse.

How could a mistake be made in the official history of the Yuan dynasty, even if it was compiled after that dynasty's downfall? Presumably the mistake occurred not in the original history but in later copies. Incidentally in the copy of the "Description of Chingis-Khan's Campaigns" used by Archimandrite Palladi for his translation of this work, it is stated that Chingis-Khan died at the age of sixty-five. However, Palladi notes that the figure, in the original, was "sixty"; "five" was added by the 19th-century Chinese scholar Ho Ch'iu-t'ao (from whom Palladi obtained the copy) in order to correlate Chingis' age at the time of his death with that at the time of his campaign against the Naimans indicated in the earlier part of the "Description." [68] It is significant that according to Tibetan tradition Chingis-Khan died at the age of sixty-one.[69] Moreover, the late Paul

63. Rashid 1A, p. 88; Grousset, p. 51.

64. Krause, *Cingis Han,* p. 41; Iakinf, p. 137.

65. Krause, *Cingis Han,* p. 41. It should be noted that according to the Chinese custom a child is considered one year old on the day of his birth; see Grousset, p. 51.

66. On the Mongol chronology see W. Kotwicz, "O chronologji mongolskiej," *RO, 2* (1925), 220–250; *4* (1926), 108–166. The Mongols eventually adopted the Tibetan sexagenary cycle, on which see A. Pozdneev, *Mongolskaia letopis' Erdeniin-erikhe* (St. Petersburg, 1833); P. Pelliot, "Le Cycle sexagénaire dans la chronologie tibetaine," *JA* (May–June 1913), pp. 633–667; Baron A. von Stael-Holstein, "On the Sexagenary Cycle of the Tibetans," *MS, 1* (1935), 277–314. Cf. George N. Roerich's introduction to *Blue Annals,* p. xxi.

67. Rashid 1A, pp. 88–89; cf. Khara-Davan, p. 17.

68. Palladi, *Kitaiskoe skazanie,* p. 195 and n. 5.

69. *Blue Annals,* p. 58.

Pelliot has recently found similar evidence in Chinese documents.[70] If we consider Chingis-Khan to have been sixty at the time of his death, in 1227, we have to take 1167 as the date of his birth. This year is again the Year of the Pig and is as admissible as 1155.

If 1167 is accepted as the date of Temuchin's birth, it means that in 1219—at the beginning of his Turkestan campaign—Chingis-Khan was fifty-two and not sixty-four as has been usually believed until recently. Chingis' strenuous activities in that campaign, which lasted for several years and was full of hardships, would certainly fit a man in his fifties better than an older man. Moreover, a birth date of 1155 would leave a hiatus in Chingis-Khan's life from the time of his marriage almost to 1200, which could not be filled in from the narrative of the Secret History.

When Temuchin was nine years old Esugay decided to arrange his engagement by negotiations rather than let his son, in due time, abduct a girl as he himself had done. For this purpose father and son started on a trip to Oelun's relatives, of the Olqonout tribe. On their way they met Dai-Sechen, a knight of the Ungirat tribe, of which the Olqonouts were a branch. He happened to have a daughter, Borte by name, a child already considered a beauty. The fathers liked each other and their respective children and a deal was promptly concluded. The boy Temuchin, as Dai-Sechen's prospective son-in-law, was to stay at his camp, according to an old Mongol custom.[71]

Pleased with these arrangements, Esugay-Bagatur set out for home alone. On the way he was invited by a group of Tatars on a spree to attend their banquet. To refuse would be contrary to steppe etiquette, and Esugay gallantly joined the carousal, in spite of the traditional feud between his clan and the Tatars. Continuing homeward afterward he felt ill and realized that the treacherous Tatars had mixed poison with his drinks. He died a few days after his return (around 1177, if Temuchin was born in 1167).

Following the instructions which Esugay gave before his death, Munlik, whom he appointed guardian of his family, summoned Temuchin home. The boy's mother Oelun proved a brave woman and tried to keep the clan together under her rule, but the task was all but impossible since her husband's relatives were not ready to accept her leadership. Within a short time all of Esugay's kinsmen and retainers, including those of the Taichiut clan, left Oelun's camp,

70. See Grousset, p. 51; Cleaves, Inscription I, p. 99.
71. Vladimirtsov, p. 48.

driving away most of her cattle. Even Munlik forsook her. Oelun was left helpless with five children (three sons besides the eldest, Temuchin, and one daughter), her husband's other wife with her children, and a few maids. Years of hardship and privation started for Esugay's family; but Oelun's spirit did not break. She took great pains to instruct Temuchin in the glorious past of his clan. The boy listened avidly and memorized all the old lays. The family's misfortunes were not over, however. Their camp was attacked by the Taichiuts, their former associates. Temuchin was taken prisoner but succeeded in escaping, with the help, he was sure, of heavenly forces.

Several years passed and the boy was rapidly becoming a vigorous young warrior. When some strangers stole eight of the family's nine horses, Temuchin rode after them on the only horse left and with the help of another youth he met on his way succeeded in getting back the animals. His new friend decided to join Temuchin's household as his companion in arms. His name was Bogurchi; later he became one of the outstanding commanders of Chingis-Khan's armies. This first success, insignificant as it may seem, gave Temuchin the much-needed feeling of self-reliance and he now decided to marry his fiancée. He probably was eighteen at the time. Dai-Sechen kept the word he had given to Temuchin's father and the marriage took place at his camp. Temuchin then took Borte to his tent. Her dowry included a precious sable fur coat, an unheard-of luxury in Temuchin's impoverished household.[72] This coat became the foundation of Te-muchin's political career. Taking it with him, he appeared at the court of Togrul-Khan, ruler of the mighty tribe of the Keraits. In Esugay's best days he and Togrul had become sworn brothers (*anda*). Temuchin now went to offer his greetings—and the fur coat—to his uncle-by-oath whom he addressed as "father." Togrul graciously promised the youth his protection (around 1185).

By placing himself under the protection of one of the mightiest Mongol rulers and thus becoming his vassal, Temuchin obtained a definite status in feudal society. In any case he was not as helpless as before—or so he thought. There is little security in the life of a knight of the steppes. Soon after Temuchin's visit to Togrul, his camp was raided by the Merkits in what may be called delayed revenge

---

72. Sable furs had a great value, especially in China. According to Marco Polo "a robe of sable, large enough to line a mantle, is worth 2,000 bezants of gold, or 1,000 at least, and this kind of skin is called by the Tatars 'the King of Furs.' " MPYC, *1*, 405; MPMP, *1*, 232.

for the kidnaping of the fiancée of a Merkit knight by Esugay about twenty years before. Because of the multitude of the attackers Temuchin made no attempt to defend his camp and galloped, with a few companions, leaving his wife behind, to nearby Burkan Mountain which belonged to the Borjigin clan and was considered sacred. Meanwhile Borte was seized by the Merkits. After receiving word that the attackers had gone home, Temuchin thanked the mountain for saving his life, taking off his belt and his cap in token of obedience to Heaven, and after prayers and nine genuflections poured out a libation of kumiss. Following that, he went to Togrul-Khan to ask help in getting back his wife. At the Khan's court he met a childhood friend, Jamuga, now an outstanding knight, Jamuga-Sechen. They became sworn brothers, and Jamuga and Togrul agreed to punish the Merkits. The attack was successful, the Merkits dispersed, and Borte rejoined her husband. During her captivity she had been forced to become a concubine of one of her captors. This did not alienate Temuchin's affection for her, especially since he must have realized that he was himself to blame for her misfortunes. However, when she gave birth to her first child, a boy whom they called Juchi, Temuchin could not be certain that the child was his and never cared much for him.

In the campaign against the Merkits Temuchin displayed much valor and made many new friends. In fact, this was the turning point of his career. Impressed by Temuchin's good relations with Togrul-Khan and his friendship with Jamuga, many of his kinsmen who had departed after Esugay's death now were ready to recognize Temuchin's leadership. Before long Temuchin was as strong and popular a leader as his father had been. As vassal of Togrul-Khan, Temuchin now embarked on haute politique and intertribal wars, in which he proved to be not only an outstanding military leader but a first-rate diplomat as well. Because of the active part that the agents of the Chin empire took in Mongol affairs, Temuchin came in contact with the Chinese and learned much of their ways in diplomacy, a fact which was to help him considerably in his future dealings with China.

The basic pattern of steppe politics was simple enough. If one tribe became unduly strong, other tribes joined against it. Variety was added by the number of clan relationships, the unity or disunity of clans within the same tribe, and the friendship or rivalry of the leaders. The ties of vassalage and loyalty to one's suzerain or sworn brother lasted only so long as they seemed politically useful to both sides and as the friendship was not marred by offense. In this mobile feudal society of the steppe each vassal, by custom, was free to defy his suzerain and to offer his services to another. Hence even if a tribal leader succeeded in building up a large khanate, his power was never firm and his state could be dissolved as rapidly as it had been established. The game could go on ceaselessly, and did—until Chingis-Khan changed the rules.

Temuchin's first move was to associate himself closely with Jamuga. They joined forces and camped together for about a year and a half. Then their relations became strained and they finally decided to part company. According to the Secret History it was Borte who advised Temuchin to separate their camp from Jamuga's. W. Barthold has attempted to interpret the break between the two leaders as a result of a basic difference in their social philosophies. He represented Temuchin as a champion of aristocracy and Jamuga as the champion of the common man. B. Vladimirtsov at first accepted this interpretation but later rejected it, rightly in my opinion.[73] There is actually no evidence of any "democratic" program in Jamuga's policies. The conflict between him and Temuchin was a clash between two aristocratic leaders vying for power. Presumably Jamuga, who had been a well-known knight at the time Temuchin appeared at Togrul-Khan's court, considered himself the natural leader in their alliance. Obviously, Temuchin could not long accept friendship on these terms.

The news of the break between the two leaders caused much excitement among the kinsmen and vassals of each. It immediately became clear that a good many of them were more impressed by the personality of Temuchin than by that of his rival. A number of influential clan leaders decided to follow Temuchin rather than Jamuga. Among them were one of Temuchin's uncles and several other chieftains of clans related to the Borjigins. One of them, Korchi, of the Baarin clan, declared that he had had a dream in which the Great Spirit revealed to him the high destiny of Temuchin. Accordingly, the assembly of clan leaders at Temuchin's court proclaimed him their khan, pledged their allegiance, and promised him the best share of booty in all their future undertakings. After this, says the Secret History, they gave their new khan a new name:

73. Vladimirtsov, pp. 83–86.

Chingis.[74] This seems a mere anticipation of later events, and, in my opinion, must be an addition made by the compiler of the Secret History to the original epic poem.

Temuchin's suzerain, Togrul-Khan, was duly informed of the decision of the Mongol clan leaders. Togrul seems to have been pleased by the honor given to his vassal and confirmed the election. Soon after that, backed by Chin diplomacy, Togrul and Temuchin undertook a campaign against the Tatars, Temuchin naturally welcoming the opportunity to avenge the death of his father. The Tatars were defeated and, in appreciation of the victory, the Chin government granted Togrul the title "wang" (king) and Temuchin that of *jaukhuri* (regional commissioner of the borderlands). From that time on Togrul-Khan was known as Wang-Khan. As for Temuchin, the title granted him was too modest to boast about.

Meanwhile Jamuga succeeded in gathering an impressive array of vassals and kinsmen and presented his claims to tribal leadership, being proclaimed Gur-Khan [75] by his followers. Wang-Khan and Temuchin-Khan decided to deal with this challenge at once and led their warriors against Jamuga. The latter's forces proved inadequate and he had to retreat quickly. Conscious now of his strength, Temuchin-Khan decided to act on his own. First he punished the Taichiuts for their former treachery. Then he turned against the remnants of the Tatars, whom he finally subjugated. Two Tatar beauties, Esuy and Esugen, became his wives. These successes immensely increased Temuchin's prestige. Wang-Khan now became suspicious of his sworn son's intentions. Nevertheless he asked him to join in the campaign he was preparing against the westernmost Mongol tribe, the Naimans, whose power was then in the ascendant; and Temuchin responded. When the campaign had started Wang-Khan changed his plans and turned back without informing his ally. Temuchin barely escaped the trap. In compensation he asked the hand of Wang-Khan's daughter. Wang-Khan refused, and the two rulers broke diplomatic relations.

In the ensuing war Temuchin depended chiefly on cunning. Wang-Khan, caught unawares when Temuchin appeared with his warriors at the Kerait camp, fled to the Naimans and was slain by them. The Keraits pledged their allegiance to Temuchin. The latter now began

74. Kozin, p. 109.
75. On the title Gurkhan see Wittfogel, p. 431.

preparations for a campaign against the Naimans, whose khan had offended him by giving refuge to Jamuga. At this juncture he started his important reforms in army organization. To forestall all possibility of future enemies catching him unawares as he had caught Wang-Khan, Temuchin created a special unit to guard his camp day and night. It consisted of 80 night guardsmen and 70 day guards. In addition a regiment of 1,000 knights (bagaturs) was organized under the command of the chieftain of the Jalair clan, one of the clans that had joined Temuchin immediately after his break with Jamuga.[76] The whole army was divided into units of thousands, hundreds, and tens.

The reorganization of his headquarters and army completed, Temuchin was ready to fight the Naimans. These were not only one of the strongest tribes of the Mongol group but one of the most civilized as well. Neighbors of the Uigurs, they used the Uigur alphabet, which was based on the Sogdian alphabet derived, in its turn, from the Syriac.[77] The Naiman khan had even a secretary and a seal of state.

Before ordering his warriors to march against the Naimans, Temuchin displayed his clan banner and had it sanctified by libations. The Naimans were defeated in 1204; their khan perished in the battle and only his son, Kuchluk, succeeded in escaping with his retinue. He fled first to the Altai region, but not feeling safe there later went to the country of the Kara-Khitans. These were a branch of those Khitans who, after the overthrow of the Khitan (Liao) Empire in North China by the Jurjen (Chin) in 1125, had gone westward and succeeded in carving out a kingdom in Transoxania [78] and the Khotan region of Chinese Turkestan (Sinkiang).[79] Meanwhile the Naimans, left without a ruler, submitted to Temuchin's leadership.

Temuchin next attacked his old enemies the Merkits and crushed them. A Merkit beauty, Kulan, became his fourth wife. Soon afterward Temuchin's rival Jamuga, who had succeeded in escaping from captivity at the time of the Naiman defeat, was seized by his own retainers and brought to Temuchin. The latter sentenced him to death, but in view of their old friendship allowed him to die "without shedding his blood." According to Mongol belief, a man's soul was in his

76. Kozin, p. 144.

77. On the Uigur script see Barthold, *Turkestan*, pp. 387–391; G. Vernadsky, "Uigurs," p. 454; Wittfogel, pp. 243, 443, 670.

78. After the Arab conquest of Turkestan, Transoxania became known as Maverannahr ("region beyond the river"), the Arabic equivalent of the name.

79. On the Kara-Khitan see Wittfogel, pp. 619–674.

blood; to kill him without letting blood was considered a favor to his soul. This favor was usually granted to members of royalty found guilty of treason, and in exceptional cases to other high state criminals. By express order of Temuchin, Jamuga's bones were deposited into a special casket with due honor.

Temuchin's self-appointed task of "gathering all of Mongolia" was now successfully completed. His generals and the leaders of the clans supporting him felt that their newly united nation and experienced army were ready for further conquest. A solemn assembly of the nation was therefore convoked to discuss the next objectives of Mongol policy and to complete the reorganization of the state. That fateful kuriltay met in eastern Mongolia near the sources of the Onon River, in the Year of the Tiger (1206).

5. The Founding of the Mongol Empire

All tribes of Mongolia—"the peoples living in the felt tents," as the Secret History puts it—were invited to attend the Great Kuriltay.[80] The diet was not, however, a "democratic" assembly; [81] "the people" were represented in it by their clan leaders. Temuchin's brothers and cousins, as well as his trusted generals, were also outstanding members. A white banner with nine tails was raised on the grounds of the gathering as the Mongol national standard.[82] Formerly a symbol or ongon of Temuchin, the clan leader, the banner now became the ongon of Temuchin, ruler of the Mongol nation. It was believed to be the visible abode of the invisible genius of his clan, now protecting the whole nation.

The first act, and main purpose, of the assembly was to proclaim Temuchin-Khan emperor (*kagan* or *kaan*) [83] and to give him the new name Chingis. There is no consensus of opinion among scholars con-

80. Secret History, sec. 202. I have followed Haenisch' translation in this case.

81. It is L. Krader's opinion that the kuriltay of 1206 was a democratic assembly; see his review of Haenisch' translation of the Secret History, *JAOS*, 70 (1950), 205.

82. On the Mongol banner see Khara-Davan, p. 46; A. P. Okladnikov, "Kon' i znamia" (as in n. 29), pp. 148–153. It was believed that Chingis-Khan's banner was the abode of his spirit (*sulde*). See Vladimirtsov, p. 145; Okladnikov, p. 151; cf. Poppe, "Opisanie," pp. 171–172.

83. On the use of the title kagan (Qakhan) among the Jou-Jan from around A.D. 50 see Gimpu Uchida, "A Study of the Jou-Jan Tribe," *ASTH*, pp. 4–5 (English summary). It should be mentioned that in Pelliot's opinion Chingis received the title of "khan" and not "kagan"; see Cleaves, Inscription I, pp. 98–99. However, the fact is that in sec. 123 of the Secret History Chingis is called kagan (Qaqan, see Kozin, p. 230); Haenisch, p. 33, translates the term into German as "chan"; for his explanation of it see Haenisch, p. 153.

cerning the origin of the name. Its derivation from the Turkish word *dengiz* (in modern Turkish *deniz*), "sea," has been suggested by Pelliot, but there seems to be hardly any reason for calling Temuchin a "sea ruler" [84] unless we take the term "sea" in the abstract sense ("limitless as the sea"). Erich Haenisch tentatively derives the name "Chingis" from the Chinese word *ch'eng* (faithful, upright, true). Chingis-Khan would then mean "the most righteous ruler." [85] Rashid ad-Din interprets "Chingis-Kagan" as the "Great Sovereign." [86] E. Khara-Davan points out that in the language of the western Mongols (Oirats or Kalmyks), "Chingis" means "strong," "robust." [87] In Khara-Davan's opinion, in Old Mongol and as applied to Temuchin "Chingis" must have comprehended the entire corporal and spiritual energy and strength of the ruler. It must be noted that according to W. Kotwicz the word Chingis does not occur in the modern language of the eastern Mongols.[88] Khara-Davan suggests that the word might have existed among the eastern Mongols in the age of Chingis-Khan but become tabu after his death.[89]

Whatever the connotations of "Chingis," the symbolic meaning of its being bestowed on Temuchin is clear. Formerly a clan leader, then the khan of the Mongols, Temuchin was now proclaimed the All-powerful Emperor. In its immediate implications, the event was first of all a challenge to the neighboring empire of the Chin. No attack on that empire could be undertaken by the Mongols without first securing the firm control over various Turkish and Tangut tribes in the borderlands between Mongolia and China as well as over those in the rear of Mongolia, in the Siberian forests. Consequently these tribes were the first to feel the impact of the mighty Mongol drive.

Obviously the main task facing the new emperor was to strengthen his army and administration; this was the mandate he received by the fact of his election. Once elected, he was given full discretion; and the kuriltay, which had started as a constituent assembly, now became a body of imperial advisers to help the ruler carry out the necessary reforms.[90] The decimal system of army organization by units of tens,

84. See Cleaves, Inscription I, p. 98; Khara-Davan, pp. 33–35; O. Turan, "Cingiz adi hakkinda," *Belleten*, 5 (1941), 267–276.
85. Haenisch, p. 153.
86. Rashid 1A, p. 65.
87. Khara-Davan, p. 32.
88. *Idem*, p. 34.
89. *Idem*, pp. 33–34.
90. The summary of the reforms and enactments of 1206 which follows is based on the Secret History, secs. 202–234.

hundreds, and thousands was now brought to perfection, and a still larger unit, the ten thousand (in Mongol, *tümen;* in Russian, *t'ma*), was created. When the units of thousands were constituted, there were found to be enough warriors to form 95 one-thousand battalions, "not counting the peoples of the forest" (who were as yet not completely subjugated).[91]

The emperor personally appointed all of the 95 noyans, the new commanders of the thousand units. Among them was Bogurchi, who as a youth had helped Temuchin get back his stolen horses; [92] Jebe, the former vassal of the Taichiuts and one-time opponent of Te-muchin; Mukali, one of those who had strengthened Temuchin's belief in his destiny at the time he was hard pressed by foes; and Subudey who was later to command the Western drive of the Mongols. Besides receiving the title of commander of the thousand, Bogurchi and Mukali were each commissioned to lead one of the newly formed ten-thousand units.

By Chingis-Khan's next order the modest palace guards unit he had instituted before his campaign against the Naimans was enlarged and reorganized to form the nucleus of the Imperial Guards (*Keshik*), ten thousand strong. The Thousand Bagaturs became one of the guards battalions. The best officers and soldiers from each army unit were selected for service in the guards. Sons of commanders of the one-hundred and one-thousand units were included automatically in the guards; others were accepted on a competitive basis. This method of composition of the guards guaranteed the loyalty and fitness of the guardsmen and had other advantages besides. Each army unit was represented in the guards, and since the units of tens, and hundreds, and thousands more or less dovetailed with the clans and groups of clans, each clan was represented in the guards. Through his loyal guardsmen and their relations in the army units, Chingis-Khan was now able to reinforce his authority over the whole Mongol people. The guards became the cornerstone of the whole army organization and administrative system of Chingis-Khan's empire. As a unit they were given many privileges. According to Chingis-Khan's ruling, a private of the guards was considered of higher rank. than any commander of the army units, including that of the thousand. Therefore any guardsman was qualified, if need arose, to

91. Following Liddel Hart's terminology, I shall call the one-hundred units squad-rons, the one-thousand units battalions, and the ten-thousand units divisions.

92. See above, sec. 4, p. 22.

command any army unit. The guards thus became something like a military academy, whose graduates received the highest commissions in the army whenever necessary.

The guards were on permanent duty even in peacetime. In time of war they formed the central division under the personal command of the emperor. Being on permanent duty they could not be expected to provide for themselves and therefore received room and board in the emperor's camp. Special palace officials (*cherbi*) were appointed to provision both the imperial family and the guards. Somewhat later the members of the imperial family were generously provided with apanages.[93] In contrast to feudal Europe, the grants consisted not in landed domains but in allotments of groups of people with their respective herds. Thus, the queen mother, Oelun, together with the ochigin, that is, Esugay's youngest brother, received 10,000 yurts (tents, and hence households or families).[94] The quotas granted to Chingis' four sons were assigned according to seniority: the eldest, Juchi, received 9,000 yurts; Jagatay (Chagatay, Chaaday) was given 8,000; Ugedey (Ogatay) and Tuluy, 5,000 each. Of Chingis' brothers, Khazar obtained 4,000 yurts; Bilgutay 1,500. A nephew, Alchiday, was given 2,000. The apanages were subject to the emperor's control, and accordingly Chingis appointed several noyans to advise each of the grantees. Thus the imperial family as an institution became part of the imperial system. The camp (*ordu*, horde) of each member of the royal house became a unit of power subordinated to the great khan.[95]

It was presumably also at this time that Chingis-Khan laid the foundations of the messenger and post-horse service (*yam*) which later was developed into one of the most useful institutions of the Mongol Empire. Another important reform was the creation of the Supreme Court, headed by Chingis' adopted brother, Shigi-Khutukhu, who proved a conscientious and competent judge.

Taken together, all these reforms and enactments constituted the basis of the new Mongol imperial law, the Great Yasa of Chingis-Khan.[96]

93. Secret History, secs. 242–243.

94. In the Secret History, sec. 242, the term *irke* is used. Kozin, p. 566, equates it to *örkö*, "family," and translates it as "yurt" (in this connotation "tent," "family"). Haenisch, and following him Ahmet Temir, the Turkish translator of the Secret History, renders the term *irke* as "men" ("*Leute*," *adamlar*).

95. On the horde (*ordu, ordo*) as an institution see Wittfogel, pp. 508–517.

96. On the Great Yasa see below, Chapter 2, sec. 6, pp. 99–110.

While Chingis had no intention of letting the shamans interfere with state affairs, he deemed it useful to emphasize his loyalty to the traditional clan cult, and appointed old Usun of the Baarin clan—a senior branch of the descendants of Alan-Qoa—chief beki.[97] Usun was given a white fur coat and a white horse. His function was "to appoint and illuminate the years and the months." Presumably he was in charge of the Mongol calendar. He also became what may be called the national augur.

At the time of Chingis-Khan's election to the imperial throne the Mongol nation was illiterate. Obviously, the new empire could not function properly without records and without a chancery. When the Naimans were defeated, their khan's secretary had been seized by the Mongols. He was brought before Temuchin who ordered his captive to explain to him the mysteries of writing and the meaning of the state seal. With his usual quick grasp of new devices and new situations, Temuchin at once realized the potential importance of literacy. He therefore ordered the captive to teach writing to a select group of his associates. The justice, Shigi-Khutukhu, was among the first Mongols to master the Uigur script used by the Naiman secretary.

The task of completing the conquest of the forest peoples was entrusted to Chingis' elder son, Juchi. Most of these peoples, including the Oirats west of Lake Baikal and the Kirghiz in the basin of the upper Enisei River, submitted to the Mongol emperor without much opposition in 1207, and in token of submission sent precious gifts—white falcons, white sables, and white horses. Since in addition to falcons and furs the Enisei region also produced grain, it represented an important economic asset for the empire. The task of training selected Mongol youth in the art of writing was greatly facilitated by the recognition of Chingis-Khan's suzerainty on the part of the idikut of the Uigurs at that time.[98] The close contact between the Mongols and the much more civilized Uigurs proved beneficial to the former in many respects. Eventually a learned Uigur became Chingis-Khan's secretary.

While the clan leaders of the forest peoples became Chingis' loyal

97. On the role of the beki in sanctioning the kagan's power see Hirosato Iwai, "Chingis Qakhan's Enthronement and the Shamans," *ASTH*, pp. 3–4 (English summary).

98. The meaning of the title of the ruler of the Uigurs, idikut (*idiqut*), is "Holy Fortune" (*iduq qut*); see Thomsen, pp. 129–130. In the Mongol inscription of 1362 the idikut is praised for "following the Will of Heaven" in submitting himself to Chingis-Khan; see Cleaves, Inscription I, p. 84.

vassals, the shamans seem to have resented the strengthening of the imperial power. The most influential shaman among the Mongols was Kokochu, elder son of the old Munlik whom Esugay just before his death had appointed guardian of his family [99] but who had deserted it in time of stress. Kokochu was known among his followers as "the Heavenly" (Teb Tengri). He tried to sow strife in the imperial family by making Chingis suspicious of the intentions of some of his brothers. For a time he succeeded, and it is even said in the Secret History that the death of Chingis' mother Oelun was hastened by chagrin over the dissension among her sons. Kokochu also seems to have attempted to play on the dissatisfaction of the commoners and serfs—both among the Mongols and among the forest peoples—with the aristocratic privileges of the clan leaders. According to the Secret History even some of Chingis-Khan's grooms and serfs were ready to go over to the shaman's side. This Chingis could not tolerate. Consequently, he made peace with his brothers and let them deal with Kokochu as they pleased. They killed the shaman "without shedding his blood," that is, by breaking his spine.[100]

6. Mongol Expansion during the Reign of Chingis-Khan

With the reorganization of the Mongol army and administration completed, and the empire reinforced with the Uigurs and forest peoples, Chingis-Khan was ready to attack the kingdom of the Tanguts, in the Ordos region and Kansu, a people of Tibetan origin. When he reached their capital they agreed to pay tribute to the Mongols; but Chingis-Khan did not insist on their complete subjection. The main objective of his raid was to weaken them and thus eliminate the danger of their attacking at the time of his projected Chinese campaign.

Careful preparations were made for that campaign, from the diplomatic as well as the military point of view. A number of spies were sent to study general conditions in the Chin empire. Uigur merchants trading with China were also instructed to collect necessary information. The basic weakness of the Chin consisted in the fact that they controlled only part of China. Moreover, the rival empire in the south—that of the Sung—was under the rule of a

99. See above, sec. 4, p. 21.
100. Kozin, p. 178.

native Chinese dynasty. The Chin were newcomers (of the Jurjen stock, as will be recalled) and in spite of their rapid assimilation with the Chinese were considered aliens by the natives. Their control extended from Manchuria to the region south of the Yellow River, including the provinces of Chihli, Hansi, Shantung, and northern Honan.[101] The original abode of the Jurjen was in northern Manchuria. Southern Manchuria was inhabited by the Khitans who had ruled North China prior to the Jurjen conquest. The loyalty of the Khitans to the Chin dynasty was questionable. All these circumstances were taken into consideration by Chingis-Khan and his advisers. Trusty agents were sent secretly to the influential clan leaders of the Khitans to prepare for future cooperation.

To the Mongols, the war against the Chin was a natural act of revenge for the support the Chin had previously given to the Tatars and especially for the humiliating execution of Ambagai-Khan some fifty years before. In the clan society of the steppes feuds last for scores of years, an offense to their forefathers being felt acutely by grandsons and great-grandsons. Acting as an embodiment of the Mongol nation, Chingis proclaimed the war holy. Before announcing the start of the campaign he retired to his tent where he spent three days in prayer, asking the Eternal Blue Sky to approve of his readiness to avenge the misfortunes of his ancestors. While their emperor prayed, the soldiers and people around his tent, in a state of great nervous excitement, called upon Heaven, shouting *Tengri, Tengri*. On the fourth day Chingis emerged and announced that Heaven vouchsafed them victory.[102]

The first China campaign of the Mongols began in 1211.[103] The armies of the Chin were more numerous, but Chingis-Khan proved a more skillful military leader than the Chin generals. The Mongol troops were divided into several army groups which acted in perfect cooperation. Being attacked in several places at once, the Chin generals had to disperse their forces; this enabled Chingis-Khan's guards to pierce the Great Wall at a point where the enemy did not expect the attack. A Mongol army division then made straight for Peking while other units reached the shores of the Gulf of Chihli. What proved to be of great importance was that the Mongols succeeded

101. Here and hereafter, unless otherwise stated, the localities and provinces of China are referred to by their modern names to avoid confusion.

102. Vladimirtsov, *Chingis-Khan*, pp. 98–99.

103. On the China campaigns see Vladimirtsov, *Chingis-Khan*, pp. 102–113; Khara-Davan, chap. 8; Martin, chaps. 5–9.

in seizing most of the imperial herds of horses kept in a region north of Peking. This deprived the Chin of the main source of remounts for their cavalry. Lacking both experience and siege engines, the Mongols at that stage made no attempt to storm strongly fortified Peking. But they were in firm control of the whole Peking area. Now Chingis' diplomacy began to bear fruit: in 1212 the Khitans revolted against the Chin, and their clan leaders recognized the suzerainty of Chingis-Khan. Two years later the Chin emperor signed a peace treaty with Chingis; according to its provisions Chingis received the Chin emperor's adopted daughter in marriage, with a fabulously rich dowry. The peace did not last long as neither side intended to keep it. The Chin emperor decided to abandon Peking and to move his capital to the southern part of his empire in order to organize a defense from there. On the way part of his troops, recruited from the Khitans, mutinied and turned back to Peking. Unwilling to let this opportunity slip away, the Mongols immediately resumed the war. Peking surrendered in 1215.

This did not bring the war to a close, since the Chin continued resistance in the southern part of their realm. Chingis-Khan's main task was achieved, however. Mongol rule was firmly established over both North China and Manchuria, and these countries became an integral part of Chingis' empire, with a far-reaching effect on the structure of the Mongol army and state. Not only did Chingis now have at his disposal a corps of Chinese army engineers but he could use the services of a body of experienced, highly cultured, and well-trained civil servants. It was with their assistance, as well as with that of the Uigurs, that the Mongols would be able to rule the world they were about to conquer. The most famous of Chingis-Khan's Chinese advisers was Eliu Chu-tsai, a descendant of the Khitan princely family, but a Chinese by education and culture.

After establishing his authority in Peking, Chingis-Khan returned to Mongolia, leaving to Mukali the task of completing the conquest of the Chin empire. His attention now turned from Chinese affairs to those of Central Asia where he had some unfinished business. It will be recalled that after the defeat of the Naimans by Temuchin in 1204 the son of the last Naiman khan, Kuchluk, escaped west, eventually reaching the kingdom of the Kara-Khitans. Before long Kuchluk took advantage of internal dissensions in the state where he was given refuge and seized power for himself. Originally a Christian of Nestorian denomination, Kuchluk was later converted to Buddhism. As the ruler of the Kara-Khitan realm he attempted to suppress both Christianity and Islam there, which aroused much opposition. Through the Uigurs Chingis-Kahn was well informed of these events.

One of the basic principles of Chingis' strategy was never to permit any of his enemies to escape final destruction. For a number of years he had seemed to forget all about Kuchluk, preoccupied by the preparation and then execution of the Chinese campaign; now, when his authority in North China was firmly established, he could afford to administer the final blow to an old foe. Consequently two Mongol divisions or tümen were sent to the Kara-Khitan region under the command of Jebe-Noyan. As soon as he entered the enemy area Jebe proclaimed complete religious freedom. The Mongols were therefore received as liberators by both Christians and Moslems. Being supported by the local population, Jebe defeated Kuchluk's troops with lightning speed. Kuchluk perished in an attempt to flee. As the result of Jebe's victory the western boundary of the Mongol Empire now reached the confines of Khorezm.

Khorezm (Khwarezm, Chwarezm) in western Turkestan, in the basin of the lower Amu-Daria River (now part of the Turkmen Soviet Republic), is one of the oldest cultural areas in the world. A high level of agriculture was made possible by an ingenious system of irrigation based on the Amu-Daria; crafts and industries had flourished in the region from time immemorial.[104] No less important was the role of Khorezm in international trade. Lying at the crossroads between China and the Mediterranean world, and between India and South Russia, Khorezm was the meeting place of commercial caravans from east and west, north and south. It may be called an island of settled civilization in the sea of steppes and deserts; Barthold aptly likens its role in steppe commerce to that of the British Isles in maritime trade.[105]

The original population of Khorezm was of Iranian stock. In the 9th and 10th centuries the country prospered under the enlightened rule of the Samanid dynasty. From the middle of the 10th century, however, the Samanid kingdom found itself under the constant and

104. See Tolstov, *Po sledam,* chap. 11.
105. W. Barthold, *Istoriia kulturnoi zhizni Turkestana,* p. 34.

ever-increasing pressure of a vast federation of Turkish tribes known as the Oguz. Historically the Oguz state was a fragment of the Turkish Kaganate which existed from the 6th to the 8th century.[106] Ethnically the Oguz represented a mixture of Turks and Iranians (Alans).[107] In the middle of the 11th century a branch of the Oguz, known as Seljuqs after their leader, established themselves in both Khorezm and Persia. Later the Seljuqs invaded Asia Minor [108] but gradually lost their control over the Middle East. One of the centers of opposition to them in Central Asia was Khorezm. Beginning in 1117 that region was ruled by a military governor, Kutbeddin Muhammad, promoted from the ranks of the Turkish mercenary troops which were usually recruited from the slaves.[109] He succeeded in founding a dynasty of able rulers; [110] originally under Seljuq suzerainty, they eventually became independent and finally assumed the old Persian title of shah. The city of Urgenj on the lower Amu-Daria River became the capital of their empire. In the last quarter of the 12th century Bukhara and north Persia were annexed to Khorezm. In the period between 1206 and 1215 the Khorezm-shah Muhammad II conquered the southern part of Persia as well as Afghanistan. He was now destined to face Chingis-Khan, and in the ensuing conflict he was found wanting.

While Muhammad II's empire was vast and prosperous, it was loosely knit and rent by internal dissensions. To the population of the newly acquired Persian provinces the Khorezm-shah was an alien; in the empire as a whole, his Iranian subjects did not mix well with the Turks. As regards religion, most of the population of the empire were Moslems but there was a perennial conflict between the Shiah and the Sunnah doctrines, and the diverging Shiah sects added their share of troubles. The peasants grumbled under the load of taxes; the merchants resented the venality of the city governors and the lack of security on the roads. There was no unified army. The holders of the fiefs (ikta) commanded the detachments of militia recruited from among their tenants. These troops were poorly trained. The Turkmen tribesmen were brave and bellicose but lacked discipline;

106. On the Turkish Kaganate see *Ancient Russia*, pp. 178–179, 182–184; on the social organization of the Turks cf. Bernshtam, chaps. 5–6.

107. Tolstov, *Po sledam*, p. 245.

108. See above, sec. 2, p. 7.

109. The role of the mercenary Turkish troops in Khorezm may be compared to the rise of the Mameluks in Egypt.

110. Tolstov, *Po sledam*, pp. 274–276; cf. Zambaur, p. 209.

the shah's Kangly (Kypchak) [111] Guards were demoralized; army technicians in charge of the catapults and other war engines were competent but their department was not integrated with the rest of the army. Besides, the shah's palace was ridden with intrigue. The shah's mother, an ambitious and dynamic woman of Kangly origin, interfered with her son's plans on many occasions and nurtured his suspicion of the most able of his sons, Jalal ad-Din, whose popularity among the people at large rose as fast as his father's prestige declined. To make things even worse, the shah's lack of tact caused him to quarrel with some of the leading mullahs.

From the Khorezmian merchants who traded with the Uigurs and Chinese, the Khorezm-shah knew of the conquest of North China by Chingis-Khan. He decided to send an embassy to the Mongol ruler with the ostensible aim of presenting his greetings. The real objective was to appraise the Mongol strength. Simultaneously, the Moslem merchants sent a huge caravan to Mongolia. Chingis-Khan received both the ambassadors and the merchants graciously and, to reciprocate, sent his envoys and a commercial caravan to Turkestan. The personnel of both the diplomatic mission and the caravan consisted mostly of Khorezmian and Bukhara merchants, subjects of Muhammad II, who were tempted by the tremendous possibilities of expanding trade with the Far East and agreed to act as Chingis' agents. Reaching the borders of the Khorezmian Empire, the caravan stopped at the city of Otrar, on the bank of the Syr-Daria River; from there the envoys proceeded to Urgenj to be received by the shah. The shah agreed to talk to them, but simultaneously the governor of Otrar—presumably acting on secret instructions from the shah—ordered Chingis' merchants killed and their goods looted. When the Mongol emperor received word of these events, he sent a new envoy to Muhammad requiring that the governor of Otrar be handed over to him. Muhammad not only refused but ordered the Mongol envoy killed. The envoy's companion was allowed to return to Mongolia but only after having his beard cut off, which was considered a grave insult. No alternative was now left to Chingis-Khan but war. He called an extraordinary session of the kuriltay at which all the neces-

---

111. In *Kievan Russia* the Kypchaks (Qypchaks) have been referred to as the Cumans, the form of the name used in Western and Byzantine sources. The Russians called them Polovtsy. In the Oriental sources they are usually mentioned as Kypchaks, and their country as Kypchak or Desht-i-Kypchak. It seems more proper to use this name in regard to the Mongol period. The eastern Kypchaks are often referred to as Kangly. See Barthold, *Turcs*, pp. 88–91.

sary dispositions for the Turkestan campaign were considered and enacted (1218). Presumably at this session the basic laws of the Mongol Empire promulgated in 1206 were systematized and approved in written code, the Great Yasa.[112]

The Mongol campaign against the empire of the Khorezm-shah was as carefully prepared as that against China.[113] Jebe undoubtedly was able to give useful advice on the basis of his raid on the neighboring country of Kara-Khitan. In addition, all the information about Turkestan available from the Moslem merchants, from the Uigurs, and from other sources was taken into consideration. If anything, Chingis-Khan, as was proved by further events, was inclined to overestimate the Khorezm-shah's strength. To round out his army, he sent an envoy to the ruler of Tangut to ask for auxiliary troops. The answer was far from friendly: "If you have not enough troops, you are not worthy of being king." This could not but be understood as a studied insult. However, with his usual self-control, Chingis decided to postpone meting out punishment to the Tanguts until after the close of the Turkestan war. The concentration of the Mongol army in northern Jungaria was completed by the spring of 1219. The main army consisted of about 100,000 horsemen; with the auxiliary troops its total strength might have been in the neighborhood of 150,000. A considerable number of Chingis' warriors were veterans of the Chinese campaign which also had served as an excellent training school for his generals. The Khorezm-shah's forces numbered around 300,000, but the majority of his troops were of inferior quality. Besides, Muhammad II lacked the stamina needed in a leader in time of duress. Many of his subjects would have welcomed the appointment of Jalal ad-Din as commander in chief, but, as has been said, Muhammad did not trust his son, being afraid that in case of victory he would seize power for himself.

Under the circumstances, Muhammad approved a plan which puzzled both his contemporaries and most of the historians of his reign. Instead of concentrating his army against the onslaught of the Mongols, he dispersed his troops, stationing most of them in the large fortified cities, such as Otrar, Bukhara, and Samarkand; only

112. On the Yasa see below, Chapter 2, sec. 6, pp. 99–110.
113. On the Turkestan campaign see Vladimirtsov, *Chingis-Khan*, pp. 125–140; Barthold, *Turkestan;* C. C. Walker, *Jenghiz Khan* (London, Luzac & Co., 1939), chaps. 4–6.

part of the Khorezmian army was assigned to the task of securing communications between the garrisons of the cities and of field maneuvering; meanwhile, orders were given to the governors of Persia to gather a reserve army there. In my opinion, Muhammad's plan of war may have been based on his appraisal of the information on Chingis' Chinese campaign reported to him by the ambassadors he had sent to Chingis prior to the break between the two rulers. At that time the Mongols proved unable to take any fortress by storm. If such was Muhammad's reason for his strategy, he gravely miscalculated. Chingis-Khan now had at his disposal a number of Chinese army engineers ready to assist him. It is not clear whether some siege engines, such as catapults, which the Mongols used in their Turkestan campaign, were actually brought from China or all were built on the spot by Moslem technicians under the supervision of Chinese. The fact is that such machines were used on several occasions. In the cases when no machines were used, the Mongols applied more elementary devices and tactics in their siege of fortified cities like Otrar and Bukhara, such as filling the moats with dirt and stones and building approaches to the walls. Presumably these works were directed by Chinese engineers or Chinese-trained Mongols. Prisoners of war and conscripted natives were used as labor. On many occasions they were also sent first to climb the city walls, suffering tremendous casualties, which concerned the Mongols very little.

In the autumn of 1219 Chingis-Khan's troops appeared before the walls of Otrar. Leaving several divisions to besiege that city, the Mongol emperor made straight for Bukhara with the choice troops of his army. On his way there, several smaller cities surrendered without a fight and were spared destruction. The Mongols ordered the city walls destroyed in each case; the population was not generally molested but had to supply a quota of laborers and to pay a moderate contribution. The authorities of the great city of Bukhara, however, decided to defend the city. Only after the garrison had left the city in an attempt to pierce the ring of the siege and had perished in the fighting did Bukhara surrender. A desperate group of warriors locked in the inner castle continued resistance for twelve days more until most of them were killed. When all was over, Chingis-Khan ordered the population to leave the city and all their possessions. The merchants and artisans were conscripted to work for the Mongols.

The rest were left to their fate and, according to some sources, most of them were slain. The abandoned city was given to the soldiers for looting, in the course of which it burned down (1220).

Bukhara became the pattern for all the enemy cities which failed to surrender without a fight. When Otrar fell, its governor—who was guilty of the murder of the merchants of Chingis' caravan—was taken alive and tortured to death. Before long Samarkand too was taken by the Mongols. Having thus lost their main fortresses and their best troops, both the Khorezm-shah and his son fled south. The difference in character between father and son was now made quite clear. Muhammad thought only of his personal safety which he hoped to enjoy on an island on the Caspian Sea. Soon after reaching the island, however, he fell ill and died. Jalal ad-Din, on the contrary, looked forward to continuing resistance and, after arriving at Gazni in Afghanistan, at once started organizing a new army. Two Mongol divisions, commanded by Jebe and Subudey, respectively, were sent south to catch the fleeing shah. Losing track of Muhammad, the Mongol expeditionary corps conquered the area along the southern shore of the Caspian Sea and reached Azerbaijan, the westernmost province of the Khorezm-shah's empire. The two generals now asked Chingis-Khan's permission to proceed north through the Caucasus in order to reconnoiter "the Western countries." Chingis approved their plans. The result was a daring raid on South Russia in 1221–23, during which a crushing defeat was administered to the Russians in the battle of Kalka.[114]

The military operations of the main Mongol armies in 1220–21 had a double objective: to capture the capital of Khorezm, Urgenj, and crush Jalal ad-Din's newly gathered army. Against the latter Chingis-Khan at first sent an army division under the command of his adopted brother Shigi-Khutukhu, the chief justice. These troops were defeated by Jalal ad-Din—the only serious reverse the Mongols suffered in the course of the Turkestan campaign. Chingis-Khan then realized the seriousness of the situation and, accompanied by his youngest son, led his main army against the Khorezmian prince. Jalal ad-Din retreated but finally accepted battle on the banks of the upper Indus River. There his army was defeated, and his wives and children were captured by the Mongols. He himself, however, plunged with his horse into the stormy river, swam to the other bank, and escaped inland, eventually reaching Delhi. For some time Chingis-Khan

114. See *Kievan Russia*, pp. 235–239.

apparently weighed the possibilities of continuing his campaign farther south and of conquering India. Both he and his advisers realized, however, the tremendous difficulties of such an undertaking and especially of crossing the high mountain ranges. Eliu Chu-tsai, among others, strongly advised against the campaign. Finally the Mongol emperor decided to abandon the idea and turned his army back.

Meanwhile his three sons—Juchi, Jagatay, and Ugedey—who were charged with capturing Urgenj, succeeded after some delay which was caused by a quarrel between Juchi and the other two. As part of the siege operations, the Mongols destroyed the main dam on the Amu-Daria River above the city, which resulted in irreparable damage to the whole system of irrigation and, consequently, to Khorezmian agriculture. Until recently, it was assumed that another result of the destruction of the great dam was the change in the course of the Amu-Daria River, which now, allegedly, turned west and discharged into the Caspian, instead of into the Aral Sea as before. Recent archeological research, however, does not confirm that theory.[115]

After completing the conquest of Turkestan, Chingis-Khan gave himself and his army a period of rest. It was at this time that he held his philosophical conversations with the Taoist monk Chang-chun.[116]

As early as 1219 Chingis heard that the Taoists were well versed in alchemy and about to discover the elixir of life. So he invited Chang-chun, who was said to be the most famous representative of the school, to visit him. Until then Chang-chun had refused such invitations, but this time he accepted and undertook the long and difficult journey. He was received with great honor at Chingis' camp. At their first meeting the emperor immediately expressed his desire to obtain the secret of long life. The philosopher answered frankly that he possessed no such secret. While disappointed, Chingis did not lose interest in the Tao doctrine and held three more conferences with Chang-chun. A Kara-Khitan officer translated the latter's words into Mongol. Chingis was pleased with the lectures and remarked that Chang-chun's philosophy could sustain man's life even if it was unable to make man immortal.

Meanwhile, measures were taken to restore order in the newly

115. Tolstov, *Po sledam*, pp. 296–316.
116. Bretschneider, *1*, 93–97; A. Waley, *Travels of an Alchemist* (London, G. Routledge & Sons, 1931), pp. 100–102, 111–120.

conquered country; a new system of taxation was established under
the competent direction of native merchants, one of whom, Mahmud
Yalavach, became one of Chingis-Khan's most trusted advisers. The
people were urged to pursue their peaceful occupations and the roads
were made safe from robbers. Thus, after the initial period of terrible
destruction was over, the country not only returned to normalcy but
even enjoyed a better administration than before. It was a long time,
however, before the irrigation system of Khorezm could be repaired.

Chingis-Khan returned to Mongolia in 1225. He was now in a
position to attend to the Tanguts for their refusal to assist him in his
Turkestan campaign. But he was in no hurry, knowing they could
not escape destruction. He took time to complete the organization of
his empire. The administrative institutions already created had now
to be adjusted to the control of the vast world conquered and more
still to be conquered. It was probably in 1225–26 that the final
version of the code of laws called the Yasa was compiled and approved.

In the autumn of 1226 Chingis-Khan set forth against the Tanguts.
The Tangut cities fell one after another; the Mongols were victorious.
But before the campaign was over Chingis-Khan was injured in a fall
from his horse and died.[117] According to his instructions, his death
was kept secret by his youngest son Tuluy who accompanied him in
this campaign, as in the Turkestan war, and who now assumed leadership of the troops in the field. Only when the resistance of the Tanguts
was finally crushed was the news announced to friend and foe.
Chingis' body was brought back to Mongolia. The exact place of
burial was kept secret; according to some sources, he was interred
in the woods of the sacred Burkan Mountain.[118]

Even after his death Chingis continued to live in Mongol history
as the guiding spirit and embodiment of the nation.[119] His name
was invoked in every state document of importance issued by his
successors; his Yasa remained the foundation of Mongol imperial
law; his collected sayings (*Bilik*) were a source of wisdom for generations to come; and his descendants alone were considered eligible

117. According to some sources, Chingis-Khan was mortally wounded by an arrow.
On his last campaign and death see E. Haenisch, "Die letzte Feldzüge Cinggis Hans und
sein Tod nach der ostasiatischen Überlieferung," *AM, 9* (1933), 503–551.

118. On the burying of the Mongol khans see Grum-Grzymailo, *2,* 64–66.

119. In the Mongol inscription of 1362 Chingis-Khan is called *Suu Jali* which means
Guiding Spirit; see Cleaves, Inscription I, p. 92 and p. 131, n. 259. Cf. Kotwicz, "Formules initiales," p. 131; Mostaert, p. 321; Poppe, "Opisanie," pp. 171–172.

to the throne. The glorification of his memory makes it far from easy for the historian properly to appraise the role of Chingis-Khan's personality in the creation of the empire. Was his success primarily the result of his own dynamic effort? To what extent was it due to the talents of his lieutenants and advisers and to the disunity of his opponents? Not every ruler knows how to profit by his enemy's mistakes; Chingis certainly made full use of them. In regard to the role of his assistants, there is no doubt that Chingis' ability to appoint the right man to the right place contributed greatly to the success of his undertakings, both in his military campaigns and in the organization of his empire. Chingis himself readily acknowledged the help given him by his marshals and secretaries of state and rewarded them generously. Still, it is obvious that he was behind all the important military and political decisions arrived at during his reign. His talent in coordinating the activities of his subordinates is beyond question. And I believe it may be safely said that both as a military leader and as a statesman he had broad vision and a sense of reality.

Chingis-Khan remained illiterate to the end of his life, and was a typical nomad in his habits and in his conception of the pleasures of life. As with all nomads, hunting was his delight; he was a connoisseur of horses; while not lewd in terms of habits of his people and of the age he lived in, he had several wives and plenty of concubines; while he warned his subjects against excessive drinking, he was not averse to wine. In some respects he was even more primitive and savage than his associates. According to Rashid ad-Din Chingis-Khan once asked his marshals what they considered man's highest enjoyment. Bogurchi said that the highest joy was to ride, in the springtime, on a good steed, with a falcon. Others also praised hunting. Chingis did not agree. "Man's highest joy," said he, "is in victory: to conquer one's enemies, to pursue them, to deprive them of their possessions, to make their beloved weep, to ride on their horses, and to embrace their daughters and wives." [120] It seems paradoxical that the man who uttered these words should have been fond of conversing with the learned men of his time and was always eager to obtain more knowledge and ready to philosophize on life and death. According to the evidence available Chingis-Khan was a healthy and robust man. Yet there are also indications pointing to the existence of a nervous strain in his personality. This must have been increased

120. D'Ohsson, *I*, Pt. 1, 306; cf. Vladimirtsov, *Chingis-Khan*, p. 166.

by many painful shocks experienced in childhood and youth. Hence his religious exaltation, his fervor in prayers during every serious crisis of his life down to the beginning of his Chinese campaign. While in his youth he personally led his followers against the enemy on many occasions and was considered a brave warrior, he seems to have lacked the chivalrous defiance of his father. He was not reckless and thought of his personal safety in situations when a typical Mongol youth would think only of combat. This was especially obvious in the case of the Merkits' attack on his camp, when he saved himself by fleeing and left his young bride at the mercy of his enemies. To be sure, his life must be saved not just for its own sake but for the sake of his great destiny, of the future empire he had to build. Still, his behavior looked very much like cowardice, even if it was only evidence of his self-control.

Vladimirtsov aptly called Chingis-Khan a "savage of genius." In his discussion of the problem of the primitive genius, Radoslav A. Tsanoff refers to the Polynesian belief in the presence, in certain outstanding and lucky men, of the weird potency which they call *mana*. This is the notion of a mysterious surplus, something "beyond the ordinary power of men, outside of the common process of nature." [121] In these terms, Chingis-Khan's faith in his universal mission may be considered a reflection of the mana which possessed him. He himself understood it as the guidance of Heaven.

There is no reliable description of Chingis-Khan's appearance. The report of the agent of the Sung who visited Peking in 1221, which has until recently been considered an important source, is now believed not to describe Chingis-Khan.[122] There is, however, a fine portrait of him, by a Chinese painter, in the series of portraits of Mongol emperors in the Imperial Palace in Peking; this was published in 1928. According to Father Antoine Mostaert, these portraits must have been made during the Yuan (Mongol) period. All the details of headgear and dress of each emperor seem authentic.[123]

---

121. Radoslav A. Tsanoff, *The Ways of Genius* (New York, Harper & Brothers, 1949), pp. 40–41, with reference to R. H. Codrington, *The Melanesians* (1891), p. 119, and R. R. Marett, *The Threshold of Religion* (2d ed. 1914), p. 105.

122. Vladimirtsov, p. 9 and n. 2.

123. Antoine Mostaert, "A propos de quelques portraits d'empereurs mongols," *AM, 4* (1927), 147–156. In a letter to me of May 3, 1951, Father Mostaert has been kind enough to give me some additional information about the portraits. As he writes: "Quant à ces portraits des empereurs et impératrices mongoles, je les ai vus dans l'ancien palais impérial à Pekin—je ne les avais pas encore vus au moment ou j'ecrivais cette note publiée dans *AM* IV. Mon impression personnelle est qu'ils datent des Iuen." Photo-

Presumably the representation of the face in each case was based on reliable descriptions if not on contemporary drawings.

7. Mongol Expansion during the Reign of Ugedey

Before his death Chingis-Khan assigned to each of his sons by his first wife, Borte,[124] a portion of the empire as his respective ulus.[125] Tuluy, as the youngest son, received the core of the Borjigin clan's possessions—the central and western part of Mongolia. Jagatay was given the area of the former Kara-Khitan realm centering in the Ili River basin. Jungaria, including the region of the upper Irtysh River, became the apanage of the third son, Ugedey. Finally, the newly conquered region north of the Aral Sea (present-day Kazakhstan) was granted to the eldest son, Juchi; after the latter's death (of which Chingis-Khan was notified shortly before his own death) it went to Juchi's second son, Batu.

In addition to receiving an ulus, each of Chingis' sons was given command of a portion of the Mongol army. Tuluy obtained the lion's share: 101,000 troops out of the total of 129,000. Neither the division of lands nor that of troops was intended to break the unity of the empire. The distribution of troops was to be valid for the period of interregnum only, pending the election of the new great khan by the kuriltay. Until then, Tuluy assumed the regency.

All the Mongol leaders agreed that only Chingis-Khan's sons were eligible for the throne; the kuriltay had merely to choose between them. It must be mentioned in this connection that while Tuluy was his father's favorite, Chingis-Khan not long before his death designated Ugedey as his successor since in his opinion Ugedey was better qualified than the other three to rule the empire. The regent apparently did not want to put any pressure on the clan leaders and allowed them ample time to consider the candidacies. The electoral

---

graphs of these portraits appeared in an album entitled *Portraits of Emperors and Empresses of China* (Shanghai, The Times Publishing Co., around 1927; inaccessible to me). The portraits may also be found in the Chinese publication *Ku-kung chou-k'an* ("Former Palace Weekly"), 1932, Nos. 131–138. (I am indebted for this reference to Francis W. Cleaves and Richard L. Walker.) Some of the portraits, including that of Chingis-Khan, have been reproduced in Father Mostaert's article quoted above. Chingis-Khan's portrait may also be found in most of his biographies published after 1928, including those by Khara-Davan and H. D. Martin.

124. Only these were considered full-fledged heirs.

125. The term "ulus" was used in different senses; it could denote "apanage," "state," and also "people" (of a state or a section of the state); see Vladimirtsov, pp. 59, 98–101.

kuriltay met in 1229. A number of its members were in favor of
Tuluy. The latter, however, refused to be a candidate and Ugedey
was unanimously elected great khan.[126]

Ugedey fully shared his father's ideas about a universal empire and
assumed his task in all seriousness. During his reign the Mongol state
definitely turned from the old habits of steppe rule to new administrative techniques. A characteristic story is told in the Chinese
history of the Mongol dynasty. After the conquest of North China
a Mongol grandee of the old school suggested to Ugedey that the
North Chinese people should be annihilated, the cities and villages
destroyed, and all lands in North China converted to pasturage. No
profit to the Mongols, he reasoned, could be extracted from the
existence of the North Chinese. Arguing against the acceptance of
this savage plan, Eliu Chu-tsai initiated Ugedey into the art of ex-
tracting profit from the nonnomad subjects of the Mongol Empire
by establishing taxes and levies on their commerce and industry and
by exploiting their iron mines and other mineral deposits. He promised huge receipts in money, fabrics, and rice.[127] Luckily for the
Chinese—and for the Mongols themselves—Ugedey accepted Eliu
Chu-tsai's program. In doing so he laid solid foundations for the
future administration of the Mongol Empire.

Ugedey profited also by the advice of his secretary of state, Chinkay, a Uigur; and of the Moslem merchant Mahmud Yalavach.
Guided by them, he took great pains to develop and improve the
institutions of the imperial administration and to strengthen the emperor's authority in internal as well as external affairs. He acted
in close cooperation with Jagatay whom, as his eldest living brother,
he consulted in all important affairs.

Before the conquest of any new country could be contemplated,
Mongol rule in China and Persia must be restored, since it was in a
weakened state in both these areas. After the death of Mukali in
1223 the Mongols' drive in China had slowed down and in 1228 they
suffered a series of reverses. Persia the Mongols had withdrawn
from even before Chingis-Khan's death; and Jalal ad-Din, who returned from Delhi at the first opportunity, was recognized as sultan
by the Persian grandees and cities. Ugedey was more concerned with
the situation in China than with Persian affairs; and consequently
the main Mongol army, under the command of Tuluy, was sent

126. On the reign of Ugedey see Iakinf, pp. 148–287; Grousset, pp. 285–301.
127. See Ratchnevsky, pp. vii–viii.

against the Chin. To guarantee the success of the campaign Ugedey made an agreement with the Sung empire in South China. The Sung proved willing to send a corps of their troops against the Chin on condition that after the joint victory the Mongols would cede to them the former Chin province of Honan. With the cooperation of the Sung the Mongols completed the conquest of the Chin empire by 1234. Tuluy died before the end of the campaign.

Simultaneously with the main drive in China other Mongol troops were sent against Korea and Persia. Korea recognized Mongol suzerainty in 1231. Three Mongol divisions commanded by Chormagan-Noyan entered Persia in 1230.[128] Fortunately for the Mongols and unfortunately for himself, the sultan Jalal ad-Din had not realized the inevitability of their impending attack on his state. Instead of preparing himself and his army for the final struggle against the Mongols, he had plunged into Near Eastern politics, trying to round out his possessions at the expense of Iraq, northern Syria, and Georgia. The natural result was that he clashed with all his western neighbors and was left without a friend when the Mongols appeared in Azerbaijan where his field headquarters was located at that time. Although caught entirely off guard Jalal ad-Din made another of those narrow escapes for which he was famous. But his efforts to organize a new army failed. Abandoned by most of his followers and betrayed by his own vizier, the sultan on his way to Anatolia was again encircled by the Mongols. He escaped once more and made for the mountains of Kurdistan, where he was killed in 1231 by brigands who did not even know who he was. "It seems to have been preordained by Fate that this bravest lion should be slain by foxes" was the comment of one Oriental writer on the sultan's death.[129]

One of the results of Jalal ad-Din's defeat was the dispersal of the remnants of his Turkmen (Oguz) troops. Many a Turkmen clan had followed Jalal ad-Din in his first retreat before the Mongol onslaught. After his return to Persia from Delhi they rallied once more to his support. Now they were again left without a leader. Some of them decided to return to Turkestan and to recognize Mongol suzerainty. Others preferred to migrate westward, to Syria and Asia Minor. Among the latter were about five hundred families led by Ertogrul.

128. On the Mongol campaigns in Persia during the reign of Ugedey see Spuler, *Iran*, pp. 35–38.
129. An-Nasawi, *Histoire du Sultan Djelal el-Din Mankobirti*, O. Houdas, trans. and ed., p. 230; cf. Grum-Grzymailo, 2, 461.

This group succeeded in reaching the Seljuq Sultanate; Ertogrul became the sultan's vassal and was granted land near Sugut, in Phrygia, close to the Byzantine borders. While the episode seemed insignificant at the time, it proved to be a major factor in the future history of the Near East since Ertogrul's son Osman eventually became the founder of the Ottoman Empire.

A much larger group of Turkmen warriors, usually referred to as "the Khorezmians," moved to Iraq and offered their services to the local Moslem rulers. Demoralized and undisciplined, they lost no chance of ravaging the country round about.[130]

With the fall of the Chin empire and with Jalal ad-Din out of the picture in Persia, the Mongols were in a position to prepare for further conquests. A session of the kuriltay was convoked in 1235 to approve plans. At that historic meeting the Mongol leaders decided to undertake four offensive campaigns simultaneously: two in the Far East, against Korea which had revolted soon after her first submission, and against the Sung empire in South China; one in the Middle East, against Iraq, Syria, Transcaucasia, and the Seljuq Sultanate in Asia Minor; and one in the West, against Europe.

The best Mongol troops were assigned for the drives against Korea and Europe; some reinforcements were sent to Chormagan-Noyan in the Middle East. Most of the army to be used in South China was conscripted from the Jurjens and North Chinese, former subjects of the Chin. War with South China became inevitable after Ugedey's refusal to cede the province of Honan to the Sung as stipulated in the treaty. Three Mongol-led armies invaded South China, but after some initial successes had to retreat; the situation became fluid and there was no drastic change in it during the last years of Ugedey's reign. The Mongols were more successful in Korea, where the resistance was broken after several years of heavy fighting (1241).

In the Middle East the Mongol forces under Chormagan-Noyan, while adequate to restore Mongol control of northern Persia, proved not strong enough for a campaign against the Caliphate of Bagdad in Iraq. The Mongols, however, succeeded in conquering Azerbaijan, Armenia, and Georgia. That last unhappy country, devastated by the Mongols in 1220–21 and once more by Jalal ad-Din in 1226, became a Mongol protectorate in 1239. The Mongols were now in a position to prepare for an attack on the possessions of the Seljuq sultans in Asia Minor, though no general drive against the Seljuqs took place in Ugedey's reign.

130. Halphen, p. 415.

It was in the West that the most spectacular Mongol successes were scored during the reign of Ugedey. The "Western lands" were considered the area of potential expansion of Juchi's Ulus. His second son and successor, Batu (Russian, Batyi), was therefore appointed commander in chief of the westward drive. It was obvious, however, that Batu's forces were not adequate for the task. According to Chingis-Khan's dispositions, in the distribution of the Mongol troops between his sons Juchi was to receive command of but 4,000 Mongol warriors; there is no evidence that any more Mongol troops were assigned him. Batu, however, was granted authority to form new army units of Turkmen tribesmen and such other Turks as happened to live within his ulus, under the command of Mongol officers. The loyalty of the Turks was yet to be tested, and in any case Batu's regional army, even when reinforced by the Turks, was still not strong enough for Western conquest. Therefore Ugedey decreed that all the other uluses of the Mongol Empire were to send contingents to Batu's assistance. The Western campaign thus became a pan-Mongol undertaking.

Batu found himself presiding over a council of princes representing all of Chingis-Khan's descendants. Prominent among them were Guyuk and Kadan, sons of Ugedey; Mongka (Mangu), son of Tuluy; and Baidar and Buri, son and grandson respectively of Jagatay. Each brought with him substantial contingents of choice Mongol troops. While Batu was the nominal head of the campaign, one of the best and most experienced Mongol generals, Subudey (Subutay), was appointed what we may call chief of staff. Subudey was well acquainted with the Russian theater of war from his previous raid on Russia in 1222–23. The Mongol core of Batu's armies was probably around 50,000 strong. With the newly formed Turkish units and various auxiliaries, the total figure may have been as much as 120,000 or even more, but because of the vastness of territories to be controlled and garrisoned as the invasion proceeded the strength of Batu's field army in his major campaign can hardly have been more than 50,000 at any given phase of the operations.

The campaign was as carefully prepared as any of Chingis-Khan's classic drives. Scouts and spies collected necessary information well in advance. It was decided that the Bulgars and other peoples on the eastern fringe of Russia, along the course of the Volga River, as well as the Kypchaks (Cumans) and other tribes of the lower Volga and the lower Don area, must be defeated first to safeguard communications and the rear of the Mongol armies operating in Russia. Most of these objectives were successfully achieved in the course of two years (1236–37). While Mongka was put in charge of the campaign against the Cumans, Batu, assisted by Subudey, undertook the conquest of the Khanate of the Volga Bulgars. The latter's capital, Great Bulgar, was destroyed in 1237. In the autumn of that year Batu's main army crossed the Volga in the Bulgar region.

It must be noted in this connection that while the first raid of the Mongols, in 1222–23, had been directed against South Russia, Subudey this time decided to conquer northeast Russia first. He may well have realized at the time of his first Russian campaign that his success in the battle of Kalka was partly due to the inactivity of the grand duke of Vladimir.[131] He must have heard then from captives that that prince was the strongest of the Russian princes. Since Subudey contemplated carrying the campaign far to the west, to Kiev and then to Hungary, he had to secure his northern flank for future operations. This made destroying the power of the North Russian princes a prerequisite for further expansion west. Paradoxical as it may seem to the modern reader, in view of our knowledge of the suffering of both Napoleon's and Hitler's armies from "General Winter," Subudey recommended winter as the best season for military operations in North Russia. As a matter of fact, winter in Mongolia itself is severe, and the Mongols were accustomed to its rigors; besides they were well protected from cold by their fur garments. The Mongol horses too could endure severe cold and when the snow was not too deep knew how to find leaves or stubble under it. The main advantage of the winter campaign was that the numerous rivers and lakes of North Russia were frozen, which greatly simplified the operations of the invaders.

While the Russians knew of the Mongol attack on the Khanate of the Volga Bulgars, they failed to realize the seriousness of the situation, probably assuming that it would take some time for the Mongols to crush the resistance of the Bulgars. Hence when Batu crossed the Volga the Russians were not ready to meet their onslaught.[132] Instead of making straight for the city of Vladimir the Mongols first attacked Riazan on the middle Oka River. The town fell on December 21, 1237. From there they drove on to Moscow. While this was

131. See *Kievan Russia*, pp. 237–238.

132. On Batu's campaign in Russia see Karamzin, *3*, 281–293 and *4*, 9–15; Soloviev, *3*, 171–176; Khara-Davan, pp. 171–176; Spuler, pp. 16–20; *ZO*, pp. 207–217; Minorsky, Caucasica III.

not yet a major Russian city, its central location made it an important objective in Subudey's strategy. By taking Moscow, which he burnt, Subudey not only outflanked Vladimir but threatened the whole north of Russia, including the wealthy city of Novgorod the Great, the financial basis of the grand duke's power.

The grand duke, Iuri II, had now no alternative but to retreat northward with his retinue to organize resistance above the upper Volga River. Trusting to the strength of the fortifications of his capital, the city of Vladimir, he left his wife and two of his sons there with a reasonably large garrison, apparently hoping that the city would withstand siege until he should be in a position to relieve it with the new army he planned to mobilize in the north. Iuri established his headquarters on the banks of the Sit' River, a tributary of the Mologa, which in turn is a tributary of the upper Volga. Taking stock of the situation, Subudey sent his vanguards northward to watch the movements of the Russian troops there, and led his main army to Vladimir. After a siege of six days the city was stormed, on February 8, 1238, and all of the survivors slain, including the grand duke's family. Vladimir was then destroyed. The Mongols immediately proceeded to the Sit' River. Outmaneuvering the Russians, they attacked the grand duke's army from several quarters. The Russians were defeated and Iuri II perished in the battle on March 4. The road to Novgorod was now open and the Mongols turned in that direction. They stopped, however, about sixty-five miles short of their goal. After careful consideration the Mongol leaders decided to turn back, being afraid of the approach of spring and the thaw which would make the roads impassable. Instead of returning as they had come—through regions where all the cities and stores of food and fodder had been destroyed—the Mongol army went straight south. While they looted boyar estates and villages on the way, they apparently by-passed the cities, avoiding any involvements which could delay their march. There was one exception, however. The small town of Kozelsk in Kaluga province, which lay straight on their way, refused to surrender. Believing that its capture would not take much time, the Mongols decided to seize it. In this case they miscalculated; the siege of Kozelsk lasted seven weeks and ended only when all of its defenders had been killed. After this the Mongols proceeded southeast to the lower Don basin. There the army was given a long period of rest, of which both men and horses were much in need. Herds of horses seized from the Cumans together with other

herds driven from Kazakhstan constituted an ample source of remounts.

In the course of the next year, 1239, only minor military operations were undertaken by the Mongols. Mongka conquered a considerable part of the Alans and Circassians in the north Caucasian
area; Batu compelled most of the Cumans finally to recognize Mongol authority. However about 40,000 Cumans, led by Khan Kotian,[133]
preferred to migrate to Hungary. They were accompanied by a number of the Alans (Iasians) of the Donets region.[134]

By 1240 Batu's armies, refreshed and reorganized, were ready to
resume their drive to the west. In the summer of that year the
Mongols took and devastated the cities of Pereiaslav and Chernigov.
Following that, Mongka, who apparently commanded the vanguard,
sent emissaries to Kiev to demand its submission. Kiev was at that
time ruled by a governor appointed by Prince Daniel of Galicia.[135]
The city seems to have contained what today we would call an "appeasement" party. To prevent any action on its part the Kievan
authorities ordered Mongka's envoys killed. This sealed the doom of
the city. Before long the Mongols were at the gates, and the city
was taken by storm on December 6, 1240 after a few days of desperate resistance. Most of the survivors were slain and the city
destroyed. A number of lesser princes and of peasant communities in
the Right Bank Ukraine [136] now recognized Mongol authority and
agreed "to till the land for the Mongols," that is, to supply millet
and other agricultural products they needed.

Most of the West Russian princes, however, preferred to seek
refuge in Hungary and Poland, which gave Batu a pretext, if any
were needed, to attack these two countries. Batu also protested against
King Béla IV of Hungary giving refuge to Khan Kotian and his
Cumans. The Mongols' main interest in Hungary was in the fact
that it constituted the westernmost extension of the steppe zone and
could serve as an excellent base for Mongol cavalry in any of its
future operations in Central Europe, as it had for Attila and his

---

133. On Kotian see *Kievan Russia*, pp. 237, 239.

134. On the migration of the Cumans to Hungary see E. Csuday, *Die Geschichte der
Ungarn* (2d ed. Budapest, 1900), *1*, 265–266; Hóman, *1*, 537–539. On the simultaneous
migration of the Alans (Iasians) see Kulakovsky, *Alany*, pp. 71–72; S. Szabo, *Ungarisches
Volk* (Budapest and Leipzig, 1944), pp. 41, 42.

135. On the earlier activities of Daniel of Galicia see *Kievan Russia*, pp. 226–227, 228–
229, 230, 237–238, 240.

136. Right Bank Ukraine is the Ukraine west of the Dnieper River.

Huns eight centuries earlier.[137] Besides, the Magyars themselves were originally nomads, and in their early history closely connected with the Turks,[138] which made them eligible to participate in the Mongol-Turkish alliance.

The Mongols had no immediate interest in Poland, but Subudey's strategy required an attack on this country in order to eliminate the potential threat to the Mongols' right flank in their operations against Hungary. Thus, by the turn of the year not only was Central Europe threatened but Western Europe as well. Much depended on the ability of the Western nations to coordinate their activities and to organize a united defense against the invaders. This, however, was easier said than done. Feudal Europe was torn by internal dissensions, and besides a major conflict was taking place at the highest level in Roman Catholic Europe—a struggle between emperor and pope, each protagonist doing all he could to undermine the prestige of the other.

It was in 1238 that news of the advance of the Mongols reached the Western nations, from two quarters, Novgorod and Syria. The English chronicler Matthew Paris relates that "the inhabitants of Gothland and Friesland,[139] dreading their [the Mongols'] attacks, did not, as was their custom, come to Yarmouth, in England, at the time of the herring-fisheries, at which place their ships usually loaded; and owing to this, herrings in that year were considered of no value, on account of their abundance." [140] Friesland was the usual designation of the Netherlands in that period; obviously that country could not in 1238 have been in any way directly affected by the Mongol invasion of Russia. However both Friesland and the island of Gothland in the Baltic Sea had close commercial ties with Novgorod, based on the treaty of 1195.[141] Novgorodian ships, as well as Gothlander and Frisian vessels, plied the Baltic and North Seas. In the light of these facts we can understand Matthew Paris' story better. As the people of Novgorod in 1238 had to prepare to defend their

137. On Attila's empire see *Ancient Russia*, pp. 137–146; E. A. Thompson, *History of Attila and the Huns* (Oxford, Oxford University Press, 1948); F. Altheim, *Attila und die Hunnen* (as above, n. 27).

138. Moravcsik, *1*, 27–28, 58–64; L. Ligeti, ed., *A Magyarság Östörténete* (Budapest, 1943); cf. *Kievan Russia*, p. 319.

139. In the Latin original, "Gothia et Frisia," *Matthaei Parisiensis Chronica Majora*, H. R. Luard, ed. (London, Longman & Co., Trübner & Co.) *3* (1876), 488.

140. Matthew Paris, *1*, 131.

141. See *Kievan Russia*, p. 121.

city against the Mongols, all the city's resources and all its able-bodied men must have been mobilized. Consequently, Novgorod merchants were not in a position either to send their ships to the North Sea or assume any obligations connected with the herring deal of that year.[142]

Simultaneously with news via the Baltic Sea, of the Mongol invasion, there came to France and England messengers from Syria with tales of the Mongol attacks in the Near East. Special ambassadors of the Saracens, "chiefly on behalf of the Old Man of the Mountain" (i.e. the sheikh of the Assassins), asked the Western nations for help.[143] To understand this move on the part of the Near East Moslems we must recall that the tension in Palestine between Moslems and Christians had subsided somewhat as a result of the conciliatory policy of Emperor Frederick II during that crusade which is usually called the sixth, although it was not recognized by the pope (because of his conflict with the emperor) as a true crusade. Frederick's policy was branded appeasement by the papists, who resented any compromise with the "infidels." For this reason, and also because the Assassins could hardly be considered respectable allies, the Saracen ambassadors in 1238 found little encouragement either in France or in England. The bishop of Winchester's reply was characteristic enough: "Let us leave these dogs to devour one another, that they may all be consumed, and perish; and we, when we proceed against the enemies of Christ who remain, will slay them, and cleanse the face of the earth, so that all the world will be subject to the one Catholic church, and there will be one shepherd and one fold." [144]

It must be noted that the aggressive spirit of the Catholic Church, as reflected in the bishop's words, was aroused not only against the non-Christian "infidels" but against the "heretics" and "schismatics" as well, including the Greek Orthodox. Therefore not only was the idea of cooperation with the Moslems in the Near East rejected by the Catholic nations but two of them, the Swedes and the Teutonic Knights, considered the moment appropriate for an attack on Russia.

142. It should be mentioned that there is considerable confusion in Matthew Paris' book concerning the names Gothia and Frisia. Emperor Frederick II's letter as transcribed by Paris (*1*, 339) says that the Tatars "reduced to a desert the countries of Friesland, Gothland, Poland, Bohemia," etc. Here, apparently, Gothia and Frisia refer to some Russian or border regions.

143. Matthew Paris, *1*, 131.

144. *Idem, 1*, 132.

Both the Swedes and the Teutonic Knights were engaged at that time in proselytizing the heathen natives—the Finns and Karelians north of the Gulf of Finland, and the Lithuanians, Letts, and Ests south of it—with sword as well as cross. Both regarded the Greek Orthodox as being as much in need of "salvation" as the pagans. Both seem to have counted on the weakness at that period of the northern Russian cities, Novgorod and Pskov. While neither city was destroyed by the Mongols, both were deprived, temporarily at least, of any support from the devastated Grand Duchy of Vladimir.

Hence in July 1240 the Swedes, led by the powerful Earl Birger, appeared at the mouth of the Neva River, in an effort to bar Novgorod's access to the sea. Before they had time to proceed farther, Novgorod's young Prince Alexander, nephew of Iuri II, led his small but determined army to the Neva and administered a severe blow to the Swedes. The latter lost a considerable part of their forces and only a few, including Birger himself, succeeded in sailing back to Finland. After this victory Prince Alexander became known as Nevsky ("of the Neva").[145] All this happened about the time of the capture of Chernigov by the Mongols.

While the Swedish venture against Novgorod was taking place the Livonian Knights directed their efforts against Pskov, but scored no decisive success in 1240. Meanwhile the Mongols attacked Poland and Silesia, and the Teutonic Order, with which the Livonian Knights were affiliated, had to answer the duke of Silesia's calls for help instead of sending troops against Pskov. On April 9, 1241 the Mongol advance corps smashed the combined Polish-German army near Liegnitz (Lehnica) in Silesia.[146] According to the Polish historian Matthew of Miechow, the victorious Mongols cut one ear off every enemy corpse they found on the battlefield; nine large bags of ears were collected.[147] Even before that the main Mongol army

145. On the battle of the Neva see Karamzin, 4, 25–28; Soloviev, 3, 186–188.

146. On Batu's Western campaigns see Grousset, pp. 298–300; Spuler, pp. 20–24; Harold T. Cheshire, "The Great Tatar Invasion of Europe," *Slavonic Review*, 5 (1926–27), 89–105; Shinobu Iwamura, "Mongol Invasion of Poland in the Thirteenth Century," *MTB*, 10 (1938), 103–157. The best account of the Tatar movements in Bohemia and Moravia is by Vaclav Novotný; see especially Novotný, 1, Pt. 3, 1005–1009. For an excellent analysis of sources and scholarly literature on the Mongol campaigns in Central Europe see Novotný, 1, Pt. 3, 715–748.

147. Matvei Mekhovsky [Mathias de Miechov], *Traktat o dvukh Sarmatiiakh* [*Tractatus de duabus Sarmatiis*] (Moscow and Leningrad, 1936), p. 54 (Russian translation, which says "ten bags") and p. 136 (Latin original, which says "nine bags"—*novem saccos*). Mekhovsky's work was first published in 1517.

crossed the Carpathian mountains and entered Hungary. On April
11 Batu and Subudey defeated the Hungarians at the confluence of
the Tisa (Tisza, Theiss) and Szajo (Solona) rivers. The Western
expeditionary corps of the Mongol army now turned from Silesia
south to Bohemia and Moravia. Having orders to march on to Hungary, this force could not waste time besieging cities. It divided into
a number of small bands, which pillaged the country as they passed.
The Bohemian king Vaclav repelled one of these bands at Kladsko,
which improved the Czechs' morale but had no effect on Mongol
strategy. Contrary to a widespread legend, no important battles were
fought in Moravia; in a week or two all the bands had traversed
the province.[148]

While the Mongols stayed in Hungary through the summer of 1241,
looting the unhappy country, King Béla attempted to organize resistance in Croatia. From Zagreb he sent frantic messages to the
pope, the emperor, and the kings urgently asking help.

Even before Béla's appeal similar messages had reached Western
nations from or on behalf of Poland and Bohemia. The count of
Lorraine wrote to the duke of Brabant describing the plight of
Poland. The duke of Brabant wrote to the bishop of Paris; and the
archbishop of Cologne to the king of England. The bishop of Paris
immediately informed Queen Blanche, mother of Louis IX, of the
contents of the letter, and she summoned her son and asked him what
he intended to do about the danger. He answered with characteristic
deep religious feeling and resignation to fate: "May comfort from
heaven raise us up, my mother. And if these people, whom we call
Tartars, should come upon us, either we will thrust them back into
the regions of Tartarus, whence they emanated, or else they shall send
all of us to heaven." [149]

After receiving news of the plight of Hungary, Emperor Frederick
II on his part sent a circular letter to all the West European rulers
urging them to help Hungary, Bohemia, and Poland. Pope Gregory
IX also issued a call for a crusade against the Mongols. Since the
feud between emperor and pope continued their respective appeals

---

148. The legend of serious defeats inflicted on the Mongols in Moravia by the
Czechs under the Moravian knight Iaroslav of Sternberg has been destroyed by Novotný's penetrating criticism. And yet the myth has been recently repeated by both
Spuler (p. 23) and Grekov (ZO, p. 217); H. T. Cheshire also mentioned Sternberg's
victory, but his study (mentioned in n. 146) appeared before the publication of Novotný's volume.

149. Matthew Paris, 1, 341.

produced less effect than they might have. Frederick warned the king of France "of the papal craft and avarice." "For, in his insatiable ambition, he [the Pope] is now purposing to bring all Christian kingdoms into subjection to him, drawing an instance from his having trodden under-foot the crown of England; and now he dares, with greater rashness and presumption, aspire to bend the majesty of the empire at his nod." [150] On the other hand, the supporters of the pope spread rumors "that the emperor had, of his own accord, plotted this infliction of the Tartars, and that by this clever letter he basely cloaked his nefarious crime, and that in his grasping ambition he was, like Lucifer, or Antichrist, conspiring against the monarchy of the whole world, to the utter ruin of the Christian faith." [151]

The natural result of all this was that King Béla received no substantial assistance from the West. The only crusade which actually took place was that of the Teutonic Knights against Pskov and Novgorod. In spite of their losses in the battle of Liegnitz, the Teutonic Order was now able to support the Livonian drive. Pskov was taken in 1241, and in March 1242 the knights marched against Novgorod. But they did not go far. Prince Alexander met and crushed them on the frozen surface of Lake Peipus in the famous "battle on the ice" (April 5, 1242).[152]

The Mongols in Hungary crossed the frozen Danube late in December 1241 and invaded Croatia, soon taking Zagreb. A detachment was sent after King Béla, who fled to Dalmatia. By the time the Mongol horsemen reached the Adriatic near Split (Spalato) the king had taken ship and reached safety on an island. The Mongols overran the Dalmatian littoral down to Dubrovnik (Raguza) and Cattaro. Another Mongol detachment was sent from Hungary to Klosterneuburg near Vienna, presumably to reconnoiter the roads to the west. The main Mongol army, after a prolonged rest in Hungary, was now poised for a new offensive in Europe. The Western nations, in view of their lack of unity, had little if any chance of withstanding the impending onslaught.

The West was unexpectedly saved by an event which took place in faraway Mongolia. Great Khan Ugedey died on December 11, 1241. When the news reached Batu, in the spring of 1242, he not only called off all preparations for an offensive but led his whole

150. *Idem, 1,* 347.
151. *Idem, 1,* 348.
152. On the "battle on the ice" see Karamzin, *4,* 30–32; Soloviev, *3,* 189–190.

army through northern Serbia and Bulgaria back to South Russia.
The reason for his withdrawal was purely political: Batu wanted to
be in a position to influence the selection of the new great khan,
especially as he himself was potentially a candidate. Moreover, in
the course of the Hungarian campaign he had quarreled with Ugedey's
son Guyuk and Jagatay's grandson Buri, both of whom had returned
in high dudgeon to Mongolia. On Batu's complaint Ugedey had
severely reprimanded both these princes. Now, after Ugedey's death,
they might be expected to take their revenge by intriguing against
Batu. Batu was obviously worried; jockeying for a strong position
in Mongol politics seemed more important to him than continuing
the conquest of Europe.

Ugedey must have been about fifty-one at the time of his death. He
seems to have wrecked his health by excessive drinking. Not long
before his death, appraising his achievements and his sins, he remarked with commendable frankness that his two main vices were
wine and lewd women.[153] As Father Mostaert has commented, Ugedey's portrait in the Yuan series shows, indeed, the features of a
habitual drunkard.[154] It may be doubted, however, that he died a
natural death. According to John of Plano Carpini he was poisoned
by an "aunt" of his son Guyuk.[155] This woman, whoever she was.
must be considered the savior of Western Europe.

153. Kozin, p. 199.
154. A. Mostaert, *AM, 4,* 147.
155. Plano Carpini M, pp. 56–57.

CHAPTER II

THE MONGOL EMPIRE

1. THE REIGN OF GUYUK

THE MONGOL EMPIRE which, until 1206, existed only as a dream in the minds of Temuchin and a few other Mongol clan leaders, took shape in the reign of Chingis-Khan. By the end of the reign of Ugedey the empire was already firmly established, with Karakorum in Mongolia as its capital. Thus within the span of thirty-five years a mighty state came into existence and presented its claims to world leadership. Within that comparatively brief space of time the Mongols conquered vast territories in Asia and Europe; in fact, as the masters of the Eurasian steppe zone, they now were in position to control all of Northern Asia and most of Eastern Europe—the Eurasian subcontinent.

While the Mongols were destined to make further territorial gains both in China and the Middle East, basically the period of Mongol conquest was over. The rulers of the empire must now consolidate and absorb what they had conquered. That task was not an easy one. Still, a tremendous effort was made to ensure the perpetuation of the empire, and during the century following the death of Ugedey, the imperial institutions functioned with reasonable efficiency and precision in most parts of the empire, in spite of all the inner conflicts.

The death of Ugedey in 1241 may be considered an important landmark in the history of both international relations and Mongol politics. While it saved Western Europe from invasion, it resulted in protracted political crisis in Mongolia. Jagatay died soon afterward, and Chingis' grandsons were left to settle the situation as they pleased, with no one in the family old and authoritative enough to impose his will on the others. Ugedey's widow, Khatun [1] Turakina (Toragana), assumed the regency, with the aim of securing the throne

1. Khatun means a noblewoman, a royal dame.

for her eldest son, Guyuk. However, strong opposition to Guyuk could be expected from many princes and clan leaders because of the animosity between him and the powerful conqueror of the West, Batu. There was much political maneuvering to be done, therefore, before the kuriltay could be gathered. In fact, the interregnum lasted four years (1242–46).

To secure her freedom of action the khatun dismissed three of Ugedey's assistants: the Chinese adviser, Eliu Chu-tsai; the Uigur chancellor, Chinkay; and the Khoresmian Moslem, Mahmud Yala-vach. Another Moslem, Abd ar-Rahman, now became the regent's chief adviser after having promised her to double the revenue from the Chinese provinces of the empire. Disillusioned and heartbroken, Eliu Chu-tsai died a few months later. As regards external affairs, the Mongol offensive was pressed during the interregnum only in the Near East. The new commander of the Mongol army in that region, Baiju-Noyan, succeeded in administering a crushing defeat to the Seljuqs in 1243, after which the Seljuq sultan became a vassal of the Mongols. Following this warning King Hethum I of Little Armenia hastened to offer his submission and aid to the Mongols. He con-trolled the region of Cilicia, opposite the island of Cyprus. Through him Mongol influence now extended to the eastern part of the Medi-terranean.

Politically, the most important development within the Mongol Empire in these years was the foundation, by Batu, of the Khanate of Kypchak in South Russia, which was subsequently to be known as the Golden Horde, with the new city of Saray on the lower Volga as its capital. One of Batu's first moves was to summon the leading East Russian princes to Saray to take their oath of allegiance as vassals. When the Mongol army led by Batu returned to South Rus-sia from Hungary most of the non-Juchid princes, with the contingents of Mongol troops they commanded, went back to Mongolia. A few, however, decided to stay in this newly conquered country which they found to their liking. Thus, the number of Mongol troops under Batu's authority increased somewhat, and of course he had at his disposal a strong and well-trained Turkish army commanded by Mongol officers loyal to him. In addition to the Central Asian Turk-men, numerous Cuman and Alan warriors joined Batu's forces.

While from the military angle Batu was powerful enough, his position in Mongol politics was rather weak, since only a small part of the Mongol army and clan leaders depended on him. He of necessity allied himself with Tuluy's son Mongka, his close friend since the European campaign. However, even their combined efforts could only postpone the pre-electoral decision on Guyuk's candidacy but not prevent it. By 1246 most of the Mongol princes and clan leaders had agreed to support Guyuk, and the electoral kuriltay then assembled at the sources of the Orkhon River near Karakorum. Pleading rheumatism, Batu refused to attend it and stayed in Saray. He agreed, however, to send to Mongolia the late Iuri II's brother Iaroslav (father of Alexander Nevsky) whom he had confirmed as grand duke of Vladimir.

Besides Iaroslav, other vassals of the Mongols, such as the Seljuk sultan Kilij-Arslan IV and King David V of Georgia were summoned to Mongolia; King Hethum I of Little Armenia was represented by his brother Sambat. And it so happened that the pope's envoy, Friar John of Plano Carpini, was also present at imperial headquarters at the time of Guyuk's election. Friar John's mission was the result of a new approach to the Mongol problem on the part of Pope Innocent IV, who had been installed in 1243. While continuing Rome's unrelenting struggle against Emperor Frederick II, this pope attempted to reassert the authority of the Catholic Church by a bold international policy based on three ideas: (1) continuation of the crusade in Palestine; (2) extension of the pope's authority over the eastern churches by diplomacy rather than by war; and (3) an understanding with the Mongols, to be achieved by converting the latter to Christianity if possible. The third point in his program proved the most significant.[2]

It must be noted that because of the unwillingness of the Western rulers (with the exception of the emperor) to come to an agreement with the Moslems, the situation in the Near East had taken a turn for the worse. In 1244 the Egyptian sultan encouraged the Khorezmians [3] to move from Iraq to Syria. In August of that year they stormed and sacked the city of Jerusalem. The pope then decided to preach a new—and seventh—crusade. To launch it he convoked a church council in 1245 at Lyon, France, which was recognized by Roman Catholics as the Thirteenth Ecumenical Council.[4] Louis IX

2. On the Eastern policies of Pope Innocent IV see J. Uminski, *Niebezpieczeństwo tatarskie w połowie* XIII *w. i papież Innocenty* IV (Lwów, 1922).

3. The Khorezmians were the remnants of Jalal ad-Din's Turkmen troops; see above, Chapter 1, sec. 7, p. 48.

4. The Greek Orthodox Church does not recognize any church council after the second Nicaean (A.D. 787) as ecumenical.

of France readily assumed the leadership of the new crusade, which however materialized but slowly. It was not until the middle of September 1248 that Louis' army was concentrated at Cyprus.

The Mongol situation was also discussed by the Lyon council, most of the information presented coming from a Russian clergyman, Bishop Peter.[5] The council attempted to rally European powers for the struggle against the Mongols but at the same time approved the pope's plan of negotiating with them. Shortly before the opening of the council the pope had dispatched several missions to contact the Mongols. Two of them succeeded in achieving their task. The Dominican Friar Ascelin and his companions went to northwestern Persia; [6] and the Franciscan Friar John of Plano Carpini accompanied by Friar Benedict of Poland reached Mongolia. Friar John left Lyon in April 1245 carrying a letter addressed "to the King and the People of the Tartars" in which the pope, speaking as head of the Christian world, reproached the Mongols for their inroads on Christian lands and, threatening them with God's wrath, exhorted them to desist from such attacks in the future and to accept Christianity. As the friars were to travel through western Russia, the pope also instructed them to admonish the West Russian princes and clergy "to return to the unity of holy mother church."

Traveling through Bohemia and Silesia Friar John came to Kraków where he and his companions stayed for several months, preparing themselves for the journey through the steppes. They were received in friendly fashion by Prince Vasilko of Volynia, who however refused to commit himself to accept Catholicism without the advice of his elder brother, Daniel of Galicia, who was at Batu's camp at that time. In February 1246 Friar John and his companions passed through devastated Kiev; in April they reached Batu's camp, were promptly received by Batu, and handed him the pope's letter. The friars assisted Batu's interpreters to translate the letter into the Russian, "Saracenic" (Persian), and "Tartar" (Mongol) languages. Batu immediately dispatched all these versions to Karakorum by special messenger and advised the Franciscans to proceed to Mongolia. They arrived at imperial headquarters on July 22 and were treated with consideration but were told that no answer could be

5. Bishop Peter's reports were also used by Matthew of Paris. It should be noted that no Bishop Peter is mentioned in the annals of the Russian church of this period, and that his identity is rather enigmatic. See Spuler, *Iran,* p. 479; Pelliot, p. 18, n. 3.
6. See Risch, pp. 43–45.

given to the pope's message before the enthronement of the khan-elect.

That event took place on August 24. The most significant moment of the ceremony was the seating of the new khan on a piece of felt upon which he was lifted up.[7] All the Mongol princes and clan leaders as well as the vassal rulers pledged their unfailing obedience to the new kagan. Friar John described Guyuk in the following words: "This emperor may be forty or forty-five years or more old;[8] he is of medium stature, very prudent and extremely shrewd, and serious and sedate in his manners; and he has never been seen to laugh lightly or show any levity, and of this we were assured by Christians who were constantly with him. We were also assured by Christians who were of his household that they firmly believed that he was about to become a Christian."[9] Most of the Christians at Guyuk's court were Nestorians, but there were also a number of Greek Orthodox—chiefly Russian artisans employed by the khan. Prominent among them was the goldsmith Cosmas (Kuzma) who was very kind to the Franciscans and supplied them with food. Before it was put in place[10] Cosmas showed the friars the emperor's throne, which he had made. "The throne was of ebony, wonderfully sculptured; and there were also [on it] gold, and precious stones, and, if I remember rightly, pearls; and one went up to it by steps, and it was rounded behind."[11] It was also Cosmas who wrought Guyuk's imperial seal.[12]

One of Guyuk's first moves was to dismiss his mother's creature Abd ar-Rahman (who was then put to death) and reinstate Chinkay and Mahmud Yalavach in their former positions.

It was with Chinkay—a Nestorian Christian—and two of his associates that the pope's envoys had to discuss the subject of their mission. When the Mongol text of the great khan's answer was ready, it was translated orally to the Franciscans who wrote it down in Latin; in addition to the Mongol original, they were also given a Persian translation of the document. Chinkay then told them that the

7. Rockhill, p. 21, n. 1 (on the basis of St. Quentin's report in Vincent of Beauvais' "Speculum historiale," Bk. 31, chap. 22). On the magic significance of the felt see L. Olschki, *The Myth of Felt* (Berkeley, University of California Press, 1949).

8. Actually, Guyuk hardly could have been over thirty at that time.

9. Rockhill, p. 29.

10. *Idem*, p. 26.

11. *Idem*, p. 24.

12. *Idem*, p. 26.

emperor proposed to send his ambassadors to Europe with them. The Franciscans took great pains to dissuade the Mongols from doing so. In the report of his mission Friar John states quite frankly several motives for refusing to let the Mongol envoys accompany him. "The first reason was that we feared they would see the dissensions and wars among us, and that it would encourage them to march against us. The second reason was that we feared they were intended to be spies." [13] After some hesitation the Mongols abandoned the project.

The khan's answer to the pope was typical of the Mongol concept of imperial power. Refusing to consider the pope's plea that he turn Christian, and rejecting the pope's right to censure him, he ordered pope and kings to come personally to Mongolia to offer homage to him. "If you resist, what do we know? Only God knows." [14]

The Franciscans left Karakorum in the middle of November 1246 and reached Lyon around All Saints Day 1247. Even before that Friar Ascelin's mission was back from Persia bringing a letter from Baiju-Noyan, Mongol commander in the Middle East, together with a letter from Khan Guyuk to Baiju-Noyan. The contents of both these documents were similar to that of the letter that Friar John brought to the pope. The relationship of the forces of West and East that confronted each other was now made clear. The pope's claims to universal leadership clashed with the equally universal claims of the Mongol emperor. Compromise or cooperation could hardly be expected between them.

Actually, however, while rigid in principle and uncompromising at the highest level, Mongol policies could be adjusted to circumstances on the local level, especially if military considerations required it. It seems that Guyuk planned to concentrate all his efforts in the Near East, at least for the time being. A new commander was sent there, Aljigiday, to replace Baiju-Noyan.[15] Aljigiday arrived at Mongol headquarters in Armenia in the middle of July 1247 with new instructions. Guyuk's new plan of expansion in the Near East seems to have been based on full cooperation with the Christians against the Moslems. The Christians around him whom Friar John mentions

---

13. *Idem,* p. 29. Three other reasons against taking along Mongol envoys are listed by Friar John in his report. *Idem,* pp. 29–30.

14. Voegelin, pp. 386–387.

15. Pelliot, "Mongols et papauté," Pt. 2, pp. 312–313.

must have supported this plan in all seriousness. It seems probable
that Guyuk himself now became a Christian—and if so a member of
the Nestorian Church. Be that as it may, as soon as Aljigiday received news of the arrival of King Louis IX at Cyprus, he sent
emissaries to coordinate their mutual efforts to "liberate" the Christians in Palestine. These envoys reached Cyprus on December 14,
1248 and were received by the French king on December 20. A
month later they embarked on their return trip accompanied by the
French mission headed by Andrew of Longjumeau. They arrived
in Aljigiday's camp some time in April or May. Khan Guyuk had
died, however, in the autumn of 1248; [16] and Aljigiday could not be
sure that his instructions were still valid. He therefore urged the
French ambassadors to go to Mongolia to see the regent.

Guyuk's reign was too short to show any definite record of successes. Knowing that in other cases every major Mongol campaign
was preceded by a period of careful preparation, we may be sure that
he did not fail to assure the future success of his Near Eastern plans.
From what we know of Guyuk, we may also be sure that he took every
possible step to strengthen imperial authority in Mongolia itself. By
doing so he must have offended many influential princes and clan
leaders. His conversion to Christianity—if we accept that—or at
least his benevolent attitude toward Christians must also have aroused
the opposition of what may be called the Old Mongol party, the
members of which still clung to their traditional beliefs.

From a political angle, relations between Guyuk and Batu were
tense from the beginning of the former's reign, partly as a result of
Batu's refusal to attend the electoral kuriltay. Guyuk kept insisting
that Batu pay him a visit. In the summer of 1248 Batu set out for
Guyuk's ulus. When he reached Lake Alakul at the confines of
Jungaria, he received news from Tuluy's widow that Guyuk was
coming half way to meet him. She added that the kagan's intentions
were evil and that Batu must be on his guard. Batu stopped at Alakul
and took precautions. Guyuk died a week's march from Batu's
camp.[17] It may be doubted that it was a natural death; probably
he was poisoned by agents of Tuluy's widow or of Batu himself.

16. According to Grum-Grzymailo, *2,* 467, Guyuk died in April 1248; according to
Tiesenhausen, *2,* 66, n. 4, in the year 646 A.H. (April 26, 1248 to April 15, 1249).

17. On the circumstances of Guyuk's death see Tiesenhausen, *2,* 66; E. Blochet, "La
Mort du Khagan Kouyouk," *ROC, 23* (1922–23), 160–171.

2. THE REIGN OF MONGKA

The death of Guyuk resulted in an even graver political crisis in Mongolia than had followed his father's death. The regency was assumed by Guyuk's widow, Khatun Ogul-Gaimish, a devoted shamanist and a superstitious and greedy woman, if we credit the sources, most of which reflect the point of view of the rival group. It is certain that the khatun lacked prestige among the Mongol chieftains. In the circumstances she was not in a position to continue her late husband's policy in the Near East, and probably did not even approve of it. Louis IX's ambassadors arrived at her court early in 1250. Instead of any promise of cooperation on equal terms, the khatun in her letter to the king demanded annual tribute from him.[18] This letter reached Louis IX in April 1251.

In the two years required for the king's ambassadors to travel to Karakorum and back, many things happened to King Louis. The Seventh Crusade ended in disaster. The French knights who had invaded Egypt and whose ranks were decimated by plague suffered a complete defeat, and Louis IX himself was taken prisoner by the Moslems in 1250. He was later set free for a huge ransom. The khatun's letter only added to his disillusionment. According to the historian Joinville, "The King regretted very much ever having sent a mission." [19]

By 1250 the heated consultations of the Mongol leaders on the succession to the great khan's throne reached a deadlock, and a complete break between the two opposing groups of the Chingisids—the descendants of Juchi and Tuluy on the one hand and those of Jagatay and Ugedey, on the other—became evident. As the latter group lacked prominent leaders, Batu and Mongka felt themselves stronger than their opponents and finally resolved to take the matter into their own hands and impose their will on the rival faction.[20] When the first session of the electoral kuriltay, which met in 1250 near Lake Isyk-Kul, in Jagatay's ulus, arrived at no decision, Batu sent his son Sartak and his brother Berke (Berkay) eastward with three army divisions to arrange for the meeting of a second session of the kuriltay

18. Voegelin, pp. 390–391.

19. Jean Sire de Joinville, *Histoire de Saint-Louis*, N. de Wailly, ed. (Paris, 1868), p. 175; cf. Voegelin, p. 381.

20. On the circumstances of Mongka's election see Grousset, pp. 306–308; Tiesenhausen, *2*, 66–67.

on the banks of the Kerulen River in Mongolia, that is, in Tuluy's ulus. The most influential descendants of Jagatay and Ugedey refused to attend this meeting, which did not prevent the rival party from insisting on the legitimacy of the session. As Batu declined the offer of the throne, Mongka was proclaimed great khan on July 1, 1251. There must have been a secret understanding between Mongka and Batu, in which Batu was promised full autonomy for his ulus. On that basis the two cousins cooperated wholeheartedly.

Mongka's first move was to crush the rival faction ruthlessly. A number of princes of the houses of Jagatay and Ugedey were accused of conspiracy against the new khan and executed or imprisoned together with their adherents. Among others Aljigiday, the Mongol commander in Persia, was summoned back to Mongolia and put to death. The chancellor, Chinkay, also had to pay with his head for his loyalty to Ugedey's house. Crafty Mahmud Yalavach was the only one of the old imperial advisers to survive. In 1252 Khatun Ogul-Gaimish was sentenced to death. The extent of Mongka's hatred of her may be seen in his defaming her memory, two years later, in an official document, his letter to Louis IX: "she was viler than a bitch," wrote the great khan to the French king.[21] To Friar William of Rubruck Mongka said that Ogul-Gaimish "was the worst kind of a witch, and that she had destroyed her whole family by her witchcraft." [22]

The transfer of the succession from the house of Ugedey to the house of Tuluy was indeed a coup d'état. While Mongka's determined policy of terror resulted in a temporary suppression of any revolt, the breach could not be healed easily and a new conflict was to occur in the reign of his successor. For the time being, however, things looked bright for the Mongol Empire since Mongka proved a capable and dynamic ruler. Two major Mongol drives were undertaken in his reign, in the Near East and in South China. In the Near East King Louis IX made another effort at cooperation. Having heard of Batu's benevolent attitude toward Christians and of the conversion of Batu's son Sartak, the king sent a new Franciscan mission to South Russia under the leadership of the above-mentioned Friar William. This time the Franciscans were instructed not to divulge their identity as diplomats but to travel as missionaries. They left Constantinople in May 1253 and arrived at Batu's headquarters on

21. Voegelin, p. 19.
22. Rockhill, p. 250.

July 31. Batu ordered one of Friar William's companions to stay in
South Russia at Sartak's court and the other two to proceed to
Mongolia.

The friars reached Mongka's camp in December 1253 and were
received by the great khan in audience on January 4, 1254. In the
report of his mission Friar William describes the reception as follows:
Mongka "was seated on a couch and was dressed in a skin spotted and
glossy, like a seal's skin. He is a little man of medium height, aged
forty-five years, and a young wife sat beside him; and a very ugly,
full-grown girl called Cirina, with other children sat on a couch after
them. This dwelling had belonged to a certain Christian lady, whom
he had much loved, and of whom he had this girl." [23] The friars were
offered drinks—choice of rice wine, "black kumiss," [24] or honey. They
chose the rice wine. Then they asked permission "to perform the service of God" for the khan and his family during their stay in Mongolia.
They referred to Batu's friendliness and Sartak's conversion to Christianity. On that occasion Mongka made a solemn declaration of his
wholehearted association with Batu: "As the sun sends its rays
everywhere, likewise my sway and that of Batu reach everywhere."
By that time, according to Friar William, his interpreter was drunk
and it became difficult to understand him. The great khan himself
appeared inebriated to the friar.[25] After the official part of the reception was over, the conversation turned to France, and the Mongols
began to question the friar, "whether there were many sheep and
cattle and horses there, and whether they had not better go there at
once and take it all." [26]

The friars were to be allowed to stay in Mongolia for two months.
Actually they stayed many more. Like John of Plano Carpini's
mission, Friar William and his companion met a number of Christian
captives in Karakorum. Among them was a woman named Pascha
from Metz in Lorraine, who was married to a Russian carpenter.
She told the friars of a "certain master goldsmith, William [Guil-
laume] by name, a native of Paris: and his family name was Buchier
[Boucher], and the name of his father was Laurent Buchier. She
believed that he had still a brother living on the Grand Pont, called
Roger Buchier." [27] Later on, in Karakorum, the friars met Guillaume
Boucher and admired the "magic fountain" he had built for the great

23. *Idem*, p. 172.
24. On the "black kumiss" see below, Chapter 3, n. 22.
25. Rockhill, p. 174.
26. *Idem*, pp. 175.
27. *Idem*, pp. 176–177.

khan's palace.[28] Friar William was received in audience once more on April 5, 1254 and then given the khan's letter to King Louis IX. He left Karakorum in August 1254 and reached Cyprus on June 16, 1255. By that time the king was already back in France, and for some reason the provincial of the Franciscan Order refused to allow Friar William to proceed there. The khan's letter and the friar's reports were sent to Louis IX through the order. When the king finally received Mongka's letter he found little encouragement in it since the great khan required his formal submission to the Mongol Empire as the basis for any further cooperation.[29]

At the time of Mongka's negotiations with Rubruck the Mongol drive in the Near East had already begun, with the great khan's brother Hulagu as supreme commander.[30] The concentration of his main army took place in Mongolia in 1253. Every effort was made to guarantee the success of the expedition. Four thousand Chinese army technicians were mobilized to man war engines capable of throwing rocks, shafts, and burning naphtha on enemy cities. Pasturage for cavalry horses and remounts was reserved for Hulagu's army all along the designated route from Mongolia to Persia. Engineers were sent ahead to build or repair bridges over the major rivers; huge stores of food and wine were established in Persia.[31]

In September 1255 Hulagu reached Samarkand and in January 1256 crossed the Amu-Daria River with choice troops; at that juncture his army was reinforced by several units of the army of the Khanate of Kypchak. Hulagu's first blow was directed against the Assassins. Within a year about a hundred castles and fortresses of the sectarians were destroyed, including their main stronghold, Alamut. Most of the members of the sect were killed or imprisoned; some entered the Mongol service. After having suppressed the Assassins, Hulagu attacked the Caliphate of Bagdad. In February 1258 Bagdad was stormed and looted and the Caliph, the last of the Abbasid dynasty, was taken prisoner and executed. While the whole Sunnite world was stunned by the news, the Shiites could not but derive some satisfaction from the ruin of the leader of the "heretics." [32]

28. *Idem,* pp. 207–208; see L. Olschki, *Guillaume Boucher* (Baltimore, Johns Hopkins University Press, 1946).

29. Voegelin, pp. 391–392.

30. On Hulagu's campaign see Grousset, *Histoire,* pp. 99–102; Spuler, *Iran,* pp. 48–53.

31. Grum-Grzymailo, *2,* 474.

32. Krymsky, *Persia, 3,* 10. V. Minorsky remarks that by destroying the Assassins, who were deadly enemies of orthodox Islam, the Mongols inadvertently contributed to the unity of Islam. Minorsky, "Middle East," p. 431.

Hulagu's next objective was Syria whose potentates were under
the suzerainty of the sultan of Egypt. Since 1250 Egypt had been
ruled by a new dynasty—the Mameluk, founded by the leader of the
former sultan's Mameluk Guards, which were recruited from foreign
captives, mostly of Kypchak extraction. The new dynasty gave Egypt
a strong rule, and since the sultan might be expected to oppose the
Mongols vigorously Hulagu had to prepare for further expansion
before actually striking. As a result, after the capture of Bagdad
there came a lull in Mongol operations in the Near East.

Meanwhile, the Chinese campaign which started in 1253 also made
good progress, under the command of another brother of Mongka,
Kubilay (Khubilay), the ablest of them all.[33] The Mongol leaders
followed a bold strategic plan according to which a strong army
group, under Kubilay's personal leadership, outflanked the center
of the Sung empire. Passing through the province of Szechwan,
Kubilay's troops entered Yunnan, and by 1257 some of them had
got as far as Tongking. Kubilay's successes and growing popularity
aroused suspicion of him at Mongka's court. In 1257 Mongka summoned Kubilay to Karakorum and sent an inspector general to South
China to investigate charges of alleged irregularities in Kubilay's
administration. A break between the two brothers seemed imminent.
However, Kubilay wisely complied with Mongka's order and returned to Mongolia, leaving Subudey's son Uriangedey in command
of the troops in the Tongking area. While the great khan was satisfied with his brother's explanations, he nevertheless decided personally to assume supreme leadership in the campaign. Kubilay was
entrusted with command of the army group which was to operate in
Hunan, Hupeh, and Anhwei; Uriangedey was ordered to proceed
northward from Tongking for a junction with Kubilay's troops. The
great khan took upon himself the task of completing the conquest
of Szechwan. On the whole, all of the operations developed successfully. Before long, however, an epidemic of dysentery occurred in
Szechwan which decimated the great khan's troops. Among its victims
was Mongka himself. He died in August 1259.

3. THE REIGN OF KUBILAY

During the reign of Mongka the princes of the houses of Jagatay
and Ugedey had no alternative but to submit to the house of Tuluy.

33. On the China campaigns under Mongka see Grum-Grzymailo, 2, 470–472; Grousset, pp. 314–317.

On the whole, the majority of the Mongols seemed definitely to have accepted Mongka's leadership. A series of outstanding military successes could not but enhance his prestige as well as that of his brothers Kubilay and Hulagu. Batu, in the West, had died around 1255.[34] His son Sartak came to Karakorum and was confirmed by Mongka as khan of Kypchak; he died, however, on his return trip to Saray, in 1256. He was succeeded by his brother Ulagchi whose reign also was very brief.[35] Presumably both Sartak and Ulagchi were poisoned by their uncle, Batu's brother Berke who assumed power in Kypchak around 1258.[36] Berke's relations with Mongka seemed to have been quite friendly, and he could be expected to remain loyal to the house of Tuluy.

So it seemed that the throne was firmly secured for Tuluy's descendants and that Kubilay, as the eldest living son of Tuluy, was the natural candidate for the imperial title. Unexpectedly, however, there appeared another candidate, Kubilay's youngest brother, Arik-Buka, whose counterclaims caused a rift in the house of Tuluy and eventually enabled the princes of the rival houses to defy the authority of Tuluy's descendants. In his capacity as ochigin Arik-Buka resided in Karakorum and was entitled to assume the regency after Mongka's death. He overstepped the bounds of his authority and without waiting for the arrival of either Kubilay or Hulagu convoked a kuriltay attended by those princes and clan leaders who were at hand in Mongolia. Among them were a few noted generals, including Alandar. Arik-Buka's obvious intention was to obtain the throne for himself.

Meanwhile Kubilay, at the news of Mongka's death, hastily concluded an armistice with the Sung, whose empire was about to collapse and who now received an unexpected respite. He then hurried north with a strong contingent of troops, to be ready for any eventuality. Owing to this precaution, when he reached Peking and heard of Arik-Buka's intentions he proved strong enough to assert his authority. His first countermove was to convoke a rival kuriltay near Dolon-Nor in northern Chihli. This gathering was attended by some of Kubilay's relatives, as well as by Ugedey's son Kadan and a grandson of Chingis' youngest brother Temuga-Ochigin. It could hardly be called legal, but neither was the one convoked by Arik-Buka. On

34. On the date of Batu's death see Pelliot, p. 29; on the dates of Sartak's and Ulagchi's reigns, pp. 34–35.
35. Whether Ulagchi was a brother or a son of Sartak is not clear. Pelliot, pp. 35–44.
36. On Berke see W. Barthold, "Berke," EI, 1, 707–709; Pelliot, pp. 47–51.

May 6, 1260 Kubilay was proclaimed great khan by his kuriltay; a couple of weeks later the other kuriltay elected Arik-Buka emperor. All attempts of Kubilay to achieve a compromise failed and war started between the two brothers. Alandar and other followers of Arik-Buka attempted to swing the armies in Szechwan and Kansu to his side but were defeated by Kubilay's generals. The next year Kubilay's army invaded Mongolia. Arik-Buka now went to Jungaria and allied himself with Alugu, a grandson of Jagatay,[37] whom Arik-Buka recognized as khan of Transoxania. Kubilay used diplomacy instead of war and succeeded in detaching Alugu from Arik-Buka. The latter finally had to surrender. He was reprimanded but pardoned by Kubilay; his associates however were arrested (1264). A few weeks later it was announced that Arik-Buka had died of an illness.[38]

Mongka's death and the ensuing troubles seriously undermined the Mongols' position in the Near East. As the death of Ugedey saved Western Europe, the passing of Mongka saved Syria. This was another drastic example of the extent to which the Mongols' politics affected their war effort. In 1259 Hulagu had made final preparations for invading Syria in force. Upon hearing of the great khan's demise, he felt that his presence at the kuriltay was more important than the Syrian campaign. He decided to go to Mongolia, taking along his best troops.

The leadership in the Syrian campaign was entrusted to an experienced general, Kit-Buka. He was a Nestorian Christian and could bid for the sympathies of the Near East Christians in his struggle against the Moslems. In René Grousset's words, this was a "Yellow Crusade." [39] Unfortunately for both Mongols and Christians the forces under Kit-Buka's command were not sufficient for the task. His main army consisted of only one division of Turkish troops led by Mongol officers. At first he scored some successes. Both Aleppo and Damascus fell to the yellow crusaders (January–March 1260). At that juncture the sultan of Egypt decided to send his best troops to Syria to stop the invaders. It will be recalled that, like their Mongol-led opponents, the Mameluk troops were also Turkish, most of them of Kypchak origin. Thus the battle between the "Mongols" and the "Egyptians" fought in Galilee on September 3, 1260 was

37. See Genealogical Table III.
38. Grum-Grzymailo, 2, 481, n. 2; Grousset, pp. 323–324.
39. Grousset, Histoire, p. 100.

actually a duel between two groups of Turkish soldiers.[40] The Mongols suffered a severe defeat; Kit-Buka himself was taken prisoner and executed. This set a limit to Mongol expansion in the Near East. Being a victory for Islam, the battle of Galilee spelled the doom of the remnants of the Western crusaders' states in Palestine.

Although Hulagu sacrificed the success of his Syrian drive in an attempt to influence the election of the new great khan, he was not able actively to interfere in Mongol high politics. The quick action of Kubilay and Arik-Buka in each convoking a kuriltay of his own made it impossible for Hulagu to attend either in view of the great distance between Persia and Mongolia. Hulagu announced his whole-hearted support of Kubilay and returned to his headquarters in Persia in order to consolidate his authority over that country and organize a new campaign against the Mameluks. These plans however had to be abandoned because of his clash with Berke, khan of Kypchak. At the time of Hulagu's war against the Assassins and the Caliphate of Bagdad the khan of Kypchak sent contingents of his troops to reinforce Hulagu's army. After the close of the campaign Berke claimed his share of the spoils, indicating that he would like to obtain Azerbaijan. The price seemed too high to Hulagu who was himself interested in Azerbaijan, among other reasons because of the excellent grazing grounds for the horses of his cavalry in the Mugan steppe. The conflict between Hulagu and Berke was accentuated by the fact that Berke sympathized with Arik-Buka; also by his becoming a convert to Islam. Negotiations between the two cousins lasted for several years without definite results. Finally Berke led his army to Transcaucasia; the battle ended in a serious defeat of Hulagu's troops (1263–64).[41]

Hulagu died in 1265, Berke in 1266. The conflict between the il-khans (Hulagu's successors) and the khans of Kypchak continued unabated, but in spite of it both the Hulagids and the Juchids recognized Kubilay as their suzerain. Both sent him contingents of troops to complete the conquest of the empire of the Sung. Thus Kubilay was able to spare Mongol warriors in the new campaign in South China which started in 1267. Most of his army consisted of soldiers conscripted in Persia and Russia. A Chinese general (from North

40. On the role of the Turkish troops in the Mameluk state see Poliak, "Caractère colonial," pp. 233–235.

41. On the relations between the khans of Kypchak and Hulagu and his descendants see below, Chapter 3.

China), Sze Tang-tse, was appointed commander in chief.[42] Kubilay's whole attitude toward China differed greatly from that of his predecessors. In 1264 he made Khan-Balyk (Peking) his capital; in 1271, following the Chinese fashion, he gave the new name Yuan to his dynasty. He considered China the most valuable part of his dominions and gradually fell under the influence of the Chinese culture, accepting Buddhism as his faith.

Kubilay's new policies were also applied to his military operations. He made every effort to spare the Chinese the horrors of war and promised peace with honor to every Chinese city that surrendered voluntarily. The policy bore fruit, and in 1276 the Mongol general Bayan took possession of Hangchow, in Chekiang, where the dowager empress with her son, the boy emperor, had sought refuge. Bayan sent them to Peking, where the boy emperor, advised by his mother, formerly ceded his imperial rights to Kubilay. The latter, on his part, generously provided for the maintenance of the last of the Sung.[43] Even after that one of the Sung princes continued resistance in Canton. It was not until 1279 that all of China submitted to the Mongol emperor.

While Kubilay's supremacy was recognized in China, his authority in the Mongol world was defied by Ugedey's grandson Kaidu (Qaidu). At the time of Mongka's coming to power, Kaidu had been among those lesser princes of the rival faction who were not considered dangerous enough to be executed. He was even granted a small apanage in the Ili region. While Kaidu must have resented the preponderance of the princes of the house of Tuluy in Mongol affairs, he realized that for the time being his resources were not sufficient to oppose them.[44] So he made the unification of the Ugedey ulus his primary objective. By 1269 he was master of Transoxania and Kashgaria, and his leadership was respected by most of his kin as well as by some princes of the house of Jagatay. Moreover, for a number of years he was careful not to oppose Kubilay's imperial authority openly. It was not until 1274 that Kaidu felt himself strong enough to assert his independence.

Kaidu's first move was to oust Kubilay's lieutenants from Kashgar, Yarkand, and Khotan. In 1276 he invaded the center of the

42. See Grum-Grzymailo, 2, 487.

43. Grousset, p. 325.

44. On Kaidu's conflict with Kubilay see Grum-Grzymailo, 2, 480-482, 488-494; Grousset, pp. 325-331. On Kaidu see also Wassaf, pp. 126-146 (German trans.).

Uigur country—the Kucha-Turfan region—to demand vassal allegiance of the idikut of the Uigurs. Kubilay reacted quickly by sending an expeditionary corps to Central Asia under the command of one of his sons, Nomogan. Before long the imperial authority was restored in Kashgaria and Khotan. But the energetic Kaidu did not consider himself vanquished. In association with a son of Mongka and with another nephew of Kubilay, Kaidu hastened to Mongolia and took possession of the former capital, Karakorum, in 1277. This event made a deep impression on many Mongol chieftains. All those who may be said to have belonged to the Old Mongol party and objected to the pro-Chinese policy of Kubilay now looked to Kaidu as their leader.

Realizing the seriousness of the situation, Kubilay sent his best general, Bayan, to Mongolia. Kaidu and his associates were defeated and Karakorum returned to Kubilay's authority in 1278. However, Kaidu was still in control of western Mongolia and a good part of Turkestan, cutting the line of communications between China and the western khanates (Persia and Kypchak). It became clear that Kubilay would have to abandon his other undertakings and concentrate his strength if he wanted to suppress Kaidu's revolt. This Kubilay was not prepared to do; he kept only sufficient forces ready to defeat Kaidu's repeated attempts to raid central and eastern Mongolia (1287–88 and 1293).

Following the conquest of South China, Kubilay turned his main attention to the peripheral states, some of which had been under the suzerainty, real or nominal, of either the Chin or the Sung dynasties. The road to Tibet had been open to the Mongols since the destruction of the Tangut Kingdom by Chingis-Khan in 1227. In the course of their subsequent wars with China the Mongols crossed the eastern section of Tibet and occupied some of its provinces. After his conversion to Buddhism Kubilay considered himself a natural protector of the monks of Tibet and in 1261 appointed the lama Pagspa (Passepa) King of the Law, investing him with spiritual and secular power in Tibet. In return the lama gave his blessing to the Yuan dynasty.[45] It was this Pagspa who designed a new Mongol alphabet, the so-called "square characters," which was used by the Mongols throughout the Yuan period.[46]

45. Grousset, *Histoire*, p. 79; Cordier, *2*, 337–338.
46. On the Mongol square writing see B. Vladimirtsov, *Sravnitelnaia grammatika mongolskogo pismennogo iazyka i khalkhasskogo narechiia* (Leningrad, 1929), pp. 22–

While relations between the Mongols and Tibet were friendly, Kubilay had to send troops to Burma and Indo-China to secure the submission of their rulers. In their expeditions to Annam, Champa, Cambodia, and Burma in the 1280's the Mongols scored a number of initial victories, but in most cases their troops suffered from dysentery and other tropical diseases, and in general the soldiers of the Mongol armies, whether Mongols, Turks, or others, could not accustom themselves to the damp climate of that new theater of war. This eventually resulted either in the defeat of the Mongols or in their withdrawal. Still, the rulers of the Indo-Chinese states were sufficiently impressed with Mongol strength, and by 1288 a number of them had recognized Kubilay's suzerainty. Only the Mongol maritime expedition to Java in 1293 was definitely repulsed and the authority of the great khan firmly defied by the rajah of Madjapahit.

That the Mongols were not a naval power was also proved by the failure of their two attempts to conquer Japan, in 1274 and 1281. For the second of these Kubilay assembled in North Chinese and Korean ports a huge flotilla to transport the expeditionary corps to Hakata on the island of Kyushu. The landing of the army took place according to plan but soon afterward the Mongol ships were destroyed or scattered by a typhoon. Cut from its bases, the army was surrounded and defeated by the Japanese. After this disaster Kubilay abandoned the idea of subjecting Japan to his power.[47]

Kubilay's attitude toward the West differed from that of his predecessors as radically as did his policy toward China. Absorbed as he was in the task of building up his Chinese empire and maintaining his control over other Mongol princes, he abandoned the idea of conquering Europe. He was the most powerful ruler in the world; most of Asia, as well as the eastern part of Europe, recognized his supreme authority. He had no incentive to expand his empire farther west; the advantages if any would be to the local khanates, not to the empire. Besides, Kubilay was realistic enough to recognize that if the European rulers agreed to collaborate with the Mongols in the Near East, it would be as his allies, not as his subjects. And in spite of his conversion to Buddhism he had a high respect for

23; A. Dragunov, "The hPhags-pa Script and Ancient Mandarin," *OGN* (1930), pp. 627–647, 755–797; M. Lewicki, "Les Inscriptions mongoles inédites en écriture carrée," *CO, 12* (1937); N. Poppe, *Kvadratnaia pismennost'* (Moscow and Leningrad, 1941).

47. Cordier, *2*, 299–301; Grousset, *Histoire*, p. 71; Franke, *Geschichte*, pp. 439–442. There is a special monograph on that episode, N. Yamada, *Ghenko, The Mongol Invasion of Japan* (New York, Dutton, 1916).

Christianity. The Nestorian Church enjoyed complete freedom in his empire and he was ready to admit Roman Catholics to his dominions as well.

From the political angle, an agreement with the Christians was especially important for the Mongol khanate in Persia since its rulers, as the il-khans,[48] were eager to continue their struggle with Egypt. As early as 1267 Hulagu's successor Abaga sent his congratulations to the pope on the occasion of the latter's victory over the Hohenstaufen, Manfred of Sicily.[49] The Nestorians in the Middle East on their part tried to promote understanding between the Mongols and the West. With Abaga's approval two Nestorian clerics attended the Fourteenth Ecumenical Council at Lyon in 1274.[50]

It is well known what an important role as intermediaries between the Mongols and the West was played during Kubilay's reign by three Venetian merchants, Maffio and Niccolo Polo and the latter's son Marco, famous as Il Milione. Maffio and Niccolo came to China for the first time in 1262. In 1266 Kubilay sent them back to Europe with a special mission to the pope, asking the dispatch to China of one hundred Christian scholars and technicians to instruct his subject in Western ways of life and religion. When the Polo brothers reached Rome, in 1269 there was no pope in office. As soon as a new pope, Gregory X, was elected, in 1271, the Polos were sent back to Mongolia with his blessings and promises of cooperation. This time young Marco accompanied his father and uncle. Marco's activities in China as well as his impressions of Kubilay's empire have been vividly described in his immortal book and are common knowledge. He reports the great khan's personal appearance in the following words. "He is of a good stature, neither tall nor short, but of a middle height. He has a becoming amount of flesh, and is very shapely in all his limbs. His complexion is white and red, the eyes black and fine, the nose well formed and well set on." [51] Marco Polo spent seventeen

48. The title "il-khan" derives from *il* (*el*) which means "people," "tribe," in old Turkish; the original meaning is "khan of a people" (of an "ulus"), that is a "regional khan." Cf. Grousset, *Extrême-Orient*, 2, 458, n. 1.

49. Spuler, *Iran*, p. 228.

50. On the role of the Nestorians in the religious life of the Middle and Far East in this period and their relations with Rome see A. C. Moule, *Christians in China before the Year 1550* (London, Society for Promoting Christian Knowledge, 1930), chap. 4; K. S. Latourette, *A History of the Expansion of Christianity* (New York and London, Harpers, 1938), 2, 331–338; Idem, *A History of Christian Missions in China* (New York, Macmillan, 1932), pp. 61–77.

51. MPYC, *1*, 356; MPMP, *1*, 204. For Kubilay's portrait see Khara-Davan, p. 187; Mostaert, *AM, 4*, 149.

years at Kubilay's court (1275–92) and was entrusted with important diplomatic missions in the Far East as well as with various administrative tasks. His success in China was an important factor in Kubilay's benevolent attitude toward the West.

The sympathetic attitude of the council of Lyon toward the idea of Mongol-Christian cooperation in the Near East was understood by the il-khans as confirmation of an alliance between themselves and the pope. Actually the West, owing to its internal dissensions, was not in a position to offer them any military assistance. The il-khans however did not abandon hope of eventually reaching an understanding with the West. In the period between 1285 and 1290 Il-Khan Argun sent several diplomatic missions to the Western rulers—to Pope Nicholas IV, Philip IV of France, and Edward I of England—urging all of them to join him in his projected attack on Egypt.[52] No military cooperation resulted from these missions, and in 1291 the Egyptian sultan Qalawun's troops stormed Acre, the crusaders' last stronghold in Palestine. On the other hand, the negotiations between the Mongols and the West prepared the ground for expanding the Catholic missions in the Middle and Far East. In 1289 Pope Nicholas IV sent the Franciscan, John of Montecorvino, with letters to Il-Khan Argun and Great Khan Kubilay. John's task was to establish the Catholic hierarchy in the Orient. He reached Tabriz in 1290 and the next year went to India to offer guidance to the Nestorian communities there. By the time he finally reached Peking Kubilay had died.

Kubilay's internal reforms were no less significant than his military and diplomatic activities. In accordance with the best Chinese traditions he encouraged the development of arts and learning. In China a council of scholars had been considered since antiquity an essential part of good government.[53] Such a council, a kind of learned academy, took shape under Kubilay and continued under his successors.[54] He also undertook the task of coordinating Mongol and Chinese institutions. In the first period after the Mongol conquest China was subjected to martial law. Mongol military commanders were in

52. On the letters of the il-khans to the Western rulers see Spuler, *Iran*, pp. 229–230; Kotwicz, "Lettres" 1, 2; E. Haenisch, "Zu den Briefen der mongolischen Il-Khane Argun und Öljeitu an den Koenig Philipp den Schönen von Frankreich," *Oriens, 2* (1949), 216–235; Cleaves, "Chancellery." Cf. Minorsky, "Middle East," pp. 434–437.

53. Escarra, p. 15.

54. See Otto Franke, "Kublai Khan und seine chinesischen Berater," *Forschungen und Forschritte, 18* (1942), 283–285; also *idem, Geschichte,* pp. 470–471.

charge of the civilian administration as well. The Mongols themselves recognized only their own law, the Yasa. This, however, was
hardly applicable to the Chinese, a settled nation with an old civilization. After the first destructive phase of the conquest was over, the
Mongol rulers had tacitly to accept the existence of native laws and
regulations in China. After the conquest of North China, the Mongol
emperors left the code of the Chin in force for the Chinese population whenever it did not patently contradict the Yasa. However, when
Kubilay felt that his rule was firmly established in North China he
decided to change the existing system of law and administration. He
abrogated the Chin code in 1271 and issued a number of new ordinances. These were contrary to the spirit of the Chinese legislation,
and Kubilay's Chinese advisers humbly but persistently pointed out
the necessity of preparing a new all-embracing code of laws. Kubilay
finally gave way, and in 1291 a draft of the future code was approved.[55]

Administratively Kubilay divided China into twelve provinces
(*sheng*). In Peking three offices of central administration were created: the Office of Government (*chung-shu-sheng*), for internal affairs; the Secret State Council (*shu-mi-yüan*), for foreign affairs
and army administration; and the Control Office (*yü-shih-t'ai*) to
supervise the work of the civil servants.[56] In F. E. A. Krause's opinion, the administrative system established by Kubilay was the best
China had so far had.[57]

Education and financial administration followed the old Chinese
patterns. When the Mongols conquered China they became acquainted with paper money; Kubilay made it the official currency of
his empire. In 1282 an important law was promulgated concerning
the issuance of paper bills, their relation to gold and silver, and the
withdrawal from circulation of damaged bills. Five years later new
regulations appeared concerning the exchange rate of paper money
for gold and silver.[58] Like his predecessors Kubilay paid great attention to the safety and improvement of the roads. In China this also

55. Ratchnevsky, pp. x–xi.
56. Krause, *Geschichte,* pp. 183–184. On the system of Mongol administration in China
under the Yuan dynasty see Cordier, *2,* 324 ff.; Ratchnevsky; Franke, *Geld;* Matsuo
Otagi, "The Census of Northern China Taken by the Mongols in the Middle of the
xiiith Century," *ASTH,* pp. 9–10 (English summary).
57. Krause, *Geschichte,* p. 184; see also Franke, *Geschichte,* pp. 470–490.
58. See Franke, *Geld,* pp. 57–82. On paper money in China under Kubilay see also
Marco Polo, MPYC, *1,* 423–426; MPMP, *1,* 238–240.

included care of the waterways. It was in Kubilay's reign that the construction of the Grand Canal connecting the mouth of the Yangtse River with that of Pei-ho was completed.[59] This, among other things, secured ample supplies of rice for the fast-growing population of Peking.

Kubilay lived to the ripe age of around seventy, an unusual life-span for one in his circumstances. He died in 1294.

4. THE YUAN DYNASTY AFTER KUBILAY

I

As we have seen, in the early period of the Mongol Empire, all of Chingis-Khan's four sons and their descendants were considered eligible for the throne, the choice of candidate to be made by the kuriltay. With Mongka's election the rights to the throne were actually restricted to the descendants of Tuluy. The contest after Mongka's death was between two members of the house of Tuluy's, no prince of any other branch being strong enough to present his claims. Still, the clash between Tuluy's oldest living son and his youngest son almost wrecked the unity of the empire and must have produced a painful impression not only on Kubilay himself but on a number of his advisers as well. A reform of the law of succession seemed imperative. This actually took place with the establishment of the Yuan dynasty in China by Kubilay. Following the Chinese pattern of power, Kubilay restricted the succession to his direct male descendants. According to Marco Polo, four of Kubilay's wives were considered his legitimate consorts, "and the eldest of his sons by the first wife ought by rights to be emperor." [60] It should be noted that this was in agreement with the traditional Chinese concept of state and society. According to that, the eldest son alone was entitled to replace the father in the family cult; the succession in the cult in turn entailed the succession in the patrimonial estate, and, at the state level, the succession in the rule.[61]

59. For Rashid ad-Din's evidence on the building of the Grand Canal see J. Klaproth, "Description de la Chine sous le règne de la dynastie mongole," *JA*, 2d ser., *11* (1833), 341–345; *Cathay, 3,* 115–116.

60. MPYC, *1,* 356; MPMP, *1,* 205. That the eldest son of the *first* wife is considered heir-apparent has been established by Moule-Pelliot; the Yule-Cordier translation has: "the eldest of his sons by those four wives."

61. See Escarra, p. 19. Among the Mongols, as we have seen (Chapter 1, sec. 3), there was a cleavage between the authority of the eldest son as head of the clan cult and of the youngest son as head of the family hearth and recipient of the father's estate.

Kubilay's eldest son was accordingly proclaimed heir apparent to the throne. As he died before his father, his son and Kubilay's grandson, Timur (whose Mongol temple name was Oljaitu and Chinese memorial title Ch'eng-tsung), was designated for the succession in 1293.[62] Presumably, in all cases when there was no clear line of succession, owing to a premature death of the eldest son, the reigning emperor was entitled to appoint his successor. The new arrangements achieved their objective in the sense that until the end of the Yuan dynasty only Kubilay's descendants were considered eligible to the throne. The order of seniority, however, was not always observed. In most cases confirmation of the new emperor by the kuriltay was held indispensable.

At the time of Kubilay's death the crown prince, Timur, happened to be in Mongolia entrusted with the task of guarding this region against any possible attack by Kaidu. Timur's mother convoked the kuriltay, which was attended by those Chingisid princes who were in or around Peking. At first, it seems, there was some opposition to Timur's candidacy.[63] The matter was settled by the commander of the Imperial Guards, Bayan, who announced that he would tolerate no opposition to Timur since the latter had been designated by Kubilay as his successor.[64] Bayan's ultimatum was accepted, and the assembly voted for Timur. He was immediately summoned to the capital and proclaimed emperor.

During the reign of Timur (1294–1307) most of the state affairs left unfinished by Kubilay were more or less satisfactorily concluded. The kings of Cambodia and Burma swore fealty to the emperor (1296–97). Keeping aloof from any further entanglements in the Pacific Ocean area, Timur was in a position to pay more attention to Mongol affairs. His troops fought a series of battles in 1297–98 with those of Kaidu and his associates. Military attacks and counterattacks were complicated by diplomatic moves and countermoves, by ever-changing combinations of princes, and by personal rivalries and betrayals. On the whole Kaidu steadily lost ground. He profited, however, by a lull, and in 1301 made a supreme effort to seize Karakorum. He was defeated, and died the same year.

62. MPYC, *1*, 360; MPMP, *1*, 206; Franke, *Geld*, p. 84. The Mongol and Chinese titles of the Yuan emperors are given here and hereafter according to A. C. Moule, "A Table of the Emperors of the Yüan Dynasty," *JNCB* (1914), p. 124. I am indebted to Richard L. Walker for calling my attention to this article.

63. D'Ohsson, *2*, 646.

64. *Idem, 2*, 645–646; cf. Cordier, *2*, 342. It should be noted that while Bayan was not a Chingisid he belonged to a prominent Mongol clan, that of Baarin.

Left without a leader, Kaidu's sons and a number of other princes of the houses of Ugedey and Jagatay agreed to recognize Timur's suzerainty and to settle all future interprincely conflicts by negotiation instead of war (1303). This important agreement was supplemented by making the il-khan of Persia a party to it. Upon the death of the Il-Khan Gazan in 1304 Timur dispatched a grand embassy to Persia to install Gazan's brother Oljaitu as the new il-khan and to inform him of the pacification of Central Asia. The khan of the Golden Horde, Tokhta, also supported the new agreement. Characteristically enough, he in his turn summoned his vassals, the Russian princes, to an assembly in Pereiaslavl, Suzdalia, where his envoy announced the decisions taken by the leading Mongol rulers.[65] The success of Timur's policy was indeed impressive and the Mongol Empire may be said to have reached the apogee of its power during his reign. All this amounted to a restoration of the unity of the empire in the new form of a pan-Mongol federation presided over by the great khan in Peking.[66]

In his internal policies as well as in his attitude toward the West Timur followed Kubilay's traditions. When John of Montecorvino finally reached Peking (1295), he was given a benevolent reception and was allowed to preach Christianity and to organize a diocese of the Catholic Church. John's labors were quite successful; in 1304 6,000 people were baptized in Peking by Roman Catholic rites. A number of them were probably not Chinese but aliens residing in China.[67] A seminary was established to teach Latin and Greek, as well as Gregorian chant, of which Timur was very fond, to 150 young men.[68] In 1305 a Catholic church was built near the imperial palace with funds supplied by an Italian merchant. Two years later Pope Clement V appointed John archbishop of China and sent three Franciscan friars to be his suffragans.[69]

In Persia the il-khans Gazan (1295–1304) and Oljaitu (1304–16) also proved willing to keep in touch with the West—although the

65. Nasonov, pp. 79–80.
66. W. Kotwicz, "Mongols," p. 2; Grum-Grzymailo, 2, 504–505.
67. According to A. C. Moule, *Christians in China* (as in n. 50), p. 150, n. 17, the number of native Chinese converted to Christianity during the Mongol period seems to have been small. Cf. K. S. Latourette, *A History of the Expansion of Christianity, 2,* 339.
68. Grousset, *Histoire,* p. 93.
69. On the Catholic missions in China see A. C. Moule (as in nn. 50 and 67), chap. 7; K. S. Latourette, *A History of Christian Missions in China,* chap. 5. For letters and reports of missionary friars from China and India see *Cathay, 3,* 3–105.

former became a Moslem early in his rule and the latter, while originally a Christian, was converted to Islam in the midst of his reign (1307). Oljaitu allowed the pope's missions to continue their work in the Orient. In 1300 King Jacob II of Aragon offered Gazan military assistance against Egypt,[70] but the offer had no practical results. Following the pan-Mongol agreement of 1303–5 Oljaitu deemed it necessary to announce the new course of Mongol policy to both Egypt and Western Europe and to urge the Moslem and Christian rulers to establish peaceful relations among all the nations of the world.[71] The significance of this appeal was not sufficiently understood in the West. King Edward II of England, in his answer, asked Oljaitu to "liberate" Palestine from the Moslems (1307).[72] From a political angle, these negotiations proved to be as futile as earlier ones had been.

II

Eight emperors ruled in the twenty-six years between the death of Timur (1307) and the accession to the throne of the last Yuan emperor, Togan-Timur (1333).[73] The reigns of most of them were short. In the absence of foreign wars and conquests in this period, it is chiefly court intrigues and personal rivalries around the throne that have caught the attention of most chroniclers. This may have been the reason for the tendency in the historical literature until recently to characterize the period—indeed the whole span between the death of Kubilay and the downfall of the Yuan dynasty in 1368—as one of decay and stagnation. Yet if we choose to turn from the palace life to the general policies of the imperial government in this period we cannot fail to notice much evidence of constructive work.

Timur left no male descendants. His cousin Ananda and his two nephews, sons of Dharmapala, contested the throne. The partisans of Ananda were defeated and, by agreement reached between Timur's nephews, Dharmapala's elder son, Kaishan (Mongol temple name Kuluk; Chinese title Wu-tsung), became emperor (1307–11).[74] The

70. Spuler, *Iran,* p. 232.
71. See Kotwicz, "Lettres" 2; Kotwicz, "Mongols," pp. 3–5; E. Haenisch, "Zu den Briefen der mongolischen Il-Khane Argun und Öljeitu an den König Philipp den Schönen von Frankreich," *Oriens, 2* (1949), 216–235.
72. Spuler, *Iran,* p. 232.
73. See Genealogical Table II.
74. Grum-Grzymailo, *2,* 506; Franke, *Geld,* pp. 83–84.

lavish spending by all sides in the electoral campaign depleted the imperial treasury to the danger point. By 1308 the deficit amounted to over seven million *ting,* as the units of paper money were called. An attempt was made to introduce silver certificates (1309) and copper money (1310). The reform was not a success, however, and in 1311 the paper money system was restored.[75] Kuluk's successor was his younger brother, Ayurparibhadra (Mongol temple name Buyantu; Chinese title Jén-tsung; 1311–20). Buyantu seems to have been a ruler of considerable ability and was assisted by a group of prominent statesmen. The firmness of his administration was clearly demonstrated when the khan of Central Asia, Esen-Buka, a descendant of Jagatay,[76] revolted against the empire in 1316.

It should be noted that Esen-Buka attempted to obtain the support of Uzbeg, khan of the Golden Horde, in his undertaking. According to the so-called "Continuation of Rashid ad-Din's Annals," Esen-Buka sent a messenger to Uzbeg to inform him that "the Kaan" (i.e. Buyantu) intended to remove Uzbeg from the throne and replace him by another Juchid prince. Upon receiving the news Uzbeg was at first very much angered and thought of joining the revolt, but his advisers succeeded in convincing him that Esen-Buka could not be trusted. Uzbeg therefore remained loyal to Buyantu.[77] The imperial armies were quick to suppress the rebellion and, after defeating Esen-Buka's forces, penetrated as far west as Lake Isyk-Kul. The victory of the imperial forces was decisive, and there was no attempt after that at opposition to the great khan by the princes of Central Asia until the fall of the empire itself.

To every government board Buyantu appointed as many Chinese officials as Mongols or other non-Chinese.[78] He also issued a decree forbidding the appointment of eunuchs to any position in the higher administration—an attempt to curb palace intrigues.[79] By another decree Buyantu exempted monasteries and other religious establishments, including the Christian, from taxes and liabilities.[80] Accord-

75. Franke, *Geld,* pp. 85–93, 102.
76. See Genealogical Table IV.
77. Tiesenhausen, *2,* 141–142.
78. D'Ohsson, *2,* 664.
79. Cordier, *2,* 345.
80. G. Devéria, "Notes d'épigraphie mongole-chinoise," *JA, 8* (1896), 396–398; Lewicki, "Les Inscriptions mongoles inédites" (as in n. 46), pp. 20–36. On the Mongol legislation in regard to the religious communities see Ratchnevsky, pp. lxviii–lxxxvi; E. Haenisch, "Steuergerechtsame der chinesischen Klöster unter der Mongolenherr-

ing to O. Kowalewski, Buyantu was a patron of arts and sciences. Scholars from Samarkand, Bukhara, Persia, Arabia, and Byzantium met at his court.[81] The legislative work which had been started under Kubilay and had progressed slowly under his immediate successors was given new impetus in the reign of Buyantu. In 1316 a code of laws was compiled, based on previously issued imperial manifestoes and decrees, ordinances, and rules of court proceedings. In 1323, in the reign of Buyantu's son and successor, Suddhipala (Mongol temple name Gegen; Chinese title Ying-tsung; 1320–23), this code was approved by a special commission.[82]

Soon after this, Gegen was assassinated, as a result of previous court intrigues. The partisans of a rival branch of Kubilay's descendants took the occasion to put on the throne their candidate, Yesun-Timur (Chinese title T'ai-ting), who was then in Karakorum. Yesun-Timur reigned for five years (1323–28). He seems to have belonged to the Old Mongol party. Presumably, the group of statesmen who had been in control of affairs in the reigns of Buyantu and Gegen now lost their influence. Their opposition to the new emperor seems understandable enough. Their motives may have been not only personal but political as well. They must have been proud of the successes they had achieved in administration and legislative work and resented the change of policy. As long as Yesun-Timur was alive and firmly on the throne, there was no chance for them to act. As soon as he died, however, the opposition came into the open and its leaders refused to recognize Yesun's son as the new emperor. They upheld instead the rights to the throne of Kuluk's sons. A brief but fierce civil war followed which resulted in the victory of the opposition. Kuluk's elder son Kusala (Mongol temple name Khutukhu; Chinese title Ming-tsung) was proclaimed emperor. He died within a few days, presumably being poisoned by the rival party. His brother Tug-Timur (Mongol temple name Jayagatu; Chinese title Wên-tsung; 1329–32) succeeded him.[83]

---

schaft," *BVSAW, 92*, Pt. 2 (1940), reviewed by H. Schurmann, *HJAS, 14* (1951), 291–306. See also Shunjô Nogami, "The Hsüan-chêng-yüan of the Mongol Dynasty of China," *ASTH*, p. 17 (English summary).

81. Grum-Grzymailo, *2*, 507, n. 2; cf. D'Ohsson, *2*, 664.

82. Ratchnevsky, pp. xvi–xvii.

83. On the Mongol names (personal name and temple name) of the emperor Wên-tsung see L. Ligeti, "Les Noms mongols de Wen-tsong des Yuan," *TP, 27* (1930), 57–61; cf. Cleaves, Inscription II, p. 52, n. 172.

III

Tug-Timur "had deep sympathy for and interest in Chinese culture. He himself composed Chinese poetry, practiced Chinese calligraphy, and painted pictures in the Chinese traditional style." [84] The revolution which put him on the throne was not a mere military putsch. The same group of statesmen that had been active under Buyantu and Gegen seems to have returned to power. El-Timur (Yan-Timur), the leader of the opposition to Yesun-Timur, became the new chancellor. He was put at the head of the legislative commission entrusted with preparing a digest of the previously issued statutes. This digest was promulgated in 1331.[85]

About the same time the Council of Scholars of Peking prepared a general map of the Mongol Empire.[86] This "map" is actually a schematic diagram of the main divisions of the empire and the chief regions and cities within each division. It is on the whole accurate, and all of the names can be identified. The three main divisions of the empire outside of China, as indicated on the map, are the Central Asian Khanate ruled by Du-lai T'ie-mu-rh (Duva-Timur, a descendant of Jagatay); [87] Persia, ruled by Bu-sa-yin (Il-Khan Abu-Said, a descendant of Hulagu); [88] and the Golden Horde, ruled by Yüe-dsu-bu (Uzbeg, a descendant of Juchi). In the northwestern part of Uzbeg's dominions we find a region called A-lo-sz; this is Russia.[89]

The map is evidence of the interest of the Peking government in imperial affairs and its consciousness of the unity of the empire. The Digest of Laws also emphasizes the seriousness of purpose and good intentions of the government in internal affairs. On the whole, the empire in this period seems to have been ruled by conscientious statesmen endowed with a certain breadth of vision.

There is some contemporary evidence showing that the unity of the empire did not exist only on the map. The memorandum on the Yuan empire prepared around 1330 by the archbishop of Saltania

---

84. Küchirô Kanda, "The Attitude of Emperor Wên-tsung of the Mongol Dynasty towards Chinese Culture," *ASTH*, p. 11 (English summary).

85. Ratchnevsky, pp. xx–xxi; Franke, *Geld*, pp. 26–27.

86. For a reproduction of this map see Bretschneider, 2.

87. Duva-Timur was Esen-Buka's younger brother.

88. See Genealogical Table IV.

89. The Chinese name for "Russia," A-lo-sz, derives from the Mongol and Turkish form, "Orus" or "Urus."

for Pope John XXII, under the title "The Book of the Estate of the Great Khan" begins with the following statement: "The Great Caan [Kaan] of Cathay [China] is one of the most puissant of all the kings in the world, and all the great lords of that country be his lieges and do him homage; and in chief three great emperors; to wit, the Emperor of Armalech [Almalyk],[90] the Emperor Boussay [Abu-Said], and the Emperor Uzbech [Uzbeg]. These three emperors send year by year live libbards, camels, and gerfalcons, and great store of precious jewels besides, to the said Caan their lord. For they acknowledge him to be their lord the sovereign." [91]

Furthermore, there was a lively trade between China and the Golden Horde in this period. According to both Al-Umari, and Ibn-Batuta (who visited Saray around 1332), plenty of Chinese goods could be bought in the bazaars of the capital of the Golden Horde. It was said that an Italian or Hungarian merchant need not travel to China to buy Chinese silk; he could easily obtain it in Saray.[92]

The presence of a strong body of Russian troops in China was another aspect of the close cooperation of the Golden Horde with the great khan in this period. It will be recalled that Kypchak, Alan, and Russian contingents formed part of Kubilay's armies.[93] After the restoration of imperial control over Central Asia in the reign of Timur, and again in the reign of Buyantu, new contingents of Kypchak and Russian soldiers must have been dispatched by the khan of the Golden Horde to China. Down to Tug-Timur's reign the units of Russian soldiers (hundreds, and possibly thousands) were distributed among several ten-thousand divisions (tümen) of the imperial army. Now a special Russian division (in Russian, t'ma) was created (1330). According to the *History of the Yuan Dynasty*, its commander (in Russian, *temnik*) received the title of "captain of the ten-thousand unit of the Life Guards [with the name of] the Herald of Fidelity." [94] He was considered an officer of the third rank in the imperial system of ranks and was subordinated directly to the

---

90. Almalyk, in the Ili River region, was, at that time, the capital of the Jagataid khans of Central Asia; see *Cathay*, 3, 87, n. 1.

91. *Ibid.*, 3, 89.

92. *ZO*, pp. 151, 157; cf. R. S. Lopez, "China Silk in Europe in the Yuan Period," *JAOS*, 72 (1952), 72–76.

93. On foreign troops in China under the Yuan dynasty see Chang Hsiang-lang, "The Rebellion of the Persian Garrison in Ch'üan-chou, A.D. 1357–1366," *MS*, 3 (1938), 611–627; cf. Franke, "Europa," p. 70. On the Alans in China see also Palladi, "Starinnye sledy khristianstva v Kitae," *VS*, 1, 47–48; Bretschneider, 2, 84–90; *Cathay*, 3, 184 ff.

94. Franke, "Europa," p. 70. Cf. Palladi, *VS*, 1, 49–50; Bretschneider, 2, 80.

Secret State Council. Lands were allotted to the Russian division north of Peking to establish a military colony there. The Russians were furnished with clothes, oxen, agricultural tools, and seeds. They were bound to supply the imperial table with every kind of game and fish found in the forests, rivers, and lakes of the country where their colony was situated. In 1331 the temnik of the Russian division was renamed "commander of the Russian Life Guard Troops," with the same title, of Herald of Fidelity. He received a silver seal of office.[95] The meaning of the change in the captain's title is not clear. It may have been the result of a decrease in the number of this group of Russian soldiers, so that they no longer constituted a full division. The alternative would be that the Russian military division was now expanded and constituted more than one division. Another entry of the same year actually mentions 600 newly recruited Russian soldiers.[96] It may be said in this connection that one more military colony of Russian and Alan troops was simultaneously established in Liao-yang province (comprising south Manchuria and parts of Korea).[97]

In addition to the soldiers drafted in Russia by the Mongol administration there, Russians captured and made slaves during punitive Mongol raids on Russia were also brought to China from time to time and settled there. In 1331 Satun (brother of El-Timur) "presented" the emperor with 16 Russian families, for which he was remunerated by the emperor's "gift" of 107 ingots (ting) of silver and 5,000 ting in paper money.[98] The Russians, in this case, were granted sheep and pastures. In 1332 Prince Chang-ki (apparently the Jagataid prince Jinkshi) presented to the emperor 170 Russian prisoners, for whom he received 72 ingots of silver and 5,000 ting in paper money. Simultaneously the chancellor El-Timur gave the emperor 2,500 Russian prisoners.[99] These were most likely Russians from the principality of Tver, captured during the punitive raids of the Mongols and the Muscovites in the winter of 1327–28.[100]

95. Franke, "Europa," p. 71.
96. *Ibid.*
97. *Ibid.*
98. *Ibid.*
99. *Ibid.* The Chinese title which Franke translates as "Prince of the Imperial House" is given by him as *chu-wang.* Bretschneider suggested that under Prince Chang-ki (Jangi), Jinkshi of the House of Jagatay was meant. In the Mongol inscription of 1362 an official by the name of Jangki (Chang Ch'i) is mentioned; his title however was duke (*kuo-kung*—the third of the eight titles of nobility), and not prince (chu-wang). See Cleaves, Inscription I, pp. 30, 83, 85; p. 40, n. 14; p. 96, n. 13.
100. See below, Chapter 3, sec. 6, p. 201.

IV

After Tug-Timur's death his seven-year-old nephew (Kusala's youngest son) was proclaimed emperor; he died within a few months and was succeeded by his elder brother, Togan-Timur (Chinese title Shun-ti, 1333–68). Soon after this El-Timur, the leading figure of Tug-Timur's reign, died. His brother Satun and the latter's friend Bayan now came to prominence. Bayan was appointed commander of the Russian Life Guards [101] in 1339; but he was sent to South China the same year and died on the way there.[102]

In the period between 1307 and 1332 Catholic missionaries had pursued their activities in Persia, India, and China. Of especial importance was the mission of the Franciscan friar Odoric of Pordenone who visited all three of these countries (1318–30).[103] In Peking Odoric was the guest of John of Montecorvino. When the latter died, around 1332, his successor to the see of Peking was the French Franciscan, Friar Nicholas, formerly a professor of the University of Paris, who brought 26 other friars with him to China. In 1336 one of these, Andrew, returned to Europe to deliver a letter from Togan-Timur to Pope Benedict XII—for the great khan continued the benevolent policy of his predecessors toward Christianity. In answer to this letter the pope sent two more missions to China; one of them was received in audience by Togan-Timur in 1342.[104]

The emperor also ordered a revision of juridical manuals, and a new digest of imperial decrees and enactments appeared in 1346.[105] But the most serious problem with which Togan-Timur's government had to cope during the first half of his reign was the protracted revolt of a river—the Yellow River (Hwang-ho). Around A.D. 1300 its course changed drastically, turning from Kaifeng eastward to discharge into the Gulf of Chihli.[106] This upset in the course of North China's main river affected the lives of millions of people, some by floods, others by depriving their fields of irrigation. After the floods,

101. Franke, "Europa," p. 72. Cf. Palladi, *VS, 1,* 50; Bretschneider, *2,* 81 (both of them refer Bayan's appointment to 1334).

102. According to Cordier, *2,* 351, Bayan fell in disgrace and was deported to South China.

103. See *Cathay, 2.*

104. Grousset, *Histoire,* p. 93; *Cathay, 3,* 213–214.

105. Ratchnevsky, p. xxi.

106. Krause, p. 189.

which occurred at intervals, came a series of famines. The situation became especially threatening in the 1330's. There was a widespread famine in 1334 and another in 1342.[107]

The great khan's government attempted to regulate the course of the river by building, or repairing, a system of dams. In 1351 the main dams broke down, and an emergency situation arose; 170,000 workers were conscripted to reinforce the river banks.[108] These and other public works undertaken by Togan-Timur's government required large funds, which meant an additional strain on the treasury. New regulations concerning paper money were announced in 1350 in an attempt to adjust the amount in circulation to the needs of the people. While in 1341 less than 1,000,000 ting was issued, the amount was doubled in 1352; in 1356 6,000,000 ting in paper money was printed.[109]

Both the elemental disasters and the deterioration of the imperial finances nourished growing dissatisfaction among the population. In all countries and all periods people are inclined to blame their government for deficiencies and troubles. This was especially true of old China since, by the traditional Chinese concept the ruler is held responsible even for the elemental disasters. Human society is considered part of the universal order. The sins of the ruler cause not only men but nature itself to revolt.[110]

.As a result the prestige of the emperor was severely damaged in North China. In South China it had never stood high because of the dynasty's alien origin. It should be noted in this connection that there was a marked difference in the attitudes of South and North Chinese toward the Yuan dynasty. Even before the Mongol conquest North China had been, on many occasions, ruled by emperors of foreign origin; and it will be recalled that the Chin dynasty—the immediate predecessor of the Yuan dynasty—was of Manchu, not Chinese, extraction. There was, then, nothing unusual for the North Chinese in accepting the rule of foreigners, especially since in each case those foreigners were ready to follow, to some extent at least, the Chinese pattern of culture. With the South Chinese the case was different, as South China had always been ruled by a native dynasty. After the overthrow of the Sung by the Mongols, they had to accept

107. Grum-Grzymailo, 2, 508.

108. *Ibid.*, Franke, *Geld,* p. 94; Eberhard, p. 268.

109. Franke, *Geld,* pp. 93–98, 103.

110. Escarra, p. 77; cf. Latourette, 2, 27. It should be noted that similar views were held in medieval Russia; see *Kievan Russia,* pp. 289–290.

the inevitable and submit to the rule of Kubilay and his successors, but in their hearts they considered the Yuan dynasty a foreign one, and their loyalty to it was questionable.

For a number of years the presence of the Mongol garrisons prevented the possibility of a general revolt in South China. Local riots and uprisings occurred, however, from time to time. Gradually the Mongol warriors settled in China—as in other countries with old cultures like Persia—lost their military ardor and in Marco Polo's words "were greatly degenerated." [111] In 1352 riots started simultaneously in various localities throughout the Yangtze area as well as in the Canton region. This movement actually amounted to a social revolution, being a rebellion of peasants and sharecroppers against the owners of large landed estates, both Mongol and Chinese.[112] By 1360 all of South China was controlled by a number of local leaders who often quarreled among themselves.

About the same time the unity of the empire was seriously endangered by the disintegration of the realm of the il-khans. Following the death of Abu-Said (1335) troubles started in Persia which resulted in a quick succession to the throne of rival candidates, each of whom was but a tool in the hands of powerful local grandees. The khans of the Golden Horde profited by circumstances and increased their pressure on Azerbaijan. Finally, in 1356, Khan Janibeg seized Tabriz, leaving his son Berdibeg there as his lieutenant. On his way home, in 1357, Janibeg died, and Berdibeg hastened to Saray to assume power,[113] leaving Persia, as Bertold Spuler puts it, in ruins.[114] Soon after the death of Berdibeg (1359) the Golden Horde itself entered a period of protracted dynastic and political crisis.[115] Jagatay's ulus in Central Asia had its share of political troubles as well. All these events seriously affected the development of pan-Mongol commerce, especially the overland trade between the Black Sea and the eastern Mediterranean area on the one hand and China on the other. This could not but affect the financial stability of the Peking regime unfavorably. Besides, the annual share of tribute

111. MPYC, *I*, 263.

112. See Franke, *Geld*, p. 2, n. 1, referring to Meng Su-ming, *Social Classes of the Yüan Dynasty* (Peking, 1938) (in Chinese). Cf. W. Eberhard's review of this study in *Orientalische Literaturzeitung* (1941), p. 540.

113. According to some sources Janibeg was killed by Berdibeg's partisans; see below, Chapter 3, sec. 6, p. 208.

114. Spuler, *Iran*, p. 137.

115. See below, pp. 245–246.

from Persia and the Golden Horde was no longer coming in, or at least not coming regularly.

To return to South China, around 1360 one of the local rival chieftains, Chu Yüan-chang, succeeded in eliminating or subordinating to himself most of the leaders of other bands. Social rebellion was now transformed into national revolution. At the moment when the Peking government was faced with this crisis, a number of clan leaders in Mongolia revolted against Togan-Timur.[116] If the latter was too much of a Mongol for the Chinese, he was too Chinese for the Old Mongol party. While the attack of the steppe Mongols on Peking was repulsed, the Peking government was compelled to keep its best troops in the north to protect the Great Wall. Under these circumstances, the rapid progress of the Chinese revolutionary forces was inevitable. In 1363 Chu Yüan-chang occupied the provinces of Hupeh, Honan, and Anhwei; in 1367 Chekiang and Kiangsi. In 1368 he defeated the Mongol army east of Peking and entered the capital in triumph. Togan-Timur fled to the Gobi desert where he died in 1369. His sons and the remnants of his army retreated to Mongolia. Meanwhile, in Peking, Chu Yüan-chang proclaimed himself emperor. The dynasty he founded became known as the Ming.

5. THE MONGOL IMPERIAL IDEA

The Mongol expansion was the result of a combination of many varied factors and motives ranging from the greed of the warriors for rich booty through a more constructive commercial imperialism of the Mongol rulers to a grandiose concept of universal empire.

It was the imperial idea which was the distinctive trait in the Mongol driving spirit of conquest, overcoming, as it did, the primitive mentality of a feudalized clan society. The Mongol emperors waged their wars with the professed aim of achieving universal peace and international stability. The goal achieved, the price for the security of mankind would be permanent service to the state on the part of each and all; this would establish an orderly way of life and social equality. The rich would serve the state to the same extent as the poor; and the poor would be protected from injustice and exploitation by the rich. According to the Armenian historian Grigor of Akanc, one of the precepts of the Yasa was "Respect the aged and the

116. Grousset, *Histoire,* pp. 261–262.

poor." [117] Ibn al-Athir says that the Mongols were harsh only to the rich.[118]

The basic concept of the nature of imperial authority was clearly expressed in the letters of the first great khans to the rulers of the West.[119] The preamble is characteristic in each case. Each letter starts with a reference to Heaven, which is followed by a reference to Chingis-Khan and to the reigning emperor. Let us consider, as examples, Guyuk's letter to the pope (1246), brought to Europe by Friar John of Plano Carpini, and Mongka's letter to Saint Louis (1254), brought by Friar William of Rubruck, as well as Mongka's edict accompanying his letter.

The Mongol original of Guyuk's letter has not been preserved, or at least not found. The letter was known for a long time only in Friar John's Latin translation; in the 1920's the Persian translation (with an admixture of Turkish phrases) was discovered. In the Latin translation the preamble reads as follows: "Dei fortitudo, omnium hominum imperator." [120] In Pelliot's French translation of the Persian text: "Dans la force du Ciel éternel, (nous) le Khan océanique du grand peuple tout entier; notre ordre." [121] It is obvious that in his Latin translation Friar John compressed the Mongol formula into a brief statement, omitting details. The Persian version seems to be much closer to the Mongol original. It must be noted that in the French translation the use of the word *océanique* ("oceanic") is questionable. It is an attempt to render the Mongol word *dalai*. Pelliot interprets it as "ocean" and compares it to the name "Chingis" which he takes for "sea," though it more likely means "all-powerful," "great." [122] Dalai, as used in Guyuk's letter, must have had the same connotation. According to E. Khara-Davan, the original meaning of dalai in the language of the Oirats (Kalmyks), is "great," "limitless"; "ocean" is but a derivative connotation.[123] As to the

117. Akanc, p. 291.

118. *ZO*, pp. 228–229.

119. For an excellent discussion of the Mongol formulas of authority in both Mongol and Chinese sources see Kotwicz, "Formules initiales."

120. Voegelin, p. 388.

121. *Idem,* 386; cf. Kotwicz, "Formules initiales," pp. 134–135.

122. See above, Chapter 1, sec. 5, p. 28.

123. Khara-Davan, pp. 33–35. According to A. de Smedt and A. Mostaert, *Dictionnaire monguor-français* (Pei-ping, 1933), p. 41, *dalai* (in Monguor dialect, *dalē*) means "sea" (*mer* in French). In A. R. Rinchine, *Kratkii mongolsko-russkii slovar'* (Moscow, 1947), p. 63, two connotations are given for dalai: (1) a sea; a great lake; and (2) uni-

phrase "du grand peuple tout entier" ("of the whole great people") in Pelliot's translation, we may compare it with the corresponding phrase on Guyuk's seal, also translated by Pelliot: "Dans la force du ciel éternel, du Khan océanique du peuple des grands Mongols, l'ordre." [124] Taking all the above into consideration, I would render the preamble as follows: "Through the virtue of the Eternal Sky [and of] the Supreme Khan of the great [Mongol] nation, our order."

Mongka's letter to King Louis IX is known only in Friar William of Rubruck's Latin version. The khan's edict which accompanied the letter gives the general juridical formula on which the international documents of Chingis' successors had to be based. As Eric Voegelin points out, this formula emanates from the Yasa.[125]

The following is the Latin version of the form of the preamble as recommended by the edict, and of the actual preamble in the letter itself.

The Edict: Preceptum eterni Dei est. In coelo non est nisi unus Deus eternus, super terram non sit nisi unus dominus Chingischan, filii [sic] Dei. Hoc est verbum quod vobis dictum est.

The Letter: Per virtutem eterni Dei, per magnum mundum Moallorum, preceptum Mangu chan.[126]

In W. W. Rockhill's English translation:

The Edict: [This is] the commandment of the Eternal God. In Heaven there is only one eternal God, and on the Earth there is only one lord, Chingis Khan, the Son of God. This is what is told you.

The Letter: Through the virtue of the eternal God, through the great world of the Moal [Mongols]. This is the word of Mongka-Khan.[127]

On the basis of the three documents as cited above (Guyuk's letter, Mongka's edict, and Mongka's letter), and taking into consideration other Mongol royal letters of the period, we may establish the

---

versal, supreme (the second meaning is characterized as "historical"). Irrespective of whether the concrete sense ("sea") or the abstract ("limitless," "universal") is the original one, it is obvious— from my point of view, at least—that in Guyuk's letter the word is used in its abstract sense. It may be added that in the Secret History (sec. 280) Ugedey is called "Dalai Kagan." Haenisch translates this title as "World Ruler" (*Weltherrscher*). F. W. Cleaves comments that here "the word 'Welt' is the equivalent of Pelliot's 'Océanique' and, I daresay, is more intelligible to the reader"; see Cleaves' review of Haenisch' German version of the Secret History, *HJAS, 12* (1949), 533.

124. Pelliot, "Mongols et papauté," Pt. 1, p. 15.
125. Voegelin, p. 412.
126. The text as restored by Wyngaert; reprinted by Voegelin, p. 391.
127. Rockhill, pp. 248–249. Trans. slightly altered by me.

following scale for the three basic elements in the Mongol concept of imperial power:

       1. God (Heaven—the Eternal Sky).

       2. Chingis-Khan (Given by Heaven).[128]

       3. The reigning emperor.

As regards point 2, Chingis-Khan is mentioned by name only in Mongka's edict—that is, in the pattern for the form of imperial letters as recommended by the Great Yasa. I am convinced, however, that in both Guyuk's and Mongka's letters Chingis-Khan is referred to, without mention of his name. In Guyuk's letter he is called the "Supreme Khan" (*Dalai-Khan*). Pelliot's insertion (in his French translation) of the word "we" (*nous*) preceding the title is not only superfluous but misleading, since it would make the title apply to the reigning emperor (Guyuk) and not to the founder of the Mongol nation (Chingis-Khan), as I am sure it should. The concluding words, "our order" (*notre ordre*), refer to the reigning emperor; in Mongka's edict the corresponding phrase is "This is what is told you"; in Mongka's letter, "This is the word of Mongka-Khan."

The two elements which are distinct in the Persian version of Guyuk's letter (the Supreme Khan and the Mongol nation) have been merged in Rubruck's Latin translation of Mongka's letter: "The great world of the Mongols." In the Mongol original we may assume the phrase to run something like "The Great Khan of all the Mongols." It is obvious that, in the Mongol pattern of thought, the Mongol nation is metaphysically connected with Chingis-Khan as its founder. In the scale of elements of power, Chingis-Khan as Son of Heaven is an intermediary between Heaven and the reigning emperor. As the Supreme Khan of the Mongol nation, he is the guiding spirit of the Mongol Empire.

The Mongol Empire, then, as the Mongol leaders understood it, was an instrument of God for establishing order on the earth. As

128. While in the Latin translation of the khan's letters edited by Christians Chingis is called "Son of God," the old Mongol formula seems to have been "Given by Heaven." It will be recalled that in Chingis-Khan's tablets of authority he is called *T'ien-t'se* in Chinese, which Tôru Haneda translates (into French) as "qu' a donné le Ciel" or "reçu du ciel," *MTB, 8,* 87. In the later period, however, with the spread of Lamaism among the Mongols, Chingis was indeed called Son of Heaven by the Mongols. At the ceremonies of the "Opening of the Seal" among the Ordos Mongols, in the addresses presented to their local prince Chingis-Khan used to be invoked as "l'incomparable fils du Ciel, ce puissant Boghda Sutu Tschingis-Khan." See A. Mostaert, "L'Ouverture du sceau," p. 321.

Eric Voegelin puts it, "The Khan bases his claim to world-domination on a divine order to which he is subjected himself. He has not only a right derived from the Order of God, but he acts under a duty." [129]

Feeling himself God's tool, the Mongol emperor, when he addressed his enemies, did not boast of the strength of his armies, but merely referred the matter to God. Here the Great Yasa of Chingis-Khan recommended the following formula: "If ye resist—as for us what do we know? The everlasting God knoweth what will happen to you." [130] As we have seen, this formula was actually used by Khan Guyuk in his letter to the pope.[131] Even if not all the nations actually recognized Mongol authority, legally, from the point of view of the first great khans, all nations were their subjects. In accordance with this principle, in their letters to the pope and to the kings both Guyuk and Mongka insisted that the Western rulers acknowledge themselves vassals of the great khan.

It was only in the reign of Kubilay that the attitude of the khans changed and a different approach to international stability was tried. The idea of complete subjection of other nations to Mongol rule was now superseded by the plan of a world federation presided over by the great khan.[132] However, even in this later period the basic concept of the divine origin of the imperial power was maintained intact. Thus we find in Il-Khan Argun's letter to the king of France (1289) a formula which is very close to the preamble of Guyuk's and Mongka's letters.

In W. Kotwicz' French translation it reads: "Par la force de l'Eternel Ciel, par le *suu* de l'Empereur, nous, Argun, disons . . ." [133]

Suu (or *sü*) means "fortune." [134] Thus we arrive at the following English version: "Through the virtue of the Eternal Sky, through the virtue of the imperial fortune, we, Argun, say . . ."

There is no preamble in Il-Khan Oljaitu's letter to the king of France dated in 1305. At the beginning Oljaitu refers to his ancestors,

129. Voegelin, p. 405.
130. Vernadsky, "Yasa," p. 345.
131. Voegelin, pp. 387–388.
132. See above, Chapter 2, sec. 4, p. 82.
133. Kotwicz, "Lettres" 1, 11.
134. See Kotwicz, *Idem* 2, 15; *idem,* "Formules initiales," pp. 144–147; P. Pelliot, "Les Documents mongols du Musée de Teheran," *Athar-e Iran, 1* (1936), 37. Cf. Cleaves, Inscription I, pp. 83, 85, 91; M. Lewicki, "Turcica et Mongolica," *RO, 15* (1949), 239–267. The concept of *sü* corresponds to that expressed in the second part of the title of the ruler of the Uigurs (idiqut), on which see Chapter 1, n. 98. For new data on the Mongol letters in the Archives Nationales, Paris, see Cleaves, "Chancellery," pp. 508–526.

up to his great-grandfather (Hulagu), and in the text of the letter, to the emperor Timur and other ruling descendants of Chingis-Khan; he also mentions Heaven's inspiration and protection.[135] It must be kept in mind that both Argun and Oljaitu were regional khans, not great khans, hence the formula they used could not but differ somewhat from that proper to the great khans.

What are the background and the origins of the Mongol imperial idea? It is obvious that it was not Chingis-Khan's invention although he became its chief exponent and symbol. He only formulated the concept which grew in his milieu, that is among the élite of the Mongol clan leaders, specifically those of the Borjigin clan and the group of clans ("bone") of which it was a branch. In a general way, the concept of Heaven (the Eternal Blue Sky) as protector of the pastoral nations was a basic belief of the Mongol and Turkish peoples.

The legend of the divine origin of Alan-Qoa's three sons points to the possibility of the influence of Christian notions on the growth of the idea of the divine foundation of imperial power among the Mongols.

Still another root of the Mongol imperial formula is the historical traditions of the former nomad empires in Mongolia and Central Asia, both Turkish (Hunnish) and Iranian. From this point of view the title "kagan" ("kaan") with which Chingis was invested at the kuriltay of 1206 is, in itself, characteristic enough, since it is an old Turkish term, used by both the Altaic Turks in the 6th to 8th centuries and the Khazars in the 7th to 9th centuries. We also find the title "supreme khan" [136] among the Danubian Bulgars in the 9th century; and they, as we know, were a fragment of that branch of the Huns which invaded Europe in the 5th century. And, indeed, the great khan of these Huns, Attila, on the occasion of the alleged discovery of Mars' sword, announced that God had appointed him ruler of the whole world.[137] The emperor of the Altaic Turks was referred to as "the Heaven-like, Heaven-born, wise Kagan." [138] In an Orkhon inscription of the 8th century a Turkish prince describes

---

135. Kotwicz, "Mongols," pp. 3-4; *idem,* "Lettres" 1, 34.
136. *Kanas üvigi,* Moravcsik, *2,* 277.
137. Priscus, chap. 4, sec. 10 (Latyshev, *Scythica et Caucasica, 1,* 839). Cf. E. A. Thompson, *A History of Attila and the Huns* (Oxford, Clarendon Press, 1948), p. 89. Priscus' version of the story of the discovery of the sword is confusing and marred by prejudice, but its significance is clear.
138. Thomsen, p. 140; Bernshtam, p. 106.

the origin of the Turkish Kaganate in the following words: "When the Blue Sky and the Dark Earth beneath it originated, men were created between, and my forefather Bumyn-Istemi Kagan sat [on the throne]." [139]

Because of the early expansion of the Alans in Central Asia and Jungaria, and the close relations between the Turkish and Iranian tribes in the Khoresm area, we may assume that Turkish (Hunnish) political thought was influenced by Iranian concepts of royal power. That the Scythians and Sarmatians of South Russia attributed divine origin to the authority of their rulers has been firmly established by Michael I. Rostovtzeff.[140] The Persian Empire, ruled in the Hunnish period by the Sassanid dynasty, was another seminary of monarchic ideas. The role of Khoresm in this respect is not to be neglected either.[141] An important channel of penetration of Iranian political ideas into the Turkish-Mongol milieu was the Uigurs, especially after they had settled in eastern Turkestan in the vicinity of the province of Sogdiana with its ancient culture.

Another, and even more important source of the Mongol ideas must be sought in Chinese political thought. It should be borne in mind that the ancient Turkish (Hunnish) Empire in Mongolia and Jungaria waged a protracted series of wars against China, which alternated with periods of peace and rapprochement. In consequence, as might be expected, the Hunnish rulers and aristocracy were subject to considerable Chinese influence. The Hunnish pattern of political thought could not but reflect some of the traditional Chinese ideas. Hence when we think of the influence of Chinese notions on the Mongol imperial idea we have to take into consideration both the ancient Chinese background of the political concepts of the nomads and the more recent Chinese influence on the Mongols in the 12th and 13th centuries. Following the conquest of China by the Mongols, the relative importance of the Chinese element in Mongol thought increased rapidly, but this was after the basic traits of the Mongol concept of imperial power had already been formulated. According to the traditional Chinese concept, the emperor is invested by the "mandate of Heaven" (t'ien ming).[142] He is the mystical link be-

---

139. Thomsen, pp. 144–145. Thomsen sees here a reference to two kagans: Bumyn and Istemi. According to W. Radloff (V. Radlov), the one kagan bears two names; see Bernshtam, p. 106.

140. M. I. Rostovtzeff, "Predstavlenie o monarkhicheskoi vlasti v Skifii i na Bospore," AK, 49 (1913), 1–62.

141. See Tolstov, Khorezm, pp. 173–187.

142. Latourette, 2, 27; Escarra, pp. 15, 128.

tween Heaven and the nation he rules.[143] This seems to be very close
to the Mongol idea of the divine origin of imperial power. However,
the Chinese concept of the mandate of Heaven was in many respects
different from the Mongol. It was part of the general pattern of the
"natural law" as the Chinese understood it, that is of the concordance
of the social order with the order of nature.[144] The emperor was
expected to conform to the basic law of nature and to "govern" as
little as possible.[145]

It may be said that the traditional Chinese idea of imperial rule
was less dynamic than the Mongol idea. On the other hand, it should
be noted that the Mongols, in the 11th and 12th centuries, had to
deal not with a native Chinese dynasty but with two foreign dynasties ruling in succession over North China, first the Khitan and then
the Chin. The Khitans seem to have been of Mongol origin and the
Chin were Manchus. The mentality of both was much closer to that
of the Mongol clan leaders than were purely Chinese concepts.[146]

To sum up, the Mongol idea of the divine origin of the imperial
power was based both on old traditions and on a more recent acquaintance with political concepts prevailing at the courts of the
Khitans and the Chin. From this vast reservoir of thought the
Mongol clan leaders of the late 12th century drew their guiding
principles, and in this intellectual milieu young Temuchin grew,
eventually to assume leadership as Chingis-Khan. What is not so
easy to explain is the intensity of feeling and the seriousness of purpose which characterize both Chingis-Khan and his close advisers.
The imperial idea not only fired their imagination but became an important factor in their life. We may perhaps best understand what
happened by comparing the emergence of Chingis-Khan's imperial
dream to a religious revival, indeed, to the birth of a new faith.
Chingis-Khan was not only its prophet; he became its embodiment.

6. THE GREAT YASA

The Mongol word *yasa* (*yasak, jasak*) means "order" or "decree."
Until recently it has been usual to speak of the Great Yasa as a
digest of Mongol customary law. This has been partly because until
recently the provisions of the Yasa dealing with criminal law and

143. Escarra, pp. 128–129.
144. *Idem*, p. 7.
145. *Idem*, p. 129.
146. On Khitan society see Wittfogel.

punishment have had more attention from historians than any other sections of the code.

No complete copy of the Great Yasa is known to have been preserved, although several Oriental writers of the 13th to 15th centuries testify that such copies existed. According to the historian Juwaini (d. 1283), a copy was kept in the treasury of each of the ruling descendants of Chingis-Khan.[147] Rashid ad-Din (1247–1318) mentions the existence of these copies on several occasions.[148] In the Persian treatise on finance ascribed to Nasir ad-Din Tusi (d. 1274) several references to the Yasa are made.[149] Makrizi (1364–1442) was told by his friend Abu-Hashim of a copy available in a Bagdad library.[150] On the basis of Abu-Hashim's information Makrizi attempted to present a full report of the contents of the Yasa. Actually, he succeeded in outlining only a part of the code, chiefly the provisions dealing with criminal law and punishments. Rashid ad-Din on his part quoted a number of ordinances and sayings of Chingis-Khan, some of which were probably fragments of the Yasa and others so-called "maxims" (bilik). For a long time modern historians dealing with the Yasa based their conclusions mainly on the information supplied by Makrizi and Rashid ad-Din. Insufficient attention was paid, until recently, to the brief summary of the Yasa made by Gregory Ab-ul-Faraj (Bar Hebraeus, 1225/26–86) or the more extensive account presented by Juwaini. But these two writers outlined the most significant division of the Yasa, that dealing with the state law of the Mongols.

In my opinion the Yasa as a whole can by no means be characterized as customary law. It was Mongol imperial law as formulated by Chingis-Khan; the Mongols themselves considered it in this light. For them it was the collected wisdom of the founder of their empire; and as we know they considered Chingis-Khan the divinely inspired Son of Heaven. The Armenian historian Grigor of Akanc compiled his story of the origin of the Yasa on the basis of what he heard from the Mongols.[151] While it cannot be considered accurate in details, it renders adequately the spirit of the Mongol attitude toward Chingis-Khan and his lifework. According to Grigor, when the Mongols "came to realize their position, being much oppressed by their

147. Juwaini, Persian text, Mirza Muhammad, ed., pp. 17–18.
148. Berezin, pp. 404 ff.
149. Minorsky, "Nasir al-Din," pp. 773, 775, 776.
150. Sylvestre de Sacy, Chrestomatie arabe (1826), 2, 160–161.
151. Akanc, pp. 289–291.

miserable and poor life, they invoked the aid of God, the Creator of heaven and earth, and they made a great covenant with him to abide by his commands. An angel appeared to them by the command of God in the guise of an eagle with golden feathers,[152] and spoke in their own speech and tongue to their chief, who was named Chankez [Chingis] . . . Then the eagle told them all the commandments of God . . . which they themselves call yasak."

Juwaini too considers the divinely inspired mind of Chingis-Khan the source of the Yasa:

Whereas the Allhighest [God] distinguished Chingis-Khan from his contemporaries with respect to his mind and intellect . . . he [Chingis-Khan], solely from the depths of his own soul and without tiresome study of [historical] annals, without conforming in details with [traditions of] antiquities, invented all the devices [of statesmanship].[153]

In both Juwaini's and al-Makrizi's opinion, the Yasa was a talisman ensuring victories on the battlefield.[154] As A. N. Poliak points out, the Mongols and the Turks ascribed to the Great Yasa a semimagic power.[155]

Without a complete copy of the Great Yasa we cannot tell in what order the provisions we do have were arranged. Presumably it began with a preamble which served as a basis for that used by Chingis-Khan's successors in their correspondence with foreign rulers. This must have contained an invocation to Heaven and mention of the Supreme Khan of the Mongol nation, Chingis-Khan. The third clause of the preamble formula, "our order," obviously must have meant Chingis-Khan's own order, since he was both founder of the nation and reigning emperor at that time. Next, as we may suppose, came the exposition of general principles and the articles on international law and the organization of the army and the state, approximately in the order in which they are outlined by Juwaini and Ab-ul-Faraj.

---

152. The eagle was an emblem of royal power among the Scythians and the Sarmatians. According to Rashid ad-Din, some of the Turkish clans venerated the eagle as their ongon; others the falcon; see Rashid 1, pp. 25–28. According to Altan Tobči, p. 124, the falcon was the ongon of the Mongol clan Kiiat-Borjigin (to which Chingis-Khan belonged). In a legend of Chingis-Khan's death it is said that he turned into a hawk and ascended into the skies, Altan-Tobči, p. 146. Cf. Kozin, pp. 68–69.

153. Vernadsky, "Juwaini," p. 37.

154. *Idem*, p. 38; Makrizi, *Khitat* (ed. 1270 A.H.), 2, 221, as quoted by Poliak, "Yasa," p. 862.

155. Poliak, "Yasa," p. 863.

I. General Precepts

The contents of this division of the Great Yasa may be tentatively reconstructed from fragments available in various redactions. The following quotations may give a general idea of it.

One must magnify and pay honor to the pure, and the innocent, and the righteous, and to the learned, and wise men, to whatsoever people they may belong; and contemn the wicked and the men of iniquity [Ab-ul-Faraj, sec. 2].[156]

The first is this: That ye love one another; second, do not commit adultery; do not steal; do not bear false witness; do not betray anyone. Respect the aged and poor [Grigor of Akanc].[157]

He [Chingis-Khan] forbade them [the Mongols] to eat anything in the presence of another without having him invited to partake in the food; he forbade any man to eat more than his comrades [Makrizi, sec. 12].[158]

Whereas Chingis-Khan did not belong to any religion and did not follow any creed, he avoided fanaticism and did not prefer one faith to the other or put the ones above the others. On the contrary, he used to hold in esteem beloved and respected sages and hermits of every tribe, considering this a procedure to please God [Juwaini, sec. 2].[159]

He [Chingis-Khan] ordered that all religions were to be respected and that no preference was to be shown to any of them [Makrizi, sec. 11].

This section of the Yasa became the foundation of the Mongol policy of religious tolerance.

II. International Law

When it is necessary to write to the rebels and to send envoys to them, do not threaten them with the strength and the great size of your army, but say only: "If ye will submit yourselves obediently ye shall find good treatment and rest, but if ye resist—as for us what do we know? The everlasting God knoweth what will happen to you" [Ab-ul-Faraj, sec. 1].[160]

It should be emphasized that from the point of view of the Yasa every nation refusing to recognize the supremacy of the great khan is considered rebel. As Eric Voegelin points out, this is contrary to our

156. From here on references to the section of Ab-ul-Faraj's outlines of the Yasa follow Budge's English version (*1*, 354–355). I have also taken into consideration Bruns and Kirsch's Latin translation.

157. Akanc, p. 291.

158. From here on references to sections of the Yasa in Makrizi's version follow Riasanovsky.

159. From here on references to sections of the Yasa in Juwaini's version are my own translation.

160. Cf. "Juwaini," sec. 1, p. 39.

concepts of international law which presuppose the existence of sovereign states: "The Mongol Empire is . . . not a state among states in this world, but an *imperium mundi in statu nascendi*, a World-Empire-in-the-Making." [161] It will be recalled that the letters of the great khans Guyuk and Mongka to the rulers of the West [162] followed faithfully the above-quoted clause of the Yasa.

An important principle of Mongol international law was the inviolability of ambassadors. Any and every case of violation of this principle by the enemy brought severe retaliation. There is, however, no explicit statement concerning this matter in the existing fragments of the Yasa.

III. Government, Army, and Administration

A. THE EMPEROR AND THE IMPERIAL FAMILY

In the extant fragments of the Yasa only one provision, that dealing with the imperial title, bears on this subject.

[The Mongols] shall not give to their kings and nobles many laudatory names or titles like the other nations, especially the followers of Islam. And to [the name of] him that sitteth upon the throne of the kingdom they shall only add one name, viz. Khan or Kaan. And his brothers and sisters and his kinsfolk shall call him by the first name given to him at his birth [Ab-ul-Faraj, sec. 3].[163]

It may be noted that the title "kaan" (kagan) in itself expresses the all-embracing fullness of the emperor's authority. At the same time, to the members of his family the emperor remains the clan leader, a close relative; hence the personal form of address recommended for his kinsfolk.

From the Secret History we know that Chingis-Khan issued special ordinances for the maintenance of the imperial household and the apanages of the members of the imperial family. Presumably the basic regulations concerning these matters were incorporated into the Yasa.

B. THE MONGOL NATION

As we have seen, in the preamble of the Khan's letters to foreign rulers, Chingis is referred to as the Supreme Khan of the Mongol nation. The pattern of this preamble must have followed that of the

161. Voegelin, p. 404.
162. See above, Chapter 2, secs. 1-2, pp. 64, 69.
163. Cf. "Juwaini," sec. 3, pp. 39-40.

preamble of the Yasa. While there is no specific clause on the authority of the nation in the existing fragments of the Yasa, some dispositions concerning the matter may have been included among the
Yasa's ordinances. In the Chinese inscription of 1338 the Mongols
are called, typically, the "state-clan" (*kuo-tsu*), that is the "ruling
nation." [164] It was through the election of the new great khan after
the death of his predecessor that the Mongol nation could express
itself politically under the empire. While, as we have seen, the electoral kuriltays did not always work smoothly, it is obvious that
there was a definite set of rules concerning their sessions, even if
the rules were not always observed. In each of the uluses of the
empire there functioned regional kuriltays to elect the regional khans.
Most of our information about those ulus assemblies relates to the
realm of the il-khans (Persia); the rules observed there seem to
follow the pattern of the great kuriltays. In all probability this pattern was included in the ordinances of the Great Yasa.

C. ARMY AND ADMINISTRATION

1. Hunting Statute. When the Mongols are unoccupied with war, they
shall devote themselves to the chase. And they shall teach their sons how
to hunt wild animals, so that they may be trained in fighting with them,
and may acquire strength, and the power to endure fatigue, and be able
to meet their enemies as they meet the wild and savage beasts in combat,
and may not spare [themselves] [Ab-ul-Faraj, sec. 4].[165]

It is obvious that the chase, besides being the most popular sport of
the Mongols, was considered by Chingis-Khan a state institution and
the basis of military training.[166]

2. Army Statute. The fighting men are to be conscripted from men who
are twenty years old and upwards. There shall be a captain to every ten,
and a captain to every hundred, and a captain to every thousand, and a
captain to every ten thousand. . . . No man of any thousand, or hundred,
or ten in which he hath been counted shall depart to another place; if he
doth he shall be killed and also the captain who received him [Ab-ul-Faraj,
secs. 5 and 7].[167]

164. See Cleaves, Inscription III, pp. 27 and 36, n. 28.
165. For a detailed description of this precept see "Juwaini," sec. 4, pp. 39–40.
166. Cf. "Juwaini," secs. 5–6, pp. 41–43.
167. Besides delineating the soldiers' duties the Yasa must also have contained regulations about their share in war booty. According to Nasir ad-Din the guardsmen
(*bagadurs*) had first choice; one-fifth of the rest belonged to the great khan; the re-
mainder was to be divided among the soldiers. See Minorsky, "Nasir al-Din," p. 774.

He [Chingis-Khan] ordered the warriors on their return from the campaign to carry out certain duties in the service of the ruler [Makrizi, sec. 20].

The creation of Imperial Guards was one of the most important of Chingis-Khan's reforms in military organization. In all probability the high position of the guards was fixed in the Yasa, although there is no mention of it in the existing fragments.

The principle of decimal organization in the Mongol army, as well as the importance of the Imperial Guards as an institution, has been already discussed.[168] Another principle, that of the attachment of each man to his place in the service, deserves attention here. The army, especially in the period of the first conquests, was the backbone of the Mongol administration as a whole. Therefore the principle of universal service, each man having his specific position to which he was bound and which he could not desert, became the foundation not only of the Mongol army but of the Mongol Empire. We may call it the Statute of Bound Service, and as is evident from al-Makrizi's statement the service was not limited to military duties. An important aspect of the obligation of service to the state was that the burden of it was to be distributed equally among all the subjects of the khan.

There is equality. Each man works as much as another; there is no difference. No attention is paid to a man's wealth or importance [Juwaini, sec. 5].

Not only men, but women as well, were bound to the service.

He [Chingis-Khan] ordered women accompanying the troops to do the work and perform the duties of the men, while the latter were absent fighting [Makrizi, sec. 19].

The Statute of Bound Service became the basis of the great khan's omnipotence, which so impressed Friar John of Plano Carpini.

There were exceptions, however, to the seemingly ironclad rules. The priests of all religions, as well as physicians and scholars, were exempt from regular duties and taxes (Makrizi, sec. 10). The services expected from them were of a different nature, spiritual or professional. In addition to this general exemption of a whole social category, individuals of other groups could receive special privileges of

168. See above, Chapter 1, sec. 5, pp. 28–29.

immunity. A recipient of such a charter of immunity was known, in Mongol, as a *darkhan* (Turkish, *tarkhan;* the term was borrowed into Russian in that form).[169] This institution acquired full significance only in the later period (14th and 15th centuries); it is not mentioned in the existing fragments of the Yasa.

Among other provisions of the Great Yasa dealing with administrative law, the following may be mentioned here: the establishment of post-horse stations (Ab-ul-Faraj, sec. 8; Juwaini, sec. 9; Makrizi, sec. 25); levies and taxes (Ab-ul-Faraj, sec. 6; Juwaini, sec. 9); the obligation of the Mongols to present their daughters (presumably also captive girls they owned) in the beauty contests, where the fairest ("moonlike girls" as Juwaini calls them) were selected as wives and concubines for the khan and the princes of royal blood (Juwaini, sec. 7; Makrizi, sec. 21).

IV. Criminal Law

Al-Makrizi's version of the Yasa provides the bulk of evidence with regard to Mongol criminal law. To this some scattered fragments from other sources may be added.

The criminal law of the Yasa had as its main objective keeping peace and order in the state and society. The general moral precept, as outlined by Grigor of Akanc, ended with the following sanction: "If a transgressor of such be found among them, the lawbreakers are to be put to death." [170] Thus, while the final goal seems to have been humanitarian in a broad sense, the law was to be enforced with ruthless severity.

Generally speaking, the Yasa recognized as crime subject to punishment the following groups of offenses: those against religion, morals, and established customs; those against the khan and state; and those against the life and interests of private persons.[171]

The main objective of punishment as understood by the Yasa was physical annihilation of the offender. Therefore punishment by death plays an important role throughout the code. As subsidiary objectives the Yasa recognized temporary elimination of the offender by imprisonment, deportation, or demotion; and his intimidation either

169. On the term darkhan (ṭarkhan) see Vladimirtsov, pp. 69, 93, 117, 164; R. N. Frye, "Tarxun-Türxün and Central Asian History," *HJAS, 14* (1951), 105–129; Menges, pp. 54–57.

170. Akanc, p. 291.

171. For details of the Yasa criminal law and punishments see Riasanovsky, pp. 31, 35–37, and Vernadsky, "Yasa," pp. 354–356.

by inflicting pain or by imposing a fine. Not only the offender himself but in some cases his wife and children were liable to punishment.

Punishment by death was prescribed for almost all types of crime. It was imposed for most of the offenses against religion, morals, or established customs; for most of the offenses against the khan and state; for some offenses against property; for a third bankruptcy; for horse stealing, when the thief was unable to pay a fine.

Punishment by imprisonment and deportation was imposed for violation of the Yasa by members of the khan's clan. Each captain of a military unit was subject to demotion if he was unable to handle his office. Soldiers and hunters were subject to punishment by inflicting pain for minor offenses against military discipline. Homicide was punishable by a fine. For horse stealing, both retaliation and a fine in kind were imposed on the offender; the alternative was death.

V. Civil Law

The evidence on the private law of the Yasa is meager. This probably is to be explained not only by the incompleteness of the existing fragments but also by the fact that such matters were regulated by customary clan law. However one important provision concerning inheritance was included in the Yasa:

From the man who is dead and hath no heir nothing shall be taken for the king, but his possessions shall be given to the man who ministered unto him [Ab-ul-Faraj, sec. 9; cf. Juwaini, sec. 10].

VI. Commercial Law

It is known that Chingis-Khan attributed great importance to commerce. Keeping commercial highways safe for international trade was one of the main objectives of his policy. Hence it is natural to surmise that the Yasa must have contained some kind of statute on trade. However, only one section on commercial law has been preserved among the fragments.

Whoever will take goods [on credit] and go bankrupt, then will take goods again and go bankrupt once more, then will take goods and go bankrupt again, shall be sentenced to death after his third bankruptcy [Makrizi, sec. 5].

The recognition of Chingis-Khan's dynamic role in the creation of the Yasa does not preclude examining the sources of his code. Both Chingis and his advisers lived in a definite environment at a definite time; their concepts and decisions naturally were conditioned by the over-all historical, economic, and social background.

The sources of the Mongol imperial idea have been discussed in the preceding section. The moral precepts announced by the Yasa were closely connected with the concept of universal empire and, partly at least, belong to the same cultural and spiritual cycle. As for the administrative statutes, they were, to a certain extent, an outgrowth of Mongol-Turkish traditions, and also show some influence of the pattern of neighboring states—those of the Chin, the Uigurs, and the Kara-Khitans. Poliak suggests that one of the sources of the Great Yasa might have been the local laws of Moslem Turkish rulers of the Middle East.[172] This is doubtful, and the hypothesis needs further proof in order to merit discussion here.[173]

In any case, the old Mongol and Turkish traditions were thoroughly revised and transformed by Chingis-Khan and his advisers, and a set of new concepts and dispositions was created. To take an example, the decimal system of army organization was an old institution among the Turks as well as among the Iranians, though it usually ran parallel with the clan and tribal organization. Chingis-Khan not only modernized the system but combined it with the principle of bound service, thus cementing it much more strongly than had anyone before him. The rigidity of the new army organization was superimposed on the fluid association of the old clans.

· The provisions of the Yasa on criminal law, were partly based on Mongol customary law; but here again norms of the law of the neighboring empires must have been taken into consideration. On the whole, the penal law of the Yasa must have been more severe than the traditional clan and tribal law of the Mongols.

Both Rashid ad-Din and Makrizi date the promulgation of the Yasa from the Great Kuriltay of 1206.[174] This, however, was only the first redaction of the code. It was supplemented by new ordinances at the kuriltays of 1210 and 1218. The code was finally revised and completed after Chingis-Khan's return from the Turkestan campaign and before his last expedition against the Tanguts, that is, around 1226.

It was Chingis-Khan's intention that the code of laws created by him should be immutable. He enjoined on his successors the duty of

172. Poliak, "Yasa," p. 863.
173. See V. F. Minorsky's note to Poliak, "Yasa," p. 875.
174. Riasanovsky, p. 10.

keeping the code intact.[175] His second son, Jagatay, known for his loyalty and firmness, was appointed guardian of the Yasa. "He ordered Jagatai . . . to see that the Yasa be observed" (Makrizi, sec. 26). Each new khan, whether ruling over the empire as a whole or over his own ulus, had to begin his reign by confirming the validity of the Yasa.[176] According to Ibn-Batuta, the descendants of Chingis-Khan had to assemble once a year together with the higher officers of each realm to ascertain that no prince of Chingis-Khan's blood had violated the Yasa during the term that had expired. Any prince who was found guilty had to be deposed.[177] "Whoever violates the Yasa shall lose his head" was a typical order of Batu, khan of Kypchak.[178]

The existence of the Great Yasa did not exclude supplementary legislation by Chingis-Khan's successors. But such legislation was not to contradict the principles of the Yasa and had chiefly local significance. Thus, the khans of the Golden Horde issued a number of charters and ordinances concerning the administration of their khanate. These were known as *yarlyk*. Characteristically enough, the yarlyks granted by the khans of the Golden Horde to the Russian church contain direct reference to the Great Yasa as authority for the immunity of the clergy from taxation.[179] There are also references to the Yasa in the codes of law of the Yuan dynasty in China.[180]

It must be noted that because of the belief of Chingis-Khan's successors in the semimagic power of the Great Yasa, the code was usually concealed by Mongol and Turkish rulers from subjugated populations as well as from foreign nations.[181] The only exception seems to have been Egypt. According to the Arabic writer, Ibn-Taghribirdi, the Egyptian amir Artash had a thorough knowledge of the Yasa.[182] Essuyuti states that the sultan Baibars intended to apply the Yasa laws and regulations in Egypt.[183] As a matter of fact, the secular law of the Mameluk realm, called As-Siyasa, was actually

175. *Bilik* (Maxims), Rashid ad-Din's version, art. 2, Riasanovsky, p. 86.
176. Juwaini, Persian text, p. 18.
177. Ibn-Batuta, *3*, 40–41.
178. Berezin, p. 404.
179. Priselkov, *Yarlyki*, p. 96; Grigoriev, *Yarlyki*, p. 124.   .
180. See Ratchnevsky, p. vii and n. 5.
181. Poliak, "Yasa," p. 863.
182. Tiesenhausen, *1*, xi–xii; cf. Vernadsky, "ZOEV," p. 82.
183. Tiesenhausen, *1*, p. xi.

based on Chingis-Khan's code.[184] Egypt, however, was a special case. The Mameluk rulers of that country were of Turkish origin and, besides, for some time considered themselves vassals of the khans of the Golden Horde.[185] As Poliak has made clear, the general organization of the Mameluk state followed the Mongol pattern.[186]

7. THE MONGOL ARMY AND ART OF WAR

The Mongol army of the 13th century was a formidable instrument of war. It was undoubtedly the best military establishment in the world of that period. Basically, it was a cavalry army accompanied by an engineer corps. Historically speaking, the Mongol army and art of war followed the age-long traditions of warfare of the steppe nomads. Under Chingis-Khan the Mongols brought the old patterns to perfection. Their strategy and tactics were the culmination of those of the earlier cavalry armies of the steppe peoples—the best of them all.

In ancient times it was the Iranians who could boast of having the best cavalry in the world: the Parthians and the Sassanids in Iran, and the Alans in the Eurasian steppes. The Iranians differentiated between heavy cavalry, with sword and spear as main weapons, and light cavalry, with bow and arrows.[187] The Alans depended chiefly on heavy cavalry. Their pattern was followed by the east German tribes associated with them—the Goths and the Vandals.[188] The Huns who invaded Europe in the 5th century were essentially a nation of archers. Because of the superiority of the Alanic and Hunnish cavalry the mighty Roman Empire proved helpless when confronted with the steady pressure of the steppe peoples. After the settlement of the Germans and the Alans in the western half of the Roman Empire and the formation of the new Germanic states, the pattern of the Alanic cavalry was followed by the medieval knights. The Mongols, on the other hand, developed and brought to perfection the Hunnish equipment and devices. But Alanic traditions also played an

184. Poliak, "Caractère colonial," pp. 235–236. Poliak, "Yasa," p. 875, suggests a linguistic connection between the terms "As-Siyasa" and "Yasa" which is unacceptable.
185. Poliak, "Charactère colonial," p. 233.
186. Poliak, "Yasa," p. 862.
187. See F. Altheim, *Weltgeschichte Asiens im griechischen Zeitalter* (Halle a.d. Saale, 1947–48), *1*, 173 f., 187 f.; *2*, 28 f.; cf. Tolstov, *Khorezm*, pp. 211 ff.
188. Vernadsky, "Sarmat. Hintergrund," pp. 368–371.

important role in the Mongol art of war, since the Mongols used heavy cavalry in addition to light cavalry.

In appraising the Mongol military establishment the following aspects need to be considered: 1. men and horses; 2. arms and equipment; 3. training; 4. organization of the army; 5. strategy and tactics.

I. Men and Horses

The "horse culture" is a basic feature of the life of the steppe nomads, and the foundation of their armies. The ancient authors who describe the ways of life of the Scythians, Alans, and Huns, and the medieval travelers who deal with the Mongols, present basically the same picture of nomadic society. Every nomad is a born cavalryman; every boy starts riding horseback in his early childhood; every youth is an accomplished horseman. What is true of the Alans and the Huns is true of the Mongols. If anything, the Mongols were more sturdy. This was partly the result of the remoteness of their country and of the slightness, in that period, of the mellowing influence of more cultured neighbors; and partly of a climate more severe than that of Turkestan, Iran, and South Russia where the Iranians lived.

In addition, each Mongol or Turk of the steppes is a born scout. In the milieu of nomadic life keenness of eyesight and visual memory for every detail of landscape develop to the highest degree. As Erenjen Khara-Davan points out, even in our times "the Mongol and the Kirghiz notices a man trying to hide behind a bush or a rock five or six versts [about four miles] away. He is able to perceive the smoke of a campfire or steam of boiling water at a great distance. At dawn, when the air is transparent, he can discern figures of men and animals at a distance of 25 versts" (around 18 miles).[189] Owing to their power of observation the Mongols, like all true nomads, have a deep knowledge of climatic and seasonal conditions, water supply and vegetation of the steppe countries. This helped them considerably in planning their campaigns.

The Mongols—in any case those of the 13th century—were endowed with astonishing powers of endurance. They could ride all day long for several days in succession, and on a minimum of food.

The Mongol horse was a worthy companion of its rider. It was able to cover long distances with brief periods of rest, and could subsist

189. Khara-Davan, p. 166.

on what tufts of grass or leaves it found on its way. The Mongol took a good care of his steed. During a campaign each horseman led from one to four remounts, riding each horse in turn. The Mongol horse was a race known to the Chinese in ancient times.[190] In the 2d century B.C. both the Chinese and the Huns became acquainted with the Central Asian race of horses, used by the Iranians. The Chinese valued these horses highly, and Chinese envoys to Central Asia reported to the emperor that the best horses there were sired by "heavenly stallions." [191] A number of Central Asian horses were imported to China and, presumably, to Mongolia as well. The Mongol horse of the 13th century must have been, then, a crossbreed. Both race and color were important to the Mongols in horses. White horses were considered sacred.[192] Each battalion of the Imperial Guards used horses of a particular color, the warriors of the Bagaturs battalion for instance riding black horses.[193] This throws light on Batu's order to the people of the principality of Riazan, at the beginning of his Russian campaign, that they give the Mongols a tithe "of everything." The tithe in horses was to be collected separately in horses of each required color: black, tawny, sorrel, and skewbald were mentioned.[194]

II. Arms and Equipment

Bow and arrow were the standard weapon of the Mongol light cavalry. Each archer usually carried two bows and two quivers. The Mongol bow was very large and of the composite type; it required a pull of at least 166 pounds, which was more than that of the English long bow; its destructive range was from 200 to 300 yards.[195]

The warriors of the heavy cavalry were armed with saber and lance, and in addition a battle ax or mace and a lasso. Their defensive armor consisted of a helmet (originally of leather, later of iron) and leather

190. It should be mentioned in this connection that until recently the primitive wild horse (*Equus Przewalskii*) still existed in Mongolia. See Grum-Grzymailo, *1*, 507–509; *idem, Opisanie puteshestviia v Zapadnyi Kitai* (St. Petersburg, 1896), *1*, 188–211. Cf. J. Hillaby, "Tough Primitive Ancestor of Horse is 'Biologically Resurrected' in Zoo," *New York Times*, November 20, 1952.

191. Groot, *2*, 12, 28, 110. Cf. McGovern, pp. 143–151; F. Altheim, *Weltgeschichte Asiens, 2*, 127.

192. See Wittfogel, pp. 214, 261.

193. Khara-Davan, p. 77.

194. *PSRL, 1*, Fasc. 3 (1928), col. 514.

195. Martin, pp. 19–20.

cuirass or coat of mail. The horses too were protected by leather headpieces and armor for shoulders and chests. The saddle was solidly built and suited for long-distance riding. Solid stirrups gave good support to the rider handling the bow.

In the winter campaigns the Mongols wore fur caps and fur coats, felt socks and heavy leather boots. After their conquest of China they wore silk underwear the year round. Each Mongol warrior carried a supply of dried meat and dried milk, a leather jug for water or kumiss, a file for sharpening arrowheads, an awl, and needles and thread.

Of artillery, before Chingis-Khan, the Mongols had none. They became acquainted with siege engines in China and met them again in Turkestan. The engines used by the Mongols were mostly of the Near Eastern types and had a range of almost 400 yards. Those casting rocks or stones, with a high trajectory, worked by a heavy counterpoise (like the trebuchets in the West). The javelin throwers (ballistas) were capable of much more accurate aim.[196]

III. Training

Training for camp life started among the Mongols in early childhood. Each boy and girl had to adapt to the seasonal migrations of the clan grazing its herds. Riding was not a luxury but a necessity. Hunting was a subsidiary occupation which, in case of loss of cattle, could become indispensable for survival. Each Mongol boy therefore began learning to handle bow and arrows at the age of three.

Hunting was also considered excellent training school for adult warriors, as we know from the inclusion of a hunting statute in the Great Yasa. The Yasa rules for the great chase make it clear that this played the role of army maneuvers.

Whoever has to fight shall be trained in arms. He should be familiar with the chase in order to know how the hunters must approach the game, how they must keep order, and how they have to encircle the game, depending on the number of hunters. When they start on a chase let them first send scouts who shall obtain information. When [the Mongols] are unoccupied with war, they shall devote themselves to the chase and accustom their army to that. The objective is not so much the chase itself as the training of warriors who should acquire strength and become familiar with drawing the bow and other exercise [Juwaini, sec. 4].

196. *Idem*, p. 30; Oman, *1*, 136 ff.; *2*, 45-46; MPYC, *1*, 121-131 (notes).

The beginning of the winter was designated as the season of the great chase. Orders were sent in advance to the troops attached to the great khan's headquarters and to the ordu, or camps, of princes of the blood. Each army unit had to supply a quota of men for the expedition. The hunters were deployed like an army, with a center and right and left wings, each commanded by a specially appointed general. Then the imperial train—the great khan himself with khatuns, concubines, and food supplies—set forth for the main theater of the chase. Around the huge area comprising thousands of square miles designated for the hunt a wide ring of the battue was formed, which gradually converged during a period of from one to three months, driving the game to the center where the great khan was waiting. Special messengers reported to the khan the progress of the operation and the location and quantity of the game. If the ring was not properly guarded and any game escaped, the commanding officers—chiliarchs, centurions, and decurions—were held personally responsible and subjected to severe punishment. Finally, the ring was locked and the center enclosed with lines of ropes around a ten-mile circumference. Then the khan entered the inner circle, which by that time teemed with bewildered, roaring animals of every kind, and opened the shooting; he was followed by the princes of the blood, army commanders, and then privates, each rank shooting in turn. The slaughter continued for several days. Finally a group of old men approached the khan and humbly implored him to grant a term of life to the remaining game. This done, the surviving animals were let out of the ring in the direction of the nearest water and grass; the slain were gathered and counted. Each hunter received his share according to custom.[197]

IV. Organization of the Army

The two basic features of Chingis-Khan's military system—the Imperial Guards and the decimal system of army organization— have been already discussed.[198] A few additional remarks seem neces-

197. See Vernadsky, "Juwaini," sec. 4, 40–41. The Persian term which occurs in Juwaini's text to denote the ring (the line of the battue) is *nerge,* on which see Steingass p. 1395. According to V. Minorsky (note to Poliak, "Yasa," p. 876), it corresponds to the Mongol term *jerge,* "a line"; on this see Pelliot, *Campagnes,* p. 143. Cf. Minorsky, Caucasica III, p. 225, n. 3.

198. See above, Chapter 1, sec. 5, pp. 28–30, and Chapter 2, sec. 6, p. 105.

sary. The guards, or ordu troops, existed before Chingis-Khan at the camps of many nomad rulers, including the Khitans.[199] Never before, however, were they so closely integrated with the army as a whole as under Chingis.

In addition to the emperor, each member of the imperial family to whom an apanage was granted had guards troops of his or her own. It will be recalled that a quota of yurts or families was attached to the ordu of each member of the imperial family holding an apanage.[200] From the population of these yurts each khatun or prince of the blood was allowed to raise troops. These ordu troops were commanded by the general (noyan) appointed by the emperor as adviser to the apanage household, or by the prince himself in case he personally held a high position in the army. Presumably a unit of these troops, depending on its size, was counted as a battalion, or a squadron, of one of the regular "thousands," especially when the prince in question had the rank of a chiliarch and commanded that thousand himself.

In the regular army the smaller units (those of tens and hundreds) usually corresponded to clans or groups of clans. A unit of one thousand could represent a combination of clans or a small tribe. In most cases, however, Chingis-Khan composed each one-thousand unit of warriors belonging to different clans or tribes.[201] The ten-thousand division (tümen) almost always consisted of different social units. It seems that this was partly at least the result of a conscious policy of Chingis-Khan, an attempt to make the larger army units loyal to the empire rather than to the old clans or tribes.[202] In agreement with this policy the captains of the larger army units—the chiliarchs and myriarchs—were appointed by the emperor personally, and Chingis-Khan's principle was to promote every talented person regardless of social background.

Before long, however, a new tendency became noticeable. The captain of a thousand or a myriad, if he had an able son, might try to secure the captaincy for him. Such instances were not infrequent among commanders of the ordu troops, especially when a prince of the blood held the captaincy himself. Cases of transfer of office from father to son are known. In each case, however, the emperor's per-

199. Wittfogel, pp. 508–517.
200. See above, Chapter 1, sec. 5, p. 30.
201. Vladimirtsov, p. 109.
202. Khara-Davan, p. 66.

sonal confirmation was required,[203] and this was not always given.[204]

The Mongol armed forces were divided into three army groups— center and right and left arms. As they always pitched their tents facing the south,[205] the left arm meant the eastern army group and the right arm the western. Special officers (*yurtchi*) were appointed to plan the disposition of troops, to direct the movements of the armies during the campaigns, and to locate the camps. They were also in charge of the activities of the scouts and spies. The office of the head yurtchi may be compared to that of quartermaster general in modern armies. The cherbi were in charge of the commissariat services.

During the reign of Chingis-Khan the whole military establishment was under the constant supervision and inspection of the emperor himself, and the Great Yasa recommended this to all future emperors.

He ordered his successors personally to examine the troops and their armament before going to battle, to supply the troops with everything they needed for the campaign and to survey everything even to needle and thread, and if any of the soldiers lacked a necessary thing the soldier was to be punished [Makrizi, sec. 18].

The Mongol army was welded from top to bottom by stern discipline to which both officers and men were subject. The captain of each unit was responsible for all his subordinates, and if he himself committed a fault his punishment was still more severe. The discipline and training of the troops and the streamlined system of organization kept the Mongol army in constant readiness for mobilization. And the Imperial Guards—the core of the army—were on duty even in peacetime.

V. Strategy and Tactics

Before a major Mongol campaign opened, a kuriltay was convoked to discuss the plans and objectives of the war. The captains of all the larger army units were present at the assembly and received the necessary instructions from the emperor. The scouts and spies who had visited the country designated for attack were questioned, and new scouts were sent, if necessary, to collect more information. The

203. Vladimirtsov, pp. 104–106.
204. See *idem*, pp. 105–109.
205. Khara-Davan, p. 72, n. 1.

area where the army was to concentrate before the campaign was then designated and grazing grounds reserved along the roads the troops would take.

Considerable attention was paid to propaganda and psychological warfare. Long before the troops reached the enemy country, secret agents there tried to convince religious dissenters that the Mongols would establish religious tolerance, the poor that the Mongols would help them against the rich, rich merchants that the Mongols would make the roads safe for commerce. One and all were promised peace and security if they surrendered without fighting, and warned of terrible retaliation if they resisted.

The army moved into the enemy country in several columns operating some distance apart. Each column consisted of five sections: center, right and left arms, rear guard, and vanguard. Communication between columns was maintained by messengers or by smoke signals. As the army advanced it left an observation corps at each major enemy fortress, while mobile troops hastened forward to contact the enemy's field army.

The basic objective of the Mongols' strategy was to surround and annihilate the main enemy army. They tried to achieve that objective—and usually succeeded—by using the device of the great chase: the ring. First they enveloped a huge area and then gradually converged and tightened the ring. The ability of the commanders of single columns to coordinate their activities was truly amazing. In many cases they were able to converge on their main objective with clock-like precision. Subudey's operations in Hungary may be considered a classic example of this method. If the Mongols, after contacting the foe's main army, were not strong enough to break its lines, they feigned a retreat; more often than not, the enemy would take it for disorderly flight and rush forward in pursuit. Then, with characteristic skill in maneuvering, the Mongols unexpectedly turned back, and their opponents found themselves surrounded, with no way of escaping the ring. The battle of Lehnica is typical of such strategy. In the battle on the Sit' River, the Russians were surrounded before they could even attempt any serious counterattack.

The light cavalry of the Mongols were the first to join battle. These harassed the enemy with constant attacks and withdrawals, and their archers decimated the foe's ranks from a distance. The movements of the cavalry in all these maneuvers were directed by their commanders through signal pennants, and, at night, through lanterns

of various colors. When the foe was sufficiently weakened and demoralized, the heavy cavalry corps was thrown against either the
center or one flank. The shock of its attack usually broke the resistance. But the Mongols did not consider their task done with
winning even a decisive battle. One of the principles of Chingis-
Khan's strategy was to pursue the remnants of the enemy to their
final destruction. Since one or two divisions were enough on such
occasions to finish the enemy's organized resistance, the other Mongol troops divided into small bands and started systematically looting the country.

It should be noted that with their first Turkestan campaign the
Mongols acquired a very effective technique for besieging and eventually storming fortified cities. If a long siege was foreseen, a wooden
wall was erected around the city at some distance to prevent supplies
entering from outside and cut the garrison off from communication
with the native armies outside. Then, with the help of captives or
conscripted natives, the moat around the city walls was filled with
fascines, stones, earth, or whatever was available; siege engines were
put in position to bombard the city with rocks, naphtha-filled con-
tainers, and javelins; and battering rams were pulled close to the
gates. Eventually, in addition to the engineer corps, the Mongols
started using infantry troops in siege operations. These were conscripted from among the natives of foreign countries previously conquered by the Mongols.

The high mobility of the army, as well as the hardiness and fru-
gality of the warriors, greatly simplified the task of the Mongol
commissariat during campaigns. A camel caravan followed each
column carrying a minimum of supplies. Basically, the army was
expected to live off the conquered lands. It may be said that in each
major campaign the Mongol army potentially had its main supply
base ahead rather than in the rear. This accounted for the peculiar
fact that in Mongol strategy seizure of huge enemy territories was
considered not only a possible but a profitable operation, even if the
armies were small. As the Mongols advanced their army grew through
their use of the population of the conquered country. City artisans
were conscripted to serve in the engineer corps or to manufacture
weapons and tools; peasants had to supply labor for besieging fortresses and driving carts. Turkish and other nomadic or seminomadic
tribes, formerly subjects of the enemy rulers, were accepted into the

Mongol brotherhood-in-arms. They were formed into regular army units under the command of Mongol officers. As a result the Mongol army more often than not was numerically stronger at the end of a campaign than on its eve. It may be recalled, in this connection, that at the time of Chingis-Khan's death the Mongol army proper was 129,000 strong. It probably never exceeded that figure. It was only by raising troops from the countries they conquered that the Mongols could subjugate and control those vast territories. The resources of each country in turn were used for the conquest of the next.

The first European who properly understood the grim significance of the Mongol army establishment and presented an outline of it was Friar John of Plano Carpini.[206] Marco Polo described the army and its operations at the time of Kubilay.[207] In modern times it has attracted the attention of but few scholars until recently. The German military historian Hans Delbrück, in his standard *History of the Art of War,* disregarded the Mongols altogether. As far as I know, the first military historian—long before Delbrück—to attempt properly to assess the boldness and inventiveness of Mongol strategy and tactics was a Russian, Lieutenant General M. I. Ivanin (1801–74). In 1839–40 Ivanin took part in the Russian campaign against the Khanate of Khiva, which incidentally proved a failure. This campaign was fought against the seminomad Uzbeks in Central Asia, that is in surroundings reminiscent of Chingis-Khan's Turkestan campaign, which must have aroused Ivanin's interest in Mongol history. His outline of *The Art of War of the Mongols and the Central Asian Peoples* was published in 1846.[208] In 1854 Ivanin was appointed Russian commissioner in charge of the affairs of the inner Kirghiz Horde and thus was able to collect more information about the Turkish tribes of Central Asia. Later he returned to his historical studies; in 1875 the revised and enlarged edition of his book was published posthumously.[209] Ivanin's work was recommended as a textbook for the students of the Imperial Military Academy.

It was only after the first World War that military historians of

206. Plano Carpini M, pp. 27–32.
207. MPYC, *1*, 260–263; MPMP, *1*, 172–175.
208. M. Ivanin, *O voennom iskusstve Mongolov* (St. Petersburg, 1846).
    209. *Idem, O voennom iskusstve i zavoevaniiakh Mongolo-Tatar i sredneaziatskikh narodov* (St. Petersburg, 1875). Inaccessible to me; there are ample quotations from this work in Khara-Davan's book.

the Western nations turned their attention to the Mongols. In 1922 an article by Henri Morel on the Mongol campaigns of the 13th century appeared in the *Revue militaire française*.[210] Five years later Captain B. H. Liddell Hart devoted the first chapter of his *Great Captains Unveiled* to Chingis-Khan and Subudey.[211] Simultaneously, a study of "the period of the great raids of the Mongols" was recommended by the chief of the British Imperial Staff to the officers of the Mechanized Brigade.[212] During 1932 and 1933 a series of articles on Chingis-Khan was contributed to the *Canadian Defence Quarterly* by Squadron Leader C. C. Walker. These were later published, in revised form, as a monograph entitled *Jenghiz Khan* (1939).[213] In Germany Alfred von Pawlikowski-Cholewa published a study of the military organization and tactics of the Central Asian horsemen in a supplement to the *Deutsche kavallerie Zeitung* (1937) and another, on the armies of the East at large, in the *Militärische Beitrage zur Geschichte des Nahen und Fernen Ostens* (1940).[214] William A. Mitchell in his *Outlines of the World's Military History*, which appeared in the United States in 1940, devoted as much space to Chingis-Khan as to Alexander the Great and Caesar.[215] Thus, paradoxically enough, interest in Mongol tactics and strategy has revived in the era of tanks and airplanes. "Is there not a lesson here for the armies of today?" asks Colonel Liddell Hart. In his opinion, "the armoured caterpillar car or light tank appears the natural heir of the Mongol horseman. . . . Further, aeroplanes would seem to have the same qualities in ever higher degree, and it may be that in future they will prove the successors of the Mongol horsemen."[216] The role of the tanks and airplanes in the second World War bore out Liddell Hart's predictions, to a certain extent at least. The Mongol principle of mobility and offensive power seems to be valid still in spite of all the difference between the world of the nomads and the world of technological revolution of our days.

210. H. Morel, "Les Campagnes mongoles au XIII-me siècle," *Revue militaire française, 92* (1922) ; as listed in Spuler, p. 504.

211. B. H. Liddell Hart, *Great Captains Unveiled* (Edinburgh and London, W. Blackwood & Sons, 1927).

212. Wittfogel, pp. 532–533.

213. Martin, p. 326.

214. Spuler, p. 503.

215. Wittfogel, p. 533.

216. Liddell Hart, pp. 32–33.

8. THE MONGOL GOVERNMENT AND ADMINISTRATION

The great khan was an absolute monarch, and his authority, at least in theory, was unlimited. As John of Plano Carpini puts it, "He has an amazing power over all his subjects." [217] According to the statement of Friar Benedict of Poland as reported by Simon of St. Quentin, when the throne was offered to Guyuk at the electoral kuriltay the latter said to the barons: "If you want me to reign over you, are you ready each one of you to do what I shall command, to come whenever I call, to go wherever I may choose to send you, to put to death whomsoever I shall command you?" They replied that they were.[218] In Rashid ad-Din's words, "Chingis was the Lord of the Constellation of Planets, autocrat of the Earth and Time, and all of the Mongol clans and tribes became his serfs and servants." [219]

Another curious formula describing the great khan's power is found in a later Mongol chronicle, Altan Tobchi (The Golden Epitome). According to this Chingis-Khan was Lord of the Five Colors.[220] To understand the full meaning of this phrase we must recall that from ancient times the Chinese designated the cardinal points by colors. Black was the color of the north, red of the south, blue of the east, and white of the west. The central area was represented by yellow.[221] Together the five colors symbolized the whole world.[222]

Since yellow is the color of gold this presumably was why the Jurjen dynasty assumed the name Chin, which means golden. The Chinese concept of the five colors was accepted by many Eurasian nomads, including the Mongols. Yellow became the imperial color.

217. Plano-Carpini M, p. 23; Risch, p. 142.
218. Rockhill, p. 21, n. 1; Risch, p. 242.
219. See Vladimirtsov, p. 99.
220. Altan-Tobči, p. 129; cf. Khara-Davan, p. 132.
221. On the Chinese system of correlating the cardinal points with colors see Groot, 1, 20; see also W. Kotwicz, "Contributions à l'histoire de l'Asie centrale," RO, 15 (1949), 169.
222. It should be noted that in Tibetan symbolism the five colors (blue, red, yellow, white, black) correspond to the five elements (wood, fire, earth, iron, and water). In the sexagenary cycle each twelve-year period was assigned a color (or element) of its own. Later on this system was adopted by the Mongols through Lamaism. However, in the characterization of Chingis-Khan's power the phrase "five colors" was apparently used in the old Chinese sense of the cardinal points.

The tent of state in the great khan's ordu became known as the Golden Horde (Orda Aurea, *Altan Ordu*). In such a tent Guyuk was placed on the throne.[223] For similar reasons the Mongol imperial family—the descendants of Chingis-Khan—were known as the Golden Kin (*Altan Urug*).[224]

All of the great khan's subjects—whether Mongols or newly conquered peoples—were bound to the service of the state and expected to be obedient to the khan's will. Yet there was at least a psychological difference in degree of obedience. The Mongols were the ruling nation and while subjects of the great khan were also the chosen people whose sovereign he was. Their clan leaders elected Chingis-Khan to the throne. Theirs were the spoils of conquest and from among them army commanders and administrative officials were chosen. While pledging their unfailing obedience to the newly elected khan Guyuk, the Mongol grandees expected him to "make largess, and rejoice in justice, and honor each of [the] princes and barons according to his rank." [225] The Turks of Central Asia and South Russia, as well as the Alans, were accepted into the brotherhood of the nations of the steppes under Mongol leadership. The settler populations conquered by the Mongols were at the bottom of the political ladder.

The highest position on that ladder was occupied by Chingis-Khan's own clan, and especially by his descendants, the Golden Kin. It was solely among the male kinsmen that future emperors and khans might be elected. While at first the whole Mongol nation, through the clan leaders, was allowed to make the choice between them, in the later period the electoral kuriltay consisted only of kinsmen. After the election of each great khan the members of the imperial family were expected to support him and his policy with all their wealth and influence. If any one of them failed in loyalty or violated the Great Yasa in any other way, he was to be admonished by the great khan, and if found recalcitrant could be imprisoned; he might not be executed, however, without his case being referred to the assembly of kinsmen.[226]

The basis of the wealth and authority of the leading kinsmen was the apanages granted to them or to their ancestors by Chingis-Khan. The legal nature of these apanages is a moot problem. B. Vladimirtsov

---

223. Rockhill, p. 22.
224. Vladimirtsov, p. 99.
225. Rockhill, p. 21, n. 1; Risch, p. 242.
226. *Bilik,* sec. 23, Riasanovsky, p. 89.

is inclined to call all of them uluses (states).[227] There is, however, a marked difference between two types of uluses. To a number of princes of the blood a quota of yurts was granted; these families were to provide for the maintenance of the grantee who, as we know, could also raise troops from among them. Each of Chingis-Khan's sons obtained such an apanage. In addition each son received a quota of the regular army battalions or thousands. This means that besides having an apanage of feudal type he also was made the ruler of his ulus; his position was that of the emperor's lieutenant commissioned to govern a portion of the empire. In this way regional khanates like those of the il-khans in Persia and the Golden Horde in South Russia came into being. Obviously, these large state-like uluses were not on the same level as the apanages of lesser princes of local importance. The latter domains became known as *injü*.[228] It goes without saying that the reigning emperor also had domains of his own and that they were, as a rule, much larger than those of his kinsmen. Hence it may be said that a not inconsiderable part of the territory and population of the Mongol Empire was subjected to a semifeudal regime rather than to the agencies of the regular state administration.

The imperial domains must have constituted a mighty economic organism. It centered around the great khan's palace. Under Chingis-Khan the palace administration consisted of four sections, each known as an ordu.[229] Under Kubilay the palace administration seems to have been centralized. The people ascribed to the imperial domains had to supply the palace storehouses with everything needed for the maintenance of the khan's household and for the khan's pleasure. The Russians settled near Peking in the 1330's, it will be recalled, had to supply game and fish for the imperial table. The Russian colony was but one of many similar supply groups. Their services were supervised by officials of the palace administration, each in charge of a special department, such as horse and cattle breeding, raising grain and vegetables, hunting and fishing. Falconry must have been an important department. In addition, artisans of every trade worked at or for the palace, including goldsmiths of the highest

227. Vladimirtsov, p. 100.

228. On the injü (*inje*) see Vladimirtsov, p. 100, n. 3; W. Radloff, *Uigurische Sprachdenkmäler* (Leningrad, 1928); S. E. Malov, "Uigurskie rukopisnye dokumenty ekspeditsii S. F. Oldenburga," *ZIV, I* (1932), 129–150; Vernadsky, "Uigurs," pp. 457–459. Of considerable importance are the Mongol inscriptions of 1335 and 1338; see Cleaves, Inscription II, p. 75 (also pp. 54–55, n. 184) and Inscription III, pp. 13, 67, 69.

229. Wittfogel, p. 517.

caliber such as the Russian, Cosmas, at Guyuk's ordu and the Frenchman, Boucher, at Mongka's court.

Let us turn now to the general state administration. It must be emphasized first of all that the Mongol Empire was created in the process of military conquest. Therefore it was but natural that the army should become the backbone of the administration, at least in the early period of the development of the empire. It was through the army officers from the myriarch down to the decurion that the great khan's orders reached the population. The officers were expected to keep in constant personal touch with the emperor: "The myriarchs, the chiliarchs, and the centurions who come to hear our thoughts at the beginning and at the end of the year and then return [to their posts] may command our troops; the state of those who sit in their yurts and do not hear these thoughts is like that of a stone that falls into deep water or an arrow shot into the reeds—they disappear. It is not fit for such men to command [*Bilik*, sec. 3]." As we know, the emperor's control of the army was exercised through the Imperial Guards. The highest officers of the guards were always available for consultation with the emperor or to receive orders from him. Presumably they formed a kind of permanent council around the emperor. Whenever necessary a plenary session of the khan's council was convoked. At such a meeting under Ugedey the great khan's brothers and senior kinsmen were present, as well as the commanders of all army units.[230]

Less conspicuous but no less important was the role of a few highly trained and experienced civilian advisers of the great khan, each of whom occupied a position comparable to that of a secretary of state or minister. At first almost all of these were non-Mongols. As we have seen, of the highest dignitaries under Chingis-Khan and Ugedey, one was a Chinese, another a Uigur, a third a Central Asian Moslem. Only the supreme justice was a Mongol. At first no one of them was given the authority enjoyed by the vizier in the Moslem Near East. It will be recalled that one, a Moslem, attempted to assume the vizier's power during Turakina's regency but fell immediately after Guyuk's accession. It was only in the later period of Mongol history, especially in the realm of the il-khans, that viziership became an important institution. In China, beginning with Kubilay, central boards of administration were developed along the Chinese pattern.

230. Secret History, sec. 280; Haenisch, pp. 147–148.

Assisted by his advisers, the emperor established the principles and chief tasks of the government; he also instructed and supervised the main agents of provincial and district administration. The latter was built around the centers of the army districts into which the country was divided.

The following statement of John of Plano Carpini may aid us to understand the basic features of Chingis-Khan's system of allocation of the army units throughout the country and his control of that system. "He [the Khan] orders where the dukes [myriarchs] shall dwell; the dukes, in turn, give the same orders to the chiliarchs; the latter to the centurions; and those to the decurions. Moreover whenever, whatever, and whoever the emperor orders, be it war, life, or death, they obey him without contradiction." [231]

The captain of each unit received a badge of his rank. Among the Turks in ancient times—and probably among the Mongols as well—bow and arrows served as badges of authority. According to Turkish historical tradition the forefather of the Turks, Oghuz-Khan, ruled that the bow be the badge of the commander of the troops of the right arm, and the arrow that of the left arm.[232] In the Hunnish Empire of the 5th century the golden bow was the emblem of authority of Attila's lieutenants.[233] According to the Secret History Chingis-Khan rewarded some of his closest followers with the right to wear the quiver and bow and arrows; [234] this equipment was known in Turkish as *sadak* or *saydak* (in old Russian, *saydak* or *sagaydak*). As every Mongol horseman was provided with quiver, bow, and arrows, Chingis-Khan must have meant in this case not the real weapons but a representation of a saydak used as an emblem of the privileged position of the wearer, especially of his status as darkhan, exempt from taxes. However, in the regular administration of the Mongol Empire it was not the bow (or quiver) which was used as a badge but the "tablet of authority" as Marco Polo calls it. This was known as *paitze* (in Russian, *baisa*). Under Chingis-Khan the badge of the functionary of the first rank was a golden tablet with tiger's head; it was inscribed in the Chinese characters which denote "The Sacred Decree of *T'ien-tsé* ('Given by Heaven'), the Emperor Chingis. Let

231. Risch, p. 142.
232. Rashid 1, p. 23.
233. Gy. László, "The Significance of the Hun Golden Bow," *AA*, *1* (1951), 91–104; J. Harmatta, "The Golden Bow of the Huns," *AA*, *1*, 105–149.
234. Haenisch, p. 102; Kozin, p. 167; cf. Harmatta (as in the preceding note), pp. 132–133.

the affairs be arranged at his will." The badge of the second rank was a plain golden tablet with the same initial formula followed by one word: "Urgent." A silver tablet with the same inscription constituted the badge of the third rank.[235] In Persia under Il-Khan Gazan (1295–1304) the badge of highest rank was round and of gold, with a tiger's head; that of second rank was similar, with a special decorative design.[236] Under Kubilay the myriarch's tablet was of gold with a lion's head engraved on it; the chiliarch's of gold or silver-gilt; the centurion's of silver. When circumstances required investing an official with the highest authority the symbol on the tablet was a gerfalcon.[237]

The camp of each of the army commanders became a center of local administration. It must be borne in mind that, unlike the Imperial Guards, the army was not on permanent duty; it was expected, however, to be able to mobilize at the first notice. For this purpose the whole country was divided into a number of military districts corresponding in size and number to the army units and called accordingly. Thus the largest districts were known as tümens (myriads); and each tümen was divided into thousands, hundreds, and tens. In each such district down to the hundred a skeleton staff of the corresponding army unit was located, to serve as the mobilization center.

The population of each district was to supply, upon notice, its quota of men and horses, with full equipment. Thus the population of each thousand had to muster, with the cooperation of the lower units, 1,000 warriors and 2,000–5,000 horses. The ratio of the quota of soldiers to the total population in the district can only be guessed at since exact figures are not available. It is assumed that the total population of Mongolia at Chingis-Khan's death was around one million. To provide a total army of 129,000 such as he had then each district must have had to furnish close to 13 per cent of its population. This figure may be compared with the proportion of the soldiers of the "ordo armies" in China under the Liao (Khitan) dynasty in the 11th and early 12th centuries. According to the Chinese sources of that period, the maximum total of these armies was 101,000 mounted soldiers; these were recruited from 203,000 households with

235. Tôru Haneda, "Une tablette du decret sacré de l'empereur Genghis," *MTB, 8* (1936), 85–91; cf. Cleaves, Inscription II, p. 55, n. 188.

236. Rashid 3, pp. 277–278.

237. MPYC, *1*, 356–357; MPMP, *1*, 203–204.

a population of 408,000 adult males.[238] The total adult population of these households must have been around 800,000. Therefore the proportion of soldiers to the total adult population was about 12½ per cent.

The figure of 129,000 for the Mongol army represented the climax of the national effort at the critical period of expansion. After the main conquest was over, the tension must have subsided. The normal total strength of the purely Mongol contingents in the imperial armies can hardly have been over 100,000. On this basis the ratio of soldiers to total population may have been about the same as in the Khitan army—not over 10 per cent. This enables us to arrive at the following tentative population figures for the military districts. The population of a hundred must have been not less and probably more than 1,000, that of a thousand 10,000 or more, and that of a tümen 100,000 or more.[239]

The district headquarters became centers of civilian as well as military administration. Through them both the system of post-horse (yam) and messenger services and the collection of taxes were organized and maintained. Hence each commander of a larger army unit became simultaneously civil governor of the district. The proper organization of the post-horse service was essential for maintaining speedy communication through messengers between the central government and its local agencies as well as for coordinating the activities of army units. Foreign ambassadors were also given the privilege of using post horses. Merchants were at first allowed to use the yam facilities without charge, but later Mongka ruled that they must travel at their own expense. The merchants, in any case, profited greatly by the safety of the roads. Post-horse stations were established at intervals along the main roads.[240] By Ugedey's order a stipulated number of riders, drivers, and other attendants as well as

238. Wittfogel, p. 515; see also pp. 55–56, 516.

239. W. Barthold says that "the tümen was the smallest administrative or taxation area," *EI, 4*, 836. This opinion may be correct for some territorial divisions in Central Asia of the later periods but is not valid for the districts of the Mongol Empire and its uluses. Barthold himself quotes Ibn-Arabshah's statement that the tümen was the area that produced 10,000 fighting men, but strangely enough ignores it in his further discussion of the problem. Barthold refers to p. 17 of the Cairo 1285 A.H. edition of Ibn-Arabshah. In S. H. Manger's edition it is *1*, 80 (Arabic text) and 81 (Latin trans.). In Manger's Latin translation the passage reads as follows: "*Taumana* [i.e., *tuman*, Persian for *tümen*] autem vulgo dicitur societas, quae educit decem milia militum."

240. According to Marco Polo, the distance between the post-horse stations was 25 miles, MPMP, *1*, 242.

horses, oxen, and wagons were to be assigned to each station. Mares and sheep were to be kept at each station to supply kumiss and meat to travelers; [241] and several horses stood ready saddled for the emperor's couriers. Every courier wore a girdle hung with bells: "And when those at the next post hear the bells they get ready another horse and a man equipped in the same way." [242]

A Yam Department was created to supervise post-horse services. The post roads were divided, for the purpose of better management, into a number of districts. The adjacent tümens had to supply everything necessary to maintain the services within each yam district.[243] The Mongol post-horse service has been described, and praised, by John of Plano Carpini, Marco Polo, and a number of other travelers. It was certainly a highly useful and well-managed institution.

To avoid misunderstandings and abuses officials and messengers traveling on business, as well as foreign ambassadors, were each given a tablet of authority similar to the badges of the captains of army units (paitze). These tablets were of different material depending on the rank of the traveler. Three silver paitze and one of iron are preserved in the Hermitage Museum in Leningrad. Tablets of lowest rank were wooden.[244] The traveler holding a higher tablet was entitled to use more horses than someone with a lower tablet. Local officials were instructed to give every assistance to the holders of tablets.[245] It would be not amiss to mention that emblems like the tablets were used in Persia long before the Mongols. When Apollonius of Tyana traveled from Ecbatana to India in the middle of the 1st century, "The guiding camel [in his caravan] bore a golden tablet on the forehead, as a sign for all they met with that the traveler was one of the king's friends and traveled with royal authorization." [246]

241. Kozin, p. 198.

242. MPYC, *1*, 436; MPMP, *1*, 247.

243. Kozin, p. 198; Ab-ul-Faraj, sec. 8; cf. P. Pelliot, "Sur *yam* ou *jam*, 'relais postal,' " *TP, 27* (1930), 192–195. W. Kotwicz' study, "contributions aux études altaiques: les termes concernant le service des relais postaux," *CO, 2* (1932), is inaccessible to me.

244. *ZO*, pp. 138–139; Rashid 3, p. 278.

245. MPYC, *1*, 15, 16, 34; MPMP, *1*, 79, 80, 90.

246. Philostratus, *The Life of Apollonius of Tyana*, Pt. 2, chap. 1. The English translation quoted here is by E. Herzfeld, *Zoroaster and His World* (Princeton, Princeton University Press, 1947), *1*, 230. F. C. Conybeare (in the Loeb Classical Library edition of Philostratus, *1*, 119) says "chain" (of gold) instead of "tablet." In the Greek original *psalion*, which may mean "chain" but as a piece of horse trappings, denotes the bit as a whole or ornaments connected with it, such as cheek pieces; see Minns, p. 75 and n. 4. In this case apparently the frontlet is meant. For pictures of Scythian horse frontlets see Minns, p. 166, figs. 54 and 55; and p. 185, fig. 78.

A notable feature of the Mongol administration was its welfare program. Assistance to the needy and poor was among the duties of the emperor. A conference of high officials and military leaders under Ugedey recommended a special tax to establish a welfare fund.[247] By a separate decree Ugedey ordered that wells be dug in arid regions to make them livable.[248] There is evidence of the existence, in the later period, of granaries and storehouses maintained by the government to assist the needy in times of famine. As has been said, the last emperors of the Yuan dynasty also instituted a program of public works to regulate the course of the Yellow River.

As regards state revenue, the main burden of taxes was imposed on the population of the conquered countries. Under Chingis-Khan the Mongols did not have to pay any taxes. Under Ugedey a tax-in-kind was introduced. From each herd of sheep one two-year-old ram was to be supplied annually for the needs of the great khan's table, and a one-year-old ewe from each hundred sheep for the welfare fund.[249] Additional taxes may have been introduced in Mongolia in the later period. However, it was not state taxes but the levies and services of various kinds to which the population of the princely domains was liable that harassed the Mongols in the 14th and 15th centuries, especially since the princely domains greatly expanded in that period. The complex of taxes-in-kind and services required from each household was known as *alban*.[250]

In contrast, the burden of taxes imposed on the conquered peoples was heavy from the very start of Mongol expansion. Each conquered nation had first of all to pay annual tribute to the Mongols, and secondly regular taxes. These were of three main kinds, according to the three main socioeconomic divisions. City dwellers (merchants and artisans) had to pay a tax known as *tamga;* [251] cattle breeders a tax on cattle (*kopchur*); [252] and the agriculturalists a land tax (*kalan*).[253] Thirdly, in addition to the main taxes there were a number of special taxes levied, and services to which the conquered peoples were liable. It must also be borne in mind that Mongol princes and army leaders received private domains in the conquered coun-

247. Kozin, p. 198. On the legislation for the benefit of the needy see also Nasir ad-Din Tusi's treatise, Minorsky, "Nasir al-Din," p. 771.
248. Kozin, pp. 198–199.
249. *Idem*, p. 198.
250. Vladimirtsov, p. 164.
251. On the tamga see below, Chapter 3, sec. 8, pp. 222–223.
252. On the kopchur see Minorsky, "Nasir al-Din," pp. 783–785.
253. On the kalan see below, Chapter 3, sec. 8, pp. 222, 223, 227.

tries. These were of the injü type; the natives living on such lands found themselves in a position close to serfdom.

On the top of all this, recruits were conscripted from each sub-jugated nation to swell the ranks of the army of the great khan as well as of the regional khan. To secure undeviating fulfillment of all the above requirements each conquered country was divided into military districts similar to those in Mongolia proper. In each such district a skeleton staff of Mongol and Turkish army officers was charged with mobilizing native soldiers for the khan's armies and with supervising the collection of taxes. To secure proper obedience from the population the commander of each military district was empowered to form, under his command, local units recruited from the natives.

Taken as a whole, the Mongol administration of the conquered countries, while oppressive, served its grim purpose of being strong enough to secure and maintain the khan's control over the natives. It was only when the khan's administration was weakened at the top level by dynastic and other troubles that the natives saw their chance to emancipate themselves from Mongol rule.

9. Inner Contradictions in the Mongol Empire

The strength and efficiency of their army and administration enabled the Mongols to maintain for more than a century after the death of Ugedey their control over the vast territories they had conquered. Throughout its existence, however, the Mongol Empire was rent with inner conflicts and faced ever-increasing troubles. While it proved its vitality on many occasions and was able to overcome many a crisis, it finally fell apart and its ruling people retired into the steppes and deserts of Mongolia.

The inner contradictions which threatened the whole structure of the Mongol Empire were many and various. First of all, there was a basic incompatibility in the principles on which the empire was built: the discordance between the imperial system and the feudal nature of Mongol society. Second, there were a lack of coordination and a number of conflicts between the empire and the local khanates as well as between some of those khanates. Third, under the primitive conditions of technology in that age the very vastness of the empire presented for its ruler a perennial problem.

Moreover there was a definite lack of proportion between the size of the ruling nation—the Mongol people—and the subjugated peoples; the ratio was about 1 to 100. And the bulk of the Mongols remained nomads and were proud of it, in contrast to the majority of their subjects. On the whole the Mongols as a nation were on a lower cultural level than some of the peoples they conquered, in spite of the fact that a Mongol élite emerged whose members, endowed with innate spiritual and intellectual abilities, greatly profited by contacts with the old civilizations of some of their neighbors and subjects.

The variety of these contacts was in itself fraught with potential danger since it broke up the original unity of the Mongol background. In terms of religious affiliation, the difference between the Mongols of the old school who remained Sky worshipers or shamanists and those who were converted to Buddhism, Islam, or Christianity resulted in loosening the spiritual ties between all these groups. Besides, the process of acculturation of the Mongols settled in each of the conquered countries was never completed. Being, in the words of Karl A. Wittfogel and Fêng Chia-shêng, a "society of conquest," the Mongols were never inclined to abandon their cultural habits and to accept wholesale those of the natives. As a result, there always remained a distinction between the society of the conquerors and that of the conquered in each of the subjugated countries, which eventually facilitated the progress of national revolution against the Mongols in most of them.

Geopolitically, the Mongol Empire consisted of two distinct parts: the Mongol–Turkish core, that is the steppes and deserts of Mongolia, Jungaria, Semirechie (the Ili River region), eastern Turkestan, Transoxania, Kazakhstan, and Kypchak; and the peripheral Mongol-ruled states with predominantly agricultural population. The steppe zone was potentially the main reservoir of Mongol military strength. Most of the rulers of the peripheral states understood this clearly. The very choice of Peking as capital of the Yuan dynasty in China and of Saray as capital of the Khanate of Kypchak is indicative of the situation. Each of these cities was located on the fringe of a peripheral state and close to the steppe zone. Only the il-khans of Persia adopted a somewhat different policy. Had they followed the same pattern as their relatives in China and South Russia, it would have been logical for them to maintain their headquarters somewhere in northern Khorasan if not in Turkmenia. Instead, they made Tabris in southern Azerbaijan their first capital. This choice must have been dictated by their political entanglements—the desire to strengthen their control of Iraq and Asia Minor in order to have a suitable base for the protracted struggle against Egypt. Later on, under the pressure of the khans of Kypchak, the il-khans moved their capital southward to Sultania in the mountainous region between Tabris and Teheran. It should be recalled that they had at their disposal a steppe island in the Mugan area in northern Azerbaijan, which they used as grazing grounds for their cavalry horses. Nevertheless, by removing their capital too far from the basic Mongol core of steppes the il-khans undermined their chances of influencing inter-Mongol politics as well as of obtaining reinforcements from the inner zone of the empire. The khans of Kypchak took advantage of this fact to strengthen their own position in Khoresm. Eventually Tamerlane, starting as a petty chieftain in Transoxania, seized the former realm of the il-khans without meeting much opposition.

In view of the central position of the Mongol core of empire and its control of the inner lines of communication, the stability of the empire depended to a great extent on the proper integration of that inner zone. Actually, the Central Asian area became the playground of Mongol feudal politics very detrimental to imperial unity. Since the inner Mongol-Turkish steppe zone was considered the common patrimony of the Mongol nation, each branch of the imperial family claimed its share of uluses and domains in that area. Most of Mongolia proper, constituting the main ulus of Tuluy's descendants, was controlled by the Yuan emperors, although, as we have seen, they had to fight on many occasions to keep their rights intact.

The originally Turkish area between Mongolia and Kazakhstan became the apanage of the descendants of Ugedey and Jagatay. Eventually the Jagataids succeeded in controlling most of that region. Owing to the process of feudal disintegration no senior prince of that branch succeeded in forming a powerful centralized state. Somewhat reluctantly the Jagataids were compelled to recognize the supremacy of the great khan. However, if the danger (from the point of view of unity of the empire) of the Jagataids blocking communication lines between Peking, on the one hand, and Saray and Sultania, on the other, was eliminated, no active support of imperial policies could be expected from the Central Asian princes. Thus, the military and political value of the steppe core of the empire was considerably reduced. The perennial conflict between the two western khanates—that of the il-khans and that of Kypchak—added its share to the troubles of the empire.

In order better to understand the complexity of Mongol inter-princely relations, a few words must be said about the claims of the princes of each branch of Chingis-Khan's descendants to a share in the exploitation of the conquered lands. As we know, in all the major Mongol campaigns, whether in China, Turkestan, Persia, or Russia, princes of all four branches of Chingis-Khan's descendants coop-erated, either personally or by sending contingents of troops. In return each expected to receive a share in the income from the newly conquered country or private domains there. Thus, according to Juzjani, Batu, khan of Kypchak, had his share of revenue from each district in Iran and his agents supervised the collection of taxes in the localities assigned to him.[254] Batu also had investments in China, in Shansi province. In the 14th century Khan Uzbeg still collected his income there.[255] The descendants of both Ugedey and Jagatay were also entitled to their quotas of the Chinese revenue. Similarly, in the western part of the Mongol Empire, the income from the Crimean ports was divided "between four khans," as the Egyptian writer Ibn-Mufaddal puts it, that is, presumably between the senior princes of the four branches of the Chingisids.[256] The effect of such partner-ship of various branches of the Chingisids in the exploitation of the empire's resources was twofold. On the one hand, it was in the interest of them all to maintain solidarity and be loyal to the great khan. On the other, claims and counterclaims at times brought con-fusion and were apt to result in discord, as in the case of the conflict between the il-khans and the khans of Kypchak.

The rapid increase of the imperial family was another factor in the changing structure of the Mongol state and society. As each branch of the Chingisids multiplied, with each prince expecting to receive an apanage, most of the pastures and yurts in Mongolia came to be distributed among the princes.[257] As a result, the "ruling nation" of the Mongols found itself subjected to the Golden Kin and the rule of princes replaced the former free association of clans each under its own leader. Thus the Mongol national base upon which the empire was built shrank considerably and lost much of its vitality.

This process also affected the structure of the kuriltay as well as that of the army. In the 14th century most of the positions of commanders of the larger army units (the tümens and thousands)

254. Tiesenhausen, 2, 15; cf. ZO, p. 71; Howorth, 2, Pt. 1, p. 172.
255. Iakinf, p. 260; Grousset, p. 537.
256. See Veselovsky, p. 46.
257. Vladimirtsov, pp. 172–173.

were filled by princes of the blood. Owing to their leading role both in Mongol society and in the army, the princes were also able to control the electoral assembly. The kuriltay at which Buyantu was elected emperor (1311) was attended by 1,400 princes.[258] In fact, the princes in the 14th century constituted a social and military oligarchy with which each emperor and khan had to reckon. In China the power of that oligarchy was to some extent neutralized by the growth of bureaucracy. Both in Persia and South Russia the oligarchy eventually shattered the government of the khans. With all that, the rise of the princes could not but affect the efficiency of the army. It actually violated two important principles of Chingis-Khan: equality in service and promotion on the basis of ability. While there must have been able generals among the princes, their monopoly of the higher offices undoubtedly prevented the promotion of many a prominent Mongol officer not belonging to the house of Chingis. Some officers, like Tamerlane, succeeded in winning power in spite of the handicaps, by the device of giving all the honors to a puppet khan of the house of Chingis and ruling in his name. Not many, however, were as successful as Tamerlane, and the frustrated attempts of those who did not succeed, like Mamay in the Golden Horde, added to the already existing confusion in government.

As we turn now to the problem of intercultural relations between the Mongols and the conquered nations we must bear in mind that the process of acculturation varied according to the historical and ethnic background of the occupied territories. In the Turkish steppe area between Mongolia and South Russia the merging of conquerors and conquered was easier and swifter than in the countries of old cultures with predominantly agricultural population. The Mongols offered military leadership to, and imposed the framework of their administration on, the Central Asian Turks. However, constituting but a minority of the total population of the area, they gradually accepted the language of the country. Characteristically, the name Chagatay (Jagatay) is used to designate the Turkish language and literature which flourished in the regions of Semirechie and Transoxania in the 15th and 16th centuries. Chagatay Turkish was the mother tongue of the dread conqueror Tamerlane, in spite of the fact that by origin he was an offspring of an old Mongol clan.

The assimilation of the Mongols by the Turks in the Central Asian area was greatly facilitated by the fact that the religious

258. D'Ohsson, 2, 663.

background of the majority of both groups was identical. While, as we know, some of the tribes of Mongolia, as well as the Turks of eastern Turkestan and Transoxania, had been for several centuries acquainted with Buddhism, Nestorian Christianity, and Islam, the majority of the Turkish tribesmen in Jungaria and Kazakhstan seem to have been Sky worshipers or shamanists in the 13th century, as were the leading clans of the Jagatay ulus. Even in the 14th century many Jagataid princes were still faithful to the traditional Mongol religious beliefs. Islam, however, was making rapid progress, and affecting both the Mongols and Turks in that area. Tamerlane, while a follower of Chingis-Khan's military doctrine, was a good Moslem, which incidentally did not make him less harsh than Chingis-Khan in his policies.

In China, as we know, Kubilay adopted Buddhism as his own faith and the official religion of the Yuan dynasty. If anything, he even strengthened it by the protection he offered the Tibetan church. Buddhism, however, was not the only religion of the Chinese, and thus only part of the Chinese people could have been favorably impressed by his action. Besides the Buddhist clergy, endowed with various privileges which amounted almost to extraterritoriality of the Buddhist monasteries, were not a mere tool of the Yuan dynasty. They soon proved to be an independent force and difficult to deal with on many occasions. Incidentally the leader of the Ming revolution, Chu Yüan-chang, was himself, for a time in his youth, a novice of a Buddhist monastery.

Even though the reigning Mongol dynasty in China accepted one of the Chinese religions, the Mongols as a group kept apart administratively and socially, from the Chinese people over whom they ruled. They clung firmly to the Mongol language. The evidence of Marco Polo is illuminating in this respect. As Wittfogel and Fêng rightly point out, in spite of his intimate acquaintance with the ruling Mongol group and his extensive travels in China, Marco Polo has little to say about the Chinese people.[259] Obviously the Mongols in China lived in a world of their own. While in their court ceremonial as well as in their administrative institutions they followed many Chinese patterns, they continued to observe the Great Yasa. And they kept many of their old ways of life and eating habits, as well as the traditional Mongol ritual of the great chase. Under Kubilay herds of white mares were kept near one of the imperial

259. Wittfogel, p. 9.

palaces to supply kumiss. They were considered sacred and the kumiss procured from their milk was for the consumption solely of the emperor, his descendants, and, as a special privilege, the members of the Khoriat clan.[260] The rules of the great chase established by Chingis-Khan were strictly observed by his successors. The description of the chase under the emperor Tug-Timur, by Odoric de Pordenone, for which the writer probably used a copy of the official instructions, is obviously based on the Yasa regulations.[261]

In one respect many Mongols in China broke with the old traditions. A number of them proved eager to obtain landed estates in the heart of China, which could not but result in their social and economic interests becoming identified with those of the upper crust of Chinese landowners. As we have seen, this was one of the contributing causes of the anti-Mongol feeling among the peasants in South China in the mid-14th century. The Mongols showed similar interest in acquiring landed estates in Persia. This tendency contributed to the rise of feudalism and local separatism in the realm of the il-khans and speeded its political disintegration.

In religion most of the peoples controlled by the il-khan had been Moslems for several centuries, although split into Shiites and Sunnites. Hulagu, founder of the dynasty of the il-khans, was a Sky worshiper. Until the conversion of his successors to Islam at the end of the 13th century, difference in religion prevented any deep assimilation of the conquerors. Moreover, in the first period of Mongol domination over Iran, both khans and Mongol grandees kept their traditional customs and habits of life as they did in China.

The cultural and ethnic background of peoples in the group of territories controlled by the khans of Kypchak was, if anything, even more complex than was the case in China and Iran. The Kypchaks (Cumans) of the Pontic steppes—or most of them—were still pagans at the time of the Mongol invasion. The Khorezmians and Volga Bulgars were Moslems. Most of the Alans in the Don area, the northern Caucasus, and the Crimea were Greek Orthodox Christians. So were the remnants of the Goths in the Crimea. The Russians (Brodniki) living in the steppe zone—in the lower Don and lower Bug areas—were also Greek Orthodox.[262] All said, it was Russia proper, the Russian federation north of the steppes, which constituted

260. MPMP, *1*, 187.
261. *Cathay, 2*, 234–237.
262. On the Brodniki see *Kievan Russia*, pp. 158, 237, 238.

the main bulwark of Greek Orthodox Christianity in the Golden
Horde.

Economically and culturally the Kypchak steppes (*Desht-i Kyp-chak*), the home of cattle breeders and dairymen, presented a marked
contrast to North Russia with its agriculture and forest industries.
The very variety of resources in south and north encouraged lively
trade between the two regions, in which the Russians as well as Volga
Bulgars were engaged. With the destruction of the Bulgar cities and
of many Russian cities by the Mongols, supremacy in commerce
passed to the Moslem merchants of Central Asia. The latter had
been under the protection of the Mongol rulers since the times of
Chingis-Khan and played an important role in Mongol finance.

In view of the diversity of religious and cultural background in
the Khanate of Kypchak, it was but natural that its khans showed
hesitation in making their final choice of religious denomination.
Batu, the first khan of Kypchak, was a Sky worshiper. His son
Sartak accepted Christianity. Batu's brother Berke was converted
to Islam. His successors went back to Sky worship, and it was only
in the 14th century that Uzbeg finally introduced Islam as the official
religion of the khanate. The financial and commercial predominance
of the Moslems in Central Asia and the Near East undoubtedly was
an important factor in the conversion to Islam of the Pontic group
of the Mongols as well as of their Turkish subjects.

It may be argued that had the khans of the Golden Horde been
converted to Christianity instead of to Islam they could have assumed, for a time at least, a position of half-assimilated rulers of
Russia similar to that of Kubilay and his successors in China. A
united Christian state with a Moslem minority could have been
established then and there. Because of the conversion of the khans
to Islam, the creation of such a state was postponed until centuries
later. Under the actual circumstances, there was, in the 14th and
15th centuries, no possibility of a far-reaching cultural fusion between the Mongols and Russians. The result was the political split
of the Golden Horde into Moslem and Christian halves.

CHAPTER III

THE GOLDEN HORDE

1. JUCHI'S ULUS

THE KHANATE OF KYPCHAK, traditionally known as the Golden Horde, was only part of a larger political body known as Juchi's Ulus. It will be recalled that not long before his death Chingis-Khan made each of his sons ruler of a portion of the empire, an ulus, under the supreme authority of the great khan. As Kazakhstan and the "western lands" to be conquered were assigned to Chingis' oldest son Juchi, that section of the Mongol Empire became known as Juchi's Ulus, or the western khanate; Marco Polo spoke of the Juchids as "the Tartars of the West."

After Juchi's death his second son, Batu, was recognized as ruler of the ulus. Following the conquest of Russia Batu, as we know, established his capital in Saray on the lower Volga. The original part of Juchi's Ulus became the apanage of Batu's older brother, Orda. It comprised a vast area including western Siberia, Kazakhstan, and the lower basin of the Syr-Daria River.[1] Two of Juchi's other sons, Shiban and Tuka-Timur, also received shares in the area. While Batu's brothers who ruled in the eastern part of Juchi's Ulus were originally under his suzerainty, later on the eastern khanate became virtually independent.

Because Juchi's Ulus was the westernmost part of the empire, we may assume that, following the system of correspondence of colors to the cardinal points, it was designated by white. According to John of Plano Carpini, during each of the four days of the ceremonies of Guyuk's election the Mongols attending the kuriltay were dressed in robes of special color. On the first day the color was white.[2] In Khara-Davan's opinion, that day symbolized the participation of Juchi's Ulus in the elections.[3] The reception on that day

---

1. *ZO*, pp. 295–296; Spuler, pp. 25, 275.
2. Rockhill, p. 19.
3. Khara-Davan, p. 199.

was held in a great tent of white velvet. Presumably, then, Juchi's Ulus as a whole was known as the White Horde. With its division into two subuluses, eastern and western, the problem of colors becomes more involved. Two names are mentioned in the sources for the subuluses—the White and the Blue Hordes—but it is not clear which color refers to which khanate.

Most scholars now agree that the eastern khanate was called the White Horde (in Turkish, Ak-Ordu), and the western the Blue Horde (in Turkish, Kök-Ordu).[4] In my opinion this interpretation is questionable. First of all we must take into consideration the evidence of the Russian chronicles. In these the western khanate (to which Russia was directly subject) is called the Great Horde (Bolshaia Orda) or just the Horde (Orda), and the eastern khanate is referred to as the Blue Horde (Siniaia Orda). The Russians, in using the name Blue were undoubtedly following their Tatar informants. Moreover the name seems logical when applied to the *eastern* khanate, since blue is the color of the east. There is no agreement in the Oriental sources about the names Blue Horde and White Horde. It is true that in some of the Persian sources such as the 15th-century chronicle called Iskander's Anonym the eastern horde is referred to as white and the western as blue.[5] However another Persian source, Kutba's poem "Khosrew and Shirin," speaks of Tinibeg, a mid-14th-century khan of Kypchak, as ruler of the White Horde.[6] The German traveler Johann Schiltberger, who visited the Khanate of Kypchak in the early 15th century, called it the Great Tartary (which corresponds to the Great Horde of the Russian chronicles) or the White Tartary (which corresponds to the White Horde).[7] It may be added that in the story of the murder of Ahmad, one of the last khans of the Golden Horde, by Khan Ibak of Tiumen in 1481 Ahmad is said to have been killed in his "white tent."[8]

It appears, then, that first Juchi's Ulus as a whole and then its western part, the Khanate of Kypchak, were known as the White Horde. And yet, in modern historiography the White Horde is called

4. Spuler, p. 25; *ZO*, pp. 261–262.

5. Tiesenhausen, *2*, 127. W. Barthold points out some confusion in the chronicler's evidence; see Barthold, *Turcs*, p. 135.

6. Tiesenhausen, *2*, 4.

7. Schiltberger, pp. 7, 33, 34. Cf. Hammer-Purgstall's remarks in Neumann's edition of Schiltberger's German text, p. 39.

8. The Ustiugian Digest of Chronicles, p. 94.

the Golden Horde. Why this name and what is its origin? As we have seen gold, representing the color yellow, was the symbol of the Mongol imperial power. At the same time yellow was geographically the color of the middle, that of the central state.

The name Golden Horde first appears in our sources to denote the imperial tent of Great Khan Guyuk. And as we are aware, Chingis-Khan's descendants were known as the Golden Kin. The rulers of the White Horde belonged to the Golden Kin, and at least one of them, the Moslem Khan Uzbeg (reigned 1313–41), used to sit in state during court receptions in what was called the "golden pavilion" (*pavillon d'or* according to the French translation of Ibn-Batuta's *Travels*).[9] The khan's throne in this pavilion was covered with gilded sheets of silver. Yet neither Ibn-Batuta, who described in detail both the pavilion and the throne, nor any other Oriental writer of the 14th and 15th centuries calls the Khanate of Kypchak the Golden Horde.

The first mention of the name Golden Horde in Russian sources occurs in the *History of the Tsardom of Kazan* (written around 1564). The author of this work, who was thoroughly familiar with the historical background of the Khanate of Kazan, derived his information in part at least from the Kazan Tatars.[10] It seems probable that after the separation of the khanates of Crimea and Kazan from the White Horde the latter could be considered a middle state in this group of three successor states, and, consequently, was called the Golden Horde in the sense of "middle horde."

Since the name Golden Horde has become traditional in historical literature, replacing it by the technically more appropriate White Horde would only lead to confusion and might cause misunderstandings. Therefore, for the sake of convenience, the Khanate of Kypchak or the White Horde will be referred to as the Golden Horde from here on.

2. The Reign of Batu and His Sons

The foundations of the Golden Horde as an autonomous state within the Mongol Empire were laid by Khan Batu after his return from his Hungarian campaign in 1242. Four years later, at the time of John of Plano Carpini's voyage to Mongolia, the outline of the new

9. Ibn-Batuta, *2*, 383.

10. The Kazan Chronicle, *PSRL*, *19*; G. Z. Kuntsevich, *Istoriia o Kazanskom Tsarstve* (St. Petersburg, 1905).

state was already taking definite shape. Southwest Russia and the Cuman steppes were under the authority of the commanders of the Mongol troops stationed there. The administration was strong, and travel was safe.

Batu's court, on the bank of the Volga River, was established "right magnificently" as John remarked. The khan and his family lived in large linen tents which had belonged to the king of Hungary. The reception at the khan's court is described by John in the following words: "He [Batu] sits in a raised place, as on the throne, with one of his wives; but everyone else [of his family], as well his brothers and his sons as others of lesser degree, sit lower down on a bench in the middle [of the tent]. All the other people sit behind them on the ground, the men to the right, the women to the left." [11]

Seven years later another traveler, William of Rubruck, described Batu's camp as "a great city stretched out about his dwelling, with people scattered all about for three or four leagues. And as among the people of Israel, where each one knew in which quarter from the tabernacle he had to pitch his tents, so these know on which side of the ordu they must place themselves when they set down their dwellings." [12] The ceremonial of Friar William's audience was similar to that of Friar John's. Of Batu's personal appearance Friar William says that "he seemed to me to be about the height of my lord John de Beaumont, may his soul rest in peace." [13] As N. M. Karamzin remarks: "What a pity that we have not had the honor of ever meeting Monsieur de Beaumont!" [14] Soon after Friar William's voyage Batu established his residence in the newly founded city of Saray.

According to archeological evidence, Batu's capital was located on the eastern bank of the Akhtuba (a channel of the lower Volga delta), around 65 miles north of Astrakhan. [15]

Of Batu's spiritual qualities the epithet *sain* given him in some of the Oriental annals as well as in Turkish folklore is an indication. This is usually understood and translated as "good." Paul Pelliot remarks, however, that the word also has the connotation of "intelligent" and that with Batu it must be understood in this sense. [16]

11. Rockhill, p. 10.
12. *Idem,* p. 122.
13. *Idem,* p. 123.
14. Karamzin, *4,* n. 49; *Notes, 4,* 30.
15. *ZO,* pp. 68–69.
16. Pelliot, p. 106.

Thus sain-khan could mean the "sensible khan" or "wise khan."

Desht-i Kypchak (the Cuman steppe) constituted the core of Batu's khanate. Its western extension was Bulgaria and its eastern was Khorezm. To the north Russia's resistance was broken, but the machinery of occupation and control was yet to be established. In the south Batu's authority extended to the Crimea and northern Caucasus. Transcaucasia occupied by the Mongols during the reign of Ugedey, and the Seljuq Sultanate in Asia Minor, conquered during the regency of Ugedey's widow, were not formally within Batu's jurisdiction. However, the Mongol troops in those regions were commanded by army generals (noyans), not by any of the Chingisid princes. Batu was then the Chingisid geographically closest to the scene of events, and a senior one at that. Under these circumstances he could be expected to take some interest in those newly conquered areas, and their rulers hastened to establish contact with him. For instance the Seljuq sultan Jias ad-Din Kai Hosrev II sent three missions to Batu. The Georgian prince David (the future king David V of Georgia) lived for some time at Batu's court as a hostage.[17]

In regard to Russia, Batu faced two main problems: to inforce the obedience of the Russian princes to his will and to organize the collection of tribute and taxes. At the time of John of Plano Carpini's journey there were no Mongol troops in North Russia; in the southwest a division under the command of Kuremsa (Qurumshi) [18] was stationed in the Dnieper region south of Kiev. There was no Russian prince in Kiev in 1246; the Kievan region, as well as part of the Chernigov region, and Podolia were under direct Mongol control. According to John, the Mongols around 1245 conscripted recruits for their army from the population of that entire area.

To extend their control farther west, north, and east, they needed the cooperation of the Russian princes. The East Russian princes were the first to pledge their allegiance. As early as 1242 Grand Duke Iaroslav I of Vladimir went to Batu's ordu and was confirmed in his office. His son Constantine was sent to Mongolia to pledge his and his father's loyalty to the regent. In 1246, as we know, Iaroslav himself went to Karakorum, where he attended the ceremonies of Guyuk's enthronement.[19] Iaroslav never returned to Russia; he fell

17. Spuler, *Horde*, p. 30; Spuler, *Iran*, p. 45.

18. In Russian chronicles, Kuremsa; for the Mongol spelling of the name see Cleaves, "Mongolian Names," pp. 433–435.

19. See above, Chapter 2, sec. 1, p. 61.

ill and died in Mongolia. According to Friar John he was poisoned by the khatun, Guyuk's mother. Both Karamzin and Rockhill doubt John's story, arguing that the great khan could always execute Iaroslav openly if he wanted to and therefore the Mongols did not need to use subterfuge.[20] However John's information, gathered from the Russians in Karakorum, is usually accurate. We must also take into consideration the tenseness of relations between Guyuk and Batu. If Guyuk considered Iaroslav Batu's tool, he might have found it necessary to get rid of him quietly. Moreover, as we know, Guyuk did not approve of his mother's policies during her regency, so there is a possibility the khatun poisoned Iaroslav to spite her son. After receiving news of their father's death, Iaroslav's sons Alexander Nevsky and Andrew went to Batu's ordu to pledge their allegiance. Batu instructed both of them to go to Karakorum to pay their respect to the great khan (1247).

Meantime Batu settled the West Russian problems in his own way. The two outstanding Russian princes he had to deal with were Daniel of Galicia and Michael of Chernigov.[21] It was characteristic of the feudal society of east Central Europe that even after the grim lesson of the Mongol invasion in 1240–41 both interprincely and international strife and rivalries continued unabated. In spite of several attempts at conciliation, the princes of Galicia were in almost perpetual conflict with the princes of Chernigov. Both Poland and Hungary tried to take advantage of the situation by supporting now one side, and now the other, with the ultimate aim of controlling Galicia themselves. This led to constant conflicts between the Hungarians and the Poles, and between both these nations and the Russians. The princes of Galicia, since they had to combine their forces now with the Poles and now with the Hungarians, several times became involved in Central European conflicts, intervening as they did in Hungarian–Czech and Czech–Polish rivalries.

In the early years of his reign Batu's attention was concentrated on the negotiations of the Mongol leaders over the future election of the new great khan; he was also preoccupied with Transcaucasian and Anatolian relations. So he did not interfere with the activities of the West Russian princes until 1245. By that time the decision had been reached in Mongolia concerning Guyuk's candidacy to the

20. Karamzin, *4,* 34–35; Rockhill, pp. 25–26.
21. On the previous relations between Daniel of Galicia and Michael of Chernigov see *Kievan Russia,* pp. 239–240.

throne. Even if Batu did not approve of it he had to accept it. He was now free to strengthen his control over West Russia.

Meanwhile, in 1245, Daniel of Galicia and his brother Vasilko of Volynia administered an overwhelming defeat to Prince Rostislav (son of Michael of Chernigov) who was supported by both the Hungarians and the Poles. This victory made Daniel the strongest ruler in east Central Europe, and Batu hastened to prevent any possible attempt on Daniel's part to assert his independence from the Mongols. He ordered Daniel to turn the administration of Galicia over to a Mongol general. Instead Daniel decided to pledge vassal allegiance to Batu personally and for this purpose went to the khan's ordu. He had to kowtow before the khan but otherwise was graciously received and shown every favor. "Do you drink our drinks—the black milk and kumiss?" Batu asked Daniel.[22] "Until now I didn't, but now I do as you order and drink it." Batu was obviously pleased. "You are now one of ours," said he, and ordered a goblet of wine to be offered the Russian prince. "You are not accustomed to milk, so drink some wine." In spite of the kind reception Daniel's pride, as well as that of his knights, was deeply wounded. "Oh, more evil than evil itself is the Tatar honor," comments the Galician chronicler. "Daniel, the great prince, the lord of the Russian land, now kneels and calls himself the khan's slave." [23]

A few months after Daniel's pilgrimage to Saray Prince Michael of Chernigov went to see Batu. He proved less fortunate than his rival. The difference in Batu's attitude toward the two princes may be explained by the fact that Daniel was much stronger than Michael and Batu found it necessary to coax him into submission. Besides, Galicia was close to Hungary and Poland, and Daniel could always seek refuge in one of these countries. Both Michael and his son Rostislav had spent several years in Hungary, and Rostislav returned there after the failure of his campaign against Daniel.[24]

22. Hyp., p. 185. Kumiss is fermented mare's milk; fermented cow's milk is called *aryan*. From milk, aryan, or kumiss the Kalmyks and other Mongols distill the spirit of milk, known as *arkhi* (or *ar'ka*). According to Khara-Davan ar'ka is prepared for home consumption and for treating friends; it is never for sale, Khara-Davan, p. 78, n. 2. Cf. MPYC, *1*, 259–260. The process of distilling milk was apparently discovered by the Mongols in the early 13th century. This is the drink which was called "cara-cosmos" (black kumiss) by William of Rubruck and "black milk" by the Russian chronicler. In Mongol and Turkish the adjective "black" in regard to water (or any liquid) means "clear," "transparent" (the spirit of milk is transparent).

23. Hyp., p. 185.

24. Rostislav married the Hungarian princess Ann, daughter of King Béla IV, and

Michael, however, preferred to go back to Chernigov, where he found himself at Batu's mercy. Moreover, Batu apparently did not trust Michael's intentions. He agreed to receive Michael only if he purified himself by walking between two fires. This was the usual Mongol procedure for foreigners seeking admission to the khan's court, based on their belief in the magic properties of fire. Daniel, incidentally, was spared it.

In addition, according to John of Plano Carpini, Batu required that Michael kowtow before the idol (ongon) of Chingis-Khan. Michael refused to comply with Batu's demands and even, in a spirit of defiance, denounced the "vile idols." For this he was executed together with one of his loyal boyars who had accompanied him to the khan's ordu and kept urging him "to win the martyr's crown." [25] Another prince of the house of Chernigov, Andrew, son of Mstislav, was executed about the same time.[26] According to John of Plano Carpini, he was punished for exporting horses abroad without license.[27]

Prince Michael's execution removed Daniel's old rival from the scene and thus strengthened his position. Moreover, by placing himself under Batu's protection as his vassal, Daniel gained prestige among the neighboring rulers, who now sought his friendship. King Béla of Hungary gave his daughter in marriage to Daniel's son Leo, and sponsored the marriage of another of Daniel's sons, Roman, with Gertrude, niece of the late duke of Austria. Roman thus became a pretender to the Austrian throne. This enabled Béla to interest Daniel in the question of the Austrian succession and to receive his military assistance against the Holy Roman Empire.[28]

It must be noted that after his return from Batu's ordu, in 1246, Daniel reorganized and re-equipped his army in the Mongol fashion. When the Austrian envoys came to his camp they were amazed to

received the principality of Machin, on the Danube River, as his fief. See S. Palauzov, *Rostislav Mikhailovich* (St. Petersburg, 1851); V. Prokofiev, "Rostislav Mikhailovich, russkii kniaz' XIII veka," *Sbornik Russkogo Arkheologicheskogo Obshchestva* (Belgrade, 1936), pp. 131 ff., as quoted by G. Ostrogorsky, "Urum-Despotes," *BZ, 44* (1951), 455.

25. There are brief accounts of the story of Michael's martyrdom in Hyp., p. 181; Laur. 2, col. 471; an expanded version in Nikon, 10, 130–133. See also John of Plano Carpini's account, Risch, pp. 67–70; Serebriansky, *Zhitiia*, pp. 110–111; Likhachev, p. 283. On the causes of Michael's execution see Grigoriev, *Yarlyki,* pp. 55–57.

26. See Baumgarten 1, Table 4, No. 64; Rog., p. 31.

27. Risch, p. 71.

28. On the relations between Daniel and Béla in connection with the Austrian affairs see Florovsky, *1,* 212–223; Pashuto, pp. 255–256.

see Daniel's horsemen clad in Mongol style cuirasses and their horses protected by headpieces and shoulder and chest armor. "And their weapons were shining." Daniel himself, however, was attired according to what the chronicler calls "the Russian custom." He wore a riding coat of Greek brocade adorned with gold lace; his boots were of green leather. His saber was incrusted with gold, and the saddle of his magnificent steed was gilded.[29]

In spite of both Béla's and Daniel's efforts, it was the candidate supported by the Holy Roman Empire, Ottokar of Bohemia (king of Bohemia since 1253), who eventually became duke of Austria.[30] As a matter of fact, Daniel did not intend to set Central Europe on fire. On the contrary, by that time he had come to the conclusion that he needed the support of the West against the Mongols. Indeed, his subservience to Batu was only a tactical move. His long-range strategy was to prepare for a struggle against the Mongols. He had to act cautiously, however, and did not make his intentions known at the start.

Daniel's first move in his new diplomatic game was to establish contact with the pope, whose authority greatly increased after the death of his bitter enemy, the emperor Frederick II, in 1250. It will be recalled that a few years earlier the pope himself, through John of Plano Carpini, urged the West Russian princes to recognize his authority. At the time of John's sojourn in Volynia (presumably, in December 1245), Daniel was at Batu's camp, and his brother Vasilko, while sympathetic to the pope's idea, refused to assume any responsibility in the matter of the union of the churches. As the friars continued their journey to Mongolia, the pope sent another cleric to Daniel to prepare the ground for a rapprochement.[31] On their way back from Mongolia John and his companion stopped in Galicia (June 1247) where Daniel and Vasilko received them "with great rejoicing." According to John both princes said "that they wished to have the Lord Pope for their particular lord and father, and the Roman Church as their lady and mistress. . . . And after that they sent with us to the Lord Pope their letters and ambassadors."[32]

---

29. Hyp., p. 187. On the Byzantine riding coat (*skaramangion*) see N. Kondakov, "Les Costumes orientaux à la cour byzantine," *Byzantion, 1,* (1924), 7–49; *idem, Ocherki i zametki po istorii srednevekovogo iskusstva i kultury* (Prague, 1929), pp. 232–240.

30. Ottokar's wife was an Austrian princess. In 1276 Ottokar was compelled to cede Austria to King Rudolph I of Hapsburg.

31. *HRM, 1,* No. 63, cf. No. 65; Pashuto, pp. 251–252.

32. Rockhill, p. 32.

There followed an exchange of embassies. Daniel agreed to prevail on the clergy and the people of Galicia and Volynia to recognize the pope as the head of their church. The pope, in his turn, promised Daniel the royal crown and the military assistance of the Roman Catholic nations.[33]

Simultaneously, Daniel entered into negotiations with Grand Duke Andrew of Vladimir (Alexander Nevsky's brother), to whom he gave one of his daughters in marriage in 1251. Andrew agreed to cooperate with Daniel but was not able to do much since, for reasons which will be explained later, he lost his throne in 1252. Thus Daniel's only hope was to receive assistance from the West. The pope duly sent him the royal emblems, and Daniel was crowned king in the city of Drogichin in 1253. However, the pope's efforts to rally the Catholic powers for a crusade against the Mongols in Daniel's aid came to nothing.

We can now return to events in East Russia. When Alexander Nevsky and his brother Andrew had appeared at Guyuk's court late in 1247 or early in 1248, the khan made Andrew grand duke of Vladimir and Alexander prince of Kiev. The latter appointment is significant for it shows that Guyuk wanted someone dependent on him to rule in West Russia. The brothers returned to Russia in 1249. Guyuk had died by that time, but there was no redistribution of princely thrones during the interregnum. While Andrew established himself in Vladimir, Alexander went to Novgorod instead of Kiev. The new metropolitan bishop of Russia visited him there in 1251. It must be noted in this connection that the former metropolitan, Joseph, had perished in Kiev in 1240. Only after an intermission of six years did Daniel of Galicia take the initiative in restoring the metropolitan's see and send his candidate, a West Russian monk named Cyril, to Nicaea [34] for the patriarch's approval. Cyril was duly ordained metropolitan of Kiev, but because of the confused situation in the Near East he did not return to Russia until 1249 or 1250. Finding Kiev completely devastated and unsuitable for the establishment of the diocesan administration, he went to East Russia instead. His disapproval of Daniel's negotiations with the pope was an additional motive for his decision. Moreover, Alexander was officially prince of Kiev even if he actually resided in Novgorod.

33. Hrushevsky, 3, 68–73; Florovsky, 1, 233–240.
34. The Byzantine patriarch moved from Constantinople to Nicaea after the establishment of the Latin Empire in Constantinople in 1204.

Meanwhile the interregnum in the Mongol Empire came to an end with the election of Mongka as the new great khan (1251). This event called for the renewal of all princely patents. However, because of the close friendship between Mongka and Batu and the wide powers Mongka had granted to Batu, the Russian princes this time had to go to Saray instead of to Karakorum for confirmation in their office. As a matter of fact Batu in his turn authorized his son and co-ruler Sartak—a Christian, apparently of Nestorian denomination—to handle Russian affairs. It was with Sartak that the Russians had to deal from now on. Alexander Nevsky went to Saray without hesitation. Andrew, however, refused to make the required journey. If he counted on Daniel's assistance in his opposition to the khan, he miscalculated; Daniel was not yet ready to take a firm stand against the Mongols. Sartak immediately sent a punitive expedition to Vladimir. Andrew met the Mongol troops near the city of Pereiaslavl-in-Suzdalia.[35] His army was defeated and he had to flee to Novgorod. From there he proceeded to Kolyvan (Revel, now known as Tallinn) and then sought refuge in Sweden. The Mongols looted Suzdalia.

Sartak now granted the patent on the throne of Vladimir to Alexander Nevsky. Alexander was greeted upon his arrival at Vladimir by Metropolitan Cyril, the clergy, and a multitude of citizens.[36] The boyars, significantly, are not mentioned in the accounts of the reception. One of the chroniclers states however that Andrew had fled to Novgorod "with his boyars." [37] Apparently the Vladimir boyars as a group supported Andrew in his opposition to the Mongols and were, at that time, opposed to Alexander and his policy of loyalty to the khan.

In order to understand better the motives of Alexander's policy it seems proper to compare them with those of Daniel. First of all, the difference in geographic background of the two realms is important. Galicia was much farther from Saray than Vladimir. Where Daniel could entertain hopes of asserting his independence from the khan, Alexander could not. Daniel, as we know, counted on support from the West. Alexander did not trust the West. It must be emphasized, in this connection, that there was a marked difference in the nature of the Western powers with which the princes had to deal. In spite

35. Pereiaslavl-in-Suzdalia, known also as Pereiaslavl-Zalesskii (Beyond the Forest).
36. Laur. *1*, Fasc. 2, col. 473; Nikon, *10*, 139.
37. Nikon, *10*, 138 (left column).

of Daniel's conflicts with Poland and Hungary the rulers of both these countries were merely his rivals (and at times his friends) rather than his enemies. Socially and psychologically Slavic Poland and half-Slavic Hungary belonged to the same Central European milieu as Galicia and Volynia. In contrast the Teutonic Knights and the Swedes whom Alexander had to face in his youth were at that time Russia's implacable enemies, permeated as they were with the crusading spirit and interest in colonial expansion with all its implications. While Daniel could hope to make Galicia a partner in a federation of friendly powers, Alexander knew that if he ever got help from the West it would be on the West's own terms. Obtaining the protection of the Teutonic Knights would entail accepting their suzerainty. Moreover, even with their help Alexander could not hope to defend Vladimir from the Mongol troops. North Russia would be split between the Teutonic Knights and the Mongols, Novgorod going to the former and Vladimir to the latter. Alexander preferred to remain loyal to the Mongols rather than divide the country.

There was also a basic difference in the attitude of Alexander and Daniel toward their respective church affiliations. For Daniel, in the Central European cultural milieu, the Roman Catholic Church was the church of the neighbors with whom he was on an equal political and social footing. Intermarriages between the West Russian princely houses and those of the neighboring Central European nations were frequent.[38] For Alexander, on the other hand, the Roman Catholic Church was represented by the knight crusaders. To this fact a difference in spiritual attitude between the two princes must be added. Alexander seems to have been a much more ardent member than Daniel of the Greek Orthodox Church, which symbolized universal truth for him. In character and personality Daniel was light-hearted and addicted to the habits and notions of Western chivalry, while Alexander was more serious in purpose and had a deeper sense of responsibility toward his country and his people. An outstanding military leader, Alexander was also a cool statesman and realistic enough to accept the inevitable course of forbearance however hard it might be. Once he had accepted this course he would not deviate from it, and he succeeded in enjoining it on his subjects, even on the rebellious Novgorodians.

Batu died around 1255 and was succeeded by his son Sartak. His

38. See Baumgarten 1, Table 11.

death did not affect the Russian princes in any way, since they were already under Sartak's authority. While new hardships were imposed on the Russian people at that time, it was not Sartak who initiated them but Great Khan Mongka. Needing more troops for his Chinese campaign as well as for the proposed conquest of the Near East, Mongka as early as 1252 ordered a new census to be taken throughout the empire, as a basis for conscripting soldiers and collecting taxes.[39] Sartak died around 1256. The new khan, Ulagchi, summoned all the Russian princes to Saray to renew their patents. Among the others the formerly recalcitrant Grand Duke Andrew of Vladimir appeared at Ulagchi's court "with many gifts." Presumably it was Alexander Nevsky who had arranged for the return of his fugitive brother from Sweden. Andrew was pardoned and appointed prince of Suzdal. While Ulagchi received his Russian vassals graciously, he confirmed the imperial order for the census and conscription.

The Mongol officials charged with these duties appeared in East Russia—in the principalities of Riazan and Murom and in the Grand Duchy of Vladimir—in 1257. Remembering well the horrors of the punitive expedition of 1252, the people of the Grand Duchy of Vladimir made no attempt at resistance. Permanent machinery of Mongol administration was now established in East Russia, and the country divided into military districts (myriads, thousands, hundreds, and tens) to facilitate both conscription and tax collecting.[40] Having thus completed the reorganization of administration in East Russia, the Mongols turned their attention to Novgorod.

At first the Novgorodians refused to let the Mongol officials enter their city. Being well aware what disaster armed resistance would bring on them, Alexander Nevsky took upon himself to convince them they must agree to the census. When the Novgorodians rejected his mediation he applied measures of coercion. Even his son Vasili, his lieutenant in Novgorod, rebelled against him on this occasion; Alexander had him arrested and deported to Vladimir, and severely punished several of his retainers. Warned that a Mongol expeditionary corps was ready to march on Novgorod, the people finally agreed to the census, on terms which will be described presently.

In 1258 the Mongol officials came to the northern metropolis

39. Spuler, p. 31. In China the census was taken in 1252; see M. Otagi, *ASTH*, pp. 9–10 (English summary).

40. Nikon, *10*, 141.

accompanied by Grand Duke Alexander Nevsky, his brother Prince Andrew of Suzdal, and Prince Boris of Rostov. By that impressive array of leading East Russian princes the Mongols apparently meant to warn the Novgorodians that they could expect no support from the Russian authorities if they renewed their resistance. In spite of this diplomatic pressure, when the officials started "counting" the inhabitants a rebellion broke out in the city. The Mongols asked Alexander Nevsky for protection, and he ordered his troops to suppress the riots. His firm stand duly impressed the Novgorodians and they finally agreed to let the Mongols proceed with the census. The terse account of these events in the First Novgorodian Chronicle reflects the range of conflicting feelings of the various groups of the population and their subdued indignation at Alexander's "appeasement" policies.[41] The proud city had to bow to the conquerors, and the required quota of soldiers was duly mustered. While this census became the basis for estimating the liabilities of the people of Novgorod, no permanent Mongol military districts were established in the area. Presumably the Novgorod authorities made themselves responsible for gathering both soldiers and taxes in the future. Some such arrangement had probably been stipulated in the preliminary negotiations. It was an important concession on the part of the Mongols, the price they paid for Alexander Nevsky's cooperation. As a matter of fact, the merchants of the Golden Horde derived substantial profits from Novgorod's Baltic trade and expected to expand them in the future. They preferred collecting golden eggs to killing the hen which laid them.

3. The Reign of Berke

The death of Ulagchi (1258) opened the way to the throne of Kypchak to Batu's brother Berke, a stern and ambitious ruler. With him a new religious element entered the politics of the western branch of the Mongols: the Islamic. Berke had been converted to Islam in his youth and made his new faith the cornerstone of his Near Eastern policies. As a Mohammedan he was in a position to enter into friendly relations with the Mameluk state of Egypt. This resulted in conflict with his cousin Hulagu, khan of the Mongols in Persia.

In the initial period of Mongol expansion in the Near East, it will be recalled, there was no clear delimitation of the spheres of in-

41. Novgorod, pp. 310–311.

fluence in the Near East of the great khan and the khan of Kypchak. Batu, as we have seen, interfered with Near Eastern affairs on many occasions. All this changed with the decision of the kuriltay of 1253 to organize a new Mongol expedition to the Near East under the command of Mongka's brother Hulagu. In terms of Mongol inter-princely politics this meant transferring the supervision of Near Eastern affairs from the descendants of Juchi to the descendants of Tuluy. At first the Juchids accepted the decision and agreed to co-operate with Hulagu by sending detachments of their troops to his assistance. But the seeds of potential discord were already sown. Much depended on the personalities of the khans of Kypchak and their specific political interests. Both Sartak and Ulagchi not only were loyal to Great Khan Mongka but were more interested in ex-ploiting their Russian dominions than in Near Eastern affairs. When Berke ascended the throne of Kypchak he pledged his full loyalty to Mongka and by the terms of his pledge had to support Hulagu's drive in the Near East. Contingents sent by Berke's predecessor Ulagchi took part in the conquest of Bagdad in February 1258.

Mongka's death in 1259 resulted in a protracted crisis in the Mongol Empire, the conflict, as we have seen, between two brother pretenders to the throne, Kubilay and Arik-Buka. In view of the incipient misunderstanding between Hulagu and Berke it was per-haps inevitable that each should support a different candidate. While Hulagu recognized Kubilay as emperor, Berke backed Arik-Buka.

The civil war between Kubilay and Arik-Buka lasted until 1264, and in this atmosphere of general uncertainty and confusion the conflict between Berke and Hulagu eventually came into the open.

A new factor entered the already complex situation in the Near East with the overthrow of the Latin Empire in Constantinople and the restoration of the Byzantine Empire in 1261 by Michael VIII Paleologus (emperor of Nicaea since 1259). This resulted in a gen-eral realignment of political and commercial trends in the eastern Mediterranean. As the Latin Empire was supported by the Venetians, Michael granted privileges to the Genoese merchants instead, which gave the latter the edge over their rivals.[42] The Empire of Nicaea had been traditionally friendly with the Mongols in Iran. Now, with the transfer of the Greek capital back to Constantinople, Michael VIII was in an advantageous position to negotiate with the Kypchak

42. Ostrogorsky, pp. 319–321; Lopez, pp. 208–213.

Mongols as well. In fact the political and commercial revolution on the Bosporus opened a convenient maritime road between Kypchak and Egypt via Byzantium which could be used for an exchange of embassies between Berke and the Mameluk sultans.

The return of the Byzantine emperor and patriarch to Constantinople was also an important event for Russia since Constantinople was much more accessible from Russia than Nicaea, and normal relations between the Russian church and the patriarch to whom it was ecclesiastically subordinated could be resumed. Politically, of course, Russia was now under the sway of the Mongols, and the khan of Kypchak became the "tsar" for the Russians. Yet the Byzantine tsar still enjoyed a degree of moral and sentimental prestige among the Russians, and was moreover in a position to influence the patriarch's policies toward the Russian church. It must be noted, however, that by his consent to recognize the authority of the pope during the short-lived church union proclaimed at the council of Lyon in 1274 Emperor Michael VIII aroused considerable opposition among the Greek Orthodox clergy both in Constantinople and in Russia. A peculiar situation developed, in which Russia's political dependence on the Mongols made her church safe from the pope's pressure. The Mongols in their turn were well aware of the possibility of using the Russian clergy as intermediaries in their relations with Byzantium. An important step toward a coordination of Russian church affairs with the Mongol administration was taken in 1261 when Berke approved the proposal, sponsored by both Alexander Nevsky and Metropolitan Cyril, to establish a Russian bishopric at Saray.[43] It must be noted in this connection that in addition to the older city of Saray, founded by Batu, Berke established a new city, also called Saray. It was situated on the eastern bank of the upper Akhtuba, close to the present-day town of Leninsk (formerly known as Tsarev), around 30 miles east of Stalingrad.[44] Old Saray, however, remained the official capital of the Golden Horde under both Berke and his successors until the reign of Uzbeg (1313–41), when the capital was transferred to New Saray.

Preoccupied with the conflict in the Mongol Empire as well as with a wide range of tortuous problems of Near Eastern policy, Berke seems to have paid less attention to Russian affairs than his predecessors. He had, however, to settle the situation in Galicia and

43. Nasonov, pp. 45–47; Makari, 4, 109–110; Golubinsky, 2, 60–61.
44. ZO, pp. 68–69.

Volynia where, as we know, King Daniel had attempted to assert his independence from the Mongols. Since the beginning of the 1250's Daniel, in addition to his other worries, was faced with the problem of checking the rapidly growing Lithuanian expansion. It will be recalled that half a century earlier his father Roman had succeeded in subduing the Lithuanian tribes closest to the confines of Volynia.[45] Now, under pressure of the Teutonic Knights from the West, the Lithuanians spread southward and eastward, coming in contact with the Russians and eventually absorbing portions of West Russian lands.

In the process of readjustment to a changed political situation the Lithuanian tribes gradually came out of their isolation; their social organization and old ways of life were greatly affected by the contact with their neighbors, which proved fruitful to them in many ways.[46] In the beginning of the 13th century the clan organization of the Lithuanians was already disintegrating. Alongside the clan there emerged local neighborhood organizations in which people of different clans, as well as those who had lost their connection with any clan, were mixed. In eastern Lithuania and Zhmud' this district organization eventually was called by the Russian term *volost'* (canton). The leading role in each such district belonged to the wealthier landowners, most of whom were connected with prominent old clans. In Prussia these local chieftains were called kings, *rikai* (cf. the Latin *rex*); in Zhmud', *kunigai* (a borrowing from the Gothic).[47] In the Russian chronicles they are referred to as princes. As regards religion, the Lithuanians still clung to their traditional heathen cult.[48] From the social and economic angle, the old Lithuanian civilization was essentially rural. The only old city built on the fringe of Lithuania in the early period was Gorodna (Grodno), founded and settled by the Russians and first mentioned in the Russian chronicles under A.D. 1128.[49]

Under the impact of the Teutonic danger many Lithuanian clan leaders saw the urgent need of reforms, especially of political uni-

45. *Kievan Russia*, p. 231.
46. On the origins of the Lithuanian state see Liubavsky, chaps. 2–3; K. Avizonis, *Die Entstehung und Entwicklung des litauischen Adels bis zur litauisch–polisch Union, 1385* (Berlin, 1932).
47. Cf. *König*, king, in modern German.
48. On the religion of the Lithuanians see *Ancient Russia*, p. 233; A. Brückner, *Dzieje kultury polskiej* (Kraków, 1930), *1*, 643–645; Liubavsky, pp. 11–12.
49. See Nasonov, *Russkaia zemlia*, pp. 56–57.

fication and creating a trained army. Many also realized the importance of fortified cities and the development of commerce. In all these respects the patterns of Russian political and social organization could be of great use to the Lithuanians. Therefore control of the nearest Russian cities and lands became an important objective of the more perspicacious Lithuanian princes. As a result, attempts on the part of the Lithuanian leaders to centralize their government developed simultaneously with their seizure of neighboring Russian cities. This was the policy specifically of Prince Mendovg (in Lithuanian, Mindaugas), who established himself around 1235 as ruler of Novgorod-Litovsk (also known as Novgorodok or Nowogródek) in so-called Black Russia.[50] Black Russia was the name for the westernmost corner of the territory of the Krivichi (Krivichians), an old Russian tribe who were the forefathers of the Belorussians.[51]

Black Russia became the foundation of Mendovg's power. In the early 1250's, in addition to Novgorodok Mendovg also controlled the cities of Grodno, Volkovysk, and Slonim. Even before that, Mendovg's nephew Tovtivil had become prince of Polotsk and another nephew prince of Vitebsk. Thus a considerable part of Belorussia was now ruled by Lithuanian princes. The Russian princes of Pinsk, in the Pripet River basin, also recognized Mendovg as their suzerain. In most of these cases the Lithuanian advance was the result not of outright conquest but of agreement with the Russians. It must be noted in this connection that Polotsk had been threatened by the Germans since the time the latter entrenched themselves in the Western Dvina basin.[52] Pinsk was in the region of Turov[53] which was devastated by the Mongols in 1240, although Pinsk itself was spared destruction at that time. After that its princes were in constant fear of a new Mongol raid. Thus both Polotsk and Pinsk were in need of protection, each from a different enemy. Because of this, together with some other cities in Belorussia they welcomed the Lithuanian princes and their retinues as efficient guardsmen. The Lithuanians were fierce warriors even if at that early time they lacked discipline and equipment; and many of the Lithuanian princes proved to be outstanding military leaders, especially after they became familiar with Russian technique and methods of training.

50. On the name Black Russia see Moszyński, 2, 1552.
51. On the Krivichians see *Ancient Russia*, pp. 324–325.
52. *Kievan Russia*, pp. 232–233.
53. On the land of Turov see *Kievan Russia*, pp. 66, 68, 74, 97, 175; A. Grushevsky, *Ocherki istorii Turovskogo kniazhestva* (Kiev, 1902).

The result of the Lithuanian penetration into Belorussia was a rapid spread of Russian culture among those Lithuanians who were in Mendovg's and Tovtivil's service and the creation of what may be called a pro-Russian party among a group of the Lithuanian princes and clan leaders. On the other hand, the continuing opposition of other princes and clan leaders to Mendovg's policy of centralization led to the formation of an Old Lithuanian party which, on many occasions, proved to be anti-Russian, both politically and culturally. In spite of his own pro-Russian orientation Mendovg remained loyal to the Lithuanian pagan cult until 1250, when he announced his conversion to Roman Catholicism. This was a purely political move calculated to obtain the pope's assistance in preventing any further attacks of the Teutonic Knights on Lithuania. Even after his conversion Mendovg continued secretly to worship the old gods.[54] The pope was naturally pleased with his conversion and sent Mendovg his blessings as well as the royal crown (1251).[55] Mendovg, on his part, ceded a portion of the Zhmud' region to the Teutonic Order.

Having derived considerable prestige from his new title and feeling more or less secure, at least for the time being, from attacks of the Teutonic Knights, Mendovg could now turn his attention to his relations with the princes of Galicia and Volynia. Both sides proved to be disposed to reaching agreement rather than going to war. Daniel needed allies against the Mongols, and Mendovg knew that his peace with the Teutonic Knights was no more than a temporary truce. Around 1251 Daniel, whose first wife had died, married Mendovg's niece (sister of Tovtivil of Polotsk). Some time afterward Mendovg's son Voishelk (in Lithuanian, Vaišelga) was baptized according to the rites of the Greek Orthodox Church, to which Tovtivil also was converted. Following his coronation Mendovg had appointed Voishelk his lieutenant in Novgorodok. Now Voishelk, with the ardor of a sincere neophyte, expressed his desire to take monastic vows and renounce his princely rights. He suggested that his father assign the principality of Novgorodok to one of Daniel's sons. An agreement along these lines was reached between Daniel and Mendovg late in 1254.[56] Daniel's son Roman (the former pretender to the Austrian throne) received the principality of Novgorodok as Mendovg's vassal. Simultaneously, a daughter of Mendovg was

54. *Ancient Russia,* p. 233.
55. *HRM, 1,* 75 (No. 85).
56. Hrushevsky, *3,* 81–82; Pashuto, p. 281.

given in marriage to Roman's brother Shvarn. Voishelk entered a Russian monastery near Novgorodok.

In accordance with the new orientation of his policies, Daniel moved his capital from Galich north to the city of Kholm, in whose settlement and development he took particular interest and of which he became very fond. As Daniel received no assistance from the West against the Mongols, he soon cooled to the idea of the church union. In 1255 the pope considered it necessary to reprimand him for his failure to establish the institutions of the Catholic Church in his dominions. The pope now decided to play Daniel and Mendovg, the two East European kings he had created, against each other, and "permitted" the Lithuanians to raid Volynia.[57] Mendovg seems to have disregarded the pope's suggestion, at least for the time being, and preferred to keep his agreement with Daniel.

Feeling strengthened through this, Daniel, around 1256, openly defied the Mongols by ousting their troops from northern Podolia, the Bolkhov land, and eastern Volynia.[58] As the attention of the Mongols was concentrated at that time on East Russian affairs, they were not in a position to reinforce their troops in the Dnieper region. Nevertheless the commander of that region, Kurumshi, was ordered to raid Galicia and Volynia. He had but few battalions at his disposal and was obliged to move "stealthily," as the Galician Chronicle puts it (around 1257). His attempts to storm the cities of Vladimir-in-Volynia and Lutsk both ended in failure. Kholm suffered severely from a fire which seems to have been the result of an accident and not of any Mongol attack. Before long the Mongols withdrew from Volynia.

Daniel could have been satisfied with the results so far of his policy of resistance to the Mongols. At this juncture, however, Mendovg changed his tactics and decided to break their agreement. In 1258 he arrested Daniel's son Roman and seized his fief in Black Russia. This event changed the whole political setup in West Russia, gravely undermining Daniel's potential strength and his chances of withstanding Mongol pressure, which was sure to be renewed. In 1259 Khan Berke replaced Kurumshi by the energetic Burunday (Borolday),[59] and assigned him more troops. Burunday decided to

57. *HRM, 1,* 83 (No. 93); Hrushevsky, *3,* 82.
58. The chronology of the Galician Chronicle for this period is very confusing. In most cases I am accepting Hrushevsky's dates.
59. On the name Borolday see Pelliot, pp. 63–64.

capitalize on the differences between the Russian and Lithuanian princes and made Lithuania the objective of his first campaign, inviting the Russian princes to support him with their troops.

From this time on the Mongols began to pay considerable attention to Lithuanian affairs. Presumably they were worried by the growing strength of Lithuania and discerned in its expansion, even at that early date, a potential threat to their rule in West Russia. The Moslem merchants of the Golden Horde must also have been interested in opening another trade outlet to the Baltic Sea through Lithuania in addition to the Novgorod route. And it was in the Mongols' interest to prevent the possibility of any further alliance between the West Russian and the Lithuanian princes which would strengthen the Russians and encourage them in opposition.

Fearing retaliation for his previous attack on the Mongols, Daniel avoided meeting Burunday, sending his brother Vasilko of Volynia to him instead. Vasilko took the most active part in the campaign against the Lithuanians, but both Daniel and his son Leo participated in it. Both Mongols and Russians seized considerable booty, the Russians being compelled to hand over most of their share to the Mongols. However, the main forces of the Lithuanians succeeded in avoiding any decisive battle, and the Russians failed to discover the whereabouts of Prince Roman and to free him. The next year Burunday led his troops to Volynia once more and ordered the Russian princes to destroy the fortifications of their main cities. Daniel escaped to Poland and Hungary, leaving his brother Vasilko and his son Leo to placate Burunday. The latter insisted on their obedience to his orders, and the Russian princes had no alternative but to destroy the fortifications of Vladimir-in-Volynia, Lutsk, Kremenets, and Lvov. The garrison of Kholm, however, refused to surrender the city without a direct order from Daniel. In retaliation the Mongols looted the Kholm district as well as several other regions in Volynia and Galicia.[60]

With this raid Burunday considered his task accomplished and withdrew his field army from Volynia, stationing it again in the middle Dnieper region. However, agents of the Mongol administration were appointed to supervise the work of collecting taxes and recruits through a network of military districts in Podolia, Galicia, and Volynia similar to those in East Russia.[61] The West Russian

60. Hyp., pp. 197–200.
61. There is no direct evidence in the sources that the military districts were estab-

princes were required to obtain the khan's patents at any change on
the throne of each principality.[62] Daniel's grand plan of resistance
was thus ruined, and he returned to his native country with a heavy
heart, now an obedient vassal of the khan. To aggravate his and his
people's misfortunes, the Lithuanians raided Volynia in 1262. About
the same time Prince Roman lost his life, probably being killed by
his captors. Daniel died in 1264, disillusioned and unhappy.

Soon after the collapse of the resistance to the Mongols in West
Russia an uprising took place in Suzdalia in East Russia (1262).
The initiative came from the cities of that region—Rostov, Vladimir,
Suzdal, and Iaroslavl. With the destruction of Vladimir by Batu's
armies in 1238 Rostov had become the largest city in Suzdalia, and
presumably it now took the lead in the movement of resistance. The
uprising was a protest against the hardships imposed on the population by the system of farming taxes widely used throughout the
Mongol Empire and applied in Suzdalia as well. The tax farmers—
mostly Moslem merchants from Central Asia—were allowed by the
Mongols to seize the delinquent taxpayers and make them work
for the interest on their unpaid taxes or even sell them into slavery.[63]

In Iaroslavl the chief agent of the tax farmers was a certain
Izosima, a Russian converted to Islam. The pressure on the taxpayers was increased with the arrival, "from the Tatar tsar," of a
head farmer whom the Suzdalian Chronicle characterizes as "a
vicious Moslem." In each of the four major Suzdalian cities the
people's assembly (veche) was convoked and the decision to rise
against the Mongols was unanimously approved. A number of the
Mongol agents and tax farmers were killed in the ensuing riots, including the renegade Izosima.

From the account of the Suzdalian Chronicle, the oldest report
on the uprising, it is plain that the Russian princes took absolutely no
part in the revolt.[64] However some of the later digests of annals, such
as the Nikon Chronicle, speak of an agreement of the princes to
fight the Mongols.[65] In the Ustiug annals an alleged appeal by Alexander Nevsky to the citizens of Ustiug to rise against the Mongols

lished in Galicia and Volynia by Burunday; however, since we know that such districts
existed later, they may have been established at the time of Burunday's raid.

62. Nasonov, p. 35.
63. Laur. 2, col. 476; Trinity, p. 327.
64. Laur. 2, col. 476; Trinity, p. 327.
65. Nikon, 10, 143.

is mentioned.[66] On this ground A. N. Nasonov finds it possible to surmise that the uprising as a whole was planned and directed by Alexander Nevsky.[67]

To explain the alleged change in Alexander's policies, from submission to resistance, Nasonov suggests that the tax farmers were sent to Suzdalia not by Khan Berke of Kypchak but by Great Khan Kubilay, and that Alexander, being aware of the strained relations between Berke and Kubilay, reckoned that his opposition to Kubilay's agents would not be against Berke's interests. Nasonov's theory is based upon his interpretation of the passage from the Suzdalian Chronicle quoted above, dealing with the arrival of the head tax farmer, the "vicious Moslem," "from the Tatar tsar"; after this last phrase the chronicler adds the words "by the name of Kutlubey." Nasonov takes the name for that of the Tatar tsar and reconstructs it as Kubilay.[68] However, the name seems to refer to the tax farmer rather than to the tsar.[69] Besides, in the Suzdalian Chronicle the great khan is usually called "kan" and not "tsar." Thus the foundations of Nasonov's theory are rather shaky. Moreover, in view of the fact that in 1262 the way from China to Russia was still barred by Arik-Buka, it is difficult to imagine that any agents of Kubilay could succeed in reaching Russia. Generally speaking, the network of the taxpayers' districts in Russia was organized jointly by Great Khan Mongka and the khan of Kypchak, Ulagchi. In 1262 the collection of taxes in Russia must have been under the joint jurisdiction of Arik-Buka and Berke. Most of the Moslem tax farmers were presumably of Khoresmian origin and thus Berke's subjects. And in any case, irrespective of who sent the tax farmers to Suzdalia in 1262, Berke was entitled to a fair share in the money collected. We can hardly agree with Nasonov that Berke could be expected to allow the revolt of the Russians against the tax collectors to go without severe punishment.

Alexander Nevsky must have understood the situation well and harbored few illusions about Berke's attitude. Obviously the up-

66. The Ustiug Chronicle, p. 48. This passage in the chronicle is a romantic story of a Tatar tax collector and the Russian girl he made his concubine. The girl converted the Tatar to Christianity by telling him that an order had come from Prince Alexander to kill all the Tatars. He believed her, was baptized, and married the girl.

67. Nasonov, pp. 52–53.

68. *Idem*, p. 51; Spuler, p. 333, n. 8.

69. Cf. Franke, "Europa," p. 69, n. 11.

rising of the Suzdalian cities was as much a surprise to Alexander as it was to the Mongols, but having insufficient armed forces at his disposal he was not in a position to contain it. In view of all this, Nasonov's theory of the support given to the uprising by Nevsky is untenable. There is no reliable evidence of any change of policies of that cautious prince. Characteristically enough, Alexander's first move after the uprising was to hasten to Berke's ordu "to implore the khan to pardon the people" of Suzdalia.[70] He hardly would have dared to face Berke had he himself been implicated in the riots.

Alexander spent several months in the Horde and succeeded in the main objective of his mission: Berke agreed not to send any punitive expedition to Suzdalia. Presumably, however, the rebellious Russian cities had to pay adequate damages.

This was Alexander's last service to the Russian people. He fell ill during his stay in the Horde and died on his way back in the city of Gorodets on the Volga River. His body was brought to Vladimir and buried there. The grief of the citizens was deep and sincere. Metropolitan Cyril expressed the general feeling when he announced that "the sun of Russia has set." And the people responded: "Woe to us! We are lost!"[71] It was Cyril who wrote the first biography of Alexander Nevsky, a brief outline of his good deeds for his country, done in the style of the lives of saints. On the basis of this, later on, an elaborate Life of Alexander was written, of which several redactions are known.[72] His memory began to be venerated almost immediately after his death. In 1380 his relics were revealed and after that time the day of his death was commemorated in the Vladimir churches as that of a saint. At the council (*sobor*) of the Russian church of 1547 Alexander was officially canonized.[73] No contemporary portrait has been preserved. In his will, written in 1356, Grand Duke Ivan II mentions, among his belongings, an icon of Saint Alexander, which, as E. E. Golubinsky thinks, must have been Alexander Nevsky's picture. If it was, it was probably painted during Ivan's reign (1353–59).[74] Alexander's helmet, of Oriental

70. Voskr., 7, 163; cf. Nasonov, p. 53, n. 1.

71. Soloviev, 3, 197.

72. For the text of the Life of Alexander Nevsky see Serebriansky; Mansikka, *Zhitie Aleksandra Nevskogo* (Moscow, 1915). Cf. Kliuchevsky, *Zhitiia*, pp. 65–70, 238, 251, 258; Likhachev, pp. 258–267.

73. Golubinsky, *Kanonizatsiia*, pp. 65, 100.

74. *Idem*, p. 65.

craftsmanship, apparently a present from the khan, is kept in the Moscow Armory.[75]

The Suzdalian uprising was all the more annoying to Berke in that it occurred when his negotiations with Hulagu had reached an impasse and war between the two cousins seemed inevitable. Diplomatically Berke was well prepared for the conflict through a friendly agreement with the Mameluk sultan of Egypt, Baybars I. It will be recalled that in 1260 the Mameluks succeeded in defeating the Mongol army sent by Hulagu to Galilee.[76] They realized, however, that the danger to Egypt from Hulagu was merely postponed and they looked to the future with apprehension. It was but natural they should turn to Berke for assistance. It must be mentioned here that because of his strained relations with Hulagu Berke ordered the Kypchak auxiliary troops sent to Persia by his predecessors to leave Hulagu. Presumably they were not in a position to return home and so made their way to Egypt. This was taken by the Mameluks as a token of Berke's good will.

In 1261 Baybars sent a letter to Berke through an Alan merchant to convince him that it was his duty as a Moslem to wage "holy war" against the heathen Hulagu in defense of Islam.[77] At the end of 1261 or early in 1262 Baybars' envoys came to an understanding with the Byzantine emperor Michael VIII, who agreed to let the embassies between Kypchak and Egypt travel via Constantinople.[78] Berke's envoys to Egypt in May 1263 used this new route. However, in the summer of that year Michael, presumably under pressure from Hulagu, changed his attitude toward the Khanate of Kypchak, and arrested both the envoys Berke sent to Constantinople and the Egyptian envoys who happened to be in Constantinople on their way to Kypchak. This breach of promise precipitated a double conflict, between Berke and Hulagu and between Berke and Byzantium.

The evidence on the war between Berke and Hulagu and their respective successors is contradictory. Most of the Persian historians dwell more on the successes of the il-khans than on their failures. The reports of the Egyptian historians, on the contrary, are favorable to the khans of Kypchak. The initial stage of the conflict is reported by Rashid ad-Din, who describes in some detail the defeat of the

75. *Drevnosti Rossiiskogo Gosudarstva, 3,* Plates 5–8.
76. See above, Chapter 2, sec. 3, pp. 72–73.
77. See Veselovsky, p. 20.
78. Spuler, p. 46.

Kypchak troops commanded by a relative of Berke, the young prince Nogay, in the Derbent region of the Caucasus, late in 1262.[79] Ibn-Wassyl, on the other hand, tells of the crushing defeat administered by Berke to Hulagu, in 662 A.H. (A.D. 1263–64). The losses were heavy on both sides. According to Ibn-Wassyl, when Berke saw the battlefield strewn with corpses he exclaimed: "Let Allah punish Hulagu who killed so many Mongols by the hand of the Mongols! Had we been united, we could conquer the whole world!" [80]

As regards Byzantium, Berke in 1264 sent to Thrace Prince Nogay who secured the cooperation against the Greeks of Berke's vassal, the Bulgarian tsar Constantine Tikh ("The Quiet"). In 1265 Constantinople itself was threatened by the combined Mongol-Bulgarian forces.[81] Still Michael was reluctant to sever his ties with the Iranian Mongols and in fact reinforced them by marrying his illegitimate daughter Maria to Hulagu's son and successor Abaga. Hulagu's death in February 1265,[82] had not ended the conflict between the Iranian and Kypchak Mongols. In 1265–66 Berke's army appeared in Transcaucasia. His vanguard troops were commanded by the dynamic Nogay, recalled from Thrace for the purpose. The young prince lost an eye in one of the skirmishes. Berke died in Tiflis (Tbilisi) during this campaign (1266) and his troops then retreated.[83]

While the Khanate of Kypchak did not derive any substantial profits from all these wars, Berke's intervention undoubtedly saved Egypt from Hulagu's attacks. It is but natural that Berke's prestige in Egypt was high. As Poliak has shown, Berke was honored as suzerain of the Mameluk state.[84] Contingents of Kypchak and Russian troops were sent from South Russia to Egypt on several occasions to reinforce the Mameluk army.[85]

4. The Reign of Mangu-Temir

Berke left no sons. Had he been in a position to appoint his successor, he would probably have designated Prince Nogay, of whom he was apparently very fond and who proved an outstanding military

79. Rashid 3, pp. 59–60.
80. Tiesenhausen, *1*, 75–76; Veselovsky, pp. 4–5.
81. Spuler, pp. 47–48; Nikov, pp. 6–8.
82. Spuler, p. 49.
83. Tiesenhausen, *2*, 76.
84. Poliak, "Caractère colonial," p. 233.
85. *Idem*, p. 234.

leader. However, the new khan had to be elected by the regional kuriltay, an assembly of the Juchid princes and highest army commanders. Genealogical seniority was not an absolute prerequisite for the candidate's election but was usually given serious consideration. Nogay could lay no claims to seniority in the house of Juchi. His father, Tatar, was a son of Boal, Juchi's seventh son.[86] And two of Batu's grandsons were still living: Mangu-Temir (Mongka-Temür) and Tuda-Mangu (Tödä-Mongka), both sons of Tugan.[87]

In view of Batu's high prestige as founder of the Khanate of Kypchak it seems natural that his grandsons were preferred to Nogay by the electoral assembly. Hence it was Mangu-Temir and not Nogay who succeeded Berke as khan of Kypchak. Since by that time Arik-Buka had surrendered to Kubilay (1264) and the latter was undisputed master of the empire, we may conclude that Mangu-Temir was confirmed khan by Kubilay (around 1267).

Nogay was, however, too prominent to disappear entirely from the stage. Besides being a Juchid he was an army commander of high rank, a myriarch. Furthermore, he had at his disposal an army of his own—his ordu troops, recruited chiefly from the tribe of the Mangkyts.[88] The main area of the Mangkyts was at that time the basin of the Iaik River.[89] Later on they became known as the Nogay Horde. Since "Nogay" means "dog," it may be presumed the dog was the totem animal of the leading clan of the Mangkyts. In Egyptian sources Khan Nogay is mentioned under a double name: Isa-Nogay.[90] Probably Isa was his personal name and Nogay his clan name (that is, the name of the clan of which he was the leader). On one occasion in 1287 Nogay stated he had received a special decree from Khan Batu to keep unity and order among his kin, after the latter's death, in the Khanate of Kypchak.[91] If this was so, Batu must have confirmed Nogay's authority over the latter's ordu troops (the Mangkyt Horde), considering them a special corps for maintaining orderly government in the khanate.

It seems that by agreement with Mangu-Temir Nogay was recognized as the acting ruler of the lower Danube region and authorized

86. Tiesenhausen, 2, 57; Pelliot, pp. 52–54.

87. For the spelling of these names see Pelliot, pp. 64–65.

88. On the Mangkyts see Rashid 1, pp. 48, 157, 186, 189–191.

89. The Iaik River is now known as the Ural River; its name was changed by order of Empress Catherine II after the Pugachev rebellion.

90. Veselovsky, p. 10.

91. Tiesenhausen, 2, 69.

to conduct diplomatic relations with both the Byzantine Empire and Egypt. According to the Byzantine historian, George Pachymeres, Nogay was sent to the Balkans by "the khans." [92] May it not be assumed from Pachymeres' use of the plural "khans" that Mangu-Temir's agreement with Nogay was confirmed by Kubilay?

For himself Mangu-Temir reserved the conduct of negotiations with Il-khan Abaga as well as the direction of Russian affairs. Since Mangu-Temir was a Sky worshiper and not a Moslem the religious motive in the previous struggle between the Golden Horde and the il-khans was now eliminated. Besides, Great Khan Kubilay must have exerted pressure on both Abaga and Mangu-Temir to settle their differences. Consequently, in 668 A.H. (A.D. 1269–70) they concluded a peace treaty which was naturally a great disappointment to Sultan Baybars.[93] The sultan was heartened however by receipt, the following year, of a friendly message from Nogay.[94]

In 1271 Nogay launched a campaign against Constantinople to compel Emperor Michael VIII to allow the sultan of Egypt and himself to use the Bosporus maritime road for their respective embassies.[95] Rather than risk a defeat, the emperor sued for peace and offered Nogay his friendship. In 1273 Michael gave his illegitimate daughter, Euphrosyne, in marriage to Nogay.[96] Thus, the house of the Paleologi now established family ties (through illegitimate princesses) with both the il-khans and the rulers of Kypchak.

Mangu-Temir's policy toward Russia was more benevolent than that of his predecessors. The chronicler noted under A.M. 6774 (A.D. 1266): "In this year Tsar Berke died and the Tatar oppression was greatly eased." [97] Apparently the farming out of taxes to the Moslem merchants was terminated and regular tax collectors appointed instead. Another act of great significance was the issuance of the immunity charter or yarlyk for the Russian church. Following the precepts of Chingis-Khan's Yasa, Mangu-Temir's predecessors had exempted Russian abbots, monks, priests, and sextons from being "counted" in the census.[98] Now the immunity privileges of the clergy

---

92. G. Pachymeres, Bk. 5, chap. 4 (Bonn ed., *1*, 344); Russian trans. (St. Petersburg, 1862), *1*, 316.
93. Tiesenhausen, *1*, 125, 353; Spuler, p. 53.
94. Veselovsky, p. 22.
95. Tiesenhausen, *1*, 359, 380; *ZO*, p. 83.
96. Also called Irene; see Spuler, p. 60.
97. Trinity, p. 329.
98. Laur. *2*, col. 475.

as a social group, including their families, were confirmed; the landed estates of the churches and monasteries with all the people employed on them were exempt from taxation; and all the "church people" were exempt from military service. The Mongol agents were forbidden, under penalty of death, to seize any church lands or to require any services from the church people. Death was also decreed for anyone guilty of defaming or vilifying the Greek Orthodox faith. To enhance the authority of the charter Chingis-Khan's name was invoked at the beginning. In return for the privileges granted, the Russian priests and monks were expected to pray to God for Mangu-Temir and his family and successors. It was emphasized that their prayers and blessings should be ardent and sincere. "And if any clergyman prays with mental reservations, he commits a sin." [99]

Presumably the original yarlyk was written in Mongol and immediately translated into Russian.[100] It will be recalled that, according to John of Plano Carpini, there had been Russian translators and scribes in Batu's chancery; and Batu's successors must have employed a number of Russian secretaries. It may also be assumed that the redaction of the yarlyk was established jointly by Mangu-Temir (or his chief Mongol secretary) and the bishop of Saray, Mitrofan, representing the Russian clergy. If so, the moral sanction against insincere prayer must have been formulated by the bishop.

By virtue of this yarlyk and a series of similar ones issued by Mangu-Temir's successors, the Russian clergy and the people under their jurisdiction were constituted a privileged group, and the foundation of the church's wealth was laid. In issuing this charter Mangu-Temir followed the traditions of Chingis-Khan and the practices of Chingis' successors in China as well as of other regional Mongol khans.[101] From this point of view his yarlyk was in accordance with the basic ideas of Mongol rule and was consistent in principle. At the same time it was a master stroke of internal policy, since it secured, to a certain extent at least, the loyalty to the khan of the best-educated social group in Russia, which enjoyed great moral prestige among

99. For the old Russian translation of Mangu-Temir's yarlyk to the Russian church see Grigoriev, *Yarlyki,* pp. 124–126; Priselkov, *Yarlyki,* pp. 94–98. On the yarlyks at large see Kurat.

100. The yarlyks issued in favor of the Russian church have been preserved in Russian translation only. On the characteristics of this translation see Grigoriev, *Yarlyki,* pp. 96–106.

101. On the great khans' charters in favor of the religious communities in China see above, Chapter 2, sec. 4, p. 84.

the people. Through the yarlyk it could be expected that the Russian spirit of resistance to the tsar would be greatly reduced.

Because of the policy of loyalty of the princes to the khan established by Alexander Nevsky in East Russia, and the breaking of the resistance of the West Russian princes during the reign of Berke, the task of controlling the Russian princes presented no special difficulties to Mangu-Temir. Following the death of Alexander Nevsky the patent on the throne of Vladimir had been given by Khan Berke to Alexander's brother, Prince Iaroslav of Tver (Iaroslav II, grand duke of Vladimir, 1263–72). His authority was renewed by Mangu-Temir. Iaroslav's successor was his brother, Prince Vasili of Kostroma (grand duke of Vladimir, 1272–76). With his death, no more sons of Iaroslav I were left, and the throne of Vladimir was assigned by Mangu-Temir to Alexander Nevsky's oldest living son, Prince Dmitri of Pereiaslavl-in-Suzdalia.

A new trend in Russia's political organization became noticeable with the accession of Iaroslav II to the throne of Vladimir. Each of Alexander Nevsky's brothers, and then each of his sons, while becoming titular grand duke of Vladimir, preferred to stay in his own apanage, coming to Vladimir for brief visits only, to expedite those state affairs which might require his presence. We witness here the temporary victory of the apanage (*udel*) principle over that of the national state.[102] It will be recalled that the succession by seniority to the throne of Kiev was shaken already in the late 12th century when the principality of Galicia in West Russia and that of Suzdalia (later the Grand Duchy of Vladimir) in East Russia, each under a princely branch of its own, became virtually independent of Kiev. Moreover, in each of the regional principalities the junior members of the princely house clung to their apanages, each trying to make his into an hereditary principality of his own. On the other hand, the senior prince in each of the regional states tended to assert his supreme authority in the region and did not consider local apanages as permanently established. All said, there is no doubt that the new "apanage regime" (*udelnyi poriadok*) which came into being in East Russia after Alexander Nevsky's death was partly the result of trends already noticeable in the preceding period. However, the victory of these trends over opposite ones was greatly facilitated by Mongol rule in Russia.[103]

102. On the apanage regime (*udelnyi poriadok*) in Russia see Kliuchevsky, *1*, 365–384; S. F. Platonov, *Lektsii po russkoi istorii* (6th ed. St. Petersburg, 1909), pp. 111–119.
103. See M. Liubavsky, *Drevniia russkaia istoriia* (Moscow, 1918), pp. 152–153.

In granting his patents to the Russian princes, the khan was guided, in part at least, by Mongol notions of the interrelation between the empire as a whole and the regional uluses, as well as of that between the regional khanate and the apanage dominions of the lesser princes. From this point of view the desire of each Russian prince to secure his hereditary rights on his local principality was quite understandable to the Mongols and considered useful for the stability of the khan's Russian dominions.

While all the Russian princes seem to have been loyal to the khan during Mangu-Temir's reign, it was the princes of the Rostov land who became his favorites. In his relations to them a definite pattern may be discerned: the khan's desire to create among the Russian princes a group whom he could trust without any reservations and whom he could use to strengthen Mongol rule in case of signs of Russian opposition to it. The choice of the Rostov region as pivot of the khan's policy in Russian affairs may be explained by his fear of the possible repetition of a popular revolt there on the pattern established in 1262. By cultivating friendly relations with the Rostov princes the khan hoped to secure the obedience to him of the Rostov land at large and to undermine the authority of the Rostov city assembly, which both he and the Rostov princes considered dangerous to their interests. It is but natural that as a reward for the loyalty of the Rostov princes the khan was only too glad to let them curb the power of the veche.

The princes of Rostov were descendants of Grand Duke Vsevolod III of Suzdalia through his eldest son Constantine, a noted patron of learning.[104] Prominent among them during Mangu-Temir's reign were Constantine's grandsons, Prince Boris of Rostov and Prince Gleb of Beloozero, as well as their cousin-in-law, Fedor, son of Prince Rostislav of Smolensk. Fedor married Princess Maria of Iaroslavl (Constantine's great-granddaughter) and received Iaroslavl as his apanage. Boris and Gleb's mother, whose name was also Maria, was a daughter of the prince-martyr, Michael of Chernigov. Well educated and deeply religious, she played an important role in the spiritual life of the élite of Rostov society.[105]

During this same reign a Juchid prince who had been converted to Christianity by Bishop Cyril of Rostov around 1259, and named

104. On Constantine (Konstantin) of Suzdal see *Kievan Russia,* p. 279. Constantine was the brother of Grand Duke Iaroslav I.

105. On Princess Maria of Rostov see Likhachev, pp. 282–285.

Peter, settled in Rostov and there married a daughter of a Mongol official whose family were already Christians. He became known in Russia as Tsarevich Peter of the Horde (Peter Ordynsky). In view of Mongol religious tolerance, change of religion did not annul Peter's rights and privileges as a Mongol prince. Hence his presence in Rostov was considered useful to promote friendly relations between the Rostov princes and the khan. Prince Boris of Rostov especially befriended Peter. According to Peter's biographer, Boris loved Peter so much that he wanted him to share all his meals and finally, with the bishop's blessing, proclaimed Peter his sworn brother.[106] Friendship is friendship and business is business. Boris was apparently a shrewd businessman. Peter, on the other hand, while very wealthy, did not know the value of money; when he decided to build a church on the shore of a lake near Rostov, Boris, to whom the land belonged, asked an extravagant price for it, which Peter paid at once. According to Peter's Life the amount was one pound of gold and nine pounds of silver.[107] Kliuchevsky comments that the transaction served as the main topic of gossip in Rostov for some time.[108]

When Peter was told of the necessity of registering a deed for the land he had bought, he said that he did not understand what deeds were for. Boris, in this case, was at least decent enough to hand over the deed to Peter. This proved very useful to Peter's descendants when, later on, Boris' grandsons had the impudence to present claims to the land.[109] In his old age Peter converted the church he had built into a monastery, endowed it, and having taken monastic vows, himself became a monk. He was canonized by the Russian church in the middle of the 16th century.[110]

The Rostov princes made frequent visits "to the Horde." In 1257 Prince Gleb went to Mongolia and was warmly received at Great Khan Mongka's court. There he married a Mongol princess who agreed to be baptized; she received the name of Theodora. When Mangu-Temir became khan of Kypchak, Gleb with a number of other Russian princes went to his ordu to receive his princely patent. He stayed "in the Horde" until 1268. In 1271 he was again at Mangu-Temir's camp. In 1277 his brother Boris with his wife and

106. There is a translation of Peter's Life into modern Russian by Buslaev, *1*, 160–165.
107. *Idem, 1,* 161.
108. Kliuchevsky, *Zhitiia*, p. 40.
109. Buslaev, *1*, 162 ff.; Kliuchevsky, *Zhitiia*, p. 42.
110. Golubinsky, *Kanonizatsiia*, pp. 110–111.

children made a pilgrimage "to the Horde." There he fell ill and died. In 1278 Gleb, who became prince of Rostov after Boris' death, sent his son Michael to Mangu-Temir, accompanied by Constantine of Uglich (son of Boris) and Fedor of Iaroslavl.[111]

Another region of Russia to which Mangu-Temir paid considerable attention was Novgorod. In this case the khan's motive was commercial: his desire to promote the Baltic trade of which Novgorod was the main channel for East Russia and the Orient. International trade was one of the bases of the prosperity of the Golden Horde and most of the khans furthered its development. In Mangu-Temir's reign the foundations were laid for its wide expansion.

While Novgorod was the most convenient northern outlet for Mongol foreign trade, the Crimean ports were of paramount importance in promotion of the Black Sea and Mediterranean commerce which was, at that time, handled chiefly by Italian merchants— the Venetians and the Genoese. Consequently both Novgorod and the Crimean ports attracted Mangu-Temir's attention. The Genoese seem to have penetrated into the Black Sea in the second half of the 12th century.[112] During the existence of the Latin Empire at Constantinople (1204–61) the Black Sea trade was all but monopolized by the Venetians. The two Polo brothers were among other Venetian merchants who came to the Crimean port of Soldaia [113] in 1260; it was the starting point for their great adventure. However, after the restoration of the Byzantine Empire by Michael VIII Paleologus, the Genoese not only returned to the Black Sea but found themselves in a more privileged position than the Venetians and saw their real chance to establish their "factories" in the Crimea. Around 1267 Mangu-Temir granted them special privileges for their trade in Kaffa (present-day Feodosia).[114] And in 1274 they established themselves in Soldaia.[115]

In a parallel development in the north, Mangu-Temir assumed the role of protector of Novgorod and of the principle of free trade in the Baltic area. After the agreement between Novgorod and Grand Duke Vsevolod III of Suzdalia (1211) only the princes of the house

---

111. Nasonov, pp. 59, 62.

112. *Kievan Russia,* p. 346.

113. Soldaia is the Italian name of the city formerly known as Sugdaea; in old Russian, Surozh; at present, Sudak. On these names as listed in his index see Vasiliev, *Goths.*

114. Bratianu, pp. 205–206. Cf. Vasiliev, *Goths,* p. 171; Lopez, p. 251.

115. Bratianu, p. 205.

of Suzdalia were considered eligible to the princely office at Novgorod.[116] Each of them, however, at the time of his election had
to sign a treaty guaranteeing the traditional liberties of the city.
Alexander Nevsky, among others, signed such a treaty, but no copy
of it has been preserved. After Alexander's death the Novgorodians
agreed to recognize his son Iaroslav II, prince of Tver and grand
duke of Vladimir, as their prince (1264). On that occasion a new
treaty was concluded between the grand duke and the city of Novgorod; its provisions were formulated in two identical charters, one
addressed by Novgorod to the grand duke and the other by the
grand duke to Novgorod (around 1265). The original of the Novgorod charter is still extant in the Russian archives.[117]

Two years later the charters were confirmed by both sides.[118]
Soon after that Iaroslav violated some of the provisions of the treaty,
and the Novgorodians demanded his immediate resignation from the
office. Not willing to comply with their demands, Iaroslav appealed
to the khan for assistance, charging the Novgorodians with rebellion.[119] To his disappointment Mangu-Temir ordered him to negotiate with the Novgorodians, and Iaroslav had no alternative but to
comply. A new treaty was signed confirming the rights and privileges
of the city. To assure its observance in the future Mangu-Temir
sent two envoys in whose presence Iaroslav pledged himself, by
"kissing the cross," to maintain its provisions (1270).[120] Simultaneously, Mangu-Temir ordered Iaroslav to let Novgorod trade with
Riga without interference. Iaroslav was obliged to notify the city of
Riga of this right.[121]

Mangu-Temir must not be taken for a champion of Novgorodian
political liberties on principle. He was merely interested in the
promotion, through Novgorod, of Baltic commerce and its extension
to the Orient. The most convenient route from Novgorod to Saray
was through the upper Volga region, that is, through the Grand
Duchy of Vladimir. Therefore, while Mangu-Temir proved ready
to protect Novgorod from any abuses by the grand duke of Vladimir,
he also insisted on the continuation of the political link between

116. See *Kievan Russia*, p. 197.
117. *SGGD*, *1*, No. 2; *GNP*, No. 1.
118. *SGGD*, *1*, No. 1; *GNP*, No. 2.
119. Soloviev, *Novgorod*, p. 104.
120. *GNP*, p. 11.
121. *Ibid.*, No. 30, p. 57.

Novgorod and the grand duke. After the death of Iaroslav II (1272) the Novgorodians elected Dmitri of Pereiaslavl as their prince. The new grand duke, Vasili of Kostroma, who claimed the Novgorod princely office for himself, appealed to the khan. The latter dispatched a battalion of Mongol troops to support Vasili's candidacy. The Novgorodians then "changed their mind," as the chronicler says, and recognized Vasili as their prince.[122] When, after Vasili's death (1276), Dmitri received the patent for the Grand Duchy of Vladimir, the khan agreed to his becoming prince of Novgorod as well.

In 1275 a new general census and levy of recruits took place in Russia. It was probably ordered in 1273 or 1274 by Great Khan Kubilay, who needed more troops for his campaigns in South China and Indo-China. Since Khan Mangu-Temir, on his part, intended to strengthen his authority in the Caucasus, fresh contingents of troops would also be useful to him. This time, in addition to East Russia, the land of Smolensk was counted. In 1281 the khan's favorite, Grand Duke Fedor of Smolensk (who by that time had returned to Smolensk from Iaroslavl), established his authority over Vitebsk which earlier had belonged to the Polotsk land. The Mongol collectors must have been sent now to Vitebsk as well.[123]

In 1277 Mangu-Temir launched a campaign against the Alans of the north Caucasus. As we know, this group of Alans, as well as other Alanic tribes in the Don basin and the Crimea, were conquered by the Mongols during Batu's campaign of 1239. After that they cooperated with the Mongols and contributed troops to the Mongol conquest of China. During the internecine wars between Berke and the il-khans the Alans of the north Caucasian group (the Ossetians) must have taken advantage of the troubles to emancipate themselves from subordination to the khan of Kypchak. Actually those who lived in the high mountain valleys had never been completely conquered by the Mongols.

Mangu-Temir ordered a number of Russian princes with their boyars and retinues to join him in his expedition against the Alans. According to the Nikon Chronicle Gleb, Boris' son Constantine, Fedor of Iaroslavl, and Andrew of Gorodets (son of Alexander Nevsky), participated in the campaign. It was successful; the Russians stormed the main stronghold of the Alans, the fortified city of

122. Soloviev, *Novgorod*, p. 106.
123. Golubovsky, pp. 304–309.

Dadakov [124] (1278), and seized rich booty of which the main share probably went to the khan. Mangu-Temir praised his Russian vassals and bestowed many gifts on them.[125]

Let us now turn to West Russian affairs. It will be recalled that after Burunday's campaign against Lithuania the relations between King Daniel of Russia and King Mendovg of Lithuania became strained.[126] Daniel died in 1264. The same year Lithuanian princes who resented Medovg's policy of centralization formed a conspiracy against him and killed him. His son, the monk Voishelk, now left the monastery to take vengeance on his father's foes. Scores of them were seized and executed, and Voishelk, with the help of his Russian troops recruited at Novgorodok and Pinsk,[127] became ruler of Lithuania. In 1267 he returned to his monastery and handed the authority over Lithuania to his brother-in-law, Daniel's son Shvarn. The political constellation seemed extremely favorable to the Danilovichi (sons of Daniel); they were now in a position to assume a leading role in the unification of West Russia and Lithuania. However, as the Volynian chronicler puts it, "Satan who had never wished well to mankind now filled Leo's heart with envy toward Shvarn." [128] Leo (Shvarn's brother) therefore killed not Shvarn but Shvarn's sponsor, Voishelk.

Voishelk's murder was naturally greatly resented by the Lithuanians, and after Shvarn's death (1270) no Danilovich stood any chance of being recognized as prince of Lithuania. The power was assumed by a native prince, Troiden (Traidenis, 1270–82); and after his death another old Lithuanian clan came to prominence.

After the conclusion of the Ossetian campaign, Mangu-Temir turned his attention to Byzantine and Egyptian affairs. Prior to this, as we know, relations with both Byzantium and Egypt had been within Nogay's competence. Apparently Mangu-Temir now decided to curb Nogay's authority. When Tsar Constantine the Quiet of Bulgaria was killed in a battle with another pretender to the throne in 1277 [129] trouble started in Bulgaria, with several candidates pre-

---

124. Presumably Dzauji-qäu (Vladikavkaz); see Minorsky, Caucasica III, p. 237.
125. Nikon, *10*, 155; Kulakovsky, *Alany*, p. 60.
126. On the events in West Russia and Lithuania in the 1260's and 1270's see Hrushevsky, *3*, 92–108; Pashuto, pp. 289–302; Paszkiewicz, pp. 100–142.
127. Paszkiewicz, p. 109.
128. Hyp., p. 204.
129. Nikov, p. 13.

senting their claims. Since Michael VIII and Nogay supported different candidates, relations between them deteriorated. It is this confusion which seems to have led to Mangu-Temir's intervention in Balkan affairs. The Russian chronicles record that Khan Mangu-Temir and Metropolitan Cyril sent Bishop Theognost of Saray [130] as their joint envoy to the emperor Michael VIII and the patriarch of Constantinople with their respective letters and gifts. This embassy must have taken place sometime in 1278 since Theognost returned to Saray in 1279.[131]

Presumably relations with Egypt were also discussed by Theognost with the emperor and the patriarch. In any case, about this time Mangu-Temir attempted to establish direct diplomatic correspondence with Egypt through Constantinople. Berke's friend, the Egyptian sultan Baybars I, died in 1277. Two of his sons reigned after him in succession, each for a brief period, and in 1279 power was assumed by Qilawun (Qalaun). In July 1280 his envoys came to Kypchak, most likely in response to a mission sent to Egypt by Mangu-Temir around 1279. By the time Qilawun's ambassadors reached Kypchak, Mangu-Temir had already died.[132]

5. THE DUAL GOVERNMENT IN THE GOLDEN HORDE: NOGAY AS CO-RULER

I

After Mangu-Temir's death his brother Tuda-Mangu was elected khan of Kypchak by the kuriltay. Thus Nogay's claims were again disregarded. However, Nogay was now strong enough to establish himself as virtual co-ruler with the new khan. In fact, from this time on the Russian chronicles, with the exception of the Rostov annals, call Nogay tsar, as they do Tuda-Mangu. In some of the Western sources Nogay is called emperor [133] and in the Egyptian annals *malik* (king).[134] It is likely that at the time of the election of Tuda-Mangu Nogay proclaimed himself khan in his own right—khan of the Nogay (Mangkyt) Horde. It is possible that, to avoid a clash be-

130. Theognost was the second bishop of Saray. The first, Mitrofan, died in 1267.
131. Nikon, *10*, 157. It was Theognost's third trip to Constantinople. Cf. Vernadsky, "ZOEV," p. 80.
132. Spuler, p. 62.
133. Golubovich, *2*, 444 (A.D. 1287); cf. Spuler, p. 64.
134. Veselovsky, 1, 50, 51.

tween the followers of Nogay and those of Tuda-Mangu, the kuriltay
which elected the latter khan of Kypchak preferred to recognize
Nogay as khan of the Mangkyts. If so, Batu's decree to Nogay mentioned before [135] must have constituted the basis for the kuriltay's
decision.

Whatever may have been Nogay's legal status, he actually became more powerful than the official khan of Kypchak, although not
powerful enough to eliminate the latter altogether. The result was
an unstable duality in government, and while at times the two khans
cooperated with each other, on several occasions they issued contradictory orders which created utter confusion, at least in Russian
affairs.

As we have seen, in the last year of Mangu-Temir's reign relations between Nogay and Byzantium had become strained because
of the Bulgarian troubles and because of Mangu-Temir's decision to
enter into direct relations with Emperor Michael VIII. Nogay's first
move after Mangu-Temir's death was to re-establish his friendship
with Michael. He offered assistance against the rebellious governor
of Thessaly and sent Michael 4,000 choice Mongol troops. The emperor was greatly pleased, but the campaign did not materialize
because of Michael's sudden death (1282).[136] Michael's son and
successor, Emperor Andronikus II, started his reign by recognizing
as tsar of Bulgaria Terter, a boyar of Cuman extraction (known as
Tsar George Terter I), who in 1280 had established his rule over a
considerable part of Bulgaria. However, when Nogay objected, Andronikus not only withdrew his support from Terter but even had
him arrested. Nogay then proclaimed a candidate of his own, another
Bulgarian boyar by the name of Smilets, tsar of Bulgaria.[137]

Presumably through his understanding with Nogay Emperor
Michael VIII concluded an agreement with Sultan Qilawun of Egypt,
guaranteeing merchants and ambassadors from and to the Golden
Horde unrestricted use of the maritime way through the Bosporus.[138]
About the same time both Nogay and Tuda-Mangu exchanged em-
bassies with Qilawun. The latter's envoys, who had been sent to
Mangu-Temir but reached Kypchak only after his death, were
warmly received by Tuda-Mangu; they returned to Egypt in 1282,

135. See above, sec. 4, p. 164.
136. Veselovsky, pp. 40–41.
137. *Idem,* p. 41; Nikov, pp. 19–21.
138. M. Canard, "Le Traité de 1281 entre Michel Paléologue et le sultan Qalaun,"
Byzantion, 10 (1935), 669–680; Spuler, p. 63.

acompanied by Tuda-Mangu's envoys.[139] The same year Nogay sent an embassy of his own to Qilawun.[140]

At this time, as before, the diplomatic correspondence between the Golden Horde and Egypt was conducted in the Mongol language.[141] On the other hand, from the religious angle, Islam, spreading from Egypt, was gradually gaining ground, not only in the Golden Horde but in the state of the il-khans as well. In 1282 Il-Khan Ahmad became a Moslem,[142] and in 1283 Tuda-Mangu announced his conversion to Islam.[143] It looked as if, with religious harmony established throughout the Near East, the political tension between the il-khans and Egypt might come to an end. More conflicts were to occur in the near future, however, especially since the conversion to Islam was not final in either the state of the il-khans or the Golden Horde.

In 1280 all the Russian princes except Grand Duke Dmitri went to the Horde to greet the new khan, Tuda-Mangu, and renew their patents. Dmitri's attention at that time was absorbed by his quarrels with the Novgorodians to whom he did "much harm" (*mnogo pakosti deia*).[144] Perhaps because of both these actions—Dmitri's failure to appear at the khan's court and his attack on the Novgorodian lands—Tuda-Mangu canceled his patent and issued a new patent on the throne of Vladimir to Dmitri's younger brother, Andrew of Gorodets and Kostroma,[145] the friend of the Rostov princes and for years a loyal vassal of Khan Mangu-Temir. As Dmitri refused to surrender the throne, a violent conflict followed. Tuda-Mangu sent Mongol troops to reinforce Andrew's retinue. The Mongols spread over the whole territory of the Grand Duchy of Vladimir, seizing or ousting Dmitri's lieutenants and soldiers and looting the country. Then they installed Andrew on the throne of Vladimir. The new grand duke entertained the Mongol princes who took part in the expedition and other Mongol army commanders at a lavish reception and banquet.[146]

139. Spuler, p. 63.
140. Veselovsky, p. 51.
141. Tiesenhausen, *1*, xi; Vernadsky, "ZOEV," pp. 81–82.
142. Spuler, *Iran*, p. 78; Spuler, *Horde*, p. 68.
143. Spuler, *Horde*, p. 68.
144. Novgorod, p. 324.
145. He received Kostroma after Grand Duke Vasili's death.
146. Soloviev, *3*, 240.

Under the preceding khans the matter would have been considered settled and Dmitri would have had either to surrender or to emigrate. Now, however, with the growth of Nogay's authority, Dmitri found a way to counteract Tsar Tuda-Mangu's dispositions. He made a pilgrimage to the camp of rival tsar, Nogay, and pledged allegiance to him. Probably Nogay had been offended by the unwillingness of Tuda-Mangu to consult him in issuing patents to the Russian princes and was now delighted to have a pretext to reassert his authority. He conferred on Dmitri the rights to the throne of Vladimir and sent a strong detachment of troops to assist him. Receiving no support this time from Tuda-Mangu, Andrew had to cede the grand duchy to Dmitri and to make peace with him. Andrew now retired to Kostroma. Dmitri pledged himself not to seek revenge on Andrew and his followers but soon violated his pledge: in 1283 two of his boyars appeared in Kostroma and arrested Andrew's leading councilor, the boyar Semen Tonilievich; they killed him after a brief interrogation.[147]

A. N. Nasonov makes the plausible suggestion that Nogay granted Grand Duke Dmitri the same privilege the city of Novgorod enjoyed: he authorized Dmitri to supervise the collection of taxes within his dominions; the Mongol officials in charge of the collection were apparently recalled. If such was the case, Nogay's intention must have been, by giving his vassals a privileged position, to attract more Russian princes to his side.[148]

While Tuda-Mangu was not strong enough to oppose Nogay openly, he did not confirm Nogay's patent to Dmitri and continued to consider Andrew the titular grand duke.[149] The Rostov princes on their part remained loyal to Tuda-Mangu. Characteristically enough, Tuda-Mangu alone is called tsar in the Rostov annals, and Nogay is referred to by name only, without any title.[150] It was Grand Duke Fedor of Smolensk (formerly of Iaroslavl) who ranked highest among the Russian princes in the khan's favor. Fedor spent several years at Tuda-Mangu's court, during which time he was entitled to stand near the khan at court banquets and hand him the ceremonial goblet, which was considered a great honor.[151] After the death of his

147. Trinity, p. 340.
148. Nasonov, p. 71.
149. *Idem*, p. 73.
150. *Idem*, p. 72.
151. See the Life of Prince Fedor in the Book of Degrees (*Stepennaia kniga*), *PSRL*, *21*, 308.

first wife, Princess Maria of Iaroslavl (around 1285), Fedor was given a Mongol princess in marriage (apparently a daughter of Mangu-Temir), who was baptized and received the name of Ann.

It has been mentioned that in 1283 Tuda-Mangu was converted to Islam. It seems that he accepted the new faith not because of political considerations but as a spiritual revelation. Psychologically it must have been a case like the conversion to Christianity of Tsarevich Peter of the Horde, who as we know eventually took monastic orders. Tuda-Mangu became a Sufi, an adept of a mystic school in Islamic thought. A great impetus to the development of Sufism was given by the Persian poet Jalal ad-Din Rumi (1207–73), who spent some time at the court of the Seljuq sultans (vassals of the il-khans) in Asia Minor, and then retired to found an order of dervishes.[152] His mystical poems enjoyed great popularity and exerted much influence in Asia Minor, Iran, and later in Ottoman Turkey. Prominent in the teachings of Sufism was the rejection of the pleasures and splendors of this world; the true Sufi had to live in poverty and purify his soul through love of all mankind and pantheistic contemplation, which was considered the essence of all religions, through which all peoples could hope for salvation.

Under the influence of Sufism Tuda-Mangu lost interest in his power and neglected state affairs, to the consternation of the leading princes and notables of his realm. Before long, rumors spread that the khan was mentally ill. Apparently Tuda-Mangu was soon asked to delegate part of his authority to his nephew Tele-Buga (Tölä-Buga). In any case Tele-Buga represented the khan in 1285 in an attempt to settle the differences between the Great Horde and the Nogay Horde. By that time Nogay had decided to extend Mongol authority westward to Hungary and invited Tele-Buga to share in this expedition.

In order better to understand Nogay's policies in regard to Hungary we must briefly consider the general nature as well as ethnic background of Nogay's realm. Within twenty years after his first appearance in the Balkans (1265–85) Nogay had succeeded in building up a prosperous empire. Its ethnic core was his own "Nogay" or Mangkyt nation, to which a heterogeneous conglomerate of other peoples was subordinated. The Nogays themselves were still nomads. Some of the subject peoples, like the Cumans, were seminomads;

152. On Jalal ad-Din Rumi see Browne 2, pp. 515–525; Krymsky, *Turkey*, pp. 5–6; R. A. Nicholson, *Rumi, Poet and Mystic* (London, G. Allen & Unwin, 1950).

others, like the Bulgarians, agriculturists. An important group among Nogay's subjects was the Alans who migrated from the Crimea and the lower Don region to Moldavia in the beginning of his reign. It will be recalled that another group of the Alans had occupied precisely the same region around A.D. 400, at which time the river Pruth became known as the Alanic River.[153] It was presumably in the 5th century that the city of Iassy (Iaşi) was founded.[154] Now it became again an important commercial town, referred to in the Russian chronicles as the Alanic Market, "Iasskii [or Asskii] Torg." [155]

Furthermore, there were many Russians in Nogay's dominions, among them the Brodniki in the lower Dniester and lower Danube regions.[156] The Russians of that area were also engaged in commerce. A list of "Russian cities" of this period in Moldavia is recorded in the Voskresensk Chronicle.[157]

Last but not least the Wallachians (Rumanians) must be mentioned. It will be recalled that the forefathers of the Rumanians had lived in the Balkan peninsula, the lower Danube area, and Transylvania since the time of the Roman Empire.[158] In the 12th century the Wallachians, together with the Cumans, took an active part in the formation of the so-called Second Bulgarian Tsardom.[159] In Transylvania the Rumanians had been under the constant influence of the Magyars. From this point of view the Mongol invasion of Hungary of 1241 may be considered an important landmark in the history of the Rumanian people, since it alleviated the Magyar pressure for a time at least.[160] As a member group in the federation of peoples ruled by Nogay, the Rumanians were able finally to establish themselves as a more or less cohesive group, first in Wallachia and later on in Moldavia. In Moldavia they lived in close contact with both the Alans and the Russians. The Rumanians adopted the Cyrillic

153. See *Ancient Russia*, p. 133.
154. *Ibid.*, pp. 133–134. In M. A. Miller's so far unpublished map of the Alanic settlements, a copy of which he kindly sent me, an old Alanic site near Iaşi is indicated.
155. Kulakovsky, *Alany*, p. 66.
156. On the Brodniki see *Kievan Russia*, pp. 158, 237, 238.
157. Voskr., 7, 240. See also Novgorod, p. 475; Nasonov, *Russkaia zemlia*, pp. 142–143.
158. See *Ancient Russia*, p. 103; *Kievan Russia*, pp. 319–320. The date of the penetration of the Rumanians into Transylvania is a moot problem. A number of historians argue that the Rumanians could not have appeared in Transylvania before 1200. See Stadtmüller, pp. 207–208 and his map 12 on p. 205.
159. On the Second Bulgarian Tsardom see F. Uspensky, *Obrazovanie Vtorogo Bolgarskogo Tsarstva* (Odessa, 1879); N. S. Derzhavin, *Istoriia Bolgarii* (Moscow and Leningrad, 1946), 2, 128–133; Mutafchiev, 2, 30–97.
160. See N. Jorga, *Histoire des Roumains et de leur civilisation* (Paris, 1920), p. 59.

alphabet, and their civilization at that time was under considerable Slavic influence.[161]

According to the Byzantine historian, George Pachymeres, all of the peoples subject to Nogay gradually came under Mongol influence, donning Tatar dress and learning the Tatar language.[162] Sociologically Nogay's empire resembled the west Scythian and Sarmatian states, as well as the Gothic Kingdom of the 4th century. Extending as it did from the Dnieper westward to the lower Danube area, it occupied approximately the same territory as the Gothic Kingdom. The country was rich in agricultural products and fish and conveniently located for carrying on extensive trade with Hungary, Lithuania, and Russia to the north, Byzantium to the south, and the Crimea to the east.

The rapid growth of Nogay's empire could not but affect the neighboring countries, especially Hungary. As we know, Hungary had been occupied by the Mongols in 1240–41. Batu's withdrawal in 1242 had prevented its inclusion in the Mongol Empire, but even after that the Mongols considered the Magyars eligible for membership in the Mongol-Turkish federation in view of their historical background. The Turkish element in Hungary was greatly strengthened by the immigration there of a strong group of Cumans in 1239.[163] A group of Alans settled with these in Hungary. The Rumanians constituted another non-Magyar element in Transylvania. With Cumans, Alans, and Rumanians in Nogay's empire, Hungary was now even more open to the influence of the peoples of the Pontic steppes than before.

The result was a revival of the old steppe traditions at the court of Hungary and among at least a section of the Magyars, and the growing influence of the Nogays and the Cumans in Hungarian affairs. The reigning king of Hungary, Ladislav (László) IV (1272–90), was of Cuman descent through his mother, a Cuman princess. It was through his Cuman relatives that László was gradually attracted to the way of life and fashions of the steppe nations. He even went so far as to imprison his consort, Queen Isabel d'Anjou, take two Nogay princesses to wife, and renounced Christianity. This naturally provoked the pope's indignation as well as consternation

161. *Idem*, chap. 5.

162. G. Pachymeres, Bk. 5, chap. 4 (Bonn ed., *1*, 344) ; Russian trans., *1*, 317 ; Veselovsky, p. 28; Vasiliev, *Goths*, p. 172.

163. See above, Chapter 1, sec. 7.

among the neighboring Christian rulers. Inside Hungary there was also much opposition to the "Tatarization" of the country. Only a small part of the Magyars were ready to follow the king along his chosen road.

It is against this background that Nogay's intervention in Hungarian affairs may be best understood. Worried by the opposition of the Christians to his rule, King László seems to have reached an understanding with Khan Nogay.[164] Nogay in his turn engaged the cooperation of Khan Tele-Buga. In the winter of 1285–86 Nogay led his army from the south through Brasov to Transylvania; Tele-Buga undertook to conquer Slovakia from the north. While Nogay's campaign was successful, Tele-Buga's army got stuck in the snow-covered valleys of the north Carpathian Mountains.[165] Having lost great numbers of both men and horses, Tele-Buga was compelled to retreat to Galicia to reorganize and reinforce his army and arrange for new supplies of horses. As herds of remounts were driven to Galicia from the Kypchak steppes, the Mongols in the spring and summer of 1286 grazed them in the Galician and Volynian fields, doing much harm to agriculture in both these regions. In addition the angry soldiers of Tele-Buga's army, disappointed in their hopes of rich booty in Hungary, looted Galicia and Volynia. But Nogay's intervention helped László keep his throne for the time being. At this juncture, however, László began to doubt the wisdom of his policies and seemed to be ready to return to Christianity. But in 1290 he was killed by the Cumans. His death signalized the final victory of Christianity in Hungary. Thus ended the dramatic career of this enigmatic and talented ruler caught between two different cultural worlds. Michael de Ferdinandy aptly compares him to Julian the Apostate while also considering him an imitator of Attila.[166]

Following the Hungarian campaign Nogay and Tele-Buga turned their attention to Poland. Their objective must have been to forestall Polish intervention in favor of the Christian party in Hungary. In the fall of 1286 Nogay appeared in Galicia with his army, and the

164. Spuler, pp. 67–68.

165. On Nogay and Tele-Buga's Hungarian campaigns see Veselovsky, pp. 30–37.

166. Michael de Ferdinandy was kind enough to give me his appraisal of the personality and historical role of László IV in a letter to me of March 6, 1952. On László IV see Michael de Ferdinandy, "Das Ende der heidnischen Kultur in Ungarn," *UJ, 15* (1935), 77; *idem, Mi Magyarok: Tiz tanulmani a Magyar történelemböl* (Budapêst, 1941), pp. 164–175; *idem, Az Istenkeresök: az Arpadhaz története* (Budapest, 1942), pp. 116–124, 220–239 (these last two works are inaccessible to me; I am indebted to their author for the reference); Hóman, *1,* 589–611; Bratianu, pp. 234–236.

two Mongol leaders, reinforced by Russian auxiliary troops under the command of the Galician and Volynian princes, attacked Poland. They again operated separately. While Nogay led his troops in the direction of Kraków, Tele-Buga advanced toward Sandomir. The Mongols succeeded in entering several Polish castles by ruse. According to the Polish chronicles, on several occasions the Russian princes who accompanied the Mongols pledged that after voluntary surrender the garrison and inhabitants would not be harmed; then in each case the Mongols violated the pledge.[167] While the Mongols seized rich booty in Poland, they did not succeed in conquering the country, and early in 1287 they returned to Galicia and Volynia, where they looted once more. The devastation of these provinces was as thorough as that of the Kievan region under Batu. As a result of the loss of population and wealth, the power of the princes of the house of Galicia was so seriously undermined as to give the grand dukes of Lithuania an advantage over them in the process of unification of West Russia.[168]

Soon after the return of his relatives from the Polish campaign, Prince Vladimir of Volynia (son of Vasilko) died after a long illness. The story of his illness and death and his biography in the Volynian Chronicle, as well as the text of his will recorded there, constitute an important body of evidence for the study of West Russian (Ukrainian) history in this troubled period.[169] According to the chronicler, Vladimir was a tall and handsome man, a lover of books, and a patron of church art. Reading his eulogy, one feels that the chronicler mourned in his person the last prince of a great age.

After Tele-Buga's return to Saray Tuda-Mangu was forced to abdicate, and Tele-Buga became khan in his own right in spite of the opposition of a group of princes and army commanders who favored Mangu-Temir's son Tokhta. Relations between Nogay and Tele-Buga had grown strained at the time of their joint campaign against Hungary and Poland when Tele-Buga complained that Nogay did not give him enough support. Now a full-fledged khan, Tele-Buga thought he could afford a more independent attitude toward Nogay, and their relations deteriorated still further.

The confusion which resulted from the lack of agreement between

167. On Nogay and Tele-Buga's Polish campaign see Veselovsky, pp. 34–37.
168. See Liubavsky, pp. 29–30.
169. Hyp., pp. 213–223.

the two khans is well illustrated by the story of the Mongol official (*baskak*) [170] Ahmad and the Kursk princes.[171] Ahmad was in charge of collecting taxes in the Kursk region. According to the story, he established two new towns there, whose population grew rapidly because of the tax exemptions granted them; numbers of craftsmen and merchants were attracted to them. In contrast, the domains of Princes Oleg of Rylsk and Sviatoslav of Lipetsk became impoverished.[172] Presently these two princes decided to complain to the tsar. As Ahmad the baskak was subordinate to Nogay, the princes addressed themselves to Tele-Buga. He ruled that the towns established by Ahmad should be destroyed. Consequently Oleg's and Sviatoslav's retainers raided and looted them.

Ahmad immediately complained to Nogay. Enraged by the action of the two princes, Nogay sent a strong detachment of troops under Ahmad's command with orders to seize Oleg and Sviatoslav as well as their boyars. Upon hearing of this punitive expedition, Oleg fled to Tele-Buga's ordu and Sviatoslav to the Voronezh woods in the principality of Riazan. Both princes, as well as Sviatoslav's boyars, succeeded in escaping, but Oleg's boyars were caught on their way east by Ahmad's soldiers and brought to the baskak's camp. Ahmad ordered their immediate execution. The domains of both princes were mercilessly looted by Ahmad's troops. The next year an agreement was reached between Tele-Buga and Nogay which allowed Oleg to return to Rylsk. Meanwhile Sviatoslav also came back, and as he was no party to any agreement he raided Ahmad's towns once more. Frightened at the possible consequences of this action, Oleg again went to Tele-Buga, who ordered him to punish Sviatoslav and sent a detachment of Mongol troops to enforce the order. Fulfilling the tsar's will, Oleg killed Sviatoslav. Sviatoslav's brother Alexander then went to Tsar Nogay to ask his protection. The tsar sent a detachment of his troops to assist Alexander. With their help, Alexander was able to seize Oleg and his two sons and killed all three of them.

This whole episode is characteristic of both the incipient decadence of Mongol rule and the demoralization which, at its worst, it caused in the Russian princes. Other similar events were to follow.

170. On the meaning of the term "baskak" see below, sec. 8, p. 220.

171. Laur., *2*, cols. 481–482; Nikon, *10*, 162–165. On the date of the episode see Nasonov, p. 70.

172. These two princes belonged to the house of Chernigov; see Baumgarten, *1*, 90. Rylsk and Lipetsk are towns in the Kursk land.

II

In the spring of 1288 Tele-Buga launched a campaign against the state of the il-khans, resuming the feud between the two branches of the Chingisids which had been started by Berke. The aim of the khan of the Golden Horde was, as before, to annex Azerbaijan. Neither this campaign nor the second one which followed in the spring of 1290 achieved any lasting results.[173] But the people of the city of Rostov took advantage of the fact that the khan's attention was concentrated on Transcaucasia to rebel in 1289 against the Mongol officials.[174] There is no evidence of any punitive expedition sent against Rostov on this occasion by Tele-Buga. Probably the revolt was suppressed by the combined efforts of the Rostov princes and the Mongol garrisons stationed in the neighboring towns.

If Tele-Buga hoped, through his war against the il-khan, to raise a prestige which had been somewhat shaken by his previous unsuccessful campaign against Hungary and Poland, he miscalculated. His failure to conquer Azerbaijan must have been severely criticized by many princes and army commanders. The leaders of the opposition may have been ready to promote Tokhta's claims on the throne. In any case Tele-Buga decided to arrest Tokhta. Warned of the danger, Tokhta fled to Nogay and asked him, as the oldest living Juchid, for protection. Nogay was only too glad to use this pretext to undermine Tele-Buga's authority. He therefore offered asylum to Tokhta in his horde and guaranteed the fugitive's safety. It was on this occasion that he mentioned Batu's decree making him moderator of the Juchid princes.[175] Nogay little realized that he was making a fatal mistake by befriending Tokhta. The man whom he befriended was eventually to bring about his ruin.

After consultation with Tokhta Nogay decided to get rid of Tele-Buga by ruse. Professing a desire to come to an agreement, he invited Tele-Buga to meet him in an appointed place. Each was to come to the meeting with a small retinue, without mobilizing his army. Tele-Buga was naïve enough to trust Nogay and fell into the trap. He was seized by Nogay's soldiers and handed over, together with several other princes who had accompanied him, to Tokhta who ordered all of them to be killed in the traditional Mongol

173. Spuler, *Iran*, p. 86; Spuler, *Horde*, 70.
174. Nasonov, p. 67.
175. Tiesenhausen, 2, 69.

way—without shedding blood, that is, by breaking their backs
(1291).[176] Nogay then proclaimed Tokhta khan of Kypchak.
Tokhta on his part, according to an Egyptian source, "gave the
Crimea" to Nogay.[177] As has been mentioned, only one-fourth of the
income of the Crimean cities was at the disposal of the khans of
Kypchak.[178] It was probably this share of his that Tokhta ceded to
Nogay.

While accepting Nogay's assistance in obtaining the throne,
Tokhta had no intention of becoming his vassal for life. Tokhta
proved to be a ruler of great ability and a man of quite different
mettle from either Tele-Buga or Tuda-Mangu. A devout Sky worshiper, he was permeated with stern Mongol traditions and believed
in pan-Mongol unity. Cautious enough to avoid an open clash with
Nogay at first, Tokhta from the very beginning of his reign started
building up a strong army and administration. But he had to make
a few more concessions to Nogay before he felt ready to oppose him.

Taking advantage of the change on the throne of the Golden
Horde, the titular grand duke Andrew, accompanied by a number
of the Rostov princes and the bishop of Rostov, went to Tokhta to
renew his patent and present his complaints against Nogay's creature,
the acting grand duke Dmitri. The latter refused to appear at
Tokhta's court, considering himself Nogay's vassal. Prince Michael
of Tver (son of Grand Duke Iaroslav II) also chose to side with
Nogay and went to him instead of to Tokhta for confirmation of his
throne. And Prince Daniel of Moscow (Alexander Nevsky's youngest
son) failed to appear at Tokhta's court. Thus, the division of
authority in the Golden Horde resulted in the formation of two rival
groups among the Russian princes. Tokhta refused to tolerate this
situation and made a vigorous attempt to reassert his authority over
all North Russia. He not only confirmed Andrew as grand duke of
Vladimir but authorized Andrew and Grand Duke Fedor of Smolensk
to depose Dmitri. As might be expected, Dmitri did not intend to
surrender the throne, and defied Tokhta's orders. The khan then
sent a Mongol army to assist his Russian vassals, under the command of his brother Tudan (Tödan) whom the Russian chronicles
call Diuden.[179] The Grand Duchy of Vladimir paid a terrible price

176. *Idem, 2,* 69–70; Veselovsky, pp. 37–38.
177. Veselovsky, p. 43.
178. See above, Chapter 2, sec. 9, p. 133.
179. Nasonov, pp. 73–77; N. Veselovsky, "Zametki po istorii Zolotoi Ordy," *ANZI,* 21,
Pt. 1 (1916), 1–10.

for Dmitri's opposition to Tokhta. Vladimir itself as well as a number of other cities, including Moscow, were mercilessly looted and the country around thoroughly devastated (1293). Only the city of Tver offered determined resistance to the invaders; to overcome it, Tokhta sent another Mongol army led by Prince Takhtamir (Tog-Temir?) which did much harm to the Tverians.[180] Meanwhile Dmitri fled to Pskov and started negotiations with Andrew. A temporary truce was agreed upon. Soon after this Dmitri died, and Andrew was recognized grand duke by most of the North Russian princes (1294).

While Nogay did not choose to intervene in Russian affairs this time, he must have been worried by Tokhta's drastic actions. He found it necessary to remind Tokhta that supreme power in the affairs of the Golden Horde still lay with Nogay. Consequently, in 1293, Nogay's senior wife, Baylak-Khatun, paid a courtesy call on Tokhta and was received with due honor. After several days of festivities she told Tokhta that his "father" (i.e. suzerain) Nogay wanted to warn him against a number of his army commanders who had formerly supported Tele-Buga and whom Nogay considered dangerous. She named twenty-three of them. Tokhta called each in turn to his tent and had them all arrested and executed one after the other.[181]

This evidence of Tokhta's loyalty reassured Nogay. He could now turn his attention to Balkan affairs in order to extend his influence to Serbia. Several local Balkan princes, including Shishman of Vidin,[182] asked his protection against King Milutin Uroš II of Serbia. Nogay sent his army into Serbia, and the king had no alternative but to acknowledge himself Nogay's vassal (around 1293).[183]

That same year a protracted war started between Genoa and Venice. In view of the wide commercial expansion of these two Italian republics in the eastern Mediterranean, their conflict affected not only the relations of each with a number of Oriental countries but international policies at large, both in Europe and Asia.[184] As we

180. Nikon, *10*, 169.

181. Tiesenhausen, *1*, 109; Veselovsky, p. 43.

182. P. Nikov, *Istoriia na Vidinskoto kniazhestvo do 1323 godina* (Sofia, 1922), pp. 47–50.

183. Nikov, *Tataro-bulgarski otnosheniia*, p. 23, refers this event to around 1292; Veselovsky, p. 42, to around 1296.

184. On the Genoese-Venetian war of 1293–99 see MPYC, Introductory Note vi, *1*, 41–44; Bratianu, pp. 263–275; Cessi, *1*, 263–265.

know, the Genoese firmly established themselves in the Crimean ports during the reign of Mangu-Temir.[185] The Venetians resented the loss of their former advantages in the lucrative Black Sea trade and before long attempted to reassert themselves in the Crimea. A Venetian consul in Soldaia is mentioned in 1287.[186] In 1291 the Venetians decided to send a mission to Nogay. They probably counted on that khan's cooperation in breaking the Genoese monopoly in the Crimea.[187] According to a historian of the Italian merchant marine, it was precisely Venetian aggressiveness in the Black Sea area which provoked the general conflict between the two Italian republics.[188] However, Nogay hesitated to take any immediate action against the Genoese. Meanwhile his relations with Tokhta became strained. In all probability the Genoese asked Tokhta for protection against both the Venetians and their sponsor Nogay. And Nogay had offered asylum and friendship to a number of Tokhta's generals who had deserted their khan. To the son of one Nogay even gave one of his daughters in marriage.

Tokhta sent an envoy to Nogay to demand explanations and, if these were not satisfactory, to threaten him with war. Nogay accepted the challenge and sent back the message: "Our horses are thirsty and we want to let them drink from the Don River." This colorful formula for declaring war has its roots in the traditional epic poetry of the steppe peoples; it was used in Scythian times and, more recently, in the "Lay of Igor's Campaign." [189] Tokhta at once led his army against the enemy. According to the Egyptian historian Rukn ad-Din Baybars the main battle of this war took place near the banks of the Ias—that is, the Pruth—River.[190] Marco Polo was told during his stay in Persia that it was fought in the plain of Nerghi.[191] *Nerge*, in Persian, means "line." [192] I believe that the name refers to the ancient fortified line between the Dniester and the Pruth rivers in Bessarabia and Moldavia, called Emperor Trajan's Wall, remnants

185. See above, sec. 4, p. 170.

186. Bratianu, p. 256.

187. *Idem*, pp. 256–257.

188. Manfroni, *Storia della marina, 2*, 103; A. Battistella, *La Republica di Venezia* (Venice, 1921), p. 165, as cited by Bratianu, pp. 256–257.

189. See G. Vernadsky, "La Geste d'Igor au point de vue historique," *Annuaire, 8* (1948), 223.

190. Tiesenhausen, *1*, 110–111; Veselovsky, p. 45. See above, subsection 1, p. 179, and n. 153.

191. MPMP, *1*, p. 486.

192. Steingass, p. 1395.

of which still exist.[193] Thus the battlefield may have been in southern Bessarabia.

The battle ended in a victory for Nogay. Tokhta fled eastward with the remnants of his troops, pursued by Nogay's army as far as the Don River. Nogay's promise came true: his soldiers actually watered their horses in the Don. Nogay now turned his wrath against the Genoese. In 698 A.H. (A.D. 1298–99) his troops looted both Kaffa and Soldaia.[194] About the same time the war between Genoa and Venice came to an end with the Genoese victory in the decisive naval battle of Curzola (September 7, 1298). Incidentally it was in this battle that Marco Polo, who had returned from China to Venice in 1295, was taken prisoner by the Genoese, and it was in a Genoese prison that he narrated his story to a fellow prisoner, Rusticiano of Pisa, who wrote it down and preserved it for posterity. Perhaps without this period of leisure in prison he might never have had time to write his story. While Genoa won the war, the provisions of the peace treaty were not harsh to Venice, and the right of the Venetians to trade in the Black Sea was recognized in 1299.[195]

By not pursuing Tokhta beyond the Don to his final destruction Nogay violated one of the major principles of Chingis-Khan's strategy. He probably overestimated his own strength; besides, he was getting old.[196] Tokhta took full advantage of the mistake. Within two years he had a new well-trained army which in 699 A.H. (A.D. 1299–1300) he again led westward. According to the Arabic sources, the main battle of this second war between Tokhta and Nogay took place at Kukanlyk (Kaganlyk). This may be identified as the Kagamlyk River in Poltava province.[197] This time fortune turned against Nogay. His army was defeated and he himself killed by a Russian soldier in Tokhta's army. The soldier brought Nogay's

193. On Trajan's Wall in Bessarabia see C. Schuchhardt, "Wälle und Chausseen im südlichen und östlichen Dacien," *AEM, 9* (1885), 202–232; V. P. Semenov, *Rossiia, 14* (St. Petersburg, 1910), 134; C. Uhlig, "Die Wälle in Bessarabia, besonders die sogenannten Trajanswälle," *Prähistorische Zeitschrift, 19* (1928), pp. 185–250.

194. Veselovsky, pp. 46–47.

195. Cessi, *1,* 265.

196. Presumably Nogay was born between 1235 and 1240.

197. For the account of the battle see Veselovsky, pp. 48–49. The Kagamlyk is a small river discharging into the Dnieper near the present-day city of Kremenchug. See P. P. Semenov, *Geografichesko-statisticheskii slovar' Rossiiskoi Imperii, 2* (St. Petersburg, 1865), 409; V. P. Semenov, *Rossiia, 7* (St. Petersburg, 1903), 311, 415, 416. According to F. K. Brun [Bruun] the battle was fought near the modern city of Odessa (see Nikov, *Tataro-bulgarski otnosheniia,* p. 32), and according to Spuler, p. 76, at the Terek River in the northern Caucasus.

head to Tokhta, expecting a lavish reward for his deed. Instead, Tokhta ordered that he be executed, commenting, "A commoner is not entitled to kill a king." [198] Obviously, Tokhta was indignant that Nogay was not given the privilege of dying without his blood being shed.

Nogay's eldest son, Chaka (Jögä), succeeded in escaping the slaughter and, with such troops as he could gather after the battle, went first to "the country of the Alans" (Moldavia) and then to Bulgaria. Tsar Smilets of Bulgaria had died late in 1298, and a period of interregnum ensued, with Terter's son Svetoslav as one of the claimants to the throne. When Chaka appeared Svetoslav recognized him as his suzerain and assisted him to ascend the Bulgarian throne at Tyrnovo (late in 1300 or early in 1301). Thus a Chingisid became tsar of Bulgaria. He did not long remain so, however. Fearing reprisals against Bulgaria on the part of Tokhta, Svetoslav soon betrayed Chaka. The conspiracy he headed proved successful, and Chaka was thrown into prison and strangled there.[199] Svetoslav then proclaimed himself tsar of Bulgaria, presumably as Tokhta's vassal.

Nogay's dynamic personality and the dramatic story of his successes and failures made him a favorite character in both Turkish and Russian epic poetry. In many a Russian *bylina* "that dog, Kalin-Tsar" (*sobaka Kalin-Tsar'*) is mentioned. It will be recalled that "nogai" means "dog" in Mongol; "kalin" in Turkish means "fat," and it is known that Nogay was fat. Thus the "dog Kalin-Tsar" of Russian *byliny* is none other than Khan Nogay.[200]

6. The Golden Horde in the First Half of the 14th Century

I

With Tokhta's decisive victory over Nogay the period of dichotomy in the government of the Golden Horde came to an abrupt end. Tokhta had at first to face a difficult situation. The country and the people were all but exhausted by the civil war. Moreover, there was a severe drought in the Pontic steppes in 1300 and the two following

198. Veselovsky, p. 49.
199. For Chaka's story see Nikov, pp. 32–49; cf. Veselovsky, pp. 55–57.
200. See O. Jensen (R. Jakobson), "Sobaka Kalin Tsar," *Slavia, 17* (1939), 82–98.

years.[201] Within a short period, however, the difficulties were over-come and conditions rapidly improved. According to the writer who continued Rashid ad-Din's *History*, Tokhta was a patient and able ruler. "In the days of his reign the countries subject to him reached a high level of prosperity, and his whole ulus became rich and con-tented." [202]

In fact, Tokhta lost no time in restoring unity of government in the Khanate of Kypchak and assuming control of its foreign relations as well as of the vassal nations and princes. After Chaka's death the Nogay Horde disintegrated; a fragment of it migrated to Russian Podolia; [203] another section recognized Tokhta's suzerainty and was allowed to remain in the Pontic steppes; these eventually became known as the Little Nogays. Other Nogay clans preferred to return to their former abodes in the Iaik River basin, north of the Caspian Sea, to join their kin who had remained there throughout Nogay's rule. These became known as the Great Nogays.

Tokhta stepped into Nogay's shoes by establishing friendly re-lations with the Paleologi in Byzantium. Friendship, as in Nogay's case, was cemented by matrimonial ties: Maria, an illegitimate daughter of Emperor Andronikus II, became one of Tokhta's wives.[204]

It should be mentioned here that at the close of the 13th century important events took place in Asia Minor whose aftermath was to affect the destinies of the Byzantine Empire and, later on, of Russia as well. In 1296 Il-Khan Gazan removed the Seljuq sultan Gias ad-Din Masud II from office. Under his successor a rebellion started in the Seljuq state which was suppressed by Gazan's troops in 1299.[205] Following that the Seljuk Sultanate disintegrated. The local amirs in Anatolia who had been the sultan's vassals during this time now had to pledge direct allegiance to the il-khan. Most of them became virtually independent, among the others Ertogrul's son Osman. To-ward the end of his reign Osman succeeded in building up a com-paratively strong state of his own. On his deathbed he had the satis-faction of receiving news that his son Orhan [206] had captured the

---

201. Tiesenhausen, *1*, 436, 513; *ZO*, p. 88.
202. Tiesenhausen, *2*, 141.
203. Spuler, p. 79.
204. *Ibid.*
205. Rashid 3, pp. 180–181.
206. The names of the Ottoman sultans are here and hereafter given in modern Turkish spelling.

important city of Brussa close to the southern shore of the Sea of
Marmora (1326). Brussa became the first capital of the Ottoman
Empire.

Tokhta entertained lively diplomatic relations with both the Egyptian sultan and the il-khans. To the latter he presented the perennial
Kypchak demands for the cession of Azerbaijan, which were declined. He also intervened in the affairs of the Gazni region in eastern
Iran (Afghanistan) and at first succeeded in putting a candidate of
his own on the local princely throne; that vassal, however, was soon
ousted.[207] Further development of the conflict between Tokhta and
Gazan was prevented by the action of Great Khan Timur, who it
will be recalled attempted to restore the unity of the Mongol Empire
in the form of a federation of all the Mongol khanates. Both Tokhta
and Gazan's successor Oljaitu approved of that plan and solemnly
pledged themselves to support it (1304–5).[208]

An important result of the peaceful relations between the Golden
Horde and the il-khans during Tokhta's reign was the revival of
trade between the two khanates. According to Wassaf, "The road
was reopened to the merchants and caravan stockholders. The Arran
region [northern Azerbaijan] was covered with tents and wagons,
and both staple commodities and refined goods flooded the markets
in rapid turnover." [209] Black Sea commerce on the contrary received
a setback because of the misunderstandings between Tokhta and the
Genoese. In 1308 Kaffa was plundered by the Mongols. In other
ports, however, trade continued unabated.

The restoration of order in the Golden Horde could not but affect
Russian affairs as well. All the Russian princes were now compelled
to obey Tokhta, since there was no rival khan to whom they could
turn for protection. Outwardly, then, Russia's subordination to the
khan was restored. And yet the old self-assurance of Mongol rule
was gone. During the preceding period of dual government in the
Golden Horde Russian awe of the implacable machinery of Mongol
administration had been considerably reduced, even if it had not yet
completely disappeared. At least the spell was broken. A number of
Russian princes discovered that while they were too weak to oppose
the united khanate they could take advantage of disagreements
among the Mongols. Even if Tokhta was now sole ruler of the Golden

207. Spuler, p. 81.
208. See above, Chapter 2, sec. 4, p. 82.
209. *ZO*, p. 89.

Horde he had to reckon in his policies, to a certain extent at least, with the grandees around his throne—the senior Juchid princes and army generals—as well as with the leading merchants and other "pressure groups." Since on many occasions there was a difference of opinion among the khan's councilors, Russian princes could always place themselves under the protection of one or another Mongol prince or official. And as there were rivalries among the Russian princes, each tried to obtain his own special patron among the Mongols, thus involving the latter in Russian quarrels. In the fierce struggle for survival between the Russian princes each of them at first thought primarily of enlarging his apanage and strengthening his control within it. If he deemed it useful, he entered into an alliance with one or more neighboring princes, but only for as long as seemed to him profitable. All methods were considered permissible in this game: force, diplomacy, ruse, intrigue at the khan's court. Eventually some of the princes became so much stronger than others that a new perspective opened before their eyes: the possibility of one of them ruling all or most of East Russia. Thus the struggle for apanages was followed by the struggle, between the leading princes, for supremacy; in this way out of the anarchy of apanages a national state gradually emerged. The process was somewhat like that of the growth of the French monarchy under the Capet dynasty after the decay of the late Carolingian era.

It will be recalled that in the early 1290's two rival alignments among the Russian princes became noticeable: the princely group centering around Rostov and the combination of princes of central Russia—those of Pereiaslavl, Tver, and Moscow. In 1294 all of them recognized, nominally at any rate, the authority of Grand Duke Andrew. Three years later, however, relations between the two princely groups became strained again and war seemed inevitable.[210] This happened at the time when Tokhta was preparing his first attack on Nogay. He considered the situation in Russia so critical, however, that he decided to intervene at once. He sent a special envoy, whom the Russian chronicles refer to as Nevrui (Nevruz?), with a strong detachment of troops, and he asked Bishop Ismail of Saray to accompany Nevrui in order to attempt conciliation. All the Russian princes were summoned to Vladimir and after a stormy conference were persuaded by Bishop Ismail to come to an agreement.[211]

210. Trinity, p. 347.
211. *Ibid.*, pp. 347–348.

Four years later new complications arose when Prince Daniel of Moscow seized the town of Kolomna which belonged to the principality of Riazan. Prince Constantine of Riazan turned to the local Mongol baskak for protection, but this did not stop Daniel, who succeeded in defeating both the Riazan and Mongol troops (1301).[212] By ruse Daniel captured Prince Constantine himself and brought him to Moscow where he kept him for several years, showing him due honor. After Daniel's death the unhappy prince was murdered by order of Daniel's son and successor, Iuri.

Encouraged by his success, Daniel in 1303 occupied Mozhaisk which had been until then part of the principality of Smolensk. Prince Ivan of Pereiaslavl died that year leaving no sons to succeed him. Grand Duke Andrew immediately sent his lieutenants to rule Pereiaslavl. Daniel was indignant since he had earmarked the city for himself and claimed that Prince Ivan had willed it to him. Consequently he ousted the grand duke's lieutenants and occupied Pereiaslavl with his own troops.

One motive may be discerned in all of Daniel's aggressive acts: his desire to round out his apanage. Kolomna lies southeast of Moscow, Mozhaisk to the west, and Pereiaslavl to the northeast. While the original territory of his apanage did not exceed the district (*uezd*) of Moscow in terms of the administrative division of modern Russia prior to 1917, Daniel came to control both the western and southeastern sections of Moscow province (*guberniia*)—the districts of Mozhaisk and Kolomna; Pereiaslavl is even outside of that guberniia. In spite of the outcry of the offended parties Daniel kept all three towns he had occupied. His tenacity in achieving his objectives laid the pattern for his successors. Their firm grip on what they had once seized greatly helped the Danilovichi eventually to become rulers of Russia.

Daniel's seizure of Pereiaslavl threw off balance the whole structure of interprincely relations, which had not been very stable even before that. Grand Duke Andrew went to the Horde to submit to the khan his complaint against Daniel's actions. Tokhta ordered a new conference of the Russian princes to be held at Pereiaslavl in the autumn of 1304, under the chairmanship of his own envoys. Among the leading Russian princes who attended were Grand Duke Andrew, Prince Michael of Tver, and Prince Iuri of Moscow, Daniel's eldest son and successor (Daniel had died in March 1304).[213] The head

212. *Ibid.*, p. 350; Nasonov, p. 80.
213. A.D. 1303 according to Ekzempliarsky.

of the Russian church, Metropolitan Maxim, also attended.[214] The conference was opened with the solemn announcement by the khan's envoys of the restoration of pan-Mongol unity and the formation of the pan-Mongol federation, to which Tokhta was a party and in which the Russian princes now became associates. The text of the pan-Mongol agreement was read, and the Russians no doubt had to swear allegiance to it.[215]

After the official part of the conference was over, local Russian affairs were discussed. With the approval of the khan's envoys, Pereiaslavl was assigned not to Grand Duke Andrew but to Prince Iuri of Moscow. This was an important indication of Tokhta's new policy with regard to Russian affairs. Tokhta's predecessors had established close ties with the Rostov princes and left the control of all other Russian principalities to the grand duke of Vladimir. Now, with the emergence of strong local states like Tver and Moscow, in Central Russia, the old policy could not be expected to work smoothly, and Tokhta had to reckon with the new situation. He therefore decided to make both the prince of Moscow and the prince of Tver his direct vassals but at the same time not to let either grow unduly strong. Thus, while Tokhta satisfied the prince of Moscow by assigning Pereiaslavl to him, his next move was in favor of the prince of Tver. In 1305 Grand Duke Andrew died,[216] and both Iuri of Moscow and Michael of Tver rushed to the khan's court, each expecting to receive the grand ducal patent. Before leaving for Saray Michael instructed his boyars to occupy Pereiaslavl. The Tver troops sent to that city were defeated, however, by Iuri's brother Ivan.[217] Meanwhile Tokhta issued the patent on the Grand Duchy of Vladimir to Michael of Tver. In compensation to Iuri Michael's claim to Pereiaslavl was denied. Combining the authority of the grand duke of Vladimir and the resources of the principality of Tver, Michael strove for supremacy in Russian affairs, and there followed a period of "cold war" between Tver and Moscow.

It seems probable that Tokhta was not satisfied with the turn of affairs in Russia and made new plans for complete political reorganization of his Russian ulus. Unfortunately information on the last years of Tokhta's reign is meager. In the Russian annals of the

214. Trinity, p. 311.
215. Nasonov, p. 79.
216. A.D. 1304 according to Ekzempliarsky.
217. Soloviev, 3, 269–270.

period there are only terse accounts of the interrelations among the Russian princes, while the Arabic and Persian chroniclers were more concerned with the relations of the Golden Horde with Egypt and Iran than with Russia. But one important hint about Tokhta's Russian plans has been preserved by the writer who continued Rashid ad-Din's *History,* in his account of the circumstances of Tokhta's death in 1312. According to him Tokhta decided personally to visit Russia; he set out by boat up the Volga River but before reaching the confines of Russia fell ill and died on board.[218] Tokhta's decision to go to Russia was unique in the history of the Golden Horde. No Mongol khan before or after him visited Russia in peacetime as a ruler, not as conqueror. Surely Tokhta's exceptional move must have been caused by his intention to introduce far-reaching reforms in the administration of his northern ulus. The nature of these reforms we can only guess.

Judging from what we know of his previous Russian policies, we may surmise that Tokhta intended to abolish the Grand Duchy of Vladimir, to make all Russian princes his direct vassals, and to assign a definite apanage to each of them, with the authority to collect taxes within his dominions. To prevent further conflicts he may also have contemplated making the interprincely conference a permanent institution. Presumably he intended personally to open its first session and then to appoint a high Mongol official (a Juchid prince, perhaps) as his lieutenant extraordinary and permanent chairman of the conference. All this (if such were Tokhta's plans) would have amounted to constituting Russia (East Russia in any case) a full-fledged partner in the Golden Horde as well as in the pan-Mongol federation. However bold and creative Tokhta's plans may have been, they fell through with his death.

II

Tokhta's successor was his nephew Uzbeg (Özbäg; ruled 1313–41); his reign is usually considered the Golden Age of the Golden Horde. Uzbeg was a Moslem, a circumstance which caused some delay in his election because of the opposition of the Old Mongol party. With his enthronement Islam became the official religion at the khan's court and gradually was adopted by most of the khan's Mongol and Turkish subjects. The conversion proved final this time. In token of his devotion to the Prophet Uzbeg built a huge mosque

218. Tiesenhausen, 2, 141.

in the city of Solkhat in the Crimea (1314) which is still standing.[219]

In his foreign policies Uzbeg was on the whole more aggressive than Tokhta. He intervened in 1324 in the Bulgaro-Byzantine conflict at the time of civil war in Byzantium, giving his support to the Bulgarian tsar, George Terter II.[220] In spite of the Mongol assistance the Bulgarian army was defeated by the Byzantines at Adrianople.[221] Later on, the Byzantine emperor Andronikus III (grandson of Andronikus II whom he dethroned in 1328) established friendly relations with Uzbeg by the familiar device of giving him his daughter in marriage. She became known as Khatun Bayalun and—an important sign of the change in religious atmosphere in the Golden Horde—had to accept Islam.[222] Around 1333 Bayalun was given permission to visit her father in Constantinople. She went—accompanied by the Arabic traveler Ibn-Batuta—and never returned.[223]

In 1330 Uzbeg intervened in Balkan affairs once more, again unsuccessfully. At that time a Byzantine-Bulgarian coalition was formed against Serbia. Both the Alans of Moldavia and the Wallachians under their voevoda (duke) John Bessarab supported the Bulgarians. Bessarab's participation in the coalition signalized the emergence of the Rumanians on the international scene. Uzbeg on his part sent 3,000 Nogay troops to reinforce the coalition. The combined allied army was 15,000 strong. The size of the Serbian army is not known; to strengthen it, the Serbian king Stephan Uroš III hired a number of Spanish and German mercenaries. The decisive battle of the war took place at Velbužd (Küstendil) on June 28, 1330 and ended in complete victory for the Serbs.[224] Serbia now became the strongest Balkan state, and soon reached its greatest size under King Stephan Uroš IV, nicknamed Dušan (1336–55).

As in Tokhta's reign, the relations between the khan and the Genoese under Uzbeg were marred by occasional conflicts. In 1322

---

219. Kulakovsky, *Tavrida*, p. 111. Solkhat is now known as Eski-Kirim in Turkish, in Russian as Staryi Krym.

220. Spuler, p. 92.

221. Jireček, *Bulgaria*, p. 289.

222. Spuler (pp. 79, 216) identifies Bayalun as Maria (Tokhta's Byzantine wife); he also thinks that she was allowed to remain a Christian, but see Pelliot, pp. 84–85.

223. Ibn-Batuta, *2*, 411–412.

224. Jireček, *Bulgaria*, pp. 293–295; Jireček, *Serbia*, pp. 361–363; Ostrogorsky, p. 361; Mutafchiev, *2*, 184–187. Cf. Spuler, p. 92. For a general outline of the development of the Slavic states in the Balkans in the 14th and 15th centuries see G. Stadtmüller, "Aufstieg und Untergang der balkanslawischen Staatenwelt," *Festschrift für Hermann Aubin* (1951), pp. 131–147.

the Mongols sacked the city of Soldaia and destroyed a number of Christian churches there. According to Ibn-Batuta this attack was the result of a clash between the Greeks and the Turks in Soldaia.[225] However, it was not the Greeks but the Genoese who represented the strongest Christian group in Soldaia at that time. Elsewhere Ibn-Batuta mentions Soldaia as a port "of the infidels," without making a distinction between the Greek Orthodox and the Roman Catholics.[226] Presumably the leading role in the Soldaia conflict belonged not to the Greeks but to the Genoese. In any case, a number of Roman Catholic churches were among those destroyed, and the pope felt it necessary to intervene, asking Uzbeg to restore them.[227] Apparently no attention was paid to his request. When Ibn-Batuta visited Soldaia, around 1333, he found there a predominantly Turkish population.[228] It must be noted in this connection that the Genoese merchants in other Crimean ports were not molested. Kaffa was again growing and from 1318 on was a see of a Roman Catholic bishop. The Genoese also established themselves in this period in both the Bosporus (Kerch) and Kherson.[229]

With Egypt Uzbeg maintained active relations. In 1314 Sultan al-Malik al-Nasir expressed his desire to marry a Juchid princess. Uzbeg readily agreed but demanded a huge price for the bride. The sultan's envoy was embarrassed since he had not enough money with him. Uzbeg graciously arranged for the leading merchants of the Golden Horde to loan the sultan the money. The preliminary agreement was signed, but it was not until 1320 that the princess, Tulunbay by name, was allowed to proceed to Cairo, escorted by a large group of notables and attendants. The cortege stopped for a few days at Constantinople where Emperor Andronikus II entertained the distinguished travelers lavishly. Tulunbay's reception at Alexandria was no less magnificent. As soon as she disembarked, the marriage contract was signed and the bride proceeded to Cairo. The marriage did not prove happy, however; the sultan divorced Tulunbay after a few days and passed her on to one of his amirs. Uzbeg did not hear of the incident and of Tulunbay's subsequent death until five years later. He was greatly offended and sent several embassies to Egypt to demand explanations (1332, 1335). Later he expressed willingness

225. Ibn-Batuta, 2, 414–415.
226. *Idem, 1,* 28.
227. Kulakovsky, *Tavrida,* pp. 106–107; cf. Vasiliev, *Goths,* p. 174.
228. Ibn-Batuta, 2, 415.
229. Kulakovsky, *Tavrida,* pp. 105–106.

to marry any of the sultan's daughters, but was informed that none
of them had reached the nuptial age.[230] Obviously Uzbeg was the
more eager of the two monarchs to establish cordial relations. As a
matter of fact, he was having a series of conflicts with the il-khans
and needed the assistance of the Mameluks.

The first period of tension between Uzbeg and Il-Khan Abu-Said
was in 1318–19. Uzbeg established his headquarters in the northern
Caucasus without any major war ensuing. In 1324–25 the il-khan's
troops penetrated into the Terek River valley in the north Caucasus,
but they were repulsed. Ten years later when Uzbeg launched a
campaign against Azerbaijan his army was stopped by the Persians.[231]

Uzbeg was highly praised by Moslem travelers and historians
for his protection and propagation of the Islamic faith, for his orderly
rule, and his promotion of trade. According to Ibn-Arabshah, a historian of the 15th century, under Uzbeg trade caravans plied safely
between the Crimea and Khoresm without need of any military escort, and all along the way food and fodder were plentiful and easily
available.[232] As has been mentioned, Uzbeg established his capital at
Berke's Saray, not far from present-day Stalingrad. Ibn-Batuta, who
visited Uzbeg's dominions around 1333, describes Saray as a large
and beautiful city with vast streets and fine markets. Six "nations"
lived in it—Mongols, Alans, Kypchaks, Circassians, Russians and
Greeks—each being assigned a section of its own. For their own
protection and that of their goods, foreign merchants stayed in a
special walled section of the city.[233] Like his predecessors, Uzbeg
spent only part of the year in the city, wandering in the other months
with his ordu. In the summer he often went to the high plateau of the
northern Caucasus, close to the mountains. His wives and the high
officials of his court always followed him. His roving ordu is described
by Ibn-Batuta as a huge city of tents on the move.[234]

Uzbeg's favorite wife was Khatun Taydula.[235] Ibn-Batuta calls
her the "Great Khatun," and he was told by persons whom he trusted
that Taydula had a peculiar constitution. Every night Uzbeg would
find her virgin once more, and for this reason he preferred her to all
his other wives.[236] Uzbeg's court was famous for the magnificent

230. Spuler, pp. 93–96; ZO, pp. 92–93.
231. Spuler, p. 93; Nasonov, p. 106.
232. Tiesenhausen, 1, 460; ZO, p. 262.
233. Ibn-Batuta, 2, 447–448.
234. Idem, 2, 380.
235. For an analysis of the name see Pelliot, pp. 101–105.
236. Ibn-Batuta, 2, 390.

receptions held every Friday at the Golden Pavilion.[237] The festival of the breaking of the fast was especially sumptuous and elaborate.[238]

In regard to Russian affairs Uzbeg's policy was less constructive than Tokhta's. He made no attempt to change things in Russia and set himself a much narrower objective: to prevent the formation of a united Russian state and to keep the balance between the Russian princes, especially between those of Tver and Moscow. He introduced one new device: as he granted the right of collecting taxes to a number of leading Russian princes, the institution of the baskaks became superfluous, so instead the khan appointed special commissioners, who may perhaps be called his political commissars, each to take care of the affairs of a Russian principality.

At the beginning of his reign Uzbeg confirmed Michael of Tver as grand duke of Vladimir. This office traditionally was combined with control over Novgorod, but the Novgorodians refused to accept Michael and invited Iuri of Moscow instead to be their prince. Michael complained to the khan, and Iuri was ordered to appear at the Horde without delay. Using funds he collected at Novgorod, Iuri was able to shower the khan and grandees with rich presents. He spent several years in the Horde and received in marriage Uzbeg's sister Konchak, who was christened Agatha. Finally Uzbeg revoked Michael's patent and made Iuri grand duke of Vladimir (as Iuri III). Kavgadyi, one of the highest Mongol officials, was appointed the khan's commissioner at Iuri's court and accompanied Iuri and Agatha to Russia. Not expecting any serious resistance on Michael's part, Iuri and Kavgadyi marched on Tver with but few troops. Michael had no difficulty in defeating them, but he was careful not to attack Kavgadyi's headquarters. While Iuri escaped to Novgorod, his Mongol wife was captured by the Tverians.[239] Kavgadyi now ordered both Iuri and Michael to proceed to the Horde. They had to travel a long way since Uzbeg was at that time in the northern Caucasus because of his conflict with the il-khan. Meanwhile Agatha died in captivity in Tver, and Kavgadyi held the Tver authorities responsible for her death.

Michael was tried by the supreme court of the Golden Horde for opposing the khan's will and for not taking proper care of his prisoner, the khan's sister. After a long trial he was sentenced to death and

237. *Idem*, 2, 383–384.
238. *Idem*, 2, 402–410.
239. Soloviev, *3*, 275; Nasonov, p. 84.

promptly executed (1319).[240] His sons at Tver had no alternative but to recognize Iuri as grand duke. They had, however, to take special precautions to prevent the people of Tver from revolting against the Mongols. An uprising did take place in Rostov in 1320; it was crushed by the Mongol general Akhmyl who was given wide powers and sent to Russia, accompanied by Iuri's younger brother Ivan, to restore order. Together they finally succeeded in breaking the rebellious spirit of the Rostovians (1322).[241]

While Uzbeg was pleased with Ivan's efficiency, he became suspicious of Iuri. Akhmyl may have received secret information from the Mikhailovichi (sons of Michael of Tver) that Iuri was withholding for his own treasury part of the taxes he collected for the khan. In any case Uzbeg deprived Iuri of the grand ducal patent and appointed Dmitri, the eldest of the Mikhailovichi, grand duke of Vladimir (1322). Iuri returned to Novgorod and after having collected more money set out once more for the khan's court. As he feared the Mikhailovichi, he chose a roundabout way from Novgorod via the Dvina land and then down the Kama River. Dmitri also hastened to the Horde. When he met Iuri, whom he considered responsible for the trial and the death of his father, he lost control of his passions and killed the Moscow prince. For thus taking the law in his own hands he was executed by order of the khan (1325). The patent to the grand duchy of Vladimir was granted to his younger brother Alexander. As a measure of precaution Uzbeg put a special commissar, Shevkal, in charge of Tver affairs.

Unfortunately for them, the Tverians could no longer suppress their anti-Mongol feelings and soon after Shevkal established his office at Tver they revolted and killed both the Mongol commissioner and most of his Mongol lieutenants and guards (1327).[242] Uzbeg immediately summoned Ivan to the Horde and ordered him to lead a punitive expedition against Tver in cooperation with Prince Alexander of Suzdal. It may be noted in this connection that after the events of 1322, the city of Rostov lost its former leadership in the Suzdalian land; instead, the cities of Suzdal and Nizhni Novgorod (now known as Gorky) came to the fore. As the Muscovite and Suzdalian troops, reinforced by Mongol detachments, approached

240. Soloviev, *3*, 276–279; Nasonov, pp. 86–88.

241. Nasonov, pp. 107–108.

242. Soloviev, *3*, 287–289; Nasonov, pp. 91–93. The Tver uprising of 1327 served as a theme for a historical tale, the "Lay of Shchelkan" [i.e. Shevkal]; see *Istoriia russkoi literatury*, 2 (Moscow and Leningrad, 1946), 103–106.

Tver, Prince Alexander fled westward. Both the city of Tver and
the whole Tverian land were mercilessly looted by the invaders, and
thousands of Tverians were captured. Some as we have seen were
brought to China.[243]

While inflicting severe punishment on Tver through Ivan, Uzbeg
apparently was reluctant to make Moscow unduly strong. Characteristically, he granted the patent on the Grand Duchy of Vladimir
not to Ivan of Moscow but to Alexander of Suzdal (1328). It was
only after Alexander's death, four years later, that Ivan was appointed grand duke of Vladimir. Several principalities, however, were
exempt from his authority: those of Tver, Suzdal, and Riazan. The
prince of each was commissioned to collect taxes and bring the money
directly to the khan, not through the grand duke. To keep himself
firmly in the khan's good graces, Ivan made frequent visits to the
Horde. Nevertheless, he was constantly watched by the khan's commissioner, Al-Buga, who established his permanent office in Moscow.[244]

To a certain extent Uzbeg could be satisfied with the outcome of
his policies. During the decade of the reign of Ivan I as grand duke
of Vladimir (1332–41) there was no major disturbance in Eastern
and Central Russia. The chroniclers noted the growing prosperity
of the principality of Moscow under the wise rule of thrifty Ivan,
nicknamed Kalita (the Money Bag). Because of the good relations
between Ivan and Uzbeg, life in the Moscow region seemed more
secure than elsewhere and the population grew rapidly. To protect
trade Ivan took energetic measures against highway robbers and,
according to the chronicler, achieved marked success.[245]

Since the grand duke had his residence in Moscow and not in
Vladimir, the head of the Russian church, Metropolitan Peter, a
dignified prelate with high moral standards, also preferred to stay
in Moscow and expressed his desire to be buried there. After his
death in 1342 [246] his tomb became a national shrine. Thus Moscow
became practically the ecclesiastical capital of Russia, although the
metropolitan still was officially known as "of Kiev and all Russia."
In obvious imitation of the metropolitan's title, Ivan I added to his
own title the phrase "and of all Russia." [247] This amplification of the

243. See above, Chapter 2, sec. 4, p. 88.
244. Nasonov, p. 110.
245. See Simeonov, under A.D. 1328; Nasonov, p. 111.
246. On Metropolitan Peter see Makari, 4, 15–21; Golubinsky, 2, 98–144.
247. Nasonov, p. 100.

grand ducal title had profound significance. It marked the beginning of the drive to unify Russia and the Moscow prince's readiness to accept leadership in it. The steady growth of Moscow presented, potentially, a serious threat to the Golden Horde. However, the forces of the khan were still so much greater than those of the princes of Moscow that Uzbeg seemed to have little reason to worry about the future, all the more in that Ivan I gave every evidence of loyalty to the khan.

It was the situation in West Russia that worried the khan at the time. There his vassals, the West Russian princes, had to face constantly rising pressure on the part of both Poland and Lithuania. It must be said that the Mongols themselves had previously undermined the strength of Galicia and Volynia by devastating that area in 1285–86. Since the late 13th century, however, the Danilovichi, especially Leo I (d. 1301) and his son Iuri I, had striven hard to improve internal conditions in their country.[248] During Iuri I's reign (1301–8) Galicia seemed on the way to recovery and he even assumed the royal title (Rex Russiae).

Meanwhile, in the thirty-odd years following the death of Troiden, the Lithuanian grand dukes succeeded in building up a strong army and administration and in uniting their Lithuanian and Belorussian provinces more closely under their rule. The combined resources and manpower of the Grand Duchy of Lithuania and Russia were skillfully used by a ruler of great abilities, Grand Duke Gedymin (Gediminas) who ascended the Lithuanian throne in 1316. During his reign, which lasted until 1341, Lithuania became a major power in Eastern Europe. An important point in Gedymin's policies was his desire to extend his authority over as many West Russian lands as possible. He preferred expanding his power by diplomacy and dynastic marriages rather than by war, but when necessary he did not shrink from using force. He devoted considerable attention to the control of commercial routes, established friendly relations with the city of Riga, and attempted to channel the Baltic trade through his dominions.[249] In this connection, it seemed important to him to establish Lithuanian control over the Russian cities along the Dnieper River (Smolensk, and eventually Kiev) on the one hand and Volynia and Galicia on the other.

248. On the history of Galicia and Volynia in the late 13th and early 14th centuries see Hrushevsky, *3*, 108–142; Paszkiewicz, *Polityka ruska*, pp. 7–45.
249. See Antonovich, *Monografii*, pp. 63–70.

Following Iuri I's death the situation in Volynia and Galicia deteriorated rapidly. Constant conflicts occurred between the princes
and the boyars. In 1323 both of Iuri I's sons died, and the Galician
throne was then offered to Prince Boleslaw of Mazovia, son of Iuri's
daughter Maria and of Prince Troiden of Mazovia (1325). He was
confirmed in his office by Khan Uzbeg and became known as Iuri II.[250]
To strengthen his international prestige he married Princess Ofka,
a daughter of Grand Duke Gedymin (1331). In addition, according
to Hrushevsky's plausible conjecture, Iuri gave his own daughter in
marriage to Gedymin's son Lubart.[251] Both of these diplomatic marriages proved more useful to Gedymin than to Iuri II, and the Mongols decided to intervene in Volynian affairs to stop the aggressive
plans of both Lithuania and Poland. In 1336 Mongol troops raided
the borderlands of Lithuania and, in the next year, Lublin in Poland.[252] In the late 1330's the Prince of Smolensk recognized Grand
Duke Gedymin of Lithuania as his suzerain and thus defied Uzbeg's
authority. Uzbeg then sent several of his East Russian vassals against
Smolensk to bring that city back to his fold (1339).[253]

The following year a serious crisis developed in Galicia. While
Iuri II seemed to have diplomatic ability and to have succeeded in
improving the international status of Galicia, he had to face constantly growing boyar opposition at home. In 1340 rumors were
spread that he intended forcibly to introduce Roman Catholicism
in Galicia; at that juncture he suddenly died, presumably being poisoned by the boyars. His death encouraged both Poles and Hungarians to present their claims on Galicia. In 1339 King Casimir the
Great of Poland concluded an agreement with King Carl Robert of
Hungary, according to which Carl Robert ceded Galicia (which
actually did not belong to him) to Casimir for life, with the provision that if he died without male heirs he would bequeath it to Carl
Robert's son Lewis. On the basis of this arrangement Casimir rushed
to Galich as soon as the news of Iuri II's death reached him. The
city, however, refused to surrender. A committee of Galician boyars
headed by their senior, Dmitri Dedko, took control of the city and
the country in the name of the prince to be elected. They then of-

---

250. For a long time historians considered Iuri II a son of Andrew of Galicia, but
more recently his identity with Boleslav has been firmly established. See Genealogical
Table VIII.

251. Hrushevsky, *3*, 139–140; *4*, 13–14.

252. Spuler, pp. 91, 97.

253. *Idem*, p. 98; Nasonov, p. 112.

fered the Galician throne to Gedymin's son Lubart who was simultaneously recognized by the Volynian boyars as prince of Volynia. If
Hrushevsky's above-mentioned hypothesis is to be accepted, Lubart
could be considered Iuri II's heir through his wife. He established
his residence in Volynia, leaving Dedko in Galich as his lieutenant.
As Lubart pledged vassal allegiance to Khan Uzbeg, a detachment
of Mongol troops was sent to protect both Galicia and Volynia from
the Poles. Casimir was obliged to retreat though he did not give up
his claims.[254]

III

After Uzbeg's eldest son, Tinibeg, had reigned briefly (1341–42)
his younger brother, Janibeg, seized power (1342–57). In his policies Janibeg on the whole followed his father's traditions, except that
he did not interfere in Balkan affairs. Uzbeg's widow, Khatun Taydula, continued to occupy a prominent position in the Golden Horde
throughout Janibeg's reign.

Like his father, Janibeg had a conflict with the Genoese and attempted to seize Kaffa from them but without success (1344). On
the other hand, he signed a commercial treaty with Venice (1347). In
the years 1349–55 Venice and Genoa were waging another war, in
which Venice was victorious. Following that, the Venetian treaty with
Janibeg was confirmed, in 1356. The Venetians received the right to
establish their trade at Solkhat upon payment of custom duties of
2 per cent of the value of the goods sold, and at Soldaia upon payment of a 3 per cent duty.[255] Relations between the Golden Horde
and Egypt continued to be friendly. As before, a considerable number
of Kypchaks and Russians were brought to Egypt either as slaves
or as auxiliary troops. Most of them, if not all, were converted to
Islam. In the period of Janibeg's reign one of the Russian soldiers
made a brilliant career in Egypt, achieving the rank of amir. His
name is given in Oriental sources as Baybuga Rus (or Urus).[256]

Four years after Janibeg's enthronement a dreadful calamity af-
flicted the Golden Horde. The plague known as the Black Death,
which seems to have originated in the Far East, penetrated to
Khorezm from China and India in the wake of the trade caravans;

---

254. Hrushevsky, *3*, 137–141; *4*, 13–28; Paszkiewicz, *Polityka ruska*, pp. 48–87.
255. Kulakovsky, *Tavrida*, p. 107.
256. L. A. Mayer, *Saracenic Heraldry* (Oxford, Clarendon Press, 1933), p. 111; Poliak,
"Caractère colonial," p. 234.

in 1346 it struck the Crimea and left 85,000 dead.[257] From the
Crimea along the Asiatic shore of the Aegean and the island of
Cyprus, the disease reached Egypt and spread into Syria. Then
by way of the Mediterranean it visited Western Europe, and heading east again by the Baltic Sea struck Novgorod and reached Moscow in 1353. Clearly it followed the main commercial routes; it
thrived in crowded markets and ships. Since trade between the
cities of the Golden Horde and Russia was extensive in this period,
it seems paradoxical that the disease should have reached Novgorod
via the Baltic Sea and not through South and Central Russia. The
fact that the South Russian steppes were thinly populated, being used
mainly as grazing grounds for the Mongol herds, may have created
a kind of safety belt through which only healthy merchants traveled
back and forth.

In the 1350's an important event took place in the Straits zone
which was to change the whole political situation in the Near East.
In 1355 a small detachment of Ottoman Turks crossed the Hellespont
and the next year firmly entrenched themselves in Gallipoli.[258]
From this base they were soon to start their conquest of the Balkan
peninsula and the destruction of the Byzantine Empire. The rise of
the military power of the Ottoman Turks and their seizure of the
Dardanelles, and later also of the Bosporus, gave them absolute
control of Black Sea commerce, since they were now in a position to
bottle up the Black Sea. The steadily weakening Byzantine Empire
which had controlled the Straits before the Turks appeared there
had presented no serious problem for the khans of the Golden Horde
who could always apply military pressure on Byzantium to secure
right of way to Egypt. The Italians, in their turn, were interested
in freedom of navigation through the Straits and obtained it from
Byzantium. As the Golden Horde thrived on trade with Egypt and
on commerce with Italy, the establishment of the Turks in Gallipoli
threatened its prosperity even if the significance of the event was
not at once understood in Saray.

Few changes occurred in Russia during Janibeg's reign. When all
the Russian princes appeared at his court in the beginning of his
reign, he granted the patent on the Grand Duchy of Vladimir to
Prince Simeon of Moscow, the eldest son of Ivan I who had died in

257. Poliak, "Caractère colonial," pp. 231–232.
258. The date as established by G. Georgiades Arnakis, "Captivity of Gregory Palamas
by the Turks and Related Documents as Historical Sources," *Speculum, 26* (1951), 111.

1341. However, the independence from Moscow of the principalities of Tver, Suzdal, and Riazan was confirmed. More than that, the princes of Riazan and Suzdal were granted the title of grand duke within their respective dominions, and within a few years the prince of Tver was given the same privilege.[259] Thus Russia was divided into several grand duchies; that of Vladimir was now practically, although not nominally, merged with the principality of Moscow. It still carried special prestige as the original grand duchy; and, as we know, beginning with Ivan I the grand dukes of Vladimir and Moscow added the words "and of all Russia" (*vseia Rusi*) to their title. Grand Duke Simeon was known as "the Haughty" (*Gordyi*). Haughty he may have been toward other Russian princes, but outwardly he was as subservient to the khan as his father used to be, and like his father he made frequent journeys to the Horde. In 1349 a situation potentially dangerous to the interests of Moscow developed: Grand Duke Olgerd (Algirdas) of Lithuania (Gedymin's son and successor) sent his brother Koriat to warn the khan of the imminent danger to the interests of both the Golden Horde and Lithuania in the growth of the Moscow state. Olgerd proposed to the khan a Mongol-Lithuanian alliance against Moscow. As soon as Simeon was informed of Koriat's arrival at the khan's headquarters, he hastened there himself and protested against Olgerd's plans. Janibeg was satisfied of Simeon's loyalty and not only declined the Lithuanian alliance but extradited Koriat to Simeon. Only after protracted negotiations, in the course of which Olgerd professed his friendly disposition toward Simeon, did the latter agree to release Koriat.[260] While Olgerd's attention was thus turned to the east, Casimir of Poland launched a new campaign against Galicia and Volynia (1349). Olgerd now had to ask Mongol aid against the Poles, who were ousted from Volynia in 1352. Galicia, however, was kept by Casimir.[261]

Simeon died of the plague in 1353 and was succeeded by his younger brother Ivan II, "the Meek" (*Krotkii*), who received the grand ducal patent without any difficulty. Leading boyars played a prominent role in the Moscow government during his reign (1353–59). Outstanding among them at that time was the Pleshcheev family. Its ancestor, Fedor Biakont, originally of Chernigov, had moved to

259. Nasonov, pp. 103–104.
260. Spuler, pp. 105–106.
261. Hrushevsky, *4*, 28–36; Paszkiewicz, *Polityka ruska*, pp. 88–135.

Moscow in the late 13th century. Since Metropolitan Theognost (Peter's successor) died of the plague at the same time as Grand Duke Simeon the metropolitan's see became vacant. With Ivan II's approval, the Moscow boyars decided to send to the patriarch of Constantinople, as Russia's candidate for the see, a member of the Pleshcheev family—Bishop Alexei of Vladimir, son of Fedor Biakont.

The prince and the boyars of Tver did not approve of Alexei's candidacy and supported another candidate, Roman, whom Grand Duke Olgerd of Lithuania sent to Constantinople with his recommendations. The patriarch solved the dilemma by appointing both men: Alexei to be metropolitan "of Kiev" (that is, actually of Moscow) and Roman metropolitan of Lithuania. Thus the Russian diocese was split in two, but the division this time proved only temporary.[262] An enlightened prelate and a deeply religious man, Metropolitan Alexei was also an outstanding statesman. Being a member of the Pleshcheev family he enjoyed considerable prestige with both the grand duke and the boyars and became the leading man in the Moscow government during the reign of Ivan II and the initial years of the reign of Ivan's son and successor, Dmitri.[263] He was also much respected at the khan's court, especially by Khatun Taydula whom he cured of an eye disease in 1357.

The same year an incident occurred in Moscow which indicates a conflict between the boyars and the commoners. On February 3, 1357 the body of the Moscow chiliarch (*tysiatsky*), Alexei Petrovich Khvost, was found on Moscow's main square with every evidence of his having been murdered.[264] It will be recalled that since the Kievan period the chiliarch, who commanded the city militia (*tysiacha*), occupied a peculiar position in the princely administration. Although chosen by the prince from among the leading boyars, he was considered the people's mouthpiece.[265] In view of this, it is understandable that the Moscow populace held the boyars responsible for Alexei Petrovich's death. Riots started in the city, and the leading boyars fled to Riazan. Most of them returned the following year, and one of these, Vasili Veliaminov, was appointed chiliarch.[266] His father, whose name was also Vasili, had served as chiliarch under Ivan I.

262. Makari, *4*, 41–47; Golubinsky, *2*, 179, 878.
263. On Metropolitan Alexei see Makari, *4*, 33–63; Golubinsky, *2*.
264. Soloviev, *3*, 327.
265. *Kievan Russia*, pp. 188–189.
266. Soloviev, *3*, 327.

Janibeg in 1356 had launched a campaign against the decaying
state of the il-khans, and became the first ruler of the Golden Horde
to conquer Azerbaijan; but on his way back from Tabriz to Saray
he died. According to Iskander's Anonym he was murdered by order
of his son Berdibeg (1357).[267]

7. STATE AND SOCIETY IN THE GOLDEN HORDE

During the first century of its existence the Golden Horde was an
ulus of the Great Mongol Empire. Descendants of Chingis-Khan
ruled the Golden Horde even after the downfall of the empire, and
when the Horde was dismembered they ruled the states which succeeded it. Mongol aristocracy was the top stratum of society in the
Golden Horde. Hence the government of the Horde was naturally
based mainly on the principles that guided the government of the empire as a whole. The Great Yasa of Chingis-Khan constituted its
legal foundation. At the same time, however, as in other parts of
the empire, the application of the general principles of Mongol
government in the Golden Horde was conditioned by the geography,
ethnic milieu, and spiritual atmosphere of the area.

Racially the Mongols were but a small minority of Golden Horde
society. The bulk of the Horde consisted of Turks. From the religious angle, the spread of Islam among both the Mongols and Turks
of the Horde was a factor of paramount importance. Gradually
Moslem institutions gained ground alongside of Mongol institutions.

Most of the Mongols of the Golden Horde were descendants of
the 4,000 troops assigned to Juchi by Chingis-Khan; they belonged
to the tribes of Khushin, Kyiat, Kynkyt, and Sayjut.[268] In addition,
there were the Mangkyts, but these as we know kept apart from the
others and, from the time of Nogay were organized as a separate
horde. As has been mentioned, the Turks were accepted as full-
fledged members of steppe society. In the western part of the Golden
Horde (west of the Volga) the Turkish element was represented
mostly by the Kypchaks (Cumans), but there were also remnants of
the Khazars and the Patzinaks. East of the middle course of the Volga,
in the Kama River basin, lived remnants of the Bulgars and the half-
Turkicized Ugrians (Bashkirs). East of the lower Volga the Mangkyts (Nogays) and other Mongol clans ruled over a number of

267. Tiesenhausen, 2, 128–129.
268. ZO, p. 100.

Turkish tribes, such as the Kypchaks and the Oguzes, most of them mixed with Iranian aborigines. The numerical preponderance of the Turks made it natural that the Mongols should be gradually Turkicized, and the Mongol language, even among the ruling classes, gave way to Turkish. Diplomatic correspondence with foreign states (like Egypt) was kept in Mongol, but most of the late 14th and 15th century documents of internal administration that we know of are in Turkish (basically Chagatay Turkish). Of nonofficial texts, a manuscript of an early 14th-century Mongol poem (written on birch bark) has recently been discovered.[269] On a lower political level than the Turks were the Russians, the Alans, and the Circassians, with their assigned quarters in the city of Saray. Tribes of Finno–Ugrian extraction like the Cheremisians, the Mordvinians, and the Meshcherians lived in the lower Oka basin, and numbers of Italians and Greeks in the Crimea and the Azov area.

Economically the Golden Horde represented a symbiosis of nomads and settled populations. The steppes of South Russia and of the north Caucasus provided the Mongols and Turks with vast grazing grounds for their herds of horses and cattle. On the other hand, some sections of the area, on the periphery of the steppes, were also used for raising crops. The Bulgar country in the middle Volga-Kama region was also fertile, with a highly developed agriculture; and, of course, West Russia (Ukraine) and the southern principalities of Central and East Russia, especially Riazan, produced grain in abundance. Saray and other large cities of the Golden Horde, with their highly developed crafts and industries and their importance as trading centers, served as contact points between nomadism and settled civilization. Both the khan and the princes lived part of the year in the cities and followed their herds during the other part. Most of them also acquired landed estates. A considerable portion of the population of the cities stayed there permanently, so that an urban class was created, consisting of various ethnic, social, and religious elements. Both Moslems and Christians had their mosques and churches in every important town. The cities played a role of primary importance in the development of the Golden Horde's foreign trade. The complex economic organism of the Horde was oriented to international commerce, and from that the khans and the grandees derived a good proportion of their income.

269. N. Poppe, "Zolotoordynskaia rukopis' na bereste," *Sovetskoe Vostokovedenie,* 2 (1941), 81–134; cf. *ZO,* p. 175.

As we know, the Golden Horde was ruled by the Juchid branch of the house of Chingis. Legally, until the downfall of the Mongol Empire the khan of the Golden Horde was a vassal of the great khan, and he was also, in a sense, a shareholder in the imperial concern, since he owned apanages in other uluses. The khan was elected by the assembly of Juchid princes, the regional kuriltay. The ceremonial of installing the new khan followed the pattern for the enthronement of the great khans. According to Johann Schiltberger, the German traveler who visited the Golden Horde in the early 15th century, "when they choose a king, they take him and seat him on white felt, and raise him in it three times. Then they lift him up and carry him round the tent, and seat him on a throne, and put a golden sword in his hand. Then he must be sworn as is the custom." [270] The ritual of carrying the new khan in the felt was known in Turkish as *khan kutermiak*.[271]

Besides functioning as electorates in the interregnum periods, the kuriltay met regularly with the khan to discuss all important matters of internal and foreign policy. Moreover the princely members of the kuriltay occupied most of the important positions in the army and administration. Eventually they became known as *oglan* (a Turkish term). As in other Mongol states, women belonging to the ruling clan—the khatuns—played an active role in political life. No less important was the fact that each member of the ruling house, including the khatuns, received an apanage which was independent of the regular state administration. Thus we may say that the Juchids ruled the Golden Horde in two ways: as sovereigns and as feudal lords.

Below the princes stood what we may call the Mongol and Turkish grandees: staff officers of the army, known originally as noyans (a Mongol term) and later on as begs (a Turkish term); and the high officials of the administration and the judiciary. Many of these were granted land estates of feudal type which were known as *soyurghal*.[272] In many cases the khan issued a charter of immunity to the grantee, exempting him and the people attached to the estate from taxes and services to the state. The holder of such an estate was known as tarkhan. Usually this term was applied to smaller land-

270. Schiltberger, p. 48.

271. Veselovsky, p. 51. In Osmanli Turkish this verb reads *gütürmek*. See Redhouse, p. 1582.

272. On the soyurghal see V. Minorsky, "A Soyurghal of Qasim b. Jahangir Aq-qoyunlu," *BSOAS*, 9 (1939), 927–960; *ZO*, pp. 136–137.

owners, since the grandees were supposed to enjoy immunity in any case. As a result of such policies, by the mid-15th century what may be called the "feudal" sector in the Golden Horde had expanded considerably at the expense of the "state" sector. This process contributed greatly to the downfall of the Horde.

The organization of the army of the Golden Horde was of the basic Mongol type established by Chingis-Khan, with its decimal division. The army units were grouped in two main formations: the right wing or western group and the left wing or eastern group. The center presumably consisted of the khan's guardsmen under his personal command. To each major division of the army a quartermaster general (*bukaul*) was attached.[273] As in the other parts of the Mongol Empire, the army formed the backbone of the khan's administration, each army unit being in charge of a particular district or section of the Horde. From this point of view we may say that, for administrative purposes, the Golden Horde was divided into the myriads, thousands, hundreds, and units of ten. The captain of each unit was responsible for order and discipline in his district. Collectively, the captains of the army units represented the provincial administration of the Golden Horde. Khan Timur-Kutlugh's immunity charter (yarlyk) of 800 A.H. (A.D. 1397–1398) issued to the Crimean tarkhan Mehmet was addressed "to the oglans of the right and the left wings; to the honorable commanders of the myriads; and to the captains of the thousands, of the hundreds, and of units of ten." [274]

For collection of taxes and other purposes a number of civil officials assisted the military administration. In Timur-Kutlugh's yarlyk tax collectors, couriers, attendants of post-horse stations, boatmen, officials in charge of bridges, and market police are mentioned. An important official was the state revenue inspector, known as the *daruga* (also spelt *doroga* in Russian chronicles). The basic meaning of the root of this Mongol word is "to press," in the sense of "to

---

273. *ZO*, p. 127. The term "bukaul" could also denote an official of lesser importance. See Radlov, p. 21; Kurat, pp. 64–65, 70–71.

274. Radlov, p. 20. In his Russian translation of the yarlyk Radlov renders the words *tümen atku bashlygh* (in the original Turkish text) as "innumerable good captains" (and on p. 22, "having ten thousand good captains"), taking the word *tümen* for a numeral. There is no doubt, however, that tümen is used here in the sense of the "myriad" as a military and administrative unit (division; in Russian, *t'ma*). Obviously the khan addresses himself here to the captains of the t'my (temniki). See, for comparison, Mengli-Geray's yarlyk, Kurat, pp. 64–65, lines 5–6.

stamp" or "to seal." [275] The term could be rendered in English as "keeper of the seal" or "sealer." The function of the daruga was to supervise the collection of taxes and to certify the amount collected.

The whole system of administration and taxation was controlled by central boards (divans). In each of these the business was actually conducted by the secretary (*bitikchi*). The chief bitikchi was in charge of the khan's chancery. Occasionally the khan intrusted the general supervision of internal administration to a special official who was called "vizier" in Arabic and Persian sources bearing on the Golden Horde.[276] Whether this was actually his title in the Golden Horde is not known. Such officials of the khan's court as the master of the table, the cup bearer, the falconers, the panther keepers, the hunters also had important roles.

The judiciary consisted of a Supreme Court and district courts. In the competence of the former were the most important cases involving state interests. It will be recalled that a number of Russian princes were tried in this tribunal. The judges of the district courts were known as *yarguchi* (*dzarguji*).[277] According to Ibn-Batuta each court consisted of eight such judges under the chairmanship of the chief justice (*amir yargu*). He was appointed by a special patent of the khan. In the 14th century the Moslem judge (*kazi*), assisted by jurists and scribes, also was present at the sessions of the district court. All matters that came under Islamic law (*Shari'a*) were referred to him.[278]

In view of the important role of commerce in the economy of the Golden Horde it was natural that the merchants, and especially those dealing with foreign markets, should be regarded with great respect by the khans and the grandees. While not officially connected with the government, the leading merchants could more often than not influence the direction of both internal affairs and foreign relations. In fact, the Moslem merchants represented an international corporation controlling the markets of Central Asia, Iran, and South Russia. As individuals, they pledged allegiance to one or another ruler according to the conjecture of the day. Collectively, they favored peace and stability in all the countries with which they had to deal. Many

275. See Pelliot, p. 72, n. 1.
276. *ZO*, pp. 128–129.
277. On this term see Smirnov, *Krymskoe Khanstvo*, pp. 43–44.
278. *ZO*, pp. 185–186.

a khan depended on the merchants financially since they commanded huge capital and were in a position to lend money to any khan whose treasury was short of funds. The merchants were also willing to farm taxes whenever requested and were useful to the khans in many other ways.

The bulk of the urban population consisted of craftsmen and workers of various sorts. In the early formative period of the Golden Horde skilled artisans captured in conquered countries became the khan's bondsmen. A quota of these was sent to the great khan in Karakorum. The majority were to serve the khan of the Golden Horde and were settled in Saray and in other cities. Most of them hailed from Khoresm or from Russia. Later on, free craftsmen too must have flocked to the industrial centers of the Golden Horde, chiefly to Saray. In Tokhtamysh' yarlyk of 1382 issued to Hoja-Beg "artisan elders" are mentioned.[279] From this it may be inferred that the artisans were organized in guilds, each craft very likely forming its own guild. Each craft had been assigned a special section of the city for its shops. According to the evidence of archeological research, there were smithies in Saray, cutlery shops, armories, factories for agricultural tools and for bronze and copper vessels.[280] A great number of workers were occupied in tanning and weaving. The weavers produced mainly woolen fabrics, although some cloth was also woven of raw cotton imported from Central Asia. A fine grade of pottery was also manufactured in Saray, mainly after the Khoresmian patterns.

Not much is known of the position of the peasants in the agricultural regions of the Golden Horde. They are mentioned in Timur-Kutlugh's yarlyk as *sabanchi* (plowmen) and *urtakchi*. The latter were sharecroppers.[281] The peasants must have been overburdened with state taxes and in some cases may have profited when assigned to an estate granted immunity. But then, no doubt, they would become subject to various manorial duties. Some of the peasants may have been freedmen, descendants of war prisoners settled on land. It was usual to turn war prisoners into slaves. Skilled artisans among them, as has been mentioned, were requisitioned by the khan. With

279. *Ibid.*, p. 153.
280. *Ibid.*, pp. 145–146; A. Iakubovsky, "K voprosu o proiskhozhdenii remeslennoi promyshlennosti Saraia Berke," *GA, 8,* Fasc. 2–3 (1931). See Sources, Archeology.
281. Radlov, p. 21. On the urtakchi see also Gordlevsky, p. 65.

others their captors could do what they pleased, employ them in their households or sell them. For Italian as well as Moslem merchants trade in slaves was a lucrative business.

8. The Mongol Administration in Russia

I

The objective of the Mongol administration in the conquered countries was twofold: to obtain recruits for the army and collect taxes for the upkeep of the state and the imperial family. The purpose of Mongol policies in Russia did not differ from that in the other lands subject to the khan's control.

The methods of application of the policies varied in different parts of Russia. In southwest Russia (Ukraine)—the Pereiaslav land, the Kievan land, and Podolia—the Mongols removed the Russian princely administration altogether, replacing it by their own direct control. In Galicia, Volynia, Smolensk, the Chernigov-Severian land, as well as in East Russia, the Mongols established their own administration alongside that of the Russian princes. Novgorod was exempt, after 1260, from the presence of Mongol agents but not from the obligation to pay taxes. Even in those Russian lands where the princes remained in power as the khan's vassals the Mongols reserved the right to place certain regions and groups of the population under their direct control. It was natural enough that in his testament Grand Duke Ivan I presupposed the possibility that some of the districts (volosti) of his principality would be taken over by the Mongols, and made tentative arrangements for this eventuality.[282] Some Russian lands were also granted in apanage to members of the Chingisid family. Thus the town of Tula, with the adjacent district, was assigned to Great Khatun Taydula.

In most of Russia, however, the Mongols allowed the native princes to continue to rule their respective principalities under the authority of the khan of the Golden Horde and the suzerainty of the great khan of Mongolia and China. As we know, each Russian prince had to receive a patent on his throne from the khan. The khan's envoy (*elchi*) then solemnly installed him. The khan could revoke the princely patent at any time if he had reason to doubt the prince's loyalty. In cases of open opposition on the part of the prince or of the people, as well as in controversies between the princes, the khan

282. *DDG*, p. 8.

sent an envoy extraordinary to Russia at the head of the necessary military force. From the time of Uzbeg on, the khan appointed a resident commissioner at the capital of each important Russian principality.

Even while the Russian princes remained in power, as the khan's vassals their administrative authority was limited, since the khans appointed their own officials to draft recruits and collect taxes. In each of the lands they conquered the Mongols hastened to ascertain the capacity to pay, by means of a census of population. The Mongol censuses in Russia were ordered by the great khan in concurrence with the khan of the Golden Horde. The first census in West Russia took place as early as 1245; the Kievan land, Podolia, and probably the Pereiaslav and Chernigovan lands were then assessed. After Burunday's punitive expedition of 1260 the census took place in Galicia and Volynia. There were two general censuses in East and North Russia. In 1258–59 the Grand Duchy of Vladimir and the Novgorod land were counted. In 1274–75 there was another census in East Russia as well as in Smolensk. After that the Mongols made no more general census, using the data of the previous ones as the basis for assessment.

In accordance with the basic principles of Mongol policy, the Mongol census (called *chislo,* "number," in Russian) had two main purposes: to establish the number of recruits to be drafted and to determine the total of taxpayers. Consequently the term "chislo" had two connotations: that of quota of recruits to be drafted [283] and that of census of population for the purpose of taxation. It is in the light of this double connotation that we should approach the problem of the numerical divisions established by the Mongols in Russia. These were identical with the basic divisions of the army and administration throughout the Mongol Empire, as discussed above.[284] The population of Russia, except for the Novgorod area and the people living on the church estates (not taxed), was divided into myriads, thousands, hundreds, and units of ten. This division was also used for the purpose of provincial administration; thus, a "thousand" denoted not only the group of people living in a certain region but the region itself. In other words, each numerical division constituted a military-financial district, a territorial unit from which a definite quota of recruits and a definite amount of taxes were re-

283. Veselovsky, p. 33, n. 1.
284. See above, sec. 7, p. 211, and Chapter 2, sec. 8, p. 127.

quired. As in Mongolia itself, the quota of soldiers which the district had to supply must have been at the basis of each numerical division. Thus a *desiatok* had to supply ten soldiers; the hundred supplied one hundred soldiers, and so on.[285]

The ratio of soldiers to the total population of the district was much lower in Russia than in Mongolia. As has been said, in Mongolia the army constituted approximately one-tenth of the total population (both male and female). At their first onslaught on Russia in 1237, the Mongols demanded a tithe "of everything," including men.[286] Thus the contingent of soldiers demanded by the Mongols from Russia was one-tenth (10 per cent) of the male population, or roughly speaking one-twentieth (5 per cent) of the total population.

On this basis, as regards the numerical divisions established in Russia by the Mongols, the population of the district known as a desiatok may be estimated at 200 (male and female) and that of a t'ma or myriad at 200,000. The number of households belonging to each desiatok must have varied according to local conditions and social habits. According to Miliukov, in 17th-century Russia the average household·consisted of 7 persons.[287] The typical household or "greater family" among the peasants in Central Russia in the 19th century comprised from 15 to 20 members.[288] If we assume that the average Russian household during the Mongol period consisted of 10 persons, the desiatok would comprise about 20 families; if we allow 20 persons to the household (which seems more likely for that period), 10 families would constitute a desiatok.

Actually the population of the numerical divisions must have varied in different parts of Russia. No general censuses were taken after the 1270's. With the subsequent fluctuations the actual population of a division must have been much lower than originally registered in some districts and substantially higher in others. Eventually, the t'ma became a unit of assessment rather than of population. On the lower level, the hundred became the basic unit in the system of assessment and taxation; and the hundreder (*sotnik*) was responsible for current matters of local taxation. The over-all tax

285. In my article in *Speculum, 26* (1951) I erroneously stated that the numerical value of each military district corresponded to the number of registered taxpayers, so that each t'ma contained 10,000 taxpayers; see Vernadsky, "Royal Serfs," p. 262. As I see it now, the 10,000 refers to the quota of soldiers each t'ma was to raise.

286. Novgorod, p. 286.

287. To be more exact, 6.9; see P. Smirnov, "Dvizhenie naseleniia moskovskogo gosudarstva" in M. Dovnar-Zapolsky, *Russkaia istoriia v ocherkakh i statiakh, 2* (Moscow, around 1910), 68.

288. See *Kievan Russia,* p. 133.

income from Russia (excluding the larger cities) was estimated according to the number of t'my (plural of t'ma), which was fixed by the original general censuses and considered permanent. The larger cities were subject to special taxes and therefore not included in the t'my system.

A list of the t'my of West Russia appears in the yarlyk of the Crimean khan Mengli-Geray issued to King Sigismund I of Poland (1507).[289] In this document Mengli-Geray confirms the earlier yarlyk of his father Haji-Geray addressed to Grand Duke Vitovt of Lithuania (around 1428). Having been rescued by Vitovt from the persecution of the rival khans, Haji-Geray "granted" to Vitovt all the former possessions of the khans of the Golden Horde in West Russia. Actually, most of them had been occupied by the Lithuanian grand dukes for several decades. In spite of this, they were still listed in the records of the Golden Horde as so many t'my, and now Mengli-Geray enumerated them all. The same list, with some variations, was repeated in King Sigismund's letter to the Crimean khan Sahib-Geray (1540).[290]

From these documents we know of the existence of t'my named after the following cities and districts: 1. Kiev; 2. Vladimir-in-Volynia; 3. Lutsk; 4. Sokal; 5. Podolia; [291] 6. Kamenets (in Podolia); 7. Braslav (in Podolia); 8. Chernigov; 9. Kursk; 10. "The Egolday t'ma" (south of the Kursk region); [292] 11. Liubutsk (on the Oka River); [293] 12. Okhura; [294] 13. Smolensk; 14. Polotsk; [295] 15–16. Riazan (at least two t'my; Riazan and Pronsk). To this list, for the first century of Mongol rule, Galicia (lost to Poland in 1349) should be added, with probably three t'my; 17. Galich; 18. Lvov; 19. Sanok. As for East Russia, it is known that in 1360 the Grand

---

289. *AZR, 1*, No. 6, 4–5. Printed from a transcript preserved in the archives of the Grand Duchy of Lithuania (*Litovskaia metrika*).

290. *AZR, 1*, No. 200, 363 (from the Litovskaia metrika).

291. Presumably, the Podolia t'ma centered around Vinnitsa.

292. On Egolday see below, Chapter 4, sec. 5, p. 301. On the Egolday t'ma see Kuczyński, pp. 78–80. This t'ma was situated in the northeastern part of the former principality of Pereiaslav. It probably replaced the original Pereiaslav t'ma.

293. Mentioned only in Sigismund's letter.

294. Mentioned only in Sigismund's letter. The name Okhura may be compared to Khukhra, a village near Akhtyrka (about 50 miles west of present-day Kharkov). The name Khukhra occurs first in the documents of the early 18th century; see D. I. Bagalei, *Ocherki iz istorii kolonizatsii stepnoi okrainy moskovskogo gosudarstva* (Moscow, 1887), p. 471.

295. It should be mentioned that Polotsk never was subject to the Mongol rule. This t'ma must have actually centered around Vitebsk, which was originally a part of the principality of Polotsk.

Duchy of Vladimir comprised 15 t'my; [296] and under Tokhtamysh 17 t'my.[297] This figure did not include the t'my of Riazan, Nizhni Novgorod, and Tver. As we have just seen, the Grand Duchy of Riazan paid for at least two t'my. The Grand Duchy of Nizhni

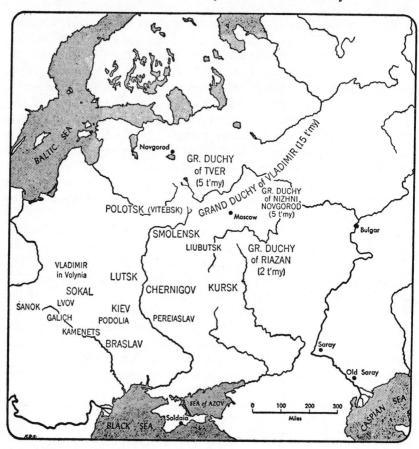

2. Taxation districts (t'my) in Russia under the Mongols

Novgorod was counted as five t'my; [298] and that of Tver must also have consisted of five.[299]

296. Rog., col. 68; cf. Nasonov, p. 98.

297. See the so-called Chronograph of 1512, *PSRL, 22*, 423; cf. Nasonov, p. 98.

298. *Piatetem*, i.e. *piat' tem*, "five t'my," *DDG*, p. 119.

299. Tver was the strongest Russian principality except for Moscow and could not have comprised fewer t'my than Nizhni Novgorod.

Thus we arrive at 27 t'my for East Russia prior to Tokhtamysh (Grand Duchy of Vladimir—15 original t'my; Riazan two; Nizhni Novgorod and Tver five each). Including the 16 t'my of west Russia,[300] the total would be 43. Allowing the average figure of 200,000 people per t'ma, the total population of all the Russian t'my as of 1275 would be 8,600,000. To this must be added the population of the regions not included in the t'my network: (1) the Russian areas in the Grand Duchy of Lithuania never subjected to the Mongols, like Black Russia; (2) Novgorod and Pskov; and (3) Tula and other apanages of the Chingisids. Besides, a number of Russians lived at that time in Saray and in Moldavia. And we must not forget the population of the larger Russian cities (not included in the t'my system), as well as that of the church estates (not subject to taxes). The grand total may be tentatively set at around 10,000,000 people.

II

An elaborate network of Mongol administrative agents was appointed in each t'ma to enforce the recruiting and tax collecting. These agents were not subordinated to the Russian princes in any way and were responsible only to the khan's government. When the numerical districts were being set up in Russia, regular Mongol army commanders seem to have been put at the head of each t'ma and each thousand. Each of these commanders had, as his associate, a tax inspector (daruga) of corresponding rank.[301] Later on, the daruga assumed full responsibility for the district. In Taydula's rescript to Metropolitan Theognost (based on Janibeg's yarlyk), three categories of darugas are mentioned: those of the volost', of the town, and of the village. Their names follow mention of "the ulus princes." The old Russian translation in this place, as in some others, is not quite clear, and it is possible that by princes darugas of the highest rank are meant. In the terminology of the old Russian translation of the khans' yarlyks, ulus seems to correspond to the t'ma; volost' to the thousand; town (gorod) to the hundred; [302] and village (selo), to the unit of ten. Of the existence of darugas of the highest rank we also know from the Russian chronicles. Thus it may

300. Not counting the Okhura t'ma, of which nothing is known for the earlier period of Mongol domination.

301. See the yarlyks issued to the Russian clergy: Grigoriev, *Yarlyki*, p. 112; Priselkov, *Yarlyki*, p. 92. In Mangu-Temir's yarlyk the tax inspector is called baskak instead of daruga: Grigoriev, p. 124; Priselkov, p. 96.

302. Apparently *gorod* here means "a small town."

be concluded that there was a daruga at the head of every numerical district at each level.

In the chronicles the darugas serving in Russia are called baskaks. This is a Turkish term whose meaning corresponds exactly to the Mongol daruga.[303] The tax inspector responsible for the whole Grand Duchy of Vladimir was known as "the great baskak" (*veliki baskak*).[304] Each baskak had a small group of Mongol and Turkish soldiers at his disposal around which he had to build up a mobile detachment to preserve order and discipline in his district. It may be mentioned in this connection that while most of the Russian soldiers recruited were periodically sent to the Golden Horde and China, a quota was retained for local needs. Each baskak detachment was assigned permanent quarters which eventually became a thriving settlement. Traces of such settlements have remained in Russian toponymics. A number of towns and villages bearing such names as Baskaki and Baskakovo are located in various regions of Russia on the territories of the former t'my.[305] When the baskak troops proved unable to cope with an emergency, such as riots of the population, the Russian princes were bound to help the baskaks, using the troops at their disposal.

It will be recalled that in the reign of Berke taxes in Russia were farmed to Moslem merchants. This system caused much suffering and later was abandoned; after that the number of tax officials was substantially increased. In the khans' yarlyks to the Russian clergy three categories or field revenue agents are mentioned: clerks (*pistsy;* Turkish, *bitikchi*); rural tax collectors (*danshchiki*); and city tax and customs duties collectors (*tamozhniki*).

There were two main categories of taxes: (1) direct taxes on the population of the rural districts; and (2) city taxes. The main direct tax was called the tribute (*dan'*). Basically it was a tithe. Originally, as we know, the Mongols demanded a tithe "of everything." In their first order men and horses were mentioned specifically (each color of horse separately). Undoubtedly cattle and agricultural products were also liable to the tithe. On one occasion, in Novgorod in 1259, the Mongols collected a tax called *tuska* which must have been heavier than the usual one, since there were bitter complaints against it. "And there was a great commotion in Novgorod," says the

---

303. Pelliot, pp. 72–73.
304. Nasonov, p. 20.
305. See Ikonnikov, 2, 863–864; and in more detail Nasonov, pp. 18–21.

chronicler, "as the damned Tatars collected the tuska and did much harm to the people in the rural districts." [306] It was apparently similar to the tax which is called *tzgu* in the Armenian chronicle of Grigor of Akanc.[307] The term "tuska" has been likened to the Turkish word *tuzghu* which is said to mean "food presented to visiting rulers or envoys." [308] On the other hand, in a Uigur document of the mid-14th century a tax called *tüshük* is mentioned, and the name may be connected with the Uigur *tüsh*, "interest" or "profit." [309] The Russian form "tuska" might have derived from either tüshük or tuzghu. In any case the tuska was an extra tax, and the indignation of the Novgorodians at this additional collection is quite understandable. The tax was introduced by the Mongols as a punitive measure after a near-revolution in Novgorod. It was never repeated, and the tithe remained the basis of the tribute. Eventually, the amount of the tithe was tabulated and the dan' was paid in silver instead of in kind. In Novgorod, in the 14th and the 15th centuries, the collection of the tax corresponding to the dan' was known as the Black Collection (*chornyi bor*). Originally it must have been paid in skins of black martens. Such payments were called "black" in contrast to payments in "white" silver. In Vasili II's reign, however, the Black Collection was assessed in silver grivnas.[310]

Besides the dan' there were a number of other direct taxes. The *popluzhnoe* (called *posokha* in North Russia) was a tax on tilled land. *Plug* (of which popluzhnoe is a derivative) means "plow"; it is a term borrowed into Russian from the German; the large heavy plow was so called in Russia. *Sokha* (from which posokha derives) is the North Russian word for "light plow." Thus the term "popluzhnoe" and "posokha" may be translated as "plow money." It may be added in this connection that the basic Slavic word for "plow" is *ralo;* it was used chiefly in South Russia. In fact, in some southern regions "ralo" was a unit of taxation in the Kievan period.[311] The yam was a special tax for the upkeep of post-horse stations. Another tax mentioned in the khan's yarlyks is *voina* ("war tax" or "soldiers'

306. Novgorod, p. 310.

307. Akanc, p. 301.

308. See S. L. Volin's explanation of the term, *Tiesenhausen, 2,* 304; also Cleaves, "Mongolian Names," p. 442.

309. See S. E. Malov's notes in V. Radlov, *Uigurische Sprachdenkmäler,* pp. 77, 300; Vernadsky, "Uigurs," p. 458. In Persian *tush* means "sustenance," "nutriment," "strength"; *tusha* means "a traveler's provision." See Redhouse, p. 610.

310. *AAE, 1,* 24.

311. *Kievan Russia,* pp. 190–191.

tax"); [312] this presumably was collected in the years when no recruits were drafted. Still another tax is called *poshlina* ("traditional
duty") in the yarlyks.[313] Both I. Berezin and B. Spuler interpret it,
in terms of the Mongol system of taxation in the Golden Horde and
other parts of the Mongol Empire, as the *kalan*. In a strictly technical sense, the kalan (a Turkish word) was a tax on land; but the
word was used in a wider sense with the connotation of "subjection"
or "servitude." As we shall see,[314] there existed in West Russia in
the Mongol and post-Mongol period a category of royal serfs known
as the *kalanny*. If we admit that "poshlina" corresponded to "kalan,"
we may take it to have been a money payment which replaced the
obligation to work in the capacity of a kalanny. The identity of
"poshlina" with "kalan" has not been definitely established, however.

In addition to the regular taxes, the khans reserved for themselves
the right of imposing an emergency tax whenever they considered it
necessary. This was known as *zapros* (an "extra demand"). It is
mentioned in the yarlyks and occasionally in the chronicles.[315] Besides, whenever the Chingisid princes and the khan's envoys traveled
in Russia, the Russians were expected to make "presents" to them
and provide them with food and their horses with fodder, as well as
to supply horses and carts for their transportation.[316]

The basic city tax was called tamga. In both Mongol and Turkish
the term "tamga" meant "emblem," specifically a clan emblem, and
hence "brand" to designate horses and other kinds of property as
belonging to the clan. As an emblem of administration, tamga denoted the design on a seal or a stamp, and then the stamp itself,
especially the stamp on goods taxed. In Persia under Hulagu and his
successors the tamga was a capital levy amounting to about 0.4
per cent of the capital: one dinar out of 240 dinars was to be paid
annually by the capitalists and merchants from their respective
capital.[317] The tamga was paid in gold or at least computed in gold.
The richest merchants (in Russian, *gosti*) were assessed individually; those of medium wealth were organized in associations which
were assessed as units. Eventually the tamga took the form of a tax

312. Grigoriev, *Yarlyki,* p. 124; Priselkov, *Yarlyki,* p. 96.
313. Berezin, p. 475; Spuler, p. 335.
314. See below, subsection III, pp. 223, 227.
315. Berezin, p. 477.
316. Grigoriev, *Yarlyki,* p. 124; Priselkov, *Yarlyki,* pp. 96–97.
317. Minorsky, "Nasir al-Din," pp. 773, 781.

on the turnover of goods and was collected as customs duties. In modern Russian *tamozhnia,* a derivative of tamga, means "custom-house." A local duty on goods, the *myt,* was also collected.[318]

In Persia of the il-khans there was a special tax on "what accrues from factories, artisans, merchants associate," as well as an additional tax on the issue of licenses in some crafts.[319] Russian crafts were apparently subject to similar taxation. It is known that in Novgorod, in 1258, all the houses in the city were counted for the purpose of collecting city taxes. The chronicler comments that the boyars arranged it so that the heaviest burden fell upon the poor.[320]

III

We may now turn our attention to those regions and districts which were put under the direct control of the Mongols. The population was organized into communes (units of ten) and groups of communes (hundreds and hordes), each of which elected its own elders: hundreders (*sotniki*) and atamans (*vatamany*).[321] *Vataman* (which is the singular form; in modern Russian, *ataman;* in Ukranian, *otaman*) is a word of Iranian origin [322] meaning "chief" (of a company).

Similar groups were established in those districts within the Russian principalities which were exempt from the jurisdiction of the Russian princes and were put under the khan's direct authority. Such groups were known in West Russia as *liudi sotnye* (hundred-men); *ordyntsy* (horde men); and *liudi kalannye* (men subject to kalan services). In East Russia the apparently similar categories were called number men (*liudi chislennye* or *chisliaki,* from *chislo,* number; that is men belonging to the numerical divisions); *ordyntsy;* and *deliui* (men subject to special services).[323] Evidence on the East Russian groups of these types is scant. Information on West Russia within the boundaries of the Grand Duchy of Lithuania is more varied but not always clear. It is only for the corresponding groups

318. On the *myt* see *Kievan Russia,* p. 191.

319. Minorsky, "Nasir al-Din," p. 775.

320. Novgorod, p. 310.

321. N. Molchanovsky, *Ocherk izvestii o Podolskoi zemle* (Kiev, 1885), pp. 156–157.

322. Vataman, leader of a vataga (company), to be derived from the Ossetian *fätäg* (leader). Vasmer, pp. 31, 172, derives both *vataman (ataman)* and *vataga* from the Turkish, which seems less likely to me.

323. On these social groups see I. A. Linnichenko, *Cherty iz istorii soslovii v iugo-zapadnoi (galitskoi) Rusi xiv–xv vekov* (Moscow, 1894); W. Hejnosz, *Jus ruthenicale* (Lwów, 1928); Z. Wojciechowski, *L'Etat polonais au moyen-age* (Paris, 1949), pp. 206–207; Vernadsky, "Royal Serfs."

in Galicia, within the kingdom of Poland, that we have at our disposal enough documentary evidence to understand the inner group structure and the functions of the hundredmen and the horde men. However, the documents available for this area belong to the post-Mongol period (the late 14th and 15th centuries). While the groups in question still existed at that time, their respective status might have been somewhat modified by the new political conditions.

To start with the hundred men—according to the Galician documents, each member of the hundred was permanently attached to the hundred commune. If he wanted to leave the commune, he had to find a substitute who would assume his duties; this substitute must be approved by the hundred authorities. At the head of the hundred (*sotnia*) was the hundreder (*sotsky*). The hundred was divided into groups of ten (*desiatki*), each headed by the decurion (*desiatsky*). The main duty of the hundredmen was to till land. Under the Polish regime the king's agent (captain, *capitaneus*) residing at the nearest castle had the authority to assign plots of land to the hundredmen. Under the Mongol regime the commune itself, under the supervision of the hundredman, must have been in charge of the distribution of land plots. The hundred owned cattle, assigning oxen and other animals to each member of the commune according to his needs. Under the Polish regime, the produce of the hundred's lands went to the granaries of the nearest royal castle. In the Mongol period the produce must have been used for the needs of the personnel of the baskak units in the adjacent districts and of the soldiers recruited there. In the late 15th century the Galician hundred communes centered around the castle of Sanok. Both hundreds and desiatki are mentioned in a number of documents of the Grand Duchy of Lithuania; but it is not always possible to ascertain which of them belonged to the special category we are now discussing. It seems that, in contrast to Galicia, not all the hundredmen in the Grand Duchy of Lithuania tilled land. Some kept bees; others may have performed duties of other kinds for the nearest grand ducal castle.

The number men or chisliaki in East Russia seem to be a group similar to the Galician hundredmen, and like them are mentioned in our sources only after the termination of the khan's authority over them. We first find them in the will of Grand Duke Ivan I, which was written around 1339. When dividing his possessions among his sons, Ivan instructed them to keep the number men under their joint control.[324] Similar clauses appear in the wills and interprincely treaties of Ivan's successors. Most of them state that the lands on which the chisliaki have been settled shall not be sold. It is obvious that the chisliaki were considered a group subject to the Moscow princely clan as a whole, not to any individual prince. We may say that they were under the authority of the grand ducal crown. Presumably they had been originally under the direct authority of the khan and then the district where they lived was granted by the khan to Grand Duke Ivan I. Since, as we know, the khan had the right to exempt certain districts from the authority of the Russian princes and subordinate them to his own administration, he must surely have had the right to return any of those districts to the Russian administration whenever he pleased to do so. The status of the chisliaki would not change with that, but the produce of their labor would go to the Grand Duchy of Moscow instead of to the khan.

The Galician horde men, like the hundredmen, were organized in communes. The term "horde" (in Mongol, *ordu;* in Russian, *orda*) as we know [325] denoted the camp or headquarters of the khan or any other members of the imperial family, as well as that of the captain of a large military unit. The horde in the present case must have been so called because it had, as a group, to perform services for the ordu of the nearest military commander. In that sense the term covered all the men liable to the special ordu services. In a narrower sense, each village commune of this type was also called a horde. People not belonging to the horde could join it if they assumed all the duties and obligations of an ordynets (member of the horde). Once a man entered the horde he had to serve for life, and his sons also. Thus the bondage of each member to the horde was permanent and hereditary. Two categories of horde officials are mentioned in the sources: the *tivuny* and *vatamany.* The former term (singular, *tivun*) is a survival from the Kievan period (*tiun*) when it was used in the sense of either the prince's steward or the judge.[326] The horde tivun was probably a judge. The vataman was the chief of the local horde unit. Presumably both the tivuny and the vatamany were elected by the people.

In the 15th and the early 16th centuries the Galician ordyntsy

324. *DDG,* pp. 8, 10.
325. On the term "ordu" see above, Chapter 1, sec. 5, p. 30.
326. *Kievan Russia,* p. 189.

lived in five villages of the Galich (Halicz) district and in ten villages of the Lvov district. Their main duties were to furnish wagons with horses for transporting loads at the king's request; to keep a relay of men at the nearest royal castle in order to expedite the moving of the wagons; to carry the king's mail up to a distance of ten miles; to supply four horsemen [327] for any campaign the king or captain of the nearest royal castle and local gentry took part in; and to graze and guard the king's cattle whenever it was specially required.[328]

According to the documents of the Grand Duchy of Lithuania, the duties of the "horde servitors" (*slugi ordynskie*), as the ordyntsy were usually called there, were of various kinds. Some of them had to take care of the dams at the water mills; others had to supply wagons for the king's envoys and messengers; still others were required to accompany, as guards, the envoys' trains to the Tatar khans. These had to appear on horseback in full armor.

The services required from the ordyntsy in Muscovy must have been similar to those performed by the horde men and horde servitors in West Russia. In the Muscovite documents the ordyntsy are first mentioned in the treaty between Grand Duke Dmitri of Moscow and his cousin, Prince Vladimir of Serpukhov, of around 1367.[329] According to this treaty the ordyntsy had to perform the same services as in the time of the respective fathers of the two signatories, a reference to the period of the reign of Ivan II (1353–59). Presumably it was at that time that the district where this group of ordyntsy lived was transferred from the khan's authority to that of the Moscow grand duke. An alternative (and less plausible) explanation would be that the group was organized by Ivan II after the Mongol pattern. In the treaty between Vasili I and Vladimir of Serpukhov (1390) appears a clause forbidding anyone to buy the lands of the ordyntsy, which indicates that they, like the chisliaki, belonged to the Crown.

Let us now consider the status of the kalannye and the deliui. In Galicia in the post-Mongol period the kalannye were hardly distinguishable from the horde men. In the Mongol period they must have constituted a separate group. The two groups kept apart in the Grand Duchy of Lithuania even in the post-Mongol period. In the

327. On that point I have to correct my former statement in "Royal Serfs," pp. 258, 264, n. 24.
328. *Ibid.*, p. 258.
329. *DDG,* p. 20.

Galician documents the kalannye are defined as "unfree men" (*homines illiberi*); also as "royal men" (*homines regales*). The derivative *kalanstvo* (the status of kalanny) denotes servitude. While attached to the royal domains, the kalannye were not slaves. They could sue in courts and serve as witnesses; they could own property. Presumably, they were descendants of the Russians taken prisoner by the Mongols in earlier times whom the khan had turned into serfs to perform various services for him. There is also a possibility that some of those prisoners had been redeemed by the king of Poland or the grand duke of Lithuania and had to work for their redeemers to compensate for the latter's expenses. Later on, in Galicia, most of the kalannye seem to have joined the horde commune. In the Grand Duchy of Lithuania the kalannye, or at least some of them, tilled land on the grand ducal estates.

The origin of the deliui must have been similar to that of the kalannye. In my opinion the term "deliui" derives from the Persian word *del* which means "center." According to the Mongol rules for the distribution of war booty, the largest quota of prisoners of war was reserved for the reigning khan in his capacity as supreme commander of the army. This quota was known in Persian as *delia-i buzurg* (the big center).[330] The khan had the right to deal with these prisoners as he pleased. Probably a number of them became the khan's serfs and were settled on plots of land or had to perform services of some kind. As has been mentioned,[331] the khans of other uluses, such as Jinkshi, for example, also received their quota of Russian captives, and some of these prisoners were brought to China and settled there. In Muscovite sources the deliui appear for the first time, together with the ordyntsy, in the above-mentioned treaty between Grand Duke Dmitri and Prince Vladimir of Serpukhov. Like the ordyntsy, then, the origin of the group may be referred to the reign of Ivan II. A district settled by the deliui may have been granted by the khan at that time to the grand duke of Moscow. However, it is also possible that the group was organized by the Russian grand dukes from Russian prisoners belonging to the *delia* group whom they had redeemed. The redeemed were assigned lands for tilling. The status of the deliui and their lands was similar to that of the ordyntsy.

---

330. Wassaf, p. 98 (Persian text); Hammer-Purgstall's German translation of this term, p. 94 (*Eidam*), is incomprehensible. See also Tiesenhausen, *2*, 82; Veselovsky, p. 16.
331. See above, Chapter 2, sec. 4, p. 88.

IV

The Mongol system of administration functioned as originally set up for about a century. It terminated in Galicia in 1349 when that country was annexed to Poland; by 1363 most of the other West Russian (Ukrainian and Belorussian) lands had recognized the authority of the grand duke of Lithuania and were also lost to the Mongols. Mongol rule over East Russia continued for one more century. Its nature, however, changed after the reform of the tax collection system in the early 14th century. Furthermore, as we shall see,[332] following the period of troubles in the Golden Horde in the 1360's and the 1370's, Mongol control weakened considerably, except for a brief period of restoration under Tokhtamysh (1382–95).

It will be recalled that some of the Russian princes in the late 13th century and all of the Russian grand dukes in the early 14th century had the privilege—and the obligation—of collecting the tribute and other taxes as the khan's commissioners.[333] The baskaks were then withdrawn and the petty tax collectors were now appointed by the Russian princes themselves. Each Russian grand duke, after collecting the money, had to deal with a special Mongol high official (daruga of the highest rank) who certified the accounts and accepted the money for the khan's treasurer. These darugas, however, stayed in Saray and not in Russia. Such a daruga in charge of the Grand Duchy of Moscow (*Moskovskii doroga*) is mentioned in the Simeon Chronicle, A.D. 1432.[334] Presumably, there were also darugas of Tver, Nizhni Novgorod, and Riazan.[335] The total sum each grand duke had to pay the khan was known as *vykhod* (literally, "going out"). This word seems to be the Russian translation of the Arabic term *kharaj*. The original connotation of the Arabic word was "tribute" in a general sense; later on it meant specifically "tax on landed property." [336]

332. See below, Chapter 4, secs. 2 and 3.
333. See above, Chapter 3, sec. 8, p. 199.
334. Simeonov, p. 171; cf. Nasonov, p. 105.
335. Nasonov, p. 105.
336. On the *kharaj* see T. W. Juynbolle, "Kharaj," *EI, 2*, 902–903; E. Mardin, "Harâc," *Islam ansiklopedisi, 4* (1949), 222–225. According to T. W. Juynbolle, the term kharaj derives from the Byzantine *choregia*. On the other hand, kharaj is close to the Arabic verb *kharaja*, "to go out." According to A. Cherbonneau, *Dictionnaire arabe-français* (Paris, 1876), *1*, 207, the causative form of this verb (Form IV), *akharaja*, means both "to cause to go out" (*faire sortir*) and "to cause to pay" (*faire payer, percevoir un impôt*). In a letter to me of December 11, 1948 Nicholas N. Martinovitch

The main part of the vykhod money derived from the dan'. Of the other taxes, the tamga was still collected but the proceeds usually remained in the grand duke's treasury. After 1360 apparently only one khan, Tokhtamysh, was able to collect the tamga.[337] The yam too was not paid to the khans regularly. The plow money was merged with the dan', which was gradually adjusted to the number of units called sokha. According to V. N. Tatishchev, the dan' was assessed on the basis of the sokha units as early as 1273; [338] but this is not corroborated by any of the chronicles and documents known to us. Tatishchev's statement, while essentially sound, may be wrongly dated. According to the chronicles, in 1384 the dan' was collected at the rate of half a ruble per farm (derevnia).[339] This unit must have corresponded to one sokha. In his letter of 1409 to Vasili I Amir Edigei said that according to his information the grand duke of Moscow collected one ruble for every two sokhas.[340] In his will, written in 1423, Grand Duke Vasili I recommended the collection of the dan' "according to the number of men and their paying capacity" (po liudem i po sile).[341] The testament of Vasili II (written in 1461 or early in 1462) contains a more exact formula: "according to the number of sokhas and men" (po sokham i po liudem).[342]

From the permit issued by the city of Novgorod to Grand Duke Vasili II to gather the Black Collection in the Torzhok district (around 1456) we know that one "plug" (heavy plow) was reckoned as two sokhas. The sokha, which we have already encountered used in the sense of "light plow," is defined as "two horses and one side horse." [343] And again, in the Nikon Chronicle: "Three obzhas constitute one sokha. The obzha is the following: one man plowing on one horse. And when a man plows on three horses with the help of two

---

called my attention to the use of the word kharaj as an interjection in the sense of "going!" In any case the translators at the khan's court must have explained the term kharaj to the Russians as coming from the verb kharaja; hence the Russian term vykhod.

337. Tokhtamysh in 1382 collected taxes both in gold and silver. The gold payments must have been the tamga.

338. Tatishchev, 4, 47.

339. Derevnia in old Russian meant originally "a field cleared from wood," hence "a farm." See Preobrazhensky, p. 180; Vasmer, pp. 341–342. In modern Russian derevnia means "a small village."

340. Nikon, 11, 210.

341. DDG, p. 61.

342. Ibid., p. 197.

343. AAE, 1, No. 32, 24.

laborers, this is one sokha." [344] Furthermore, as mentioned in the Novgorodian document, four men without horses also constituted one sokha. The unit of taxation in nonagricultural occupations was a sokha too. According to the same document, the tanning vat is reckoned as one sokha; the fishing seine is one sokha; the large pan or *tsren* used for evaporation in salt works, is reckoned as two sokhas; the smithy is one sokha.

All this refers to the Novgorodian sokha. In Moscow in the 16th and 17th centuries the term sokha was applied to a much larger unit. It seems, however, that in the 15th century the Moscow sokha was a unit of the same size as in Novgorod.[345] Consequently, for the agricultural districts, at any rate, three may be considered the minimum number of men in each sokha. Three men with their respective families and dependents might make up a group of about twenty people. This would correspond to a large homestead of a family commune ("greater family").

The annual amount of the vykhod is not mentioned in our sources. The payments decreased considerably during the troubles in the Golden Horde in·the 1360–70's. Tokhtamysh restored the original rates, but after his downfall the vykhod was not paid regularly. The unpaid balance remained in the treasuries of the Russian princes, mainly in that of the grand duke of Moscow. We find some figures bearing on the vykhod in the princely wills and interprincely treaties, but these figures were intended for calculating the share of each prince in the payments and do not indicate the sum total of the vykhod. In his will, written in April or May 1389, Grand Duke Dmitri Donskoy set the quota of the dan' to be collected by each of his five sons from his apanage per thousand rubles of the vykhod.[346] In Dmitri's treaty with his cousin Prince Vladimir of Serpukhov (March 1389) the latter's share is defined in proportion to each 5,000 rubles of the vykhod.[347] This figure is repeated in Vasili I's treaty with Vladimir of Serpukhov (1390).[348] In another treaty between the same princes (1401 or 1402) 7,000 rubles is taken as a basis for the interprincely accounting.[349] In Prince Vladimir's will

344. Nikon, *12*, 184; see also *Sofiiskii vremennik* (1821), *2*, 194.
345. S. Veselovsky, *Soshnoe pismo, 1* (Moscow, 1915), 43.
346. *DDG*, pp. 35–36.
347. *Ibid.*, p. 31.
348. *Ibid.*, p. 38.
349. *Ibid.*, p. 44.

(also written in 1401 or 1402), the figure 5,000 is again mentioned.[350] In the will of Prince Iuri of Zvenigorod and Galich (1433) 7,000 appears once more.[351] It is obvious that none of these figures covers the total of the vykhod.

The only possible way to estimate the sum total of the vykhod, even tentatively, is to use the tax rate established by Tokhtamysh in 1384 as a basis. At that time the dan' was collected at the rate of one poltina (half a silver ruble) per farm, that is, per sokha, or for about twenty people.[352] In terms of the numerical divisions of the population established by the Mongols, the sokha may be reckoned as one-tenth of the desiatok. There were 1,000 desiatki in a t'ma, corresponding to at least 10,000 farms (or sokhas). At the rate of half a ruble per sokha this would mean collecting 5,000 silver rubles per t'ma.[353] This figure might have been set as the quota required from each t'ma.[354] If more was actually collected, the surplus went to the grand duke's treasury; if less, the grand duke had to make it good from the surplus of the other t'my or from his own pocket. Counting the Grand Duchy of Vladimir as 17 t'my (under Tokhtamysh) we arrive at the figure of 85,000 silver rubles as the total of the dan' paid by the Grand Duchy of Vladimir in 1384. If the other East Russian grand duchies paid at the same rate, Riazan must have paid 10,000 rubles, and Nizhni Novgorod and Tver 25,000 rubles each. The total figure for East Russia, except for Novgorod the Great, would be 145,000 rubles. The tamga collections should be added to this.

The amount paid by Novgorod the Great is hard to estimate on the same basis since Novgorod was outside of the t'my network. The main source of the khan's income from Novgorod must have been the tamga (in the periods when it was paid), not the dan'. As to the dan', I am inclined to think that Novgorod's basic provinces were assessed as five t'my. While it was left to the Novgorodians themselves to collect the tax, they might have found it more convenient to consider each province as corresponding to a t'ma. Indeed, it is possible that

350. *Ibid.*, p. 49.

351. *Ibid.*, p. 74.

352. Trinity, pp. 427–428; Nikon, *11*, 85.

353. The Muscovite silver grivna (ruble) of around 1400 weighed 92 grams; see G. B. Fedorov, "Dengi moskovskogo kniazhestva," *MIAS, 12* (1949), 157.

354. This is probably the meaning of the figure "5,000 rubles" mentioned in the princely charters.

the organization of the so-called *piatiny* (fifths) [355] in Novgorod took final shape in the Mongol period in connection with the assessment system adopted then.

355. On the *piatiny* see *Kievan Russia*, p. 204; K. A. Nevolin, "O piatinakh i pogostakh novgorodskikh," *ZRGO, 8* (1853) ; Nasonov, *Russkaia zemlia,* pp. 117–126.

CHAPTER IV

THE DECLINE OF THE GOLDEN HORDE AND THE RESURGENCE OF RUSSIA

1. THE TWO RUSSIAS

I

IN THE FIRST half of the 14th century the Golden Horde reached the height of its prosperity. However, after the death of the Khan Berdibek (1359) a protracted political crisis began in the Horde which lasted about two decades, greatly undermining the authority of the khans and shattering their grip on the tributary peoples, including Russia. The Russians profited by the circumstances and attempted to assert their independence. In the west, under the guidance of the grand duke of Lithuania, they reconquered much of the territory formerly occupied by the Mongols and even, for a time, reached the Black Sea. In the east, under the grand duke of Moscow, they succeeded in administering a crushing defeat to the army of the one among the rival khans who seemed strongest at the time.

The formation, in this period, of two mighty states, the Grand Duchy of Lithuania, controlling the resources of West Russia, and the Grand Duchy of Moscow (nominally, of Vladimir), controlling a large and ever-increasing portion of East Russia, is a fact of paramount importance in Russian history. It resulted in the division of the Russian lands between Lithuania and Muscovy. Eventually, because of the union of Lithuania with Poland, a lengthy conflict between Poland and Moscow was to evolve. Political division was accentuated by social and cultural changes, and contributed a great deal to a gradual split of the formerly united Russian nation into three peoples—the Great Russians (at present called simply Russians) in the east, the Little Russians (Ukrainians) and the White Russians (Belorussians) in the west. For a long time, however, the people of each of the three branches continued to call themselves just Russians.

The political division between West and East Russia resulted partly from the failure of the Mongol khans to give adequate protection to the Russians in the west against the encroachments of Poland and Lithuania. As long as both West and East Russia were under the control of the khan, both were parts of the same political body, the Golden Horde. But after Nogay's downfall the khans of the Golden Horde paid less attention to the position of their West Russian dominions than to their control over East Russia. While Uzbeg found it necessary to protect Galicia from the attack of the Polish king Casimir the Great in 1340, his successor Janibeg was not able to ward off Casimir's second onslaught on Galicia in 1349 and only helped the Lithuanian prince Lubart to oust the Poles from Volynia. Lubart, however, although formally a vassal of the khan, actually represented the interests of the growing Lithuanian state and potentially was an enemy of the Mongols. Thus we may say that the Mongol power in West Russia started crumbling in 1349. Soon after the beginning of the troubles in the Golden Horde Grand Duke Olgerd of Lithuania launched a successful campaign against the Mongols with the object of establishing control over Kiev and Podolia. His advance met but feeble resistance, and in 1363 he defeated the forces of three Mongol princes at the Blue Waters (*Sinie Vody*) near the mouth of the Bug River and reached the shores of the Black Sea.[1]

While Olgerd's successors eventually lost the access to the Black Sea, they kept both Kiev and Podolia, although after Olgerd's death his son, Prince Vladimir of Kiev, had to recognize the khan's suzerainty and pay him tribute. Most of West Russia was in any case freed from the Mongols, whose authority over it was now replaced by that of Lithuania and Poland. Mongol suzerainty over East Russia was to continue for about one more century. This in itself was another factor in accentuating the differences in the historical development between East (or Great) and West (Little and White) Russia.

As regards these names, Little Russia (*Malaia Rus'*, later on used in the form *Malorossiia*), seems to have originated in the late 13th or the early 14th century. When in 1303 the patriarch of Constantinople, at the insistence of King Iuri I agreed to institute a metropolitan's see at Galich, the new prelate received the title of Metropolitan

1. Spuler, pp. 116–117.

of Little Russia (in Greek, Μικρὰ 'Ρωσία; in Latin, Russia Minor).[2] The following eparchies (besides Galich) were subordinate to him: Vladimir in Volynia, Kholm, Peremyshl, Lutsk, and Turov. Thus the name Little Russia was applied, in this period, to Galicia, Volynia, and the Turov land. That it was not confined to ecclesiastical matters but acquired a political meaning as well is clear from one of Iuri II's charters (issued in 1335) in which he calls himself "Duke of Little Russia" (*Dux Russiae Minoris*).[3]

The origin of the name "White Russia" (in Russian, *Belaia Rus'*, later, *Belorussiia;* in Polish, *Biala Ruś*) is not clear.[4] It would be tempting to connect it with the early Sarmatian background. As we know, a Sarmatian-Slavic tribe which established itself in Galicia in the early Middle Ages was known in the 9th century as the White Khorvatians, meaning, according to the Chinese color system, the West Khorvatians. It is possible that another western Sarmatian tribe made its way, in the early period, to the upper Dnieper region. It will be recalled that a branch of the Alanic group of the Sarmatians was known as the Whites (Aorsi), or the White Alans (Alanorsi).[5] There is, however, no definite evidence to support any hypothesis of the Sarmatian origin of the name White Russia. Besides, the name should be bracketed with "Black Russia" (*Chernaia Rus'*, *Ruś Czarna*), a region occupied by the Lithuanians at an early stage in the formation of the Grand Duchy of Lithuania.[6] These two names seem to have formed an onomastic pair and thus must be examined together. A possibility of explaining the terms in the light of their religious background has been mentioned in the folkloristic literature, in any case for White Russia. It has been suggested that the name "White Russia" was connected with the cult of the White God (Belbog), an alleged pagan deity of the Slavs.[7] Now in Slavic mythologies a Black God (Chernobog) is also mentioned occasion-

2. Moszyński, *2,* 1552. On the creation of the Galich diocese see Golubinsky, *2,* 100–101; Hrushevsky, *3,* 112–113.

3. Hrushevsky, *3,* 137, n. 2; Moszyński, *2,* 1552.

4. See Moszyński, *2,* 1551; N. P. Vakar, "The Name 'White Russia,'" *ASEER, 8* (1949), 201–213.

5. On the White Khorvatians (White Croats) see *Ancient Russia,* pp. 167, 321; F. Dvornik, *The Making of Central and Eastern Europe* (London, Polish Research Center, 1949), pp. 266–267, 283–285, 291–292. On the Aorsi see *Ancient Russia,* pp. 82, 87–89.

6. On the name Black Russia see Moszyński, *2,* 1552; cf. above, Chapter 3, sec. 3, p. 155.

7. Vakar (as above, in n. 4), pp. 204–205.

ally; using the same approach as with White Russia we would have to consider Black Russia the sphere of the cult of the Black God. However, the authenticity of the deities Belbog and Chernobog is questionable.

Another approach, through the Slavic terminology of social relations, has also been suggested. It has been pointed out that the Slavic word "white" (*belyi*) has the connotation of "free" (in regard to property, "nontaxable"); and the word "black" (*chernyi*) that of "unfree" ("taxable").[8] From this point of view, Black Russia would be so called because of its early subjugation to Lithuania, in contrast to free White Russia. The theory does not seem plausible since White Russia, as we know, was absorbed by the Lithuanians also, only a little later than Black Russia. According to still other explanations, Black and White Russia took their names from the color of dress of their inhabitants. This seems to be the simplest explanation, but it is perhaps too casual. Besides, the difference in color of dress might have had some historical meaning.

All said, the problem of the origin of the names White and Black Russia cannot be considered adequately solved. As a new suggestion, I would like to point out that in the course of the 8th and 9th centuries the Norsemen penetrated the basins of all the rivers discharging into the southern and eastern sections of the Baltic Sea, from the Oder in the west to the Dvina in the east. As we know, Black Russia lies in the upper Nieman River basin and White Russia in the basin of the Dvina and (through portages) of the upper Dnieper.[9] Now, it should be mentioned in this connection that the Irish chroniclers, speaking of the Vikings, distinguish between White Foreigners (*Finngaill*) and Black Foreigners (*Dubhgaill*). This is usually assumed to be a distinction between "fair Norwegians" and "black Danes." However, T. D. Kendrick considers that distinction "of only dubious ethnological value."[10] In my opinion the distinction must have been based not on the hair color of the respective vikings but on the color

8. Moszyński, *2*, 1552; Vakar, p. 210.

9. On the expansion of the Vikings in the southeast Baltic area see T. J. Arne, *La Suède et l'Orient* (Upsala, 1914); B. Nerman, *Die Verbindungen zwischen Skandinavien und dem Ostbaltikum* (Stockholm, 1929); idem, "Swedish Viking Colonies on the Baltic," *ESA, 9* (1934), 357–380; F. Balodis, "Ein Denkmal der Wikingerzeit aus Semgallen," *ESA, 9,* 399–404; H. Jänichen, *Die Wikinger im Weichsel-und Odergebiet* (Leipzig, 1938); O. Scheel, *Die Wikinger* (Stuttgart, 1938), pp. 194–209; M. Vasmer, "Wikingerspuren bei den Westslaven," *ZOG, 6* (1932), 1–16, idem, "Wikingerspuren in Russland," *AWB, 24* (1931), 3–28.

10. T. D. Kendrick, *A History of the Vikings* (London, Methuen & Co., 1930), p. 275.

of their dress and armor. On the Oseberg textiles there is a representation of a warrior with a white shield.[11] As far as I know, nothing in our sources indicates any color specially ascribed to the Swedes. Presumably the Blacks and the Whites were special corporations among the vikings. The Blacks apparently predominated among the Danes and the Whites among the Norwegians. Both corporations might have existed among the Swedes. On the basis of the above considerations I am inclined to think that the region known as Black Russia was, at a certain time, let us say in the 9th century, controlled by the Black Vikings and the area called White Russia by the White Vikings. This would be a possible explanation of the origin of the names.

The name "Great Russia" (*Velikaia Rus'*, later on *Velikorossiia*) occurs for the first time in the charter issued by the Byzantine emperor John Kantakuzen to Prince Lubart of Volynia in 1347, to confirm the abolition of the metropolitan's see of Galich. The emperor ruled that "in all of Russia—Great and Little—there be one metropolitan, that of Kiev." [12] It may be added that in the middle of the 17th century the tsar of Moscow, Alexei (second tsar of the Romanov dynasty), made all three names of Russia official by including them in his title: "Tsar of all Great and Little and White Russia" (1654).

II

In Muscovy a centralized autocracy of the tsars was gradually built up. By contrast, in the Grand Duchy of Lithuania an aristocratic regime eventually came to being. Even at the early stages of its growth the grand duchy was not a centralized state but a political federation under the military guidance of the grand duke. That federation, from its very inception during the reign of Mendovg, consisted of both Lithuanian and Russian lands. During the reign of Gedymin all of White Russia and portions of Ukraine recognized the authority of the grand duke of Lithuania. Under Olgerd that authority

11. My interest in the Black and White Vikings was stimulated by the lecture on "The Vikings in Europe" Johannes Broensted gave at the Yale Art Gallery on October 27, 1948. For the picture of the viking with the white shield see Bjorn Hougen, "Oseberg-funnets billedev," *Viking, 4* (1940), 104. I am indebted to Harald Ingholt for referring me to this publication and to Miss Alexandra Kalmykow who at my request studied the copy of it in the Avery Library, Columbia University, and ordered a photostat for me of the pertinent picture.

12. *RIB, 6*, Suppl. No. 6, p. 30.

extended over all of Ukraine except for Galicia which, as we know, was seized by Poland.

In that process of political absorption of West Russia by Lithuania, a number of local Russian princes kept their apanages, and most of the boyars their estates. Large principalities, however, such as Kiev and Volynia, were assigned to Lithuanian princes—descendants of Gedymin. As a matter of fact, Kiev after its destruction by the Mongols in 1240 was for a number of years under their direct control, and when in the early 14th century the Mongols allowed a Russian prince to rule in Kiev, they chose one of the lesser princes (probably of the house of Chernigov). The fact that the old tradition of princely succession in Kiev was thus broken made it easier for Olgerd to establish one of his sons (Vladimir) as prince of Kiev. In the case of Volynia, the old reigning house of Roman (father of Daniel and Vasilko) being extinct, there could be no objection on that count to the intrusion of Gedymin's son Lubart; and moreover, as has been mentioned, he could claim a degree of relationship with the old reigning house through his wife.

As the Lithuanian grand dukes added more Russian lands to their dominions, they left intact all the traditional Russian social and political institutions. The Russian language and "the Russian faith" were in no way disturbed. On the contrary, the influence of Russian civilization spread to Lithuania proper. For example, a number of the words in the Lithuanian language pertaining to church and church service have been borrowed from the Russian.[13] While in the 14th century the bulk of the Lithuanians were still pagans, many Lithuanian princes were converted to Greek Orthodoxy, especially since a number of them had Russian wives. Although Olgerd, for political reasons, was anxious not to disclose his church affiliations, there is ground to believe he was a Greek Orthodox; all of his sons accepted the Russian faith without concealing it, even if some of them, like Iagailo, later on shifted to Roman Catholicism for political reasons. Russian influence was also strong in shaping the Lithuanian adminis-tration. In the principalities of Vilno and Troki—which constituted the core of the grand duke's dominions—Russian terms such as *gorodnichi* (town chief), *tivun* (judge), *koniushi* (master of the stables) were used to designate the offices of various administrative agents. In the realm of social relations, the Russian term "boyar"

13. See A. Senn, "Notes on Religious Folklore in Lithuania," *Slavic Studies*, A. Kaun and E. J. Simmons, eds. (Ithaca, Cornell University Press, 1943), pp. 164–165, 174–175.

made its way to Lithuania,[14] although it eventually acquired there a somewhat different connotation. Even more significant was the fact that the Russian language became the main vehicle of the chancery of the grand dukes. Even much later, in the 16th century, when Russian was to a great extent replaced by Latin in the official documents, the Lithuanian Code of Laws (first published in 1529) was compiled in Russian (Old Belorussian). In fact, it was a Russian code of laws made valid for the whole grand duchy.

While the Lithuanians were indomitable warriors, the Russian subjects of the grand duke also played a prominent role in his army; and especially in the initial period of the country's growth the Russians contributed a great deal to the organization of the Lithuanian military establishment. As evidenced by German chroniclers like Peter of Dusburg and Wigand of Marburg, the Russians took an active part in Lithuania's struggle against the Teutonic Knights.[15] The Teutonic threat to the new Lithuanian state continued throughout the 14th century, and much energy on the part of the Lithuanian grand dukes was needed to parry the danger from that quarter. By agreement Grand Duke Olgerd and his brother Keistut (Kestutis) each assumed a special task. While Keistut, who was a great military leader, undertook to direct the struggle against the knights, Olgerd, a cunning politician, was free to concentrate his attention on Russian and Polish affairs.[16]

After Olgerd's death (1377) his son Iagailo (in Lithuanian, Jogaila; in Polish, Jagiello) was recognized as grand duke, though not without some opposition. Before long, however, a conflict developed between Keistut and Iagailo. The latter seized his uncle by ruse and had him stealthily strangled in the castle of Krevo (1381). Since Keistut was a popular hero of the Lithuanians, especially of those of the old school (he remained heathen to his death and his body was cremated according to the old pagan rites), his death produced a painful impression and resulted in much opposition to Iagailo on the part of many influential princes and boyars. Moreover, Iagailo now had to assume himself the task of defending his country against the Teutonic Knights, for which he proved not strong enough. A way out of the difficult situation seemed to have been found when the

14. Liubavsky, p. 41.

15. Dusburg, *SSRP, 1,* 162, 284, 287; Wigand, *SSRP, 2,* 454–455, 475. Cf. Antonovich, *Monografii,* pp. 40–41.

16. For a penetrating characterization of Olgerd and Keistut see Antonovich, *Monografii,* pp. 83–93.

Poles (who in their turn were struggling with the knights) suggested uniting the forces of the two nations through a diplomatic marriage. Iagailo was to marry Queen Hedwig (Jadwiga) of Poland and become king of Poland while remaining grand duke of Lithuania. Iagailo and the leading Lithuanian boyars accepted the offer and on August 15, 1385 in the castle of Krevo Iagailo signed the instrument of the union for himself as well as on behalf of all the local princes of the grand duchy. He then was accepted into the Catholic Church, receiving the name of Vladislav (Wladyslaw).

The Krevo union (ratified in 1386) was much more than a dynastic or personal union.[17] It amounted to a complete incorporation of Lithuania into Poland. Roman Catholicism was to become the official religion of Lithuania; the Lithuanian noblemen, after their conversion to Catholicism, were to enjoy all the rights and privileges of the Polish nobility. While this last clause was quite agreeable to both Lithuanian and Russian boyars, the Russians immediately objected to any attempt to curb the rights of the Greek Orthodox Church. And both Lithuanians and Russians resented the plan to destroy the identity of the grand duchy as a separate state. For these reasons King Vladislav-Iagailo was unable to enforce the conditions of the Krevo union upon his peoples and in 1392 had to recognize the leader of the opposition, his cousin Vitovt, son of Keistut (in Lithuanian, Vytautas; in Polish, Witold), as grand duke of Lithuania for life under his suzerainty.

In the field of international relations the most important fruit of the Polish-Lithuanian union was the decisive victory of the combined Polish and Lithuanian-Russian troops over the Teutonic Knights at Tannenberg in East Prussia (1410). Three years later a new treaty of union was signed between Poland and Lithuania, at Gorodlo. While the principle of incorporation of Lithuania into Poland was reasserted, it was agreed that after Vitovt's death the Lithuanian boyars (*pany*) and gentry (*szlachta*) would elect as their next grand duke only a candidate acceptable to the king of Poland. This meant that their right to elect their grand duke was recognized in principle, although with some formal limitations. Actually the Grand Duchy of Lithuania enjoyed complete autonomy under Vitovt, who toward the end of his life became the most powerful ruler in Eastern Europe.

17. On the Krevo union see O. Halecki, *Dzieje unji jagiellonskiej* (Kraków, 1919), *1;* Liubavsky, pp. 45–53; I. I. Lappo, *Zapadnaia Rossiia i ee Soedinenie s Polshei* (Prague, 1924), pp. 100–106.

III

Moscow is first mentioned in the Russian annals A.D. 1147. At that time it was but a small town centering around one of the manors of Prince Iuri I of Suzdal.[18] Several years later that prince built a castle on the high bank of the Moscow River, the nucleus of the Kremlin. By the time of the Mongol invasion the town must have been grown up considerably, for it was ruled by a prince, a son of Grand Duke Iuri II.

The growth of Moscow started soon after its destruction by the Mongols in 1238. Like the rise of Tver in the same period it was partly the result of the shift of population caused by the Mongol raids. While in their first onslaught on Russia the Mongols destroyed Moscow and looted the Tver region, the devastation of the central area of East Russia was not as thorough as that of Suzdalia and Riazan. In subsequent years too Moscow and Tver on the whole suffered less than Suzdalia from the punitive expeditions of the Mongols.

The influx of people to the Moscow and Tver regions was not caused exclusively however by the Mongol threat to the more exposed regions. The favorable location of the two cities for trade was also a factor. Both lie in the western part of the Russian "Mesopotamia," the area between the upper Volga and the Oka rivers. This region is in the center of the system of Russian riverways: on the one hand the tributaries of the upper Volga and Oka connect it with the tributaries of the upper Dnieper, and on the other hand the upper Oka and its tributaries lie near the upper stretches of the Donets and Don and their tributaries.[19] Tver is situated at the confluence of the Volga and the Tvertsa, and the latter's sources lie very near to the sources of the Msta, which discharges into Lake Ilmen. Thus Tver is at the entrance of the riverway from Novgorod to the Volga system.

Kliuchevsky in Lecture 21 of his famous *Course of Russian History* [20]—that lecture which can truly be called a classic—has pointed out the importance of the fact that Moscow commands the inner line of communications between the upper Volga and the upper Oka, up

18. On the history of the city of Moscow see I. E. Zabelin, *Istoriia goroda Moskvy* (Moscow, 1905); *Moskva v ee proshlom i nastoiashchem* (Moscow, 1910–12), 12 vols.; "Materialy i issledovaniia po arkheologii Moskvy," *MIAS,* 7 (1947) and *12* (1949).

19. See R. J. Kerner, *The Urge to the Sea* (Berkeley, University of California Press, 1943), pp. 35–38, 107–114.

20. Kliuchevsky, *Kurs, 2,* 3–27.

the Shosha River (a tributary of the Volga) and the Lama (tributary of the Shosha), and then, with a short portage, down the Istra and the Moskva. The importance of this riverway is evidenced by the early

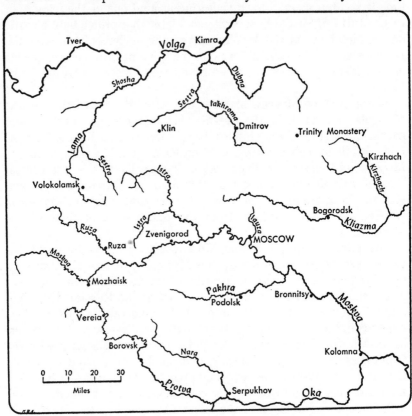

3. Rivers of the Moscow region
(before the digging of the Volga-Moscow Canal)

growth of the town of Volokolamsk (the Lama Portage), halfway between the upper Volga and Moscow. From Moscow, further to the south, merchants could easily descend the Moscow River to the Oka, at whose confluence lies the town of Kolomna, which we have seen was coveted and eventually seized by Prince Daniel of Moscow. While at the beginning of the 14th century it might have seemed that the chances of Moscow and Tver for supremacy were about equal, toward the end of the century there could be no doubt that Moscow was leading the race, and in fact winning it. What were the reasons?

First of all, it may be pointed out that Moscow's position at the hub of inner ways of communications within the "Mesopotamia" not only gave her considerable advantage in trade but was of primary strategic importance in warfare. Then, as has been said, under Metropolitan Peter Moscow became the ecclesiastical capital of Russia, and all subsequent attempts of the Tver princes to transfer the metropolitan's see to their own city failed. No less important was the fact that on more than one occasion Novgorod preferred to side with Moscow rather than with Tver. This may partly be explained by their fear that the prince of Tver, as their immediate neighbor, would be more inclined to suppress their liberties and would have more facilities to do so if he wished to, than the prince of Moscow. So it happened that in most of the conflicts between Tver and Moscow the latter could count on Novgorod's support. That support was not so much military as financial. From Novgorod the Moscow princes obtained vast funds which not only expanded their treasury reserves but could be used to promote their interests at the khan's court.

Last but not the least, the Moscow princes knew much better than those of Tver how to make use of their resources and advantages. There are two schools of thought in Russian historiography in regard to the personal characteristics of the Moscow princes. Platonov emphasizes their talents and shrewdness as an important factor in the rise of Moscow.[21] Kliuchevsky, on the other hand, considers them just so many mediocrities who owed their success to favorable historical circumstances. According to him, no Moscow prince prior to Ivan III had a marked personality of his own; each was merely a replica of the same family type. They were all "one so much like another that the observer at times hesitates to determine which of them was Ivan and which Vasili." [22] Irrespective of the abilities of the Moscow princes, it is hard to agree with Kliuchevsky's caustic characterization of the "Ivans" and "Vasilis." Indeed, in my opinion at least, almost every Moscow prince had striking traits which distinguished him from the others. Consider the daring and aggressive Iuri III and his quiet and patient brother Ivan I. Contrast the "meek" Ivan II with his courageous and dynamic son, Dmitri Donskoy. Note the difference between Dmitri's son Vasili I, a cunning diplomat, and the latter's son Vasili II, a ruler of no outstanding abili-

21. S. F. Platonov, *Uchebnik russkoi istorii* (reprinted in Prague, 1924), *1*, 103–104.
22. Kliuchevsky, *Kurs, 2,* 51 (a few lines earlier Kliuchevsky also names Simeon and Dmitri in the same connection).

ties and yet tenacious and persevering, undaunted by misfortune. There was abundant variety within the family type that Kliuchevsky speaks of. On the other hand, we may agree with Kliuchevsky that most of the Moscow princes were good businessmen, efficient managers of their estates and properties. In that trait he sees a sign of the narrowness of their interests and lack of statesmanship.

As a matter of fact, any political aspirations of the Russian princes in that period had to revolve in the small sphere of a subjugated nation. To revolt aganst the khan's administration would be a bold policy—but would it be a constructive one? The Tver princes tried it and lost. The submission of the Moscow princes to Mongol authority down to the period of the Great Trouble in the Golden Horde was a grim necessity. That they followed the traditions of their forefather, Alexander Nevsky, in that respect, is evidence of their political wisdom, not of narrowness of interests. Being restricted in their political actions by the self-imposed policy of loyalty to the khans, the Moscow princes naturally had to concentrate on economic activities. By getting rich and by adding new cities and territories to their dominions, they accumulated the resources necessary for a future rebellion. When Dmitri Donskoy saw a chance for successful resistance to the Mongols in the 1370's he did not hesitate to strike. Dmitri's rebellion proved premature, however, and Moscow's fight for complete independence was postponed once more.

While giving credit to the Moscow princes for their role in the rise of the Muscovite state, we should not forget that their success was due to a great extent to the support of both the boyars and the church. With the growth of Moscow, more and more boyars were attracted to the court of the grand duke of Moscow and Vladimir, since to serve him became more profitable than to serve minor princes. Besides, a number of Lithuanian princes and West Russian princes and boyars found their way to Moscow whenever they were dissatisfied with conditions at home, after Olgerd's death and even more after Iagailo's attempt to enforce the incorporation of Lithuania into Poland and to curb the rights of the Greek-Orthodox Church in West Russia.

2. THE GREAT TROUBLE IN THE GOLDEN HORDE AND THE REBELLION OF THE MUSCOVITES

I

The Great Trouble (in Russian, *Velikaia Zamiatnia*) started as a family feud, a conflict between Janibeg's three sons Berdibeg, Kulpa, and Nevruz (Naurus in Russian sources). It will be recalled that in all probability Berdibeg ascended the throne by killing his father.[23] If so, the subsequent opposition to him on the part of his brother Kulpa and a number of the grandees is quite understandable. In 1359 a palace revolution took place in the Golden Horde, led by Kulpa; Berdibeg was killed and Kulpa proclaimed khan. It should be noted that Kulpa's two sons bore Russian names—Michael and Ivan; the former name was popular among the Tver princes, and the latter among those of Moscow. There is no doubt that both of Kulpa's sons were Christians. Their conversion must have offended the Moslem majority of princes and grandees and helped Janibeg's youngest son Nevruz to lead another palace revolt, in which both Kulpa and his sons were murdered (around 1360). The conflict between Janibeg's sons thus came to an end by the process of elimination of the two eldest, and Nevruz seemed to have a fair chance to restore the line of succession of the khans of the Uzbeg family.

However, the dynastic crisis in the Golden Horde lowered the morale of the Juchids as a clan; and the khans of the eastern part of Juchi's Ulus—descendants of Orda, Shiban, and Tuka-Timur— thought it opportune to enter the melee in their turn, lured by that fabulous reward of success, the wealth of the Golden Horde accumulated during the period of its prosperity. This wealth seemed to lie within the reach of any adventurous Juchid. Thus started the second phase of the Great Trouble. In 1361 a descendant of Shiban by the name of Khidyr (Khyzr) was secretly invited by some of the grandees of the Golden Horde to assume the throne. At the approach of Khidyr's army Nevruz was treacherously seized by his own lieutenants and handed over. Khidyr immediately ordered Nevrus and his whole family executed. Among the princes and princesses slain at that time was "the Great Khatun," Taydula. After a brief reign Khidyr was murdered by his own son, Temir-Khodja, who succeeded

23. See above, Chapter 3, sec. 6, p. 208.

in keeping the throne for only five weeks,[24] as some of the remaining descendants of Uzbeg tried to regain power. They could not agree among themselves, however. In 1362 one of them, Keldi-Beg by name, ruled in Saray, and another, Abdullah, in the Crimea. That same year still another Juchid prince, Bulat-Temir (presumably of an eastern branch of the Juchids) seized the Bulgar region in the middle Volga basin.

None of the Juchid princes so far mentioned seems to have had outstanding ability either as an army leader or a statesman. But such a leader appeared among the non-Juchid Mongol generals of the Golden Horde. His name was Mamay. Having no right to the throne he had to use one of the Juchids as a puppet khan. Hence Mamay backed Abdullah against Keldi-Beg. However, in spite of all Mamay's efforts he was not able to take Saray away from a series of rival khans, such as Mürid, 1362–63 and Aziz-Khan (son of Temir-Khodja) 1364–67. After Abdullah's death, around 1370, Mamay put on the throne still another Juchid prince, Muhammad-Bulak (called Mamat-Saltan in Russian sources). Actually, Mamay's authority was recognized only in the western part of the Golden Horde—west of the Volga River. Within a few years he succeeded in restoring order in this territory. In a sense Mamay's realm was a replica of Nogay's empire, though it did not extend as far west. After 1363, as we know, the section of the Black Sea shore between the Bug and the Dniester was controlled by Grand Duke Olgerd of Lithuania. In Moldavia a new Rumanian state, independent of Wallachia, was in process of formation. It was ruled by a series of local chieftains, except for the period 1372–77, when a nephew of Olgerd, Iuri, son of Koriat, occupied the throne.

It will be recalled that during some of the earlier crises in the Golden Horde or during its conflicts with other Mongol khanates the great khan of China was able to act as moderator. As we know, however, in 1360 all South China was in open rebellion against the great khan, and in 1368 the Yuan dynasty was overthrown, to be replaced by the native Chinese Ming dynasty. This proved the end of the pan-Mongol empire, and the local Mongol khanates now were left without any central authority, to deal with local conflicts as best as they could on the basis of their own resources.

While the Golden Horde was for a time all but paralyzed by inner discord, two new centers of Mongolo-Turkish power were

24. Nikon, *10*, 233.

formed in Central Asia: one in southern Kazakhstan, at Sygnak, on the lower Syr-Daria River; and another at Samarkand in Transoxania. At Sygnak the mightiest of Orda's descendants, Urus-Khan, established his court around 1360.[25] More and more Juchid princes and Mongol generals recognized him as their suzerain. "Urus" is Turkish for "Russian." Presumably Urus-Khan's mother was a Russian princess. Apparently he was prepared to press his claims on Russia on that ground.

Out of a protracted period of hopeless confusion and a maze of local conflicts, the dynamic personality of Timur (Tamerlane) emerged in Transoxania, in the 1360's.[26] Timur was born at Kesh in the year of the Mouse, A.D. 1336. He belonged to an old Mongol clan, that of the Barlas, and claimed to be a descendant of the mythical ancestress of the Mongols, Alan-Qoa.[27] He was not a Chingisid, however, which means that he did not belong to the Golden Kin and had no right to the throne. Even when he became all-powerful, he had to exercise his rule, like Mamay, through puppet khans of the house of Chingis.

Timur's role in history is often compared to that of Chingis-Khan. There is no doubt that to his contemporaries he seemed even mightier. And, indeed, in achieving his objectives, Timur was as ruthless as Chingis, and even more cruel in a highly developed way. As a military leader he was apparently Chingis-Khan's peer. In statesmanship, however, he was less constructive. While, like Chingis-Khan, he was guided by the idea of world conquest, the immediate motive of his campaigns was desire for more power and booty rather than promotion of universal peace. There was also a difference in the religious and cultural background of the two world conquerors. At the time of Timur's birth the members of his clan, while proud of their Mongol lineage, were already Turkicized. They spoke Turkish and most of them were converted to Islam. While Chingis-Khan was a "heathen" Timur was a Moslem. His religious affiliation helped him a great deal at the time of his campaigns in the Near East; on the other hand it made his attitude toward the non-Moslem peoples more narrow than that of Chingis. It may also be said that instead of promoting the pan-

25. On Sygnak see *ZO*, pp. 305–310.

26. On Timur (Tamerlane) see Barthold, *Ulugbek*, pp. 12–18; Bouvat, pp. 11–76; Grousset, *Empire des steppes*, pp. 486–534; W. J. Fischel, trans., *Ibn-Khaldun and Tamerlane* (Berkeley, University of California Press, 1952).

27. E. Herzfeld, "Alongoa," *Der Islam, 6* (1916), 317–318; cf. above, Chapter 1, sec. 4, p. 18.

Mongol movement originated by Chingis-Khan, Timur on the one hand continued the pan-Islamic traditions of the caliph and on the other gave a powerful impulse to the pan-Turanian movement of the future.[28]

The first important landmark in Timur's rise to power was his establishment as a local ruler of his native city of Kesh, in 1360. There followed a period of civil war in Transoxania during which Timur supported now one side and now the other. He was hardly more than a chieftain of a band of adventurers at this time. In one of the numerous skirmishes in which he took part he was wounded in the right leg and became lame for life. Hence his nickname, "The Lame Timur"; in Turkish, Temir-Aksak; in Persian, Timur-Leng, from which comes the English form Tamerlane. This troublesome period in Tamerlane's life came to an end when he succeeded in defeating and killing his former suzerain, Hussein, and became ruler of Transoxania, with Samarkand as his capital. He was now ready to start building an empire of his own. The old Mongol Empire had crumbled to pieces just two years before he seized Samarkand. To enhance his prestige Tamerlane in a shrewd diplomatic move acknowledged himself a vassal of Hong Wu, the first Chinese emperor of the Ming dynasty.[29] In this way, he obtained imperial sanction of his future conquests. In a sense this move was along the same lines as his former devices in the petty conflicts of Transoxania. To be a vassal of a powerful ruler added to his prestige; to overthrow that ruler and to seize power for himself was the next step in the game. And, indeed, that was what Tamerlane intended to do, in due time, with his Chinese suzerain. Death prevented him from crowning his victories by the conquest of Peking.

Appraising the political situation in Central Asia after his seizure of Samarkand, Tamerlane decided first of all to establish his control over the Turks of Kazakhstan; in other words, over the eastern part of Juchi's Ulus. This meant eventual conflict with Urus-Khan. As Tamerlane did not want to risk an immediate attack on Urus-Khan, he attempted to sap the latter's power from within, by acquiring friends among the princes and military leaders of his retinue. Time was required for this policy to bear fruit, and Tamerlane waited

28. See L. Cahun, *Introduction à l'histoire de l'Asie: Turcs et Mongols des origines à 1405* (Paris, 1896). On the influence of this book "on certain chauvinistic circles in Turkey" see Browne 3, 14–15.

29. See Krymsky, *Persia, 3,* 21.

quietly for several years before making any decisive move. Meanwhile Urus-Khan, unaware of these schemes, started his march westward, leaving his son Kutlug-Buka to rule in Sygnak. Around 1372
his army reached the lower course of the Volga River, and the next
year it occupied the two Sarays. After entering New Saray Urus-
Khan proclaimed himself khan of the Golden Horde. He was the
strongest adversary Mamay had had to face so far and there seemed
little chance for Mamay to keep in power. However, at this juncture
the results of Tamerlane's intrigues appeared: Prince Tokhtamysh,
one of the ablest of Urus-Khan's lieutenants, deserted him and went
to Tamerlane for protection and assistance.

Tokhtamysh is usually identified as a nephew of Urus-Khan, and
consequently a descendant of Orda. However, according to a 15th-
century genealogy called the *Muizz* Tokhtamysh' ancestor was not
Orda but another of Juchi's sons, Tuka-Timur.[30] In any case, Tokhtamysh was a Juchid of good standing. As could be expected, Tamerlane received the fugitive Mongol prince with due honor and recognized him as ruler of Sygnak. With troops and equipment received
from his new suzerain Tokhtamysh launched a campaign against
Urus-Khan's son Kutlug-Buka. The latter was killed in the first
battle, yet his troops won the day. Tokhtamysh fled to Samarkand.
Soon after, a prominent Mongol general of the Mangkyt tribe, Idigu
(in Russian sources, Edigey), also deserted Urus-Khan's camp and
offered his services to Tamerlane. For the time being Tokhtamysh
and Edigey served the same master, although later on they split
apart.

Receiving news of his son's death in the battle and of Edigey's
desertion, Urus-Khan hastily returned to Sygnak and sent a mes-
senger to Tamerlane with the demand that both Tokhtamysh and
Edigey be extradited to him. Tamerlane refused, and war followed
between them. This time Tamerlane personally led his army to
Sygnak, but the campaign was indecisive (1376). The next year
Urus-Khan died and was succeeded by his youngest son, Timur-
Melik.

Tamerlane let Tokhtamysh try his luck once more in another
campaign against the new ruler of Sygnak. At last he was victorious
and captured Sygnak in 1377. He had more ambitious plans, how-

30. Tiesenhausen, *2*, 61. According to *Muizz* Urus-Khan was also a descendant of
Tuka-Timur, through another of the latter's sons. It seems, however, that the derivation of his descent from Orda is more reliable.

ever—to become khan of the Golden Horde as well and thus establish himself as ruler over the whole of Juchi's Ulus. As he acknowledged himself Tamerlane's vassal, the latter was ready to continue to support him in all these undertakings. By 1378 Tokhtamysh' army reached the Volga, and soon he entered Saray. A clash with Mamay was now inevitable.

II

In the initial period of the Great Trouble the Russian princes continued to act as they were accustomed to and asked each new khan to renew their patents. With the rapid changes on the throne of the Golden Horde it sometimes happened that the khan in power had no time to issue the new patents, and the Russians had to wait in the Horde for the next khan to do so.

When the power was divided between two, or sometimes more, rival khans, a situation like that in the time of Nogay evolved. Then the Russians were able to play one khan against another in their own diplomatic game. The result was a decline of the khans' prestige and the growth of independent spirit among the Russians. There is no mention in Russian chronicles of any of Kulpa's decisions about Russian affairs. He reigned only about five months, and by the time the Russian princes appeared in the Horde they had to deal with the new khan, Nevruz. The latter confirmed most of the local princely patents. He refused to assign the grand ducal patent to Ivan II's young son Dmitri of Moscow (born 1350), and instead appointed Dmitri of Suzdal grand duke of Vladimir. The Moscow boyars were indignant since they were wont to regard the grand duchy as the traditional patrimony of the princes of Moscow. The compiler of the Trinity Chronicle comments that Dmitri of Suzdal's acceptance of the Vladimir throne was contrary to the principle of succession from father to son.[31]

As soon as Nevruz was killed by Khidyr the Moscow boyars took their boy prince to the new khan's court. They did not succeed in obtaining the patent for Dmitri and were only too glad to have left the Horde before the new palace revolution there. Dmitri of Suzdal went to the Horde in his turn to have his patent reaffirmed and witnessed the riots. He considered himself lucky to have survived and hastily returned home. Presumably the Russian word *kuterma* ("bustle," "senseless disorder") originated in an impression of these

31. Trinity, pp. 376–377.

riotous and futile enthronements of the khans (with the ritual of "carrying in the felt"—*kutermiak*—observed each time) and the subsequent palace revolutions.

When Mürid became khan of Saray the two Dmitris resumed their attempts to obtain the grand ducal patent each for himself. Remembering their recent experiences neither of them went to Saray personally but each sent his plenipotentiaries (*kilichei*) to the khan. The latter issued the patent to Dmitri of Moscow. As Dmitri of Suzdal was reluctant to part with his office, the Moscow boyars, taking their prince with them, led the Moscow army against Pereiaslavl where Dmitri of Suzdal assembled his forces. There was no battle, for the Suzdal grand duke fled to his apanage. Dmitri of Moscow was then solemnly enthroned at Vladimir.

At that juncture the ruler of the western section of the Golden Horde, Mamay, found it necessary to demonstrate the right of the khan he supported—Abdullah—to have his say in Russian affairs. Mamay's envoys brought to Moscow Abdullah's patent confirming Dmitri as grand duke of Vladimir. The Moscow boyars did not object to receiving a second patent for their prince and showed due honors to Mamay's envoys (1363). But their action offended khan Mürid of Saray, who had issued the first patent. He ruled that Dmitri of Moscow had forfeited his rights to Vladimir, and issued a new patent in favor of Dmitri of Suzdal. The latter rushed to Vladimir but was able to stay in power only twelve days. This time the Muscovites not only ousted the Suzdal prince from Vladimir but stormed Suzdal as well. Dmitri of Suzdal had to abandon all claims to the throne of Vladimir.

For the time being the Muscovites seemed to have restored the former preponderance of their city in East Russia. Moreover, in view of the weakening of the Golden Horde they felt more independent of Mongol tutelage. They had eliminated the threat to the authority of Moscow from the princes of Suzdal, and, in their opinion, that could serve as a warning to the princes of Tver as well. And yet before long the princes of Tver made another attempt to wrest leadership in Russian affairs from Moscow. Not relying on the Mongols under the circumstances, they now turned for assistance to the rising power in West Russia, the Grand Duchy of Lithuania. Grand Duke Olgerd, it will be recalled, had suggested to the Mongols an alliance against Moscow as early as 1349, but his plan fell through. Olgerd grew much more powerful and as we know he now controlled a

section of the Pontic steppe which he took from the Mongols in
1363. This put him in an advantageous position for negotiating
eventually with the Mongols (some of whom entered his service).
Later on, under his successor Iagailo, a degree of Mongol–Lithuanian
cooperation against Moscow was achieved. For the time being, however, the Mongols seemed to be of little use, and Olgerd turned his
attention to Tver as a possible ally.[32]

Relations between Olgerd and Moscow became strained after
1363. For several years, however, there was no open warfare between them, partly because Olgerd's potential allies, the princes
of Tver, were absorbed in local rivalries. A series of internecine
skirmishes occurred between Vasili, grand duke of Tver and prince
of Kashin (son of Grand Duke Michael I, the unfortunate rival of
Iuri III of Moscow), and his nephew, Prince Michael of Mikulin. In
1368 Grand Duke Dmitri of Moscow offered his mediation in the
conflict. However, when Michael of Mikulin came to Moscow he
was immediately arrested, apparently on the instigation of his cousin
Eremei of Dorogobuzh. After he had made some concessions to
Eremei Michael was released. He left in high dudgeon and appealed
to Olgerd for assistance.

The rulers of Moscow had been worried by the possibility of
Olgerd's intervention during all these years of the Tverian crisis.
They thought it wise to take some measures of precaution, the most
important of which—and one which proved quite timely—was replacing the wooden fortifications of the Kremlin by stone walls in
1367. Olgerd was apparently ready to attack Moscow when Prince
Michael appeared at his court. Before long Olgerd led a combined
Lithuanian–Russian army westward. He was a past master at secret
war moves. The Moscow army was not on war footing when Olgerd,
after defeating some weak vanguard detachments of Moscow troops
on the way, appeared before the new Kremlin walls (November
1368). While he was not able to storm the Kremlin, his troops
mercilessly looted the country around Moscow. It was the first
enemy invasion Muscovy had suffered since 1293. Prince Michael,
backed by Olgerd, was recognized as grand duke of Tver (Michael
II), an ominous event from the point of view of the Moscow poli-
ticians. The blow to Moscow was not mortal, however, and in 1370,

32. On the relations between Lithuania, Tver, and Moscow in 1368–75 see Soloviev, *3*,
336–347; A. E. Presniakov, *Obrazovanie velikorusskogo gosudarstva* (Petrograd, 1918),
pp. 298–306; Paszkiewicz, pp. 414–426; Nasonov, pp. 127–134.

profiting by the fact that Olgerd, together with his brother Keistut, was that year engaged in fighting the Teutons in Prussia, Moscow troops plundered the region of Tver. The grand duke of Tver fled to Lithuania and once more implored Olgerd to help him.

Olgerd appeared again before Moscow in December 1370 but once more failed to storm the Kremlin. He then offered to sign a peace treaty; Dmitri, however, agreed only to a truce, until the Day of Saints Peter and Paul (June 29), 1371. Disappointed in his hopes, Michael of Tver now went to Mamay and obtained the new puppet khan Muhammad-Bulak's patent on the Grand Duchy of Vladimir. Mamay's special envoy, Sary-Khoja, was authorized to put Michael on the throne. However, the people of Vladimir, acting on Dmitri's instructions, refused to accept either Michael or Sary-Khoja. Instead the latter was invited to come to Moscow, was feted and showered with presents, and then sent back to Mamay. On his advice Mamay invited Dmitri to pay him a visit in the Horde. Dmitri arrived at Mamay's court with rich gifts for Mamay, the khan, the khatuns, and princes. As a result, Mamay agreed to arrange for the cancellation of Michael's patent, and Dmitri was confirmed grand duke of Vladimir. On this occasion Dmitri offered to pay 10,000 rubles to the creditors of Michael's young son Ivan who at that time resided in the Horde. The offer was accepted, the money paid, and Dmitri took the Tverian prince to Moscow where he was kept until his father paid Dmitri back in full. This episode, as Soloviev rightly remarks, shows clearly how much greater Moscow financial resources were than those of Tver.[33]

While Tver affairs seemed to be settled in favor of Moscow, a new challenge to Moscow came from Riazan. The motives for the opposition of Grand Duke Oleg of Riazan to Dmitri are not clear. Most likely, it was a projection of Mongol rivalries into Russian affairs—if we suppose that Oleg was a vassal not of Muhammad-Bulak but of the khan of Saray. In any case a war started between Moscow and Riazan. The Muscovite army was commanded by a Lithuanian prince who had become Grand Duke Dmitri's brother-in-law, Dmitri Bobrok-Volynsky, son of Koriat, husband of Princess Liubov of Moscow.[34] He was apparently a military leader of great ability in strategy and proved the outstanding Russian general of

33. Soloviev, *3*, 341.
34. The name of Bobrok-Volynsky's wife is given by different authorities as Liubov, Ann, and Maria. Presumably it was Liubov.

the period. Oleg's troops suffered a severe defeat. His cousin Prince Vladimir of Pronsk took advantage of the situation and proclaimed himself grand duke of Riazan (1371). The next year, however, he was ousted by Oleg. This clash between Moscow and Riazan proved unfortunate for the cause of Russian unity since in the subsequent war between Moscow and the Mongols Oleg was to side with the latter.

In 1372 Grand Duke Michael of Tver concluded another alliance with Olgerd and attacked the apanages of some of his relatives, lesser Tverian princes whom he considered so many Moscow stooges. Dmitri of Moscow had no alternative but to defend his friends. This new conflict between Tver, backed by Lithuania, on the one hand and Moscow on the other lasted for three years. During this period there appeared elements of opposition to Dmitri in Moscow itself. In 1374 when the tysiatsky (chiliarch) Vasili Veliaminov died Dmitri made no new appointment to fill his office. As we know, a conflict between the boyars and the tysiatsky (Veliaminov's predecessor) had taken place in Moscow seventeen years earlier. Now Dmitri decided to abolish the office altogether.

It should be noted that with the Mongol system of conscription and the decline of the role of the veche, the city militia (tysiacha, thousand), which was headed by the tysiatsky, had lost its former importance (except in Novgorod). The princely court (*dvor*) became the anchor of the new organization of the Russian army. In connection with this, a new office was instituted, that of quartermaster general (*okolnichi*). In the Moscow documents the okolnichi is first mentioned in Grand Duke Simeon's treaty with his brothers Ivan and Andrew (around 1350–51).[35] Both the Moscow tysiatsky and the okolnichi signed this treaty as witnesses. Now, with the abolition of the tysiatsky's office, the okolnichi became the grand duke's main assistant in military affairs.

Ivan Veliaminov, Vasili's son, who apparently had expected to be appointed his father's successor, fled to Tver together with a rich merchant by the name of Nekomat. The latter is called "Surozhanin" in our sources, which means that he was engaged in trade with the city of Surozh (Soldaia) in the Crimea. Both of them urged Grand Duke Michael to attack Moscow, apparently trying to convince him that he would find enough support among the populace. More than that: both of them went from Tver to Mamay. Nekomat returned

35. *DDG*, p. 11.

to Tver with the khan's patent on the Grand Duchy of Vladimir issued to Michael.[36] Ivan Veliaminov stayed with Mamay for several years.

None of these devices worked, however; the Muscovite troops smashed the resistance of the Tverians. Receiving no help from either the Lithuanians or the Mongols and disappointed in his hopes for an uprising in Moscow, Michael had to sue for peace. According to the peace treaty of 1375, Michael acknowledged himself "the younger brother" (i.e. vassal) of Dmitri.[37] Furthermore he promised never to claim for himself either the Grand Duchy of Vladimir or Novgorod; he agreed to the independence of one of the Tverian local principalities, Kashin; and he assumed the obligation to support Moscow with the Tverian troops in her future wars. This obligation covered Moscow's eventual conflicts with the Mongols as well as those with Lithuania. Michael thus had to break his friendship with Olgerd.

As a result of this treaty Dmitri emerged the recognized suzerain —on paper at least—of all East Russia except Riazan.

III

Mamay's annulment of Dmitri's patent on the Grand Duchy of Vladimir and his abortive appointment of Michael of Tver as grand duke (1375) indicated an important change in the Mongol ruler's policies toward Russia. They were evidence of Mamay's fear of the growing power of Moscow. Nekomat, who must have been well informed about Moscow's plans, succeeded finally in convincing Mamay that Moscow's expansion must be stopped now or never. An episode which occurred in 1374 was further evidence of Dmitri's defiance of Mongol authority. In that year Mamay sent his envoys and a detachment of about 1,500 troops to the city of Nizhni Novgorod, presumably to compel Prince Dmitri of Suzdal to sever his vassal allegiance to Dmitri of Moscow. The arrival of the embassy became a signal for the city's revolt against the Mongols. Most of Mamay's emissaries and soldiers were killed, and the senior envoy was taken prisoner together with his personal guards. Until now Russian princes had proved ready to suppress the popular revolts and assist the Mongols in restoring their authority. This time Grand Duke Dmitri of Suzdal—undoubtedly acting on instructions of his

36. Soloviev, 3, 345.
37. For the text of the treaty see *DDG,* pp. 25–28.

suzerain Dmitri of Moscow—approved the citizens' action. The
captive Tatars [38] were interned as a group in Nizhni Novgorod. The
next year Prince Vasili (son of Dmitri of Suzdal) ordered that the
prisoners be divided into smaller units and confined in separate
towns. When they refused to obey and tried to resist all of them were
slain.[39]

Upon receiving news of these events Mamay sent another detachment of troops to plunder the southern districts of the principality
of Nizhni Novgorod, restricting his action for the time being to
this local raid. He realized that it would be futile to try to suppress
local revolts one by one since he had to face a graver danger—the
impending rebellion of Grand Duke Dmitri himself. Large-scale
preparations, both military and diplomatic, were needed if the Mongols were to be victorious. As for Mamay's potential allies, Tver was
obviously lost, for a while at least. Riazan could be used against
Moscow but it was not strong. It was therefore to the Grand Duchy
of Lithuania that Mamay turned for assistance. Time was needed to
persuade cautious Grand Duke Olgerd to renew his costly struggle
against Moscow; and when Olgerd died, in 1377, trouble started in
Lithuania. It was not until 1380 that Olgerd's son and successor
Iagailo felt himself secure in the saddle and ready to cooperate with
the Mongols.

A new complication arose for Mamay when Tokhtamysh occupied
Saray and was obviously preparing to continue his drive westward
(1378). Mamay now faced a dilemma. He could either launch a
campaign against Tokhtamysh and let Moscow grow stronger, or try
to defeat Moscow first and then, reinforced with Russia's resources,
turn his attention to Tokhtamysh. He chose to do the latter.

Grand Duke Dmitri of Moscow was also hastily preparing for the
coming test of power. His victory over Tver had made him more
confident of success than before. He could count on the support of
large groups of the Russian people for his policies. In the major
Russian cities opposition to the Mongols had never been entirely
subdued. Now, when the princes sanctioned rebellion, that old
spirit flared up more vigorously than ever. Most of the boyars ad-
vocated bold action, and some church prelates were now willing, if

38. The Russian chronicles use the name Tatars (and not Mongols) throughout. After
the downfall of the Mongol Empire the Turkish (Tatar) element in the Golden Horde
came to the fore. Because of this, from now on I shall use the name Tatars occasionally
and later, for the period after 1419, regularly.

39. Trinity, pp. 396, 398.

necessary, to proclaim a "holy war." When Metropolitan Alexei died in 1378—before events had reached a climax—Abbot Sergius of the Holy Trinity Monastery, a venerated *starets* (elder),[40] became the spiritual leader of Russian Orthodoxy. His refusal to accept the nomination for the metropolitan's see only enhanced his moral prestige among the people at large, who considered him saintly (he was canonized by the Russian church in 1452).

It should not be imagined, however, that there was complete unanimity among the Russians, even in Moscow. Nekomat's attitude was typical of the richest merchants, those who dealt with the Crimea. Some of the boyars too had misgivings about the wisdom of Dmitri's policy. One of them, Ivan Veliaminov, as we know, deserted with Nekomat. There must have been others who, while remaining loyal to Dmitri, did not approve of his policies. Among them was Fedor Koshka, the ancestor of the Romanovs. Years later, in his letter of 1409 to Grand Duke Vasili I (Dmitri's son and successor) the Mongol ruler Edigey praised Koshka for his friendly feelings toward the Horde (*dobraia duma k Orde*).[41]

Koshka started his career under Dmitri. At the time of Dmitri's campaign against Mamay, in 1380, Koshka was left in Moscow to command its garrison. This may be an indication of his lukewarm attitude toward the war. It is possible that men like Nekomat and Koshka felt that time worked for Russia and that it would be more profitable to her to remain within the framework of the Golden Horde as an autonomous state than to start a premature rebellion and, even in case of success, pay a terrible price for achieving independence.

Disregarding all warnings Grand Duke Dmitri, then in his prime, proceeded with his bold plans. His first move was to anchor his left flank on the middle Volga River, extending his control of its course as far down as possible. In order to achieve this he sent his best general, Prince Dmitri Bobrok, with a strong detachment of troops reinforced by the Suzdal army, to the Bulgar region, east of the middle Volga. The main city of that region—also called Bulgar (in Russian, Bolgary)—offered strong resistance. It is noteworthy that the Tatars used firearms: according to the chronicler they "sent

40. On the role of the "startsy" in Russian religious life see G. Vernadsky, *A History of Russia* (3d revised ed. New Haven, Yale University Press, 1951), p. 213; H. Iswolsky, *The Soul of Russia* (New York, Sheed & Ward, 1943), pp. 19–21, 33–34, 80–89; S. I. Chetverikov, *Optina Pustyn'* (Paris, 1926).

41. Nikon, *11*, 212.

thunder from the fortress walls." But the Russians captured the city, and the local Tatar princes had to pledge vassal allegiance to Dmitri. The Russians collected war indemnities of 5,000 rubles from the city and appointed their own officials—a tax collector (doroga) and a customs inspector (tamozhnik).[42]

The Bulgar region belonged not to Mamay but to the Saray khan, Arab-Shah (son of Bulat-Temir). He was greatly worried by the Russian advance, and the next year led his troops into the southern sections of the principality of Nizhni Novgorod. He caught the combined Muscovite and local Russian troops off guard and defeated them on the banks of the Piana River, after which his forces hastened to Nizhni Novgorod and plundered it. Arab-Shah was not able to exploit his success, however, since at that juncture his capital, Saray, was taken by Tokhtamysh. Mamay now stepped into the struggle. Encouraged by news of the Russian disaster, he sent a strong army against Moscow under the command of his ablest lieutenant, Prince Begich. The Russians, under the leadership of Grand Duke Dmitri, the okolnichi Timothy Veliaminov, and Prince Vladimir of Pronsk, met the Mongol troops in the northern part of the principality of Riazan, on the banks of the Vozha (a tributary of the Oka). In the ensuing battle the Russians successfully used the classic Mongol tactics of enveloping the enemy army from both flanks, the Mongols suffered a severe defeat, and their remnants fled south in disorder (1378). The next year the Muscovites apprehended Ivan Veliaminov, who by that time had stealthily returned to Russia. He was publicly executed in Moscow (August 30, 1379) by Grand Duke Dmitri's order. According to the chronicler, "a multitude of people were present at the execution and many of them wept as they thought of his [Veliaminov's] noble nature and past greatness." The chronicler himself explains Veliaminov's revolt against the grand duke as a scheme of Satan.[43]

IV

The victory at the Vozha River naturally caused great elation in Moscow, but at the same time there was much apprehension about the future. Everybody knew that the climax was yet to come.

In fact, dismayed as he was at the news of Begich's defeat, Mamay

---

42. *Ibid.*, *11*, 25. In the Nikon Chronicle the city of Bolgary is identified as Kazan, which is a later interpolation.

43. *Ibid.*, *11*, 45.

had no way to keep in power but to make a supreme effort to crush
Moscow. He hired mercenary troops from among the Genoese, the
Circassians, and the Alans to reinforce his army. In contrast to the
old Mongol armies of only cavalry, he decided to use foot soldiers
as well. The Genoese infantry had a high reputation as a well-
equipped and trained corps. He also reached full understanding
with Grand Dukes Oleg of Riazan and Iagailo of Lithuania. It was
agreed that in case of victory the territory of the Grand Duchy of
Vladimir would be divided between Riazan and Lithuania; Oleg and
Iagailo would rule the conquered Russian lands as the khan's vassals.[44] The Riazan troops were to support Mamay's army on its way
north; Iagailo promised to join them at an appointed place—in the
basin of the upper Don—late in July 1380. When his army was ready
to march on Moscow, Mamay sent emissaries to Dmitri to demand
that he resume his vassal allegiance to the khan and agree to pay
tribute much heavier than he had paid before 1375.

On the advice of Metropolitan Cyprian (Alexei's successor)
Dmitri did not reject the ultimatum at once but sent his own envoys
to Mamay for further negotiations. However, at the borders of the
principality of Riazan these envoys were told that Mamay's army
was already on the move. They immediately sent a messenger to
Dmitri to advise him of the situation and to ask for further instructions. Understanding that there was now no alternative to war,
Metropolitan Cyprian approved Dmitri's decision to offer resistance.
Messengers were immediately sent to all the major cities urging them
to mobilize as fast as possible. Local princes were invited to Moscow
for conferences, and there all the troops available were ordered to be
concentrated at Kolomna by August 15. Grand Duke Dmitri made
a pilgrimage to the Trinity Monastery to ask Abbot Sergius' blessing;
and the abbot sent two monks, Peresvet and Oslebia, to encourage the
troops.

Most of the local Russian princes of the Grand Duchy of Vladimir
—such as those of Beloozero, Ustiug, Kostroma, Rostov, and Iaroslavl—led contingents of their troops to Kolomna. The princes of
Suzdal and Nizhni Novgorod remained at home, presumably being
assigned to guard the middle Volga region, the strategic anchor of the
left flank of the Russian theater of war. Novgorod the Great was
exempt, by treaties, from the duty of sending her troops outside the
Novgorod region. Tver was bound to send auxiliary forces by the

44. *Ibid., 11,* 46–48.

Treaty of 1375, but actually did not send any. Thus that provision
of the treaty of which Dmitri was especially proud proved useless
to him at the time when he needed it most. He could rest assured, however, that Tver did not support the Mongols either. All said, the
people of the Grand Duchy of Vladimir were alone in taking a firm
stand against Mamay.

How large was Dmitri's army? The Nikon Chronicle says 400,000,
which of course is greatly exaggerated. Since for the purpose of
gathering tribute and recruits for the Mongols the Grand Duchy
of Vladimir was divided into fifteen t'my, it could muster 150,000
soldiers at best.[45] Hardly more than one-third of them could have
been actually mobilized at short notice. Moreover, those needed for
the supply and communication services, and those assigned to garrison duty in Moscow and some other cities must be subtracted.
Hence Dmitri's field army could not have been over 30,000 strong.
Mamay's army was apparently about the same size. It had, however, a much greater proportion of cavalry troops, which, in terms
of that age and area, was to its advantage.

By the end of July Mamay's army had reached the plain situated
between the upper Don and its tributary the Nepriadva, near Kulikovo Pole (Snipes' Field), in the Epifan district of Tula province—
according to the 19th-century administrative division of Russia.
There Mamay stopped to await the arrival of Iagailo with his Lithuanians. The latter, however, was late for the rendezvous. Meanwhile
two of Iagailo's brothers who had refused to accept his authority,
Prince Andrew of Polotsk and Prince Dmitri of Briansk, decided to
support Dmitri. Both with their retinues joined Dmitri at Kolomna.
At the war council meeting there late in August both princes insisted
that the Russian army should cross the Don and attack Mamay's
troops before Iagailo joined them (he was then only about 25 miles
away). They were known as skilled military leaders, and their advice prevailed, coinciding as it did with a message from Abbot Sergius
encouraging the army to fight for church and country. The Russian
army was ferried over the Oka River by September 1 and over the
much narrower upper Don six days later.

As soon as the Russians crossed the Don they found themselves
face to face with the Mongols. The bloody battle of Kulikovo Pole
took place on September 8.[46] Because of the numerical superiority of

45. See above, Chapter 3, sec. 8, p. 218.
46. On the battle of Kulikovo Pole see Trinity, pp. 419–420; Nikon, pp. 55–66;

the Mongol cavalry, the Russians were not able to use enveloping tactics. Dmitri however placed a strong detachment of his choice troops in ambush in a nearby forest close to the Don, under the command of his courageous and loyal cousin Prince Vladimir of Serpukhov, with Prince Dmitri Bobrok as adviser. As commander in chief of the main army Dmitri appointed the boyar Michael Brenok. The grand duke himself chose to fight in the ranks.

According to the chronicles the battle was preceded, in the heroic fashion of the chivalry of steppe warfare, by the challenge of a Tatar bogatyr', Temir-Murza, to any Russian to dare to fight a duel with him. Peresvet, one of the two monks sent by Abbot Sergius, accepted the challenge.[47] He galloped full speed against the Tatar, and both were killed in the terrific impact of their collision. Then the general battle started along a seven-mile front.[48] In about four hours it became plain that the advantage was on Mamay's side; the Russian infantry was all but cut to pieces, and the Russian cavalry too was having a difficult time. Two horses in succession were killed under Grand Duke Dmitri. As the Mongols were preparing for a final onslaught, Dmitri Bobrok told Prince Vladimir, commander of the detachment in ambush who had long been itching to take part in the battle, that the moment to strike had come.

The sudden appearance of fresh Russian troops changed the situation at once. Mamay was the first to take flight, and his whole army soon followed him in complete disorder. The Russians chased them several miles and seized Mamay's camp with all its equipment and supplies. Further pursuit was out of the question because of the great losses of the Russians and exhaustion of the survivors. The Tatar casualties were as high as the Russian, each army losing about half its men. When Prince Vladimir, back from pursuit of the fleeing Mongols, stood on the corpse-strewn battlefield for a roll call, many prominent leaders did not answer. Among the slain were the commander in chief Michael Brenok, Prince Fedor Belozersky, and a

---

Karamzin, *5*, 70–76; Soloviev, *3*, 358–360; Kolankowski, pp. 19–20; Nasonov, p. 134; *ZO*, pp. 242–243, 292–294.

47. It should be noted that in medieval Russia, in contrast to the medieval West, it was quite unusual for the clergymen personally to participate in the fighting. The Peresvet and Oslebia case is thus exceptional. Another notable exception, in the later period, was the active participation of the monks in the defense of the Trinity-Sergius Monastery against the Poles in 1608–10.

48. According to the Nikon Chronicle the battle front was ten verstas long. One versta is approximately two-thirds of a mile.

number of other princes and boyars, as well as the Monk Oslebia. For some time it was feared that Grand Duke Dmitri himself had perished in the melee. Finally they found him lying under a tree, apparently dead. He proved to be alive, however, not even seriously wounded, but just stunned.

Dmitri's first concern was the potential threat of the Lithuanian army; he was soon reassured, however, by the news that Iagailo was making hastily for home with all his troops. Grand Duke Oleg of Riazan also fled to Lithuania, and from there later started to negotiate. Dmitri agreed to his return on condition that he acknowledge himself Dmitri's vassal.

There was great rejoicing in Russia at the news of the victory, together with great sorrow at the number of the dead. Immediately after his triumphal return to Moscow, Dmitri made another pilgrimage to the Trinity Monastery; Abbot Sergius officiated in a solemn service for all the Russian soldiers who had lost their lives at Kulikovo Pole. The church authorities then appointed the Saturday on or before October 26 (the Day of St. Dmitri of Salonike, Grand Duke Dmitri's patron saint) as a memorial day to be observed annually "as long as Russia exists." Dmitri's prestige reached its pinnacle. He was referred to as Donskoy—"of the Don." The battle of the Don fired the imagination of the Russians, even if later events somewhat marred its significance. A poem dedicated to it was written by a contemporary Russian writer (probably the priest Sofonia) with the title "Zadonshchina" ("Deeds beyond the Don"). From the literary point of view it is a rather pale imitation of the 12th-century "Lay of Igor's Campaign." [49] A number of legends connected with the battle were included in the late compilations of Russian annals, such as the Nikon Chronicle; they were also used in the numerous stories devoted to the battle, generally known under the name of "Mamayevo Poboishche" ("The Mamay Carnage").

The battle of the Don represented the supreme spiritual and material effort of which East Russia was capable at the time. If the

---

49. It should be mentioned that according to the French scholar André Mazon it is the "Lay of Igor's Campaign" which should be considered an imitation of the "Zadonshchina," and not vice versa. Mazon's theory is unacceptable to me. See A. Mazon, *Le Slovo d'Igor* (Paris, 1940); *idem*, "Le Slovo d'Igor," *RES, 21* (1944), 5-45. Mazon's thesis has been refuted by Roman Jakobson; see H. Grégoire, R. Jakobson, M. Szeftel, J. A. Joffe, "La Geste du Prince Igor'," *Annuaire, 8* (1948). For Mazon's answer see *SEER, 27* (1948-49), 515-535; for Jakobson's recent article on the problem see "The Puzzles of the Igor' Tale," *Speculum, 27* (1952), 43-66.

troubles in the Golden Horde had continued, it would have secured immediate independence for Russia. Actually, however, unity and strong government were restored in the Horde soon after Mamay's defeat. Almost without a respite Russia had to face a new and even harder test. And that test, because of the heavy losses of 1380, she proved unable to pass.

3. TOKHTAMYSH AND TAMERLANE

I

The defeat at Kulikovo Pole was a severe blow to the Mongol power but not a mortal one. Mamay lost no time in organizing a new army for another expedition against Moscow. At that juncture, however, he had to face a greater danger: the onslaught of a rival Mongol leader, Tamerlane's vassal Tokhtamysh, the ruler of Saray. The clash between the two armies took place in 1381 on the banks of the Kalka River near the spot where the Russians had first been defeated by the Mongols in 1223.

This second battle of the Kalka resulted in a complete victory for Tokhtamysh' troops. Following the debacle, most of the Mongol princes and generals who had up to now recognized Mamay as their leader went over to the conqueror's side. Mamay, with a few followers, escaped to the Crimean port of Kaffa, at that time controlled by the Genoese. He succeeded in taking with him most of his gold and jewelry, by means of which he probably hoped to hire new troops or at least secure a decent living for himself and his retinue. The Genoese let him in, but soon after killed him and seized his treasure. The Russian chronicler commented philosophically: "And thus ended in evil the evil Mamay's life." [50]

With his victory over Mamay Tokhtamysh became sovereign of both the eastern and western sections of Juchi's Ulus—in fact one of the mightiest rulers of the period. It was but natural that he considered it his duty to restore the Golden Horde's authority over Russia. One of his first moves was to confirm the alliance Mamay had made with Lithuania. He sent his envoy to notify Grand Duke Iagailo of his accession to power. As we know, before the battle at Kulikovo, Iagailo had acknowledged himself a vassal of the khan. While the text of Tokhtamysh' charter to Iagailo of 1381 has

50. Nikon, *11*, 69.

not been preserved, we may assume from a later yarlyk of his (1393) that he declared his suzerainty, as the khan of the Golden Horde, over the grand duke of Lithuania.[51] At the same time Tokhtamysh notified Grand Duke Dmitri of Moscow, as well as other Russian grand dukes and princes, of his victory over their mutual enemy Mamay. Neither Dmitri nor any other Russian prince considered it proper to pay a personal visit to Tokhtamysh; all of them, however, sent special envoys (kilichei) to the new tsar with their greetings and many gifts. While this action might be taken to be renewal of the vassal submission of the Russian princes, Tokhtamysh understood that the Russians did not intend to resume their former obligations toward the Golden Horde. His next move therefore was to send an envoy extraordinary to Moscow to reaffirm his authority. The envoy got as far as Nizhni Novgorod and was not allowed to proceed further. The failure of this mission convinced Tokhtamysh that the only way to bring Moscow to obedience was war. He immediately started preparations to attack Russia.

Tokhtamysh by no means underestimated the strength of the Russians. He saw his only chance in secrecy and speed. So he concentrated his troops—all cavalry—beyond the Volga and occupied the city of Bolgary (Bulgar) as Batu had done when he first attacked Russia. Then he ordered the seizure of all the Russian merchant flotillas on the river—he needed the boats for ferrying his army across—and the arrest of the merchants so that none could inform the Russian princes of the impending attack. Incidentally, as Iakubovsky rightly remarks, this episode shows that the Volga shipping was, at that time, controlled by the Russians.[52]

When Tokhtamysh' army appeared on the western bank of the middle Volga, the Russians were caught completely by surprise. Both Grand Duke Oleg of Riazan and Grand Duke Dmitri of Suzdal and Nizhni Novgorod found themselves compelled to assume a policy of benevolent neutrality toward the invader if not of active cooperation with him. The grand duke of Suzdal hastened to send his two sons, Simeon and Vasili, to Tokhtamysh' camp. Oleg of Riazan supplied the Mongols with guides on condition that they spare his principality.

Gloom and consternation prevailed in Moscow when the news of

51. The text of the yarlyk of 1381 has not been preserved, but there is a reference to it in that of 1393. For a transcription of the text of the latter see Kurat, p. 147; for a Russian translation see Radlov, 6. Cf. ZO, pp. 323–324.

52. ZO, p. 326.

Tokhtamysh' approach reached the city.[53] Since it was too late to order a general mobilization, many princes and boyars recommended immediate surrender as the only way to avoid complete ruin. Grand Duke Dmitri disregarded their advice. He decided to let the city of Moscow defend herself as best she could behind her stone walls, and meanwhile to organize a relief army in the northern regions of his dominions. He went himself to Kostroma and sent his cousin Vladimir of Serpukhov to Volokolamsk, to protect the road to Novgorod. Much depended on the attitude of Grand Duke Michael of Tver, but he kept an ominous silence.

It will be recalled that Grand Duke Olgerd of Lithuania had tried twice to storm the new stone walls of Moscow and failed. Probably Dmitri hoped the Mongols too would fail, especially as the Moscow garrison was now equipped with firearms, both cannons and hand-guns. The latter must have been of the type the Russians became acquainted with at Bulgar in 1376. That Dmitri was confident of Moscow's capacity to withstand the Mongol attack may be inferred from the fact that he allowed his wife—Grand Duchess Evdokia—Metropolitan Cyprian, and some of the major boyars to stay in the city.

However, as soon as he left the capital dissension broke out among the people. The wealthy wanted to follow the grand duke to safety. The commoners wanted to stay and resist the invaders. Those of the wealthy who tried to escape were killed and their property looted by the angered commoners. A general assembly (veche) met with the commoners in complete control. They manned the walls, forbidding anyone to leave the city. Exception was made only for the metropolitan and the grand duchess with their respective retinues. While they received a permit to go north, they were not allowed to take their treasure along. The grand duchess hastened to Kostroma to join her husband. The metropolitan, however, preferred to go to Tver. Not trusting any of the local boyars, the veche elected as commander of the Moscow garrison a Lithuanian prince by the name of Ostei whom the Nikon Chronicle calls a grandson of Olgerd. He succeeded in restoring order in the city and started hasty preparations for defense. People were apparently impressed with his efficiency and self-assurance, and more refugees from the neighboring towns and rural districts hurried to Moscow.

On August 23, 1382 Tokhtamysh' army appeared before the walls

53. The basic Russian accounts of Tokhtamysh' invasion are the following: Trinity, pp. 422–425; Simeonov, pp. 131–133; Nikon, *11*, 71–81.

of the city. The Muscovites seem to have been unanimous now in their decision to fight. The chronicler, however, noted the difference in attitude between the "good people" who prepared themselves for death by praying to God and the "wicked people" who looted the cellars of the wealthy and fortified themselves with drink. For three days and nights the Mongols attacked the city furiously but were unable to take it. Then Tokhtamysh decided to use deceit and on August 26 proposed a truce, asking only "small gifts" as the price of lifting the siege. The two Suzdal princes who accompanied him vouched for the sincerity of his offer.

The Muscovites were naïve enough to believe them. As the gates were opened and the procession of Moscow notables led by Prince Ostei went to greet the tsar, the Mongols fell upon them and cut them to pieces. Meanwhile other bands of Mongols rushed to the city. There followed terrible carnage and looting. The conquerors seized the grand ducal treasury as well as the accumulated riches of the boyars and wealthy merchants. Precious gold vessels and crosses, jewel-bedecked fabrics and other art objects were seized in the churches. The chronicler recorded with special grief the loss of books, explaining that a multitude of books had been brought to the Moscow churches from the neighboring towns and villages in an attempt to save them from the invaders. All were thrown away or burned by the Tatars. When the looting ended the city was set on fire. "Until then the city of Moscow had been large and wonderful to look at," lamented the chronicler, "crowded as she was with people, filled with wealth and glory . . . and now all at once all her beauty perished and her glory disappeared. Nothing could be seen but smoking ruins and bare earth and heaps of corpses." [54]

As soon as news of the disaster reached Tver, Grand Duke Michael sent his envoy to Tokhtamysh with rich presents. The tsar received him graciously and issued his patent to Michael for the Grand Duchy of Tver. Meanwhile the Mongols spread over the territory of the principality of Moscow, looting both towns and villages. But when they approached Volokolamsk Prince Vladimir counterattacked and turned them to flight. Simultaneously, Tokhtamysh' scouts reported that Grand Duke Dmitri had gathered a considerable force at Kostroma. On the basis of these reports Tokhtamysh ordered retreat, having every reason to be satisfied with the results already achieved. On the way back the Mongols looted Riazan principality,

54. Nikon, *11*, 78–79.

which had remained neutral during the war. When Grand Duke
Dmitri and Prince Vladimir returned to what was left of Moscow,
they wept at sight of the destruction. Dmitri's first order was to bury
all the corpses still unburied. He paid one ruble for interring eighty
bodies. The total expense came to 300 rubles, from which it may be
deduced that 24,000 were buried at that time. Dmitri's next move
was to punish Grand Duke Oleg of Riazan for what he considered
his treason. The unhappy principality of Riazan, which had just
suffered at the hands of Tokhtamysh' troops, was now looted once
more by the Muscovites. So Oleg's attempt to sit on the fence brought
only ruin to his people.

While Dmitri could take some grim satisfaction in having punished
the grand duke of Riazan, he was not able to re-establish his suzerainty over Riazan; nor could he restore Moscow's supremacy over
Tver. All the achievements of his diplomacy of the 1370's in interprincely relations came to nothing. For some time the grand duke
of Moscow seemed to have lost even the support of the church, which
had so far been one of his main assets in interprincely conflicts. It
was to Tver, not to Dmitri's temporary residence in Kostroma, that
Metropolitan Cyprian went when he left Moscow on the eve of its
siege. Dmitri now sent two boyars to Tver to invite Cyprian to
return to Moscow. While Cyprian came, reluctantly, he was apparently unwilling to promise Dmitri his support against Tver. A
sharp conflict arose between the grand duke and the metropolitan,
and as a result Cyprian went to Kiev which still was nominally the
metropolitan's see. He thus avoided having to take a firm stand in
the controversy between Moscow and Tver. Kiev, however, was controlled by the grand duke of Lithuania, and the political consequences
of the metropolitan's siding with Lithuania could have been even more
ominous to Moscow than his supporting Tver.

All in all, the heavy sacrifices made by the Russians in resisting
the Mongols in the 1370's now seemed to have been made in vain.
The political atmosphere in Russia in 1383 reminds one of the
earlier period of Mongol domination: most of the Russian princes
hastened to the Horde to offer their pledge of submission to the new
tsar and to receive patents from him. Among them were Grand Duke
Michael of Tver with his son Alexander, and Prince Boris of Gorodets, brother of Grand Duke Dmitri of Suzdal. The latter's son Vasili
had already been in the Horde, having had to accompany Tokhtamysh
in the tsar's retreat from the ruins of Moscow. Dmitri of Suzdal

himself was not able to go because of illness (he died not long after). Grand Duke Dmitri of Moscow failed to appear personally but sent his eldest son Vasili to represent him.

As might be expected, the grand duke of Tver presented his claims to the Grand Duchy of Vladimir. Had Tokhtamysh recognized these claims, the political situation in Russia would have become similar to that in the early 14th century, and Tver would have had another chance to try to assume leadership of all East Russia. Tokhtamysh, however, did not intend to replace Moscow's supremacy by that of Tver. He preferred to keep East Russia divided into several grand duchies, being confident of his ability to hold a balance between them, especially since Moscow now seemed exhausted and humiliated. The tsar therefore confirmed Michael's patent as grand duke of Tver but the patent on the Grand Duchy of Vladimir was granted to Dmitri of Moscow. To enforce the obedience of both Tokhtamysh kept both Michael's son Alexander and Dmitri's son Vasili in the Horde as hostages. Since Tokhtamysh was Tamerlane's vassal and Tamerlane the vassal of the Ming emperor of China, Moscow was now again—legally at least—under the supreme authority of Peking as she used to be in the age of the Yuan dynasty.

All the Russian principalities were required to resume regular payments of tribute and other taxes at the rates established during the reign of Janibeg, which were much higher than those of the period of the Great Trouble in the Horde.[55] The people of the Grand Duchy of Vladimir had to pay heavy indemnities either in gold (the tamga) or in silver (the tribute) in 1384. The Novgorodians were subject to the Black Collection. Furthermore, Russia had again to supply contingents of troops to the tsar's army whenever he requested it. While there is no definite evidence in Russian sources of the renewal of conscription, it is known from Persian sources that Russian troops constituted part of Tokhtamysh' grand army of 1388.[56]

II

Russia's future looked black indeed in 1383. By one stroke Tokhtamysh had restored Mongol control over Russia, and the Golden Horde now seemed stronger than it had ever been. It looked as if

55. Janibeg's rates of taxation are mentioned in Edigey's letter of 1409 to Vasili I, *SGGD*, 2, 16.
56. *ZO*, p. 338.

the Russians must resume their subservient attitude to the Mongols for many years to come, until they could accumulate new strength. The decline of the authority of the grand duke of Moscow and Vladimir, which resulted in lessening the degree of national unity previously achieved, was another unfortunate factor in the situation.

Actually, Russia succeeded in recovering her autonomy and promoting her national unity much faster than could have been expected. That the course of history proved more favorable to Russia than it had looked at first was not the result (or at least not only) of Russia's own efforts but of the intervention of a third power—Tamerlane's (Timur's) Central Asian Empire, its victory over the Golden Horde, and the subsequent resumption of the process of disintegration within the Golden Horde itself.

The open conflict between Tokhtamysh and Timur began four years after Tokhtamysh seized Moscow. However, friction between the two rulers had been evident since 1383. The conflict had two aspects, personal and geopolitical. From the psychological angle, while Tokhtamysh was indebted to Timur for his initial successes, after his victory over Russia he considered himself a mightier ruler than his suzerain and behaved like an independent khan. As early as 1383 he had ordered money with his name on it coined in Khorezm, whose suzerainty Timur also claimed. From the geopolitical angle, the conflict between Tokhtamysh' state and Timur's empire was a revival of the old antagonism between the Golden Horde and the empire of the il-khans of the late 13th and the 14th centuries. The similarity of the diplomatic aspects of the early and the new contest was clearly shown by Tokhtamysh' attempt to secure the cooperation of the Mameluks. In 1385 he sent envoys to Egypt to prepare the way for an alliance, just as the earlier Juchids had done.

The two main regions disputed by the Golden Horde and the Central Asian Empire were Khorezm in Central Asia and Azerbaijan in Transcaucasia. Both were autonomous when the conflict between Timur and Tokhtamysh started. Each was ruled by a local dynasty, Khorezm by the Sufis and Azerbaijan by the Jalayrs. In 1385 Timur undertook a campaign against Azerbaijan. While he defeated the Jalayr troops at Sultaniah he did not complete the conquest of the country, and soon returned to Persia. Timur's campaign showed the weakness of the local Azerbaijan rulers, and Tokhtamysh decided to take advantage of the situation. In the winter of 787 A.H. (A.D. 1385–86) Tokhtamysh seized Tabriz by the same wile that had tricked the

Moscovites three years earlier. The city was looted and destroyed as thoroughly as Moscow had been. This raid opened Timur's eyes to the seriousness of the threat he had to face from the Golden Horde. As soon as Tokhtamysh withdrew north Timur appeared in Azerbaijan with a strong army. In the winter of 788 A.H. (A.D. 1386–87) Timur's vanguard troops clashed in Daghestan with Tokhtamysh' army. While the battle was indecisive Tokhtamysh ordered a retreat.

There is no doubt that from the very beginning of the clash between the two Mongol rulers the Russian princes, who had excellent information on what was going on in the Golden Horde, understood the implications of the incipient conflict for Mongol-Russian relations. Any trouble in the Golden Horde could mean a relaxation of Mongol control over Russia. The first to profit by the new situation was Vasili of Moscow, Grand Duke Dmitri's son, who was kept in the Horde as a hostage. In the fall of 1386 he escaped with the help of some Mongol officials friendly to him. He went first to Moldavia and then, by way of Germany, to Lithuania, where he asked Prince Vitovt for protection. Vitovt at that time felt slighted by his cousin, King Iagailo of Poland, and was preparing to rebel. Looking for allies in the future struggle, he secretly negotiated with the Teutonic Knights. He now decided to use Vasili as a means of establishing friendly relations with Moscow. He made Vasili promise to marry his daughter Sophia, then about sixteen, when the time should be opportune. After this pledge Vitovt showed Vasili every honor and helped him return to Moscow through Polotsk. Vasili appeared in his native city on January 19, 1387 accompanied by several Lithuanian princes and boyars.[57]

Had Tokhtamysh' position been secure, he would probably have required that Vasili be punished for his escape. However, the tsar could not afford to be harsh with Moscow as he was about to launch a new campaign against Timur. This time Tokhtamysh led his troops not to Transcaucasia but across the Volga and the Iaik rivers to Central Asia. His plan was to attack Transoxania, the heart of Timur's dominions. He succeeded in reaching Bukhara but was unable to storm the city. After his troops had looted all the country round he turned back.

Timur in retaliation entered Khorezm and devastated the prosperous city of Urgenj, the hub of Central Asian commerce. The next move in this battle of giants who in their fury destroyed everything

57. They are called "Poles" in Nikon, *11*, 91.

in their path was made by Tokhtamysh. In 1388 he gathered a huge army into which, according to the Persian historian Sharaf ad-Din, he drafted soldiers from all the peoples of Juchi's Ulus, including Russians, Bulgars, Circassians, and Alans.[58] It apparently included contingents of both Muscovite and Suzdalian troops, the former under the command of Prince Vasili of Moscow and the latter under that of Grand Duke Boris of Suzdal and Nizhni Novgorod. Once more Tokhtamysh penetrated deep into Central Asia. An indecisive battle took place on the banks of the Syr-Darya River in the early spring of 1389; then Tokhtamysh turned back and retreated to Kazakhstan in order to reorganize his army. The two Russian princes accompanying him, Boris and Vasili, were allowed to return home.

Soon after Vasili reached Moscow his father, Grand Duke Dmitri, died (May 19, 1389). Three months later Vasili was solemnly installed on the throne of the Grand Duchy of Vladimir by Tokhtamysh' envoy, Prince Shikhmat. About the same time three important Mongol officials appeared in Moscow expressing their desire to become Christians and to serve the new grand duke. They were probably Vasili's old friends, who had helped him to escape from the Horde. They were baptized in Moscow amid popular rejoicing. This event was symptomatic enough. It evidenced the feeling among some of the Mongol grandees that the grand duke of Moscow sat firmer in the saddle than their own khan and that Moscow was a safer place to live than Saray.

Vasili's prestige was greatly enhanced by his marrying Vitovt's daughter Sophia as well as by the return to Moscow of Metropolitan Cyprian. Both these events took place in 1390. At that time Vitovt was in Prussia, having concluded an alliance with the Teutonic Knights against Iagailo. The rapprochement with Vasili proved a skillful diplomatic move for Vitovt. Fearing to be caught between two fires—Prussia and Moscow—Iagailo had to reconsider his attitude toward Vitovt, and finally in 1392 the two cousins made an agreement which recognized Vitovt as grand duke of Lithuania. Following that he immediately broke relations with the knights. His relations with Moscow, however, continued to be friendly for some time.

III

In 1391 the conflict between Tokhtamysh and Timur entered its decisive phase. Annoyed by Tokhtamysh' devastating raids on

58. Tiesenhausen, 2, 156.

Transoxania, Timur decided to go after his adversary in his own dominions. In February 1391, after careful preparations, he concentrated an army said to be of 200,000 men at Otrar on the Syr-Darya River, and gathered a kuriltay which approved his plans, at which the commanders of the units received final instructions. The army reached Saryg-Uzen (Sary-Su) in Kazakhstan in April, where water was ample, and paused to rest. Conscious of the historic importance of his campaign, Timur ordered an inscription to be carved on a nearby rock to record his camping there (April 28, 1391).[59]

The army Timur led to Kazakhstan was a formidable war machine.[60] Every detail of its organization and equipment was based either on the best Mongol military traditions or on Timur's own previous experience. While he followed the general principles of the decimal army organization and of stern discipline laid down by Chingis-Khan, Timur introduced some important innovations in both strategy and tactics. Among other things, he assigned an important role to infantry. To enable his foot soldiers to withstand cavalry attacks, he created a corps of experienced sappers. On the battlefield his infantry was well protected by trenches which were fortified with huge shields. The whole army was divided into seven corps, two of which formed a reserve that the commander in chief could throw in any direction depending on the course of the battle, to support either the center or a flank. The center was made much stronger than in the Mongol armies of old, in fact stronger than in Timur's own earlier armies.

In May Timur ordered his army to organize a great battue, partly to replenish food stocks and partly to give his officers and men final training. It was successful in both repects. Then Timur led his army north to the region of the upper Tobol River where, according to the intelligence reports, part of Tokhtamysh' army was stationed. By the time Timur's soldiers reached the Tobol, however, Tokhtamysh' troops had withdrawn west to the Iaik River. It was obvious that Tokhtamysh wanted to avoid a decisive battle as much as Timur

59. *ZO*, p. 357.

60. There is an old but still useful study of the organization of Timur's army by M. Charmoy, "Expédition de Timour-i-lenk ou Tamerlan contre Toqtamiche," *Mémoires de l'Académie Impériale des Sciences de St. Petersbourg*, 6th ser., *3* (1836), 89–505. It should be noted, however, that in addition to the authentic sources he used, Charmoy also took into consideration an apocryphal treatise, the so-called "Timur's Institutions." Recently, strange to say, Ferdinand Lot has based his whole account of Timur's army on "Timur's Institutions" (Lot, *2*, 353–370). There is an excellent brief outline of Timur's military establishment by A. Iu. Iakubovsky in *ZO*, pp. 339–354.

desired one. While Timur proceeded hastily to the Iaik Tokhtamysh retreated once more; and it was only in the middle Volga area, in the region of Samara (Kuibyshev), that Timur's troops reached their enemies' main camp. This time no orderly retreat was possible for Tokhtamysh; he had to accept battle on June 18, 1391 on the banks of the Kondurcha River, a tributary of the Sok (which in turn is an eastern tributary of the Volga north of present-day Kuibyshev). The bloody battle ended in a complete rout of Tokhtamysh' army. Tokhtamysh himself escaped with but a few followers. Immense booty was seized by the conquerors.

Contrary to Chingis-Khan's principles, Timur made no attempt to pursue Tokhtamysh beyond the Volga, apparently thinking him no longer dangerous. However, he agreed to let two important leaders from Juchi's Ulus who had sided with him against Tokhtamysh— Prince Timur-Kutlugh (a grandson of Urus-Khan) [61] and the amir Edigey—leave him and go to Kypchak, presumably counting on their opposing Tokhtamysh if he tried a comeback. By the close of the year Timur returned triumphantly to his capital of Samarkand. Feeling secure now from Tokhtamysh' inroads, he agreed to restore the city of Urgenj in Khorezm which he had destroyed three years earlier.

It soon became clear that Timur had underestimated Tokhtamysh' personality and resources. While he had lost the whole eastern part of Juchi's Ulus (east of the Iaik River) he still controlled its western part, the Golden Horde proper. Most of the princes and grandees of the Golden Horde remained loyal to their khan. We hear nothing of the activities, in this period, of Timur-Kutlugh and Edigey. Presumably they did not as yet dare to oppose Tokhtamysh openly.

Much depended on the attitude toward the khan of both Moscow and Lithuania. To keep Moscow on his side Tokhtamysh had to alter his Russian policies drastically. Instead of keeping a balance between the four Russian grand duchies he now saw his only chance of retaining control over East Russia in making concessions to the strongest duchy—that of Moscow. Grand Duke Vasili immediately took advantage of the new situation by asking the tsar to let him annex to Moscow the whole grand duchy of Nizhni Novgorod. The ground for this claim was carefully prepared by the Moscow boyars, who held secret negotiations with the boyars of Nizhni Novgorod behind the back of their grand duke, Boris. Vasili personally ap-

61. See Genealogical Table VI.

peared in Tokhtamysh' camp and showered both tsar and grandees with presents. After receiving the patent on the throne of Nizhni Novgorod he returned to Moscow accompanied by the tsar's special envoy, who was then sent to Nizhni Novgorod together with the leading Moscow boyars. Grand Duke Boris, abandoned by his fol-lowers, was promptly arrested. Nizhni Novgorod had to accept a lieutenant of Vasili's as governor. Vasili was then again invited to Tokhtamysh' camp and treated "with great respect, such as no Russian prince had ever been shown." [62] In addition to Nizhni Novgorod the tsar granted him the principalities of Gorodets, Meshchera, and Tarusa. In return the grand duke of Moscow agreed to continue to recognize Tokhtamysh as his sovereign. Moscow, however, was now stronger than she had ever been, and an important step had been made toward the unity of East Russia, even if it was achieved by means of dubious morality.

Tokhtamysh now turned his attention to Lithuania and Poland. He sent envoys to King Iagailo of Poland demanding that he re-affirm his loyalty and agree to pay tribute from Kiev, Podolia, and some other West Russian regions. Since Vitovt was now grand duke of Lithuania, Tokhtamysh' envoys had to talk to him as well. An agreement satisfactory to Tokhtamysh was reached, although the details are not known. He also resumed relations with the Mameluks whom he still hoped to enlist as allies against Timur.

Feeling greatly encouraged by his diplomatic achievements and having drafted and trained a new army, Tokhtamysh decided to resume a limited offensive against Timur in the Caucasus. In the autumn of 1394 his troops passed Derbend and appeared in the region of Shirvan, looting everything along their path. Upon news of this Timur sent an envoy demanding that Tokhtamysh withdraw his troops and once more recognize Timur's suzerainty. This Tokh-tamysh refused to do. The final clash between the two rulers became inevitable.

IV

In February 1395 Timur set out northward from Transcaucasia to Daghestan, along the western shore of the Caspian Sea. In April his army established a fortified camp in the Terek River valley, from which it faced Tokhtamysh' main forces. The clash occurred on April 15. For many hours the issue of the battle was not clear, but

62. Nikon, *11*, 148.

finally Timur's reserve regiments entered the contest and broke the resistance of the enemy. As in 1391, Timur's soldiers seized immense riches in Tokhtamysh' abandoned camp. But this time Timur attempted to pursue Tokhtamysh who, fleeing with a small retinue across the lower Volga, sought refuge in Bulgar on the middle Volga. Timur too crossed the Volga but soon lost track of the fugitive. He ordered Prince Kairichak-Oglan (Urus-Khan's son), whom he apparently intended to install as vassal ruler of the Golden Horde, to establish order in the region of the lower Volga.

Timur returned to the western bank of the Volga and crushed the sporadic resistance of Tokhtamysh' amirs on the lower Don. Then after resting his troops a few weeks he started a new campaign—this time against Russia. His army marched north up the course of the Don in two columns, one advancing in the plains east of the river and the other on the western side. In July both columns reached the southern districts of the principality of Riazan. The western column, under Timur's personal command, stormed the city of Elets. The prince of Elets was taken prisoner and the inhabitants of the city either slain or enslaved. After the capture of Elets Timur established his camp there, letting his troops plunder the country around. Presumably he sent scouts and spies north and awaited their reports.

The Russians, well informed of the course of the previous struggle between Timur and Tokhtamysh, were prepared for any eventuality. The army of the Grand Duchy of Vladimir (which now included the former Grand Duchy of Nizhni Novgorod) was mobilized in June and July. Early in August Grand Duke Vasili concentrated his main forces at Kolomna. A strong garrison was left in Moscow under the command of Prince Vladimir of Serpukhov, the hero of the battle of Kulikovo Pole. By letting that able and popular prince take charge of the defense of Moscow, Vasili apparently hoped to prevent the repetition of riots of the city populace such as had taken place at the time of Tokhtamysh' invasion.

Vasili's main strategic plan was apparently to defend the line of the Oka River rather than cross it and advance southward as his father, Dmitri Donskoy, had done. In order to raise the spirits of his soldiers and especially to reassure the Muscovites, Vasili asked Metropolitan Cyprian to have brought to Moscow the venerated icon of Our Lady which had been kept in the Vladimir Cathedral since the mid-12th century and was considered miracle-working. According to the legend it was painted by St. Luke the Evangelist. (In the opinion of art historians it is actually the work of an 11th-century Byzantine painter.) [63] Cyprian approved Vasili's plan and sent his clerics to Vladimir to bring the icon to Moscow. It was taken from the cathedral on August 15, the holy day of the Dormition of Our Lady. A solemn cortege of clergy and laymen accompanied it on its way to the capital. The cortege appeared before Moscow on August 26, the thirteenth anniversary of the seizure of the city by Tokhtamysh' troops. The people of Moscow led by Prince Vladimir, Metropolitan Cyprian, church dignitaries, and boyars went out to meet it. After solemn litanies the icon was brought to the cathedral and set up there. The whole procedure seems to have had a very heartening effect on the Muscovites. It was undoubtedly an important psychological event which helped to strengthen religious feeling among the Russians and their will to resist.

It so happened that the day the icon of Our Lady of Vladimir reached Moscow Timur announced the termination of his campaign and ordered a retreat. The story spread among the Russians, that as Timur lay asleep that day he had a vision which terrified him. He saw in the skies a Lady in purple vestments leading an innumerable host to guard the road to Moscow. When he awoke, he was trembling and for a long time could not explain to his courtiers what had happened to him.[64]

As a matter of fact, Timur must have heard by this time of the readiness of the Russians to defend themselves and of the strength and good organization of their army. He must have known that it was only by catching them off guard that his rival Tokhtamysh had succeeded in defeating them thirteen years earlier. Timur could hope to defeat them but he must have realized that his own army would suffer great losses. Besides, the campaign would have taken time and led him too far from the center of his empire.

While Timur did not reach Moscow, he made the best publicity he could out of his campaign. His occupying the southern outskirts of the principality of Riazan was represented as the conquest of Russia. Stories of this kind, told by Timur's officers who had participated in the campaign, were used by the Persian historian Sharaf ad-Din, who lived at the court of Timur's son Shahrukh and completed his *Book of Victories* twenty years after Timur's death. In describing the

63. On the icon of Our Lady of Vladimir see A. I. Anisimov, *Vladimirskaia ikona Bozhiei Materi* (Prague, 1928).

64. Nikon, *11*, 160.

campaign of 1395 Sharaf ad-Din stated that Timur reached Moscow ("Mashkaw") and seized rich booty there.[65] Not only Sharaf ad-Din's contemporaries in Central Asia but some modern Orientalists as well have taken his story at face value. Both Edward G. Browne in his *History of Persian Literature* and L. Bouvat in *L'Empire Mongol* repeat his statement.[66] And yet, granted that it would have been too much trouble for these two scholars to consult Russian literature on the subject—"Slavica non leguntur" (Slavic can't be read)—they could easily have consulted Gibbon for a right appraisal of Sharaf ad-Din's mistake.[67]

On his way home Timur seized and looted the city of Azak (present-day Azov) at the mouth of the Don and devastated the land of the Circassians in the western part of the north Caucasus. From there he turned, in the winter of 1395–96, to the lower Volga region and burned the two main centers of the Golden Horde—Astrakhan and New Saray or Berke's Saray. Well satisfied with his handiwork, Timur returned to Samarkand and soon started planning his Indian campaign. It took place in 1398–99 and netted fabulous treasures.

4. THE RULE OF EDIGEY

I

The results of Timur's campaigns against the Golden Horde were catastrophic for the latter from the economic point of view as well as the military. The prosperity of the Horde depended on international commerce, especially on trade with the Far East. The great caravan roads from China and India converged at Urgenj, and from there the routes led to Old Saray (whose role had been assumed by Astrakhan since about 1360) and New Saray. From Astrakhan goods were transported to Azov (Tana) where Italian merchants took them in charge for further shipping. All of these great trading centers— Urgenj, Astrakhan, Saray, Azov—were destroyed by Timur during his struggle with Tokhtamysh. Timur intended apparently not merely to defeat his rival's armies but to sap the commercial strength of the Golden Horde by rerouting the Chinese and Indian trade with the West from the north Caspian and Black Sea regions to Persia and Syria. He hoped thus to deprive the Horde of the benefits of the

65. Tiesenhausen, 2, 180.
66. Browne 3, 192; Bouvat, p. 50.
67. Gibbon, 2, 1237.

Far Eastern trade and to obtain all these profits for his own empire. He succeeded to a considerable extent in this undertaking. According to the Venetian envoy Giosafato Barbaro, who visited the Golden Horde in 1436, Azov's former trade in silk and spices was all but extinct, and those goods were now going through Syria.[68] The Crimean ports—Kaffa and Soldaia—were also affected by the dislocation of the Oriental commerce. They continued to trade with the Golden Horde and Russia (until the late 15th century when the Venetian and Genoese factories in the Crimea were closed by the Ottoman Turks), but that trade was more restricted in scope than the Far Eastern.

Commerce was not the sole branch of economics of the Golden Horde which Timur disrupted. The major cities he destroyed were centers not only of trade but of crafts and industries of various sorts. All these were now ruined. The effect of Timur's campaigns on the Golden Horde was thus like that of Batu's campaign on Russia. The destruction of the main cities eliminated the leading cultural groups of society, in terms both of economics and of intellectual life and technology.

The effect on the development of the Golden Horde could not but be disastrous. The cultural level of the Kypchak state was lowered drastically. While its former progress had been based on a symbiosis of nomadism and city culture, the nomads were now left temporarily at least to their own resources. They still constituted a strong military power but lacked the benefits of the cultural leadership of the cities. Among other things, they now had no proper arsenal of war. This was the period of an important change in military technique— the rapid spread of firearms. While its neighbors, including Muscovy and Lithuania, started producing firearms, the Golden Horde for the time being had no means of doing so. True, firearms were still in the experimental stage and of but limited use, but as a characteristic facet of general technical progress they were important. It was only on the periphery of the Golden Horde—in the Bulgar region in the basin of the middle Volga River, and in the Crimea—that city culture continued to flourish. Before long, however, these two regions showed a tendency to emancipate themselves from the nomadic core of the Horde and eventually each of them served as a base for local khanates, those of Kazan and of the Crimea. All said, there is no doubt that after the blows administered by Timur, the economic and tech-

68. *ZO*, p. 376.

nological foundations of the Golden Horde shrank catastrophically. A political and military revival of the Horde still proved possible but not for long, in view of the rapid growth of neighboring states such as the Ottoman Empire, Muscovy, and Lithuania.

As soon as Timur withdrew to Samarkand, the persevering Tokhtamysh dashed back to the Kychak steppes and attempted to rebuild his power. He went first to the Crimea, which he apparently decided to make his main base. Owing to its geographic location the Crimean peninsula could be defended against even a superior enemy. During the debacle of 1395 the Genoese had seized power in the Crimea.[69] Tokhtamysh attacked the Genoese forces and stormed Kaffa, where he probably seized considerable riches. He certainly needed money to rebuild his army and state. At first he met with some success in promoting his plans and before long issued a call to all the Mongol grandees and princes who had not yet rejoined him to do so. By 1398 he felt strong enough to attempt to restore his authority over Russia, and sent an envoy to Prince Oleg of Riazan.

At this point, however, trouble started again in the Golden Horde. Tokhtamysh' rivals, Timur-Kutlugh and Edigey, finally succeeded in organizing a revolt against him. The majority of the Mongol grandees deserted their sovereign and proclaimed Timur-Kutlugh the new khan. Edigey became co-ruler. Both sent envoys to Timur to pledge vassal allegiance to him.[70] Meanwhile Tokhtamysh, at the head of several thousand troops who remained loyal to him, galloped to Kiev and asked Grand Duke Vitovt to help him regain his throne. Timur-Kutlugh also sent envoys demanding that Tokhtamysh be extradited to him. Vitovt was thus faced with a momentous decision.

After consulting the boyar council (*pany-rada*) of the grand duchy, he decided to intervene in favor of Tokhtamysh. As a matter of fact, for the past few years Vitovt and his advisers had watched the evolution of Mongol policies with ever-increasing interest. It must be borne in mind that a number of Lithuanian-Russian princes considered the Golden Horde Russia's main enemy and were ready to support every effort of either Moscow or Lithuania to combat the Mongols. To this group belonged Prince Andrew of Polotsk, Dmitri of Briansk, and Dmitri Bobrok. As we know, in the 1370's when Grand Duke Dmitri of Moscow assumed the leadership in Russia's opposition to the Mongols, all three of them supported him and took

69. *Ibid.*, pp. 377–378.
70. Tiesenhausen, *2*, 125.

an active part in the battle of Kulikovo. When the East Russian princes were compelled once more to bow their heads before the khan, Prince Andrew returned to Polotsk, which had meanwhile been occupied by his brother Skirgailo. The latter arrested Andrew and imprisoned him in a castle in Poland (1386). When in 1393 Andrew succeeded in escaping, he became Vitovt's vassal. Dmitri of Briansk also sided with Vitovt. We do not know exactly when Dmitri Bobrok shifted his allegiance from the grand duke of Moscow to the grand duke of Lithuania; in 1389 he was still in Moscow and signed Dmitri Donskoy's will as a witness; in 1399 he was in Vitovt's retinue. These three princes enthusiastically supported Vitovt's anti-Mongol plans.

During the winter of 1397–98 Vitovt led his army down the Dnieper River and is said to have reached the shore of the Black Sea.[71] The local Tatar hordes he met on his way did not put up any strong resistance. Very likely they were not in favor of the khan's government (Tokhtamysh still being khan at that time). Thousands of them surrendered and were settled in the Troki region. The main object of the campaign seems to have been reconnoitering. At that time Vitovt could hardly expect to find himself in a position to crush the Mongols. But the civil war in the Horde and Tokhtamysh' appeal for support changed the whole picture. Vitovt now could hope, using Tokhtamysh as a puppet khan, to establish his own suzerainty over all the Golden Horde.

Once his decision was made Vitovt started careful preparations for a campaign which, he hoped, would end in the conquest of the Golden Horde. He asked both Poland and the Knights of the Teutonic Order for help. The king of Poland, Iagailo, agreed to send a few troops but much fewer than Vitovt expected. In order to obtain the knights' support, Vitovt ceded to them part of Samogitia (Zhmud'). For this consideration they agreed to send a choice and well-equipped detachment of troops to participate in the campaign.[72] There is no information about Vitovt's negotiations with Moscow, but in any case Moscow remained neutral. Grand Duke Vasili of Moscow had, indeed, good ground for being suspicious of his father-in-law's intentions. In 1395 Vitovt had seized Smolensk and arrested most of its princes. While Smolensk was not subordinated to Moscow, the grand duke of Moscow could not but be worried by the strengthening of Lithuanian control over it. Even more threatening was Vitovt's intent to es-

71. See A. Barbashev, *Vitovt 1* (St. Petersburg, 1885), 95; Kolankowski, pp. 70–71.
72. Spuler, p. 138.

tablish his suzerainty over Novgorod. In 1398 he arranged with the
Teutonic Order for a joint campaign against Pskov and Novgorod. In
case of success the knights were to receive Pskov, and Vitovt Novgorod. These plans now had to be abandoned because of the new
turn in Mongol affairs.

The bulk of Vitovt's forces in his steppe campaign of 1399 consisted
of the Lithuanian and West Russian army and Tokhtamysh' Tatars.
The Lithuanian-Russian army was well organized and equipped with
cannon. The rulers of the Golden Horde were also well prepared for
the contest. Instead of waiting for the enemy deep in the steppes, as
Subudey had done in 1223, Timur-Kutlugh and Edigey decided to
advance toward the middle course of the Dnieper in the general direction of Kiev. Early in August 1399 the t vo enemy armies faced
each other on the banks of the Vorskla (a tributary of the Dnieper),
probably not far from where the city of Poltava was one day to be
built and where Peter the Great would defeat the Swedes in 1709.

According to the Nikon Chronicle, Khan Timur-Kutlugh proposed an agreement to Vitovt instead of fighting. Vitovt demanded
that the khan acknowledge himself his vassal and that Vitovt's name
appear on the coins of the Golden Horde. Edigey rejected Vitovt's
demands in behalf of Timur-Kutlugh and in turn demanded that his
tamga (clan emblem) be stamped on the Lithuanian coins. There
was now no way out but war. A fierce battle raged for several hours.
Vitovt's troops seemed on the verge of victory over the main Mongol
army commanded by Edigey when Timur-Kutlugh's reserve squad-
rons attacked the Lithuanians from the rear. Tokhtamysh' Tatars
were the first to take to flight, and soon Vitovt's whole army was in
confusion. While Vitovt himself succeeded in escaping with a few
followers, a great number of Lithuanian-Russian princes perished in
the battle, among them Andrew of Polotsk, Dmitri of Briansk, and
"Dmitri Koriatovich" (Bobrok-Volynsky).[73] "And who could count
all the Lithuanians, and the Russians, and the Poles, and the Germans slain on that day?" commented the chronicler bitterly.

Chasing the remnants of Vitovt's defeated army, Timur-Kutlugh
made straight for Kiev and established his camp before the city.
Detachments of his army spread all over the Kievan land and Podolia,
looting towns and villages and seizing thousands of captives. Kiev
had to pay 3,000 rubles ransom. The lower Bug River basin, which
had been conquered by Olgerd in 1363 and had given Lithuania an

73. Nikon, *11*, 174-175.

outlet to the Black Sea, was now again occupied by the Mongols and was assigned as grazing grounds for a section of Edigey's Mangkyt (Nogay) Horde.

Even after that catastrophe Tokhtamysh did not abandon his attempts to regain power in the Kypchak steppes. Vitovt offered Tokhtamysh' soldiers landholdings in Lithuania if they would give him military service. While a great number of them accepted the offer, Tokhtamysh returned to the steppes with a small band of loyal followers and started guerrilla warfare against Edigey. After being defeated in several encounters he fled east and found refuge in Tiumen in western Siberia.[74] From there he sent an envoy to his former suzerain, Timur, asking him once more for protection and offering alliance against Edigey. Tokhtamysh' envoy was received graciously by Timur in the city of Otrar in January 1405. Timur was about to start his campaign against China. He was obviously worried by the rapid rise of Edigey's power and, in order to prevent the possibility of an attack by Edigey on Central Asia during his absence he was glad to use Tokhtamysh against Edigey as he had used Edigey against Tokhtamysh ten years before. Neither Timur nor Tokhtamysh was destined to benefit by their new alliance. Timur died in Otrar on February 18, 1405. Tokhtamysh must have died in Tiumen about the same time or soon after. In any case his name is not mentioned after that date in the sources available to us.

II

Edigey belonged to an old Mongol family of the White Mangkyt (Ak-Mangkyt) clan.[75] The Mangkyts, as we know, formed the nucleus of the Nogay Horde. Their support greatly helped Edigey in seizing power in the Golden Horde—as it had helped Nogay about 130 years earlier. Edigey's position was more difficult than Nogay's, however, since he was not a Chingisid. True, Edigey claimed to be a descendant, through an ancestress, of the first caliph, Abu-Bakr.[76] This might have been impressive enough for the Moslems. But although most of the Mongol princes and grandees in Juchi's Ulus had

74. On Tokhtamysh' last years see *ZO*, pp. 383–384.

75. On Edigey see Barthold, "Edigey"; P. M. Melioransky, "Skazanie ob Edigee i Tokhtamyshe," *ZRGO, 19* (1905), Suppl., pp. 1–23 (Kirgiz text, pp. 1–39); *ZO*, pp. 379–405.

76. See B. S. Ischboldin, "O rode Izhboldinykh," *Novik* (mimeographed ed., 1945), pp. 35–36. The author of this study, now on the faculty of St. Louis University, is a descendant of Edigey.

embraced Islam by that time, they did not discard all their Mongol traditions. Politically, now as before, only the descendants of Chingis-Khan were considered eligible to the throne of the Golden Horde. Edigey therefore found himself in the same position as Mamay and Tamerlane. The only way he could rule was through puppet khans. He himself had to be satisfied with the title of amir. Timur-Kutlugh, the first khan he created, was a drunkard and died in 1400.[77] His cousin Shadibeg was then elected khan with Edigey's approval.[78] According to the Persian historian, Muin ad-din Natanzi, Shadibeg spent all his life in revels and pleasures.[79] Edigey at first had no difficulty in ruling through him.

After having defeated Vitovt's army and cut Lithuania off from the Black Sea, Edigey concentrated on restoring order and discipline in the Golden Horde. As Muin ad-din puts it, Edigey established "refined customs and great laws." [80] By the former he probably means strict ceremonial forms of obedience for the grandees to the khan; by the latter the Yasa with all its implications, including a severe system of taxation. An interesting aspect of Edigey's policies was his attempt to stop the trade in Turkish slaves. Even before the Mongol invasion Cuman children were exported to Egypt where they were trained for the Mameluk corps. The practice continued in the late 13th century and throughout the 14th. Now, according to al-Makrizi, Edigey forbade "the Tatars" to sell their children into slavery abroad.[81] By the Tatars Makrizi presumably means not only the Cumans but all the Turks subject to the Golden Horde. Edigey probably wanted to prevent any decrease in the numerical strength of the Turks as the backbone of the Golden Horde. As a result of this policy the number of slaves imported to Syria and Egypt from the Golden Horde decreased sharply. Later on, the trade was resumed, with Circassian instead of the Turkish children exported. Accordingly the Mameluk corps in the 15th century was recruited mainly from the Circassians.[82] It should be emphasized that Edigey's policy in this case could not be interpreted as a desire to curb the foreign trade at large. On the contrary, he was fully aware of the importance of developing the commerce of the Golden Horde, and in particular of restoring trade

77. *ZO*, p. 391.
78. See Genealogical Table VI.
79. Tiesenhausen, *2*, 133.
80. *Ibid.*
81. *Idem, 1*, 474; Barthold, "Edigey," p. 23.
82. Poliak, "Caractère colonial," pp. 241–242.

routes to Central Asia. Taking advantage of Tamerlane's death
(1405), he seized Khorezm in 1406.[83]

After the reorganization of his state Edigey felt himself strong
enough to handle the Russian problem. As a matter of fact, East
Russia became practically independent with Tokhtamysh' final defeat by Timur. It was only in 1400 that Grand Duke Ivan of Tver
(son of Michael II) found it necessary to send his envoys to Edigey.
He may have been impressed by the latter's victory over Vitovt. Two
years later Prince Fedor of Riazan (son of Oleg) went to the Horde
and received the patent on the throne of Riazan (which had become
vacant after Oleg's death). However, immediately after Fedor's return from the Horde, he concluded a convention with Grand Duke
Vasili of Moscow by which he pledged himself not to give any assistance to the Mongols and to inform Vasili of any threatening moves
by Edigey.[84] As for Grand Duke Vasili, under various pretexts he
discontinued sending tribute to the Horde and paid no attention to
the complaints of the khan's envoys about it. Such an attitude Edigey
could not tolerate for long.

In view of these circumstances it was unfortunate for Moscow that
in 1406 a conflict began between Vasili and his father-in-law Vitovt.
The conflict was caused by the renewal of Vitovt's pressure on Smolensk, Pskov, and Novgorod. Encouraged by Vitovt's defeat at the
Vorskla River in 1399, the anti-Lithuanian party in Smolensk raised
its head. In Smolensk, as in Tver and Novgorod, the boyars favored
the aristocratic system of government of Lithuania; the commoners,
on the contrary, were against it. In 1401 the people of Smolensk
revolted, killed the Lithuanian lieutenant, and called former Grand
Duke Iuri back to the throne.[85] Vitovt immediately dashed to Smolensk but failed to take it. Nor was he more successful three years
later. It was only in 1405, when he was able to concentrate a strong
army equipped with cannon, that he succeeded in storming the city
and re-establishing his rule over it. He then attacked the land of
Pskov (February 1406). The Pskovians turned to the grand duke
of Moscow for help. Meanwhile Vitovt demanded that Novgorod accept a cousin of his, Lugven (son of Olgerd), as its prince. Grand
Duke Vasili now deemed it necessary to stop Vitovt's aggression.
Edigey was delighted when he heard of the impending war between

83. *ZO*, p. 392.
84. *DDG*, pp. 52–53; Nasonov, p. 141.
85. Golubovsky, pp. 332–333.

Muscovy and Lithuania since it could not but weaken both of them. He gladly offered his help to Vasili. The help was accepted and a detachment of Tatar troops joined the Muscovite army. There was no battle, however, and a truce was soon negotiated. The following year Novgorod accepted Prince Lugven as military commander, but he was not allowed to reside in the city and had to live in a neighboring town. The war between Vasili and Vitovt flared anew, to end soon with another truce. In July 1408 a leading Lithuanian prince, Svidrigailo (Švitrigaila) (son of Olgerd), deserted Vitovt and entered the service of Vasili. There was great rejoicing in Moscow. For his support or "feeding" Svidrigailo received the city of Vladimir with the adjacent districts, Pereiaslavl, Volokolamsk, Rzhev, and half of Kolomna.[86] Worried by Svidrigailo's move, Vitovt led his troops against Moscow for the third time. As in the preceding campaigns, there were no major battles, and an armistice was signed in September 1408.

While Vitovt restored his control over Smolensk and put a Lithuanian prince in command of the Novgorod troops, Grand Duke Vasili attempted to establish control over Tver. Ivan, the reigning grand duke of Tver, showed no desire to accept Vasili's leadership, so Vasili decided to help a rival Tverian prince, Iuri of Kholm, to obtain the khan's patent on the throne of Tver. In 1407 Iuri came to Moscow and from there, with Vasili's blessings, went to the Horde. As soon as Grand Duke Ivan received news of this move he too hastened to the khan's court.[87] At the time of Ivan's arrival at the Horde troubles were starting there. Annoyed by Edigey's tutelage, Khan Shadibeg attempted to assert his own sovereignty. As a matter of fact, opposition was growing in the Horde to Edigey's policies of centralization and increased taxation. The dealers in slaves who traded with Egypt must have been especially indignant. Shadibeg attempted to get rid of Edigey by heading the opposition movement. A brief but violent civil war started in the Horde.[88] Edigey defeated his opponents and put on the throne a new khan, Pulad (called Bulat-Saltan in Russian chronicles).[89] Shadibeg fled to Astrakhan.

As soon as order was restored the assembly of Mongol grandees presided over by the new khan ruled to confirm the patent of Grand

86. Nikon, *11*, 204.
87. *Ibid.*, *11*, 198, 201.
88. *Ibid.*, *11*, 201–202; Nasonov, pp. 141–142; *ZO*, pp. 391–392.
89. According to Sharaf ad-Din Yazdi, Pulad was Shadibeg's son; Tiesenhausen, *2*, 146. Cf. *ZO*, p. 393.

Duke Ivan on Tver. Iuri's claims were denied. Not satisfied with the decision, Iuri went to Astrakhan and received a patent on the principality of Kashin (the most important of the local Tverian principalities) from fugitive Khan Shadibeg.[90] Ivan, however, refused to recognize the validity of this patent. Vasili's scheme thus fell through, and his relations with Ivan of Tver became even more strained than before, to Edigey's entire satisfaction.

Edigey's next move was to replace Grand Duke Fedor of Riazan, whom he did not trust, by Prince Ivan of Pronsk. In the summer of 1408 Ivan occupied Riazan with the help of a Tatar army. Fedor appealed to Vasili, who sent a detachment of troops to help the deposed prince. In spite of this, Fedor's army was defeated by Ivan's forces. Soon after, however, presumably through Vasili's mediation, the rivals came to a friendly agreement, and Fedor returned to Riazan.[91] In this case Vasili succeeded in checking Edigey's intervention in Russian affairs. Edigey now decided the time had come to strike at Moscow itself.

Like Tokhtamysh at the time of his raid on Moscow, Edigey knew that his only chance of success lay in the complete secrecy of his preparations for the campaign. Fearing that some of the friends of Moscow in the Golden Horde would notify Vasili of his gathering a strong army, Edigey sent a messenger to Moscow to explain that Khan Bulat-Saltan planned to wage war against Lithuania. This must have been in October 1408. By that time Vasili had signed an armistice with Vitovt and demobilized the army he had used in the Lithuanian campaign. The armies of both adversaries in that campaign must have been small.

Hence the Muscovites were completely unprepared when in November Vasili received news from a friendly Tatar grandee that Edigey was about to attack Moscow with a strong army.[92] There was no time left for any large-scale mobilization. Vasili went to Kostroma to gather the forces of the northern districts of his realm, while Prince Vladimir of Serpukhov again assumed command over the Moscow garrison.

Edigey's army appeared before the walls of Moscow on December 1. The first attempt of the Tatars to storm the city was unsuccessful. Edigey then established his headquarters a few miles outside Moscow

90. Nasonov, p. 142. Shadibeg died soon after.
91. Nikon, *11*, 203–204.
92. *Ibid.*, *11*, 205.

and let his troops loot the countryside. At the same time he sent envoys to Tver, ordering Grand Duke Ivan to bring his artillery to Moscow. Ivan promised and pretended to set out for Moscow but soon returned to Tver. Apparently he was unwilling to take chances and feared reprisals on the part of the grand duke of Moscow. Edigey, without artillery, abandoned hope of storming Moscow and decided to take it by siege. The siege continued for several weeks without success, and finally Edigey offered to lift it for 3,000 rubles indemnity. Receiving that sum, he led his troops back to the steppes.

While Edigey failed to take Moscow, he had succeeded in devastating a considerable part of the principality and thus greatly weakening the material resources of the grand duke. And he had restored the independence of the principality of Nizhni Novgorod, granting its throne to Daniel, son of Boris who, it will be recalled, was deposed in 1392.[93] Yet in spite of the devastation and suffering caused by Edigey's raid, it did not achieve its main objective: the power of the grand duke of Moscow was not broken. Not only did Vasili continue to defy the suzerainty of the khan but he even gave refuge in Moscow to Tokhtamysh' sons whose claims to the throne of the Golden Horde were a source of considerable worry to Edigey. The amir complained bitterly to Vasili of his unfriendliness in a caustic letter in 1409, but that was all he could do for the time being.[94]

Edigey's raid on Moscow, however, greatly enhanced his prestige in the Moslem world. When his envoys, together with those of Bulat-Saltan, appeared in Herat at the court of Tamerlane's son Shahrukh, in 1409, they were given a magnificent reception. In the same year the Egyptian sultan sent his envoys to Bulat-Saltan.[95] Edigey seemed to have achieved the zenith of his glory. And yet the days of his power were numbered. The forces of opposition, defeated in 1407, soon rallied. The puppet khan Bulat-Saltan died in 1410 and was succeeded, with Edigey's approval, by Timur-Kutlugh's son, Timur-Khan. In order to strengthen his hold on the new khan, Edigey gave him one of his daughters in marriage. But within a few months Timur-Khan turned against his father-in-law. Edigey was defeated and fled to Khorezm (1411). Timur-Khan derived no benefits from his victory, however, since he himself was soon ousted by Tokhtamysh' son Jalal ad-Din.

93. Nasonov, p. 143.
94. *SGGD*, 2, No. 15; a variant in Nikon, *11, 209–210.*
95. *ZO,* pp. 396–397.

Everyone now turned against Edigey, including Tamerlane's son Shahrukh, whose army occupied Urgenj (the capital of Khorezm) in 1414. This did not end Edigey's career, however. With a small retinue he returned to the Kypchak steppes and succeeded in establishing a principality of his own, probably in the Crimea. In 1416 his wife made a pilgrimage to Mecca with an escort of 300 horsemen.[96] The same year, according to the 15th-century Polish historian Jan Dlugosz, Edigey raided Kiev. Three years later he sent envoys to Vitovt offering the Lithuanian grand duke an alliance against Tokhtamysh' sons.[97] Before such an alliance could materialize, he was killed in a skirmish with Tokhtamysh' son Kadyr-Berdi.

Edigey's dramatic career made him a favorite hero of Turkish epic poetry, especially of the epos of his own people, the Nogays.[98] While many of his contemporaries suffered from his greed for power, the Nogay poets saw in him a valiant knight of the steppes and praised him for his audacity and chivalry.

III

As Edigey's power declined, that of Vitovt rapidly increased. It was Vitovt who derived the greatest benefits from Edigey's raid on Moscow of 1408. Indeed, while causing great harm to the Russians, Edigey failed to subjugate Muscovy. At the same time, however, the blow to Moscow was serious enough to prevent any renewal of her opposition to Lithuania. This was well understood by Svidrigailo, who in 1409 gave up hope of Muscovite support of his ambitious plans and decided to return to Lithuania. When he entered his native country, however, he was arrested and imprisoned for nine years.

Upon his release, he received Novgorod-in-Severia and Briansk in apanage, through the mediation of Sigismund of Germany. Feeling himself safe from any danger on the part of Muscovy, Vitovt was now able to concentrate on the struggle with the Teutonic Order, acting in close cooperation with King Iagailo. In 1410 the combined Polish and Lithuanian-Russian armies defeated the knights in the double battle of Grunwald and Tannenberg. The order was never able fully to recover from this blow.

Vitovt next turned his attention to Tatar affairs. With his assistance Tokhtamysh' son Jalal ad-Din succeeded in establishing himself in

96. Tiesenhausen, *1*, 442; *ZO*, p. 404.
97. *ZO*, pp. 403–404.
98. See Barthold, "Edigey," p. 18.

the Golden Horde. The ensuing troubles in the Horde enabled Vitovt not only to continue to interfere in steppe affairs but also to extend his hold on the lower Dnieper region. In 1412 he built a number of forts and established trading posts along the right bank of the Dnieper from Kiev down to the Black Sea.[99] He continued this policy to the end of his reign, with the double objective of preventing the Tatars from raiding the Kievan land and Podolia and of building up a military base for further penetration into the steppes.

The situation in the Dnieper steppes was fluid at this time. None of the rival khans was able to exercise full authority over the local Tatar princes. A number of semi-independent Tatar groups formed that called themselves Cossacks.[100] Some of them were hired by Vitovt to strengthen the garrisons of the forts he established. He also used similar Russian (Ukrainian) groups in addition to his regular troops. These Ukrainian frontiersmen became known as Cossacks too.[101] The main system of frontier settlements established by Vitovt centered around the town of Cherkasy, situated about half-way between Kiev and the Dnieper cataracts. Cherkasy is the old Russian form of the name Circassians. Probably a group of Circassians had been settled on the opposite side of the Dnieper in the 11th century by Prince Mstislav of Tmutorokan.[102] There is no evidence, however, that the town of Cherkasy existed before the 15th century.[103] From the late 1400's on the Ukrainian Cossacks were called Cherkasy by the Muscovites.

Another important aspect of Vitovt's policies in this period was his interest in the affairs of the West Russian church. His approach was purely political. He wanted to be sure that the church would not side with the grand duke of Moscow in case of a conflict between Muscovy and Lithuania. So Vitovt, like Olgerd before him, insisted on

99. Spuler, p. 149; cf. B. Spuler, "Mittelalterliche Grenzen in Osteuropa, I. Die Grenze des Grossfürstentums Litauen im Südosten gegen Türken und Tataren," *JGOE, 6* (1941), 157–158.

100. See below, sec. 5, pp. 291–292, for the explanation of the term.

101. The Ukrainian Cossacks are first mentioned by that name in the sources in the late 15th century. On the origin of the Cossacks in Ukraine see Hrushevsky, 7 (1909), 74–82; M. Liubavsky, *Oblastnoe delenie i mestnoe upravlenie Litovsko-Russkogo Gosudarstva* (Moscow, 1892), pp. 531–532; D. Doroshenko, *Narys istorii Ukrainy* (Warsaw, 1932), *2,* 144–160.

102. See *Kievan Russia,* p. 78.

103. In a late West Russian chronicle Cherkasy is mentioned in connection with Gedymin's alleged seizure of Kiev around 1320, but the authenticity of the story has been questioned. See Antonovich, *Monografii,* pp. 47–49; Kuczyński, pp. 48, 307.

his right to select the candidate to the metropolitan's see whenever it became vacant. Metropolitan Cyprian, whose relations with the Lithuanian rulers had been friendly, died in 1406. Vitovt then sent the Greek-born bishop Theodosius of Polotsk to Constantinople, asking the patriarch to ordain him metropolitan for Russia. The Byzantine authorities, however, disregarded the recommendation, and in 1408 selected for the office another Greek, Photius, who reached Kiev in 1409 and then went to Moscow.

Before long Vitovt expressed his dissatisfaction with Photius' policies, and in 1414 he forbade Photius to interfere in the affairs of the West Russian church. Then he asked the patriarch's permission to elect a separate metropolitan for West Russia. He recommended for this post Gregory Tsamblak, a learned monk of Rumanian extraction, born in Tyrnovo, Bulgaria, and a relative of Metropolitan Cyprian.[104] Receiving no answer from Constantinople for more than a year, Vitovt convoked the council of West Russian bishops, and Gregory was elected metropolitan (1416). Vitovt then attempted to establish better relations between the two Christian churches within his realm, the Greek and the Roman. At his request the new metropolitan agreed to attend the sessions of the Sixteenth Ecumenical Council at Constance. Gregory arrived there in February 1418 when the council was about to close. His mission had no tangible results. Soon after his return to Kiev he resigned from office, for reasons which are not clear, and retired to Moldavia (1419). Vitovt's church policy proved a failure.

5. THE GOLDEN HORDE, LITHUANIA, AND MUSCOVY,
1419–39
I

After the passing of Edigey from the historical scene the process of disintegration of the Golden Horde entered a new phase which resulted in the formation within Juchi's Ulus of several hordes, each of which eventually achieved independence. One of them was the Nogay Horde which established itself firmly in the Iaik River basin. While the Mongol clan of the Mangkyts occupied a leading position among the Nogays, sections of the Kypchaks and other Turkish tribes

---

104. On Gregory Tsamblak see Makari, *4*, 88–101; Barbashev, *Vitovt* (as in n. 71), pp. 131–135; Golubinsky, *2*, 377–388, 882; E. Turdeanu, "Grégoire Camblak," *RES, 22* (1946), 46–81.

also joined this horde. East of the Nogays, in Kazakhstan, two other hordes were in process of formation, the Uzbeks and the Kazakhs (the latter often referred to as the Kirghiz).[105] Each of them represented a mixture of Mongol clans with native Turkish tribes which were themselves a mixture of Turks and Turkicized Iranians.

The name Uzbek is identical with that of the famous 14th-century Khan Uzbeg of the Golden Horde, only spelt differently. Whether there is a historical connection between the people and the khan is a disputed question.[106] In my opinion it is improbable. According to Paul Pelliot the name Uzbeg (*Özbäg*) means "master of one's self" (*maître de* [*sa*] *personne*),[107] that is a "free man." Uzbek for a nation would then mean "a nation of free men." If so, the meaning is close to that of Kazakh. The form Kazakh, now officially adopted in the Soviet Union, is a variant of *Kazak,* which in several Turkish dialects means "free man," "free adventurer," [108] and hence "frontiersman." In its basic connotation it was applied both to the groups of Tatar, Ukrainian, and Russian frontiersmen (the Cossacks) and to the whole Central Asian people of the Kirghiz (Kazakhs). While the meaning of the term kazak has been well established, its origin is not clear. I am inclined to think it should be connected with the ethnic name Kas which forms the basis of the name Kasog (or Kosog), under which the Circassians of the north Caucasian area are mentioned in the early Russian chronicles. About the mid-15th century the Russians started calling these people Cherkasy (in modern Russian, Cherkesy), from which, presumably, the English form Circassians originated.

The name Cherkas is a contraction of Chahar-Kas.[109] *Chahar* means "four" in Persian. Hence Chahar-Kas means Four Kas or Four Kas Clans. It must be mentioned in this connection that the Circassians, as well as the Alans, were considered first-rate warriors. Detachments of soldiers of both these peoples were drafted or hired by the Mongol khans to serve as their guards on many occasions.

---

105. On the formation of the Uzbek and Kazakh states see Barthold, *Turcs,* pp. 185–188, 193–194; Grousset, *Empire des steppes,* pp. 556–563; M. Abdykalykov and A. Pankratova, eds., *Istoriia Kazakhskoi SSR* (Alma-Ata, 1943), chaps. 5, 7. Cf. B. G. Gafurov, *Istoriia tadzhikskogo naroda* (Moscow, 1949), chaps. 17, 18.

106. See *ZO*, pp. 298–302.

107. Pelliot, p. 92.

108. Radlov, *Versuch, 2,* 363–365.

109. See J. Marquart [Markwart], "Über das Volkstum der Komanen," *AWGA,* N.S., *13,* No. 1 (1914), 141.

The Circassian soldiers were probably not merged with the Mongols and Turks in the Mongol armies but formed their own autonomous units, or military fraternities of a sort. Later the name Kas might have been applied to such fraternities among the frontiersmen of Turkish, Russian, and Ukrainian origin as well.

The Uzbek Horde consolidated itself in the 1420's; the Kazakh Horde was organized about thirty years later. In the late 15th century the Uzbeks started a migration southward into Transoxania which was completed early in the 16th century. The Kazakhs remained masters of the steppes north and east of the Aral Sea, which gave their name to that region (Kazakhstan).

The same process of disintegration of old empires and formation of new local khanates was going on simultaneously in the western part of Juchi's Ulus, that is in the Golden Horde proper. It resulted eventually in breaking the Golden Horde into three separate states: the Khanate of Kazan (formed in 1445), that of the Crimea (1449), and the remnants of the main horde at Saray. After the final dissolution of the Golden Horde in 1502, Astrakhan attempted to take over Saray's historical role as a center of the Lower Volga Khanate.

II

In 1419 the throne of the Golden Horde passed from Tokhtamysh' children to a descendant of Tuka-Timur, Ulug-Mahmed (Big Mahmed, perhaps in the sense of the Elder Mahmed). Actually his authority was recognized only in the western part of the Golden Horde. The lower Volga region was controlled by Tokhtamysh' son, Kepek (Kibäk). Even in the western part of the Kypchak steppes the rule of Ulug-Mahmed was not firm; a number of Tatar princes refused to obey him. Under the circumstances, it is understandable that Ulug-Mahmed turned to the grand duke of Lithuania for support. Vitovt was thus able to further his policy of intervention in the affairs of the Golden Horde through khans friendly to him. He now emerged as the most powerful ruler in Eastern Europe, and the Grand Duchy of Lithuania became the most important factor in East European policies. Vitovt's influence was felt even in Central European affairs, of which the focal point was at that time the Hussite movement in Bohemia. Both the Hussites and Emperor Sigismund attempted to influence Vitovt, each in their, or his, favor. In 1421 a Czech delegation visited Vitovt offering him the crown of Bohemia. He accepted in principle and sent his relative Sigismund

Koributovich (son of Olgerd's son Koribut) to Bohemia as his lieutenant with a detachment of 5,000 Lithuanian–Russian troops.[110]
Later on, disagreements rose between the Hussite leaders and Vitovt,
chiefly because of the king of Poland's objections to the cooperation
between Lithuania and Bohemia. Under Iagailo's pressure Vitovt
broke off relations with the Czechs, and Sigismund Koributovich fled
from Bohemia. The whole plan to unite Bohemia with Lithuania
and West Russia thus fell through.

In the Golden Horde the unsteady balance of power among the
local khans was upset by the invasion, in 1422, of Khan Barak
(grandson of Urus-Khan) from Kazakhstan into the lower Volga
region. Within two years both Mahmed and his rival, Kepek, were
defeated by Barak's Uzbeks. Ulug-Mahmed's cousin Davlet-Berdi
also failed in his attempt to withstand the invader. All three defeated
khans had to flee west. Kepek raided the Russian cities of Riazan and
Odoev (1424) but was not able to establish himself firmly in those
regions. Ulug-Mahmed fled to Lithuania to ask Vitovt for protection.
Davlet-Berdi took advantage of the general confusion to seize the
Crimea (around 1425).[111]

Meanwhile Barak, after causing all this havoc, returned to Kazakhstan, his baggage train laden with booty (1425). He now felt
strong enough to proclaim himself an independent khan—of the
Uzbeks. Tamerlane's grandson Ulug-Beg, who reigned in Samarkand
and considered Barak his vassal, was indignant at this and two years
later personally led his army to Kazakhstan to reconquer it. Barak
defeated him (1427.)[112] Soon after, however, a conspiracy of Uzbek
amirs was formed against Barak and he was assassinated (1428).
The next khan elected—Abul-Khair, a descendant of Shiban—
reigned from 1428 to 1468, succeeded in consolidating the Uzbek
state, and founded the Shibanid dynasty.

To return to Crimean affairs, in 1426 Davlet-Berdi, trying to
strengthen his hold of the Crimea, sent a letter to the sultan of
Egypt, informing him of the troubles in Kypchak and offering alliance. Ulug-Mahmed, however, soon ousted Davlet-Berdi from the
Crimea and, with the help of the powerful local Tatar family of
Shirin, established his own headquarters there (1427). With this
the name of Davlet-Berdi disappeared from history. It is known,

110. Florovsky, *1,* 285, 286, 296, 306.
111. See *ZO,* pp. 410–412.
112. Barthold, *Ulugbek,* pp. 85–86.

however, that about 1428 Khan Haji-Geray fled to Lithuania and asked Vitovt for protection. V. D. Smirnov plausibly suggests that the one khan may have had two names, and was known first under the former, later under the latter.[113]

Ulug-Mahmed's political triumph was marred by an epidemic of plague, which started in the West, not in the Orient. In Russia it first struck at Novgorod, then penetrated to Moscow, and finally to the Kypchak steppes. His first diplomatic move was to establish friendly relations with the Ottoman sultan Murat II.[114] A year after that the khan sent an envoy to Cairo to negotiate an alliance with the Mameluks. While there is no evidence that either side profited from these negotiations, the arrival of ships from the Crimea at a time when the plague was visiting the Kypchak steppes proved unfortunate for Egypt for it introduced the disease there.[115]

While Ulug-Mahmed thought it premature at that time to assert his authority in East Russia, he watched Muscovite policies closely and could derive considerable satisfaction from events in Moscow as he could expect to obtain a suitable pretext for intervening in Russian affairs béfore long. When Grand Duke Vasili I died, in 1425, his son, also called Vasili,[116] was only ten years old. In his will Vasili I made his father-in-law Vitovt, as well as his brothers Andrew and Peter and his second cousins Simeon and Iaroslav (sons of Vladimir of Serpukhov), guardians of his widow and son.[117] Vasili I's brother Iuri, next to him in seniority, was excluded from guardianship. Iuri's apanage consisted of Zvenigorod, a town west of Moscow, and the rich city of Galich, northeast of Kostroma beyond the Volga.[118] Iuri was an ambitious and wealthy ruler and an enthusiastic builder. His reign brought prosperity to his residence, Zvenigorod. The city grew rapidly, was embellished by new churches and fortified with new strong walls.[119] Probably Vasili I was suspicious of Iuri's political designs and did not trust him. And indeed, Iuri refused to accept the validity of Vasili's will and presented his own claims to the grand ducal throne. When they were rejected by Metropolitan

113. Smirnov, *Krymskoe Khanstvo*, pp. 229–234.

114. Kurat, p. 9.

115. Spuler, p. 159.

116. Vasili II was Vasili I's third son. The first two died before their father. See Baumgarten 2, Table 2.

117. *DDG*, p. 62.

118. Not to be confused with Galich (Halicz) in Galicia.

119. *MIAS, 12*, 125–133.

Photius and the boyars, Iuri set out for Galich in dudgeon and started gathering an army there. This was the beginning of a protracted political crisis in Muscovy, in fact the first and only case of internecine war between the descendants of Ivan Kalita.

The crisis was dynastic in form and political in content. Iuri based his claims on the old idea of clan rule that the throne had to be occupied according to genealogical seniority within the framework of the grand ducal clan as a whole, instead of on the principle of succession from father to son within the same family. Politically, Iuri's action was a protest against the subordination of all the princes to the prince of Moscow; he sought equality of the princes. In other words, he was in favor of the federative organization of Russia of the late Kievan type as against the domination of the grand dukes of Moscow over all other princes.

Iuri's army was stopped by the troops of Moscow. Then Metropolitan Photius went personally to Galich to admonish the rebellious prince and plead for unity. Peace was restored and both sides agreed to refer the conflict to the khan for decision. No term was specified for this appeal, and actually the government of Moscow was able to postpone getting the decision. The dowager Grand Duchess Sophia went to Smolensk to ask her father Vitovt for protection, which he promised her. Under these circumstances Iuri preferred not to press the matter and for some time held his peace.

While Vitovt agreed to support and guide his grandson's rule over the Grand Duchy of Vladimir, he lost no opportunity of extending, or trying to extend, his direct control over all other parts of North and East Russia. In 1426 he waged a war against Pskov with the help of Tatar auxiliary troops sent to him by Ulug-Mahmed. His attempt to storm the town of Opochka proved a failure, however. He then concluded peace with Pskov after collecting an indemnity of 1,450 rubles. The next year he undertook a campaign against Novgorod and early in 1428 reached the town of Ostrov. The pride of Vitovt's artillery was a huge cannon cast by a German master, Nicholas; it had a name, Galka or Jackdaw, and was drawn by forty horses. Its first discharge shattered the main tower of the fortress of Ostrov but also burst Galka itself, killing Nicholas as well as a number of Lithuanians who stood around.[120] Novgorod sued for peace which Vitovt granted for an indemnity of 10,000 rubles.

While Vitovt derived substantial financial profit from these two

120. Nikon, *12*, 8.

wars, he did not succeed in subjugating either Novgorod or Pskov. From this point of view he was much more successful with Tver and Riazan. In 1427 he concluded a treaty of alliance with Tver, in which Grand Duke Boris recognized Vitovt as his lord; Vitovt, however, promised not to interfere with local Tverian affairs.[121] Two years later both Grand Duke Ivan IV of Riazan and Grand Duke Ivan II of Pronsk acknowledged themselves Vitovt's vassals. Each addressed Vitovt not only as his lord (*gospodin*) but also as his sovereign (*gospodar*).[122]

Having thus strengthened his control over East Russia and re-plenished his treasury with the money of Novgorod and Pskov, Vitovt now felt prepared to take the initiative in a bold attempt to solve the urgent international problems faced by the rulers of Eastern and Central Europe. At his invitation a conference of these rulers and their representatives and advisers met in Lutsk, Volynia, in 1429. Among those present were Sigismund, emperor of the Holy Roman Empire, and Iagailo, king of Poland. The pope, the Byzantine emperor John VIII, the king of Denmark, the Teutonic Order, and the voevoda of Moldavia each sent representatives. A number of Russian princes, including the grand duke of Tver, also attended the conference.[123] All enjoyed the lavish reception and entertainments offered by their mighty host. The chroniclers recorded with awe the amounts of food and drink consumed by the guests. From the business angle, however, the congress was not as successful as it was socially.

The main items on the agenda were the Turkish-Byzantine prob-lem, the relations of the Roman Catholic and Greek Orthodox churches (which was connected with the Byzantine question); the Hussite question; and the relations of Poland and Lithuania. It soon became obvious that there was no unity of approach among the various members on any problem; besides, some were interested only in a specific item on the agenda and were not prepared to discuss the others. It is easy to understand why no decisions were reached.

121. *DDG*, pp. 62–63.

122. *Ibid.*, pp. 67–69. According to the editors the treaty was signed "around 1430." It was probably concluded in 1429.

123. On the Lutsk conference see Baron M. Taube, "Mezhdunarodnyi kongress na Volyni v xv stoletii," *Russkii vestnik*, 255 (1898), 133–151; *idem*, "Etudes sur le dével-oppement historique du droit international dans l'Europe orientale, Académie de Droit International," *Recueil des cours*, 1 (1926), 468–469; Hrushevsky, 4, 134–135, 430; Kolankowski, pp. 153–154; Florovsky, 1, 294.

Everybody agreed that the Byzantine Empire was about to crumble under the pressure of the Ottoman Turks if no assistance were forthcoming from the European powers. However, the pope would agree to preach a crusade to save Constantinople only if the Greek schismatics would become Roman Catholics. For Vitovt this was naturally a delicate question, since most of his subjects—the Russians—were such schismatics. Emperor Sigismund also preferred cooperation of the two churches to formal subjection of the East to the West. As he said, half jokingly: "They [the Greek Orthodox] have the same faith as we and differ from us only by the beards and wives of their clergymen. But nobody should blame them for this, since while the Greek priest is satisfied with one wife our Latin priests each keep ten or more 'wives.' " [124]

Sigismund suggested that a section of the Teutonic Order be moved to the Danube area to assume military leadership in the struggle of the Europeans against the Turks. Both Poland and Moldavia immediately objected. Poland had had enough trouble with the Teutonic Knights in the north of her dominions and could hardly be expected to help them bar her own access to the Danube. The Polish attitude in this question irritated Sigismund and he became even more favorable than before to Lithuania's desire to achieve complete independence from Poland. He proposed that Vitovt be crowned king of Lithuania. The Poles again objected. Sigismund did not abandon the project, however, and promised to send Vitovt the royal crown the next year.

When that year, A.D. 1430, came, coronation festivities began in Vilno. All of Vitovt's Russian allies and vassals appeared personally, including Grand Duke Vasili II of Moscow and the grand dukes of Tver, Riazan, and Pronsk. Metropolitan Photius also considered it proper to come to greet Vitovt, inasmuch as he wanted to discuss with him certain matters concerning the West Russian church. The Teutonic Order and the Tatars sent their representatives as well.[125] To the great disappointment of both Vitovt and his guests, the crown did not arrive; Emperor Sigismund's messengers were detained by the Poles. One by one the embarrassed guests took leave of their host and set out for home. Two weeks later Vitovt fell from his horse and died as a result of the accident. He was eighty years old.

---

124. Dlugosz, *11*, 515; quoted by Taube, *Russkii vestnik, 255,* 147.
125. Kolankowski, pp. 160–161.

III

Vitovt's death caused a protracted political crisis in both Lithuania and Muscovy. Had the Golden Horde been united and strong, the Tatars could easily have taken advantage of the situation. But they were divided among themselves, and they only added at times to the confusion of Lithuanian and Muscovite affairs.

Soon after Vitovt's death an assembly of Lithuanian and West Russian princes and boyars elected his cousin Svidrigailo grand duke of Lithuania. Their acting without previous agreement with the Poles was contrary to the terms of the Gorodlo convention of 1413, so the Poles refused to recognize the election as valid and proposed Vitovt's brother Sigismund. His chances seemed slight at first, but before long he was able to play upon the differences between the Lithuanian and the Russian party in the grand duchy.[126]

While Svidrigailo was a Roman Catholic, he was at first very popular among the West Russian princes and boyars since he did not distinguish between Roman Catholic and Greek Orthodox in appointing members of his council and high dignitaries. But this caused considerable resentment among the Lithuanian grandees who dubbed him pro-Russian. In 1432 a conspiracy of the Lithuanian boyars was formed against Svidrigailo. He succeeded in escaping, but Sigismund was proclaimed grand duke in Vilno. Svidrigailo retired to the Russian provinces of the grand duchy and rallied his supporters. A dangerous situation developed which could end in breaking the grand duchy into Lithuanian and Russian halves. Even the staunchest Lithuanian nationalists understood the need to compromise with the Russians. So Sigismund issued a charter (*privilei*) which abrogated the clause of the Gorodlo convention that denied political rights to the Greek Orthodox. In spite of this move most of the Russian princes continued at first to support Svidrigailo, but he soon grew suspicious of their loyalty and tried to improve his position by an agreement with the Teutonic Knights.

He also opened negotiations with Rome to unite the West Russian church with the Roman. Although Metropolitan Gerasim seemed to be ready to discuss the matter of church union, Svidrigailo arrested

126. On the political struggle in Lithuania following Vitovt's death see Hrushevsky, *4*, 161–195; Kolankowski, pp. 164–211; Liubavsky, pp. 64–71; A. I. Voldemar, "Natsionalnaia bor'ba v Velikom Kniazhestve Litovskom v xv–xvi vekakh," *ANORI, 14*, Pt. 3 (1910), 162–170.

him, accusing him of treason (Gerasim had probably been negotiating with Sigismund). Intending to suppress all opposition to him by drastic measures, Svidrigailo ordered that Gerasim be burned at the stake (July 1435). Instead of intimidating the Russians this action infuriated them. Deprived of Russian support, Svidrigailo was defeated by his opponent in the battle of the Sventa River, September 1435. He was allowed to keep Kremenets and part of Volynia and Podolia as his apanage, however. Sigismund's control over the grand duchy seemed now to be firmly established. The net outcome of this civil war was favorable to the Greek Orthodox, that is to the Russians, since they now received equal rights with the Roman Catholics.

It should be noted that at the time of the civil war in Lithuania two Tatar khans rose against Ulug-Mahmed vying for control of the Golden Horde. They were Said-Ahmad, a son of Tokhtamysh,[127] and Küchük-Mahmed (Little Mahmed or the Younger Mahmed), grandson of Timur-Kutlugh. Actually the Golden Horde was now split into three hordes. Two of the rival khans intervened in Lithuanian affairs: Ulug-Mahmed supported Sigismund and Said-Ahmad made an agreement with Svidrigailo.

Meanwhile, in Muscovy the conflict between Vasili II and Iuri of Galich flared anew. Iuri decided to take advantage of the fact that Vitovt's death had deprived Vasili of his most powerful protector. Moreover, Iuri had friendly relations with Svidrigailo through the house of Tver (Svidrigailo's wife was a Tverian princess). Encouraged by the changed political situation in Lithuania, Iuri renewed his claims on Moscow and demanded that the matter be submitted to the khan's decision. Consequently in 1432 both Iuri and Vasili appeared before the Supreme Court of the Golden Horde. Iuri was confident of success since he had a powerful friend in the Horde—the Crimean prince Tegin Shirin who also was a friend of Svidrigailo. The Moscow boyar Ivan Vsevolozhsky, Vasili II's chief adviser at that time, succeeded, however, in arousing Khan Ulug-Mahmed's suspicions of the sincerity of Shirin's intentions. Vsevolozhsky pointed out that a triple alliance between Shirin, Iuri, and Svidrigailo could be dangerous to the khan's interests.[128] The Supreme Court's decision, approved by the khan, was favorable to Vasili, who received the grand ducal patent. To make some amends

127. According to *ZO*, p. 414.
128. Nikon, *12*, 15–16.

to Iuri he was granted the principality of Dmitrov (a town north of Moscow) in addition to those of Zvenigorod and Galich.[129]

Vasili returned to Moscow accompanied by the khan's envoy, a Juchid prince, who ceremonially installed him on the grand ducal throne. This was the first time this event took place in Moscow and not in Vladimir. Moscow thus became the official capital of the grand duchy.

Iuri did not intend to accept the khan's verdict. No sooner was he back in Galich than he started gathering an army. He was greatly encouraged by the appearance of a new supporter, his former opponent at the court, the boyar Vsevolozhsky, who had deserted Vasili for personal reasons: Vasili had promised Vsevolozhsky to marry his daughter, but after returning from the Horde he married Princess Maria, daughter of one of his guardians, Iaroslav (son of Vladimir of Serpukhov), instead. Probably his mother had insisted that he marry a princess and not a mere boyar's daughter.

After Vsevolozhsky's desertion there was apparently no one left in Moscow competent to guide the young grand duke. The Muscovites were caught unawares when in April 1433 Iuri appeared before their city. Vasili surrendered and Iuri proclaimed himself grand duke, granting the town of Kolomna to Vasili as his apanage. This proved a mistake on Iuri's part. While the Muscovites did not actively defend Vasili, their sympathies still lay with him, and before long most of the Moscow notables were moving to Kolomna. Unable to withstand the psychological strain of this passive resistance, Iuri returned to Galich.

The crisis seemed to be over, but now Vasili decided to complete his victory by ousting Iuri from Galich. However Iuri, with the help of auxiliary troops sent by the free city of Khlynov (Viatka), defeated the Muscovites and once more occupied Moscow (1434). Vasili escaped to Nizhni Novgorod, and there planned to go to the Horde to ask the khan for protection. Iuri now felt himself much more secure than at the time of his first occupation of Moscow. He hastened to conclude treaties of alliance with the Mozhaisk princes as well as with Grand Duke Ivan of Riazan. Iuri's relations with the Tver princes were friendly and he could also count on the assistance of Viatka and at least diplomatic support from Svidrigailo. But Iuri was not destined to exploit the advantages of his position; he died on June 6, 1434 at the age of sixty.

129. The principality of Dmitrov reverted to the grand duke of Vladimir by escheat when Prince Peter of Dmitrov died in 1428 leaving no sons.

His eldest son, Vasili, surnamed Kosoy (The Squint), proclaimed himself grand duke. He obviously had no chance of keeping the throne, and even his own brothers, Dmitri Shemiaka and Dmitri Krasny (The Handsome), did not recognize him but called Vasili II back instead. Peace was thus restored, but not for long. Vasili Kosoy did not abandon his claims. In the ensuing war he was defeated, taken prisoner, and blinded by order of Vasili II. This cruel act, by which the grand duke sought to crush opposition to his rule once and for all, greatly shocked Russia. Blinding rival pretenders to the throne was a familiar practice in Byzantium. In Russia there had been only one such case, in the 12th century.[130] In the not too distant future Vasili II was to pay dearly for his cruelty, but for the time being he triumphed over his opponents. The first stage of the Muscovite civil war was over.

While both Lithuania and Moscow returned to a degree of stability, the confusion in the Golden Horde continued. In the western part a struggle was going on between Said-Ahmad and Ulug-Mahmed. There were also smaller Tatar groups which preferred recognizing the suzerainty of the grand duke of Lithuania to that of the rival khans. At the head of one such group was Egolday (called Jeholday in Polish sources) who, around 1438, founded a vassal principality bearing his name south of the region of Kursk.[131] The lower Volga region was controlled by Khan Küchük-Mahmed. Under his pressure and that of Said-Ahmad Ulug-Mahmed was compelled to withdraw north with the remnants of his horde. In 1437 he occupied the town of Belev on the upper Oka River. This region, the northern section of the former land of Severia, was at that time under Lithuanian suzerainty. Nevertheless Grand Duke Vasili II, worried by the appearance of the Tatars close to the confines of Muscovy, decided to drive them out and sent a detachment of troops under the command of the two Dmitris, the late Iuri's sons. The first encounter ended in favor of the Russians, and Ulug-Mahmed sued for peace. He expressed his willingness to become an ally of Moscow and to guard the frontiers of Russia against mutual enemies. The Russians rejected his offer and insisted he withdraw from Belev. The war was resumed and this time the Russians were defeated.[132]

Ulug-Mahmed remained master of Belev. About his next moves there is much uncertainty in the scholarly literature. Most historians

130. See *Kievan Russia*, pp. 90–91.
131. Kuczyński, p. 184; cf. Spuler, p. 160.
132. Nikon, *12*, 24–25.

suppose that soon after his victory at Belev Ulug-Mahmed must
have led his horde to the Bulgar region beyond the middle Volga
and established himself in Kazan. I differ with this view. In my
opinion Veliaminov-Zernov has convincingly shown that the Khanate of Kazan was founded by Ulug-Mahmed's son Mahmudek, in
1445, not 1438.[133] What is certain is that in 1439 Ulug-Mahmed
appeared before Moscow.[134] But he must have come there from Belev
and not from Kazan. The Muscovite army had been demobilized after the unfortunate Belev expedition, and Vasili II, following the
pattern his father and grandfather set, went to the Kostroma region
as soon as he got news of the approach of the Tatars in order to gather
an army beyond the Volga. He left his brother-in-law, Prince Iuri
Patrikeevich (a descendant of Gedymin), in command of the Moscow
garrison. Ulug-Mahmed's army stood ten days before Moscow without being able to storm it. Then he retreated to Kolomna, which he
burned, and presumably went back to Belev. On their way the
Tatars looted the country and did a great deal of harm to the Russians, yet Ulug-Mahmed's raid showed that the Tatar strength was
ebbing.

A number of Tatar princes were now ready to enter either Muscovite or Lithuanian service. As we have seen, before his victory at
Belev Ulug-Mahmed himself proposed to use his whole horde to
protect the Russian frontiers. At the time of his Moscow campaign
or soon after, one of the Juchid princes of his horde, Berdidad, went
over to Vasili II with his followers. Other Tatar chieftains were
soon to follow his example.

6. The Ottoman Turks, Byzantium, and Moscow

I

While the Golden Horde in the mid-15th century was disintegrating, another Moslem Turkish state, that of the Osmanlis (Ottoman
Turks) was rapidly rising. The Osmanlis had acquired a firm foothold
in the Balkan peninsula in the second half of the 14th century. Their
successes, like those of the Mongols in the initial period of the
Mongol Empire, may be explained by their strong military organiza-

133. Veliaminov-Zernov, *1*, 11–13. A. N. Kurat is in favor of the date 1438 and considers Ulug-Mahmed the first khan of Kazan, Kurat, p. 28.
134. Voskr., *8*, 7; Tverian Chronicle, *PSRL, 15*, 491.

tion and the inner weaknesses and lack of unity among the peoples they threatened.[135]

In the past the Osmanlis, like the Seljuks in whose wake they came to Asia Minor, had been horsemen. In the mid-14th century an important military reform was effected: an infantry corps was created known as the "new army" (*yeniçeri*)—the dreaded Janissaries.[136] We have seen that about the same time the Central Asian emperor Timur used infantry in his major campaigns, and that in conditions of steppe warfare. In the mountainous regions of the Balkan peninsula where the Ottoman Turks penetrated in the 1360's, the infantry proved to be even more efficient. Since no self-respecting Turk would deign to fight on foot, the Janissaries were recruited from the Christian peoples conquered by the Turks. A quota of Christian boys, aged ten to twenty, was levied at regular intervals or whenever necessary, to be converted to Islam and to receive thorough military training. They were forbidden to marry and so their corps (*ocak*) became their home. According to Turkish historical tradition the Janissary corps was instituted by Orhan (1326–59). In contemporary sources it is first mentioned in the second half of the 14th century. Originally it was small, hardly more than 1,000 strong. By 1450 it comprised about 5,000 men, and by 1550 10,000. While most of the "tribute children" were impressed into the Janissaries, some of them were also employed in the sultan's military and civil administration, occupying the highest positions in it. In contrast to the Janissaries, the Ottoman cavalry (spahis) consisted originally mostly of Turks, in any case of free Moslems. A spahi guard regiment of about 3,000 men was on permanent duty at the sultan's court. Other spahis were assigned fiefs (*timar*) in the conquered lands and were mobilized whenever necessary. In addition irregulars could be sum-

135. On the background and formation of the Ottoman Empire, besides the well-known old histories of the Ottoman Empire by J. Hammer-Purgstall and J. W. Zinkeisen and the more recent works of N. Iorga and H. A. Gibbons, see Krymsky, *Turkey*, pp. 10–21; R. P. Blake and W. L. Langer, "The Rise of the Ottoman Turks and Its Historical Background," *AHR*, 37 (1932), 468–505; M. F. Köprülü, *Les Origines de l'Empire Ottoman* (Paris, 1935); P. Wittek, *The Rise of the Ottoman Empire* (London, The Royal Asiatic Society, 1938); G. G. Arnakis, Οἱ Πρῶτοι Ὀθωμανοί (Athens, 1947), reviewed by R. L. Wolff in *Speculum*, 26 (1951), 483–488; Stadtmüller, chap. 18. For a survey of the Oriental sources for the Ottoman history see Togan, pp. 223–228.

136. On the Janissaries see Zinkeisen, *1*, 118, 124, 127, 132; C. Huart, "Janissaries," *EI*, *2*, 572–574; Oman, *2*, 342–343, 357; J. K. Birge, *The Bektashi Order of Dervishes* (London, Luzac & Co., 1937), pp. 46–48, 66, 67, 69, 74–75; N. Weissmann, *Les Janissaires* (Paris, 1938). On the tribute children see Zinkeisen, *3*, 215–231 and *4*, 166; J. H. Mordtmann, "Dewshirme," *EI*, *1*, 952–953.

moned, both horse (*akinci*) and foot (*azab*), but these were more skillful in the art of plunder than in that of war.

The inner strength of the Ottoman drive did not depend only on material factors. The spiritual factor was of great importance. During the incubation period of the Ottoman state in Asia Minor in the late 13th and early 14th centuries the Osmanlis were greatly influenced by the Akhi fraternity, which was based on craftsmen's unions. This fraternity contributed much to a spiritual revival among the urban classes in Asia Minor and to the spread of Islam among the Christians there.[137] On the whole, the religious policy of the sultans in the early period of the Ottoman Empire was one of toleration. Except for the tribute children, there was no forcible conversion of conquered peoples to Islam. Each religious group among the sultan's non-Moslem subjects was left under the supervision of the head of its church. Yet the position of the non-Moslem population (*rayah*) was precarious, and there were many cases of voluntary conversion to Islam. Once converted, the former Christian would become a full-fledged member of Ottoman society. In Asia Minor the Akhi fraternity was active in proselytizing. By 1350 numbers of Greeks in Nicaea, Brussa, and other towns in Asia Minor had been converted. Later on, in the Balkans, many Serbs became Moslems, especially in the southern part of Serbia and in Bosnia, as well as some Bulgarians (the so-called Pomaks).

On the eve of the Ottoman conquest of the Balkan peninsula the Christian powers there were weak. The Byzantine Empire—what was left of it—was torn by internal dissension. Moreover economically it was in the clutches of the Venetians and, politically, pressed by the Slavs. The great Serbian ruler Stephan Dušan attempted to create a Slavo-Greek empire, to infuse new blood in the veins of decaying Byzantium, and even proclaimed himself tsar of the Serbs and the Greeks. A considerable part of Bulgaria was included in Stephan's empire. That empire, however, proved short-lived and rapidly disintegrated after Stephan's death (1355). The Greeks seemed to be saved from Slavic domination; the Bulgarians regained their independence; Macedonia became a separate kingdom, and Serbia proper broke into two halves: the kingdom of Bosnia and the principality of North Serbia. The city of Belgrade (Beograd) was seized by the Hungarians.

137. On the Akhi fraternity see Gordlevsky, chap. 9; G. G. Arnakis, "Captivity of Gregory Palamas," *Speculum, 26* (1951), 113–114, 117–118.

Not feeling themselves strong enough as yet to storm Constantinople, the Osmanlis outflanked it by taking Adrianople, which they made their capital, shortening its name to Edirne (1361). Two years later the Turks occupied Philippopolis (Plovdiv) in southeast Bulgaria. At the close of the 1360's King Vukašin of Macedonia challenged the authority of the sultan, successfully at first, but he was defeated and perished in battle in 1371. His son Marko Kraljević (King's Son), a hero of the Serbian epos, could hold Macedonia only as the sultan's vassal. Having obtained control of Thrace, southeast Bulgaria and Macedonia, the Osmanlis, after careful preparation, invaded the Sredets (Sophia) region in northwest Bulgaria (1385).[138] Sultan Murat I's next move was to attack Prince Lazar's North Serbian realm. The Serbian army was defeated in the fateful battle of Kosovo Pole (Black Thrushes' Field) in 1389. Four years later Murat's son and successor, Bayazit I, completed the conquest of Bulgaria by storming Tyrnovo (Trnovo), the old Bulgarian capital.

Bulgaria was annexed to the Ottoman Empire and a number of spahis were installed there as holders of military fiefs. Macedonia retained her limited autonomy until the death of Marko Kraljević and then followed the path of Bulgaria. Serbia fared better, being granted a far-reaching autonomy which lasted until 1459.

Prior to the Turkish conquest considerable cultural progress had been made, in both Bulgaria and Serbia which found expression in art and in literature. Stephen Dušan's famous Code of Laws (*Zakonnik*) of 1349 represented another facet of the intellectual achievements of the Balkan Slavs of this period. The religious and literary revival in Bulgaria was sponsored by Patriarch Euthymius who held office from 1375 to the Turkish conquest of Tyrnovo.[139] This spiritual ferment spread from Bulgaria into Russia. Both Metropolitan Cyprian and Metropolitan Gregory Tsamblak were natives of Tyrnovo. Other Bulgarians and Serbs made their way to Russia in the course of the 15th century.

The Turkish conquest put an abrupt end to the blossoming of Bulgarian thought. The patriarchate was abolished and the church in Bulgaria was placed under Greek control and guidance. In this

138. Date according to F. Babinger, *Beiträge zur Frühgeschichte der Türkenherrschaft in Rumelien (14–15 Jahrhundert)* (Munich and Vienna, 1943), p. 78.

139. On the religious and literary movements in Bulgaria in the 14th century see N. S. Derzhavin, *Istoriia Bolgarii* (1946), 2, 133–153; E. Turdeanu, *La Littérature bulgaire de XIV-me siècle et sa diffusion dans les pays romains* (Paris, 1947); Mutafchiev, 2, 242–253.

respect, as well as in regard to her administration, Serbia was better off than Bulgaria. In fact, the Osmanlis themselves were to a certain extent influenced by Serbian culture. Serbian became an accepted language at the sultan's court along with Greek, and many official documents of the Ottoman Empire in the late 14th to 16th centuries were written in Serbian. The popularity of Serbian at the sultan's court was partly a result of the high position of Serbian princesses in the sultan's harem. Prince Lazar's daughter Olivera (called Mileva in Serbian folksongs) was Bayazit I's favorite wife, and some of Bayazit's successors also impressed Serbian girls into their harems.[140]

II

The advance of the Osmanlis in the Balkans greatly worried the peoples of Central and Western Europe, especially the Hungarians who found themselves directly threatened by the Turks. King Sigismund of Hungary (the future emperor of the Holy Roman Empire) belonged to the house of Luxembourg and through it was in close relations with most of European royalty. His appeals to the other Roman Catholic rulers resulted in a pan-European crusade against the Turks in which English, French, Polish, Czech, Italian, and German knights participated side by side with the Hungarians. According to an eyewitness, the German soldier Schiltberger, the crusaders' army was 16,000 strong. From an analysis of all evidence available, Ferdinand Lot has recently arrived at a much lower figure, not over 9,000.[141] The Turkish army was hardly more numerous but was much better led. The Serbs under Despot Stephan (Prince Lazar's son) [142] loyally supported their suzerain Bayazit in that war. The decisive battle of Nikopol ended in the complete defeat of the crusaders (1396). Grief and panic spread at the European courts when the news of the battle was received. Constantinople was now considered lost, and Rome itself seemed to be threatened. Within a few years, however, Bayazit's attention turned from the West to the East. A conflict took place between him and Timur. At Ankara in Asia Minor the Osmanlis and their allies the Serbs were defeated by Timur's veterans, and Bayazit himself was taken prisoner (1402).

That catastrophe almost shattered the young Ottoman Empire.

140. See Krymsky, *Turkey*, pp. 15–18.
141. Lot, *2*, 222, 460.
142. Despot (*despotes*), "potentate," "lord," is a late Byzantine title used by some of the Balkan rulers.

Several years passed before one of Bayazit's sons, Mehmet I (1402–21), succeeded in restoring order and discipline. Under his son and successor Murat II (1421–51) the empire once again became a formidable power. The days of Constantinople seemed to be numbered. The Byzantine government's sole hope was to receive assistance from the West. It soon became obvious that such assistance could be obtained only at the price of the union of the Byzantine church with the Roman under the supreme authority of the pope. In the complex of Christian Trinitarian dogmas the main obstacle to the union from the Greek point of view was the "Filioque" clause in the Roman creed. In the old Niceno-Constantinopolitan Creed approved by the Second Ecumenical Council (A.D. 381) the dogma of the procession of the Holy Ghost from the Father had been formulated.[143] In the West a different interpretation of the interrelation of the three persons of the Trinity eventually prevailed: that of the double procession of the Holy Ghost from Father and Son. The addition of the phrase "and Son" (Filioque) was approved by a number of church councils in Spain, France, and Germany in the late 8th and early 9th centuries.[144] Several Greek theologians proved ready to consider the Western point of view on the basis of philosophical arguments. Prominent among them was Bishop Bessarion of Nicaea, a sophisticated scholar imbued with the spirit of Renaissance. The majority of the Greek clergymen clung, however, to the Eastern traditions. In the grim circumstances of those days, there was hardly chance for a free and dispassionate theological discussion of the problem. Feeling himself under Damocles' sword, the Byzantine emperor urged the clergy to make as many concessions to the Roman church as possible. Politics prevailed over religious feelings.

It will be recalled that the problem of assistance to Constantinople was discussed at the international conference at Lutsk in Volynia in 1429. No decision was taken. The discussion was resumed at the Seventeenth Ecumenical Council which opened in Basel in 1431. To make the situation even more confused, a conflict developed between that council and Pope Eugenius IV. In 1437 the pope ordered the sessions at Basel to be closed and the council to move to Ferrara in

143. Denzinger, *Enchiridion,* p. 38. See also A. E. Burn, "Creeds (Ecumenical)," *Hastings' Encyclopedia of Religion and Ethics,* 4, 239–240. For the theological background of the doctrine see G. Florovsky, *Vostochnye otsy IV veka* (Paris, 1931); *idem, Vizantiiskie otsy V–VIII vekov* (Paris, 1933).

144. Denzinger, *Enchiridion,* p. 38; A. Palmieri, Filioque, *Dictionnaire de théologie catholique,* 5, 2309–2343.

Italy. The majority of the members refused to obey; they remained in session at Basel and elected an antipope, Felix V. So two councils were now at work, each claiming to be the Seventeenth Ecumenical Council. That which began in 1438 at Ferrara later moved to Florence and is therefore usually referred to as the Ferrara-Florence council. Eventually, Eugenius IV succeeded in restoring his authority in Central Europe, and under his successor, Nicholas V, the remnants of the Basel council voted to dissolve (1449). The Ferrara–Florence council was in session from 1438 to 1443 and then moved to Rome where it completed its work in 1445.[145] Its decisions became valid for the whole Roman Catholic Church.

To return to the initial period of the conflict between Pope Eugenius IV and the Basel council, each side claimed to have sole authority in dealing with the Greek problem. Finally, the Byzantine emperor John VIII accepted the invitation of the pope and personally led the delegation of Greek clergy to Ferrara. Being a part of the Byzantine patriarchate, the Russian church was entitled to be represented at Ferrara. But it had troubles of its own at this time. Metropolitan Photius had died in 1431. The Moscow government and clergy favored an East Russian bishop, Iona of Riazan, as his successor. The grand duke of Lithuania, Svidrigailo, supported a West Russian bishop, Gerasim of Smolensk, who went to Constantinople and was there appointed metropolitan of all Russia (1434). The Byzantine authorities may have thought that a West Russian bishop would be more inclined to the idea of church union than an East Russian. As we know, the next year Gerasim was executed in Vitebsk by order of the same Svidrigailo who had backed him at first. The metropolitan's see of Russia was vacant again. The government of Moscow now sent Bishop Iona to Constantinople asking the emperor and the patriarch to recognize him as the new metropolitan. This the Byzantine authorities refused to do and instead, appointed a Greek (or Hellenized Slav), Isidor (born in Salonike). Isidor came to Moscow in 1437 and, after some hesitation, was accepted there as metropolitan. Before long he disclosed his intention to go to the Ferrara council. Both Grand Duke Vasili II and the Moscow clergy were at first suspicious of the proposed negotiations with the Roman church.

145. For a detailed account of the work of the Ferrara-Florence council see G. Hofmann, "Die Konzilsarbeit in Ferrara" (Florenz, Rom), *OCP, 3* (1937), 110–140, 403–455; *4* (1938), 157–188, 372–422; *5* (1939), 151–185; *8* (1942), 5–39; *15* (1949), 71–84; *16* (1950), 358–376.

Finally, however, after Isidor swore not to betray Orthodoxy, the Moscow authorities let him go to Italy. He was accompanied by Bishop Avraami of Suzdal and about a hundred clerics and laymen.

In spite of the opposition of the Greeks of the old school to any change of the Creed, most of them, under the pressure of Emperor John, had reluctantly to agree to the Roman formula which, on the Greek side, was supported by both Bessarion of Nicaea and Isidor of Russia. The supremacy of the pope was also recognized.[146] Bishop Mark of Ephesus was the only Greek prelate who refused to sign the declaration of union. The union with the Greeks was announced in the papal bull ("Laeterentur coeli") of July 6, 1439.[147] Both Bessarion and Isidor were then made cardinals. Union with the Armenians was promulgated in November 1439, and with the Jacobites in 1441.

However expedient church union might have been for Byzantine diplomacy, it shattered the spiritual unity of the Greeks and added to the tension within the empire. While the emperor and some of the church prelates supported the union, most of the clergy and laity opposed it. An ominous sign of demoralization caused by the religious conflict was the spread of a Turcophile and defeatist mood among the Orthodox Greeks. A characteristic saying of the "man in the street" illustrating this tendency has been recorded in Ducas' chronicle: "It is better to fall into the hands of the Turks than into those of the Franks." [148] Much depended now on the ability of the "Franks" to give the necessary assistance against the Turks. The pope honored his pledge and a new crusade was organized in 1444. This time neither English nor French could participate since they were at war with each other. A number of German and Czech knights volunteered, but essentially the crusade was conducted by two nations, Hungary and Poland, with some assistance from Wallachia.[149] According to the papal collector, Andreas de Palatio, who took part

146. For a survey of the older literature of the Florentine union see Krymsky, *Turkey*, pp. 40–42. Cf. Golubinsky, *2*, 433–441; Hrushevsky, *5*, 519–521, 657–661; A. M. Amman, S.J., *Storia della Chiesa Russa e dei paesi limitrofi* (Torino, 1948), pp. 119–128; Z. V. Udaltsova, "Bor'ba vizantiiskikh partii na florentiiskom sobore," *Vizantiiskii vremennik, 3* (1950), 106–132.

147. For the Latin text of the "Decretum pro Graecis" see Denzinger, *Enchiridion*, pp. 235–236.

148. Ducas, *Historia Byzantina* (Bonn ed.), p. 291.

149. For a survey of literature of the Varna crusade see Krymsky, *Turkey*, pp. 50–56. See also O. Halecki, *The Crusade of Varna* (New York, Polish Institute of Arts and Sciences, 1943), reviewed by J. Bromberg, *Speculum, 20* (1945), 247–250.

in the expedition, the crusaders' army consisted of 16,000 horsemen, not counting the Wallachians. The modern French historian, Ferdinand Lot, argues for a much lower figure, 4,800 at most.[150] His figure seems too low in this case. The core of the Turkish army—the Janissaries and spahi guardsmen—was about 8,000 strong. The number of mobilized provincial spahis is unknown. On the whole the Turkish army hardly was more numerous than that of the crusaders. In the battle of Varna the Turks were once more victorious (1444). The young Polish king Vladislav III lost his life in the melee.

Historically speaking, the catastrophe at Varna sealed the fate of Constantinople. The task of storming the "Imperial City" was undertaken by Murat II's son and successor, Mehmet II after careful preparations. The siege began on April 5, 1453. By that time Constantinople was almost a ghost city. Owing to the protracted economic and political crisis, its population which in the old times must have reached 500,000 or more now was hardly a tenth of that figure.[151] Besides, owing to the religious split, the people were in a state of mental confusion. In 1451 the Uniate patriarch of Constantinople had been ousted by the Greek clergy and fled to Rome. The next year, under the pope's pressure, Emperor Constantine XI had to accept Cardinal Isidor as the pope's legate. On December 12, 1452 the Roman Mass was performed in the Cathedral of St. Sophia. From that day the people shunned the church.

Constantinople's fortifications were still formidable but their very vastness—a twelve-mile circuit—presented a problem for the few defenders. Emperor Constantine had at his disposal less than 5,000 Greek soldiers. The pope sent 200 soldiers and the Genoese condottiere Giovanni Giustiniani brought with him 700 men, of whom only 400 were properly armed.[152] For the Turkish army various sources give figures ranging from 80,000 to 400,000. Even 80,000 is probably exaggerated, unless we count the irregulars. In addition to the numerical superiority of his troops, Mehmet II had the advantage of a strong artillery directed by foreign experts (a Transylvanian and a Hungarian are mentioned among them). With such a disproportion of forces the defenders had no chance; that the siege lasted almost seven weeks is an indication of their valor. Constantinople was finally

150. See Lot, 2, 229–230.

151. See A. M. Schneider, "Die Bevölkerung Konstantinopels im xv Jahrhundert," *AWGN* (1949), pp. 233–234; reviewed by H. Ritter, *Oriens, 3* (1950), 147.

152. Lot, 2, 233–234. For a survey of the literature and sources of the siege and conquest of Constantinople by the Osmanlis see Krymsky, *Turkey,* pp. 68–73.

stormed on May 29, 1453. Most of the defenders, including Emperor Constantine himself, perished in the last battle. Cardinal Isidor was taken prisoner by the Turks. As soon as the plundering was over order was restored, and Constantinople became the Ottoman capital. The Cathedral of St. Sophia and a number of other Christian churches were turned into mosques. The Greek church as an institution was not molested. Greeks were invited and encouraged to return to the city and their church was promised protection. The council of Greek bishops elected Gennadius Scholarius the new patriarch. While previously he had favored an agreement with Rome, later on, under the influence of Mark of Ephesus, he became a staunch supporter of Greek traditions and an antagonist of the church union. Sultan Mehmet II expressed his desire to have the new patriarch installed with old Byzantine ceremonial. The sultan personally handed the crosier to the new patriarch,[153] taking the place of the Byzantine autocrats who had formerly done it. Ironically enough a champion of Islam, Fatih Mehmet (Mehmet the Conqueror), now assumed the role of protector of the Greek faith, which the last two Byzantine emperors had failed to play properly.

III

Both the acceptance of the church union by the Greeks and the fall of Constantinople deeply affected the course of Russian church history as well as the development of Russian political thought. Apparently Metropolitan Isidor did not keep the government of Moscow informed of the progress of the debates at the Ferrara-Florence council. In 1440 Isidor, now a cardinal and apostolic legate, returned to Russia. He went first to Kiev where he spent the winter; Prince Alexander issued him a charter confirming his authority over the church estates in the Kievan region. In March 1441 Isidor appeared in Moscow. He officiated at a solemn Mass in the main cathedral of Moscow—that of the Dormition of Our Lady—invoking the name of the pope. After the service he read the Florentine declaration of the church union. This caused great commotion among the Muscovites. Isidor was prevented from conducting any further church services and confined in a cell in the Chudov Monastery in the Kremlin,[154] pending the decision of the

153. Phrantzes, *Chronicon* (Bonn ed.), pp. 305–307.
154. The Chudov Monastery was founded by Metropolitan Alexei in honor of the miracle (*chudo*) of St. Michael at Chone. See N. P. Kondakov, *The Russian Icon*, E. H. Minns, trans. (Oxford, Clarendon Press, 1927), p. 136.

council of Russian bishops which met immediately. In the Nikon Chronicle as well as in the Book of Degrees (*Stepennaia kniga*) the initiative in the opposition to Isidor is ascribed to Grand Duke Vasili II. Both these historical works were written in the second half of the 16th century, in the reign of Ivan IV; both are permeated with a strong monarchic tendency. As M. A. Diakonov has convincingly shown, contemporary evidence indicates that it was the Russian bishops rather than the grand duke who first rallied the Muscovites against the union.[155] In any case the council of bishops rejected the Florentine declaration and refused to recognize Isidor as metropolitan unless and until he recanted. Isidor was unwilling to change his position. The Russian authorities let him leave Moscow quietly; later on it was explained that he had "escaped." [156] He went to Tver, where he was arrested by order of Grand Duke Boris and kept in prison for several months. Released early in 1442, Isidor made for Lithuania seeking Grand Duke Casimir's protection. The latter, however, supported the Basel church council against Pope Eugenius and recognized the antipope, Felix V. He therefore refused to accept Isidor, who had no alternative but to return to Rome.

This matter settled, the Russians were at a loss what to do next. They had at the moment no intention to make a final break with Constantinople. It must be said that in their subsequent moves the Russian bishops, as well as Grand Duke Vasili under their guidance, showed much self-restraint and caution. Soon after the rejection of the union the grand duke signed a letter addressed to the Byzantine emperor and the patriarch, explaining his and the bishops' reasons for not recognizing Isidor. Pointing out that Isidor had been ordained metropolitan without consultation with the Russian authorities, Vasili II asked the emperor and the patriarch to agree, in view of the troubled international situation, to the election of the new metropolitan by a council of Russian bishops, the prelate elected to receive the patriarch's blessings.[157] This letter was never sent since information reached Moscow that both the emperor and the patriarch had definitely accepted the union. Two years later a new version of the letter was prepared but this again was not expedited.[158] The Russians

---

155. Diakonov, *Vlast;* pp. 55–57; V. Valdenberg, *Drevnerusskie ucheniia o predelakh tsarskoi vlasti* (Petrograd, 1916), pp. 171–173.

156. Golubinsky, *2,* 457; Valdenberg, p. 171; Hrushevsky, *5,* 526.

157. *RIB, 6,* cols. 526–535.

158. *Ibid., 6,* cols. 529–530, n. 1.

waited five more years. Only after they had become convinced that the Byzantine authorities had no intention of repudiating the union did the Russians decide to act. The government of Moscow consulted both Grand Duke Casimir of Lithuania and Prince Alexander of Kiev to learn if they would recognize Moscow's candidate to the metropolitan's see, Bishop Iona of Riazan, if he were elected to the office. After receiving affirmative answers from both Casimir and Alexander, the grand duke convoked the council of bishops, and on December 5, 1448 Iona was elected metropolitan of all Russia.[159]

Even that action was not construed at first as a rejection of the authority of the patriarch of Constantinople. In his sermons and epistles Metropolitan Iona took pains to explain that he accepted the election only in view of the abnormal circumstances and that in the future, provided the Byzantine authorities would return to Orthodoxy, the Russians would always ask the patriarch's blessing. Actually, the emancipation of the Russian church from the patriarch's authority became final. The fall of Constantinople, indeed, ended the church union there and restored Orthodoxy, but at the same time it overthrew the whole Byzantine system of a "symphony" of church and state. The dependence of the Greek church on an "infidel" ruler made renewal of their subordination to the Greeks psychologically and politically difficult for the Russians, especially as Russia itself was on the eve of emancipation from the Moslem khans. The net result was that the Russian church became autocephalous owing to the course of international events rather than by conscious effort on its part.

The political consequences of the fall of Constantinople were as far-reaching as the religious. The grand duke of Moscow now found himself the leading independent Greek Orthodox ruler—in fact, almost the only such ruler in the whole Greek Orthodox world. Whether he wanted it or not, he was now expected to act as protector of the Greek faith. This proved the starting point for a complex current of political thought, both in and outside Russia; among the speculations based on it was the significant idea of the shift of the center of true Orthodoxy from the Second Rome (Constantinople) to the Third Rome—Holy Moscow.

159. Golubinsky, 2, 484–485.

7. Muscovy, Lithuania, and the Tatars during the Second Half of Vasili II's Reign

I

In 1440 Grand Duke Sigismund of Lithuania fell victim to a conspiracy of the Lithuanian grandees. They accused him of tyranny and of intending to undermine the rule of the aristocracy in Lithuania. It seems that after his victory over Svidrigailo in 1435 Sigismund had grown suspicious of his boyar supporters and attempted to rule through the officials of his court, appointing a number of them to key positions in the army and administration. Sigismund's assassination resulted in a new political crisis in the grand duchy which appeared at first to be even more serious than that of the early 1430's.[160] The majority of the Lithuanian boyars or pany preferred Iagailo's son Casimir for the throne. Iagailo had died in 1434 and his son Vladislav III (Casimir's elder brother) was now king of Poland. Vladislav agreed to let Casimir go to Lithuania but only as his lieutenant, not as a grand duke. This caused new parleys and much delay, and meanwhile new candidates to the throne appeared, among them Sigismund's son Michael and the aged Svidrigailo. A rebellion took place in Smolensk and another in Kiev. The people of Smolensk elected Prince Iuri of Mstislavl as their sovereign. Kiev recognized Michael, who was also elected by the people of Samogitia (Zhmud') as their prince.

In these difficult circumstances the Lithuanian aristocracy once more showed their tenacity, sense of statesmanship, and strength. Their leader at that time was Ian Gashtovt (Gasztold) who became young Casimir's chief adviser. Under his guidance Casimir (recognized as grand duke by the Lithuanians) succeeded within two years in reuniting most of the seceded lands. Smolensk was brought to submission by force of arms and then pacified by the grand duke's charter which guaranteed local autonomy. Kiev was given a vassal prince of her own, Alexander (Olelko), son of Vladimir. It will be recalled that Vladimir (son of Olgerd) had ruled in Kiev before the abolition of the local principalities by Vitovt. The problem of Zhmud'

---

160. See Hrushevsky, *4*, 195–207; Kolankowski, pp. 226–247; Liubavsky, pp. 72–81; Voldemar (as above, n. 126), pp. 171–174. See also A. Lewicki, "Powstanie Swidrygielly," *Rozprawy Akademii Umiejetnosci* (Historical and Philosophical Section), *29* (1892), inaccessible to me; O. Halecki, *Ostatnie lata Swidrygielly i sprawa Wolynska* (Kraków, 1915).

was settled by negotiation: the Zhmud' land recognized Casimir in return for new guarantees of autonomy. Finally, in 1445 the non-agenarian Svidrigailo also pledged his loyalty to his nephew. Only Michael continued guerrilla warfare against Casimir, finding supporters now in one region and now in another.

A new complication arose when King Vladislav III of Poland perished in the Varna crusade (1444). The next year Casimir was elected king by the Polish *Seim*. The Lithuanians, however, were not willing to let Casimir accept the Polish crown since they were afraid that this would result in the subordination of Lithuania to Poland. They agreed to it only after Casimir signed a pledge to keep a separate administration for Lithuania. Although the Poles refused to approve this guarantee, Casimir issued a new charter for the grand duchy confirming the rights and privileges of both the Lithuanian and Russian lands. This privilei of his (1447) became the cornerstone of the constitutional government of the grand duchy.[161] Soon after Casimir was crowned king of Poland at Kraków. Thus the union of Poland and Lithuania was restored in one ruler for both nations, but Lithuania actually remained a separate state. This indeed amounted to abrogation of the original Krevo union of 1385.

The Poles had to recognize the fait accompli even if they took exception to its legality. However, their refusal to confirm Casimir's pledge aroused doubts in the minds of many Lithuanians and West Russians about the desirability for the grand duchy of having a common ruler with Poland. These feelings increased Michael's chances. In 1446 Michael concluded an agreement in Moldavia with Khan Said-Ahmad.[162] Backed by the Tatars, Michael occupied a number of towns in the Severian region including Novgorod and Briansk (1448–49). But he was not able to withstand the pressure of Casimir's army for long and had to abandon Severia and flee abroad, eventually finding refuge—and death—in Moscow.

II

Just when Casimir won the first round in his struggle for power in Lithuania (1445), the internecine war between Vasili II and his opponents was resumed in Muscovy. The unhappy turn of the struggle

161. For the text of Kazimir's *privilei* see Vladimirsky-Budanov, *Khristomatiia, 2,* 20–31. The date 1457 in Vladimirsky-Budanov's edition refers to the confirmation of the privilei; it was originally issued in 1447.

162. Kolankowski, pp. 272–273.

between the Russians and the Tatars encouraged the leader of opposition, Prince Dmitri Shemiaka, openly to defy Vasili.

In the winter of 1443–44 a strong group of Tatars led by the Juchid prince Mustafa attacked the land of Riazan. Presumably this group belonged to the Saray horde ruled by Khan Küchük-Mahmed. Grand Duke Vasili hastened to send a detachment of his troops, reinforced by the Mordvinians, on snowshoes to help Riazan. These troops, together with the Riazan Cossacks (also on snowshoes) succeeded in destroying the whole Tatar army. Mustafa and a number of Tatar princes were killed in the battle, and the remnants of the Tatar army were captured.[163] Incidentally, this is the first mention of the Rus- sian Cossacks in our sources. Other groups of them were to be organized before long.

Soon after, a new threat arose from another Tatar horde, that of Ulug-Mahmed. In 1444 that khan led his horde from Belev down the Oka River and established himself, as the chroniclers have it, in "Old Novgorod Nizhni." [164] All the historians who mention this episode assume that by that name the old site of the city of Nizhni Novgorod (the former capital of the grand duchy by that name) is meant.[165] I have serious doubts of this. Ulug-Mahmed might have pitched his camp not at the old site of Nizhni Novgorod (at the confluence of the Oka and Volga rivers) but much higher up the Oka, at the old site of the fortress Gorodets.[166] The town of Gorodets was destroyed by the Mongols in 1376, at the time of their raid on the area around Nizhni Novgorod; [167] the old fortress was abandoned after that and a new one built about 1,400 yards up the river. That new fortress was then called the New Lower Castle, *Novyi Nizovyi Gorod*.[168] The adjective nizovyi is a synonym of nizhni. It is the old site of this Novgorod Nizhni which I believe Ulug-Mahmed occupied in 1444. The Russian garrison in the new castle was now besieged by the Tatars. It should be mentioned in this connection that about eight years later Grand Duke Vasili II granted Gorodets to Ulug-Mahmed's son Kasim. If Ulug-Mahmed occupied Gorodets in 1444, it is possible that Kasim could claim it as his patrimony.

163. Nikon, *12*, 61–62.

164. *Ibid.*, *12*, 62–63.

165. See especially Karamzin, *Notes*, *5*, 226–227, n. 322.

166. Not to be confused with Gorodets-on-the-Volga. *Gorodets* is a derivation of *gorod* (town, castle).

167. On that raid see above, sec. 2, p. 256.

168. Veliaminov-Zernov, *1*, 41; D. Ilovaisky, *Istoriia Riazanskogo Kniazhestva* (Moscow, 1858), p. 259.

There is one more argument against identifying the city occupied by Ulug-Mahmed in 1444 as Nizhni Novgorod. As we shall see presently, in the late summer of 1445 Dmitri Shemiaka signed a treaty with the descendants of Vasili Kirdiapa (one of the last independent Suzdal and Nizhni Novgorod princes) in which he agreed to restore to them the principality of Nizhni Novgorod and to recognize them as princes there. This was one of Shemiaka's moves directed against Vasili II. At that time he hoped that Ulug-Mahmed would issue him the patent on the throne of Moscow. He would hardly dare to promise Nizhni Novgorod to the Suzdal princes if it had been occupied by Ulug-Mahmed. So I would rather assume, as a working hypothesis at any rate, that Ulug-Mahmed established himself, in 1444, at the old site of Gorodets-on-the-Oka and not at that of Nizhni Novgorod.

Ulug-Mahmed's next move, in the winter of 1444–45, was to attack Murom (which lies about halfway between Gorodets and Nizhni Novgorod). This attack was repulsed by the Muscovite troops under the personal command of Vasili II. The grand duke was not able, however, to relieve the Russian garrison besieged in Gorodets. The Russians therefore abandoned it, setting the castle on fire before leaving. Ulug-Mahmed now was able to send part of his army, under the command of his sons Mahmudek and Yakub, against Suzdal where Vasili had gone from Murom. However, by the time Vasili received news of the new Tatar advance he was back in Moscow. He immediately returned to Suzdal with a small force. His vassal Tatar prince, Berdidad, followed behind at some distance. On July 7, 1445, without waiting for Berdidad's auxiliary troops, Vasili II attacked the army of Ulug-Mahmed's sons which was 3,500 strong. According to the chronicles, Vasili had only 1,500 troops under his command. The Tatars won the day and the wounded Vasili was taken prisoner.[169] Thus a casual encounter between two small forces, a mere skirmish as it were, unexpectedly proved an event of great historical importance. The Tatar princes themselves had not expected such a success and did not know what to do with their prize. They did not attempt to exploit their victory and after looting Suzdal and the country around retreated to Murom which their father had by this time occupied. Ulug-Mahmed too seems to have been puzzled with the situation and, instead of attempting a campaign against Moscow, led his horde and his prisoner to Kurmysh, by-passing Nizhni Novgorod. Kurmysh lies about halfway between Nizhni Novgorod and Kazan. Probably Ulug-Mahmed

169. Nikon, *12*, 64–65.

had by that time decided to establish himself in Kazan and was moving in that direction. However, he stopped at Kurmysh for several months to determine Vasili's fate.

When the news of the grand duke's capture reached Moscow, panic and consternation spread among the people. As the city was hastily preparing for the Tatar attack which was considered imminent, a huge fire started, apparently by accident. Dowager Grand Duchess Sophia and Grand Duchess Maria fled to Rostov accompanied by the boyars. Left to themselves, the commoners took matters into their own hands as they had at the time of Tokhtamysh' raid in 1382. The fortifications which had been damaged by the fire were repaired; nobody was allowed to leave the city; discipline was restored, and the citizens' militia put on a war footing.[170] It is interesting to note that while the Moscow commoners, both before and after this episode, failed to take any active role in the struggle between Vasili II and his cousins, they were now, as before, the first to unite against the Tatar danger. Obviously there was not much difference from the point of view of their interests between this or that Russian prince, but the danger of subjection to a foreign invader was acutely felt by all of them and served as a stimulus for intermittent revival of the veche tradition.

Meanwhile Dmitri Shemiaka tried to exploit the political situation for his own benefit. As has been mentioned, he had made an agreement with the princes of Suzdal to give them back the principality of Suzdal–Nizhni Novgorod.[171] This was in line with his father Iuri's political program of federation. Khan Ulug-Mahmed, in his turn, seems to have favored the idea of setting Dmitri Shemiaka on the Moscow throne. Some time early in September the khan sent Begich, his envoy, to Galich for preliminary negotiations with Dmitri. Dmitri, as might be expected, received him with great cordiality and sent him home accompanied by an agent who was instructed to urge the khan not to let Vasili return to Moscow.

Vasili, on his part, kept urging the khan to release him. He had probably been joined in captivity by some of his courtiers who could have brought him money to make presents to the khan and the khan's family. Besides, Vasili was ready to promise the khan a substantial ransom, to be collected after his return to Moscow. In any case, he succeeded in gaining the friendship of two of Ulug-Mahmed's sons, Yakub and Kasim, and of several Tatar princes and grandees. For

170. *Ibid., 12*, 65.
171. *DDG*, pp. 119–120.

some unknown reason, Begich's journey to Dmitri took more time than was expected. Vasili's friends in the Horde used the envoy's long absence to make Ulug-Mahmed suspicious of Dmitri's intentions. Rumors were spread that Begich had been killed by Dmitri's order. In any case, on October 1, Ulug-Mahmed announced his decision in favor of Vasili.[172]

Vasili was set free and his patent on the throne of Moscow was confirmed by the khan. He had to promise under oath, though, to pay a ransom of 25,000 rubles, according to the Pskovian Chronicle; [173] the Novgorodian Chronicle gives the much higher figure of 200,000 rubles,[174] but this probably refers not merely to Vasili's personal ransom but to all the payments required from Russia. Apparently, besides the ransom, Vasili promised to collect both the tribute and the tamga at the high rates established by Tokhtamysh. To secure collection, several Tatar princes and high officials, with their retinues, were to accompany the grand duke to Moscow. Vasili immediately sent ahead a courier, Andrew Pleshcheev, to announce his return to the capital. On the way Pleshcheev met the grooms of Begich, now returning to the khan (Begich himself traveled up the Oka by boat). Pleshcheev reported this to the nearest Muscovite military commander, Prince Vasili Obolensky, who immediately arrested Begich. Dmitri's agent who accompanied Begich succeeded in escaping.

Ulug-Mahmed's decision to set Vasili free has been severely criticized in modern times by the German scholar Bertold Spuler: "Ulug-Mahmed wantonly threw away a fine chance of completely subjugating the Grand Duchy of Moscow!" [175] As a matter of fact, Ulug-Mahmed might have understood the situation better than his 20th-century adviser. Tokhtamysh' times were over. With the breaking up of the Golden Horde and the expansion of Russian economic strength, the balance of forces had changed in Russia's favor. Ulug-Mahmed's horde was apparently not numerous. He had scarcely more than 10,000 warriors under his command. He must have realized that the victory of his sons at Suzdal was entirely accidental. Under the circumstances he could not seriously think of conquering Russia by force of arms or of keeping her subjugated by mere force.

172. Nikon, *12*, 66.
173. The First Pskovian Chronicle, p. 47.
174. Novgorod, p. 426.
175. Spuler, p. 165.

His only chance was to use Vasili as his agent for collecting from Russia a huge indemnity by means of which he could build up a khanate of his own out of the immediate reach of the Muscovite troops. His decision was probably the most profitable he could make. The only factor he did not take into consideration was his eldest son, Mahmudek. Enticed by the riches to be collected from Russia, Mahmudek decided to use them himself instead of letting his father use them. He killed his father and led the horde to Kazan, where he proclaimed himself khan in the fall of 1445. He probably would have killed his brothers Yakub and Kasim as well, but they ran away, to the land of the Circassians, as the chronicler puts it. What he meant by Circassians will become clear from subsequent events. A number of other princes and grandees also left Mahmudek and went over to Khan Said-Ahmad.

III

Vasili returned to Moscow on November 17. He could be reasonably satisfied with the outcome of events. He had retained his throne and his realm,˙ ceding no territory to the khan. Moreover, after Ulug-Mahmed's assassination and Mahmudek's retirement to Kazan, the immediate danger was over. The Tatar princes sent by Ulug-Mahmed to collect the indemnity were not bound by allegiance to his son and some of them at least could be induced to enter Vasili's service, to be rewarded with the money they collected. Other Tatar princes and grandees who did not agree to follow Mahmudek to Kazan were now lured to Russia by the attractive conditions offered by Vasili. The arrival of Tatar officials in Russia in great numbers was at first an incidental result of Vasili's defeat and captivity. But the process continued as a result of Vasili's deliberate policies. He quickly saw in the use of Tatar vassals a new method of dealing with the Tatar hordes in the neighborhood of Muscovy; he engaged "loyal" Tatars to fight the outside Tatars. Besides, Vasili had long since realized the advantage of having a new body of loyal servitors whom he could use to suppress any opposition on the part of his Russian subjects to his internal policies.

That opposition was rallying rapidly, and it was precisely Vasili's generosity toward the Tatars which was seized upon by his enemies as the most convenient point in their propaganda against him. As could be expected, Prince Dmitri Shemiaka became the moving spirit of that propaganda. He succeeded in getting the full support of Prince Ivan Mozhaisky, and both of them persuaded the grand duke of Tver to maintain at least benevolent neutrality in the coming struggle. Even the Nikon Chronicle, which is permeated with monarchic traditions and on other occasions emphasizes Vasili's popularity among the Muscovites, admits that this time many of the Moscow boyars and rich merchants and even some of the monks entered the conspiracy against him.[176] The propaganda sponsored by Dmitri Shemiaka seems to have produced its effect.

Rumors were spread that Vasili had failed to make public the main clause in his agreement with Ulug-Mahmed. It was alleged that by that clause Ulug-Mahmed was to become tsar of Moscow and Vasili to be installed in Tver as his vassal prince.[177] It is against this background that the origin of the epithet "Temnyi" under which Vasili became known in the last years of his reign may best be explained. The usual connotation of the word (now pronounced *tiomnyi* when used in this sense) is "dark." As we shall see, Vasili was blinded in 1446 by his opponents. It has been suggested that he was called Temnyi because of his blindness. Ushakov in his *Dictionary of the Russian Language* points out that in some "regional" dialects "temnyi" means "blind." He does not refer to any particular region, however, and the only example of this connotation he submits is precisely "Vasili Temnyi" which he interprets as "Vasili the Blind." [178] On the other hand, no such connotation of the word is indicated in Sreznevsky's *Dictionary of the Old Russian Language.* But there existed, in Old Russian, an identical word with an entirely different meaning: *temnyi*, derived from t'ma (myriad).[179] The captain of the myriad of the Mongol army was called "temnik" in Russian; the adjective referring to an officer or prince when he was appointed such a captain was "temnyi." In the late period of the Golden Horde most of the temniks were Tatar princes. They were known in Russian as "the prince captains of the myriad" (*temnye kniazia*). In view of the above-mentioned rumors concerning a secret agreement between Vasili and Ulug-Mahmed, it seems most likely that, in order to ridicule Vasili, his opponents dubbed him a "prince

176. Nikon, *12*, 67.
177. *Ibid.*
178. D. Ushakov, *Slovar' russkogo iazyka, 4* (Moscow, 1940), 647.
179. Sreznevsky, *3*, col. 1085.

captain of the myriad" (*temnyi kniaz'*), implying that he had become a mere vassal prince of the khan and an official of the Tatar army. Hence Vasili Temnyi (and not Tiomnyi).

In February 1446 Vasili decided to make a pilgrimage to the Trinity Monastery. The conspirators used his absence from Moscow for the coup d'état. On February 12 Dmitri Shemiaka and Ivan Mozhaisky appeared before Moscow; the gates were opened by their "fifth column" inside the city, and they entered without opposition. They arrested the two grand duchesses, as well as some of the boyars, and seized the grand ducal treasury. Dmitri was proclaimed grand duke of Moscow. The victors then sent one of the new grand duke's boyars with a detachment of troops to the Trinity Monastery to arrest Vasili, which he did without difficulty. Faithful attendants succeeded, however, in spiriting away to safety Vasili's two sons, Ivan (the future grand duke Ivan III) and Iuri, aged six and five respectively. They found a protector in Prince Ivan Riapolovsky who fled with them to Murom.

Vasili was immediately brought to Moscow and, on February 16, blinded by order of Shemiaka and Mozhaisky (in some chronicles, the name of Grand Duke Boris of Tver is also mentioned in this connection). The following statement of his guilt was made to Vasili on this occasion: he has loved the Tatars excessively; he has granted them Russian towns for feeding; he has showered them with gold and silver; he has blinded Prince Vasili Kosoy.[180] Vasili and his wife were then deported to Uglich; his mother was exiled to Chukhloma, a remote town north of Galich. His boyars—at least those who happened to be in Moscow—went over to Dmitri Shemiaka. Two princes of Vasili's retinue, Vasili of Serpukhov (his brother-in-law) and Simeon Obolensky, fled to Lithuania. On the other hand, a number of "boyar sons" (*deti boyarskie*), a group of gentry in the grand duke's service, who might have been expected to be more loyal to Vasili than the boyars, pledged allegiance to Shemiaka. As further events showed, however, they proved as a group more ready to give support to Vasili than any other social class. At that moment, however, of all Vasili's servitors among the gentry only one, Fedor Basenok, openly defied Shemiaka. He was promptly arrested but succeeded in escaping from prison and, gathering a number of other boyar sons loyal to Vasili, fled with them to Lithuania where he joined Prince Vasili of Serpukhov. The latter had been well received

180. Novgorod IV, 443.

by King Casimir, who granted him Briansk and several other Severian towns in apanage.

Dmitri Shemiaka's next move was to get hold of Vasili's sons, princes Ivan and Iuri. Since their guardian Riapolovsky refused to hand them over, Shemiaka asked Bishop Iona of Riazan (the future metropolitan) to mediate, promising under oath not to harm the boys in any way. Under Iona's guarantee Riapolovsky agreed to let him take the princes to Moscow. Shemiaka at first received them with kindness and entertained them at dinner. Two days later, however, he sent them to Uglich to be imprisoned with their parents. Riapolovsky was naturally very indignant and, together with Prince Ivan Striga-Obolensky, started gathering a detachment of Vasili's former servitors, most of whom had apparently remained loyal to the deposed grand duke. Their plan was to attack Shemiaka's garrison in Uglich and to set Vasili and the whole grand ducal family free. Shemiaka, however, received news of the conspiracy in time through a spy and sent troops against Riapolovsky. After a few skirmishes Riapolovsky and Striga-Obolensky fled to Lithuania and joined Prince Vasili of Serpukhov who was in Mstislavl at the time.

Meanwhile Bishop Iona kept reproving Dmitri Shemiaka for imprisoning Vasili's sons contrary to his promise. Finally Shemiaka agreed to set free not only the young princes but their father as well. He went personally to Uglich and announced his willingness to grant Vasili the city of Vologda as his apanage if Vasili would pledge under oath to acknowledge him as grand duke. The oath was duly administered, and Shemiaka entertained his former prisoners at a lavish dinner. Several days later Vasili with his family set out for Vologda.

Even if Vasili had meant to keep his pledge not to revolt against Shemiaka, he could hardly have done it because of the pressure of his supporters. As soon as it became known that Vasili was at liberty, a psychological reaction against Shemiaka's rule became evident everywhere. Vasili's former boyars who had entered Shemiaka's service now left him and moved to Tver, to await further developments in neutral territory. A number of boyar sons did not bother about seeking a neutral area but fled from Moscow to the Monastery of St. Cyril in the Beloozero region where Vasili II went in pilgrimage from Vologda. At St. Cyril Abbot Trifon absolved Vasili II from his pledge to Shemiaka on the ground that it had been given under duress. Vasili's boyars in Tver were engaged in important parleys

with Grand Duke Boris, who finally agreed to invite Vasili to Tver
for a personal talk. A friendly understanding was reached between
Boris and Vasili, and the former's daughter Maria was betrothed to
the latter's son Ivan.

Meanwhile those of Vasili's supporters who had joined Prince
Vasili of Serpukhov in Mstislavl set out for Moscow. At Elnia (which
lies southeast of Smolensk) they met a strong detachment of Tatars
whom they at first took for enemies and were ready to fight. It
turned out, however, that these Tatars were friends. They were led
by Ulug-Mahmed's sons Kasim and Yakub who, having heard of
Vasili II's misfortunes, had decided to help him.[181] As we have seen,
these two Juchid princes had fled after their father's assassination,
to the land of the Circassians (Cherkasy). It is usually accepted that
this meant the Circassians in the north Caucasus, but if so it would
be hard to explain why the princes appeared at Elnia, so far west of
Moscow. The usual route from the north Caucasus to Moscow was
up the Don River, through the land of Riasan. It is therefore much
more likely that Kasim and Yakub sought refuge not among the
Circassians of the north Caucasus but in the Cherkasy region in the
basin of the middle Dnieper, where as we know Tatars and Ukrainians used to meet and the nucleus of the future Ukrainian Cossacks
was being formed. On this assumption the appearance of the two
princes at Elnia becomes quite understandable.

The two groups of Vasili's adherents, Russians and Tatars, now
joined forces and hastened to Moscow. Meanwhile Dmitri Shemiaka
and Ivan Mozhaisky concentrated their army at Volokolamsk from
where they could guard both the Tver and Mozhaisk roads. In spite
of this, one of Vasili II's boyars, Michael Pleshcheev, succeeded in
stealing into Moscow with a small body of troops. Shemiaka's lieutenants in Moscow either fled or were arrested, and the people were
ordered to swear allegiance to Vasili II. The position at Volokolamsk
now became untenable and Shemiaka and Mozhaisky hastily retreated to Galich. Vasili II decided to pursue them and led his troops
to Iaroslavl where he was joined by Kasim's and Yakub's Tatars.
His forces were now so much stronger than those of his adversaries
that he could count on their submission and sent the boyar Vasili
Kutuzov to Shemiaka to ask for the release of his mother, Grand
Duchess Sophia, then still imprisoned in Chukhloma. Without await-
ing the results of Kutuzov's mission, Vasili II returned to Moscow,

181. Nikon, *12*, 72.

on February 17, 1447 almost exactly a year after being blinded there.

Being on the verge of complete defeat, Shemiaka set the grand duchess free, and with Mozhaisky appealed to Prince Vasili of Serpukhov to mediate with Vasili II. Early in July 1447 a preliminary truce treaty was concluded between the two rebel princes and Vasili of Serpukhov. Under the latter's sponsorship, Shemiaka and Mozhaisky agreed to petition Grand Duke Vasili II to let each of them keep his patrimony (except that Shemiaka would give up Zvenigorod). They in their turn promised to return the grand ducal jewels and other valuables they had taken away from Moscow. They also promised not to attack or harm Vasili's vassals in any way—the tsarevichi (Kasim and Yakub), the other Tatar princes, and their troops.[182] Two months later a formal peace treaty was signed between Vasili II and Prince Ivan Mozhaisky. The latter addressed the grand duke as his lord and acknowledged himself his "younger brother" (i.e. vassal).[183] Shemiaka, however, having gained the time he needed so much, did not hasten to surrender. Instead he sent agents to Novgorod and Viatka to urge these two free cities to help him against Vasili II. He even dispatched an envoy to Mahmudek, the khan of Kazan, urging him to break off relations with Vasili.[184]

IV

Vasili reigned for fifteen years after his return to power. This comparatively brief span of time may be considered a significant period in Russian history. In it the foundations, both ideological and material, were laid for the Tsardom of Moscow. As we have seen, the election of Metropolitan Iona by a council of Russian bishops (1448) signalized the emergence of the national Russian church. In the realm of politics, the consolidation of the Grand Duchy of Moscow was almost completed. Most of the apanages of the descendants of Ivan Kalita were now in the hands of the grand duke. The old capital, Vladimir, had been reduced to the status of a provincial town. Outside of Muscovy proper, the Grand Duchy of Riazan became a vassal state of Moscow (1447), and the liberties of Novgorod the Great were substantially curbed (in 1456). Inside Muscovy, the boyar council was discredited by the lack of unity and

182. *DDG*, No. 46, pp. 140–142.
183. *Ibid.*, No. 48, pp. 146–148.
184. *AI*, *1*, 80.

determination among its members at the time of the preceding crisis and, historically speaking, lost the opportunity (if there ever was one) to limit the authority of the grand duke in its own favor. Also in this period East Russia, actually, if not yet formally, emancipated herself from Tatar domination. While the Moscow government continued to recognize the supreme authority of the khan in principle, it did not allow the nominal suzerain to interfere in Russian internal affairs in any way. And while the tribute was still collected, only token payments ever reached the khan, and even those were paid irregularly if at all. A share of the tribute now went to Vasili's Tatar vassals, but this represented payment for services rendered and in that sense was not a waste of money. The bulk of the tribute collected remained in the grand duke's treasury and became one of the main sources of state revenue.

Obviously Muscovy was much stronger by the end of Vasili's reign than she had been at its beginning. The credit for the success of her policies hardly belongs to Vasili himself, however. It will be recalled that in the first part of his reign Vasili II, even when he came of age, while he displayed personal courage and tenacity (as well as cruelty) on several occasions, never showed particular ability as a statesman and military leader. In the second part of his reign he was handicapped by his blindness. The constructive achievements of the latter part of his reign are explained by the firm support given him by the church, the "servitor princes," [185] the gentry, and the "loyal" Tatars. It was fortunate for Moscow's destinies that a number of gifted statesmen and generals emerged at this time from various groups of Vasili's supporters. Outstanding among them were the head of the Russian church, Metropolitan Iona, a wise and tactful old man; the grand duke's brother-in-law, Vasili of Serpukhov (whom Vasili II paid with base ingratitude); a prince of Lithuanian origin, Ivan Patrikeev (son of Prince Iuri Patrikeevich); two princes of the house of Riurik in Vasili II's service—Vasili Obolensky and his son Ivan Striga-Obolensky; and the boyar son, Fedor Basenok. It should be mentioned that while members of several boyar families, like the Koshkins, the Kutuzovs, and the Pleshcheevs, acquired considerable influence on state affairs toward the end of Vasili's reign, none of them in that period seems to have been equal in ability to the men of other groups mentioned above, except perhaps for Constantine Bezzubtsev, grandson of Fedor Koshka.

185. See below, Chapter 5, sec. 4, p. 368, for explanation of the term.

Two urgent tasks faced Vasili II's government after his return to power: that of crushing the resurgence of Shemiaka's opposition and protecting Muscovy from the attacks of the Tatar hordes. To handle them both successfully it was essential for Moscow to eliminate any possibility of a "third front" in the west. Therefore one of the government's first moves was to arrange a nonaggression pact with Lithuania. The ground for such a convention was prepared by King Casimir's approval of Iona's candidacy for the metropolitan's see. Iona probably participated in the subsequent political negotiations as well. The Moscow–Lithuanian treaty of friendship and nonaggression was signed on August 31, 1449. According to its provisions Grand Duke Vasili II and King Casimir pledged each to live in peace with the other and not to support the other's enemies. Specifically, Casimir promised not to help Shemiaka, and Vasili not to give refuge to Michael (Sigismund's son). Each ruler was to assist the other in his fight against the Tatars. In addition, it was agreed that the Grand Duchy of Tver was within the Lithuanian sphere of influence; [186] Grand Duke Boris of Tver accordingly signed a special treaty with King Casimir.[187]

The specific provisions of the Moscow–Lithuanian treaty were not kept scrupulously by either side, or at least not for long. In 1450 Michael was given refuge in Moscow. (He died there the next year, of poison—presumably administered by Lithuanian agents.) Four years later Shemiaka's former associate, Prince Ivan Mozhaisky, was received and granted lands by Casimir. Moscow countered by attempting to detach Tver from Lithuania, and around 1456 a pact of friendship was concluded between Vasili II and Boris of Tver. In spite of these mutual violations the Moscow–Lithuanian treaty served its main purpose by making Muscovy secure from attack from the west during a critical period of his history. On the whole, relations between Vasili II and Casimir remained friendly to the end of Vasili's life, and in his will the grand duke of Moscow made "his brother" the king of Poland guardian of his widow and his sons.

With Shemiaka the Moscow government decided to try persuasion before having recourse to force of arms. On December 29, 1447 five Russian bishops, including the metropolitan designate Iona, signed an appeal urging Shemiaka to end the civil war and recognize Vasili II as grand duke. Shemiaka in a message to the Novgorodians had

186. *DDG*, p. 161.
187. *Ibid.*, pp. 163–164.

once more accused Vasili of letting his vassals the Tatars rule over a number of Russian cities. The bishops retorted that Shemiaka himself was responsible for the presence of the Tatars on Russian soil, since Vasili II was not in a position to get rid of them while civil war was going on in Russia. They guaranteed that the practice of granting Russian towns to the Tatars for feeding would be terminated and the Tatars settled outside of Russia as soon as Shemiaka pledged obedience to Vasili.[188]

The bishops' appeal brought results. Not being ready as yet for war, Shemiaka made a solemn pledge to acknowledge himself Vasili's vassal and never revolt against him. As events proved, the pledge was a stratagem. As soon as he felt ready to continue the struggle he broke his word. In 1449 he attacked Kostroma but was repulsed by the Muscovite troops under the command of Prince Ivan Striga-Obolensky and Fedor Basenok. A year later Vasili II sent a strong army to Galich under the command of Prince Vasili Obolensky, supported by the tsarevichi Kasim and Yakub with their Tatars. Shemiaka's troops were defeated and Shemiaka himself fled to Novgorod. Even then, however, he was not discouraged and in the winter of 1451–52, gathering a new army (increased no doubt by Novgorodian and Viatka volunteers), he besieged Ustiug, an important trading center in northern Russia. Strong Muscovite forces were immediately sent there under the command of Prince Vasili of Serpukhov, Prince Simeon Obolensky, and Fedor Basenok. Tsarevich Yakub also participated in the expedition. Once more Shemiaka fled to Novgorod. The next year he was poisoned there by a Muscovite agent. When news of his death reached Vasili II, the latter showed "indecent joy" as Karamzin puts it.[189] Fearing that the same fate was in store for him, Shemiaka's former associate, Prince Ivan Mozhaisky, fled to Lithuania (1454). His apanage, as well Shemiaka's, was annexed to Moscow. His appetite whetted by these acquisitions, Vasili now awaited a pretext to seize Serpukhov and Borovsk as well. These towns constituted the apanage of his brother-in-law Vasili. In July 1456 the latter was arrested and imprisoned in Uglich. He was charged with treason but no specific evidence of guilt was ever presented.[190] He died in prison in 1483.

The assistance given Shemiaka by Novgorod and Viatka irritated

188. *AI, 1*, 79.
189. Karamzin, *5*, 342.
190. Nikon, *12*, 112; Karamzin, *5*, 346–347.

the Muscovites, and relations between Vasili II and the two free cities became tense. In 1456 Vasili declared war on Novgorod. The Muscovite troops, led by Prince Ivan Striga-Obolensky and Fedor Basenok, stormed the prosperous city of Staraia Rusa, meeting with but weak resistance. Then they defeated the Novgorodian army sent to rescue Rusa. Novgorod sued for peace, which was granted for 8,500 rubles indemnity. Worse still, Novgorod had to agree to severe restrictions on her liberties. Two years later Vasili II sent a detachment of troops against Viatka, but the expedition proved a failure. In another campaign against the Viatka land in 1460 two towns were seized by the Muscovites and their inhabitants compelled to pledge allegiance to Vasili.

To return to Tatar affairs, it will be recalled that after the assassination of Khan Ulug-Mahmed by his son Mahmudek a number of Tatar princes and generals of Ulug-Mahmed's horde went over to Khan Said-Ahmad, who controlled the Crimea and the steppes east of the Dnieper. The Moscow government also recognized Said-Ahmad and at once paid him the current quota of tribute.[191] This action angered Mahmudek, now khan of Kazan, who considered himself entitled to receive the tribute from Russia after his father's death. In November 1447 Mahmudek sent a strong army against Muscovy, which was repulsed. Before long relations between Moscow and Said-Ahmad also became tense. As we have seen, Said-Ahmad at this time was supporting Michael's claims to the throne of Lithuania against Casimir. Casimir retaliated by sponsoring a rival Juchid prince, Haji-Geray (who had lived in Lithuania since 1428). In 1449 Haji-Geray seized the Crimea and established himself firmly there, founding the Geray dynasty which ruled until the late 18th century.[192]

In view of the rapprochement that year between Lithuania and Moscow, the Muscovite government now felt it could afford a less subservient attitude toward Said-Ahmad. Presumably the tribute payments were discontinued. In any case Said-Ahmad found it necessary to send a detachment of his mobile troops to attack Moscow. This force reached the banks of the Pakhra River (about 20 miles southwest of Moscow), looting the country on its way and taking many prisoners including Princess Obolensky (wife of Vasili Obolensky). However, Tsarevich Kasim with his troops (stationed in

191. *AI, 1,* 80.
192. Spuler, p. 168; Smirnov, *Krymskoe Khanstvo,* p. 207.

Zvenigorod at that time) promptly counterattacked, defeated the invaders, freed the prisoners, and retrieved the loot (1449). The next year news reached Moscow that another Tatar army, led by Prince Melim-Berdi, was approaching the land of Riazan from the south. This group apparently belonged to Küchük-Mahmed's horde centered around Saray. Vasili II sent an expeditionary Russo-Tatar army under the command of the boyar Constantine Bezzubtsev and Tsarevich Kasim deep into the steppes to stop Melim-Berdi. The two armies met at the banks of the Bitiug River (an eastern tributary of the Don). Melim-Berdi's troops were defeated and their remnants fled south.

In 1451 Moscow itself was threatened by Said-Ahmad's horde. At the news of its approach Vasili II decided to go north to the upper Volga region to gather more troops. He went to Kimra with his eldest son Ivan (then aged eleven); his wife with the youngest children he sent farther down the Volga, to Uglich. In Moscow Vasili left his mother with his second son Iuri, Metropolitan Iona, and many boyars and boyar sons. The Moscow garrison was well provided with artillery and handguns. The Tatars appeared before Moscow on July 2 and set fire to the houses in the suburbs outside the city walls; when they tried to storm the citadel they were repulsed. The battle raged until evening, and during the night the Tatars hastily retreated. The next morning they were gone, to the amazement and rejoicing of the Muscovites, who ascribed their panic to the miraculous intercession of the Holy Virgin.[193]

V

We have seen that in 1447 five Russian bishops solemnly promised that after the end of Shemiaka's resistance the loyal Tatars would be evacuated from the Russian towns given them for feeding. With Shemiaka's flight from Ustiug, early in 1452, the civil war was definitely over, and the time had come to honor the pledge. One of the bishops, Iona, was now the head of the Russian church and, we may say, spiritual leader of the Moscow government. Iona was conscientious and honest, and we may be sure that he earnestly urged Vasili to terminate the stay of the loyal Tatars in Russia. On their part, the people in the towns subject to those Tatars undoubtedly reminded the government of the bishops' pledge.

The high officials of Vasili's administration must have given the

193. Nikon, *12*, 76–77.

problem serious consideration. Once it was decided in principle that the loyal Tatars should be settled outside of Russia, the question arose where to settle them. This problem was approached mainly from the strategic point of view. While the Tatar raids of the preceding years had all been repulsed, they had been harassing enough, and a device had to be found to make it more difficult for the Tatars to penetrate deep into Russia. The best solution seemed to be to establish a network of advance posts along the southern border of Russia, close enough to the Tatar-controlled steppes so that Russia's military leaders could both watch the movements of the Tatars and repulse them when they came. As we know, there were three Tatar hordes at this time, each constituting an ever-present threat to Russia: the Khanate of Kazan, that of Saray, and that of the Dnieper. (The fourth, that of the Crimea, represented no danger to Moscow for the time being.) We do not know what measures, if any, were taken at this time to strengthen the advance defenses against Said-Ahmad's Dnieper horde. The town of Gorodets-on-the-Oka was chosen as site of the main advance post to deal with the encroachments of both the Kazan and Saray hordes. And now the two problems, the evacuation of the loyal Tatars and the strengthening of the steppe defenses, were tied together: it was decided to use those Tatars to man the main advance post in the southeast. Tsarevich Kasim—who as we remember could probably consider Gorodets in a sense his patrimony—agreed to assume the leadership of this group. Thus, late in 1452 or early in 1453 a new Tatar khanate arose, under the tutelage of Moscow—that of Tsarevich Kasim. Later on, after Kasim's death, the town of Gorodets was renamed Kasimov in his honor (1471), and the khanate (or tsardom as the Russians called it) became known under that name.[194] While Gorodets was an old Russian town, by the mid-15th century few Russians were left there. The country around was populated mainly by the Meshcherians and the Mordvinians, both tribes of Finnish extraction. Thus, no protest on the part of the Russians need be expected against the establishment of the new khanate.

As a matter of fact, the creation of the Tsardom of Kasimov satisfied both the loyal Tatars and the Russians; inside Russia it eliminated the main cause of opposition to Vasili II's regime; and it undoubtedly strengthened Russian defenses against the steppe Tatars. But it had even more significant implications. It at once

194. On the creation of the Tsardom of Kasimov see Veliaminov-Zernov, *1*, chap. 1.

raised Moscow's prestige in the Tatar world and made it psycho-logically easier for an ever-increasing number of the outside Tatars to enter the grand duke's service, both individually and in groups. Moreover, the khan of Kazan was Kasim's brother, and there was a possibility that Kasim could eventually claim the throne of Kazan for himself.

Information on the inner organization of the Tsardom of Kasimov in this period is scant. From a later document, Ivan III's treaty with the grand duke of Riazan of 1483, we know that Kasim had several Tatar princes under his authority; of administrative officials, treas-urers (*kaznachei*) and sealers (*dorogi*) are mentioned. They col-lected tribute (*yasak*) and other taxes (*obroki i poshliny*) from the tsarevich's Meshcherian and Mordvinian subjects. On his part the grand duke of Riazan was obligated to pay an annuity to Kasim. Any misunderstanding between them was to be referred to the grand duke of Moscow.[195]

The creation of a vassal Juchid khanate under the authority of the grand duke of Moscow signalized the end of the era of Mongol domination over Russia and the beginning of a new epoch—that of Russia's claim for leadership in the Eurasian world. The Mongol yoke was broken. On his deathbed Vasili II did not hesitate to bequeath "his patrimony," the Grand Duchy of Moscow, to his eldest son without reference to the khan's prerogatives. It was left to that son, Ivan III, formally to announce Russia's emancipation from the remnants of the Golden Horde, which he did in 1480.

195. *DDG*, No. 76, p. 284.

CHAPTER V

THE MONGOL IMPACT ON RUSSIA

1. PRELIMINARY REMARKS

I

THE PROBLEM of the role played by the Mongols in Russian history has been discussed by many historians in the course of the last two centuries, but no consensus of opinion has been reached.[1] Among the historians of the older generations N. M. Karamzin, N. I. Kostomarov, and F. I. Leontovich attributed great importance to the Mongol impact on Russia. Karamzin coined the sentence: "Moscow owes its greatness to the khans"; he also noted the extinction of political liberties and the deterioration of morals in Russia, which he considered a result of Mongol oppression.[2] Kostomarov emphasized the role of the khans' yarlyks in strengthening the authority of the Moscow grand duke within his realm.[3] Leontovich made a special study of the Oirat (Kalmyk) codes of law in order to demonstrate the influence of the Mongol law on the Russian.[4] In contrast, S. M. Soloviev denied the importance of Mongol influence on the internal development of Russia, and in his *History of Russia* almost disregarded the Mongol element except for its disruptive aspects— invasions and wars. While mentioning briefly the dependence of the Russian princes on the khan's patent and the collection of taxes, Soloviev expressed the opinion that "we have no reason to assume any great influence [of the Mongols] on [Russia's] internal administration as we do not see any traces of it."[5] Soloviev's former student and successor in the chair of Russian history at the University of Moscow, V. O. Kliuchevsky, made a few general remarks on the

1. For brief summaries of opinions on the role of the Mongols in Russian history see *ZO*, pp. 249–258; Diakonov, *Ocherki*, pp. 193–196; Riasanovsky, pp. 261–278.

2. Karamzin, *5*, 365–384.

3. N. I. Kostomarov, *Nachalo edinoderzhaviia v drevnei Rusi,* in his Collected Works (*Sobranie sochinenii*) (St. Petersburg, 1905), *5*, 41–47.

4. F. I. Leontovich, *Drevnii oiratskii ustav vzyskanii* (Odessa, 1879).

5. Soloviev, *4*, 179.

importance of the khans' policies for the unification of Russia but otherwise paid little attention to the Mongols.[6] Among the historians of Russian law and institutions, M. A. Diakonov followed Soloviev's ideas although he expressed his views more cautiously.[7] M. F. Vladimirsky-Budanov admitted but a limited influence of Mongol law on the Russian.[8] V. I. Sergeevich on the other hand followed Kostomarov's line of argument as did P. N. Miliukov to some extent.[9]

A quarter of a century ago the role of the Mongols in Russian history was reappraised by the philologist Prince Nicholas Trubetskoy;[10] his conclusion was that the origins of the Muscovite state cannot be properly understood without considering the political and moral principles on which the Mongol Empire was built. Trubetskoy's point was made even more emphatically by Erenjen Khara-Davan, author of a penetrating biography of Chingis-Khan.[11] On the other hand, V. A. Riasanovsky and B. D. Grekov returned to Soloviev's position. Riasanovsky, like Leontovich, made a careful study of Mongol law but minimized its importance for Russia.[12] Grekov stated his opinion as follows: "The Russian state with Moscow at its head was created not with the assistance of the Tatars but in the process of a hard struggle of the Russian people against the yoke of the Golden Horde."[13] Obviously we have here a slightly different aspect of the problem. It is logically possible to deny any positive influence of Mongol institutions on Russian ones and yet to recognize the importance of the Mongol impact on Russia's development, even if it were merely negative.

The problem of the Mongol influence on Russia is many-sided indeed. We face here a complex of important problems rather than just one question. We have first of all to consider the immediate effect of the Mongol invasion—the sheer destruction of cities and population; then the effects of the conscious policy of the Mongol rulers on various aspects of Russian life. Besides, certain important changes took place in Russia as unintended results of this or that

6. Kliuchevsky, 2, 18–22, 38–39, 44–45.
7. Diakonov, Ocherki, pp. 148–149.
8. Vladimirsky-Budanov, Obzor, pp. 101–103.
9. Sergeevich, 2, 35–38, 252–256; Miliukov, Ocherki, 1, 165–166.
10. I. R. [= Prince Nicholas Trubetskoy], Nasledie Chingiskhana (Berlin, 1925).
11. Khara-Davan, pp. 198–226.
12. Riasanovsky, pp. 261–278.
13. ZO, p. 256.

turn of Mongol policy. Thus the inability of the khans to stem the Polish and Lithuanian drives obviously was a factor in the division between East and West Russia. Furthermore, in certain cases the influence of the Mongol pattern on Muscovy achieved its full effect only after the latter's emancipation from the Mongols. This may be called influence through delayed action. Moreover, in some respects, the direct Tatar influence on Russian life increased rather than decreased after Russia's emancipation. It was only after the breakup of the Golden Horde that throngs of Tatars entered the service of the Moscow rulers. Finally, the Tatar danger did not disappear after Ivan III's defiance of the Golden Horde. For almost three more centuries Russia had to mobilize a considerable part of her army every year on her southern and southeastern borders; this affected the whole political and social system of Muscovy.

II

A convenient method of gauging the extent of Mongol influence on Russia is to compare the Russian state and society of the pre-Mongol period with those of the post-Mongol era, and in particular to contrast the spirit and institutions of Muscovite Russia with those of Russia of the Kievan age.

It will be recalled that the political life of the Russian federation of the Kievan period was based on freedom. The three elements of power, the monarchic, aristocratic, and democratic, counterbalanced each other, and the people had a voice in the government throughout the country.[14] Even in Suzdalia, where the monarchic element was the strongest, both the boyars and the city assembly or veche had their say in affairs. The typical prince of the Kievan period, even the grand duke of Suzdal, was merely head of the executive branch of the government and not an autocrat.

The picture changed completely after the Mongol period. First of all, in the 16th and the early 17th centuries, instead of a pan-Russian federation all of whose member states enjoyed a similar constitution, we find a sharp division between East Russia (Muscovy) and West Russia (included in the Polish–Lithuanian Commonwealth); in addition, on the southern fringe of each of the two Russias there emerged military states of the new type—the Cossack hosts. These represented the old Russian democratic tradition although it now assumed a peculiar form, that of a warriors' fraternity. The aristo-

14. *Kievan Russia,* chap. 7.

cratic element of power was not only continued in West Russia but was even more accentuated under Polish influence and became the foundation of West Russian (Ukrainian and Belorussian) political life. As for East Russia, it obviously promoted and developed the monarchic element to a high degree. To say, however, that the Tsardom of Moscow merely followed the tradition of Andrew Bogoliubsky and some of the other Suzdalian princes would be to underestimate the significance of the change. With all their monarchic tendencies the Suzdalian princes never succeeded in becoming absolute rulers of their land.

The authority of the tsar of Moscow, both ideological and actual, was immensely stronger than that of his Suzdalian forerunners. While the 16th century witnesed the growth of monarchical institutions throughout the European continent, the process nowhere went so far and fast as in East Russia. When the envoy of the Holy Roman Empire, the Austrian Baron Sigismund von Herberstein, arrived at Moscow in 1517, he felt that he entered a different world, politically. He noted that Grand Duke Vasili III surpassed all other monarchs in the extent of his power over his subjects.[15] The Englishman Giles Fletcher who visited Moscow some seventy years after Herberstein's first voyage came to the conclusion that "the state and form of their government is plaine tyrannicall, as applying all to the behoofe of the prince, and that after a most open and barbarous manner." [16]

No less deep was the contrast between pre- and post-Mongol periods in the realm of social relations. The very foundations of Muscovite society were different from those of the Kievan age.

The society of Kievan Russia may be called, with certain reservations, a free society. There were slaves but they were considered a separate group, outside the pale of the nation. The situation was similar to that in ancient Greece: slavery coexisted with the freedom of the bulk of society. The government functioned on the basis of the cooperation of free social classes: the boyars, the city people, and the "men" (*liudi*) in the rural districts. True, there was a group of peasants, the so-called *smerdy,* who were under the prince's special

---

15. Herberstein, p. 20.

16. Fletcher, p. 26. It should be noted that Fletcher presented a somewhat distorted picture of the Muscovite government and political life of the late 16th century. He underestimated the actual authority of the boyar council, paid no serious attention to local self-government in North Russia, and was not aware of the Russian counterpart of the Etats-Généraux—the *Zemsky Sobor.* See S. M. Seredonin, *Sochinenie Dzhilsa Fletchera kak istoricheskii istochnik* (St. Petersburg, 1891), pp. 217–244, 278–280, 283–287.

jurisdiction, but even they were freemen. There was also a group of the half-free (the so-called *zakupy*) whose position eventually became similar to slavery, but their enslavement was the result of indebtedness, that is of the unrestricted interplay of economic forces, not of government action.[17]

In the Tsardom of Moscow of the 16th and 17th centuries we find an entirely new concept of society and its relation to the state. All the classes of the nation, from top to bottom, except the slaves, were bound to the service of the state. Ironically enough, the slaves were the only group free from governmental regimentation. This Muscovite system of universal service to the state was aptly called *krepostnoy ustav* (statute of bound service) by Cyril Zaitsev.[18] Both the former apanage princes and the boyars now became permanent servitors of the tsar, as did the lower gentry such as the boyar sons and the *dvoriane* (courtiers). Attempts at resistance to the new regime on the part of the princes and the boyars were crushed by Tsar Ivan IV at the time of the *oprichnina* terror.[19] Through the institution of military fiefs (*pomestia*) the tsars controlled both the gentry's landed estates and the army. The necessity to provide the pomestia with labor resulted in the establishment of serfdom, at first only of a temporary nature, on the estates of the gentry (1581). That peasant serfdom was made permanent and sanctioned by the Code of Laws (*Ulozhenie*) of 1649. It was also by provisions of the Ulozhenie that the townspeople (*posadskie liudi*) were finally organized into so many closed communes, all of whose members were bound by mutual guarantee to pay taxes and to perform special kinds of services imposed on them. Both the free peasants on state lands and the serfs, as well as the townspeople, were considered the lowest class of the tsar's subjects, free of military or court service but bound to pay heavy taxes and, in some cases, to compulsory labor (*tiaglo,* "burden"). Thus a distinction arose between the *sluzhilye liudi* (men liable to "service" in the technical sense of military and court service) and the *tiaglye liudi* (men liable to tiaglo). The "service" (in the above sense) became eventually a characteristic of the noble-

17. *Kievan Russia,* chap. 6.
18. K. Zaitsev, *Lektsii po administrativnomu pravu* (Prague, mimeographed ed., 1923), 2, 154–155.
19. The oprichnina regime was inaugurated by Tsar Ivan IV in 1564 with the creation of a body of special guards or political police at the court to combat treason. The word oprichnina means "separate" or "private" household or court. See G. Vernadsky, *A History of Russia* (Yale University Press, 1951 ed.), pp. 67–69.

man; the "burden" that of a commoner. That distinction became a basic feature of the social regime of the Tsardom of Moscow in the 17th century, and assumed even sharper forms in the St. Petersburg empire of the 18th century.

On the basis of the above brief comparative survey of the characteristic features of the state and society of Kievan Russia and those of Muscovite Russia, it is evident that the gulf between the two regimes was deep indeed. We have before us two different sociopolitical systems. It is obvious that the change could not have come overnight. In fact, the process of transformation of the free society into a service-bound society started during the Mongol period although it was not completed until as late as the mid-17th century.

The question which we now have to consider is the role of the Mongols in that process. To ascertain this we must examine briefly the changes that occurred in the Russian national economy, politics, and social organization during the Mongol period.

2. The Effect of the Mongol Conquest on Russia's National Economy

I

The wholesale looting and destruction of property and life in Russia during the Mongol invasion of 1237–40 was a staggering blow which left the Russian people stunned, and for a time disrupted the normal course of economic and political life. It is hard to estimate the Russian casualties but they must have been tremendous, and if we include the vast throngs of civilians, both men and women, who were enslaved by the Mongols they can hardly have been less than 10 per cent of the total population.

The cities suffered most in the debacle. Such old centers of Russian civilization as Kiev, Chernigov, Pereiaslav, Riazan, Suzdal, and the somewhat younger Vladimir-in-Suzdalia, as well as a number of other towns, were thoroughly destroyed, and the first three named above lost their former importance for several centuries. Only a few major cities in West and North Russia such as Smolensk, Novgorod, Pskov, and Galich (Halicz) escaped devastation at that time. The Mongol policy of conscripting master craftsmen and skilled artisans for the khan's service added a new burden even for those cities which had been spared physical destruction during the first period of the conquest. A quota of the best Russian jewelers and craftsmen was sent to the great khan. As we have seen, Friar John of Plano Carpini met one of them, the goldsmith Kuzma, in Guyuk's camp. Many others were requisitioned by the khan of the Golden Horde for his personal service as well as to build and embellish his capital, Saray. Artisans of various kinds—smiths, armorers, saddlers, and so on—were also assigned to the ordus of the members of the house of Juchi as well as to those of the major commanders of the Mongol armies in South Russia.

The dispersion of Russian master craftsmen in the Mongol world all but exhausted, for a time, Russia's own reservoir of skilled man power and could not but disrupt the continuity of industrial tradi-tions.[20] With the closing of the enamel shops of Kiev in 1240 and the murder or abduction of their artisans, the Russian art of making cloi-sonné enamel which had reached such a high level in Kievan Russia disappeared altogether. In the course of the 14th century some Li-moges enamels were imported, and late in the century champlevé enamels were made in Moscow; in the 16th century the Moscow craftsmen started producing cloisonné enamels, but these are rather coarse and bear no comparison to the Kievan types.[21] The production of filigree works (skan') stopped for almost a century, after which it was resumed under the influence of Central Asian patterns.[22] Speci-mens of Central Asian jewelry like Monomach's Crown [23] were brought to Moscow and some of the Russian master artisans who worked with jewelry in Saray (and possibly in Urgenj as well) suc-ceeded in returning to Russia in the mid-14th century; when later on both Saray and Urgenj were destroyed by Timur, some of the crafts-men of the Khorezmian school who happened to survive the catas-trophe might have been engaged by the grand duke of Moscow.

The niello technique too went out of use after the Mongol invasion and became popular again only in the 16th century. Nor is there evidence of production in Russia of glazed polychrome ceramics, including decorative tiles, in the late 13th and the 14th centuries. Specimens of it reappear in the 15th century. Production of glass bracelets, as well as of glass, carnelian, and bronze beads and some other ornaments was also completely disrupted.[24]

20. See Rybakov, pp. 525–538.
21. *Idem*, pp. 535–536.
22. *Idem*, pp. 641–646.
23. On Monomach's Crown see below, sec. 6, p. 386.
24. In *Kievan Russia*, p. 116, I made an erroneous statement that "there is no definite evidence that glass was produced in Kievan Russia." At the time of writing I was not

Another serious casualty of the Mongol conquest was the art of stone cutting and fretwork. The last masterpiece of that sort was the stone reliefs in the Cathedral of St. George in Iuriev-Polsky in Suzdalia, which were completed just a few years before the Mongol onslaught.[25] The building crafts in general suffered a serious setback in East Russia. Fewer stone buildings were erected in the 1st century of Mongol domination than in the century before, and the quality of the work deteriorated markedly.

Russian industrial production in general was also seriously disrupted by the Mongol invasion and Mongol policies toward craftsmen. Even Novgorod was affected at first, but it recovered early; its industrial depression lasted about half a century. In most of East Russia the depression persisted a full century. Only in the mid-14th century, when Mongol control over Russia eased considerably, did the revival of certain branches of industry, especially the metallurgical, became noticeable. Throughout the 15th century most of the city crafts made a rapid progress.[26] Not only Tver and Moscow but some of the smaller towns like Zvenigorod became lively industrial centers.[27]

The disappearance of the city crafts during the first century of Mongol domination left for a time a serious gap in the fulfillment of consumers' demands. The villagers had to depend on what they could produce at home. Princes, boyars, and monasteries had no alternative to sponsoring crafts on their own estates. They tried to train their slaves or tenants and to attract skilled artisans to their domains to work for them. As we know, the people on the church estates were exempt from taxes and other levies by the Mongols. While the princely domains did not enjoy such immunity, a prince, if he had good relations with the khan, could often arrange, even during the first harsh decades of Mongol conquest, that at least some of the artisans in his domains should not be conscripted into the khan's service. Eventually the princes and bishops succeeded in redeeming some of the captive craftsmen; and a number of others were able to flee from the Mongols and return to Russia. Thus quite a few smiths, potters, carpenters, cobblers, and tailors settled on princely and monastery es-

---

acquainted with the newest evidence of archeological research which has been since presented by B. A. Rybakov.

25. See *Kievan Russia*, p. 260.
26. Rybakov, pp. 595 ff.
27. On Zvenigorod industries see *MIAS, 12* (1949), 127–131.

tates. When the grand ducal manor became a large city, as in the case of Moscow, these artisans and many more continued to work for the grand ducal palace instead of for the market. This growth of manorial industries was a characteristic feature of the Russian economy of the 14th to 16th centuries.

II

Agriculture was less affected by the Mongol invasion than were the industrial crafts. In those parts of southern Russia which were subject to their direct control the Mongols themselves encouraged raising crops, such as millet and wheat, for the needs of their army and administration.[28] In other parts of Russia it was the agricultural population which paid the bulk of the tribute collected by or for the Mongols, and so the Mongols had no motive for disrupting the productivity of agriculture. The same was true of hunting and fishing. The mining of iron and the production of salt (by evaporation) also continued unabated, especially as most of the deposits of near-surface iron ore (which alone was mined in Russia in the Mongol period) and most of the saltworks were located in the Novgorod territory; those in the northern part of the Grand Duchy of Vladimir also were beyond the immediate reach of the Mongols.

The steady growth of agriculture in East Russia in the Mongol period resulted in making it the leading branch of the national economy. Its expansion in the central and northern parts of the country was an aspect of the movement of the population, in the first period of Mongol domination, to the areas which seemed safest from encroachment, such as the regions around Moscow and Tver. The northeastern sections of the Grand Duchy of Vladimir beyond the Volga, chiefly the regions of Kostroma and Galich, were also rapidly colonized. With the increase of population, more and more forests were cleared to make tilling possible. While in the newly cleared areas the *podseka* technique was applied,[29] in the central regions the three-field system of crop rotation prevailed.[30] Three main types of plow were used in East Russia and in Novgorod in this period: the

28. See Chapter 1, sec. 7, p. 52, and Chapter 3, sec. 8, p. 224.

29. *Podseka* means "cutting." The yield of a patch of ground was high in the first two or three years after trees had been cut and underbrush burned, but subsequently the patch had to lie fallow for several years. See *Kievan Russia*, p. 108.

30. N. Rozhkov, *Obzor russkoi istorii s sotsiologicheskoi tochki zreniia*, 2 (St. Petersburg, 1905), 137–138. See also P. P. Smirnov, "Obrazovanie russkogo tsentralizovannogo gosudarstva v xiv–xvi vekakh," *Voprosy istorii* (1946), Fasc. 2–3, pp. 77–79.

heavy plow (*plug*), the improved sokha (wooden plow with iron plowshare), and the light wooden sokha. The "plug" apparently was not often used; the light sokha (drawn by one horse) was typical of the northern forest regions. Around Moscow the improved sokha, drawn by three horses, seems to have been the standard implement. Recently the historian P. P. Smirnov has suggested that in the reign of Ivan I an entirely new type of sokha was invented which gave much impetus to Muscovite agriculture. Smirnov even considers that invention to have been one of the main causes of the rise of the Muscovite state.[31] The theory is ingenious but there is not enough evidence to support it.[32]

Horse and cattle breeding had only a limited importance in the peasant economy of East Russia, and the methods of tending cattle were on the whole primitive. The princes, however, and especially the grand dukes of Moscow, were interested in raising cattle and, in particular, horses. The master of the stables (koniushi), as we know, was an important official in the grand ducal administration. In the wills of the grand dukes of Moscow stallions and herds of mares, saddle horses, and harness horses are mentioned frequently.[33] Obviously horse breeding was a major branch of the grand ducal economy. For one thing, the grand duke needed horses to build up the cavalry squadrons of his army.

Let us now glance at the development of commerce in Russia during the Mongol period. As we know, control of the commercial routes was an important aspect of Mongol policy, and international trade constituted one of the foundations of the Mongol Empire, as well as of the Golden Horde. The khans of the Golden Horde, and especially Mangu-Temir, did much to promote the trade both of Novgorod and of the Italian colonies in the Crimea and the Azov area. The Mongol regional governors also patronized commerce, as the story of Baskak Ahmad shows.[34]

Hence it might have been expected that Mongol domination would

31. Smirnov (as in n. 30), pp. 76–77.

32. For criticism of P. P. Smirnov's theory see I. I. Smirnov, "O putiakh issledovaniia russkogo tsentralizovannogo gosudarstva," *Voprosy istorii* (1946), Fasc. 4, pp. 30–44; V. Mavrodin, "Neskolko zamechanii po povodu stat' i P. P. Smirnova," *Voprosy istorii* (1946), Fasc. 4, pp. 45–54; S. Iushkov, "K voprosu ob obrazovanii russkogo gosudarstva v XIV–XVI vekakh," *Voprosy istorii* (1946), Fasc. 4, pp. 55–67; K. Bazilevich, "K voprosu ob istoricheskikh usloviiakh obrazovaniia russkogo gosudarstva," *Voprosy istorii* (1946), Fasc. 7, pp. 26–44.

33. See DDG, 8, 14, 16.

34. See above, Chapter 3, sec. 5, p. 343.

be favorable to the expansion of Russian trade. On the whole it was, but not throughout the period. In the first century of Mongol dominance Russian internal commerce suffered a serious setback because of the disruption of city crafts and the resulting inability of the cities to satisfy the demands of the villagers. As for foreign trade, in the reign of Berke it was all but monopolized by the powerful corporations of Moslem merchants of Central Asian origin. Only in the reign of Mangu-Temir were Russian merchants given their chance— but they knew how to use it. As has been mentioned, in Uzbeg's reign (1314–41) there was a large Russian colony in Saray, and merchants must have constituted the core of it. From the story of the execution of Grand Duke Michael of Tver in Uzbeg's camp in the north Caucasus (1319), it is known that a number of Russian merchants lived there at that time. According to the story, they wanted to place Michael's body in a nearby church but were forbidden by the Mongols to do it.[35] As we know from the account of Tokhtamysh' campaign (1382), by that time the Russians controlled the Volga shipping. The Russian chronicles of the period display a good knowledge of the geography of the Golden Horde and on various occasions mention not only Saray but other commercial centers like Urgenj and Astrakhan. Information about them must have been supplied by the merchants.

The Russians were also well acquainted with the Italian colonies in the Azov region and the Crimea. Indeed, it was with the city of Surozh (Soldaia) that Russian merchants of the period did their most profitable business. That group became known as Surozhane ("the Surozh dealers"). The Surozhane are first mentioned in the Volynian Chronicle on the occasion of the death of Prince Vladimir, son of Vasilko, in the city of Vladimir-in-Volynia in 1288. The chronicler relates that his death was regretted not only by the prince's relatives and the citizens of Vladimir but also by the merchants then residing in the city—the Germans, the Surozhane, the Novgorodians, and the Jews.[36] In the 14th century the Surozhane played an important role in Muscovite commerce. In fact most of the Moscow gosti, as the members of the top layer of the Muscovite merchant class were known,[37] were Surozhane.[38]

35. Nikon, *10*, 186.
36. Hyp., p. 220.
37. On the term *gost'* see *Kievan Russia*, p. 317.
38. See V. E. Syroechkovsky, "Gosti-Surozhane," *GA, 127* (1935).

Owing to the free trade policies of Mangu-Temir and his successors, Russian trade with the West also expanded during the Mongol period. Novgorod entertained a lively and profitable commerce with the Hanseatic League. Moscow and Tver traded with Novgorod and Pskov as well as with Lithuania and Poland, and through them with Bohemia and Germany. Since woolen cloth was an outstanding item of import to Russia from the West, the Moscow merchants dealing with the West were known as "the clothiers" (*sukonniki*). In the earlier period, as we know, Novgorod received cloth of fine quality from Ypres.[39] In the 14th and 15th centuries clothing industries developed in Central Europe, especially in Saxony, Bohemia, and Moravia. It was from Bohemia and Moravia that most of Moscow's imported cloth came in the 16th century, but there is no evidence of similar large-scale exports from those countries to Russia in the 15th century.[40] Locks manufactured in Tver were exported from East Russia to Bohemia in the 14th and 15th centuries.[41]

3. THE IMPACT ON GOVERNMENT AND
ADMINISTRATION

I

Juridically speaking, Russia had no independent government in the Mongol period. The great khan of Mongolia and China was considered suzerain of all Russian lands, and as we know, at times actually interfered with Russian affairs. For practical purposes, however, the khan of the Golden Horde was the supreme ruler of Russia—its "tsar" as the Russian annals called him. No Russian prince was entitled to rule over his land without the required patent of authority from the khan.

Such were the legal aspects of the situation. Actually, as has been seen from the story of Mongol-Russian relations told in the two preceding chapters, inner Russian political life was never stifled but only curbed and deformed by Mongol rule. As the Mongol Empire fell to pieces and the Golden Horde itself was weakened, native political forces in Russia emerged from beneath the Mongol superstructure and assumed more and more vigor. The traditional interrelation of

39. *Kievan Russia*, pp. 120, 343.
40. See Florovsky, *2*, 141–142; *idem*, "*Českomoravské a slezské soukenictvi a výhodoevropský trh*," *ČČH*, *46* (1940), 2–5.
41. Rybakov, p. 600; Florovsky, *2*, 208–210.

these forces, however, had been completely upset by the Mongol invasion, and the relative importance and very nature of each of the three elements of power underwent a drastic change. Here, as in the sphere of the national economy, the decline of the role of the cities constituted a fact of paramount importance.

From the political angle, the destruction of most of the major cities of East Russia during the Mongol invasion was a crushing blow to the urban democratic institutions which had flourished in the Kievan period all over Russia (and continued to flourish in Novgorod and Pskov during the Mongol period). Moreover, it was from the population of those cities which escaped the destruction or were restored that the only determined opposition to Mongol rule we know of came during the first century. While the princes and boyars succeeded in adapting themselves to the conquerors' requirements and establishing a modus vivendi with them, the townspeople, especially the artisans, who lived under the constant threat of conscription, seethed with indignation at every fresh oppressive measure introduced by the new rulers. Because of this, the Mongols on their part were determined to crush the opposition of the cities and to eliminate the veche as a political institution. For this task, as has been seen, they engaged the cooperation of the Russian princes, who were themselves afraid of the revolutionary tendencies of the veche in Rostov as well as in a number of other cities.

The cooperation of the Mongols and the princes prevented the general spread of city rebellions in the second half of the 13th century and quelled the sporadic and isolated revolts which flared up from time to time in Rostov and elsewhere. The authority of the veche was thus drastically curbed, and by the mid-14th century it had ceased to function normally in most East Russian cities and could be discounted as an element of government. When in the 1370's the East Russian princes began to resist the Mongols, at least one cause of friction with the veche was eliminated. As in the case of the arrest of Mamay's envoys in Nizhni Novgorod in 1374, the anti-Mongol activities of the veche of that city were approved by the local prince. On the whole, however, both princes and boyars continued to be suspicious of the riotous spirit of the veche. While they asked the townspeople to cooperate with them against the Mongols, they intended to keep the leadership in their own hands. Consequently the veche was all but eliminated as a permanent branch of the government. As we have seen, the princes even succeeded in doing away

with the representation of the interests of commoners in their administration by the tysiatsky; in 1375 that office was abolished. It
was not so easy to eradicate the veche, however. While not allowed
to function in normal times, it rose again as soon as the princes and
boyars failed in their leadership. The temporary seizure of power
by the commoners of Moscow at the time of Tokhtamysh' invasion
is a typical example of the revival of the veche in time of crises even
if that revival did not last long in each case.

Another important effect on social and political life of the decline
of the cities was the increase in relative importance of the large landed
estates in Russia's political setup. Even in the pre-Mongol period,
as we know, the manor as a sociopolitical institution was in the
ascendant.[42] In the 12th century both princes and boyars owned
large landed estates from which they derived substantial profits.
Political life, however, still centered around the cities, and most of
the princes were more concerned with their political than with their
economic activities. The situation changed in the Mongol period.
With the limitation of their political rights by the Mongols, the
princes could not but become more interested in the management
of their estates. With the decline of the cities, agriculture and other
branches of exploitation of the natural resources of the land and the
forests came to the fore. The result was that in Muscovy the grand
duke's domains became the chief foundation of both his economic
power and his administration. Not only were his landed estates
one of the main sources of his revenue; they also became the core
of his dominions in the administrative sense. The whole concept of
princely power was now modified by patrimonial habits.

Boyar ownership of land also grew steadily in this period. On the
whole it may be said that the boyars had greater influence on state
affairs in the Mongol age than before. Previously only the Galician
boyars had succeeded in dominating political life; their political
aspirations increased rather than decreased in the first half of the
14th century and, as we know, their conflict with the last duke of
Galicia, Iuri II, precipitated his downfall and opened the gate to
Lithuanian and, soon after, Polish domination.

In contrast to Galicia where the boyars constantly and consciously
opposed the prince, the boyars in East Russia were ready to support
the expansion of the grand duchy or principality of whose ruler they
were councilors, especially since such expansion was profitable to

42. *Kievan Russia,* pp. 202–204.

themselves both as a class and as individuals. When it became clear that the Moscow princes led the race for power among the Russian rulers, more and more boyars offered their services to the prince of Moscow. By promoting the expansion of Moscow the boyars consciously or unconsciously served the cause of unification of Russia. In many cases they were able to persuade boyars of other principalities to accept the leadership of the prince of Moscow. As an incentive, such outside supporters of the growth of Moscow were promised positions at court, which meant admittance to the ruling circle of Moscow boyars.

As in the Kievan period, when we speak of the boyar council we have to differentiate between its plenary session, which was convoked only on important occasions and in which all the leading boyars participated, and the inner circle, or prince's cabinet, which was in permanent session. In the grand duke's cabinet in the Mongol period the chief officers of state and court administration took part, among them the "great lieutenant" of Moscow and the quartermaster general (okolnichi); so did the boyar heads of administrative departments of princely domains, who were called "departmental boyars" (*boyare putnye*). The other major boyars members of the cabinet were known as the "great boyars" (*bolshie boyare*) or the *boyare vvedennye* ("boyars admitted [to the prince's palace]"). Until the office of chiliarch was abolished, he was also a permanent member of the inner council.

In spite of all their influence on the course of state affairs and in spite of the growth of their landed estates, the Muscovite boyars did not succeed, during the Mongol period, in clearly defining their political rights. What factors prevented their building up firm, constitutional guarantees for the functioning of their council? The existence of the supreme Mongol power was certainly a leading one. As the authority of the Russian princes, including the grand duke of Moscow, derived from the khan's patent, the prince could always ask the khan for protection against any internal opposition. The power of the veche was curbed by the combined efforts of khan and princes. The boyars must have known very well that in case of any violent conflict with them the prince could be expected to appeal to the khan. When the Golden Horde was strong the khan's patent was not a mere scrap of paper; it was a mandate. Another check on the potential political aspirations of the East Russian boyars in the Mongol period was the attitude of the city people, especially the lower classes. In spite of the decline of the veche as an institution, the townspeople could not be discounted altogether as an element in Russian politics. And they could be expected to object violently to the establishment of any kind of aristocratic constitution. While repeatedly frustrated by the grand duke in their attempts to revolt prematurely against the Mongols, the commoners did not oppose the princely power in principle, since the grand duke as head of the armed forces was the only leader they could look to to head a successful national revolution against the Mongols in the future. In contrast, the commoners were suspicious of the boyars as a group and did not trust them. The antiboyar riots in Moscow in 1357 [43] are an example of this. In any case, from the point of view of the commoners the prince was a lesser evil than the boyars, and the boyars realized that in any conflict between them and the prince the latter would be supported not only by the khan but by the townspeople as well.

Furthermore, psychologically the very freedom the boyars enjoyed as a class made any clear definition of boyar rights superfluous from the point of view of most of them. As in the Kievan period, any East Russian boyar, if not satisfied with the prince, could sever his ties and enter the service of another prince (except when the two princes were at war). By doing this he would not forfeit his landed estates, since they were not his fief but his patrimony. Usually this principle of free service worked in favor of the prince of Moscow since service at his court offered more attraction and more chance of profit than that of any other Russian ruler of the period. The principle of boyar freedom and full rights for the boyars on their estates was confirmed in a number of interprincely treaties of the 14th and first half of the 15th century. [44]

Future events were to bring bitter disappointment to the East Russian boyars in their reliance on their traditional freedom. What they thought was solid rock beneath their feet had turned to sand by the close of the 15th century. That freedom of service which was an aspect of the federative constitution of Kievan Russia proved incompatible with the interests of the growing Moscow monarchy. With the change in political atmosphere, violations by the grand duke of the principle of freedom of service became almost unavoidable. Some violations of this sort occurred in the Mongol period. The

43. See above, Chapter 3, sec. 6, p. 207.
44. See *DDG,* pp. 40, 42, 52, 55.

first notable instance was the case of Ivan Veliaminov. When he left Moscow and went over to the prince of Tver, in 1374, his estates were confiscated, and later on, when he was caught by the Muscovites, he was executed.[45] It may be argued that this was a moment of sharp political conflict and of national emergency, but still the violation of principle cannot be denied. Another similar episode occurred in 1433 when the Moscow boyar Ivan Vsevolozhsky went over to Grand Duke Vasili II's rival, Iuri of Galich. His estates too were confiscated.[46] This was again a period of sharp conflict, of a civil war in which both sides disregarded not only treaties but moral precepts as well. Yet as a result of such repeated actions a tendency developed at the court of Moscow to deny the right of boyars to leave at will and under all circumstances. Those boyars who tried to use their freedom in a time of crisis were now considered deserters or traitors. The new notion gained ground rapidly, and by the early 16th century—when Moscow absorbed all the regional principalities—the Moscow boyars found themselves bound to the grand duke's service. Besides, at the time of the oprichnina, many of them lost their patrimonial estates and were granted fiefs (pomestia) instead.

II

There were two main aspects to the growth of the grand ducal power in East Russia in the Mongol period: the strengthening of each grand duke's authority within his grand duchy and the expansion of the strongest grand duchy at the expense of its neighbors. As a result of the first process, the Moscow grand duke eventually became an absolute sovereign (*gosudar'*) of his realm, or we might say autocrat, although the Russian term *samoderzhets* (autocrat) around 1500 had a different connotation, that of independence of the ruler from foreign suzerainty. The second process led to the establishment of the national state and to the victory of the principle of monocracy (*edinoderzhavie*). As the two trends merged, the Moscow grand duke (later, tsar) was endowed with that full power which was to amaze both Herberstein and Fletcher.

The unification of East Russia was a protracted process which continued, with ups and downs, throughout the Mongol period and

45. See above, Chapter 4, sec. 2, p. 258; cf. Diakonov, *Vlast'*, pp. 175–176.

46. See Diakonov, *Vlast'*, p. 177. According to the Tverian Chronicle, when Vsevolozhsky was later seized by the Muscovites, he was blinded by order of Vasili II (*PSRL, 15,* 290). There is no such report in other chronicles, and the accuracy of the Tverian Chronicle in this case may be questioned.

was completed only in the early 16th century during the reign of Vasili III. It has often been asserted in the historical literature that the khan himself contributed to the unification by making the grand duke of Moscow his chief tax collector. On the basis of the actual story of Mongol-Russian relations told in the two preceding chapters we know that this view is erroneous or at least exaggerated. The khans understood well the dangerous implications of giving too much power to a single Russian prince. Consequently, in the first half of the 14th century the khan sanctioned the division of East Russia into four grand duchies and commissioned each of the four grand dukes to collect taxes within his realm. It was only in 1392 that Khan Tokhtamysh, being in a desperate situation and needing the assistance of Vasili I of Moscow, authorized him to annex the Grand Duchy of Nizhni Novgorod. The two other grand duchies, Tver and Riazan, remained intact at that time. In addition to keeping Russia politically divided, the Tatars, whenever they were afraid of the growing power of some Russian prince, tried to sow seeds of discord between him and his potential allies. If a conflict followed, they were in a position either to offer their mediation, and thus reassert their authority, or to punish the prince of whom they were suspicious. The Russian princes were well aware of this crafty device, and in several of the interprincely treaties of this period we find a clause by which the signatories bound themselves not to listen if the Tatars attempted to set one of them against the other. But the Russians did not always have the good sense to carry out their good intentions.

It will be recalled that the ruler of Moscow was not the only grand duke who strove to unify the country. The grand dukes of Tver were no less ambitious, if less fortunate, and before long a new claimant appeared—the grand duke of Lithuania. The attempts at unification of East Russia on the part of these leading grand dukes cannot be explained solely by their personal ambitions. The grim political situation required unity of the nation's effort; without it the task of freeing Russia from Mongol rule could not be achieved. This was well understood not only by many princes but by most of the people— boyars and commoners alike. They instinctively felt that only a strong ruler could lead them to victory, and they were ready to support such a ruler. When it became plain that the grand duke of Moscow was becoming stronger than the others, increasing numbers of boyars and commoners, even in the other grand duchies, looked to his leadership. From this point of view Dmitri Donskoy's victory at Kulikovo Pole, although followed by a new period of humiliation, was an important step toward the growth of national consciousness.

The struggle for supremacy between the Russian grand dukes and princes went through various stages. Each grand duke tried first to secure his authority over the apanage princes of his own house and then to jockey for a better position in the community of East Russian princes at large. The gamut of the political interrelations between the grand dukes and princes is well reflected in the interprincely treaties of this period—a number of the originals are still extant in Russian archives. Political equality or subordination was usually expressed in these treaties in terms of kinship, even if the terms did not correspond to the actual family relationship of the signatories. Thus in the treaties of 1367 and 1374 Prince Vladimir of Serpukhov, cousin of Dmitri Donskoy, was referred to as "younger brother" of the latter, and in the treaty of 1389 as Dmitri's "son." Both terms were used to denote vassal ties; the degree of subordination was increased in 1389. In 1375 the grand duke of Tver acknowledged himself a "younger brother" of the grand duke of Moscow; in 1382 the grand duke of Riazan did the same. On the other hand, when two or more princes concluded an alliance on terms of equality, each called the other "brother."

More formal terms of vassal subordination were introduced by Grand Duke Vitovt of Lithuania in his treaties with East Russian princes. Thus, in the treaty of 1427 Grand Duke Boris of Tver recognized Vitovt as his lord (gospodin). About two years later the grand duke of Riazan called Vitovt both his "gospodin" and "gospodar" (sovereign). The first of these two terms was promptly picked up and used by Vasili II in his treaty with Vasili of Serpukhov (1433). The latter had to address his Moscow namesake as his "lord [gospodin], elder brother and father"—a curious combination of political and kinship terms. A year later the Mozhaisk and Vereia princes recognized Vasili II as their gospodin, in this case omitting kinship terms. From that time on the term gospodin was used in most of Vasili II's treaties with the apanage princes. In 1448 (or early in 1449) the Moscow chancery attempted to make a step forward by defining the authority of the grand duke of Moscow in regard to the apanage princes. In the treaty with a Suzdal prince Vasili II was called the former's "gospodar." This formula was not repeated, however, in any of Vasili's subsequent treaties. But Vasili II's son, Ivan III, made full use of it, demanding in 1478 that the Novgorodians recognize him as their gosudar' (which is the Great Russian variant of the West Russian form "gospodar").[47] The recognition of the term by the Novgorodians meant the end of Novgorod's independence.

Let us now examine the rise of the grand ducal power in the Grand Duchy of Vladimir and Moscow, the one which succeeded in absorbing all the others. From the point of view of Mongol law, the authority of the grand duke of Moscow, as well as that of the other Russian grand dukes and princes, was based primarily on the khan's patent. As we know, in the Kievan period only princes of the house of Riurik were entitled to occupy the Russian princely thrones. The Mongols accepted the principle of the exclusive rights of the Riurikovichi (descendants of Riurik)—in those Russian lands which were not put under the direct authority of the khan. Since the Mongols themselves were ruled by the Golden Kin, the Russian principle of a single ruling house was close to their own concepts. It may be mentioned in this connection that when, in the 14th century, the new dynasty of Gedymin was recognized in West Russia the Mongols agreed to deal with some of the Gedyminovichi as well. In this case, however, the khan's new vassals emancipated themselves quickly from the Mongol power, and the "submission" of Iagailo to Mamay's puppet khan and then to Tokhtamysh was in essence an alliance rather than vassalage.

The recognition by the Mongols of the rights of the Riurik dynasty was a wise step which saved them from much trouble. It also made it easier for the Russians to accept Mongol suzerainty. The Riurikovichi continued to rule Russia—to the extent that they were allowed to—but they now ruled on the basis of both their genealogical rights and the khan's investiture. The old principle of assigning thrones by genealogical seniority, which had already declined in the late Kievan period, now became even less valid, both because the khans often disregarded it in assigning the princely patents and because conditions in Russia changed considerably. The patrimonial principle of the transfer of power from father to son in each principality now came to the fore; nowhere did it prove as vital as in the principality of Moscow and, after the virtual merger of Moscow with Vladimir, in the Grand Duchy of Vladimir and Moscow. The patri-

47. See Preobrazhensky, p. 153; Vasmer, p. 300. The term *gospodar* derives from the old Slavic *gospod'*, "lord" (also "God," the sense in modern Russian). Preobrazhensky, pp. 151–152; Vasmer, pp. 299–300. According to Vasmer, the root of the second syllable in *gospod'* is the Indo-European *potis* (which in Latin means "capable of," "mighty").

monial principle, then, may be considered the psychological basis of the power of the house of Daniel (the Danilovichi) of Moscow. While they first applied it to the principality of Moscow, they soon extended it to the Grand Duchy of Vladimir as a whole.

As has been mentioned, from the practical point of view the grand duke's domains constituted one of the important foundations of his power. The intermingling of the grand duke's manorial rights with his authority as a ruler has led many historians and jurists, like Boris Chicherin, for example, to speak of the complete victory of private law over public and the disappearance of all notions of statehood in Muscovy of this period. To prove his theory Chicherin refers to the testaments of the Moscow princes.[48] The theory may seem convincing at first glance but is indeed an example of oversimplification of historical reality. One has to be cautious in applying abstract legal patterns to the interpretation of medieval notions and terminology. Actually the prince's authority was not entirely submerged in the sphere of his private interests. A clear expression of the gradual growth of the idea of the state may be found in the preference given by each Moscow ruler to his eldest son. Then as later there was no rule of primogeniture in the provisions on intestate inheritance in the Russian codes, and so the idea of *majorat* did not influence the institutions of the Russian private law. The landed estates, whether princely or boyar, were divided equally between all the sons, with special provisions made for the maintenance of mother, widow, or daughters.

This rule even in regard to state domains prevailed in most East Russian principalities of the Mongol period, but not in Moscow. Even in Moscow, to be sure, each prince was bound by family traditions to grant an apanage to each of his sons, but, in contrast to the other principalities, he usually made the share of the eldest son, the heir to the throne, larger than those of the others. At first the material advantage of the eldest son was not very conspicuous. As a matter of principle, however, the disposition was of great importance, as any succeeding prince could easily raise the ratio in favor of his eldest son. According to the will of Dmitri Donskoy, who left five sons, the share of the eldest in the payment of each 1,000 rubles of Mongol tribute (which is an indication of the revenue each received from his share of lands) was 342 rubles (instead of the 200 rubles it would

48. B. Chicherin, "Dukhovnye i dogovornye gramoty velikikh i udelnykh kniazei," in his *Opyty po istorii russkogo prava* (Moscow, 1858), see especially pp. 233–237, 242.

have been if the shares had been equal). Dmitri's grandson, Vasili II, assigned 14 cities to his eldest son, Ivan III, as against 12 which were divided among the four other sons. Ivan III carried the same principle even further, leaving his eldest son 66 cities and to the four others together only 30. The motive of these dispositions was to secure the dominance of each succeeding ruler among his kin, if not yet complete unity of princely government. As the arrangements were contrary to the spirit of Russian private law, we may see in them elements of the state law.

When the Golden Horde weakened, the grand duke of Moscow felt himself secure enough not only to bequeath shares of his dominions to his sons but also to appoint the successor to the grand ducal throne itself. Dmitri Donskoy was the first to "bless" his eldest son Vasili I with the Grand Duchy of Vladimir. But Vasili did not ascend the throne without receiving the khan's patent. When Vasili I made his will he did not dare to dispose of the grand duchy. As we know, his son Vasili II gained the throne with great difficulty, against the opposition of his uncle Iuri. After that he twice lost and twice recovered it. To secure the rights of his eldest son, Ivan III, Vasili II proclaimed him grand duke and co-ruler late in 1448 or early in 1449. Because of this and of the increase of his power in the second half of his reign, Vasili II had no hesitation in "blessing" Ivan III with his "patrimony," the grand duchy. The latter ascended the throne on the basis of that blessing, not bothering about confirmation from the khan.[49]

III

In the Kievan period the main branches of princely administration were the judiciary, the military, and the financial. The prince was the chief justice and commander of the army, and his agents collected the taxes and court fees. After the Mongol invasion the supreme direction of all administrative functions was assumed by the tsar, the Mongol khan. The authority of the Russian princes shrank considerably. The princes now had to obey the khan's orders, and their administrative competence in their own realms was strictly limited; they could exercise it only within the narrow sphere of affairs left to their discretion by the Mongols.

As regards the judiciary, all the Russian princes were now under the authority of the khan and of the Supreme Court of the Mongols,

49. Nikon, *12*, 115.

and as we know a number of them were executed by order of the khan for real or alleged state crimes. The khan also settled most major litigation among the Russian princes. Russians drafted into the Mongol army were subject to Mongol military law.

Moreover, all litigation between Russians and Mongols was subject to trial in the Mongol court. There was for example the case of the descendants of Prince Boris of Rostov versus the descendants of Tsarevich Peter of the Horde. Peter, as we know, became a Greek Orthodox, and so were his descendants. From the khan's point of view, however, they remained Mongols and of the royal blood at that. So when Boris' descendants tried to seize the lands belonging to the monastery founded by Peter, the latter's grandson appealed to the khan. The Mongol court upheld the rights of Peter's descendants in this case, which, it may be added, was a just settlement of the controversy. Although in this affair the interests of a monastery were involved, it was tried as a civil suit. As a general rule, however, the church was protected by the khan's yarlyk against any infringements upon its rights and privileges. The violators, if they were Mongols, were subject to the Mongol courts. If they happened to be Russians, the Russian princes were probably bound to punish them. If the prince failed to act, the church undoubtedly could appeal to the khan.

With his juridical prerogatives firmly established at the higher level, the khan did not interfere with litigation among the Russian boyars and commoners, allowing the prince in each given locality to continue his judicial functions. Because of such policies, of all the branches of princely administration the judiciary was the one least affected by Mongol rule. And yet, as the Russians became familiar with Mongol criminal law and the Mongol courts, they proved ready to accept some of the patterns of Mongol jurisprudence. Even Vladimirsky-Budanov who, on the whole, tends to minimize Mongol influence on Russia, admits that both capital punishment (unknown to the *Pravda Russkaia*—Russian Law code—of the Kievan period) the corporal punishment (applied only to slaves in the Kievan period) entered Muscovite law under Mongol influence.[50] According to the provisions of the Dvina Land Charter of 1397 issued by Grand Duke Vasili I of Moscow, each thief was to be branded; for the third theft the penalty was death by hanging.[51] The death penalty by beheading

50. Vladimirsky-Budanov, *Obzor*, p. 361.

51. Dvina Land Charter, art. 5, *MRL*, p. 58. To my translation there of art. 5 the sentence "And each thief shall be branded" should be added.

was also established for traitors, as may be seen from the Veliaminov case. In Ivan III's *Sudebnik* (Code of Laws) of 1497 capital punishment was ordered for the following categories of crimes: [52] sedition, theft of church property; homicide; *podmet*, that is, leaving things at another's house in order subsequently to accuse him of theft; [53] and arson. An inveterate murderer and brigand known to society as such (*vedomyi likhoi chelovek*) could also be executed if implicated in any serious crime.

It should be mentioned in this connection that in the same period capital punishment was introduced in the city of Pskov. In this case, however, it was not Mongol but Western law which served as a pattern. Owing to their geographical position and lively trade with the German cities, both Novgorod and Pskov were much more open to Western influences than Moscow. As a matter of fact, the penal law of England, France, and Germany in the late Middle Ages and early modern period was as harsh or even harsher than Mongol criminal law. Both capital and corporal punishment were prescribed for a variety of crimes. In Germany decapitation and hanging were the usual forms of execution of a criminal; and many other methods of inflicting death were in use, such as burning at the stake, burying alive, drowning, the wheel, quartering, and piercing with a pole.[54] In Pskov capital punishment was ordered for four kinds of crimes that were considered most offensive: theft in the precincts of the Pskov Kremlin, horse stealing, spying, and arson.[55] The form of execution was not mentioned in the Pskov charter; it was probably either decapitation or hanging, depending on the nature of the crime. In Novgorod in the same period drowning criminals in the Volkhov River seems to have been the preferred form of execution.

It was also during the Mongol period and presumably under Tatar influence that torture became a regular part of Muscovite criminal procedure. The Sudebnik of 1497 prescribes that the suspect be tortured without either prejudice or connivance; the main object of the torture apparently was to obtain both confession and information about accomplices. The official in charge was instructed, however, not to let the victim make any slanderous accusations against innocent persons.[56] It would not be amiss to note that torture was widely

52. Sudebnik, 1497, art. 9, Vladimirsky-Budanov, *Khristomatiia*, 2, 85.
53. See Herberstein's comment on this article, Herberstein, p. 83.
54. R. Schröder, *Lehrbuch der deutschen Rechtsgeschichte* (4th ed. Leipzig, 1902), p. 756.
55. Pskov Charter, art. 7, *MRL*, p. 63.
56. Sudebnik, 1497, art. 36, Vladimirsky-Budanov, *Khristomatiia*, 2, 94.

used in the West in this period. In the 14th century it was recommended by the Roman Catholic Church in the trials of heretics. In
the 15th century it was habitual both in France and Germany to
use torture at the interrogation of criminals. In France both the
secrecy of criminal procedure and the use of torture were legalized by
the ordinances of 1498 and 1539.[57] In Germany Emperor Charles V
tried to limit the use of torture in his Ordinance on Criminal Law
(Halsgerichtsordnung) (1532) but failed to stop the abuses. The
Pskovians did not follow the new pattern in this respect; torture was
not sanctioned by Pskovian law.

While some influence of Mongol penal and trial law on Muscovite
law can hardly be denied, there is no positive evidence of the Russians' borrowing from the Mongols any outstanding feature of court
organization. We might note though that a minor official of the local
courts in northern Russia in the 16th and 17th centuries was known
as yaryga, which is obviously derived from the Mongol jargu (dzargu,
yargu), "judge." [58]

IV

In matters of taxation and army conscription the khan exercised
full and direct power in Russia for more than half a century. The
post-horse service (yam) established by the Mongols they used for
their own needs. The khan also reserved for himself the right of
coinage. Under this system, which lasted intact down to the early
1300's, the Russian grand dukes and princes retained only fragments
of their former authority in matters of military and financial administration. Each prince was allowed to keep a small contingent of troops
—his retinue—and to collect some minor local taxes as well as the
manorial taxes. One hardly can speak of independent princely administration for this period. The situation changed when the grand
dukes were commissioned to collect the Mongol tribute, as well as
the tamga, within the confines of their principalities, on their own
responsibility, though at first under the supervision of a Mongol commissar. Presumably the grand dukes also supervised the conscription
of soldiers for the khan's army, and the post-horse service. The basic
system of military and financial districts, the t'my, was left intact,

57. A. Esmein, Cours élémentaire d'histoire du droit français (13th ed. Paris, 1920),
pp. 851–853.
58. On the term jargu see above, Chapter 3, sec. 7, p. 212; Smirnov, Krymskoe Khanstvo, pp. 43–44.

but now the grand duke's tax agents (danshchiki) collected the tribute instead of the Mongol baskaks. The conscription of craftsmen seems to have been discontinued. The grand dukes encountered no difficulties in collecting taxes since during the sixty-odd years of immediate Mongol control the people were cowed into obedience and well trained in the performance of their duties to the state.

While the princes were merely the khan's commissioners and were constantly under the control of Mongol officials, the abandonment of the old system yet had significant results. The princes were again allowed to perform their administrative functions, even if they had to follow the Mongol pattern of administration which they had no authority to change. In fact they soon discovered that the new system could be financially profitable to them, since after paying the quota of tribute required for each t'ma they could turn whatever surplus there was into their own treasuries. As the number of t'my of the Grand Duchy of Vladimir was greater than that of any other grand duchy, the Moscow rulers profited most from the situation.

With the revolt of Dmitri Donskoy against Mamay, and even more after the fall of Tokhtamysh, a new phase opened in Mongol–Russian relations: one of considerable autonomy of the Russian lands. The grand dukes and princes continued to acknowledge themselves the khan's vassals and paid him tribute—not always regularly—but they took over the internal administration of their principalities almost without interference from the khan. The princes now began to coin their own money, with the khan's name on it, to be sure, in addition to their own.[59] The foundations of the Mongol administrative system were not changed, however, since the grand dukes found them convenient and efficient. So it was on the basis of the Mongol patterns that the grand ducal system of taxation and army organization was developed in the late 14th to 16th centuries.

As regards taxation, the dan' (tribute) remained the main source of revenue, and the sokha the basic unit of assessment. The tamga now definitely took the shape of customs duties on imported goods; in addition, there were the local customs duties or myt. Fees and tolls of various kinds, most of them probably established by the Mongols, were also collected at each stage of the transportation of goods; and there were taxes on the sale of cattle and horses, such as the *privi-*

59. On the Russian coinage of the late Mongol period see G. B. Fedorov, "Dengi moskovskogo kniazhestva vremeni Dmitriia Donskogo i Vasiliia I (1359–1425)," *MIAS*, *12* (1949), 144–185.

aznoe or fee for roping cattle, the *rogovoe* or horn tax, and the *piatno* for branding horses.

All the moneys collected were kept in the grand duke's treasury (*kazna*) and managed by the treasurer (*kaznachei*). The fact that both these Russian terms are borrowed from the Turkish is a clear indication that the institution itself was created after the Mongol pattern.

Another important source of grand ducal revenue was court fees. In the administration of justice only major cases were referred to the grand duke personally. Most of the crimes and suits were in the competence of his lieutenants (*namestniki*). The most important of these was the "grand lieutenant" (*bolshoi namestnik*) of the city of Moscow. There was also a lieutenant in each major town and a district chief (*volostel*) in each rural district. Each had assistants— sometimes his slaves—known as judges (*tiuny*) and reporters (*dovodchiki*). A person dissatisfied with the decision of the minor judges could appeal to their superiors (*volosteli* and *namestniki*), and then, if need be, to the grand dukes. Actually, the latter procedure was not easy because of the distance and the costs connected with appearing at the prince's court.

Since there was not enough money in the grand ducal treasury to pay salaries to all the above officials, the grand duke had no alternative to letting them "feed themselves" off the district to which they were appointed. The roots of this "feeding system" (*kormlenie*) go back to the Kievan period [60] but it became universal only in the Mongol period. The officials themselves—the lieutenants and district chiefs—were known as *kormlenshchiki*. The amount of food and other items the people had to supply to them was established by custom and later on regulated by law. Usually the newly appointed namestnik or volostel expected some "entrance food" (*v'iezzhii korm*) at the time he took up his office; after that he expected supplies sent to him (or money payments instead) three times a year (at Christmas, at Easter, and on the Day of Saints Peter and Paul [June 29]). Besides he was entitled to collect, within his region, custom's duties, court fees, and fees for marriage licenses, of which he kept a good share for himself.

60. On the kormlenie system see *Kievan Russia*, p. 190; Kliuchevsky, *1*, 376–377; *2*, 356–361; Kliuchevsky, *Boyarskaia Duma*, pp. 110–119; Vladimirsky-Budanov, *Obzor*, pp. 192–194; G. Lantzeff, *Siberia in the Seventeenth Century* (Berkeley, University of California Press, 1943), pp. 19–24; S. B. Veselovsky, *Feodalnoe zemlevladenie v severo-vostochnoi Rusi* (Moscow and Leningrad, 1947), *1*, 263–280.

More often than not the kormlenshchiki tried to exact as much food and money from the people subject to their authority as they could. Then the people complained to the grand duke, who might recall a too covetous kormlenshchik and appoint another to replace him. But the new one could prove even worse than his predecessor. This was one reason the kormlenie appointments were usually for a short term, two or three years at most. There was constant pressure on the grand duke, from those agents who had so far failed to occupy a lucrative post, to let them "feed themselves"; and the grand duke had to apply a system of rotation in office to satisfy everybody. In regard to major lieutenancies, there was an additional reason for short-term appointments: the grand duke did not want any of his lieutenants to become too powerful and so was reluctant to grant permanent tenure to anyone or risk letting the office become hereditary.

In addition to their judicial functions the lieutenants and district chiefs, as the grand duke's agents, had general administrative authority, the former over the townspeople, the latter over the population of the state lands. On the other hand, the grand ducal domains, the boyar estates, and the church lands were not within their sphere of competence, being ruled and managed by the grand duke's stewards, the boyars, and the church authorities, respectively. Thus the whole territory of the grand duchy actually consisted of two sections, one ruled by what may be called state officials and the other by manorial administration. Since the grand duke's domains in this period constituted one of the bases of his material power, their administration was as important as the general state administration.

The whole system centered around the grand ducal court (dvor). The main official in charge of it was the *tiun dvorski,* also known simply as *dvorski* (majordomo). Later on the term *dvoretski* (from *dvorets,* "palace") was used to denote this office. The functions of the dvorski were manifold. First of all, he was head of the personnel of the grand ducal court: the *slugi* (servitors) and *dvoriane* (courtiers).[61] He assigned services to each of them and provided for their maintenance. Many of them received landholdings for the duration of their service. Second, the dvorski was the judge and administrator of the peasants settled in the grand ducal estates. Third, he was the treasurer of the domains. The money collected from the popula-

61. Kliuchevsky, *Boyarskaia Duma,* pp. 101, 108–110; Sergeevich, *1,* 466–477.

tion of the domains was kept separate from that in the state treasury (as we may call the kaznachei's office).

With the rapid expansion of the grand ducal economy, a number of special departments of administration of the domains were created, known as *puti* (which is the plural of *put'*, literally, "way," "road"), each headed by a special official (*putnik*) subordinate not to the dvorski but directly to the grand duke. These departments were those of falconry, the stables, the hunt, and food and drink.[62] Most of these offices had existed in the Kievan period. Each major prince of the Kievan era had, among the officials of his household, a master of the stables, of the hunt, and so on. But the whole system of offices of the princely household was apparently not as elaborate in the Kievan period as it became in Muscovy in the Mongol and especially post-Mongol periods. Nor did these particular officials of the princely domains play as important a role in the princely administration in the Kievan era as in the Mongol.

It may be asked if the puti, as they were organized during the Mongol period, were not built up under a certain influence of Oriental patterns. The term *put'* is in itself significant in this regard since there is no evidence of its use in this connotation ("department of princely administration") prior to the Mongol period.[63] Might it not be considered a Russian equivalent of some Oriental term? The Turkish words *türe* and *yol* are of interest in this connection. "Yol" is the exact counterpart of the Russian "put'," its basic connotation being "way," "road," "path." But it may also mean "method," "habit," "rule," "law." "Türe" means "habit," "custom," and also "customary law," "code of laws," "regulation." [64] In the Turkish version of the Persian story of the Seljuqs ("Seljuq-nama"); the legendary forefather of the Oghuz Turks defines the türe as "ways and pillars" (*yol ve erkyan*), that is institutions and regulations, and orders his sons to tread "the path" of the türe. He then establishes the seniority of army officers of the right arm and the left arm and the place of each at banquets. He adds that all the offices of adminis-tration should be distributed among the Turkish clans according to the traditional regulations.[65] While the term "way" (yol) is not used in the Turkish text quoted above in the specific sense of the Russian

---

62. Kliuchevsky, *Boyarskaia Duma*, pp. 102–108, 121–123.
63. Sreznevsky, *2*, 1738–1739.
64. Redhouse, p. 608; Gordlevsky, p. 52.
65. M. T. Houtsma, ed., *Recueil des textes relatifs à l'histoire des Seldjoucides, 3* (Leyden, 1902), 204–205; cf. Gordlevsky, p. 53.

"put'," the general psychological background of the terminology seems to be analogous. The corresponding Arabic term (which was borrowed into both Persian and Osmanli Turkish) is *tarik* ("road," "way," "method," "a hierarchy," "a line of service and promotion"). The basic Persian word for "way" is *rah;* it may also mean "pattern," "rule," "custom." [66] In Rashid ad-Din's version of the story of the Turks, Oghuz-Khan states that "the way [rah] of the right arm is higher" (than that of the left). In this case rah apparently means "rank of offices" or "line of service." [67]

Besides his administrative functions, the head of each put' also had judicial authority over the people who worked in his department. For the same reason as in the case of the namestniki and volosteli, the putniki received no salary from the grand ducal treasury but were rewarded by shares in the income derived from each put'. In some cases the shares of a putnik amounted to 50 per cent of the collections, either in money or in kind. In view of the considerable profits which could be derived from the office of the putnik, and the important role of the putniki in the grand ducal cabinet, it was but natural for the candidate for the office usually to be selected from among the boyars. These became known as boyare put-nye.

Let us now consider the changes which occurred in the Russian army organization during the Mongol period. There can be no doubt that the Russians—who first met the Mongols as enemies and then became, for a long period, their subjects—acquired a thorough knowledge of the Mongol army system and could not but be impressed with its efficiency. It will be recalled that a number of Russian princes with their retinues had to participate in various campaigns undertaken by Mongol khans. Suffice it to refer here to the role of the Rostov princes in Mangu-Temir's expedition against the Alan mountaineers in 1277–78 and the participation of the Moscow and Suzdal princes in Tokhtamysh' expedition against Timur a century later. Besides, scores of thousands of Russians were drafted into the Mongol army at regular intervals if not yearly. Hardly any of those who were taken to China and settled there ever had a chance to return to Russia, but some of those used by the khans of the Golden Horde in South Russia, as for example by Tokhta against Nogay in 1298–99, might be expected to make their way back home

66. Redhouse, p. 1239; Steingass, p. 565.
67. Rashid I, 23 (Russian trans.); *VOT,* 7 (1861), 29 (Persian text).

after the close of the campaign and to tell the Russian authorities about their experiences.

Hence it was unavoidable that the Russians should introduce some Mongol patterns into their own army. For example, the standard division of the Muscovite army of the late 15th and the 16th centuries into five large units certainly followed the Mongol setup. Those units were known in Russian as *polki*.[68] They were as follows: the center (*bolshoy polk*, literally the big division); the right arm division (*pravaia ruka*); the left arm division (*levaia ruka*); the advance guard (*peredovoy polk*); and the rearguard (*storozhevoy polk*). The phrases right arm and left arm correspond to the Turkish *ong kol* and *son kol*. As with the Mongols, the right arm unit was considered more important in the Muscovite army than the left arm.

The Russians familiarized themselves with the Mongol tactic of enveloping the enemy on both flanks (the Vozha River battle of 1378 is a good example of this). Furthermore, they introduced some Mongol armor and weapons into their own army. It will be recalled that as early as 1246 Daniel of Galicia's troops were equipped after the Mongol fashion. In their war against Riazan, in 1361, the Muscovites used the lasso quite successfully. The equipment of the Muscovite troops of the 16th century also shows definite Mongol influence.

The Russian army of the Kievan period consisted of two main parts: the prince's retinue (*druzhina*) and the city militia under the authority of the chiliarch (tysiatsky). The rural population was not subject to mobilization and as a rule did not take any part in the campaigns. The Mongol invasion changed the whole picture. First of all, for the needs of their own armed forces, the Mongols established a rigid system of universal conscription, including in it the entire rural population. Second, by destroying or depopulating the Russian cities and curbing the authority of the veche, they shattered the foundations of the city militia system; the tysiatsky now had little to do as an army chief, and as we know the office itself was eventually abolished.

Simultaneously, although not under any direct Mongol pressure, the princely retinue changed its nature. In the Kievan period the druzhina consisted of two groups.[69] The senior retainers eventually became the backbone of the boyar class. The junior retainers were known collectively as *grid'*, a term of Norse origin (meaning "home"

68. In modern Russian *polk* means "regiment."
69. *Kievan Russia*, p. 138.

in Norse). They occupied minor positions in the princely court. The druzhina as a whole was based on the principle of free companionship. The prince's authority was maintained by his popularity with its members, the *druzhinniki,* as well as by his qualifications for leadership. The druzhinniki followed him only so long as they were willing to. As a military institution, the druzhina represented originally a united group in which senior and junior members cooperated closely. In the second half of the 12th century a process of differentiation started, and each of the two groups became a distinct unit with its own characteristics. By that time every outstanding boyar (senior member of the druzhina) had built up his own retinue. The junior druzhinniki now constituted the core of the prince's own following. As such they were known collectively as the prince's court (dvor). This process of differentiation of the two strata of the druzhina assumed even more rapid tempo in the Mongol period. The very term druzhina now became obsolete. The sources of the period speak of the boyars and the dvor as of two entirely different groups. The prince, when he went to war, was assisted by the boyars (and their respective retinues), but it was his dvor which now became the main source of his strength in the military sense. For the Mongol period, then, the prince's dvor must be considered the cornerstone of the Russian army organization.[70] As a matter of fact, the dvor was not unlike the ordu of the Chingisid princes. That the Russians of the period were aware of the parallel between the two institutions may be seen from an entry in the Nikon Chronicle, A.D. 1426. In that year, answering Grand Duke Vitovt's call for assistance in his campaign against Pskov, Khan Ulug-Mahmed sent Vitovt his ordu troops; the chronicler translates the term as "the khan's dvor."[71]

While the prince's dvor was, in a sense, an outgrowth of the grid' of the Kievan period, it was different in many respects from its prototype. The dvoriane were not the grand duke's companions, they were his servitors. And, in contrast to the boyars, they were bound to service, some of them for a term, others for life.

In connection with the decline of the city militia and the growth of the dvor, a new office was created, that of the okolnichi (quartermaster general), whose functions corresponded to those of the bukaul

70. The military aspect of the prince's court (dvor) has been so far neglected in Russian historical literature. See Peter Struve's penetrating remarks on this problem, Struve, p. 35.
71. Nikon, *12,* 7.

in the army of the Golden Horde. The okolnichi is first mentioned in
Smolensk in 1284.[72] This was during the reign of Grand Duke Fedor
who, as we have seen, spent many years at the khan's court, married
a Mongol princess, and, in general, might be called a "Mongolophile."
Presumably he created the office of okolnichi after the Mongol pattern of army administration. In Moscow the office is first mentioned
in 1350–51; [73] in Riazan in 1356.[74] It should be added that in the
16th century the term okolnichi acquired a different connotation, that
of a member of the Boyar Duma of the second rank.

After the decline of the Golden Horde the grand dukes of Moscow
became able to use, whenever necessary, the system of universal
conscription established by the Mongols. It was on the basis of the
Mongol system that Dmitri Donskoy succeeded in mobilizing the
army with which he defeated Mamay at Kulikovo Pole. His son
Vasili I used general conscription once more when he prepared to
meet Tamerlane's invasion. In the 16th century conscription was
used on several occasions. At that time it became known as the
posokha, since the required quota of recruits was assessed per
sokha.

A few words should be said here about the introduction of firearms
into Russia. The Russians first became acquainted with them at the
siege of Bulgar in 1376. After seizing that city they must have studied
the samples of Bulgarian artillery they had captured. Not satisfied
with this, they apparently made inquiries in the West and obtained
a number of cannon of Western type to reinforce the defenses of
Moscow. In any case, at the time of Tokhtamysh' raid on Moscow
in 1382 the garrison had both cannon (*pushki*) and handguns
(*tiufiaki*) at their disposal. While later on Tokhtamysh was able to
take Moscow by ruse, in the 15th century the city successfully with-
stood all the Tatar attacks, and artillery thus proved its usefulness.
In addition to the pushki and tiufiaki, a new type of light cannon
appeared, known as *pishchal* (plural, *pischali*). In East Russia it is
first mentioned in Tver (1408), and later also in Moscow (1451).
The original Muscovite handgun (tiufiak) must have been of the
Oriental type. The term itself was borrowed from the Turkish
(*tüfek*); the Turkish word was in its turn a borrowing from the
Persian. In Persian *tup* means "cannon" and *tupang* "little can-

72. Sergeevich, *1*, 458.
73. *DDG*, p. 13.
74. *AI, 1*, No. 2.

non." [75] As a matter of fact, none of the Mongol leaders of the late 14th century (not even Tamerlane) equipped their armies with firearms. Presumably Bulgar, as well as some of the large cities of Central Asia, equipped themselves with guns on their own initiative. At that time firearms were used both in Persia and India,[76] and Bulgar could easily obtain them via Khorezm. It must be borne in mind in this connection that the Muscovite handgun could not have been imported from the West since at that time Western Europe was just experimenting with hand firearms and they were but rarely used. In England hand firearms began to be produced in small quantities around 1375 (the term "handgun" first occurs in English sources in 1386). In Germany "handcannon" are mentioned in Augsburg in 1381. All of them were very cumbersome. It was only in the 1420's that a greatly improved handgun (which may be called the predecessor of the musket) was widely used by the Czechs in the Hussite wars.[77]

The cannon, in contrast to the handgun, must have been borrowed by the Russians from the West. The Russian words for "cannon" and "light cannon" (pushka and pishchal) are both borrowings from the Czech language.[78] Presumably, then, the first cannon imported to Russia came from Bohemia, or in any case were manned by Czech artillerists. In the middle of the 15th century firearms were manufactured in East Russia, probably in both Moscow and Tver. At that time the best guns were apparently produced in Tver. Of the Tver cannon founder Nicholas Krechetnikov it was said (around 1453) that such a skillful master could not be found even among the Germans.[79] In 1475 a number of first-rate Italian mechanics and founders were engaged by Ivan III and the Moscow armament plant was greatly expanded.

4. SOCIAL CHANGES

I

The changes which occurred in East Russia during the Mongol period in the position of the social classes were not as drastic as those in government and administration, but no less significant. It may be said

75. See V. Mavrodin, "O poiavlenii ognestrelnogo oruzhia na Rusi," *VLU* (1946), No. 7, 72.

76. *ZO*, p. 353.

77. Oman, 2, 228–229.

78. Florovsky, 2, 325. In modern Czech *puška* means "rifle."

79. Rybakov, p. 603.

that throughout the Mongol period the foundations of the old social order—the free society—were gradually and persistently chipped away without at first affecting the façade. At the time when Ivan III announced Russia's emancipation from the Mongol power and conquered Novgorod, the framework of the new structure was all but ready, and the new order, that of a service-bound society, became clearly noticeable. This is especially true of the position of the old upper class of Russian society, the boyars; paradoxical as it may seem, the process of their subordination to the monarch was completed sooner than the regimentation and enserfment of the lower classes.

Moscow boyardom consisted of varied and heterogeneous elements. Some of the boyars of the 14th and 15th centuries belonged to the old boyar clans of the Grand Duchy of Vladimir. Among them were the Buturlins, the Cheliadnins, the Kutuzovs (all three of these families claiming originally to be of German descent), the Morozovs, the Veliaminovs (these were of Varangian ancestry), and the Vorontsovs. Quite a number of the Moscow boyar families were of West Russian origin. To this group belonged the Pleshcheevs and the Kvashnins. Besides the West Russians, a number of Lithuanians and, later on, Poles entered the service of the grand dukes of Moscow. It must be borne in mind that when our sources refer to families of "Polish and Lithuanian origin," they mean that they hailed from Poland and Lithuania, but their exact ethnic origin is not always clear. Some of the boyars were Polonized West Russians. Others claimed to be of "Prussian" origin. As by the end of the 13th century Prussia, originally a Baltic (Lithuanian) country, had been thoroughly Germanized, "Prussian" origin must in this case have meant German. To this group the Khvostovs, the Romanovs (originally known as the Koshkins and then as the Zakharins), and the Sheremetevs belonged.[80] The Golovins and the Khovrins were of Greek descent. Last, but not least, some of the best boyar families of Moscow were of "Tatar" (Mongol or Turkish) origin. Prominent among them were the Veliaminov-Zernovs (not to be confused with the original Veliaminovs). The Saburovs and the Godunovs were branches of this family. The Arsenievs and Bakhmetevs established themselves in Russia in the late 14th and mid-15th centuries respectively.

By 1450 the position of the boyars as a class was seriously undermined by the appearance of a new aristocratic group, that of the

80. According to A. I. Sobolevsky, the name Sheremetev derives from "Sarmatian."

servitor princes (*sluzhilye kniazia*), as well as by the steady growth of the lower gentry (the dvoriane) which centered around the grand duke's dvor.

The formation of the class of the servitor princes was a protracted historical process, and the class itself was as heterogeneous as that of the boyars. In the course of the 14th and 15th centuries a number of East Russian princes, all descendants of Riurik, found it convenient or necessary to cede or sell their sovereign rights to the grand duke of Moscow. Among them were some of the princes of the house of Rostov, as well as those of Nizhni Novgorod and Suzdal. In addition, a number of the Riurikovichi whose principalities were situated in the land of Severia (mostly in the upper Oka River basin) found themselves in the no man's land between Muscovy and Lithuania and threatened by both these powers. Some of them pledged their allegiance to the grand duke of Lithuania but others, like the Obolenskys, for example, chose to enter the service of the grand duke of Moscow. A number of Lithuanian princes, descendants of Gedymin (the Gedyminovichi), being for various reasons dissatisfied with the state of affairs in Lithuania, also went to Moscow. Among them were the Patrikeev princes (descendants of Gedymin's son Narimunt). Lastly, as we know, some of the Juchid princes entered Russian service during the reign of Vasili II; these were known as the tsarevichi or even as the tsars, if they happened to have reigned in their own name in Kazan or Siberia before coming to Moscow. In the 1500's they ranked highest among the princes serving the tsar of Moscow. In the course of the 16th and 17th centuries lesser Tatar nobility, such as the Kudashev and Engalychev princes, following in the wake of the Juchids, found their way to Moscow; so did some members of the Circassian and Georgian nobility, like the Cherkassky and the Imeretinsky princes.

Following the annexation of the last regional principalities during the reign of Ivan III and Vasili III, all the East Russian Riurikovichi, both regional grand dukes and apanage princes, faced the alternative of emigrating or entering the service of the grand duke of Moscow. Most of them chose the latter course. By 1550 the process of formation of the group of servitor princes was all but completed. Outstanding among the Russian princely families of the house of Riurik who established themselves in Moscow were the princes Belozersky, Dolgorukov, Kurbsky, Shchepin-Rostovsky, Lobanov-Rostovsky, Obolensky, Shakhovskoy, Shuisky, Volkonsky, and many others. Of no lesser social standing were the Gedyminovichi, such as the princes Golitsyn, Kurakin, Mstislavsky, Trubetskoy, and a number of others.

The princes who entered the grand ducal service performed the same political and military functions as the boyars. Eventually they formed the top layer of the boyar class. The respective positions of the princely and boyar families in the service as well as on the social ladder were regulated in the 1500's by a complicated system known as *mestnichestvo* (place order) which was based on the official Genealogical Directory prepared for the tsar (*Gosudarev rodoslovets*) and the lists of state and army officials (*Razriadnye knigi*).[81] On the basis of these two registers the tsar was expected to choose his councilors and to appoint high officials of his army and administration. Records of the previous service of members of the boyar and princely families were consulted, together with genealogical seniority, to establish their respective positions in the service according to precedent. No member of any boyar or princely family would agree to serve in a position lower than a man he considered socially inferior. For the Boyar Duma the tsar was also bound by custom to choose new members from the very top of the boyar and princely class. Within that group, however, he had more freedom of choice for the Duma than for the army and administration. The tsar had the final selection of members of the Duma and decided to what rank each belonged. Precedent, of course, played an important role in his decision in each case. The term "boyar" now acquired a new connotation, that of a member of the Duma of the first rank (whether prince or boyar in the old sense of the word). Members of the second rank were okolnichi.

The mestnichestvo system confirmed the privileged position of the boyar and princely class in the Muscovite government and administration and offered certain guarantees to the group as a whole. Even the oprichnina terror instituted by Ivan IV, while shattering the boyar class, did not succeed in abolishing the mestnichestvo. On the other hand, the old freedom of service of the boyars was completely extinguished as all of them were now bound to serve the tsar. As has been mentioned, the limitations on boyar freedom started in the reign of Dmitri Donskoy. As we have seen, under the old order the boyar's rights on his landed estates were not connected in any way

81. On the mestnichestvo see Kliuchevsky, *2*, 149–166; A. I. Markevich, *O mestnichestve* (Odessa, 1879).

with his service. From the time of Dmitri Donskoy on a boyar's estates could be confiscated if the grand duke ruled that he had committed treason. As a rule, however, the old principle of boyar freedom
was still recognized and confirmed in the interprincely treaties of the
first half of the 15th century. In this respect there was a marked
difference between the boyars and the servitor princes.

While the princes were socially superior to the boyars, they were
actually less free politically. The princes had to offer permanent
loyalty to the grand duke and sign a pledge not to seek service
elsewhere. If they broke their promise they would forfeit their estates. In Grand Duke Vasili II's treaty of 1428 with his uncle Iuri
we find a characteristic clause in which Iuri promised not to accept
into his service the grand duke's servitor princes with their estates.[82]
The limitation of the rights of the servitor princes became a precedent
for curbing the privileges of the boyars as well. Toward the end of
Ivan III's reign both boyars and princes found themselves in the
same boat. In his Testament (1504) Ivan III ruled that no servitor
prince and no boyar should leave his son and successor's service; if
any did, he forfeited his estates.[83]

It would not be amiss now to glance at the ethnic origins and
composition of the Russian nobility as a whole (including boyars
and princes) as it consolidated itself in the 17th century. According
to N. P. Zagoskin's computation, 229 Russian noble families were
of "West European" (including German) origin; 223 of Polish and
Lithuanian origin; 156 of "Tatar" and other Oriental origin. Against
those families of alien ancestry, 168 families belonged to the house of
Riurik; 42 were of unspecified "Russian" origin; and 97 families of
uncertain ancestry.[84] Some of the families of so-called Polish–
Lithuanian ancestry must have been West Russian. Still, the families
of Russian origin were obviously a minority. Zagoskin's figures refer
to the later period. It must be borne in mind that the influx of "Tatar"
families into the Russian nobility greatly increased after the reign of
Vasili II. The majority of Russian noble families of West European
and Polish origin settled in Russia only in the 17th century and some
of them even later. Therefore the proportion of families of Russian
origin in the composition of Moscow boyardom must have been
higher in the Mongol period than later.

82. *DDG*, p. 65.
83. *Ibid.*, pp. 356–357.
84. Vladimirsky-Budanov, *Obzor*, p. 123, n. 1.

II

At a lower social level, the East Russian gentry of the Mongol period consisted of two main groups: the free servitors (*slugi volnye*) and the service-bound servitors, who were under the authority of the majordomo of the grand ducal court (*slugi pod dvorskim*) and eventually became known as the dvoriane. It was a special category of the free servitors that was known as the boyar sons—the impoverished branches of boyar families. The term first occurs in the Novgorod Chronicle, A.D. 1259,[85] but it seems that the group itself was consolidated and assumed importance only in the first half of the 15th century. Both the slugi volnye and the boyar sons enjoyed the same freedom of service as the boyars; both owned patrimonial estates which they kept even if they left the prince's service. Their estates (especially those of the boyar sons) were probably much smaller than the boyar domains, and their manorial rights less comprehensive. Most of the free servitors must have been petty army officers. They lost their freedom of service at about the same time as the boyars.

Most of the dvoriane ("slugi pod dvorskim") were freemen, but some were originally the grand duke's slaves. All of them were bound to service. The slaves, of course, might escape but could not legally terminate their service of their own will. The freemen could specify the term of their service when entering it. Quite a number of them must have served for life. Some served in the prince's army (dvor in the military sense). Others performed various duties at court and in the management of the grand ducal domains. At the lowest level of this social group stood those employed in the princely domains as apiculturists, gardeners, hound keepers, beaver catchers, and so on. A number of the dvoriane received maintenance from the grand duke. Others were granted small landed estates as temporary holdings. If and when they ceased to serve the grand duke, they had to quit their lands. Here we are at the sources of that important institution of the Muscovite period—the military fief (pomestie).

As a social group, the "slugi pod dvorskim" of the Mongol period deserve the historian's special attention not only because of their important role in the growth of the wealth and power of the Moscow grand dukes but also because this class proved the nucleus of the Russian gentry and the chief support of the tsar in his conflict with

85. Novgorod, pp. 82, 310.

the boyars. When the political independence of the boyars was broken by Tsar Ivan IV in the second half of the 16th century, the status of the dvoriane of the Mongol period became the pattern for the subsequent relationship between the tsar and the nobility at large. An important source of the power of the Moscow tsar was his control of the landed estates of the army officers through the pomestie system.[86] And as has been said, it is in the landholdings of the grand ducal dvoriane of the Mongol period that at least some of the roots of the pomestie system may be discerned. Thus, while that system assumed definite shape only in the post-Mongol period—in the 16th century—the Mongol age may be called its incubation period. The rise of the *dvorianstvo* (that is, of the dvoriane collectively) became obvious by the middle of the 16th century when the tsar created the third rank of Duma membership, that of the "Duma squire" (*dumnyi dvorianin*), to which the dvoriane could be appointed. This gave the dvorianstvo a voice in the highest council of the tsardom. In the course of the 17th century the position of the top layer of the dvoriane came close to that of the boyars. In the 18th century the two groups merged, with the result that in imperial Russia the term "dvorianin" acquired the connotation of "nobleman" and "dvorianstvo" that of nobility.

III

While military service became the main duty of the nobility and gentry and the basis of their bondage to the state, the townspeople and peasants were subject to tiaglo. Their main duties were to pay taxes and to supply labor whenever required by the state. The consolidation of the tiaglo-bound social classes (which numerically constituted the bulk of the nation) was completed in the course of the 17th century. The long-drawn-out process started, however, in the Mongol period. The basic factor at the initial stage of the process was the system of universal taxation and army conscription imposed on Russia by the Mongols.

In the Kievan period the citizens of the large towns were free from taxes; and they formed their own militia (*tysiacha,* "thousand") in

86. The pomestie system will be discussed in Volume *4* of this series. On the pomestie see K. A. Nevolin, *Polnoe sobranie sochinenii* (St. Petersburg, 1857), *4*, 191–261; Kliuchevsky, *2*, 230–242; Vladimirsky-Budanov, *Obzor,* pp. 566–574; S. V. Rozhdestvensky, *Sluzhiloe zemlevladenie v moskovskom gosudarstve XVI veka* (St. Petersburg, 1896); Veselovsky, *Feodalnoe zemlevladenie* (as above, n. 60), pp. 281–313; Eliashevich, *1*, 368–377; *2*, 21–57.

which they served as free citizens, not as conscript soldiers. Conscription and taxation introduced by the Mongols, coupled with the curbing of the veche, basically changed the status of the urban class in East Russia. (Novgorod and Pskov, it will be recalled, succeeded in maintaining their autonomy, and their citizens kept their full political and individual rights throughout the Mongol period.) When East Russia emancipated herself from the Mongols, the grand duke of Moscow did not revoke the Mongol system of taxation and conscription but used it for the needs of his own government. That system was now further expanded: in 1478 Novgorod was annexed to Moscow, and in 1510 Pskov. The old free institutions of the two cities were then abolished.

With the disintegration of the political freedom of the East Russian cities, the economic differentiation between wealthy and poor citizens assumed new significance. The top layer of the Muscovite merchants, the gosti and sukonniki, became a privileged minority high above the bulk of the townspeople. In the course of the 16th century that top layer was divided into three groups: (1) the gosti, the richest wholesale merchants; (2) the gosti hundred (*gostinnaia sotnia*), a corporation of the less rich gosti; (3) and the sukonniki hundred (*sukonnaia sotnia*), the corporation of the sukonniki. All of them were exempt from direct taxes as well as from any compulsory labor services. For the privileges they enjoyed the merchants of these three groups had to assist the tsar in the financial administration of the tsardom and the collection of the indirect taxes.

Deprived in this way of their most valuable element, the tiaglo-bound mass of the burghers was organized in two groups: the "middle" burghers (*serednie*), such as retail merchants and master artisans; and the "junior" burghers (*molodshie*), also known as the "black" people (*chernye liudi*), that is, the petty artisans and the half-skilled and unskilled workers. They formed the so-called "black hundred" (*chernaia sotnia*). Most of the middle and junior burghers lived outside the city proper, in the *posad* (town settlement). By 1550 they were known as the *posadskie liudi* ("townspeople" in the specific sense of the tiaglo-bound middle and lower classes of the urban population). The scale of compensation for offenses against the honor of the people of various classes established in Ivan IV's Sudebnik gives an adequate notion of the difference in social and economic position of different urban groups.[87] The fine for offending

87. Sudebnik, 1550, art. 26, Vladimirsky-Budanov, *Khristomatiia, 2,* 129–130.

against the honor of a gost' was 50 rubles; against the honor of a middle-class burgher, 5 rubles; for offending the honor of a lower-class "posadski" 1 ruble was sufficient.

In the 17th century, following the crisis of the Time of Troubles, the Moscow government took steps to bind the townspeople to their communes. In 1613 it ordered the posadskie who had fled from the capital during the troubles forcibly returned to Moscow; in 1619 a general ordinance was issued that all the posadskie who had migrated earlier should return to their respective towns all over Russia.[88] By the provisions of the Code of Laws (Ulozhenie) of 1649 the commune was finally consolidated as a closed group to which all of its members were permanently bound. Any member who left the commune without the government's permission was to be punished by deportation to Siberia.[89] In 1658 the death penalty was established for moving from one posad to another.[90]

The process of regimentation and enserfment of East Russian peasants was similar to that of the East Russian townspeople. The Mongol system of taxation and conscription was its starting point. The logical conclusions were drawn by the Muscovite government itself. In the Kievan period, it will be recalled, people of the rural classes as a general rule were not subject to military service. The petty landowners (liudi and *svoezemtsy*) [91] were not liable to the direct tax (tribute),[92] but the state peasants (smerdy) [93] were. In the Mongol period the smerdy, as a separate group, continued to exist only in the Novgorodian land. In West Russia the term smerdy gradually went out of use under the Lithuanian regime. In East Russia it was not used at all in the Mongol period. Presumably many of the former West and East Russian smerdy joined the service communes established by the Mongols, such as the "hundreds" (in that specific sense) and the "hordes." The term liudi (in the specific sense of the small landowners) also disappeared from parlance in the Mongol period. While small landowners still existed in East Russia,[94]

88. Vladimirsky-Budanov, *Obzor*, p. 129.

89. *Sobornoe Ulozhenie tsaria Alekseia Mikhailovicha* (Moscow, 1907), chap. 19, see especially arts. 1–11, 13, 18–20.

90. Vladimirsky-Budanov, *Obzor*, p. 130.

91. On the liudi and svoezemtsy see *Kievan Russia*, pp. 143–144.

92. *Ibid.*, p. 191.

93. On the status of the smerdy see *ibid.*, pp. 143–146.

94. On the small landowners in East Russia of the Mongol period see Eliashevich, *1*, 247.

their number must have decreased considerably. Some must have joined the prince's dvor; others sank to the rank of peasants. In the Novgorodian and Pskovian lands, however, the class of petty land-owners continued to occupy a prominent position throughout the Mongol period. In Novgorod they were known as svoezemtsy if each owned land individually; in case of cooperative ownership they were called *shabry* (in Pskov, *siabry*).[95]

In East Russia, from about the middle of the 14th century on, the peasants were called simply "Christians" (*khristiane* or *krestiane*).[96] According to Peter Struve the new term was introduced by the church.[97] And indeed the earliest East Russian document using the word "khristiane" in the sense of "peasants" is Metropolitan Cyprian's charter to the Monastery of St. Constantine (1391). In this he called the tenant farmers of the monastery Christians, probably wishing to emphasize their spiritual rather than legal dependence on the monastery. The term was repeated, either in this form or in the form "krestiane," in a number of church documents and soon became quite familiar in the sphere of church-land relations. Since the monasteries by that time owned a considerable proportion of land in East Russia, the new term for "peasants" was eventually accepted in regard to other categories of land as well.[98] It was used in the Code of Laws of 1497 [99] as well as in that of 1550.[100]

Besides the church and monastery estates there were three other categories of lands settled by peasants: (1) the "black" lands, that is taxable state lands; (2) the grand ducal domains; (3) and the estates of the servitor princes and boyars. In the first century of Mongol domination there was an important difference between the status of the peasants on the monastery lands and of those on the lands of other categories. As we know, the church and its estates were exempted by the khan from taxation and other duties. Hence the peasants on monastery lands were liable only to manorial services for the monastery and not to state tiaglo. In contrast, the peasants on other lands were subject to both tribute and conscription. Para-

95. On the term siabry see *Kievan Russia*, p. 134.
96. The Russian word khristiane ("Christians") derives from "Christ" (*Khristos*); krestiane from "cross" (*krest*). In Old Russian krestiane originally meant "Christians"; in modern Russian it means "peasants."
97. Struve, pp. 78–84.
98. Eliashevich, *1*, 23.
99. Art. 57, Vladimirsky-Budanov, *Khristomatiia, 2*, 102 (*khristiane*).
100. Art. 88, *idem, 2*, 173 (*krestiane*).

doxical as this may seem, the immunity of the church was curbed after the decline of the Golden Horde and the rise of the authority of the Moscow grand duke. The church now had to turn to the grand duke for confirmation of its privileges. A number of grand ducal charters were issued granting the church administrative immunity but subjecting the peasants on the church estates to the yam and sokha taxes. As a result, by 1500 the status of the monastery peasants approached that of the other categories of peasants.

Although tiaglo-bound, the peasants of all categories were still personally free in the Mongol period. Moreover, the East Russian peasant of this period was not a mere tenant on somebody else's land but had his own right, the "toiler's right" (trudovoe pravo), on the piece of land he actually tilled. Whether he tilled a piece of "black" land or a grand duke's or a boyar's land, nobody could legally remove him from his farm, and his rights on it were recognized by the courts—as long as he continued to work on the land and paid his taxes.[101] The difference between the position of the peasants settled on black lands and those on the church or private lands was that the former had to pay only state taxes while the latter had to pay manorial duties as well, or to work for the manor in accordance with the custom. To equalize the position of the two groups the "black" peasants paid taxes at a higher rate than the manorial peasants. Each peasant had a right to quit his farm and move to another estate after settling all his accounts at the end of the agricultural cycle, that is late in the autumn. On the black lands he was usually required to find a substitute who could assume his share of the tiaglo. By the mid-15th century St. George's Day, November 26, was considered the proper day for terminating the peasant's liability. This date was legalized by the Codes of Law of 1497 and 1550.

The peasant's freedom of movement could of course be encumbered by private indebtedness to the lord of the manor. As a result of the agricultural crisis of the mid-16th century cases of such indebtedness became more frequent. It was not the private indebtedness of some peasants, however, but the new policies of governmental control of the landed estates which proved the most serious threat to the peasants' freedom. With the establishment of the pomestia on a large scale in the middle of the 16th century the government faced the problem of supplying labor to the pomeshchiki (holders of these fiefs) and saw no alternative to binding the peasants settled on them

101. Eliashevich, 1, 59–65.

to the pomestia lands, at first as a temporary measure (1581). By the provisions of the Code of Laws of 1649 serfdom was established on all kinds of non-black lands and made permanent. The peasants on the black lands retained their former status, but were now permanently bound to their respective communes.

5. SPIRITUAL LIFE

I

In medieval Russia, as in the medieval West, the Christian church played a leading role in the nation's spiritual life. Therefore, especially after the victory of Islam in the Golden Horde, there was little occasion for direct Mongol influence on Russia in the religious sphere. Indirectly, however, the Mongol conquest affected the course of development of the Russian church and the spiritual culture in various ways. The first shock of the Mongol invasion was as painful to the church as to the other aspects of Russian life and culture. Many outstanding clergymen, including the metropolitan himself, perished in the destroyed cities; many cathedrals, monasteries, and churches were burned or looted; hosts of parishioners were killed or enslaved. The city of Kiev, the metropolis of the Russian church, was so devastated that for many years it was unfit to serve as the center of the church administration. Of the eparchies, Pereiaslav suffered most and the bishopric there was closed.

It was only after the issuance of Mangu-Temir's immunity charter to the Russian clergy that the church found itself on firm ground once more and could gradually reorganize; as years went by, it became even stronger in some respects than before the Mongol onslaught. Indeed, ruled by Greek metropolitans or by Russian metropolitans ordained in Byzantium, and protected by the khan's charter, the church in Russia was in this period less dependent on the princely power than in any other period of Russian history. In fact the metropolitan on more than one occasion served as arbiter in interprincely disputes. This was also a period in which the Russian church was able to build up a strong material basis for its activities. As the church lands were immune from interference by state authorities, either Mongol or Russian, they attracted an increasing number of peasant settlers, and the ratio of their production to the total agricultural output rose steadily. This was especially true of the monas-

tery estates. A degree of prosperity achieved by the church toward
the end of the first century of Mongol domination greatly helped in
the performance of its spiritual activities.

Among the tasks the church faced in the Mongol period, the first
was that of giving spiritual advice and moral support to the embit-
tered and exasperated people, from princes to commoners. Connected
with this was a more general mission—to complete the Christianization of the Russian people. In the Kievan period Christianity became
firmly established among the upper classes and the townspeople.
Most of the monasteries founded in that period were located in the
cities. In the rural districts the Christian layer was rather thin, and
the remnants of paganism were still unconquered. Only in the Mongol
period did the rural population of East Russia become more thoroughly Christianized. This was achieved both by strenuous efforts
of the clergy and by the growth of religious feeling among the
spiritual élite of the people themselves. Most of the metropolitans
of this period spent much time traveling throughout Russia trying
to correct deficiencies in church administration and to direct the
activities of the bishops and priests. Several new eparchies were
organized, four of them in East Russia, two in West Russia, and one
in Saray. The number of churches and monasteries grew steadily,
especially after 1350, both in the cities and the rural districts. According to Kliuchevsky, about thirty monasteries were founded in
the first century of the Mongol period and five times as many more
in the second century.[102] A characteristic trait of the new monastic
movement was the initiative shown by individuals, young men of
ardent religious spirit who took monastic orders in order to go to
"the wilderness"—deep into the woods—for hard work in primitive
conditions as well as for prayer and meditation. The disasters of the
Mongol invasion and of the interprincely strife as well as harsh conditions of life in general were conducive to the development of this
mentality.

When a former hermitage grew into a large, crowded, and wealthy
monastery surrounded by prosperous peasant villages, the original
hermits, or the new monks of like spirit, would find the changed
atmosphere stifling and would leave the monastery they had created
or helped to expand, and establish another hermitage deeper in the
woods or farther north. In this way each monastery served as a

102. V. O. Kliuchevsky, *Ocherki i rechi* (Moscow, around 1915), p. 210. On the role
of the monasteries in the Mongol period at large see Kliuchevsky, *Kurs, 2,* 260–280.

nursery for several more. A pioneer and the most venerated leader of this movement was St. Sergius of Radonezh, founder of the Trinity Monastery about 40 miles northeast of Moscow. His saintly personality was a source of inspiration even to those who never met him, and the influence of his lifework on following generations was immense. St. Sergius became a symbol of faith—an important factor in the religious life of the Russian people.[103] Among other outstanding leaders of Russian monasticism of this age were St. Cyril of Beloozero, and Saints Zosima and Savvati, founders of the Solovki Monastery on the island of that name in the White Sea. Incidentally, the new monasteries played an important role in the colonization of the northern regions of Russia.[104]

Several of the northern monasteries were located in the area of the Finno–Ugrian tribes, and these people were now Christianized as well. The mission of St. Stephan of Perm among the Zyrianians (now called the Komi) was especially productive in this respect. A gifted philologist, Stephan not only mastered the Zyrianian language but even created a special alphabet for it which he used to spread religious literature among the natives.[105]

Another important aspect of the religious revival in East Russia in the Mongol age was church art. This period witnessed the blossoming of Russian religious painting, in the form of both frescoes and icons.[106] An important role in this artistic renaissance was played by the great Greek painter Theophanes, who stayed in Russia for around thirty years, to the end of his life and career. Theophanes worked first in Novgorod and then in Moscow. While both his masterpieces and his personality were admired by the Russians, he cannot be called the founder of either the Novgorod or the Moscow school of icon painting. The Russian painters profited greatly by his free brush-stroke technique but they did not attempt to imitate his individualistic and dramatic style. The greatest Russian painter of this period was Andrew Rublev, who spent his youth in the Trinity

103. Kliuchevsky, *Ocherki i rechi*, pp. 199–215.

104. See V. O. Kliuchevsky, "Khoziaistvennaia deiatelnost' Solovetskogo monastyria," *Opyty i issledovaniia* (2d ed. Moscow, around 1915), pp. 1–36.

105. On St. Stephan of Perm see Makari, *4*, 138–149; *5*, 236–240; Golubinsky, *2*, 262–296.

106. On Russian painting of the Mongol period see M. Alpatov and N. Brunov, *Geschichte der altrussischen Kunst* (Augsburg, 1932), pp. 285–346; M. Alpatov, *Andrei Rublev* (Moscow and Leningrad, 1943); N. P. Kondakov, *The Russian Icon*, E. H. Minns, trans. (Oxford, Clarendon Press, 1927); P. P. Muratov, *Les Icones russes* (Paris, 1927); D. T. Rice, *Russian Icons* (London and New York, King Penguin Books, 1947); L. Ouspensky and W. Lossky, *Der Sinn der Ikonen* (Bern, Switzerland, 1952).

Monastery and later painted for it his famed icon, "The Old Testament Trinity." The charm of Rublev's creations lies in the serene quiet of the composition and the symphony of delicate colors. There is a certain similarity between his works and those of his contemporary, the Italian painter Fra Angelico.

Less spectacular but no less significant must have been the development of church singing in this period, of which unfortunately we know little. Most of the manuscripts of the diatonic *znamenny* chant known to us belong to the post-Mongol age, ranging as they do from 1450 to 1650.[107] The prototype of this znamenny chant was introduced to Russia in the 11th century by Byzantine singers. In the post-Mongol age the Russian chant differed from the Byzantine pattern in many ways. As Alfred J. Swan points out, "during its growth on Russian soil and adaptation to Russian conditions [the znamenny chant] come into close relation with the Russian folksong." [108] Presumably the Mongol age was the incubation period of the final stage of the znamenny chant. It was also at the end of the Mongol period that another chant, the so-called *demestvenny,* made its appearance. It became fashionable in the 16th century.[109]

In literature the spirit of the church found expression first of all in the bishops' sermons and in the lives of saints, as well as in the biographies of certain Russian princes who, it was felt, deserved to be .canonized, so that their biographies were written in the style of the lives of saints.[110] The underlying idea of most of these works was that the Mongol yoke was a visitation of God for the sins of the Russian people and that only true Christianization could lead the Russians out of their plight. The sermons of Bishop Serapion of Vladimir (1274–75) are typical of this attitude. He blamed for Rus-

---

107. On the znamenny chant see V. Stasov, "Zametki o demestvennom i troestrochnom penii," in his Collected Works (*Sobranie sochinenii*), *3,* 107–128; N. Findeisen, *Ocherki po istorii muzyki v Rossii* (Moscow and Leningrad, 1928), *1,* 97–103; A. J. Swan, "The Znamenny Chant of the Russian Church," *Musical Quarterly, 26* (1940), 232–243, 365–380, 529–545.

108. Swan (as in n. 107), p. 365.

109. On the demestvenny chant see Stasov (as in n. 107); Findeisen (as in n. 107), pp. 247–251; M. S. Pekelis, ed., *Istoriia russkoi muzyki* (Moscow and Leningrad, 1940), *1,* 85–86.

110. On the Russian hagiographic literature of the Mongol period see I. Nekrasov, *Zarozhdenie natsionalnoi literatury v severnoi Rusi* (Odessa, 1870); Kliuchevsky, *Zhitiia;* A. P. Kadlubovsky, *Ocherki po istorii drevne-russkoi literatury zhitii sviatykh* (Warsaw, 1902); N. P. Barsukov, *Istochniki russkoi agiografii* (St. Petersburg, 1882); E. V. Petukhov, *Russkaia literatura, drevnii period* (Iuriev, 1912), pp. 93–95, 112–125; G. P. Fedotov, *Sviatye drevnei Rusi* (Paris, YMCA Press, 1931).

sia's sufferings primarily the princes who had sapped the nation's strength by their constant quarrels. But he did not stop at that. He reproved the common people for clinging to remnants of paganism as well as for their superstitions, and urged every Russian to repent and become Christian in spirit and not in name only.[111] Among the princes of the first century of Mongol rule the lives of Grand Duke Iaroslav and his son Alexander Nevsky are of special interest. Iaroslav's biography has been preserved only in fragments. It was conceived as a national tragedy in the first act of which Iaroslav happened to be a leading actor. In the introduction the happy past of the Russian land was admiringly described. Probably it was to be followed by a description of the catastrophe which befell Russia, but that part has been lost. The introduction has been preserved under a separate title, the "Lay of Russia's Ruin" (*Slovo o pogibeli zemli russkoi*).[112] It is perhaps the highest achievement of Russian literature of the early Mongol period. In the Life of Alexander Nevsky the emphasis is on the military valor he displayed in the defense of Greek Orthodoxy against the Roman Catholic crusade.[113]

As in the Kievan period, the clergy of the Mongol age played an important role in the compilation of the Russian chronicles. The work all but stopped after the Mongol invasion. The only chronicle written between 1240 and 1260, known to us in part, was that of Rostov. Its editor was Bishop Cyril of that city. As D. S. Likhachev has convincingly shown, Cyril was helped by Princess Maria, daughter of Michael of Chernigov and widow of Vasilko of Rostov. Both her father and her husband were killed by the Mongols, and she devoted herself to charities and literary work.[114] In 1305 a chronicle was compiled in Tver. This was partly copied in 1377 by the Suzdal monk Laurentius (the writer of the so-called Laurentian Codex). In the 15th century there appeared in Moscow historical works of a wider scope, like the Trinity Chronicle (started under the direction of Metropolitan Cyprian and completed in 1409) and the even more ambitious digest of annals compiled under the editorship of Metropolitan Photius around 1418. The latter served as a basis for further

111. On Serapion of Vladimir see Petukhov (as in n. 110), pp. 84–86; *idem, Serapion Vladimirskii* (St. Petersburg, 1888) ; M. Gorlin, "Sérapion de Vladimir, prédicateur de Kiev," *RES, 24* (1948), 21–28.

112. M. Gorlin, "Le Dit de la ruine de la Terre Russe et de la mort du Grand-Prince Jaroslav," *RES, 23* (1947), 1–33.

113. See above, Chapter 3, n. 72.

114. Likhachev, p. 283.

work which resulted in the great digests of the 16th century—the Voskresensk and the Nikon chronicles. Novgorod, throughout the 14th century and down to her fall, was a center for the writing of her own historical annals. It should be noted that many of the Russian chroniclers, and especially the editors of the Nikon Chronicle, showed excellent knowledge not only of Russian events but of Tatar affairs as well.

II

In the Russian lay literature of the Mongol age, both written and oral, a twofold attitude toward the Tatars can be noticed. On the one hand there was a feeling of repulsion, of opposition to the nation's oppressors, on the other a psychological undercurrent of attraction to the poetry of steppe life. Recalling the longing of a number of 19th-century Russian writers such as Pushkin, Lermontov, and Leo Tolstoy for the Caucasus and the picturesque life of the Caucasian mountaineers is helpful in understanding this mentality.

Owing to the tendency to repulsion, the byliny of the pre-Mongol age were revised to fit the new situation, and the name of the new enemy—the Tatars—was substituted for that of the old (the Cumans). Simultaneously new byliny and historical legends and songs were created dealing with the Mongol phase of Russia's struggle against the steppe peoples. Batu's destruction of Kiev and Nogay's raids on Russia served as topics for contemporary Russian folklore.[115] The Tatar oppression of Tver and the revolt of the Tverians in 1327 not only were recorded in the chronicles but apparently constituted the basis of a special historical tale.[116] And of course, as has been mentioned, the battle of Kulikovo Pole became the subject of a variety of patriotic stories, parts of which were used by the chroniclers and which later were recorded in full in writing. Here we have a case of merging of the oral and written forms of the old Russian literature. The "Zadonshchina," whose topic belongs to the same cycle, is obviously a piece of written literature.[117]

---

115. A. S. Orlov, *Drevniaia russkaia literatura XI–XVI vekov* (2d ed. Moscow and Leningrad, 1939), pp. 141–145; N. K. Gudzii, *Istoriia drevnei russkoi literatury* (2d ed. Moscow, 1941), pp. 225–226, 318–321; R. Jakobson, "Sobaka Kalin Tsar" (as above, Chapter 3, n. 200); D. S. Likhachev, *Natsionalnoe samosoznanie drevnei Rusi* (Moscow and Leningrad, 1945), pp. 78–81.

116. See above, Chapter 3, n. 242.

117. See above, p. 262. For the text of the "Zadonshchina" see P. Simoni, ed., "Zadonshchina," *ANORS, 100*, No. 2; J. Frček, *Zadonština* (Prague, 1948).

As to the element of attraction, the poetry of steppe life and warfare was already felt by the creators of byliny in the pre-Mongol age. This same psychological process continued now. Even in the patriotic tales of Kulikovo Pole the chivalry of the Tatar knight whose challenge was accepted by the monk Peresvet was noted with obvious admiration. In the pre-Mongol Russian byliny there are undeniable close parallels to the Iranian and early Turkish heroic songs.[118] In the Mongol age Russian folklore also was influenced by "Tatar" (Mongol and Turkish) poetic patterns and themes.[119] Presumably Russian soldiers drafted into the Mongol armies were the means of acquainting the Russians with Tatar heroic poetry. Tatars settled in Russia must also have brought Tatar motifs into Russian folklore.

The enrichment of the Russian language with words and terms borrowed from Mongol and Turkish or from Persian and Arabic through Turkish was still another aspect of the same process of cultural osmosis. By 1450 the Tatar (Turkish) language had become fashionable at the court of Grand Duke Vasili II of Moscow, which was strongly resented by many of his opponents. Vasili II was accused of excessive love of the Tatars "and their speech" (*i rech ikh*).[120] It was typical of the period that a number of Russian noblemen in the 15th, 16th, and 17th centuries assumed Tatar surnames. Thus a member of the Veliaminov family became known as Aksak (which means "lame" in Turkish) and his descendants as the Aksakovs.[121] Similarly, one of the Shchepin-Rostovsky princes was called Bakhteiar (*bakhtyar* in Persian means "fortunate," "rich"). He was the forefather of the Bakhteiarov princes, a line which became extinct in the 18th century.

A number of Turkish words entered the Russian language before the Mongol invasion, but the real influx started in the Mongol age and continued in the 16th and 17th centuries. Among the terms borrowed from Mongol and Turkish (or through Turkish from Arabic and Persian) in the sphere of administration and finance, such words as *dengi* (money), *kazna* (treasury), *tamozhnia* (customshouse) may be mentioned here. Another group of borrowings is

---

118. See *Kievan Russia,* pp. 250–251.
119. See V. V. Stasov, "Proiskhozhdenie russkikh bylin," in his Collected Works (*Sobranie sochinenii*) (St. Petersburg, 1894), *3,* 948–1260.
120. Novgorod IV, 125–126.
121. Prince P. Dolgorukov, *Rossiiskaia rodoslovnaia kniga, 4* (St. Petersburg, 1857), 44, 71.

connected with trade and merchandise: *bazar* (bazaar), *balagan* (booth), *bakaleia* (groceries of certain kinds), *barysh* (profit), *kumach* (red cloth), and others. Among the borrowings for clothing, headgear, and footwear are the following: *armiak* (peasant overcoat), *bashlyk* (a kind of hood), *bashmak* (shoe). Naturally enough, an important group of borrowings is that connected with horses, their color, and their breeding; for instance *argamak* (thoroughbred steed), *bulanyi* (dun), *tabun* (drove of horses). Many other Russian words denoting household objects, food and drink, as well as fruit and vegetables, metals, and precious stones also were borrowed from Turkish or from other Oriental languages through Turkish.[122]

A factor in Russian intellectual and spiritual development whose importance is hard to evaluate is the role of the Tatars who settled in Russia and were converted to Christianity, and of their descendants. The case of Tsarevich Peter of the Horde, founder of a monastery in Rostov, has been already mentioned. There were other similar instances. A prominent 15th-century Russian religious leader who also founded a monastery, St. Pafnuti of Borovsk, was grandson of a baskak. In 'the 16th century a boyar son of Tatar extraction, Bulgak by name, was ordained priest and after that there was always a priest in the family, down to Father Sergius Bulgakov, a well-known Russian theologian of the 20th century.[123] And there were other outstanding Russian intellectual leaders of Tatar extraction like the historian N. M. Karamzin and the philosopher Peter Chaadaev.[124] Judging from his name, Chaadaev must have been of Mongol ancestry, for Chaaday is a contraction of the Mongol name Jagatay (Chagatay). Presumably Peter Chaadaev was a descendant of Chingis-Khan's son Jagatay.[125] It is both paradoxical and typical of

122. On the Russian words of Oriental (Tatar) origin see F. Miklosich, "Die türkische Elemente in den südost-und osteuropäischen Sprachen," *AWV* (Vienna, 1884–90) pp. 34, 35, 37, 38; L. Wanstrat, *Beiträge zur Charakteristik des russischen Wortschatzes* (Leipzig, 1933), pp. 63–82, 97–98; Menges, Preobrazhensky, and Vasmer are also to be consulted. An etymological dictionary of the Oriental loan words in old and modern Russian is being prepared at the University of California by P. A. Boodberg and K. H. Menges (see Menges, p. 6).

123. Father Sergius Bulgakov, *Avtobiograficheskie zametki* (Paris, YMCA Press, 1946), p. 15. Besides the priestly Bulgakov family there were two noble Bulgakov families in Russia, both of them also of Tatar origin, one known since the 14th century and the other since the 16th.

124. See M. Vasmer, "Der Name Čaadajev," *ZSP*, *17* (1941), 340.

125. Vasmer (as in n. 124), pp. 340–341. On Chaadaev see C. Quénet, *Tchaadaev et ses Lettres philosophiques* (Paris, 1931); A. Schelting, *Russland und Europa* (Bern, 1948); V. V. Zenkovsky, *Istoriia russkoi filosofii* (Paris, YMCA Press, 1948), *1*, 157–179; N. O.

the melting pot of Russian civilization with its heterogeneous ethnic elements that the "Westernizer" Chaadaev was of Mongol extraction and the "Slavophile" Aksakov family was of Varangian ancestry (a branch of the Veliaminovs).

6. THE AFTERMATH

I

When East Russia emancipated herself from the authority of the khan she emerged much stronger than before the Mongol invasion. All of "Great Russia" was now politically united under the guidance of the grand duke of Moscow and, to emphasize his independence of foreign rule as well as his authority in the internal affairs of the country, he assumed the titles of autocrat (samoderzhets) and tsar. The Jesuit Antonio Possevino, one of the shrewdest diplomats of the second half of the 16th century and well acquainted with East European affairs, was apparently right when he commented that the "haughtiness" of the Moscow rulers was the result of their emancipation from Tatar domination.[126] The two titles "tsar" and "autocrat" were used occasionally in the latter part of the reign of Ivan III and more frequently in the reign of Vasili III.[127] Ivan IV was officially crowned tsar with the sanction of the church (1547). In his subsequent polemics against Prince Kurbsky Ivan IV used "autocrat" in the sense of a ruler absolutely supreme in the internal affairs of the country.

It will be recalled that the title "tsar" was first applied by the Russians to the Byzantine emperor and then to the Mongol khan also. It so happened that at the time Russia was shedding the already half-broken fetters of the khan's control the Byzantine Empire was destroyed by the Ottoman Turks. Ivan III's marriage to Sophia Paleologus, a niece of the last Byzantine emperor and the pope's ward, could be understood as his becoming heir to the Byzantine tsars. The pope and the Venetians who wanted to solicit Russian help against the Osmanlis lost no time in pointing out the significance of the marriage from this point of view. The Russians themselves were aware of its implications but did not attribute too much value to the

Lossky, *History of Russian Philosophy* (New York, International Universities Press, 1951), pp. 47–51.

126. V. O. Kliuchevsky, *Skazaniia inostrantsev o moskovskom gosudarstve* (2d ed. Moscow, 1918), p. 83.

127. Diakonov, *Vlast'*, pp. 134–136.

event.[128] However, they used the Byzantine traditions in many other ways. Russian political thought had been influenced by Byzantine doctrines from the time of Russia's conversion to Christianity. Yet no elaborate theory of monarchy was built up by the Russians during the Kievan period, since the Russian political background was at that time quite different from the Byzantine. Then conditions changed, a strong centralized state came into being in Muscovy, and the Russian literati could turn for inspiration to those currents in Byzantine thought which they had neglected earlier. There is no doubt that the Muscovite monarchic theories of the 16th century reflected the Byzantine doctrine in many respects.[129]

More than that, the Muscovites now attempted to find historical evidence for claiming a direct connection between the Byzantine and the Russian monarchies. Among various semihistorical and pseudohistorical arguments which were brought forward was the assertion that Vladimir the Saint at the time of his conversion was crowned tsar by the emperor and the patriarch of Constantinople. Another popular story had it that Prince Vladimir Monomach received the insignia of tsardom from the Byzantine emperor. On the basis of that legend the jeweled and fur-trimmed crown of the Moscow rulers became known, in the 16th century, as Monomach's Crown (*Shapka Monomakhova*). Herberstein was the first foreign observer of Russian affairs who connected the crown with the name of Monomach.[130] Ivan IV's testament is the first Russian document to refer to it as Monomach's Crown.[131] The crown had been kept in the treasury of the Moscow grand dukes since the reign of Ivan I and mentioned in their wills as the Golden Crown (*Shapka Zolotaia*).[132] It was probably given to Ivan I by Khan Uzbeg. The crown is a masterpiece of Central Asian art of the late 13th or early 14th century.[133]

It is hard to tell whether the Muscovites themselves seriously believed in the stories of the crownings of Vladimir the Saint and

128. Likhachev, *Natsionalnoe samosoznanie drevnei Rusi* (as in n. 115), p. 97.

129. Diakonov, *Vlast';* Valdenberg, *O predelakh tsarskoi vlasti* (as above, Chapter 4, n. 155).

130. Herberstein, p. 32.

131. *DDG*, p. 433.

132. *Ibid.*, p. 8.

133. A. A. Spitsyn, "K voprosu o Monomakhovoi shapke," *ORSA, 8*, Pt. 1 (St. Petersburg, 1906), 146–184; Rybakov, pp. 642–643. For a picture of Monomach's Crown see *Drevnosti Rossiiskogo Gosudarstva, 2*, Plates 1, 2; J. S. Martin, *A Picture History of Russia* (New York, Crown Publishers, 1945), p. 25.

Vladimir Monomach. In any case they did not put all their eggs in the Byzantine basket, being well aware of the historical connection between the Tsardom of Moscow and the Golden Horde. And indeed it was but natural for the Muscovite ruler to take the title of his former suzerain. Moreover, when the Russian counterattack started and the Russians conquered the khanates of Kazan and Astrakhan (in 1552 and 1556 respectively), the Russian tsar could claim to have become heir to at least two of the Golden Horde succession states. The implications of the conquest were emphasized by the Moscow government in its effort to obtain for its ruler recognition of the title of tsar from the king of Poland. A Russian note handed to the Polish and Lithuanian ambassadors in 1556 stated in addition to the Byzantine argument, along the lines of the two stories above, that besides the Russian land God gave Ivan IV the tsardoms of Kazan and Astrakhan, "and the throne of Kazan and Astrakhan has been a tsar's see from the origins." [134] It may be added that a 17th-century Muscovite writer, Gregory Kotoshikhin, who was thoroughly familiar with his country's institutions and traditions, also considered the conquest of Kazan and Astrakhan the historical foundation of the Tsardom of Moscow.[135]

An important aspect of the continuity of Mongol traditions in the Muscovite monarchy was the Mongol influence on the etiquette of diplomatic negotiations. Many a Western envoy to Muscovy complained of the stiff and ridiculous formalities of the diplomatic ritual. As a matter of fact, when we look back now on those mutual offenses and claims and counterclaims about etiquette by the Russian and Western diplomats of the 16th and 17th centuries, some of the notions of the Western envoys seem to us as absurd as the Muscovite. At the root of the misunderstandings lay the fact that Westerners and Russians followed different bodies of rules, and that the Russian ceremonial reflected the Mongol pattern in many respects.[136]

The basic Muscovite concept of the duties of a government toward foreign ambassadors and of the rights of ambassadors with respect

---

134. Diakonov, *Vlast'*, pp. 142–143.

135. G. Kotoshikhin, *O Rossii v tsarstvovanie Alexeia Mikhailovicha* (3d ed. St. Petersburg, 1884), p. 1.

136. N. I. Veselovsky, "Tatarskoe vliianie na posolskii tseremonial v moskovskii period russkoi istorii," *Otchet St. Peterburgskogo Universiteta za 1910 god* (St. Petersburg, 1911), Suppl. pp. 1–19. For a general outline of the Muscovite diplomatic ceremonial and methods of conducting diplomatic affairs see V. P. Potemkin, ed., *Istoriia diplomatii, 1* (Moscow, 1943), 235–250.

to the government in the country of their destination differed markedly from the Western concept. From the Mongol point of view—shared by the Muscovites—an ambassador was a guest of the ruler to whom he was accredited. That ruler had to provide him, and his suite, with free transportation, lodgings, food and drink, and to guard his safety. While the Westerners did not object to free lodgings and food, they protested on many occasions that Moscow's care for their safety amounted to keeping them constantly under guard. On the other hand, the Russian ambassadors who had to travel in the West were indignant when they had to pay—and sometimes exorbitantly—for their transportation and maintenance. In both Mongol and Muscovite diplomatic ceremonial much attention was paid to mutual gifts. Not only did the rulers exchange presents but ambassadors were expected to offer appropriate gifts to the ruler they visited. A Muscovite rule, patterned on Mongol etiquette, forbade any foreign envoy to be armed when received in audience by the tsar. Many a Western ambassador resented being required to part with his sword before entering the audience hall, but all had to comply with the rule. When the foreign envoy entered Russia he was met at the frontier by a special official (*pristav*). Muscovite (as well as Tatar) etiquette required that envoy and pristav dismount simultaneously to greet each other in the name of their respective sovereigns. Then the pristav rode at the right of the ambassador. For reasons hard to understand, the Westerners objected violently to these two rules and tried every possible device to circumvent them. Most however had to accept the inevitable.[137]

The familiarity of the Muscovites with Mongol ways of diplomacy helped them greatly in their dealings with Oriental powers, especially with the succession states of the Golden Horde. In a sense Russia herself was such a succession state, and after the breakup of the Golden Horde the ruler of Russia seemed to be entitled to present his claims for leadership in the Mongol-Tatar sphere. Since as we have seen the so-called Golden Horde was actually known as the White Horde, the tsar of Moscow, as successor of the khans of this horde, was now called the "white tsar." As late as the 18th and 19th centuries the Russian emperor was still the white khan (*tsagan khan*) to the Kalmyks and the Buriats.[138] The feeling among many

137. It would not be amiss to mention that the Muscovite etiquette in foreign relations was abolished by Peter the Great and the Western body of rules introduced instead. In the 18th and 19th centuries Russian diplomatic ceremonial was identical with the Western.

138. Khara-Davan, p. 199.

Turkish and Mongol tribes that the Russian tsar was the successor of the Mongol khans created a favorable situation psychologically for the extension of the tsar's rule over those tribes. Moscow diplomats consciously or subconsciously took advantage of the situation. In this sense it may be said, as Prince Nicholas Trubetskoy did, that the Russians inherited their empire from Chingis-Khan.

II

The emancipation of East Russia from Mongol rule was the result of a combined effort of the Moscow grand dukes, the church, the boyars, the gentry, and the commoners—in fact of the whole nation. The new monarchy which was created in the tortuous process of emancipation was based on principles alien to the Russians of the Kievan period. All classes of East Russian society were now subordinated to the state. It might have been expected that once the goal of emancipation was achieved the Muscovite regime would relax and at least some of the old liberties would be restored. Actually, as we know, the opposite happened. Regimentation of the social classes progressed unchecked and reached its peak about 1650, two centuries after the end of the Mongol rule.

Why this seeming historical paradox? The answer is obvious: the precarious position of the Moscow monarchy on the international scene and the constant danger of war. In the southeast and south Muscovy was still threatened by the Tatars; in the west the struggle for power between Moscow and Lithuania (after 1569, between Moscow and Poland) continued to flare up at almost regular intervals; in the northwest, after having annexed Novgorod, the Moscow government had to take over the task previously performed by the Novgorodians, that of containing the pressure of the Livonian Knights and of Sweden in the area of the Gulf of Finland and Karelia. When Moscow defied the authority of the khan of the Golden Horde, there still remained several Tatar succession states, and the Tatars continued to raid the southern and eastern provinces of Muscovy almost yearly, looting and seizing thousands of captives. Thus the drain on Russian resources increased rather than decreased after the emancipation of the grand duke of Moscow from Mongol rule. There were no natural boundaries in the steppes between Muscovy and the Tatars, and the Moscow government had to keep the whole frontier constantly guarded. Both the Kasimov Tatars and the frontiersmen and Cossacks proved useful, but regular army troops had to be mobilized every year as well. An elaborate system of fortified defense lines was built up, but on many occasions the Tatars would pierce them and pour into the country between and behind them. Under the circumstances, the only way to solve the problem seemed to be to establish firm Russian control of the steppes, by either conquest or diplomacy. From the geopolitical point of view, Ivan IV's dash down the Volga to Astrakhan was an important move since it cut the steppe zone into two sectors, each of which could now be taken care of separately. But that was only the beginning of Russia's bid for sovereignty over the peoples of the steppes. The process continued throughout the 17th and the 18th centuries, ending, in the south, with the annexation of the Crimea in 1783.

The struggle in the west, while not continual and not as exasperating as the process of containing the Tatars, was on the whole no less costly since it required, in the periods of acute crises, stronger and better-equipped armies and more expenditure for armament plants. The situation was certainly not propitious for any relaxation of governmental controls. On the contrary, new taxes were required and the taxation system was to be tightened rather than liberalized. The creation of the new army based on the pomestie system raised the problem of supplying agricultural labor to the pomestia, and this, as we have seen, led to serfdom. As a result of all this, the regimentation of the social classes which started during the Mongol period and was originally based on the Mongol principles of administration, was carried further and completed by the Muscovite government. Autocracy and serfdom were the price the Russian people had to pay for national survival.

ABBREVIATIONS

AA Acta Archaeologica Academiae Scientiarum Hungaricae.
AAE Akty Arkheograficheskoi Ekspeditsii.
Abaev V. I. Abaev, *Osetinskii iazyk i folklor, 1* (Moscow and Leningrad, 1949).
Ab-ul-Faraj Gregory Ab-ul-Faraj, *Chronographia*, E. A. W. Budge, trans. See Sources.
AEM Archäologisch-epigraphische Mitteilungen aus Österreich-Ungarn.
AHR American Historical Review.
AI Akty istoricheskie.
AIK Annales de l'Institut Kondakov.
AIZR Arkhiv iuzhnoi i zapadnoi Rossii.
AK Arkheologicheskaia Kommissiia, *Izvestiia.*
Akanc Grigor of Akanc, History of the Nation of the Archers, R. P. Blake and R. N. Frye, eds. and trans., *HJAS, 12* (1949), 269–399.
Altan-Tobči "Altan-Tobči," Galsan Gomboev, trans., *VOT, 6* (1858).
AM Asia Major.
AN Akademiia Nauk, *Izvestiia.*
Ancient Russia G. Vernadsky, *Ancient Russia* (New Haven, Yale University Press, 1943).
Annuaire Annuaire de l'Institut de Philologie et d'Histoire Orientales et Slaves.
ANORI Akademiia Nauk, Otdelenie Russkogo Iazyka i Slovesnosti, *Izvestiia.*
ANORS Akademiia Nauk, Otdelenie Russkogo Iazyka i Slovesnosti, *Sbornik.*
Antonovich, *Monografii* V. B. Antonovich, *Monografii po istorii zapadnoi i iugo-zapadnoi Rusi* (Kiev, 1885).
ANZ Akademiia Nauk, *Zapiski.*
ANZI Akademiia Nauk, *Zapiski po istoriko-filologicheskomu otdeleniiu.*
ASAW Abhandlungen der Sächsischen Akademie der Wissenschaften zu Leipzig (Phil.-hist. Klasse).
ASEER American Slavic and East European Review.
ASTH Asiatic Studies in Honour of Tôru Haneda (Society of Oriental Research, Kyoto University, 1950).
AW Ateneum Wilenskie.
AWB Preussische Akademie der Wissenschaften, Berlin, *Sitzungsberichte* (Phil.-hist. Klasse).

AWGA Akademie [formerly: Gesellschaft] der Wissenschaften in Göttingen, *Abhandlungen* (Phil.-hist. Klasse).

AWGN Akademie [formerly: Gesellschaft] der Wissenschaften in Göttingen, *Nachrichten* (Phil.-hist. Klasse).

AWV Akademie der Wissenschaften, Vienna, *Denkschriften* (Phil.-hist. Klasse).

AZR *Akty zapadnoi Rossii.*

Barthold, "Edigey" W. Barthold, Otets Edigeiia, *TO, 1* (1927), 18–23.

Barthold, *Turcs* W. Barthold, *Histoire des Turcs de l'Asie centrale* (Paris, 1945).

Barthold, *Turkestan* W. Barthold, *Turkestan Down to the Mongol Invasion* (London, 1928).

Barthold, *Ulugbek* W. Barthold, *Ulugbek i ego vremia* (Petrograd, 1918).

Baumgarten 1 N. de Baumgarten, Généalogies et marriages occidentaux des Rurikides russes du x-me au xiii-me siècle, *OC, 35* (1927).

Baumgarten 2 N. de Baumgarten, Généalogies des branches régnantes des Rurikides du xiii-me au xvi-me siècle, *OC, 94* (1934).

Belleten Türk Tarih Kurumu, *Belleten.*

Berezin I. N. Berezin, Ocherk vnutrennego ustroistva Ulusa Dzhuchieva, *VOT*, 8 (1864).

Bernshtam A. Bernshtam, *Sotsialno-ekonomicheskii stroi orkhonoeniseiskikh Tiurok VI–VIII vekov* (Moscow and Leningrad, 1946).

Blue Annals G. N. Roerich, ed., *The Blue Annals*, Pt. 1 (Calcutta, 1949).

Bouvat L. Bouvat, *L'Empire mongol, 2-me phase* (Paris, 1927).

Bratianu G. I. Bratianu, *Recherches sur le commerce génois dans la Mer Noire au XIII–ME siècle* (Paris, 1929).

Bretschneider E. Bretschneider, *Medieval Researches from Eastern Asiatic Sources* (London, 1888; 2d ed. 1910). 2 vols.

Browne 2 E. G. Browne, *A Literary History of Persia from Firdawsi to Sa'di* (London, T. Fisher Unwin, 1906; reprinted, Cambridge, Cambridge University Press, 1928).

Browne 3 E. G. Browne, *A History of Persian Literature under Tartar Dominion* (Cambridge, Cambridge University Press, 1920).

BSOAS *Bulletin of the School of Oriental and African Languages.*

Buslaev F. I. Buslaev, *Sochineniia, 1–2* (St. Petersburg, 1908–10).

BVSAW *Berichte über die Verhandlungen der Sächsischen Akademie der Wissenschaften zu Leipzig* (Phil.-hist. Klasse).

BZ *Byzantinische Zeitschrift.*

CAH *Cambridge Ancient History.*

Cathay Colonel Sir Henry Yule, *Cathay and the Way Thither*, new edition by Henri Cordier (London, Hakluyt Society, 1914–16). 4 vols.

ČČH *Český Časopis Historický.*

Cessi R. Cessi, *Storia della Republica di Venezia* (Milano, 1944). 2 vols.

Chteniia Moscow, Universitet, Obshchestvo Istorii i Drevnostei, *Chteniia.*

Cleaves, "Chancellery" F. W. Cleaves, A Chancellery Practice of the Mongols, *HJAS, 14* (1951), 493–526.

Cleaves, Inscription I F. W. Cleaves, The Sino-Mongolian Inscription of 1362, *HJAS, 12* (1949), 1–133.

Cleaves, Inscription II F. W. Cleaves, The Sino-Mongolian Inscription of 1335, *HJAS, 13* (1950), 1–131.

Cleaves, Inscription III F. W. Cleaves, The Sino-Mongolian Inscription of 1338, *HJAS, 14* (1951), 1–104.

Cleaves, "Mongolian Names" F. W. Cleaves, The Mongolian Names and Terms in the *History of the Nation of the Archers* by Grigor of Akanc, *HJAS, 12* (1949), 400–443.

CO Collectanea Orientalia.

Cordier H. Cordier, *Histoire générale de la Chine* (Paris, 1920). 4 vols.

DDG S. V. Bakhrushin and L. V. Cherepnin, eds., *Dukhovnye i dogovornye gramoty velikikh i udelnykh kniazei XIV–XVI vekov* (Moscow and Leningrad, 1950).

Denzinger, *Enchiridion* H. Denzinger and C. Bannwart, *Enchiridion symbolorum* (14th and 15th ed. Freiburg, 1922).

Diakonov, *Ocherki* M. A. Diakonov, *Ocherki obshchestvennogo i gosudarstvennogo stroia drevnei Rusi* (4th ed. St. Petersburg, 1912).

Diakonov, *Vlast'* M. A. Diakonov, *Vlast' moskovskikh gosudarei* (St. Petersburg, 1889).

D'Ohsson M. D'Ohsson, *Histoire des Mongols* (Paris, 1824). 2 vols. This (first) edition only has been accessible to me.

Eberhard W. Eberhard, *Chinas Geschichte* (Bern, 1948).

EI *Encyclopaedia of Islam.*

Ekzempliarsky A. V. Ekzempliarsky, *Velikie i udelnye kniazia severnoi Rusi v tatarskii period* (St. Petersburg, 1889–91). 2 vols.

Eliashevich V. B. Eliashevich, *Istoriia prava pozemelnoi sobstvennosti v Rossii,* 1–2 (Paris, 1948–51).

ES Brockhaus-Efron, *Entsiklopedicheskii slovar'.*

ESA Eurasia septentrionalis antiqua.

Escarra J. Escarra, *Le Droit chinois* (Peking and Paris, 1936).

FEQ Far Eastern Quarterly.

Fletcher G. Fletcher, *On the Russ Commonwealth* (London, Hakluyt Society, 1856).

Florovsky or Florovsky, *Chekhi* A. Florovsky, *Chekhi i vostochnye slaviane* (Prague, 1935–47), 1, 2.

Franke, "Europa" H. Franke, Europa in der ostasiatischen Geschichtsschreibung des 13. und 14. Jahrhunderts, *Saeculum, 2* (1951), 65–75.

Franke, *Geld* H. Franke, *Geld und Wirtschaft in China unter der Mongolen Herrschaft* (Leipzig, 1949).

Franke, *Geschichte* O. Franke, *Geschichte des chinesischen Reiches, 4* (Berlin, 1948).

GA   Gosudarstvennaia Akademiia Istorii Materialnoi Kultury, *Izvestiia*.

Gibbon   E. Gibbon, *The Decline and Fall of the Roman Empire* (New York, Modern Library, n.d.). 2 vols.

GNP   S. N. Valk, ed., *Gramoty Velikogo Novgoroda i Pskova* (Moscow and Leningrad, 1949).

Golubinsky   E. Golubinsky, *Istoriia russkoi tserkvi* (Moscow, 1900–17). 2 vols., each in two parts.

Golubinsky, *Kanonizatsiia*   E. Golubinsky, *Istoriia kanonizatsii sviatykh v russkoi tserkvi* (2d ed. Moscow, 1903).

Golubovich   G. Golubovich, ed., *Biblioteca Bio-bibliografica della Terra Santa e dell' Oriente Franciscano* (Quaracchi, 1906–27). 5 vols.

Golubovsky   P. V. Golubovsky, *Istoriia smolenskoi zemli* (Kiev, 1895).

Gordlevsky   V. Gordlevsky, *Gosudarstvo Seldzhukidov Maloi Azii* (Moscow and Leningrad, 1941).

Grekov, *Krestiane*   B. D. Grekov, *Krestiane na Rusi s drevneishikh vremen do XVII veka* (Moscow and Leningrad, 1946).

Grigoriev, *Yarlyki*   V. Grigoriev, *O dostovernosti yarlykov dannykh khanami Zolotoi Ordy russkomu dukhovenstvu* (Moscow, 1842).

Groot   J. J. M. de Groot, *Chinesische Urkunden zur Geschichte Asiens* (Berlin and Leipzig, 1921–26), 1–2.

Grousset   R. Grousset, *L'Empire Mongol* (Paris, 1941).

Grousset, *Empire des steppes*   R. Grousset, *L'Empire des steppes* (Paris, 1939).

Grousset, *Extrême-Orient*   R. Grousset, *Histoire de l'Extrême-Orient* (Paris, 1929). 2 vols.

Grousset, *Histoire*   R. Grousset, *Histoire de l'Asie, 3* (Paris, 1922).

Grum-Grzymailo   G. E. Grum-Grzymailo (Grumm-Grzhimailo), *Zapadnaia Mongoliia i uriankhaiskii krai* (Leningrad, 1914–30), *1, 2,* and *3,* Pt. 1, Pt. 2.

Haenisch   E. Haenisch, *Die geheime Geschichte der Mongolen* (Leipzig, 1948).

Halphen   L. Halphen, *L'Essor de l'Europe, XI–XIII-me siècles* (Paris, 1932; 3d ed. Paris, 1948).

Herberstein   Baron S. Herberstein, *Zapiski o moskovitskikh delakh*, A. I. Malein, trans. (St. Petersburg, 1908).

HJAS   Harvard Journal of Asiatic Studies.

Hóman   B. Hóman and Gy. Szekfü, *Magyar Történet, 1–2* (Budapest, 1941–42).

Howorth   H. H. Howorth, *History of the Mongols* (London, Longmans, Green & Co., 1876–1927). 4 vols.

HRM   Historica Russiae monumenta, A. Turgenev, ed.

Hrushevsky   M. Hrushevsky (Grushevsky), *Istoriia Ukrainy-Rusi* (Kiev and Lvov, 1903–31). 9 vols.

Hyp.   Hypatian Codex (1st ed. *PSRL, 2*).

Iakinf   Iakinf (Bichurin), monk, trans., *Istoriia pervykh chetyrekh khanov iz doma chingisova* (St. Petersburg, 1829).

Ibn-Batuta   C. Defrémery and B. R. Sanguinetti, eds. and trans., *Voyages d'Ibn-Batoutah* (Paris, 1853–58). 4 vols.

IIM   Akademiia Nauk, Institut Istorii Materialnoi Kultury, *Kratkie soobshcheniia*.

Ikonnikov   V. S. Ikonnikov, *Opyt russkoi istoriografii* (Kiev, 1891–1908). 2 vols.

IMT   Istoricheskii Muzei, *Trudy*.

JA   Journal asiatique.

JAOS   Journal of the American Oriental Society.

JGOE   Jahrbücher für Geschichte Osteuropas.

Jireček, *Bulgaria*   H. Jireček, *Geschichte der Bulgaren* (Prague, 1876).

Jireček, *Serbia*   C. Jireček, *Geschichte der Serben, 1* (Gotha, 1911).

JNCB   Journal of the North China Branch of the Royal Asiatic Society.

JRCAS   Journal of the Royal Central Asian Society.

Karamzin   N. M. Karamzin, *Istoriia Gosudarstva Rossiiskogo* (6th ed. St. Petersburg, A. Smirdin, 1851–53). 12 vols.

Karamzin, *Notes*   *Primechaniia k istorii Gosudarstva Rossiiskogo* (6th ed. St. Petersburg, A. Smirdin, 1852–53). 12 vols.

Khara-Davan   E. Khara-Davan, *Chingis-Khan kak polkovodets i ego nasledie* (Belgrade, 1929).

Kievan Russia   G. Vernadsky, *Kievan Russia* (New Haven, Yale University Press, 1948).

Kliuchevsky or Kliuchevsky, *Kurs*   V. O. Kliuchevsky, *Kurs russkoi istorii* (American Council of Learned Societies Reprints, Russian Series, No. 14). Reproduction of the 1937 Moscow edition. 5 vols.

Kliuchevsky, *Boyarskaia Duma*   V. O. Kliuchevsky, *Boyarskaia Duma drevnei Rusi* (4th ed. Moscow, 1909).

Kliuchevsky, *Zhitiia*   V. O. Kliuchevsky, *Drevnerusskie zhitiia sviatykh kak istoricheskii istochnik* (Moscow, 1871).

Kolankowski   L. Kolankowski, *Dzieje Wielkiego Księstwa Litewskiego za Jagiellonów* (Warsaw, 1930), *1*.

Kotwicz, "Formules initiales"   W. Kotwicz, Formules initiales des documents mongols au XIII-me et XIV-me siècles, *RO, 10* (1934), 131–157.

Kotwicz, "Lettres" 1.   W. Kotwicz, En marge des lettres des il-khans de Perse, *CO, 4* (1933).

Kotwicz, "Lettres" 2.   W. Kotwicz, Quelques mots encore sur les lettres des il-khans de Perse, *CO, 10* (1936).

Kotwicz, "Mongols"   W. Kotwicz, Les Mongols, promoteurs de l'idée de paix universelle au début du XIII-e siècle, *La Pologne au VII-e Congrès*

International des Sciences Historiques (Warsaw, 1933), pp. 1–6 (of the reprint).

Kozin   S. A. Kozin, ed. and trans., *Sokrovennoe skazanie, 1* (Moscow and Leningrad, 1941).

Krause, *Cingis Han*   F. E. A. Krause, *Cingis Han* (Heidelberg, 1922).

Krause, *Geschichte*   F. E. A. Krause, *Geschichte Ostasiens* (Göttingen, 1925), *1*.

Krymsky, *Persia*   A. Krymsky, *Istoriia Persii, eë literatury i dervishskoi teosofii* (Moscow, 1909–15). 3 vols.

Krymsky, *Turkey*   A. Krymsky, *Istoriia Turechchyny* (Kiev, 1924).

Kuczyński   S. M. Kuczyński, Ziemie czernihowsko-siewierskie pod rządami Litwy, *TISU, 33* (1936).

Kulakovsky, *Alany*   Iu. Kulakovsky, *Alany po svedeniiam klassicheskikh i vizantiiskikh pisatelei* (Kiev, 1899).

Kulakovsky, *Tavrida*   Iu. Kulakovsky, *Proshloe Tavridy* (2d ed. 1914).

KUO   Kazan, Universitet, Obshchestvo Arkheologii, Istorii i Etnografii, *Izvestiia.*

Kurat   A. N. Kurat, *Topkapı Sarayi Müzesi Arşivindeki Altın Ordu, Kırım ve Türkistan Hanlarına ait yarlık ve bitikler* (Istanbul, 1940).

La Monte   J. L. La Monte, *The World of the Middle Ages* (New York, Appleton-Century–Crofts, 1949).

Latourette   K. S. Latourette, *The Chinese, Their History and Culture* (New York, Macmillan, 1934). 2 vols.

Laur.   Laurentian Codex of the Russian annals.

Likhachev   D. S. Likhachev, *Russkie letopisi* (Moscow and Leningrad, 1947).

Liubavsky   M. K. Liubavsky, *Ocherk istorii litovsko-russkogo gosudarstva* (2d ed. Moscow, 1915).

Lopez   R. Lopez, *Storia delle colonie genovese nel Mediterraneo* (Bologna, 1938).

Lot   F. Lot, *L'Art militaire et les armées au Moyen Age en Europe et dans le Proche Orient.* (Paris, 1946). 2 vols.

McGovern   W. M. McGovern, *The Early Empires of Central Asia* (Chapel Hill, University of North Carolina Press, 1939).

Makari   Makari (Bulgakov), Metropolitan, *Istoriia russkoi tserkvi* (St. Petersburg, 1888–91). 12 vols.

MAR   Arkheologicheskaia Komissiia, *Materialy po arkheologii Rossii.*

Martin   H. D. Martin, *The Rise of Chingis Khan and His Conquest of North China* (Baltimore, Johns Hopkins Press, 1950).

Matthew Paris.   See Paris, Matthew.

Menges   K. H. Menges, *The Oriental Elements in the Vocabulary of the Oldest Russian Epos, The Igor Tale.* Preface by R. Jakobson. Supplement to *Word,* Monograph No. 1 (New York, 1951).

MIAS Akademiia Nauk, Institut Istorii Materialnoi Kultury, *Materialy i issledovaniia po arkheologii SSSR.*

Miliukov, *Ocherki* P. Miliukov, *Ocherki po istorii russkoi kultury, 1* (7th ed. Moscow, 1918).

Minns E. H. Minns, *Scythians and Greeks* (Cambridge, Cambridge University Press, 1913).

Minorsky, Caucasica III V. Minorsky, Caucasica III, The Alan capital Magas and the Mongol campaigns, *BSOAS, 14* (1952), 221–238.

Minorsky, "Middle East" V. Minorsky, The Middle East in Western Politics in the 13th, 15th, and 17th Centuries, *JRCAS, 27* (1940), 427–461.

Minorsky, "Nasir al-Din" M. Minovy and V. Minorsky, Nasir al-Din Tusi on Finance, *BSOAS, 10* (1942), 755–789.

Minorsky, *Tadhkirat* V. Minorsky, ed. and trans., *Tadhkirat al-Muluk: A Manual of Safavid Administration* (London, Luzac & Co., 1943).

Moravcsik Gy. Moravcsik, *Byzantinoturcica* (Budapest, 1942–43). 2 vols.

Mostaert, "L'Ouverture du sceau" A. Mostaert, "L'Ouverture du sceau" et les adresses chez les Ordos, *MS, 1* (1935), 315–337.

Moszyński K. Moszyński, *Kultura ludowa Slowian, 2,* Fasc. 1–2 (Kraków, 1934–39).

MPMP Marco Polo, trans. Moule and Pelliot. See Sources.

MPYC Marco Polo, trans. Yule and Cordier. See Sources.

MRL G. Vernadsky, trans., *Medieval Russian Laws* (New York, Columbia University Press, 1947).

MS Monumenta serica.

MSOS Mitteilungen des Seminars für orientalische Sprachen (Berlin).

MTB Memoirs of the Research Department of the Toyo Bunko (Tokyo).

Mutafchiev P. Mutafchiev, *Istoriia na bulgarskiia narod* (Sofia, 1943–44). 2 vols.

Nasonov A. N. Nasonov, *Mongoly i Rus'* (Moscow and Leningrad, 1940).

Nasonov, *Russkaia zemlia* A. N. Nasonov, *"Russkaia zemlia" i obrazovanie territorii drevnerusskogo gosudarstva* (Moscow, 1951).

Nikon The Patriarch Nikon Chronicle.

Nikov P. Nikov, *Tataro-bulgarski otnosheniia* (Sofia, 1921).

NORAO Russkoe Arkheologicheskoe Obshchestvo, Numizmaticheskoe Otdelenie, *Zapiski.*

Novgorod The First Novgorodian Chronicle (1950 ed.).

Novgorod IV The Fourth Novgorodian Chronicle.

Novotný V. Novotný, *České dějiny, 1,* Pt. 3. (Prague, 1928).

OAK Otchet Arkheologicheskoi Kommissii.

OC Orientalia christiana.

OCP Orientalia christiana periodica.

OGN Akademiia Nauk, Otdelenie Gumanitarnykh Nauk, *Izvestiia.*

Oman   Ch. Oman, *A History of the Art of War in the Middle Ages* (2d ed. London, Methuen & Co., 1924). 2 vols.

OO   Odessa, Obshchestvo Istorii i Drevnostei, *Zapiski*.

ORSA   Russkoe Arkheologicheskoe Obshchestvo, Otdelenie russkoi i slavianskoi arkheologii, *Zapiski*.

Ostrogorsky   G. Ostrogorsky, *Geschichte des byzantinischen Staates* (Munich, 1940).

Palladi, "Kitaiskoe skazanie"   Palladi (Kafarov), Archimandrite, trans., Starinnoe kitaiskoe skazanie o Chingiskhane, *VS, 1* (1877), 149–202.

Paris, Matthew   Matthew Paris, *English History*, trans. from the Latin by J. A. Giles (London, H. C. Bohn, 1852–54). 3 vols.

Pashuto   V. T. Pashuto, *Ocherki po istorii galitsko-volynskoi Rusi* (Moscow, 1950).

Paszkiewicz   H. Paszkiewicz, *Jagiellonowie a Moskwa, 1* (Warsaw, 1933).

Paszkiewicz, *Polityka Ruska*   H. Paszkiewicz, *Polityka ruska Kazimierza Wielkiego* (Warsaw, 1925).

Pelliot   P. Pelliot, *Notes sur l'histoire de la Horde d'Or* (Paris, 1950).

Pelliot, *Campagnes*   P. Pelliot and L. Hambis, eds. and trans., *Histoire des campagnes de Gengis Khan* (Leyden, 1951), *1*.

Pelliot, "Mongols et papauté"   P. Pelliot, Les Mongols et la papauté, Pts. 1–2, *ROC, 23* (1922–23), *24* (1924). Only these two parts have been accessible to me.

Plano Carpini M   Ioann de Plano Carpini, *Istoriia Mongalov*, A. I. Malein, trans. (St. Petersburg, 1911).

Poliak, "Caractère colonial"   A. N. Poliak, Le Caractère colonial de L'Etat Mamelouk dans ses rapports avec la Horde d'Or, *REI*, 1935, 231–248.

Poliak, "Yasa"   A. N. Poliak, The Influence of Chingis-Khan's Yasa upon the General Organization of the Mameluk State, *BSOAS, 10* (1942), 862–876.

Poppe, "Opisanie"   N. Poppe, Opisanie mongolskikh 'shamanskikh' rukopisei Instituta Vostokovedeniia, *ZIV, 1* (1932), 151–200.

PPS   *Pravoslavnyi palestinskii sbornik*.

Preobrazhensky   A. Preobrazhensky, *Etymological Dictionary of the Russian Language* (New York, Columbia University Press, 1951). Reproduction of the Russian edition.

Priselkov, *Yarlyki*   M. D. Priselkov, *Khanskie yarlyki russkim mitropolitam* (Petrograd, 1916).

PSRL   *Polnoe sobranie russkikh letopisei*.

RA   *Revue archéologique*.

Radlov   V. Radlov, Yarlyki Toktamysha i Temir-Kutluga, *VOZ, 3* (1889), 1–40.

Radlov, *Versuch*   W. Radloff [V. Radlov], *Versuch eines Wörterbuches der Türk-Dialekte* (St. Petersburg, 1893–1911). 4 vols.

Rashid 1 Rashid ad-Din, Sbornik letopisei, I. N. Berezin, trans., *VOT*, *5* (1858).
Rashid 1A *Idem, VOT, 13* (1868).
Rashid 1B *Idem, VOT, 15* (1888).
Rashid 3 Rashid ad-Din, *Sbornik letopisei, 3*, A. A. Romaskevich, E. E. Bertels, and A. Iu. Iakubovsky, eds., A. K. Arends, trans. (Moscow and Leningrad, 1946).
Ratchnevsky P. Ratchnevsky, *Un code des Yuan* (Paris, 1937).
Redhouse J. W. Redhouse, *A Turkish and English Lexicon* (new impression, Constantinople, 1921).
REI Revue d'études islamiques.
RES Revue des études slaves.
Riasanovsky V. A. Riasanovsky, *Fundamental Principles of Mongol Law* (Tientsin, 1937).
RIB Russkaia istoricheskaia biblioteka.
Risch Johann de Plano Carpini, *Geschichte der Mongolen und Reisebericht*, F. Risch, trans. (Leipzig, 1930).
RO Rocznik Orientalistyczny.
ROC Revue de l'Orient chrétien.
Rockhill W. W. Rockhill, ed. and trans., *The Journey of William of Rubruck . . . with two accounts of the earlier journey of John of Pian de Carpine* (London, Hakluyt Society, 1900).
Rog. The Rogozhsky Chronicle (*Rogozhsky letopisets*).
Rybakov B. A. Rybakov, *Remeslo drevnei Rusi* (Moscow, 1948).
SA Sovetskaia arkheologiia.
Schiltberger J. Buchan Telfer, ed. and trans., *The Bondage and Travels of Johann Schiltberger* (London, Hakluyt Society, 1879).
Schmidt W. Schmidt, *Der Ursprung der Gottesidee, 9*, Die Asiatischen Hirtenvölker, die primären Hirtenvölker der Alt-Türken, der Altai- und der Abakan-Tataren (Münster and Freiburg, 1949).
Secret History. See Kozin (Russian trans.) and Haenisch (German trans.).
SEER The Slavonic and East European Review (London).
Serebriansky, *Zhitiia* N. Serebriansky, *Drevnerusskie kniazheskie zhitiia* (Moscow, 1915). Also in *Chteniia.*
Sergeevich V. I. Sergeevich, *Drevnosti russkogo prava* (St. Petersburg, 1908–11). 3 vols.
SGGD Sobranie gosudarstvennykh gramot i dogovorov (St. Petersburg, 1813–94). 5 vols.
Siyaset-nama B. N. Zakhoder, trans., Siyaset-nama, *Kniga o pravlenii vizira XI stoletiia Nizam al-Mulka* (Moscow and Leningrad, 1949).
Simeonov The Simeonov Chronicle (*Simeonovskaia letopis'*).
SK Seminarium Kondakovianum (Prague).
Smirnov, *Krymskoe Khanstvo* V. D. Smirnov, *Krymskoe Khanstvo pod verkhovenstvom Ottomanskoi Porty* (St. Petersburg, 1887).

Soloviev   S. M. Soloviev, *Istoriia Rossii s drevneishikh vremen* (1st ed. Moscow, 1851–79). 29 vols.
Soloviev, *Novgorod*   S. M. Soloviev, *Ob otnosheniiakh Novgoroda k velikim kniaziam* (Moscow, 1845).
Spuler or Spuler, *Horde*   B. Spuler, *Die goldene Horde* (Leipzig, 1943).
Spuler, *Iran*   B. Spuler, *Die Mongolen in Iran* (Leipzig, 1939).
Sreznevsky   I. I. Sreznevsky, *Materialy dlia slovaria drevnerusskogo iazyka* (St. Petersburg, 1893–1912). 3 vols.
SSRP   Scriptores rerum prussicarum (Leipzig, 1861–63), *1–2*.
Stadtmüller   G. Stadtmüller, *Geschichte Südosteuropas* (München, 1950).
Steingass   F. Steingass, *A Comprehensive Persian–English Dictionary* (London, Kegan Paul, Trench, Trübner & Co., 1892; 2d impression 1930).
Struve   P. B. Struve, Nabliudeniia i issledovaniia iz oblasti khoziastvennoi zhizni i prava drevnei Rusi, offprint from *Sbornik Russkogo Instituta v Prage, 1* (Prague, 1929).
TAS   Trudy Arkheologicheskikh S'ezdov.
Tatishchev   V. N. Tatishchev, *Istoriia rossiiskaia, 1–4* (St. Petersburg, 1768–84).
Thomsen   V. Thomsen, Alttürkische Inschriften aus der Mongolei, *ZDMG, 78* (1924), 121–175.
Tiesenhausen   V. G. Tiesenhausen [Tizengauzen], ed. and trans., *Sbornik materialov otnosiashchikhsia k istorii Zolotoi Ordy, 1* (St. Petersburg, 1884); *2* (Moscow and Leningrad, 1941).
TISU   Travaux de l' Institut Scientifique Ukrainien (Warsaw).
TO   Tavricheskoe Obshchestvo Istorii, Arkheologii i Etnografii (Simferopol), *Izvestiia.*
Togan   A. Z. V. Togan, *Tarihde usul* (Istanbul, 1950).
Tolstov, *Khorezm*   S. P. Tolstov, *Drevnii Khorezm* (Moscow, 1948).
Tolstov, *Po sledam*   S. P. Tolstov, *Po sledam drevnekhorezmiiskoi tsivilizatsii* (Moscow and Leningrad, 1948).
TP   T'oung Pao.
TPS   Transactions of the Philological Society.
Trinity   The Trinity Chronicle (*Troitskaia letopis'*), M. Priselkov's reconstruction.
UJ   Ungarische Jahrbücher.
Vasiliev, *Goths*   A. A. Vasiliev, *The Goths in the Crimea* (Cambridge, Mass., Mediaeval Academy of America, 1936).
Vasmer   M. Vasmer, *Russisches etymologisches Wörterbuch* (Heidelberg, 1950–   ). Not yet completed.
Veliaminov-Zernov   V. V. Veliaminov-Zernov, *Issledovanie o Kasimovskikh tsariakh i tsarevichakh* (St. Petersburg, 1863–87). 4 vols.
Vernadsky, "Juwaini"   G. Vernadsky, Juwaini's Version of Chingis-Khan's Yasa, *AIK, 11* (1939), 33–45.
Vernadsky, "Royal Serfs"   G. Vernadsky, The Royal Serfs (*Servi Regales*)

of the "Ruthenian Law" and Their Origin, *Speculum, 26* (1951), 255–264.

Vernadsky, "Sarmat. Hintergrund"   G. Vernadsky, Der sarmatische Hintergrund der germanischen Völkerwanderung, *Saeculum, 2* (1951), 340–392.

Vernadsky, "Uigurs"   G. Vernadsky, Notes on the History of the Uigurs in the Late Middle Ages, *JAOS, 56* (1936), 453–461.

Vernadsky, "Yasa"   G. Vernadsky, The Scope and Contents of Chingis-Khan's Yasa, *HJAS, 3* (1938), 337–360.

Vernadsky, "ZOEV"   G. Vernadsky, Zolotaia Orda, Egipet i Visantiia v ikh vzaimootnosheniiakh v tsartstvovanie Mikhaila Paleologa, *SK, 1* (1927), 73–84.

Veselovsky   N. I. Veselovsky, *Khan iz temnikov Zolotoi Ordy Nogay i ego vremia* (Petrograd, 1922).

VLU   Vestnik Leningradskogo Universiteta.

Vladimirsky-Budanov, *Khristomatiia*   M. F. Vladimirsky-Budanov, *Khristomatiia po istorii russkogo prava* (St. Petersburg and Kiev, 1908–15). 3 vols.

Vladimirsky-Budanov, *Obzor*   M. F. Vladimirsky-Budanov, *Obzor istorii russkogo prava* (7th ed. St. Petersburg and Kiev, 1915).

Vladimirtsov   B. Ia. Vladimirtsov, *Obshchestvennyi stroi Mongolov,* (Leningrad, 1934).

Vladimirtsov, *Chingis-Khan*   B. Ia. Vladimirtsov, *Chingis-Khan* (Berlin–St. Petersburg–Moscow, 1922).

Voegelin   E. Voegelin, The Mongol Orders of Submission to European Powers, 1245–1255, *Byzantion, 15* (1941), 378–413.

Voskr.   The Voskresensky Chronicle (*Voskresenskaia letopis'*).

VOT   Russkoe Arkheologicheskoe Obshchestvo, Vostochnoe Otdelenie, *Trudy.*

VOZ   Russkoe Arkheologicheskoe Obshchestvo, Vostochnoe Otdelenie, *Zapiski.*

VS   Vostochnyi sbornik, 1 (St. Petersburg, 1877).

Wassaf   *Geschichte Wassaf's,* J. Hammer-Purgstall, ed. and trans. (Vienna, 1856).

Wittfogel   K. Wittfogel and Fêng Chia-shêng, *History of Chinese Society: Liao* (Philadelphia, American Philosophical Society, 1949).

Wyngaert   A. van den Wyngaert, *Itinera et relationes fratrum minorum saeculi XIII et XIV* (Quaracchi, 1929).

Zambaur   E. Zambaur, *Manuel de généalogie et de chronologie pour l'histoire de l'Islam* (Hanovre, 1927). 2 parts and volume of tables.

ZDMG   Zeitschrift der Deutschen Morgenlandischen Gesellschaft.

Zinkeisen   J. W. Zinkeisen, *Geschichte des Osmanischen Reiches in Europa* (Hamburg, 1840–63). 7 vols.

ZIV   Zapiski Instituta Vostokovedeniia.

ZMNP   Zhurnal Ministerstva Narodnogo Prosveshcheniia.

ZO   B. D. Grekov and A. Iu. Iakubovsky, *Zolotaia Orda i ee padenie* (Moscow and Leningrad, 1950).

ZOG   *Zeitschrift für osteuropäische Geschichte.*

ZRGO   *Zapiski Russkogo Geograficheskogo Obshchestva.*

ZSP   *Zeitschrift für slavische Philologie.*

SOURCES *

I. Inscriptions

AKCHOKRAKLY, O., Staro-Krymskie i otuzskie nadpisi XIII–XV vekov, *TO*,
1 (1927), 5–17.
—— Staro-Krymskie nadpisi, *TO*, *3* (1929), 152–159.
BLOCHET, E., Les inscriptions de Samarkand, I. Le Gour-i-mir ou Tombeau
de Tamerlan, *RA*, ser. 3, *30* (1897), 67–77, 202–231.
BONAPARTE, PRINCE ROLAND, *Documents de l'époque mongole* (Paris,
1895). Inaccessible to me.
CHAVANNES, E., Inscriptions et pièces de chancellerie chinoises de l'époque
mongole, *TP*, *5* (1904), 357–447; *6* (1905), 1–42; *9* (1908), 297–425.
CLEAVES, F. W., Inscriptions I–III. See Abbreviations.
*CLEAVES, F. W., The Sino-Mongolian Inscription of 1346, *HJAS*, *15*
(1952), 1–123.
DEVÉRIA, G., Notes d'épigraphie mongole-chinoise, *JA*, ser. 9, *8* (1896),
94–128, 395–443.
HANEDA, T., Une tablette du décret sacré de l'empereur Genghis, *MTB*, *8*
(1936), 85–91.
KEMAL, IA., Nadpis' na portale "Mecheti Uzbeka" v gorode Starom Krymu,
TO, *1* (1927), 202–204.
KOTWICZ, W., Mongolskie nadpisi na Erdzeni-dzu, *Sbornik Muzeiia Antro-
pologii i Etnografii*, *5*, Fasc. 1 (Petrograd, 1918), 205–214.
LEWICKI, M., Les Inscriptions mongoles inédites en écriture carrée, *CO*, *12*
(1937).
MURAYAMA, S., Über die Inschrift auf den "Stein des Čingis," *Oriens*, *3*
(1950), 108–112 (tables 1–2).
ORLOV, A. S., *Bibliografiia russkikh nadpisei XI–XV vekov* (Moscow and
Leningrad, 1936).
PONOMAREV, A. I., Popravki k chteniiu nadpisi Timura, *Sovetskoe Vostoko-
vedenie*, *3* (1945), 222–224.
POPPE, N. N., Karasakpaiskaia nadpis' Timura, Gosudarstvennyi Ermitazh,
Trudy Otdela Vostoka, *2* (1940), 185–187.
RYBAKOV, B. A., K bibliografii russkikh nadpisei XI–XV vekov, *Istoricheskie
zapiski*, *4* (1938), 250–256.
SPITSYN, A. A., Tatarskie baisy, *AK*, *29* (1909), 133–134.

* The asterisk items are titles of publications which reached me too late to be taken
into consideration in the preparation of this volume.

II. Coins

1. Mongol

BLAU, O., and STICKEL, J. G., Zur mohammedanischen Numismatik und Epigraphik, I. Über einige mohammedanische Münzen, *ZDMG, 11* (1857), 443–459.

BLOCHET, E., Les Monnaies mongoles de la Collection Decourdemanche, *ROC, 11* (1906), 50–59, 113–129.

DROUIN, E., Notice sur les monnaies mongoles faisant partie des documents de l'époque mongole publiés par le prince Bonaparte, *JA*, ser. 9, 7 (1896), 486–544.

FRÄHN, C. M., *Recensio numorum muhammedanorum Academiae Imperialis Scientiarum Petropolitanae* (St. Petersburg, 1826).

—— *Über die Münzen der Chane vom Ulus Dschutschis oder der Goldenen Horde* (St. Petersburg, 1832).

GRIGORIEV, V. V., Monety Dzhuchidov, Genueztsev i Gireev, *OO, 1* (1844). Inaccessible to me.

—— Neskolko novykh vidov i variantov dzhuchidskikh monet, *VOT, 8* (1864), 319–354.

—— Opisanie klada iz zolotoordynskikh monet naidennogo bliz razvalin Saraya, *Zapiski St. Peterburgskogo Arkheologichesko-Numizmaticheskogo Obshchestva, 2* (1850), 1–63.

LANE-POOLE, S., *Catalogue of the Oriental Coins in the British Museum, 6: The Coins of the Mongols* (London, 1881); additions to *6* in *10* (1890), 81–138.

LIKHACHEV, A. F., Novyi klad dzhuchidskikh monet, Russkoe Arkheologicheskoe Obshchestvo, *Izvestiia, 8* (1877), 37–43.

MARKOV, A. K., *Inventarnyi katalog musulmanskikh monet Ermitazha* (St. Petersburg, 1896).

—— O monetakh Khana Nogaia, Moskovskoe Numizmaticheskoe Obshchestvo, *Trudy, 3* (1905). Inaccessible to me.

—— Serebrianaia moneta dinastii Argunidov, *Numizmaticheskii sbornik, 2* (Moscow, 1913), 319–320.

MASSON, M. E., Monetnyi klad XIV veka iz Termeza, *Bulletin de l'Université de l'Asie Centrale, 18* (Tashkent, 1929), 53–66.

SAVELIEV, P. S., Monety Dzhuchidov, Dzhagataidov, Dzhelairidov i drugie, *VOT, 3* (1858), 203–528.

—— Spisok zolotoordynskikh monet iz goroda Uveka, *KUO, 2* (1880), 171. Inaccessible to me.

SORET, F., Lettre à M. le professeur H. Brockhaus sur quelques monnaies Houlaguides, *ZDMG, 16* (1862), 417–426.

—— Neizdannye vostochnye monety, *VOT, 2* (1856), 68–112, 304–328; *4* (1859), 285–314.

TIESENHAUSEN (Tizengauzen), V. G., Numizmaticheskie novinki, *VOZ*, *6* (1892), 241–257.
—— Vostochnye monety N. P. Linevicha, *VOZ*, *4* (1889), 302–312.
VASMER, R., O dvukh zolotoordynskikh monetakh, *Zapiski Kollegii Vostokovedov*, *2* (1926), 109–112.

2. Russian

FEDOROV, G. B., Dengi Moskovskogo Kniazhestva vremeni Dmitriia Donskogo i Vasiliia I, *MIAS*, *12* (1949), 144–185.
KAUFMAN, I. I., Russkii ves, ego proiskhozhdenie i razvitie, *NORAO*, *1*, Fasc. 1 (1906), 93–183.
—— Serebrianyi rubl v Rossii, *NORAO*, *2*, Fasc. 1–2 (1910), 1–268.
MARKOV, A. K., O tipakh russkikh monet xv veka, *NORAO*, *1*, Fasc. 4 (1910), 130–137.
ORESHNIKOV, A. V., *Russkie monety do 1547 goda* (Moscow, 1896).
TOLSTOY, COUNT I. I., Dengi velikogo kniazia Dmitriia Ivanovicha Donskogo, *NORAO*, *1*, Fasc. 4 (1910), 139–154.
—— Monety velikogo kniazia Vasiliia Dmitrievicha, *NORAO*, *2*, Fasc. 3–4 (1913), 1–84.

III. ARCHEOLOGY

1. The Golden Horde and Central Asia

BALLOD, F., *Privolzhskie Pompei* (Moscow and Petrograd, 1923).
—— *Staryi i Novyi Saray* (Kazan, 1923).
BARTHOLD, W., Arkheologicheskie raboty v Samarkande letom 1924 goda, *GA*, *4* (1925), 119–132.
—— Novye dannye o samarkandskikh pamiatnikakh, *VOZ*, *25* (1921), 83–88.
BASHKIROV, A. S., and BODANINSKY, U., Pamiatniki krymsko-tatarskoi stariny, *Novyi vostok*, 8–9 (1925), 295–311.
BERNSHTAM, A. N., Chuiskaia dolina, *MIAS*, *14* (1950), 140–141 and Plates 91–94.
BLOCHET, E., *Musulman Painting XIITH–XVIITH Century*, C. M. Binyon, trans. (from the French), with an introduction by Sir E. Denison Ross (London, Methuen & Co., 1929).
BODANINSKY, U., Tatarskie mavzolei "durbe" v Krymu, *TO*, *1* (1927), 195–201.
BOROZDIN, I. N., Solkhat, *Novyi vostok*, 13–14 (1927), 271–301.
DENIKE, B., *Zhivopis' Irana* (Moscow, 1938).
ELISSÉEV, S., and others, *Histoire universelle des arts*.
    Arts musulmans–Extrême Orient (Paris, 1939). Pt.: Les Arts musulmans, by Georges Salles, pp. 54–62: "L'Art mongol et l'art timouride." Pt.: L'Art de la Chine, by S. Elisséev, pp. 351–356: "L'Epoque Yuan."

GORODTSOV, V. A., Rezultaty arkheologicheskikh issledovanii na meste goroda Madzhar, *TAS, 14*, Pt. 3, 199. Inaccessible to me.

IAKUBOVSKY, A. Iu., *Feodalizm na Vostoke. Stolitsa Zolotoi Ordy Saray Berke* (Leningrad, 1932).

―― Razvaliny Sygnaka, Gosudarstvennaia Akademiia Istorii Materialnoi Kultury, *Soobshcheniia, 2* (1930), 123–159.

―― Razvaliny Urgencha, *GA, 6*, Fasc. 2 (1930).

MARKEVICH, A. I., Poezdka v Staryi Krym, *Izvestiia Tavricheskoi Uchenoi Arkhivnoi Kommissii, 6* (1888).

―― Staro-Krymskie drevnosti, *Izvestiia Tavricheskoi Uchenoi Arkhivnoi Kommissii, 17* (1892).

NEVOSTRUEV, K. I., O gorodishchakh Volzhsko-Bolgarskogo i Kazanskogo Tsarstv, *TAS, 1* (1869). Inaccessible to me.

PILIAVSKY, V., *Urgench i Mizdakhan* (Moscow, 1948). Reviewed by B. Nikitine, *JA, 239* (1951), 255–256.

Samarkandskie mecheti, Fasc. 1, Mechet' Gur-Emir (St. Petersburg, 1905).

SMIRNOV, A. P. Bania XIV veka v Velikikh Bolgarakh, *IIM, 6* (1940), 82–88.

―― Issledovanie gorodishcha Suvar, *SA, 4* (1937), 330–332.

―― Suvar, *IMT, 16* (1941). Inaccessible to me.

SMIRNOV, Ia. I., ed., *Vostochnoe serebro* (St. Petersburg, 1905). The following numbers in this album belong to the Mongol period: 173–180, 194–198, 220–225, 227–240, 242, 244, 245, 297, 300, 321, 322.

SMOLIK, J., Die timuridischen Baudenkmäler in Samarkand aus der Zeit Tamerlans (Vienna, 1929). Inaccessible to me.

SPITSYN, A. A., K voprosu o Monomakhovoi shapke, *ORSA, 8*, Pt. 1 (1906), 146–184.

―― Tatarskie kurgany, *TO, 1* (1927), 149–153.

STASOV, V. V., *Miniatiury nekotorykh rukopisei vizantiiskikh, bolgarskikh, russkikh, dzhagataiskikh i persidskikh* (St. Petersburg, 1902).

TALITSKY, M. V., Verkhnee Prikam'e v X–XIV vekakh, *MIAS, 22* (1951), 33–96.

[TIESENHAUSEN, V. G.] Materialy dlia bibliografii musulmanskoi arkheologii. Iz bumag V. G. Tizengauzena, K. A. Inostrantsev and Ia. I. Smirnov, eds., *VOZ, 16* (1906), 079–0145, 0213–0416.

TOLSTOV, *Khorezm* (see Abbreviations), pp. 154–170.

TOLSTOV, *Po sledam* (see Abbreviations), pp. 274–295.

VESELOVSKY, N. I., Nadgrobnyi pamiatnik Timura v Samarkande, *TAS, 7*, Pt. 2 (1891), 67–72. Inaccessible to me.

―― Proizvodstvo arkheologicheskikh raskopok. Kubanskaia Oblast', *OAK* (1905–6), pp. 69–75.

Viatkin, V., Otchet o raskopkakh observatorii Ulug-Beka v 1908 i 1909 godakh, *Izvestiia Russkogo Komiteta po Izucheniiu Srednei Azii*, ser. 2, No. 1 (1912). Inaccessible to me.

Zhukovsky, V. A., Drevnosti Zakaspiiskogo Kraia, razvaliny Starogo Merva, *MAR, 16* (1894).

2. Russia

ALPATOV, M., and BRUNOV, N., *Geschichte der altrussischen Kunst* (Augsburg, 1932). Plates in a separate volume.

ARTSIKHOVSKY, A. V., ed., Materialy i issledovaniia po arkheologii Moskvy, Pts. 1–2, *MIAS, 7* (1947); *12* (1949).

—— and RYBAKOV, B. A., Raskopki na Slavne v Novgorode Velikom, *SA, 3* (1937), 179–193.

GRABAR, I., *Istoriia russkogo iskusstva* (Moscow, n.d., around 1912), *1*, 205–302, 322–330; *6*, 151–262.

KARGER, M. K., *Arkheologicheskie issledovaniia Kieva* (Kiev, 1951).

LOUKOMSKI, G. K., *L'Architecture religieuse russe du XI-me siècle au XVII-me* (Paris, 1929).

NEKRASOV, A. I., *Ocherki po istorii drevnerusskogo zodchestva XI–XVII vekov* (Moscow, 1936).

PORFIRIDOV, N. G., *Drevnii Novgorod* (Moscow and Leningrad, 1947).

RYBAKOV. See Abbreviations.

SOLNTSEV, F. G., illustrator, *Drevnosti rossiiskogo gosudarstva* (Moscow, 1849–53). 6 vols.

STROKOV, A. A., Otchet ob arkheologicheskikh rabotakh v Staroi Russe v 1939 godu, *Novgorodskii istoricheskii sbornik*, B. D. Grekov, ed., *7* (1940), 19–31. This is the only volume of *NIS* available to me.

—— Raskopki v Novgorode v 1940 godu, *IIM, 11* (1945), 65–73.

—— and BOGUSEVICH, V. A., Predvaritelnyi otchet o raskopkakh v Novgorode v 1939 godu, *Novgorodskii istoricheskii sbornik, 7*, 3–18.

TARAKANOVA, S. A., K voprosu o krepostnykh stenakh Pskova, *IIM, 13* (1946), 77–80.

VORONIN, N. N., *Drevnerusskie goroda* (Moscow and Leningrad, 1945).

—— *Ocherki po istorii russkogo zodchestva* (Moscow, 1934). Inaccessible to me.

IV. DOCUMENTS

A. Documents of the Mongol Empire and of the Regional Khanates

I. THE GREAT YASA OF CHINGIS-KHAN

No full authentic text has been preserved.
For partial accounts of the contents see the following:
AB-UL-FARAJ, Latin trans. by Bruns and Kirsch, *1*, 449–451.
  English trans. by Budge, *1*, 354–355.

JUWAINI, Persian text, Mirza Muhammad, ed., pp. 16–25; for English trans., see Vernadsky, "Juwaini."

MAKRIZI, Al-, Excerpt on the Yasa, Silvestre de Sacy, ed. and trans., *Chrestomatie arabe*, 2 (1826), 160–164.

Russian trans., Berezin (see Abbreviations), pp. 409–413.

English version, Riasanovsky (see Abbreviations), pp. 83–85.

RASHID AD-DIN, see below.

2. CHINGIS-KHAN'S MAXIMS (BILIK)

RASHID 1B, pp. 120–131; English trans. by Riasanovsky, pp. 86–91. See also Berezin (as in Abbreviations), pp. 484–487.

3. DOCUMENTS OF THE GREAT KHANS AND OF THE REGIONAL KHANS

ABEL-RÉMUZAT, M., Mémoires sur les relations politiques des princes chrétiens, et particulièrement des rois de France, avec les empereurs mongols, *Mémoires de l'Institut Royal de France*, 6–7 (1822–24).

*CLEAVES, F. W., The Mongolian Documents in the Musée de Téhéran (forthcoming in *HJAS*).

HAENISCH, E., Zu den Briefen der mongolischen Il-Khane Argun und Öljeitu an den König Philipp den Schönen von Frankreich, *Oriens*, 2 (1949), 216–235.

KOTWICZ, "Lettres" 1, 2. See Abbreviations.

*MOSTAERT, A., and CLEAVES, F. W., Trois documents mongols des Archives Secrètes Vaticanes (forthcoming in *HJAS*).

PELLIOT, P., Les Documents mongols du Musée de Teheran, *Athar-e Iran*, *1* (1936), 31–44.

—— *Mongols et papauté* (see Abbreviations), *1*, 15–16.

VOEGELIN. See Abbreviations.

4. THE YARLYKS OF THE KHANS OF THE GOLDEN HORDE

BEREZIN, I. N., *Khanskie Yarlyki* (Kazan, 1850–51). 3 vols. Inaccessible to me.

—— Tarkhannye yarlyki Krymskikh Khanov, *OO*, *8* (1872). Inaccessible to me.

—— Yarlyki krymskikh khanov Mengli-Gireiia i Muhammed-Gireiia, *oo*, *8* (1872). Inaccessible to me.

GRIGORIEV, *Yarlyki*. See Abbreviations.

GRIGORIEV, V. V., and IARTSOV, I. O., Yarlyki Tokhtamysha i Seadet-Gireiia, *OO*, *1* (1844). Inaccessible to me.

KURAT. See Abbreviations.

OBOLENSKY, PRINCE M. A., ed., *Yarlyk Khana Zolotoi Ordy Tokhtamysha k polskomu koroliu Iagailu 1392–1393 g.* (Kazan, 1850). Inaccessible to me.

Priselkov, *Yarlyki*. See Abbreviations.

Radlov. See Abbreviations.

Samoilovich, A. N., Neskolko popravok k izdaniiu i perevodu yarlykov Tokhtamysh-khana, *TO, 1* (1927), 141–144.

—— Neskolko popravok k yarlyku Timur-Kutluga, *AN*, 1918, pp. 1109–1122.

B. Documents of the Russian Lands and of the Grand Duchy of Lithuania

I. INTERNATIONAL AND REGIONAL TREATIES; PRINCELY WILLS

Bakhrushin, S. V., ed., *Dukhovnye i dogovornye gramoty kniazei velikikh i udelnykh* (Moscow, 1909).

—— and Cherepnin, L. V., eds., *Dukhovnye i dogovornye gramoty velikikh i udelnykh kniazei XIV–XVI vekov* (Moscow and Leningrad, 1950).

Goetz, L. K., ed., *Deutsch-russische Handelsverträge des Mittelalters* (Hamburg, 1916).

Sobranie gosudarstvennykh gramot i dogovorov, 1–2 (Moscow, 1813–19).

2. LAWS

The Charter of Dvina Land (1397). Old Russian text, *AAE, 1*, No. 13; reprinted in Vladimirsky-Budanov, *Khristomatiia, 1*, 121–126. English trans., *MRL*, pp. 57–60.

The Charter of the City of Pskov (1397–1467). Phototypic reproduction of the MS, *Pskovskaia Sudnaia Gramota* (St. Petersburg, 1914); first edition, N. N. Murzakevich, ed. (Odessa, 1847; reprinted, 1868); reprinted, Vladimirsky-Budanov, *Khristomatiia, 1*, 128–162; modern Russian trans. by L. V. Cherepnin, and A. I. Iakovlev, *Istoricheskie zapiski, 6* (1940), 237–299. English trans., *MRL*, pp. 61–82.

3. DOCUMENTS OF NOVGOROD AND PSKOV

Bakhrushin, S. V., ed., *Pamiatniki Velikogo Novgoroda* (Moscow, 1909).

Valk, S. N., ed., *Gramoty Velikogo Novgoroda i Pskova* (Moscow and Leningrad, 1949).

4. DOCUMENTS OF THE GRAND-DUCHY OF LITHUANIA

Danilowicz, I., *Skarbiec Dyplomatow* (Wilno, 1860–62). 2 vols.

Dovnar-Zapolsky, M. V., Akty litovsko-russkogo gosudarstva, *Chteniia* (1899), Pt. 4.

Litovskaia metrika (Register of the Grand Duchy of Lithuania). Most of the documents of these files belong to the post-Mongol period.

Akty litovskoi metriki, F. I. Leontovich, ed. (Warsaw, 1896–97). 2 vols.
Litovskaia metrika, *RIB, 20* (1903), *27* (1910), *30* (1914).
LIUBAVSKY (see Abbreviations), pp. 297–376.
PASZKIEWICZ, H., ed., *Regesta Lithuaniae, 1* (Warsaw, 1930). Inaccessible to me.
PROCHASKA, A., Codex epistolaris Vitoldi, *Monumenta medii aevi historica res gestas Poloniae illustrantia, 6* (1882).
Volumina Legum, 1 (St. Petersburg, 1859). Inaccessible to me.

5. DOCUMENTS OF THE RUSSIAN CHURCH

PAVLOV, A. S., ed., Pamiatniki drevnerusskogo kanonicheskogo prava, *RIB, 6* (1880).
PRISELKOV, M. D., and VASMER, M. Otryvki V. N. Beneshevicha po istorii russkoi tserkvi XIV veka, *ANORI, 21,* Pt. 1 (1916), 48–70.

6. COLLECTIONS OF MISCELLANEOUS DOCUMENTS OF THE MONGOL AND POST-MONGOL PERIODS

Akty istoricheskie (St. Petersburg, 1841–42). 5 vols.
Akty iuridicheskie (St. Petersburg, 1838).
Akty otnosiashchiesia k istorii iuzhnoi i zapadnoi Rossii (St. Petersburg, 1863–92). 15 vols.
Akty otnosiashchiesia k istorii zapadnoi Rossii (St. Petersburg, 1846–53). 5 vols.
Akty sobrannye Arkheograficheskoiu Ekspeditsieiu (St. Petersburg, 1836). 3 vols.
Arkhiv iugo-zapadnoi Rossii (Kiev). Ser. 1, *1–9* (1859–93); ser. 2, *1* (1861); ser. 3, *1–3* and *5* (1863–1902); ser. 6, *1, 2, 4, 6* (1876–1911); ser. 7, *1–2* (1886–90).
Historica Russiae monumenta, A. I. Turgenev, ed., *1* (St. Petersburg, 1841).
Russkaia Istoricheskaia Biblioteka (St. Petersburg, 1872–1927). 39 vols.

V. CHRONICLES

A. Mongol and Tibetan

1. The Secret History of the Mongols (*Monghol-un Niuča Tobča'an;* Chinese paraphrase: *Yüan Ch'ao Pi Shi*). Mongol text edited by E. Haenisch, *Mangchol un Niutscha Tobtscha'an* (Leipzig, 1935–39) 2 vols.; by S. A. Kozin (see below), pp. 203–302; by P. Pelliot (see below), pp. 5–120. Russian trans. by Palladi (Palladius) Kafarov, Starinnoe mongolskoe skazanie o Chingiskhane, *Trudy chlenov Rossiiskoi Dukhovnoi Missii v Pekine, 4* (1866), 23–160; by S. A. Kozin, *Sokrovennoe skazanie, 1* (Moscow and Leningrad, 1941), 79–199.
German trans. by E. Haenisch, *Die geheime Geschichte der Mongolen* (Leipzig, 1948).

French trans. (of sects. 1–185) by P. Pelliot, *Histoire secrète des Mongols* (Paris, 1949), pp. 121–196.
Turkish trans. by A. Temir, *Moğollarin Gizli Tarihi* (Ankara, 1948).
2. *The Blue Annals* [Tibetan], Pt. 1, G. N. Roerich, ed. and trans. (Royal Asiatic Society of Bengal, Monograph Ser., No. 7, Calcutta, 1949).
3. Altan Tobči (The Golden Epitome).
Edited and trans. into Russian by Galsan Gomboev, *VOT, 6* (1858), pp. 1–116 (Mongol text) and pp. 117–197 (Russian trans.)
*Edited by F. W. Cleaves, preface by A. Mostaert (Cambridge, Harvard University Press, 1952).
4. SANANG-SECEN, *History of the East Mongols*. Ed. and trans. into German by I. J. Schmidt, *Geschichte der Ost-Mongolen und ihres Fürstenhauses verfasst von Ssanang Ssetsen* (St. Petersburg, 1829).

B. Chinese

1. History of Chingis-Khan's Campaigns (*Wu Ch'in Cheng Lu*). Russian trans. by Palladi (Palladius) Kafarov, Starinnoe kitaiskoe skazanie o Chingiskhane, *VS, 1* (1877), 149–202. French trans. by P. Pelliot and L. Hambis, *Histoire des campagnes de Gengis Khan, 1* (Leyden, 1951).
2. History of the Yuan Dynasty (*Yüan Shi*). Partial Russian trans. by Iakinf (Hyacinthus) Bichurin, *Istoriia pervykh chetyrekh khanov iz doma Chingisova* (St. Petersburg, 1829); partial German trans. by F. E. A. Krause, *Cingis Han* (Heidelberg, 1922).

C. Arabic and Persian

1. IBN AL-ATHIR, *Chronicon*, C. J. Tornberg, ed., *12* (Leyden, 1853).
Partial Russian trans. by A. A. Kunik, Vypiska iz Ibn-el-Atira o pervom nashestvii tatar na kavkazskie i chernomorskie strany s 1220 po 1224 god, *Uchenye Zapiski Imperatorskoi Akademii Nauk po I i III otdeleniiu, 2*, Fasc. 4 (1854), 636–668.
2. AN-NASAWI, MUHAMMAD.
Histoire du Sultan Djelal ed-Din Mankobirti, prince du Kharezm, O. Houdas, ed. and trans., *Publications de l'Ecole des Langues Orientales Vivantes*, ser. 3, *9* (1891), Arabic text; and *10* (1895), French trans.
3. Juwaini, Ala ad-Din Ata Malik, *Tarikh-i Jahan Gusha* (History of the World Conqueror), Mirza Muhammad, ed. (Leyden and London, Gibb Memorial Series, 1912).
Chapter on the Great Yasa trans. into Russian by V. F. Minorsky, Appendix I to G. Vernadsky, *O sostave Velikoi Yasy Chingis Khana* (Bruxelles, 1939), pp. 40–50; into English by G. Vernadsky, *AIK, 11* (1939), 33–45.
Excerpt on Mongol Campaigns in the West, trans. by J. A. Boyle, Minorsky, Caucasica III, pp. 222–223.

4. Rashid ad-Din, Fadla'llah, *Jami at-Tawarikh* (Collection of Chronicles).
Vol. *1*. Introduction and History of Chingis-Khan.
Persian text, I. N. Berezin, ed., Sbornik letopisei, istoriia Mongolov,
VOT, 7, 13, 15 (1861–88).
Russian trans., I. N. Berezin, *VOT, 5, 13, 15*.
*New Russian trans., A. A. Semenov, ed. Pt. 1, A. A. Khetagurov, trans.;
Pt. 2, O. I. Smirnova, trans. (Moscow and Leningrad, 1952).
Excerpt on Western Campaigns, trans. into English by V. F. Minorsky,
Caucasica III, pp. 224–228.
Vol. *2*. History of Chingis-Khan's Successors.
Persian text, E. Blochet, ed., *Djami el-Tévarikh* (London, Gibb Memorial
Series, 1911).
Partial French trans., H. J. Klaproth, *JA*, ser. 2, *11* (1833), 335–358 and
447–470.
English version of the above, *Cathay* (see Abbreviations), *3*, 105–133.
Vol. *3*. History of the Mongols in Persia.
Persian text, M. Quatremère, ed., *Histoire des Mongols de Perse, 1* (Paris,
1836); K. Jahn, ed., *Tarih-i-mubarak-i Gazani des Rašid al-Din. Ge-
schichte der Ilhane Abaga bis Gaihatu* (Prague, 1941); K. Jahn, ed.,
Geschichte Gazan-Hans (London, Gibb Memorial Series, 1940).
French trans., M. Quatremère (as above).
Russian trans., A. K. Arends. See Abbreviations.
5. WASSAF. See Abbreviations.
6. NIZAM AD-DIN SHAMI, *Zafar-nama* (Book of Victories).
Tauer, F., ed., *Histoire des conquêtes de Tamerlan, intitulé Zafarnamah*
(Prague, Oriental Institute, 1937).
Excerpts in Russian trans., Tiesenhausen, *2*, 105–125; *Materialy po
istorii Turkmen* (see No. 11 below), *1*, 511–524.
7. Sharaf ad-Din Ali Yazdi, *Zafar-nama* (Book of Victories).
Persian text, Mawlawi Muhammad Ilahdad, ed., *The Zafarnamah* (Cal-
cutta, 1885–88). 2 vols.
French trans., Petis de la Croix, F., *L'Histoire du Timur-Bec connu sous
le nom du Grand Tamerlan* (Paris, 1722).
English trans. (from the French), *The History of Timur-Bec, known by
the name of Tamerlain the Great, Emperor of the Monguls and Tatars*
(London, 1723). 2 vols.
Chapters on Timur's campaign against Tokhtamysh of 1391, French
trans. by M. Charmoy, Expédition de Timour-i-lenk ou Tamerlan contre
Toqtamiche, *Mémoires de l'Académie Impériale des Sciences de St. Petersbourg*, ser. 6, *3* (1836), 172–243.
8. IBN-ARABSHAH, AHMAD, Life and Deeds of Timur.
S. H. Manger, ed. and trans. (into Latin), *Ahmed Arabsiadae vitae et
rerum gestarum Timuri, qui vulgo Tamerlanes dicitur, historia* (Leeuwar-
den, 1767–72).

English trans., J. H. Sanders, *Tamerlane or Timur the Great Amir* (London, 1937). Inaccessible to me.

French trans. of chap. 8 (Timur's expedition against Tokhtamysh of 1391) by Charmoy (see No. 7 above), pp. 419–421.

9. Ibn-Khaldun, Autobiography.

Chapter on Ibn-Khaldun's meeting with Timur in 1401, W. J. Fischel, ed. and trans., *Ibn-Khaldun and Tamerlane* (Berkeley and Los Angeles, University of California Press, 1952).

10. Tiesenhausen (Tizengauzen), V. G., ed. and trans., *Sbornik materialov otnosiashchikhsia k istorii Zolotoi Ordy: 1*, Arabic Sources (St. Petersburg, 1884); *2*, Persian Sources, Romaskevich and S. L. Volin, eds. (Moscow and Leningrad, 1941).

Selected excerpts from the above listed and other Arabic and Persian writers, with Russian trans.

11. Volin, S. L., Romaskevich, A. A., and Iakubovsky, A. Iu., eds., *Materialy po istorii Turkmen i Turkmenii, 1* (Moscow and Leningrad, 1939), 469–541.

Selection of Arabic and Persian sources bearing on the history of Central Asia in the Mongol period, in Russian translation.

12. HAYDAR DUGHLAT, MIRZA MUHAMMAD, *Tarikh-i-Rashidi*.

English version, N. Elias, ed., E. D. Ross, trans., *A History of the Moghuls of Central Asia* (London, S. Low, Marston & Co., 1895, re-issue, 1898).

D. Armenian, Georgian, Greek, Syriac

1. ARMENIAN AND GEORGIAN

BROSSET, M. F., *Histoire de la Géorgie, 1* (St. Petersburg, 1849).

DULAURIER, E., Les Mongols d'après les historiens armeniens, *JA*, ser. 5, *11* (1858).

GRIGOR OF AKANC, History of the Nation of the Archers, R. P. Blake and R. N. Frye, eds. and trans., *HJAS, 12* (1949), 269–399.

Russian trans. by K. Patkanov, *Istoriia Mongolov inoka Magakiia* [i.e. Grigor of Akanc] (St. Petersburg, 1871).

PATKANOV, K., *Istoriia Mongolov po armianskim istochnikam* (St. Petersburg, 1873–74). 2 vols.

[VARDAN] *Vseobshchaia istoriia Vardana Velikogo*, N. Emin, trans. (Moscow, 1861).

2. GREEK

CHALCOCONDYLES, L., *Historiarum demonstrationes*. I. Bekker, ed. (Bonn, 1843); E. Darkó, ed. (Budapest, 1922–27). 2 vols.

DUKAS (DUCAS), *Historia byzantina*, I. Bekker, ed. (Bonn, 1834).

GREGORAS, NIKEPHOROS, *Historia romana*, L. Schopen and I. Bekker, eds. (Bonn, 1829, 1830, 1855). 3 vols.

Russian trans., P. Shalfeev, *Rimskaia istoriia Nikifora Grigory*, *1* (St. Petersburg, 1862).

PACHYMERES, GEORGIOS, *De Michaele et Andronico Palaeologis libri XIII.* I. Bekker, ed. (Bonn, 1835). 2 vols.
Russian trans., V. N. Karpov, ed., *Georgiia Pakhimera istoriia o Mikhaile i Andronike Paleologakh*, *1* (St. Petersburg, 1862).

PHRANTZES, GEORGIOS, *Chronicon.* I. Bekker, ed. (Bonn, 1838); J. B. Papadopoulos, ed. *1* (Leipzig, 1935).

3. SYRIAC

AB-UL-FARAJ, GREGORY (Bar Hebraeus), *Chronographia.*
Latin trans., P. Bruns and G. G. Kirsch, eds. and trans. (Leipzig, 1788).
English trans., E. A. W. Budge, ed. and trans. (London, 1932).

E. Russian

The Chronography (*Khronograf*) of 1512, *PSRL, 22*, Fasc. 1 (1911).
The V. D. Ermolin Chronicle (*Ermolinskaia letopis'*), *PSRL, 23* (1910).
The Galician and Volynian Chronicle. See the Hypatian Codex.
The Gustynsky Monastery Chronicle (*Gustynskaia letopis'*). Published as Appendix to the Hypatian Codex, *PSRL, 2* (1843), 233–373.
The Hypatian Codex. Contains the Book of Annals (see *Kievan Russia*, p. 371); the Kievan Chronicle; and the Galician and Volynian Chronicle. Published in *PSRL* and separately. *PSRL, 2*, 1st ed. 1843 (does not include the Book of Annals); 2d ed. 1871; Fasc. 1, 3d ed. 1923. Separately, A. Shakhmatov, ed. (1908).
The Kazan Chronicle (*Kazanskii letopisets*), *PSRL, 19* (1903).
The Laurentian Codex. Contains the Book of Annals and the Suzdalian Chronicle. Published in *PSRL, 1*, 1st ed. 1846; 2d ed. Fasc. 1: The Book of Annals (1926); Fasc. 2: The Suzdalian Chronicle (1927); Fasc. 3: The Continuation of the Suzdalian Chronicle (1928).
The N. A. Lvov Chronicle (*Lvovskaia letopis'*), *PSRL, 20*, Pts. 1–2 (1910–14).
The Patriarch Nikon Chronicle (*Patriarshaia ili nikonovskaia letopis'*), *PSRL, 9–13* (1862–1906).
The Novgorodian Chronicles.
The First Novgorodian Chronicle, *PSRL, 3* (1841); separately, *Novgorodskaia letopis' po sinodalnomu kharateinomu spisku* (St. Petersburg, 1888); *Novgorodskaia pervaia letopis'*, A. N. Nasonov, ed. (Moscow and Leningrad, 1950).
English trans., R. Mitchell and N. Forbes, with an introduction by C. R. Beazley, in *Camden Third Series, 25* (London, 1914).
Latin trans. of the section of the First Novgorodian Chronicle containing a narrative of the Fourth Crusade, A.D. 1204 [1950 ed., pp. 46–49;

variant, pp. 240–246], C. Hopf, ed., *Chroniques greco-romanes inédites ou peu connues* (Berlin, 1873), pp. 93–98. Inaccessible to me.

Spanish trans., based on the Latin, Sara Isabel de Mundo, La Cuarta Cruzada segun el cronista Novgorodense, *Anales de historia antigua y medieval,* 1950 (Buenos Aires, 1951), pp. 135–141.

The Second Novgorodian Chronicle, *PSRL, 3* (1841); 2d ed. A. F. Bychkov, *Novgorodskie letopisi* (St. Petersburg, 1879).

The Third Novgorodian Chronicle, Bychkov, *op. cit.*

The Fourth Novgorodian Chronicle, *PSRL, 4* (1848); 2d ed. Fascs. 1–3 (1915–29).

The Pskovian Chronicles, *1.* The First Pskovian Chronicle (*Pskovskaia pervaia letopis'*), A. N. Nasonov, ed. (Moscow and Leningrad, 1941).

The Rogozhsky Library Chronicle (*Rogozhskii letopisets*), *PSRL, 15* (2d ed.), Fasc. 1 (1922).

The St. Sophia Annals (*Sofiiskii Vremennik*), P. M. Stroev, ed. (St. Petersburg, 1820). 2 vols.

The N. Simeonov Chronicle (*Simeonovskaia letopis'*), *PSRL, 18* (1913).

The Suzdalian Chronicle. See the Laurentian Codex.

The Synodal Printing Office Chronicle (*Tipografskaia letopis'*), *PSRL, 24* (1921).

The Trinity Monastery Chronicle (*Troitskaia letopis'*). Text reconstructed by M. D. Priselkov, *Troitskaia letopis'* (Moscow and Leningrad, 1950).

The Tverian Chronicle (*Tverskaia letopis'*), *PSRL, 15* (1863).

The Ustiugian Digest of Chronicles (*Ustiuzhskii letopisnyi svod*), K. N. Serbina, ed. (Moscow and Leningrad, 1950).

The Voskresensky Monastery Chronicle (*Voskresenskaia letopis'*) *PSRL, 7–8* (1856–59).

The West Russian Chronicles (*Zapadnorusskie letopisi*), *PSRL, 17* (1907).

VI. Travels

AGREFENI, ARCHIMANDRITE, *Khozhdenie* (Itinerary to Jerusalem), Archimandrite Leonid, ed., *PPS, 48* (1896).

AVRAAMI, Bishop of Suzdal, *Otryvki* (Fragments of a Journey to Florence), A. Popov, *Istoriko-literaturnyi obzor drevne-russkikh polemicheskikh sochinenii protiv latinian* (Moscow, 1875), pp. 400–406. Inaccessible to me.

[BARBARO,GIOSAFAT], *Travels to Tana and Persia by Josafa Barbaro and Ambrogio Contarini,* W. Thomas, trans., Lord Stanley of Alderley, ed. (London, Hakluyt Society, 1873).

BATUTA, IBN, *Travels.* See Ibn-Batuta (Abbreviations).

BENEDICT THE POLE, Friar, *Relation of Journey to Mongolia.*
Latin text, Wyngaert, pp. 134–143.
English trans., Rockhill. See Abbreviations.

Friar Benedict was a member of John of Plano Carpini's mission.

EPIFANI, Monk, *Skazanie o puti k Ierusalimu* (Tale of the Journey to Jerusalem), Archimandrite Leonid, ed., *PPS, 15* (1887).

GONZÁLEZ DE CLAVIJO, R., *Embajada a Tamorlan*, F. López Estrada, ed. (Madrid, 1943).

Russian trans., I. I. Sreznevsky, ed. Dnevnik puteshestviia ko dvoru Timura v Samarkand v 1403–1406 godakh, *ANORS, 28* (1881).

English trans., C. R. Markham, *Narrative of the Embassy of Ruy Gonzales de Clavijo to the Court of Timur* (London, Hakluyt Society, 1859).

IGNATI OF SMOLENSK, Deacon, *Khozhdenie* (Itinerary to Jerusalem), S. V. Arseniev, ed., *PPS, 12* (1887).

JOHN OF PLANO CARPINI, *History of the Mongols and Journey to Mongolia*.
Latin text, Wyngaert, pp. 27–130.
English trans. (of the *Journey* only), Rockhill. See Abbreviations.
German trans., Risch. See Abbreviations.
Russian trans., D. Yazykov, *Sobranie puteshestvii k Tataram* (St. Petersburg, 1825), pp. 7–63; A. I. Malein, *Ioann de Plano Karpini, Istoriia Mongalov; Vilgelm de Rubruk, Puteshestvie v vostochnye strany* (St. Petersburg, 1911), pp. 1–62.

JULIAN, FRIAR, and Other Hungarian Missionaries, *Journey to Great Hungary*.
Bendefy, L., ed., Fontes authentici itinera fr. Iulianii (1235–38) illustrantes, *Archivum Europae Centro-Orientalis, 3* (1937), 1–52. Cf. J. Bromberg, Zur Geographie der Reisen des Dominikaners Julian, *Finnischugrische Forschungen, 26* (1940), Anzeiger, pp. 60–73.
Anninsky, S. A., ed. and trans. (into Russian), Izvestiia Vengerskikh missionerov XIII–XIV vekov o Tatarakh i vostochnoi Evrope, *Istoricheskii Arkhiv, 3* (1940), 95–112; Russian trans., pp. 77–94.
*Sinor, D., Un voyageur du treizième siècle, le Dominicain Julien de Hongrie, *BSOAS, 14* (1952), 589–602.

LANNOY, GHILLEBERT DE, *Oeuvres*, Ch. Potvin and J. Ch. Houzeau, eds. (Louvin, 1878), pp. 9–72.

MICHAEL, Bishop of Smolensk, and SERGIUS, ARCHIMANDRITE, Khozhenie Piminovo v Tsargrad (Bishop Pimin's Journey to Constantinople), *PSPL, 11*, 95–104.

ODORIC OF PORDENONE, Travels.
Latin text, Wyngaert, pp. 413–495.
English trans., H. Yule and H. Cordier, *Cathay* (see Abbreviations), *2*.

POLO, MARCO, Travels.
The Book of Ser Marco Polo, the Venetian, Colonel Sir Henry Yule, trans., 3d ed. revised by H. Cordier (London, J. Murray, 1903). 2 vols.
The Description of the World, trans. and annotated by A. C. Moule and P. Pelliot (London, G. Routledge & Sons), *1* (1938).

SCHILTBERGER, HANS, Travels.

German editions: (1) K. F. Neumann, ed., Fallmerayer and Hammer-Purgstall, commentators, *Reisen des Johannes Schiltberger aus München in Europa, Asia und Afrika von 1394 bis 1427* (München, 1859); (2) V. Langmantel, ed., *Hans Schiltbergers Reisebuch* (Tübingen, 1885).

English trans., Commander J. Buchan Telfer, *The Bondage and Travels of Johann Schiltberger* (London, Hakluyt Society, 1879).

Russian trans., F. Brun, Puteshestvie Ivana Shiltbergera, *Zapiski Novorossiiskogo Universiteta, 1* (Odessa, 1867). Inaccessible to me.

SIMEON OF SUZDAL, HIEROMONK, *Isidorov Sobor i khozhenie ego* (Journey to the Council of Florence), A. Popov, *Obzor* (see Avraami, above), pp. 344–359. Inaccessible to me. Cf. *PSRL, 8,* 100–106.

VARSONOFI, HIEROMONK, Khozhdenie k sviatomu gradu Ierusalimu (Itinerary to Jerusalem), S. O. Dolgov, ed., *PPS, 45* (1896).

WILLIAM OF RUBRUCK, FRIAR, Journey to Mongolia.

Latin text, Wyngaert, pp. 164–332.

English trans. See Rockhill (Abbreviations).

German trans., F. Risch, *Wilhelm von Rubruck: Reise zu den Mongolen 1253–1255* (Leipzig, 1934).

Russian trans., A. I. Malein (see John of Plano Carpini), pp. 65–178.

ZOSIMA, HIERODEACON, *Xenos sirech Strannik* (Xenos i.e. Wanderer), Kh. M. Loparev, ed., *PPS, 24* (1889).

BASIC BIBLIOGRAPHY

I. HANDBOOKS

BIRGE, J. K., *A Guide to Turkish Area Study* (Washington, D.C., American Council of Learned Societies, 1949).

Encyclopaedia of Islam (London, Luzac & Co., 1913–36). 4 vols. Turkish ed., revised and enlarged, *Islam ansiklopedisi, 1*—(Istanbul, 1940—). Not yet completed.
Articles on Turkish subjects rewritten by Turkish specialists and greatly expanded.

PHILIPS, C. H., *Handbook of Oriental History* (London, Royal Asiatic Society, 1951).

STRAKHOVSKY, L., ed., *A Handbook of Slavic Studies* (Cambridge, Harvard University Press, 1949).

TOGAN, A. ZEKI VELIDI, *Tarihde usul* (Istanbul, 1950).

II. BIBLIOGRAPHICAL OUTLINES AND REVIEWS

Bibliografiia Vostoka. 1, Istoriia (1917–1925), D. N. Egorov, ed. (Moscow, 1928).

FRANKE, H., Neuere Gesamtdarstellungen der Geschichte Chinas, *Saeculum, 1* (1950), 318–323.

GLAZER, S. S., Bibliography of Periodical Literature on the Near and Middle East (reprinted from *The Middle East Journal*). *1* (1947)—

GROUSSET, R., *Histoire de l'Extrême-Orient, 2, Eléments de bibliographie,* chap. 3, Les Mongols, 672–677.

KERNER, R. J., *Northeastern Asia, a Selected Bibliography* (Berkeley, University of California Press, 1939). 2 vols.

—— *Slavic Europe: A Bibliography* (Cambridge, Harvard University Press, 1918).

KRAUSE, F. E. A., Die Epoche der Mongolen, *MSOS, 26-27* (1924), 46–49.

Library of Congress, *Monthly List of Russian Accessions* (Washington, D.C.), *1* (1948)—

LOEWENTHAL, R., A Bibliography of Near and Middle Eastern Studies published in the Soviet Union from 1937 to 1947, *Oriens, 4* (1951), 328–344.

—— Works on the Far East and Central Asia published in the U.S.S.R., 1937–47, *FEQ, 8* (1948–49), 172–183.

POPPE, N., Russische Arbeiten auf dem Gebiet der Mongolistik 1914–24, *AM, 1* (1924), 676–681.

SPULER (see Abbreviations), pp. 455–525: Verzeichnis des Schrifttums.

SPULER, *Iran* (see Abbreviations), pp. 465–502: Verzeichnis des Schrifttums.

III. HISTORICAL GEOGRAPHY AND ETHNOGRAPHY

AHMAD, N., *Muslim Contribution to Geography* (Lahore, 1947).

ARISTOV, N. A., Zametki ob etnicheskom sostave tiurkskikh plemen i narodnostei, *Zhivaia starina*, 1896, *3–4*. Reviewed by W. Barthold, *VOZ*, *11* (1899), 341–356.

BARTHOLD, W., *Istoriia izucheniia Vostoka v Evrope i Rossii* (St. Petersburg, 1911; 2d ed. Leningrad, 1925).

German ed., Ramberg-Figulla, E., trans., *Die geographische und historische Erforschung des Orient* (Leipzig, 1913).

French ed., *La Découverte de l'Asie*, B. Nikitine, trans. and annotator (Paris, 1947).

—— *Orta Asya Türk tarihi hakkında dersler* (Istanbul, 1927.).

German ed., *12 Vorlesungen über die Geschichte der Türken Mittelasiens*, Th. Menzel, trans. (Berlin, 1935).

French ed., *Histoire des Turcs d'Asie centrale*, M. Donskis, trans., (Paris, 1945).

—— Svedeniia ob Aralskom more i nizoviakh Amu-Dar'i s drevneishikh vremen do XVII veka, *Izvestiia Turkestanskogo Otdela Russkogo Geograficheskogo Obshchestva*, *4* (1902).

German ed., H. von Foth, trans., *Nachrichten über den Aral-See und den unteren Lauf des Amu-Darja von den ältesten Zeiten bis zum XVII Jahrhundert* (Leipzig, 1910).

—— Turks, Historical and Ethnografic Survey, *EI, 4*, 900–908.

BAZILEVICH, K. V., ed., *Atlas istorii SSSR, 1* (Moscow, 1950).

BEAZLEY, C. R., *The Dawn of Modern Geography* (London, J. Murray), *3* (1906).

BERNSHTAM. See Abbreviations.

CASTREN, M. A., *Ethnologische Vorlesungen über die altaischen Völker* (St. Petersburg, 1857).

CURTIN, J., *A Journey in Southern Siberia, the Mongols, Their Religion and Their Myths* (Boston, Little, Brown & Co., 1909).

CZAPLICKA, M., *The Turks of Central Asia in History and at the Present Day* (Oxford, Clarendon Press, 1918). Reviewed by W. Barthold in *Zapiski Kollegii Vostokovedov, 1*, 506–511.

GRUM-GRZYMAILO. See Abbreviations.

HALECKI, O., Geografja polityczna ziem ruskich, Polski i Litwy 1340–1569, *Sprawozdania Towarzystwa Naukowego Warszawskiego, 1–2* (1917).

HAZARD, H. W., compiler, *Atlas of Islamic History* (Princeton, Princeton University Press, 1951).

HENNIG, R., *Terrae incognitae, 3–4* (Leyden, 1938–39).

HERRMANN, A., *Historical and Commercial Atlas of China* (Cambridge, Mass., Harvard University Press, 1935).

IVANOVSKY, A. A., Zur Anthropologie der Mongolen, *Archiv für Anthropologie, 24* (1896).

KATANOV, N. F., Etnograficheskii obzor turetsko-tatarskikh plemen (Kazan, 1894). Inaccessible to me.

KERNER, R. J., *The Urge to the Sea: the Course of Russian History* (Berkeley and Los Angeles, University of California Press, 1942).

KERVYN, L. M., *Moeurs et coutumes mongoles* (Gembloux, 1949).

KOZLOV, P. K., *Mongolia i Amdo i mertvyi gorod Khara-Khoto* (Moscow and Petrograd, 1923).

—— *Mongolia i Kam* (St. Petersburg, 1905–7). 5 vols.

KUCZYŃSKI. See Abbreviations.

KUZNETSOV, S. K., *Russkaia istoricheskaia geografiia* (Moscow, 1910).

LIUBAVSKY, M. K., *Obrazovanie osnovnoi gosudarstvennoi territorii velikorusskoi narodnosti* (Leningrad, 1929).

MARQUART (MARKWART), J., Über das Volkstum der Komanen, *AWGA*, N.S., *13*, No. 1 (1914), 25–238.

MORAVCSIK. (See Abbreviations).

NASONOV, A. N., *"Russkaia zemlia" i obrazovanie territorii drevnerusskogo gosudarstva* (Moscow, 1951).

PALLAS, P. S., *Sammlungen historischer Nachrichten über die Mongolischen Völkerschaften* (St. Petersburg, 1776–1801). 2 vols.

PELLIOT, P., A propos des Comans, *JA*, 11th ser., *15* (1920), 125–185.

PYPIN, A. N., *Istoriia russkoi etnografii* (St. Petersburg, 1890–92). 4 vols.

RADLOFF, W. (Radlov, V.), *Ethnographische Übersicht der Türkstämme Sibiriens und der Mongolei* (Leipzig, 1883). Inaccessible to me.

RIASANOVSKY, V. A., *Customary Law of the Mongol Tribes* (Harbin, 1929).

SEREDONIN, S. M., *Russkaia istoricheskaia geografiia* (Petrograd, 1916).

SPULER, B., Mittelalterliche Grenzen in Osteuropa, I.
Die Grenze des Grossfürstentums Litauen im Südosten gegen Türken und Tataren, *JGOE*, *6* (1941), 152–170.

VAMBERY, H., *Das Türkenvolk* (Leipzig, 1885).

VLADIMIRTSOV. See Abbreviations.
French ed., M. Carsow, trans., *Le Régime social des Mongols; le féodalisme nomade* (Paris, 1948). Preface by R. Grousset.

ZAMYSLOVSKY, E., *Uchebnyi atlas po russkoi istorii* (2d ed. St. Petersburg, 1887).

ZELENIN, D., *Russische (ostslavische) Volkskunde* (Berlin and Leipzig, 1927).

IV. Source Study

1. Mongol and Tibetan Sources

Cleaves, F. W. Chancellery. See Abbreviations.

—— The Expression *Dur-a Qočarulčaju* in the Letter of Öljeitü to Philippe le Bel, *HJAS, 11* (1948), 441–455.

—— The Expression *Jöb Ese Bol in the Secret History of the Mongols, HJAS, 11* (1948), 311–320.

Haenisch, E., Der Stand der Yüan-pi-schi-Forschung, *ZDMG, 98* (1944).

—— Untersuchungen über das Yüan-ch'ao pi-shi, *ASAW, 41*, No. 4 (1931).

Kotwicz, Formules initiales. See Abbreviations.

Laufer, B., Skizze der mongolischen Literatur, *Keleti Szemle, 8* (1907), 165–261.

2d ed. in Russian, revised and enlarged by B. Ia. Vladimirtsov, *Ocherk mongolskoi literatury* (Leningrad, 1927). Second ed. inaccessible to me.

Mostaert, A., A propos du mot *širolga* de *l'Histoire secrète des Mongols, HJAS, 12* (1949), 470–476.

—— Sur quelques passages de *l'Histoire secrète des Mongols*, *HJAS, 13* (1950), 285–361; *14* (1951), 329–403. To be continued.

Pelliot. See Abbreviations.

Roerich, G. N., The Author of the Hor-chos-hbyun, *Journal of the Royal Asiatic Society* (1946), 192–196.

—— *The Blue Annals, 1*, i–xxi.

—— Kun-mkhyen Chos-kyi hod-zer and the Origin of the Mongol Alphabet, *Journal of the Royal Asiatic Society of Bengal. Letters* (1945), 52–57.

—— Notes on Central Asia, Greater India Society, *Journal, 13* (1946), 73–76.

Vladimirtsov (see Abbreviations), pp. 5–26.

2. Arabic and Persian Sources

Barthold, W., *Iran* (Tashkent, 1926).

—— *Musulmanskii mir* (Petrograd, 1922).

—— *Turkestan*. See Abbreviations.

Blochet, E., *Introduction à l'histoire des Mongols de Fadl Allah Rashid ed-Din* (London, Gibb Memorial Series, 1910).

Brockelmann, C., *Geschichte der arabischen Literatur* (2d ed. Leyden, E. J. Brill, 1943–49). 2 vols.

Browne 3. See Abbreviations.

Krymsky, *Persia* (see Abbreviations), *3*, 33–80.

Martinovitch, N., Die verlorene Handschrift von Rašid ad-Din, *Artibus Asiae, 5* (1935), 213–220.

Storey, Ch. A., *Persian Literature, a Bio-bibliographical Survey* (London, Luzac & Co., 1927–39). 2 vols., vol. *2* in three parts.

Wüstenfeld, F., Die Geschichtsschreiber der Araber, *AWGA, 28–29* (1882–83).

3. Russian Sources

Berezhkov, N., *Litovskaia metrika kak istoricheskii istochnik, 1* (Moscow and Leningrad, 1946).

Cherepnin, L. V., *Russkie feodalnye arkhivy* xiv–xv *vekov* (Moscow, 1948–51). 2 vols.

Iasinsky, M. N., *Ustavnye zemskie gramoty litovsko-russkogo gosudarstva* (Kiev, 1889).

Ikonnikov, V. S., *Opyt russkoi istoriografii* (Kiev, 1891–1908). 2 vols., each in two parts.

Kochin, G. E., *Materialy dlia terminologicheskogo slovaria drevnei Rossii* (Moscow and Leningrad, 1937). Inaccessible to me.

Leontovich, F. I., Istochniki litovsko-russkogo prava, Warsaw, Universitet, *Izvestiia*, 1894, Fasc. 1. Inaccessible to me.

Likhachev, D. S., *Russkie letopisi* (Moscow and Leningrad, 1947).

Nasonov, A. N., Letopisnye pamiatniki tverskogo kniazhestva, *OGN*, 1930, 709–738, 739–772.

Priselkov, M. D.; *Istoriia russkogo letopisaniia* xi–xv *vekov* (Leningrad, 1940).

Shakhmatov, A. A., *Razyskaniia o sostave drevneishikh letopisnykh svodov* (St. Petersburg, 1908).

Tikhomirov, M. N., *Istochnikovedenie istorii SSSR s drevneishkih vremen do kontsa* xviii *veka* (Moscow, 1940).

Valk, S. N., *Sovetskaia arkheografiia* (Moscow and Leningrad, 1948).

V. Genealogy and Biography

1. Mongol

GENEALOGIES

Lane-Pool, S., *The Mohammedan Dynasties* (Westminster, A. Constable & Co., 1894).
   Russian ed., W. Barthold, trans. and annotator, *Musulmanskie dinastii* (St. Petersburg, 1899).

Muizz al-Ansab fi Shajarat Salatin Moghul (Glorification of the Genealogies of the Mongol Sultans). See Storey, *2, 298*, and Tiesenhausen, *2, 29.*
   Excerpts in Russian trans., Tiesenhausen, *2, 41–63.*

Zambaur, E., *Manuel de généalogie et de chronologie pour l'histoire de l'Islam* (Hanovre, 1927). 2 vols. and a volume of tables.

BIOGRAPHIES

Chingis-Khan

BARTHOLD, W., Chingis-Khan, *EI, 1*, 856–862.

ERDMANN, F., *Temudschin der Unerschütterliche* (Leipzig, 1862).

FOX, R., *Genghis Khan* (New York, Harcourt, Brace & Co., 1936).

GRENARD, F., *Gengis-Khan* (Paris, 1935).

GROUSSET, R., *Le Conquérant du monde* (Paris, 1944).

LAMB, H., *Genghis Khan, the Emperor of All Men* (New York, R. M. McBride & Co., 1927).

MARTIN, H. D., *The Rise of Chingis Khan and His Conquest of North China* (Baltimore, Johns Hopkins Press, 1950).

PRAWDIN, M., *Tschingis-Chan und sein Erbe* (Stuttgart and Berlin, 1938).

VLADIMIRTSOV, B. Ia., *Chingis-Khan* (Berlin, Petrograd, and Moscow, 1922).

English ed., Prince D. S. Mirsky, trans., *The Life of Chingis-Khan* (Boston and New York, Houghton Mifflin & Co., 1930).

WALKER, C. C., *Jenghiz Khan* (London, Luzac & Co., 1939).

Nogay

VESELOVSKY. See Abbreviations.

Timur (Tamerlane)

BOUVAT, L., Timur Lang (Tamerlane), *EI, 4*, 777–779.

IBN-ARABSHAH. See Sources, V, C. 8.

LAMB, H., *Tamerlane the Earth Shaker* (New York, R. M. McBride & Co., 1928).

Ulug-Beg (Ulugbek)

BARTHOLD, W., *Ulugbek i ego vremia* (Petrograd, 1918).

Turkish ed. [Kurat], A. Nimet, trans., *Uluğ-Bey ve zamani* (Istanbul, 1930).

2. Russian and Lithuanian

BARSUKOV, A. P., Obzor istochnikov i literatury russkogo rodosloviia, *ANZ, 54* (1887), Suppl.

BAUMGARTEN 1, 2. See Abbreviations.

BENZ, E., ed., *Russische Heiligenlegenden* (Zurich, 1953).

DOLGORUKOV, PRINCE P. V., *Rossiiskaia rodoslovnaia kniga* (St. Petersburg, 1855–57). 4 vols.

EKZEMPLIARSKY. See Abbreviations.

KONECZNY, F., Jagiello i Witold, *Przewodnik naukowy i literacki, 20* (1892).

LOBANOV-ROSTOVSKY, PRINCE A. B., *Russkaia rodoslovnaia kniga* (2d ed. St. Petersburg, 1895). 2 vols.

PROCHASKA, A., *Król Wladyslaw Jagiello* (Kraków, 1908).

PUZYNA, J., Korjat i Korjatowicze, *AW, 7* (1930), 425–454.

PUZYNA, J., Korjat i Korjatowicze oraz sprawa podolska, *AW, 11* (1936), 61–97.

Rodoslovnaia kniga kniaziei i dvorian rossiiskikh i vyezzhikh (Moscow, 1787). 2 vols. Contains the so-called Velvet Book (*Barkhatnaia kniga*).

Russkii biograficheskii slovar' (St. Petersburg, 1896–1918). 25 vols. Not completed.

SMOLKA, S., Kiejstut i Jagiello, *Pamiętnik Akademii Umiejętnosci* (Phil. and Hist. Sec.), 7 (1889).

STADNICKI, K., *Bracia Wladyslawa Jagielly* (Lwów, 1867).

—— *Olgierd i Kiejstut* (Lwów, 1870).

—— *Synowie Gedymina* (Lwów, 1881).

VITOVT, Biographies of,

BARBASHEV, A., *Vitovt* (St. Petersburg, 1885–91), 2 vols. Vol. 2 inaccessible to me.

PFITZNER, J., *Grossfürst Witold von Litauen als Staatsmann* (Prague, 1930).

WOLFF, J., *Kniaziowie Litewsko-ruscy od końca czternastego wieku* (Warsaw, 1895).

—— *Ród Gedymina* (Kraków, 1886). Inaccessible to me.

ZOTOV, R. V., *O kniaziakh chernigovskikh po liubetskomu sinodiku* (St. Petersburg, 1892).

GENEALOGICAL TABLES

THE PURPOSE of the following tables is not to give the full genealogy of each ruling house but to help the reader to identify the rulers mentioned in this volume.

I. THE HOUSE OF CHINGIS-KHAN

Numbers indicate the order of succession of the great khans

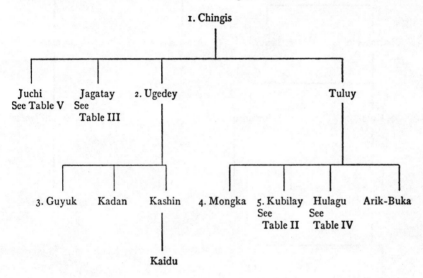

II. THE HOUSE OF KUBILAY

Numbers indicate the order of succession of the great khans

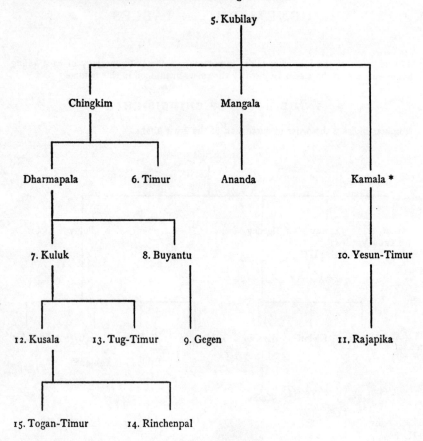

* According to Zambaur, Kamala was a son of Chingkim.

III. THE HOUSE OF JAGATAY

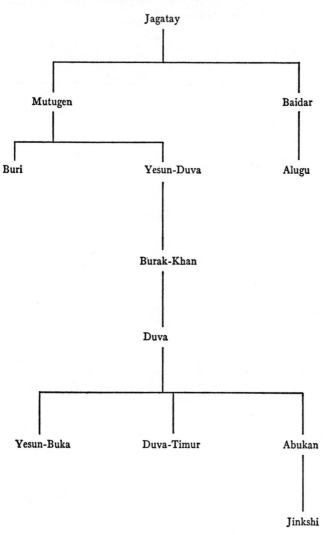

IV. THE IL-KHANS OF PERSIA

Numbers indicate the order of succession

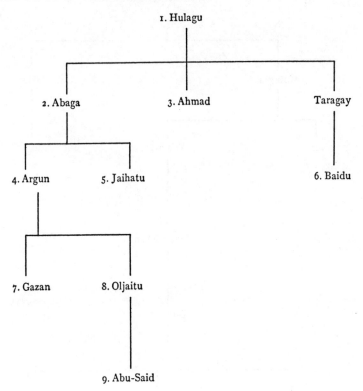

V. THE HOUSE OF JUCHI

Numbers refer to the order of succession of the khans of the Golden Horde

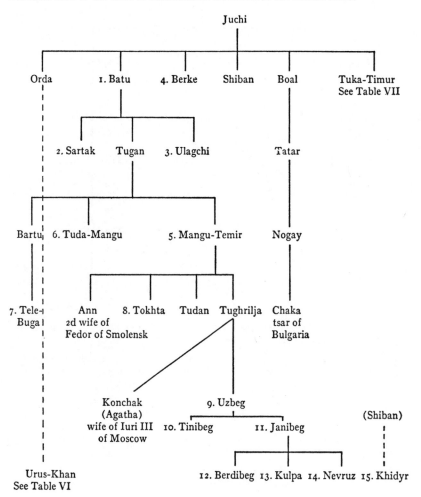

VI. THE HOUSE OF URUS-KHAN *

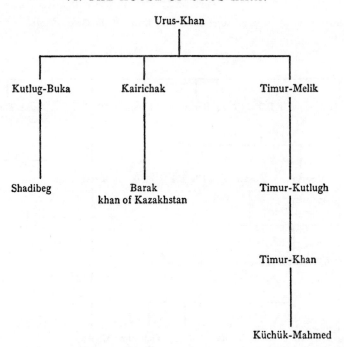

* According to Zambaur, Urus-Khan was a descendant of Orda; according to *Muizz*, a descendant of Tuka-Timur.

VII. THE HOUSE OF TUKA-TIMUR

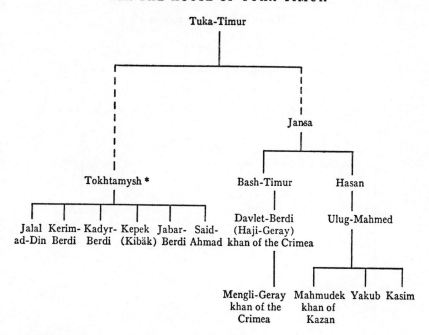

* According to *Muizz*, Tokhtamysh was a descendant of Tuka-Timur; according to Zambaur, a descendant of Orda.

VIII. THE HOUSE OF GALICIA AND VOLYNIA

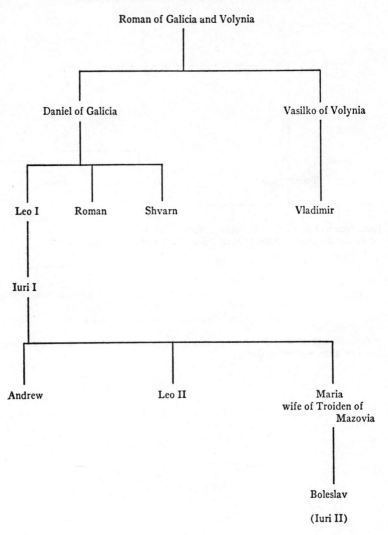

Roman of Galicia and Volynia

Daniel of Galicia

Vasilko of Volynia

Leo I   Roman   Shvarn

Vladimir

Iuri I

Andrew   Leo II   Maria
wife of Troiden of
Mazovia

Boleslav

(Iuri II)

IX. THE HOUSE OF GEDYMIN OF LITHUANIA

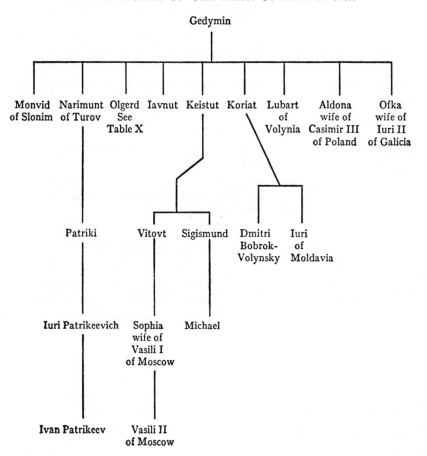

X. THE HOUSE OF OLGERD OF LITHUANIA

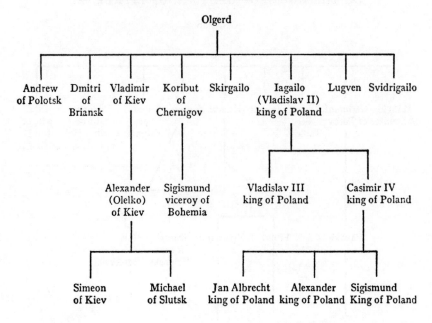

XI. THE HOUSE OF MOSCOW

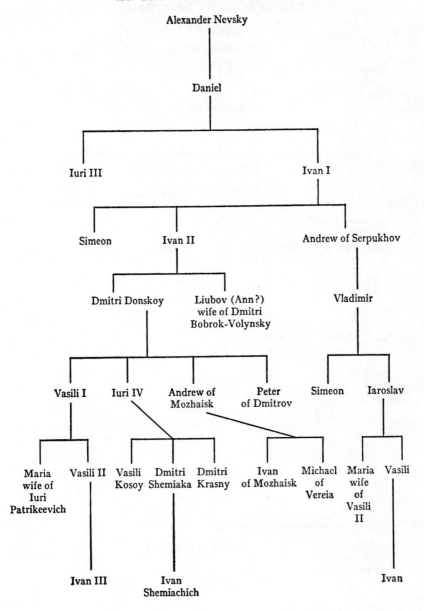

XII. THE HOUSE OF TVER

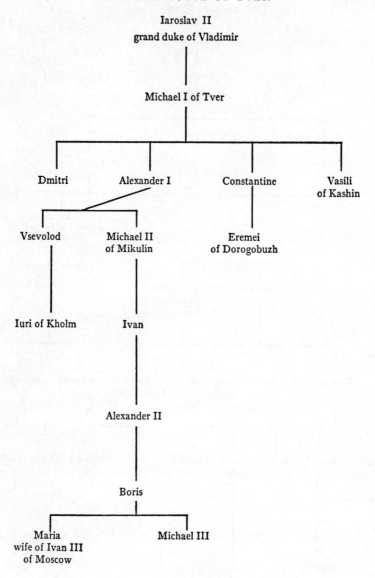

Iaroslav II
grand duke of Vladimir

Michael I of Tver

Dmitri   Alexander I   Constantine   Vasili
of Kashin

Vsevolod   Michael II   Eremei
of Mikulin   of Dorogobuzh

Iuri of Kholm   Ivan

Alexander II

Boris

Maria   Michael III
wife of Ivan III
of Moscow

GENERAL INDEX

INDEX OF AUTHORS CITED

SOMERSET COUNTY COLLEGE LRC

3 3666 00061 8651

DK
40
V44   VERNADSKY   47341
v.3   A history of Russia,

SOMERSET COUNTY COLLEGE
LIBRARY
North Branch, New Jersey